Signifyin(g),
Sanctifyin',
&
Slam Dunking

■ ■ ■ ■ ■ ■

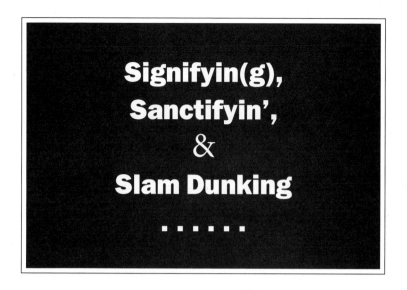

Signifyin(g), Sanctifyin', & Slam Dunking

A Reader in African American Expressive Culture

edited by GENA DAGEL CAPONI

University of Massachusetts Press   Amherst

Copyright © 1999 by

The University of Massachusetts Press

All rights reserved

Printed in the United States of America

LC 99-18345

ISBN 1-55849-182-1 (cloth); 183-x (pbk.)

Set in Adobe Minion by Keystone Typesetting, Inc.

Printed and bound by Thomson-Shore, Inc.

Library of Congress Cataloging-in-Publication Data

Signifyin(g), sanctifyin', and slam dunking : a reader in African
american expressive culture / edited by Gena Dagel Caponi.

p.   cm.

Includes bibliographical references and index.

ISBN 1-55849-182-1 (cloth : alk. paper). — ISBN 1-55849-183-x
(pbk. : alk. paper)

1. Afro-Americans—Social life and customs.

2. United States—Civilization—Afro-American influences.

3. Popular culture—United States. 4. Afro-American dance.

5. Afro-Americans—Music.

6. Afro-American aesthetics. 7. Afro-Americans—Language.

8. Afro-Americans—Sports.   I. Caponi, Gena Dagel, 1953–   .

E185.86.S575   1999

305.896073—dc21   99-18345

CIP

British Library Cataloguing in Publication data are available.

Previously published chapters in this anthology are reproduced as they
originally appeared except that notes and bibliographical references
that follow the essays have been standardized.

IN MEMORY OF

WILLIAM DILLON PIERSEN

(1942–1996)

Contents

Acknowledgments

The idea for this anthology arose during a conversation with William D. Piersen, colleague and friend. Bill was killed in an automobile accident on December 30, 1996, along with his wife, Charlotte, and their sixteen-year-old daughter, Katie. The memory of Bill's generosity, liveliness, and curiosity fueled my work on this volume, and I dedicate it to him.

My editor Clark Dougan has been so consistently enthusiastic and encouraging that in moments of self-doubt I have questioned his judgment, but on the whole I'm grateful for his faith. I'm even more grateful for his guidance throughout this project. Joel Dinerstein has been an especially strong sounding board, and I thank him for his straight talk, ideas, and friendship. I am grateful to Richard Crawford for his careful reading, faithful correspondence, and amiable collaboration. Thanks go to the anonymous readers for this volume, and I particularly thank Samuel A. Floyd, Jr., John Gennari, Guthrie P. Ramsey, Jr. and Siva Vaidhyanathan, whose suggestions strengthened the book. I appreciate the financial assistance of the University of Texas at San Antonio, and I am grateful to my colleagues there. I thank Joe Piersen and the Piersen family for their gracious support. Finally, thanks to Angie, Cindy, Linda, and Melissa for their friendship and coffee, and, as always, to my family—my parents, Maff, Pete, and Tom—for everything else.

Signifyin(g),
Sanctifyin',
&
Slam Dunking

. . . . . .

Introduction

The Case for an African American Aesthetic

GENA DAGEL CAPONI

． ． ． ． ． ． ．

Ralph Ellison once wrote, "Without the presence of Negro American style our jokes, our tall tales, even our sports would be lacking in the sudden turns, the shocks, the swift changes of pace (all jazz-shaped) that serve to remind us that the world is ever unexplored, and that while a complete mastery of life is mere illusion, the real secret of the game is to make life swing."[1]

In his memoir *Upside Your Head! Rhythm and Blues on Central Avenue*, white rhythm and blues artist Johnny Otis wrote, "I never had to instruct my horn players how to phrase a passage. . . . The music grew out of the African American way of life. The way mama cooked, the Black English grandmother and grandfather spoke, the way daddy disciplined the kids—the emphasis in spiritual values, the way Reverend Jones preached, the way Sister Williams sang in the choir, the way the old brother down the street played the slide guitar and crooned the blues, the very special way the people danced, walked, laughed, cried, joked, got happy, shouted in church. In the final analysis, what forms the texture and adds character to the music is the African American experience."[2] Otis believed all these things were connected, and he called this connection the "African American way of life."

Is there anything particularly African American about this way of life other than the fact that African Americans are living it? What might be served by identifying African American style? What is this "black" in "black culture"?

The readings in this volume may not answer these questions, but they raise them persistently. The essays that follow come from a broad range of disciplines and cover many years, but each considers expressive culture—whether music, dance, sport, or oral expression—from the perspective of cultural aesthetics. A set of aesthetic principles emerges from these readings, a way of doing things that seems remarkably consistent over time and across different forms of cultural expression. The aesthetic underpinning that links so many forms of African American expression is one that has profoundly shaped American cultural life.

Perhaps in no arena of present-day cultural life in this country is the African American aesthetic so visibly on display as in sports. Yet scholars have rarely considered the hardwood court, gridiron, or baseball diamond within the expressive domain in which literature, music, dance, and speech exist. A major reason surely is that sports feature bodies more prominently than minds. Yet, if chess is recognized as an intellectual activity, then it seems sensible to accord intellectual status to those who use their bodies with comparable strategic purpose, though with much greater physical virtuosity. Surely athletics count as "fields of humanly significant action," and especially so in black culture, since they provide "the only extensive field of survey for analyzing black male ambition in a context where its expression has had an enormous impact on America culture at large."[3]

According to Gerald Early, boxing has attracted more commentary from African American intellectuals than any other sport, because of a long history of participation by black fighters within the sport, because of its inherent symbolism, and because three of the most powerful black male presences in the twentieth century have been boxers: Jack Johnson, Joe Louis, and Muhammad Ali.[4] For Early, African American prizefighting has a powerful role in expressing and constructing blackness in American culture.[5] "The importance of the black fighter as a symbol, political and social, and as a kind of running commentary, critical and complementary, in the whole matter of what it means to be a black American takes on a greater power, a more compelling insistence, with the black masses—both lower class and bourgeoisie—than the comparable instance of the white fighter for the white masses in defining meaning for the white American."[6] Within the blatant racialism and latent eroticism intrinsic to the sport's most celebrated competitions, the prizefighter is both blues hero and theorist, performing athletic statements on the meaning and transcendence of African American dislocation.

Discussions of aesthetics are rare in histories of sport, but when historians consider the contributions of African American players, such comments leap off the page. In a chapter entitled "The Black Myth: Basketball As Jazz," Michael Novak wrote, "Basketball, although neither invented by blacks nor played only by blacks, came to allow the mythic world of the black experience to enter directly, with minimal change, into American life. The game is corporate like black life; improvisatory like black life; formal and yet casual; swift and defiant; held back, contained, and then exploding; full of leaps and breakaway fluid sprints."[7] Novak also talked about the "cool, shaded mask" the basketball player must "put on," for basketball is a game of feint. Novak said what has now become indisputable—"the game becomes more black with every passing year"—and he was describing the aesthetics of the game, not the players.

In the basketball volume of *A Hard Road to Glory*, subtitled "Putting the Record Straight: Forgotten Facts," Arthur Ashe similarly documented the "distinctive 'black' style of play" that developed in the 1940s, one "that featured speed, uncommon jumping ability, and innovative passing skills." It was this "black style" that "produced results and was extremely exciting to watch," and in 1951 forced white professional leagues to admit black players.[8]

The black style Ashe and Novak describe evolved from a cultural willingness to improvise, from a cultural imperative to adapt, and in reaction to a rule change. Until 1937, players returned to midcourt after every goal for a new tipoff. But that year, the National Basketball Committee eliminated the center jump, which sped the game up and made full-court basketball possible for the first time. Faster, running teams immediately benefited from this move, and African American players were among the first to take advantage of a full-court strategy called the "race-horse move," today known as the fast break. For years the fast break was so closely associated with African American players that it was called simply "Negro ball."

In *Elevating the Game*, Nelson George noted other contributions to a black aesthetic in basketball. Slam dunking personalizes the act of scoring and is a form of stylization; verbal intimidation—trash-talking—falls within the tradition of satire; and intimidation through improvisation has many parallels in musical and verbal arts. Yet this style, which has so many connections to other forms of African American expression, was derogatorily termed "schoolyard ball." As George says, "because of schoolyard experimentation, *all* players now do things once thought impossible."[9] When novelist John Edgar Wideman played for the University of Pennsylvania in the 1960s, he missed the "spontaneity, the free-form improvisation and electricity of the playground game.... 'Playground move' was synonymous with bad move. Not *bad* move, but something undisciplined, selfish, possibly immoral. Twenty years later, coaches are attempting to systematize and teach the essence of the game invented on the playgrounds."[10]

Perhaps the most important innovation that historians do not yet appreciate as coming from "Negro ball" is the jump shot. Most still credit one of several renegade white players with developing the one-handed jump shot, yet there is much evidence to suggest that the jump shot evolved along with the fast-break style in the late 1930s and 1940s, and that African American players pioneered this move as well.[11] Clarence "Big House" Gaines was coach for forty-six years at Winston-Salem State and witnessed the development of the jump shot. He explains, "Shooting with one hand is a natural reaction. If a player's got good hands and good skills and he's running, he's not going to stop and use two hands. The jump just came along with [the fast break]."[12] Yet white coaches resisted the jump shot for two decades. When Nat Holman, coach at City College of New York, saw his first jump shot in the late 1930s, he declared, "That's not basketball. If my boys ever shot one-handed, I'd quit coaching."[13] In his autobiography, former Boston Celtics player and coach Bill Russell describes playing ball in the 1950s when coaches routinely benched players for taking "Negro" jump shots.[14] Today this move is so essential to basketball that we cannot imagine the game without it. And basketball's most visible icon, Michael Jordan, calls his fan club simply "Jump, Inc."

In *A Hard Road to Glory* Arthur Ashe showed how African American athletes changed the style of play and coaching in every sport they entered in great numbers. "Within five years of Jackie Robinson's entry into the major leagues, Blacks took over the stolen base category and made it a weapon of intimidation it hadn't been since the Ty Cobb era. We're used to playing an in-your-face game," Ashe wrote.[15] In some cases, the "in-your-face" style was so intimidating that rules were changed to eliminate it. The National Collegiate Athletic Association banned the slam dunk in 1967 because of Kareem Abdul-Jabbar's (then Lew Alcindor) performances for UCLA, and the move didn't return until Julius Erving ("Dr. J") and others helped popularize it in the American Basketball Association of the 1970s. Likewise, professional football has banned "excessive celebration" after touchdowns, a rule scholar Joel Dinerstein ironically terms "illegal use of black culture." But as George notes, despite the contributions of African American athletes in many sports, "perhaps only boxers (Joe Louis, Sugar Ray Robinson, Muhammad Ali) have so radically remade a sport as African-Americans have basketball."[16]

To Gerald Early's 1989 list of "the three black persons who have exercised the greatest influence upon our social reality and our mythical selves"—Joe Louis, Jack Johnson, and Muhammad Ali—many would now add a fourth figure: Michael Jordan, the most recognizable American worldwide. As Louis before him, Jordan is "a symbol of national unity."[17] But Jordan has transcended Louis's role as "a representative of American manhood and masculinity": he is the one whom boys and girls across the country and the world want to be like.[18]

In their essays in this volume on Michael Jordan, John Edgar Wideman and Michael Eric Dyson focus on him as the athlete whose domination of the game makes it impossible to ignore the ways in which African American players have shaped the game. Wideman says Jordan's remarkable star power grows out of a particularly African American willingness to "elevate the game." Jordan has taken this urge to shine to a national level, but Wideman has seen it on the playground as well, when a fellow player executed a move so spectacular that "Glory reflected instantly on all of us because he was one of us out there in the game and he'd suddenly lifted the game to a higher plane."[19]

Composer Olly Wilson notes similar occasions in black music performance and calls them "soul focal moments." In a soul focal moment, the player performs the unexpected with virtuosity, elevates the community through his or her individual effort, and the community bursts into spontaneous applause, responding as one body. Michael Eric Dyson's identification of African Americanisms in Jordan's style of play (pp. 407–416, this volume) captures three necessary ingredients of the soul focal moment: the will to spontaneity, stylization of the performed self, and edifying deception. Such moments unite the community in appreciation, wonder, and inspiration; Jordan, master of the soul focal moment, becomes, in Wideman's words, "the truest prophet of what might be possible."[20]

The virtuosic individual performance is a social act, inspiring the team and the community. In *Race Matters*, Cornel West describes a "mode of being in the world" that he calls a "jazz freedom fighter." The jazz freedom fighter galvanizes others through "individuality . . . promoted in order to sustain and increase the *creative* tension with the group—a tension that yields higher levels of performance to achieve the aim of the collective project."[21] Reconfigured in this way, what was once derisively called "hot-dogging" becomes community building, whether the "hot-dogger" does it *for* anyone else or not. And when a performer does excel in a moment of brash and unexpected virtuosity, ordinary time and gravity disappear. Louis Armstrong and Billie Holiday bend time beyond constraints of meter, measure, and tempo; Julius Erving leaps clean from the foul line to the basket for a dunk, altering the physics of everyday life, along with our understanding of human limitations. These "soul focal moments"—what Ralph Ellison calls "true jazz moments"[22]—are moments of transcendence and fusion for all involved: transcendence of the ordinary, and of the boundaries between community and individual. In these moments all, including observers, are participants. The individual who is the catalyst for such a moment is the ultimate team player.

"Hot-dogging" is also called "showing off" (or more derogatorily, "showboating") and "showiness" has always been a part of African American expressive style. William D. Piersen discusses at length the showiness of African American festive style in various eighteenth-century New England parades and processions (pp. 417–433, this volume). Such events did not, in his words, "try to approximate the region's European American regard for uniformity." Roger Abrahams, too, notes with regard to early African American ring dancing and play, "Each player is encouraged to *show off* in some way, either through some kind of individualized dance step . . . or through strutting, teasing, flirting, and wiggling, with everyone else clapping, commenting, and joking in support. This is the point. For while the player is at the center he or she is never alone; rather there is constant commentary and support by the ring."[23]

Occasionally coaches, players, and fans bemoan the disappearance of a "team spirit," supposedly diminished by individual virtuosity or one-on-one body-dialogue. Yet to do so is to miss the balancing act in African American artistic expression altogether, to notice only the tightrope walker and ignore the crowd standing in a circle around the performer, not only cheering him or her on, but holding up the rope as well. From another perspective, while the slam dunking and one-on-one competitions may temporarily distract attention from a team organization, they nevertheless take place within a larger organic community that is following every nuance, a community that in each action, and each comeback, is being resurrected, strengthened, and dignified. In such a game, style is more important than the score. And when the game is stylish, everybody wins.

White players have consciously adopted the "showy" moves they have observed in black basketball. Bob Davies, who played for Seton Hall from 1941 on, recalled his early exposure to basketball in his hometown of Harrisburg, Pennsylvania. "When I was a kid I couldn't afford to pay to see the high school team, so we would look through a crack in the door. The only thing I could see was the foul-lane area and the basket on the other end of the court. I'd see these great black players jump in the air, throw the ball, hit somebody with a pass, or shoot the ball, and I guess that stuck in my mind. I think that's what helped me to become a playmaker."[24] "Pistol" Pete Maravich learned such moves at his father's insistence. Observing black teams in the late 1950s, Clemson University coach Press Maravich told his son they held the key to the game. Anyone who wanted to compete in the future needed to copy the black players' moves, advice that Boston Globe columnist Bob Ryan said turned Maravich into "a freak."[25] To this day writers describe Maravich's African American–inspired ball-handling as "flamboyant," comparing him to Bob Davies and African American players such as Magic Johnson and Marques Haynes of the Harlem Globetrotters.[26]

The remaking of basketball in the shape of the African American aesthetic is an obvious case of subversion of the dominant culture by subordinate African Americans. But it is only one of many ways in which a largely Western European cultural tradition has shifted shape in American culture, conforming to an increasingly African American aesthetic. In postindustrial management philosophy, basketball has replaced football as the sports metaphor of choice. Bernard Avishai, of Monitor management consultants, urges companies to turn from football's "division of labor" organization style to basketball-like "teams of knowledge workers, acting creatively, improvisationally, and in reasonable harmony."[27] Management expert Peter Drucker believes the new model for corporation structure in information-based industries will be that of the jazz combo, in which members must not only cooperate but contribute equally and attempt to sense the direction of the group.[28] In a postindustrial culture, industrial aesthetics fail and new—African American—models emerge.

That an African American aesthetic not only survives but thrives and often has been the vanguard of American cultural expression is a powerful testament to its vitality and power. Yet few studies stress such qualities. More often, the perspective has been pathological, what Ralph Ellison called the "fakelore" of American social science, stressing problems in African American history and race relations rather than the strengths and joys to be found in an American cultural life that has been shaped by African and African American contributions. In 1995, American Studies scholar Shelley Fisher Fishkin surveyed over one hundred books and articles in thirteen different fields published since 1990 on African American culture.[29] Yet the integration of such work into our common understanding of America lags far behind. Generally speaking, at a conscious and institutional level most Americans refuse to acknowledge or do not recognize the African-derived aesthetic they have unconsciously adopted as their own.[30]

A Cultural Aesthetic

The idea of an African American aesthetic is controversial; to some the term sounds dangerously like a racial essentialism—a perpetuation and justification of outmoded notions of race. As writer John Edgar Wideman puts it, "Our stories, songs, dreams, dances, social forms, style of walk, talk, dressing, cooking, sport, our heroes and heroines provide a record . . . so distinctive and abiding that its origins in culture have been misconstrued as rooted in biology."[31] A second problem with the notion of cultural style is that it appears to fly in the face of differences in class, region, generation, and gender. Do an eighty-year-old east Texas cotton farmer and a south Philadelphia adolescent girl practice the same cultural style?

Such objections assume a static cultural style. But the readings in this volume discuss something more malleable and fundamental than a cultural style. They approach the issue at a structural level, the level of cultural aesthetics. Through cultural expressions such as dance, religion, music, and play, societies articulate and transmit the ideas, values, and beliefs that bind people together.

Within the very body of the expression—the form of the music, the shape of the dance, the worship practices of the religion—are embedded cultural values. The structure of cultural expression—the cultural aesthetic—reflects and supports the ethics of the society, reinforces its values and philosophy. Varieties of cultural expression are "manifestation[s] of the culture as a whole, the visible sign of its unity [that] reflects or projects the 'inner form' of collective thinking and feeling."[32] They are, in the words of anthropologist John Szwed, "models of social behavior that reflect strategies of adaptation to human and natural environments."[33] They emerge from a particular culture in a particular way, and they carry with them what musicologist Gary Tomlinson calls "archaeological rules of formation," which means their structure has evolved over time in relation to their social function.[34]

In an essay entitled "Aesthetics and Cultural Studies," Ian Hunter defines aesthetics as "a self-supporting ensemble of techniques and practices for problematizing conduct and events."[35] These techniques and practices form the archaeological structure on which cultural expression rests. Discussing African American music and dance, Albert Murray uses the phrase "technology of stylization" to describe the same idea, whereas ethnomusicologist Steven Feld calls aesthetics "the iconicity of style."[36] The African American aesthetic is a set of techniques and practices—a technology of stylization—that recur over time and across different forms of cultural expression. Even as forms of cultural expression develop and evolve, the underlying structure changes; yet some fundamental elements remain the same. An aesthetic is a constellation of such traits, a set of factors that are not incidental, occasional, or ornamental but which serve as the foundation of an art form.

The idea of an African American aesthetic is not new; neither is the notion that this aesthetic has African origins. Anthropologists, sociologists, and historians have debated the presence of Africanisms in African American cultures at least since the early part of this century.[37] The most noted work on the subject prior to the 1960s was Melville Herskovits's *The Myth of the Negro Past* (1941). With regard to existing musicological and historical scholarship in the area of Africanisms, Herskovits noted dryly "a certain significant malaise concerning the point."[38] He concluded that the "myth of the Negro past"—that African culture died on its journey across the Atlantic—persisted because "the existence of survivals has been denied rather than investigated." For Herskovits, such "failure . . . to face the question of Africanisms" was fundamentally anti-intellectual. When scholars ignore the existence of a body of knowledge, they fail to "apply to their study all the resources of their disciplines."[39]

Today the terms of the debate have changed. The fields of African American studies, black studies, and diasporic studies exemplify interdisciplinary and

Introduction

comparative cultural studies in the Americas, and many scholars note connections among African aesthetics, the American experience, and African American cultural expression in their own fields. Yet still we lack a common—that is to say interdisciplinary—ground on which the various arguments might engage each other.

This volume maps a territory on which scholars of African American expressive culture might meet. The readings in this book (1) call attention to points of convergence in music, dance, athletics, and other expressive forms; (2) use these points of convergence to plot an interdisciplinary cultural (and structural) aesthetic; (3) show this aesthetic at work in African American expressive culture; and (4) underscore the influence of the African American aesthetic in American culture.

An African-Derived Cultural Aesthetic?

In view of the number of cultures and peoples populating the immense continent of Africa, discussing an African cultural aesthetic might seem reductive. Certainly West and Central Africa are regions of many countries and separate cultures with distinct histories and traditions. Yet among the ethnically varied Africans to whom African Americans may trace their origins, scholars customarily note "common orientations to reality," "underlying principles," "aesthetic patterns," and "value systems."[40] For all of these cultures, religion is the central value system, and scholars of religion agree that various African peoples share a religious orientation to such a degree that one may speak of "African" religion and philosophy. As John S. Mbiti says, "there are sufficient elements which make it possible for us to discuss African concepts of God as a unity and on a continental scale."[41] Albert J. Raboteau asserts that "similar modes of perception, shared basic principles, and common patterns of ritual were widespread among different West African religions."[42]

In philosophy too, as Fred Lee Hord and Jonathan Scott Lee demonstrate in their survey of the subject, fundamental precepts recur in cultures across Africa. Perhaps the most common of these is the "meaning of individual life in community," a concern that remains central "across the great temporal and spatial reaches of the African Diaspora."[43] Central, too, is the aesthetic structure through which Africans transmitted and maintained the practice of balancing individual and community needs.

In the majority of cultures across Africa, group rituals were performed in a circle, dancers danced in a circle, and individuals performed solos in the center before returning to the surrounding circle of community. The circle helped to keep everybody involved, active, and interdependent. In addition to the circle, African rituals used the following: *(1) rhythmic and metric complexity; (2) individual improvisation and stylization; (3) dialogic interaction or call-and-response; (4) active engagement of the whole person and the whole community; (5) social commentary or competition through indirection and satire; and (6) development of a group consciousness or sensibility—the invisible conductor.*[44] Such strategies helped shape the structure of African music, dance, storytelling, and play. Separately, they may be found elsewhere, but taken together they form the basis of most African cultural expressions—the basis of African aesthetics.

African Music and Dance Aesthetics

There are more readings on music in this book than on any other form of expression. Music is the key to the aesthetic we are discussing, the fulcrum of African culture and the expression that sustained African aesthetic principles in the Americas. As Nathan Irvin Huggins writes, "Almost every African event occurred within its own music—religious ceremonies and rites, alike. But everything was a religious ceremony: initiations, marriages, healing, planting, harvesting, battles, funerals. History itself, the grandeur of the people, their heroes and chiefs, were recalled in song."[45] For ethnomusicologist and drummer John Miller Chernoff, African music laid the foundation of African culture, mediating between African men, women, and children and their communities. As he explains in *African Rhythm and African Sensibility*: "The stability and continuity of musical forms and associations suggest that music in Africa can be considered a formal institution."[46] For all the differences among the musics of African cultures, Chernoff finds common traits: rhythmic emphasis and complexity; the principle of call-and-response; connection of music to dance and the body; rhythmic linking of music and language; timbral variations; and formal reliance on tradition combined with insistence on individual stylistic variations. Since so many later writers have accepted Chernoff's conclusions and built upon them, they seem worth further discussion.[47]

"Music . . . provides a basis for thinking about and ensuring the integrity of the group," writes Chernoff.[48] This group sensibility was constantly reinforced through musical practice. The most important structural principle of African music, present in music of all Africans, is that of *rhythmic complexity*—multiple rhythms and meters operating simultaneously. Polyrhythmic and polymetric music creates interdependence, because it forces all participants to be aware of each other—of their place in the rhythmic field in relation to others and to the whole.

Unlike a Western approach, in which musicians find their place in the music by following a central beat, marked either by a baton-wielding conductor or by participants tapping their toes in unison, African players find their places in relation to other musicians, because in African music "there are always at least two rhythms going on. . . . There seems to be no unifying or main beat."[49] Eventually all the musicians, including non-performers who also participate through hand-clapping, must find the rhythmic center that holds the music together, even though that center itself is not being played. For Chernoff this rhythmic center constitutes an "additional rhythm" that drummers feel and hear with their inner ears, but do not play. For A. M. Jones this is "metronome sense," and for Richard Waterman, a "subjective beat." Abraham Adzenyah, of the University of Ghana Dance Ensemble and Wesleyan University, terms it the "hidden rhythm," while for John Blacking it is the "rhythm of an *invisible conductor.*"[50] Similarly, Bess Lomax Hawes called the principle that held together African American children's games and dances the "rhythmic bond." For Charles Keil and Steven Feld, this idea of "participatory consciousness" is best captured by the word *groove.*[51] The invisible conductor is an elusive presence the group calls forth and sustains through constant vigilance and attention to rhythmic relationships.

All who have studied African music agree that the rhythms and multiple meters require *active engagement* to sustain both a strong sense of individual rhythm and an attention to the unvoiced and unifying rhythm of the group. Everyone plays a part in the rhythmic field, either by contributing calls and cries, clapping, stamping, or drumming, or by imaginatively constructing the hidden rhythm at the center of the field, or both. Actively engaged in finding the rhythmic center, each person is thus engaged in finding a place within the group.

As a structural device, *call-and-response* ensures interdependence through participation. A leader calls to the group and the group responds. One soloist calls to another, or one part of the group calls to another. The response may vary from one call to the next, or it may remain the same, as in a refrain.[52] The dialogue continues from one to another, and every member of the group remains involved. The call-and-response structure assures that responsibility for the music will be exchanged constantly, from individual to group, and back again.

The principle of *improvisation within traditional forms* sustains a balanced tension between the individual and the community. The African aesthetic constantly pressures one to innovate within a traditional structure—a rhythmic pattern, for instance—so that each musical event blends history and the contemporary approach of the musicians performing at the time.[53] For the master drummer, improvisation does not generate new rhythms but varies the "organization and form given to the already existing rhythms."[54] Improvisation or individual variation must respect the integrity of the group and may, in Chernoff's words, "vary only within the boundaries determined by [one's] place in the ensemble."[55] Improvisation is relational; a master drummer uses improvisation not for self-aggrandizement but to "isolate or draw attention to parts of the ensemble."[56]

Along with improvisation comes the development of a unique personal style within the tradition, an individual trademark, or *stylization*.[57] Chernoff suggests that in African drumming, a musician's "*style* of organizing his playing" adds the "extra dimension of excitement" that makes the occasion a success.[58] For the point of improvising is to add a personal perspective to the tradition, to give the collective effort a unique voice, rooted in the moment. Improvisation is personal interpretation within the tradition, whether through the slightest of vocal slides or scoops, or the most elaborate retelling of a traditional tale, but stylization occurs when one man or woman appropriates the tradition through a particular improvisational device and exceptional skill in that technique.[59]

Each of these African aesthetic principles aids in the process of developing and maintaining an interactive and interdependent social community. African identity develops within a "living web of interrelationships," in the context of family and community.[60] Kwame Anthony Appiah observes of contemporary Africans: "The African asks always not 'who am I?' but 'who are we?' and 'my' problem is not mine alone but 'ours.'"[61] For Africans, identity is a geometric concept: it can be defined only in relation to others. The European believes, "I think, therefore I am." The African believes, "I participate, therefore I am," or as Hord and Lee reiterate, "I am because we are."[62]

Inseparable from African music, African dance preserves and transmits certain African cultural ideas and value. In many cases, the dance itself is a form of faith, "worship converted into sound and motion, performed in the open air."[63] In "An Aesthetic of the Cool: West African Dance," Robert Farris Thompson explains the intellectual properties of dance. For Thompson, "the traditional choreographies of tropical Africa constitute . . . complex distillations of thinking, comparable to Cartesian philosophy in point of influence and importance."[64]

Thompson identifies West African dances as "key documents of aesthetic history." Further, he noted, "they are nonverbal formulations of philosophies of beauty and ethics." The specific traits Thompson includes in his aesthetic of West African dance are "the dominance of a percussive concept of performance; multiple meter; apart playing and dancing; call-and-response; and, finally, the songs and dances of derision."[65]

Clearly here are many correspondences to African music. Percussive dominance, multiple meters, and playing and dancing apart contribute to, or result from what I have called *rhythmic complexity*, and the songs and dances of derision depend on the pervasive mode of satire or *ironic troping* in African expressive culture. As in music, West African dance embodies an aesthetic that nurtures the individual while sustaining the community. Even while moving to multiple-metered music, dancers add rhythmic complexity through percussive dancing that features stamping, slapping and striking the body, playing rattles and hand-drums, and creating a thick musical texture or "tonal mosaic."[66] The drummer-musicians themselves also dance. Such a complex rhythmic field forces all dancers to define their individuality while situated within the group, in a way that makes African music-dance "a communal examination of percussive individuality."[67] Although performance unifies different forms of human expression such as music, dance, body art, and visual art in a communal celebration, it is also an occasion for many simultaneous individual interpretations, a particularly African solution to the problem of balancing individual and community.[68]

Like African music, African dance encourages improvisation and individual variation, an attribute that allowed dancing to evolve and flourish even when transplanted to the Americas. Perhaps it is this built-in tendency to adjust and adapt that explains the dominance of the African aesthetic in American dance. For American dance confounds the "melting-pot" notion, in which "the culture of an early majority swallows up the culture of later minorities."[69] In both American concert and social dance, evolution has been primarily—some scholars would say exclusively—motivated by aesthetic dimensions that are clearly African.

Ring Shout

How did African music and dance elements become part of African American culture? Can we be certain that African American music and dance preserve African elements? Skeptics of cultural continuity suggest that rather than continuing to make music in the African tradition, transplanted Africans were imitating folk music of other cultures with whom they might have come in contact. In his 1925 collection of spirituals (the preface of which is excerpted in this volume), James Weldon Johnson anticipated this question. "What music did American Negroes hear to imitate? . . . Some of them may have heard a few Scotch songs in this country, but it is inconceivable that this great mass of . . . Negro songs could have sprung from such a source." As to the proposal that Negro spirituals are an offshoot of nineteenth-century white religious music, Johnson responded ironically, "Now if ignorant Negroes evolved such music as *Deep River, Steal Away to Jesus, Somebody's Knockin' at Yo' Do', I Couldn't Hear Nobody Pray*, and *Father Abraham* by listening to their masters sing gospel hymns, it does not detract from the achievement but magnifies it."[70]

According to Dena J. Epstein in *Sinful Tunes and Spirituals*, a wealth of information on transplanted Africans in many colonies, both British and French, demonstrates the "continuous existence of native African musics, recognized by contemporary European travelers as displaying distinctive qualities": "syncopation, call-and-response form, strong rhythm, or repeated short melodic phrases."[71] In modifying practices of African arts and institutions, Africans began to redefine themselves and thus to shape a new culture.[72] During the Middle Passage ethnically distinct Africans began the cooperative efforts that would form new communities, through the bonding of shipmate ties, or through the enforced shipboard drumming, dancing, and singing performed for exercise.[73] Contrary to ideas about Africans leaving all musical instruments behind, many Africans did take instruments. The most common were various drums and the guitar-like instrument known as a banza. Africans from a variety of cultures found themselves dancing to a different drummer, as it were, and drummers and musicians were forced to find ways of making music in common. In the erasing of intra-African cultural barriers, African American culture was born.

Many scholars attribute the survival of African features in African American expression to a particular cultural institution, the religious ritual called the "ring shout." In this ritual, participants shuffled single-file, counterclockwise in a circle to rhythmic accompaniment, gradually increasing in tempo and intensity.[74] As Sterling Stuckey shows in *Slave Culture: Nationalist Theory and the Foundations of Black America*, the African American ring shout is a variation on the religious burial dances common to central and western African cultures and perpetuated in all parts of the United States by African Americans.[75] For Africans, the circular form of rituals honoring ancestors traced the cycles of birth, death, and rebirth. The continuous circular path across the earth had many variations in African and African American performances, sometimes mournful, sometimes celebratory,[76] but always the circle moved counterclockwise, mimicking the four moments of the sun from east, to overhead, to west, and into oblivion beneath the earth.[77]

One of the values common to nearly all African groups was honoring the dead and their departed spirits. Just as in Africa, where the ecstatic ring rituals eliminated barriers between earthly participants and the spirit world, in the Americas ring shouts were the way that Africans from various ethnicities could join in a ceremony so universal in meaning as to efface cultural barriers.[78] Harold Courlander describes the ring shout as "a cluster of thinly disguised and diluted elements of West African religious practices," and even among former Africans who had been in the New World for many years, the counter-clockwise movement of the ring dance remained a "recognizable and vital point of cultural convergence."[79] In Stuckey's view, "the use of the circle for religious purposes in slavery was so consistent and profound that one could argue that it was what gave form and meaning to black religion and art."[80]

In African religious traditions, where "all forms of music involved bodily movement," dance was integral to the worship experience.[81] Those with a European background who observed the ring shout often misunderstood its religious nature, seeing only the increasingly frenetic dance and not compre-hending it as a form of worship. Music historian Eileen Southern pinpoints the ring shout as a key to understanding a distinctively African expressive style, saying, "Nowhere in the history of the black experience in the United States was the clash of cultures—the African versus the European—more obvi-ous than in the differing attitudes taken towards ritual dancing and spirit possession."[82]

The ring shout is by no means a thing of the distant past. James Weldon Johnson remembered seeing this dance many times in the late nineteenth century:

> A space is cleared by moving the benches, and the men and women arrange themselves, generally alternately, in a ring, their bodies quite close. The music starts and the ring begins to move. Around it goes, at first slowly, then with quickening pace. Around and around it moves on shuffling feet that do not leave the floor. . . . The music is supplemented by the clapping of hands. As the ring goes around it begins to take on signs of frenzy. The music, starting, perhaps, with a Spiritual, becomes a wild, monotonous chant. The same musical phrase is repeated over and over one, two, three, four, five hours. The words become a repetition of an incoherent cry. The very mo-notony of sound and motion produces an ecstatic state. Women, screaming, fall to the ground prone and quivering. Men, exhausted, drop out of the shout. But the ring closes up and moves around and around.[83]

John and Alan Lomax observed and recorded the ring shout through the 1950s in Louisiana, Texas, and Georgia, and Marshall Stearns witnessed it in South Carolina in the 1950s where it persists to this day.[84]

The ring shout provided an organized venue for cultural continuity, and an explanation for the means by which African ideas about social organization passed into the formal African American cultural institution of religion. In the ring shout were many parts of the aesthetic I have described: call-and-response and rhythmic complexity to unify the group, individual improvisation within a group, emphasis on style over form, and most of all, integration of music and dance (use of the whole body, or bodily engagement). Ring shout music and aesthetics provided the basis for African American music and religious practices in contemporary Holiness or Sanctified and black Baptist churches.[85] The modern Rock Elijah, characteristic of Holiness churches, is a rhythmic shuffling down the aisles, occasionally to music, accompanied by chanting, shouts of praise, and hand-clapping, and often culminating in speaking in tongues or other manifestations of the gifts of the spirit. Such music and movement help bring believers into communion with the Holy Spirit and each other and are part of the means by which souls are saved or sanctified. For scholars C. Eric Lincoln and Lawrence H. Mamiya, the contemporary shout of the Holiness or Sanctified churches "is to gospel and its cult what the ring-shout was to the spiritual and the slaves, and what spirit possession was to African sacred song . . . a spiritual possession experience in which the worshipper 'gets happy' or is 'anointed by the spirit' and praises God in paroxysmal dance."[86]

Many African American performers claim the Sanctified church as part of their spiritual and artistic grounding. Dizzy Gillespie wrote, "The Sanctified church's rhythm got to me as it did to anyone else who came near the place. People like James Brown and Aretha Franklin owe everything to that Sanctified beat. I received my first experience with rhythm and spiritual transport going down there to the well every Sunday, and I've just followed it ever since."[87] Such performers, and many before them, carried the Sanctified aesthetic and beat into the secular music of boogie-woogie, jump blues, rhythm and blues, and, of course, many eras and styles of jazz.

But distinguishing between the secular and the sacred is more in keeping with a European Protestant than an African value system. The same aesthetic that informed African American sacred rituals permeated secular practices, from work songs, folk songs, and children's games to secular dances and folk narration.[88] In her comprehensive 1971 history, *The Music of Black Americans*, Eileen Southern notes many occasions to which African music and dance were integral, including holiday celebrations, birthdays of public figures, Election Day, Pinkster Day (Pentecost Sunday), and dancing contests at slave festivals.[89] As Roger Abrahams says, "these very same traits were also present in the afterdinner entertainments—the forming into a ring, the singing and moving together," and became the essence of slave festivals and holiday celebrations.[90]

Apparently there were secular ring shouts, too. Pianist James P. Johnson remembers them in late-nineteenth-century New Brunswick, New Jersey: "I'd wake up as a child and hear an old-fashioned ring-shout going on downstairs. Somebody would be playing a guitar or jew's-harp or maybe a mandolin, and the dancing went to 'The Spider and the Bed-Bug Had a Good Time' or 'Susie.' They danced around in a shuffle and then they would shove a man or a woman out into the center and clap hands."[91]

Through call and response, rhythmic and metrical complexity, body connectedness, satire, stylization and, most of all, improvisation within a collective setting, Africans and African Americans formed community, balanced the needs of the individual against those of the community, and kept community united in ritual and play.

African-derived American Culture

MUSIC

Although listeners wondered about African origins of African American music, one of the earliest scholars to do so in writing was music critic and scholar H. E. Krehbiel. Inspired by the dancing of Dahomeans at the World's Fair in Chicago in 1893, Krehbiel concluded in *Afro-American Folksongs: A Study in Racial and National Music* (1914) that the folk songs of his study contained "essential elements" from Africa that were not the result of the "negro's innate faculty for imitation" but rather reflected "peculiarities of scale and structure" that must have come from Africa.[92] Krehbiel's attribution of "innate rhythmical capacity" to Africans sits poorly today, but Krehbiel also asked serious questions about the African origins of unusual melodic intervals, complicated rhythmic figures, the persistent associations between music and dance, and the predominance of satire songs or "musical lampooning."[93] Krehbiel apologized for a lack of "adequate material" for detailed study of African influences on African American music. "Who has gone to Africa to capture a melody?" he asked. "No one. Yet a few scores or hundreds of phonographic records of music would be worth more to science and art to-day than a thousand stuffed skins of animals robbed of life by the bullets of a Roosevelt."[94]

Though James Weldon Johnson did not go to Africa to stalk melodies, it was in keeping with Krehbiel's suggestion that he and his brother J. Rosamond Johnson (the popular song-writing team composed "Lift Every Voice and Sing," commonly known as the African American National Anthem) published *The First Book of Negro Spirituals* (1925) and *The Second Book of Negro Spirituals* (1926), two volumes important not only for the music they captured but for the remarkable preface (excerpted in this volume), a daring cultural assessment of "America's only folk music" and an assertion of its Africanness.

Other writers from the twenties wrote around the connections between African American music and dance and Africa. Henry O. Osgood's *So This Is Jazz* (1926) suggested that the physicality of jazz musicians' playing linked them to "the 'ring shout,' the dances of religious frenzy or ecstasy, without question of African origin."[95] But Osgood followed this train of thought no further. Maud Cuney-Hare's *Negro Musicians and Their Music* (1936) began with chapters on African music and African song, and she supposed that "the feelings of the Negroes in America were expressed in the manner of the primitive music of Africa," who voiced their "homesickness in a medium familiar to them."[96] Cuney-Hare identified "intricacy of rhythm" and satire as elements found in "true African song," but did not try to pin down what exactly accounted for the distinctive sound of Negro music.[97]

In *The Myth of the Negro Past* (1941) anthropologist Melville Herskovits criticized Krehbiel for his insufficient data (which Krehbiel himself had admitted). Krehbiel failed to make "detailed study of African musical style," and instead relied "on what he could glean from travelers' accounts and other nonmusical works."[98] Reluctant to assert positive Africanisms without more substantial study of African music, Herskovits nevertheless noted three important traits of African music: the integration of song and dance throughout Africa, the call-and-response pattern, and the prominence of the rhythmic element in African music.[99]

A decade and a half later, Marshall Stearns tallied Africanisms in his *The Story of Jazz*: "complicated rhythms, the use of the falsetto break, blue tonality, and the inevitable call-and-response pattern," and the preponderance of satire in what he called "signifying songs." He heard these songs of "loving insults" in New Orleans, and noted, "In West Africa, these numbers are called songs of allusion and the people at whom they are directed actually pay the singers to stop singing and go away." Stearns also commented on competitiveness in jazz, illustrated with an incident from a concert. "Following trumpeter Dizzy Gillespie, the saxophonist Charlie Parker astonished his colleagues at a Carnegie Hall concert in 1950 by repeating Gillespie's complicated phrases, wringing them out, and hanging them up to dry with additional embellishments—in the same time interval."[100] Not until the 1980s did scholars again note this connection between the "signifying" songs of allusion and the competitive "signifying" of jazz musicians.[101] On top of these fresh interpretations, Stearns made the even more stunning assertion that since 1900, the "over-all direction" of American popular music had "switched from European elements *dominating*

African elements to European elements *being influenced* by a new combination dominated by African elements."[102]

Two more books of the 1960s continued the search for Africanisms, each focusing on a different type of music. In *Negro Folk Music, U.S.A.* (1963) folklorist Harold Courlander repeated Herskovits's findings, mentioned the use of falsetto (as had Stearns), and added timbral variations as an African feature.[103] In 1968, Gunther Schuller's *Early Jazz* analyzed rhythm, form, harmony, melody, timbre, and improvisation in American jazz, finding African characteristics in all. Schuller identified African "democratization of rhythmic values," or accenting weak beats, along with polymetric and polyrhythmic time relationships in the African American approach to rhythm, as well as a highly developed ability to feel subtle rhythmic deviations. Structural Africanisms Schuller identified included the call-and-response pattern, repeated refrain, and chorus format, while he noted African parallel fourths, fifths, and thirds in scalar and melodic patterns. As for timbre, Schuller noted not only timbral variations but the way in which African and African American musicians use timbral variation to establish individuality.[104] But it was a book by a poet that made the biggest waves in African American music in that decade.

In one sense, *Blues People* (1963) by Amiri Baraka (then LeRoi Jones) repeated observations of Krehbiel, Herskovits, and Cuney-Hare, as he identified African rhythmic qualities, vocal techniques, antiphonal technique, competitive games and songs, and indirection or "a tendency towards obliquity and ellipsis."[105] But where previous writers had focused on one genre of African American music in isolation, such as jazz or folk music, Baraka insisted that any form of African American music had to be studied in relation to all others and within a larger cultural context. For Baraka "the survival of the *system* of African music is much more significant than the existence of a few isolated and finally superfluous features."[106] Toward the end of his book, Baraka stated, "The idea of the Negro's having 'roots' and that they are a valuable possession, rather than the source of ineradicable shame, is perhaps the profoundest change within the Negro consciousness since the early part of the century."[107] This idea alone would have made Baraka's book revolutionary, but like Stearns, Baraka went beyond claiming African ancestors for African American music and extended this heritage to the whole of the United States: "The notable fact is that the only so-called popular music in this country of any real value is of African derivation."[108]

Scholars at the Symposium in Black Music held at Indiana University in 1967 agreed that all kinds of African American music are related and that similar practices may be found in gospel music, jazz, work songs, and the blues. They defined black music as "music which is, in whole or significant part, part of the musical tradition of peoples of African descent."[109] Then, in 1971, Eileen Southern published *The Music of Black Americans: A History*, beginning with a section on African heritage and continuing with an emphatic declaration: "The prevailing 'myth of the Negro past'—that enslavement caused the blacks to lose their every vestige of the African heritage—is nowhere more firmly refuted than in the areas of music and dance and, more specifically, than by the occurrence of the slave festivals."[110] Southern also noted the important role women played in sustaining African traditions through singing and storytelling.

Finally, to the now-familiar principles of rhythmic and metrical contrast (or complexity), percussive approach, call-and-response, and engagement of the body, composer Olly Wilson added the useful phrase the "heterogeneous sound ideal" (see pp. 160, this volume) to describe a musical approach that values and strives to create a "kaleidoscopic range of dramatically contrasting qualities of sound (timbre) in both vocal and instrumental music."[111] Thus Baraka's idea of a unified body of heterogeneous musical styles reappeared in Wilson's theory of sound itself in music of African origins, and as it turns out, the concept of heterogeneity has been fundamental to developing a sense of African American expressive culture as a unified field of study.

As the 1960s marked an upswing in the effort to define "black music" in a rigorously theoretical fashion, it was also a period of intentionally interdisciplinary approaches to the study of African American culture. Following *Blues People*, Baraka reexamined African American literature in light of African American music and decided the two forms had been developing in contrary directions. According to Baraka in his essay "Myth of a Negro Literature," African American writers such as Jean Toomer, Richard Wright, Ralph Ellison, and James Baldwin were mere imitators of "white models" and "cultivators" of white middlebrow and middle-class literary values.[112] By contrast, he argued in *Blues People*, African American musicians had developed a truly black form of expression that owed nothing to white oppressors.[113] Throughout his 1966 *Home* and 1969 volume *Black Fire*, edited with Larry Neal, Baraka continued to argue against black literature produced in the shadow of "double-consciousness," claiming black music as the model for all African American artists. "Listen to James Brown scream," Baraka and Neal demanded. "Ask yourself then: Have you ever heard a Negro poet sing like that?"[114]

While Baraka and Neal argued for black music and against black literature, they were busy creating black theater, a development which, in C. W. E. Bigsby's words, "placed drama at the heart of the Black Arts movement."[115] Baraka's 1964 play *Dutchman* explored in dramatic parable the aesthetic of political and social alienation, and his Black Arts Repertory Theater in Harlem was the midwife to the Black Arts movement of the 1960s. In his 1964 manifesto "The Revolutionary Theatre," Baraka proposed the guiding principles for a radical theater that would focus on black subjects and unify and motivate a black audience.[116] As Kimberly W. Bentson notes, Baraka's manifesto sketched the trajectory of what might be considered the aesthetic of modern black drama: the movement from *mimesis*, or representation of an action, to *methexis*, that is, communal participation in the action. Bentson describes the process as a shift from drama to ritual, one that transforms the spectator to a "participatory member of tribal or, in this case, national ceremony which affirms a shared vision."[117] Recent symposia organized by August Wilson and Ed Bullins on the subject of black theater continue to explore the issues Baraka set forth in his 1960s writings.[118]

In critical theory, Baraka was instrumental in the creation of what became the "black aesthetic" of the 1970s, as well as the "vernacularism" of the 1980s, demanding that African American literature and music be examined in the context of the culture that gave rise to it, with particular focus on the oral traditions of storytelling, sermonizing, and music of all sorts—sacred and secular.[119] Following Baraka, Addison Gayle, Jr., formalized the idea of black aesthetic theory in his two anthologies *Black Expression* and *The Black Aesthetic*.[120] In *The Black Aesthetic*, Gayle renewed Baraka's oppositional stance: "The serious black artist of today is at war with the American society as few have been throughout American history."[121] As Gayle defined it, the black aesthetic had a strong prescriptive and political agenda, "a corrective—a means of helping black people out of the polluted mainstream of Americanism, and offering logical, reasoned arguments as to why [a black writer] should not desire to join the ranks of a Norman Mailer or a William Styron."[122] Later generations of African American cultural critics have continued to work from a vernacular position, which Gayle called the logical conclusion of the black aesthetic: "unique art derived from unique cultural experiences mandates unique critical tools for evaluation."[123] Significantly, this black aesthetic was not yet Africanized. The sole African-based essay in *The Black Aesthetic* was Ortiz W. Waltons's "Analysis of the African and the Western Aesthetics."

Going beyond theorizing a black aesthetic, Albert Murray's *Stomping the Blues* appeared in 1976 as the full embodiment of this position. But as Murray had already established in *The Omni-Americans*, his intent was not to examine the nature of African American arts but to put the whole of American culture in its proper perspective. For Murray, African American music, dance, and writing are so deeply embedded in and expressive of the American experience that they constitute the prototypical American expression. With the title *Stomping the Blues*, Murray assumed interconnectedness between music and dance, and the book's thematic (rather than chronological) organization and jazzlike writing style reinforced the notion that the meaning of African American music is to be found within a social context. (See pp. 96–109, this volume.)

Likewise, although literary critic Houston Baker concentrated on the links between music and literature in *Blues, Ideology, and Afro-American Literature*, he emphasized the connectedness of all African American cultural expressions. Here Baker set forth a vernacular theory of African American literature. Rejecting the European universalist approach, Baker instead proposed a study of literature that connected it to the blues and examined both within the African American cultural matrix.

In particular, Baker used the blues as a "trope"—a recurring set of images and ideas—to describe the overwhelmingly synthetic nature of African American cultural expression. "Combining work songs, group seculars, field hollers, sacred harmonies, proverbial wisdom, folk philosophy, political commentary, ribald humor, elegiac lament, and much more, they constitute an amalgam that seems always to have been in motion in America."[124] Baker suggested adopting Michel Foucault's approach, focusing on the discourse—rather than a body of knowledge—and its fundamental unit, the statement, describing African American writers such as Toni Morrison, Jean Toomer, and others as literary performers of the African American musical vernacular.[125]

Henry Louis Gates, Jr., continued the interest in vernacularism in his 1987 volume *Figures in Black: Words, Signs, and the 'Racial' Self*, in which he proposed a theory of interpretation based on the African American (discursive) vernacular tradition of "signifying." *The Signifying Monkey* (1988) is Gates's fullest explication of this theory. "Signifyin(g)" (the parenthetical "g" denotes the African American vernacular practice) is a satirical African American oral tradition that assumes many forms, such as "marking, loud-talking, testifying, calling out (of one's name), sounding, rapping, playing the dozens."[126] Signifyin(g) can be taunting, teasing, or insulting. But it operates indirectly, through metaphor and simile, often claiming only to be repeating what one has heard "through the grapevine." One can signify on another through an individual comment, but more often signifyin(g) takes place within a competitive context, in which each player tries to outperform the previous one, as Charlie Parker signified on Dizzy Gillespie. To "signify" is to repeat, revise, reverse, or transform what has come before, continually raising the stakes in a kind of expressive poker, as in "I'll see your insult and raise you one more." Signifyin(g) is inherently dialogical, to use Mikhail Bakhtin's word, always existing within a relationship with an other.

Gates's extension of this category of "black rhetorical tropes" to a theory of culturally specific literary analysis was both resonant and multi-functional. As it is possible to signify in different ways and at different levels, so it is possible to theorize *through* signifying.[127] And music scholars were quick to signify on Gates. Samuel A. Floyd, Jr., who has actively promoted the idea of "integrative studies," was one of the first music scholars to apply Gates's theoretical work to African American music, seizing Sterling Stuckey's idea of the ring shout as the institution through which Africanisms in African American music were transmitted.[128]

In 1991, Floyd published the article "Ring Shout! Literary Studies, Historical Studies, and Black Music Inquiry" (reprinted in this volume), in which he detailed "musical practices from throughout black culture [that] converged in the spiritual"—practices he called, after Gates, Baker, and musicologist Lawrence Kramer, "tropes."[129] In his *The Power of Black Music* Floyd refined and categorized these ideas and others to outline what is nothing less than an aesthetic of African American music. Continuing in the vein of Baraka, Wilson, and Gates, Floyd proposed a vernacular theory of African American music, one that insisted on the "compelling cultural and musical continuity . . . between all the musical genres of the black cultural experience."[130]

For Floyd, musical signifying is "troping": "the transformation of preexisting musical material by trifling with it, teasing it, or censuring it. Musical Signifyin(g) is the rhetorical use of preexisting material as a means of demonstrating respect for or poking fun at a musical style, process, or practice through parody, pastiche, implication, indirection, humor, tone play or word play, the illusion of speech or narration, or other troping mechanisms.[131] As with verbal signifying, musical signifying may be synchronic—a response in the musical moment—or diachronic—a dialogue with historical predecessors. When a congregation or chorus responds to the gospel singer's "I was guilty" with the affirmative "Guilty!" or "Huh!" they are signifyin(g) in the moment. When Ella Fitzgerald inserts "A tisket, a tasket" in a song performance she is signifyin(g) diachronically on her first hit record. When Charlie Parker plays the "Woody Woodpecker" theme in the middle of a solo, he may be signifyin(g) on the craziness of the moment or on American popular culture in general.

In *To Be or Not . . . to Bop*, Dizzy Gillespie explains that he owed much of his playing to Roy Eldridge, who derived his playing from Louis Armstrong. "I hardly ever listened to Louis, but was always aware of where Roy's inspiration came from," Gillespie said. At the same time, Gillespie explained, he developed his own style. "A style of playing is only the way you get from one note to another, since the same notes are there for everybody. How you get from one note to another is the style."[132] Further, Gillespie recognized that younger trumpet players would carry his influence forward, absorbing what they could and modifying it to their own purposes. "If he's younger than me and playing trumpet, he's following in my footsteps," Gillespie said.[133] The evolution Gillespie describes is one of diachronic signifyin(g). Yet at any given moment of playing, while Gillespie was building on the legacies of Armstrong and Eldridge, and creating a legacy of his own, he was responding to all the forces of the moment—musical, critical, economic, and the listening audience—and signifyin(g) on them, synchronically.

"Call-Response" is Floyd's master trope, emphasizing the inherently dialogical nature of African American music. He offers the phrase, "Dance, Drum, and Song," as a way of describing total engagement in music—body and song—or the trope of the whole person. But he also uses the phrase to discuss African and African American music's communal context, as an element of African American cultural unity, and as an expression of an African world view. The concept of "Dance, Drum, and Song" could be used as a structural trope for the African American body-centered aesthetic of interrelatedness. Floyd prefers the term "cultural memory" to that of aesthetic, insisting that though an aesthetic may provide a mechanism for transferring expressive culture, "the arbiters in all things human are the people: only they have memories."[134] The term underscores Ralph Ellison's comment in *Shadow and Act* that "Negro American consciousness is not a product (as so often seems true of so many American groups) of a will to historical forgetfulness. It is a product of our memory, sustained and constantly reinforced by events, by our watchful waiting, and by our hopeful suspension of final judgment as to the meaning of our grievances."[135]

DANCE

The opening pages of Marshall and Jean Stearns's *Jazz Dance* (reprinted in this volume) describe a meeting in the 1950s of dancers from three different countries: Asadata Dafora from Sierra Leone, West Africa; Geoffrey Holder from Trinidad, West Indies; and Al Minns and Leon James from the Savoy Ballroom, New York. Minns and James began with a demonstration of twenty or so African American dances from their repertory, and the "astonishing" results were that no sooner had the African Americans begun a dance than the Trinidadian or African dancer would jump to his feet and execute a "related version of his own." When Dafora performed the Shika dance of Nigeria—called the Banda in Trinidad, and the Oleke in West Africa—Stearns recognized the American Shimmy.[136] Parts of the Lindy, or Jitterbug, could be found in a Shango dance from the West Indies and in a dance of the Ejor people of Africa. The Charleston resembled a dance Trinidadians call King Sailor and West African Ibo people call the Obolo. When Minns and James performed the

Snake Hips, introduced by Earl Tucker at the Cotton Club in Harlem in the 1920s, Holder and Dafora agreed that the dance was the same as one called the Congo in Trinidad and Africa.[137]

As in African dance, vernacular American dances of African origin are flat-footed dances that favor gliding, dragging, or shuffling steps.[138] As African dances featured bent knees and waist, so it is with African American–influenced dance.[139] African dance is centrifugal: it explodes outward from the hips. The leg moves from the hip, not from the knee. Likewise, shoulder and head movement appear as the end result of motion beginning at the hips. The pelvic thrust itself is unknown in European usage, either in vernacular or classical dance. Yet the pelvic thrust is the soul, if not the heart, of American popular dance, as anyone knows who is remotely aware of the censored Elvis Presley appearance on the Ed Sullivan Show.[140] It is equally important in modern American "art" dance, from Martha Graham to George Balanchine to Geoffrey Holder. When so many specific African dance movements survive in American dance, we must suspect the underlying aesthetic has also survived.

Kariamu Welsh Asante, former artistic director of the National Dance Company of Zimbabwe, makes no distinction between African and African American cultural forms, stating, "Africans are all people of African descent." Asante identifies the foundations of the African dance aesthetic as seven "senses": polyrhythm; polycentrism; curvilinear form, shape, and structure; dimensionality; epic memory; repetition; and holism. Most of these "senses" are self-explanatory; the fourth—dimensionality—is another variation on the idea of the "invisible conductor." Asante's dimensionality refers not to "measured dimension" but to "perceived dimension," a "something extra that is present in harmony with the music, dance, or sculpture." It is the dimension audience members create as they reverberate with the dancers and musicians in the moment of performance.[141]

In *Digging the Africanist Presence in American Performance*, Brenda Dixon Gottschild similarly uses "Africanist" to mean all forms of expression bearing an African influence. For her Africanist aesthetic in performance, Gottschild lists general principles: (1) Africanist art and dance embrace conflict; (2) is polycentric and polyrhythmic; (3) is full of "high-affect juxtaposition"—the development of contrast beyond accepted European standards; (4) is full of power, vitality, flexibility, drive, attack, and intensity; and (5) follows the aesthetic of the cool.[142]

The most extensive survey of African American vernacular dance to follow Marshall and Jean Stearns's *Jazz Dance* is Jaqui Malone's *Steppin' on the Blues: The Visible Rhythms of African American Dance*.[143] Vernacular dance is one of America's "most important contributions to world culture," says Malone, yet even dance historians ignore it.[144] Malone identifies the hallmarks of American vernacular dance as "improvisation and spontaneity, propulsive rhythm, call-and-response patterns, self-expression, elegance, and control," and she traces these elements to their African American and African origins.[145] Malone's list includes four of Thompson's five traits of African music and dance (dominance of a percussive concept of performance, multiple meter, apart playing and dancing, call and response). She devotes a separate chapter to the importance of satire in early African American music and dance, calling on Thompson's fifth element: songs of allusion/dances of derision.

Malone emphasizes the link between African dance and African music. "Most European conceptions of art would separate music from dance and both music and dance from the social situations that produced them," says Malone. Africans, on the other hand, "experience music as part of a multidimensional social event," in which "articulating the beat through motor response" helps everyone feel more involved.[146] Malone agrees with Albert Murray that African American dance halls serve as secular temples "where rituals of purification, affirmation, and celebration are held."[147]

Hip hop has inspired new thinking about African American popular dance as part of a cultural movement that extends from music and dance to clothing and graphic art. Like other forms of expressive culture in African America, hip hop places a premium on developing a new, individual style. Fab Five Freddy, an early rapper and graffiti writer, says, "You make a new style. That's what life on the street is all about. . . . That's what makes it so important, that's what makes it feel so good—that pressure on you to be the best. Or to try to be the best. To develop a new style nobody can deal with."[148] Thus the dialogue between the individual and community continues through stylistic innovations.

Hip-hop combines a fistful of African American aesthetic factors. The rhymed satirical patter takes off from children's rhyming plays and games and adult signifyin(g) poems; the dancing is an athletic stylization of many forms of African American dance, from children's "jumps" to, occasionally, tap. Early break dancers arranged themselves in a circle, with the soloist in the middle. The circle maintains support, but also exerts pressure on the soloist to perform with ever-increasing virtuosity or stylistic uniqueness. In the tradition of African dance and the ring shout, soloists return to their place in the circle. Hip hop dance is competitive, using the community in its traditional functions of support and confrontation, for the good of the performance.

Tricia Rose identifies a set of aesthetic coordinators in the hip hop expressions of rap music, break dancing, and graffiti. Specifically, she refers to a conceptual framework of flow, layering, and ruptures in line to describe the general continuities of movement composed of many disjunctures.[149] Rap music layers a rhythmic text on dominantly percussive music which emphasizes breaks and ruptures. Yet the overall effect is of a piece that could flow forever, as long as the artists continue to create verses. Similarly, the overall flow of hip hop depends on many popping, snapping, quick, and disjointed individual movements, strung together one after the other like a pop-bead necklace. Spray-painted graffiti, a flowing medium in itself, uses letters that slant forward, flow into each other, and yet assault the eye through dramatic colors and sudden visual ruptures. Individuals build on the past, striving for uniqueness, for innovation within convention, using rhythmic complexity, voice and body, in dialogue with others.

As Shane White and Graham White point out in *Stylin': African Expressive Culture from Its Beginnings to the Zoot Suit* (1998)—see their contribution to this volume, pp. 434–452—the aesthetic on which hip hop builds represents not only an alternative set of cultural values but a long history of "provocation" and "celebration."[150] Generations of African Americans admired a parade Marshall's "improvisational skill, his physical dexterity, his unexpected changes of direction and dramatic juxtaposition of different marching steps or sequences."[151] In public celebrations appeared the "totality of black style": improvisation, yes, but also "vibrancy, aliveness, and constant surprise," parody and ironic reversal, and heterogeneous diversity."[152] From cross-cultural study, Alan Lomax concluded that parades and other public celebrations—the nonverbal performance tradition—preserved the African aesthetic "virtually intact in African America." Lomax's description of this aesthetic is remarkably similar to Rose's description of hip-hop: "velocity and changefulness . . . making the most use of marked shifts of level, direction, limb use, pacing, and energy in dance . . . along with the greatest facility in shifting style collectively in close coordination."[153] Recent scholarship on the ways in which black men, women, and children have presented their bodies offers much support for the existence of a "distinctive and identifiable African American aesthetic."[154]

SIGNIFYIN(G)

As Henry Louis Gates, Jr. has noted, irony is a principal characteristic of signifying. So has satire been a staple of African expressive culture. Africans improvised satirical songs about private grievances and personal gossip, and marked by social and political criticism. Satirical songs were part of many rites, but were also sung during informal evening entertainments and during group work. Such songs reduced stress by airing frustrations publicly, in a socially approved way. Satire was important to managing communal equilibrium and functioned as a kind of "communal psychological medicine."[155]

Satire survived in the Americas and has been documented in songs from St.

Christopher, Jamaica, Haiti, Cuba, Brazil, and Trinidad. In jazz, soloists often add satire by "quoting" from popular tunes or jazz standards, commenting, or signifyin(g), on the present situation through musical references. The persistence of the satirical mode manifests a cultural preference for drama as a way of getting ideas across. In the United States, satirical dramas, or play-acting, were part of Saturday night dances in Charleston in 1772.[156] The "cake-walk," a staple of minstrelsy and nineteenth- and twentieth-century ragtime song and dance, was originally a Sunday African American burlesque of stiff-bodied white dancers, and it persists in the exaggerated drum major's strut. Satirical folk tales abound, providing clever social criticism and also allowing individuals to put a unique stamp on a collective text.

Jumps—children's dances and games—use irony and satirical spins in their chanted or sung rhymed texts; "thus all dramatic conflict is worked through in public," said Bess Hawes. Zora Neale Hurston wrote, "If a man or woman is a facile hurler of threats, why should he or she not show their wares to the community? Hence the holding of all quarrels and fights in the open. One relieves one's pent-up anger and at the same time earns laurels at intimidation. Besides, one does the community a service."[157]

In his classic study *Deep Down in the Jungle*, Roger Abrahams identified two groups of "good talkers," preachers and street-corner bards, whom he declared hated each other.[158] The street corner bard, or "man of words," is a signifier, specializing in satirical toasts (stories), insults, and joking, but with command of a traditional store of material, an improvisational impulse, and an urge toward developing a personal style that greatly resembles the efforts of his counterpart, the preacher. For the most part, this early work of Abrahams offered a psychosocial interpretation of narrative folklore, with only a hint that some of this cultural endowment may have owed something to African traditions.

A later piece by Abrahams, "Rapping and Capping: Black Talk as Art" analyzed certain black speaking styles (elsewhere called "signifyin[g]") as art and discussed displays of verbal virtuosity as performances of a cultural style.[159] Abrahams also identified African antecedents for this perspective. Most important, Abrahams spent some time on the effect of such "performances" on the audience, the community. "The attention of the audience is gained through a willingness of the performer to involve himself totally in the performance and to call for the audience to do so as strongly. This the artful talker does by 'dancing' his talk, by dramatizing himself and his argument in physical ways."[160] The verbal performer combines body and words and draws attention to himself to engage the sensibility of his audience. Emphasizing Robert Farris Thompson's phrasing, Abrahams called this expressive style an "'aesthetic of the cool': a program of interaction which stresses ability to assert verbal control in the midst of noise and contest, through an ability to keep your wits about you and to capitalize on whatever verbal opportunities arise."[161] Abrahams thus identifies dialogic interaction, individual virtuosity and style, and improvisation as keys to this "cool" aesthetic.

Henry H. Mitchell described several elements of a unique "Black style" of preaching in his book, *Black Preaching*, all of which stem from what he called "freedom of expression" and "ritual freedom." Freedom of expression within the African American church (he focused on the Baptist, Methodist, and Church of God in Christ as "Black" churches) gives "high importance to the feelings of the individual" and allows men, women, and children in the worship service to express their devotion and emotion in their own unique ways. Ritual freedom, or the eschewing of a formal agenda, allows worshipers and worship leaders to adjust their practice to the demands of the moment. Mitchell believed such freedoms within African American churches counteracted limitations of freedom of expression in all other areas of life. For Mitchell, a preacher, the African American aesthetic in religious experience was a form of active resistance to oppression. Through freedom of expression and ritual freedom, "interpretation is enriched and selfhood asserted and strengthened as it may be in few places in the Black world." Great emphasis on "personal style" is one of the hallmarks of Black preaching. As Mitchell puts it, developing a "striking mannerism or trademark" may not be a necessity for the Black preacher, "but it is certainly not a handicap." In the Black pulpit, "individuality is celebrated."[162]

Though Mitchell believes there are some similarities between African American music and African American preaching, he does not believe rhythm is one of them. But the call-and-response "pattern" and the "ensuing dialogue" it creates is "the epitome of creative worship." Mitchell further suggests that call-and-response is a reason for the persistence of so many Africanisms in African American culture. "Mass participation works to increase retention," he asserts.[163] Although some white churches, such as southern white Pentecostal churches, also engage in active response during sermonizing, Mitchell stressed that African American responses are much more widely varied—not only "Amen," but also "Tell it!" "That's right!" "Un-huh!" and "So true!"

Mitchell also noted the use of musical tone or chanting in preaching, similar to Olly Wilson's notion of "timbral variation," which usually enters a sermon toward the end, near a climactic moment. Nearly every American has heard the "I Have a Dream" speech of Martin Luther King Jr. (August 28, 1963). In this speech, King stresses his points through timbral variations. The repeated phrase "I have a dream" serves as punctuation, hypnotic suggestion, and call to action. His delivery is so repetitive that one fairly sways to each return of the phrase, "I have a dream."[164] Thus King uses the African techniques of timbral variation, bodily movement, and end-repetition—a kind of call-and-response—to stir the listener, draw his audience into a unified community, and simultaneously connect his contemporary speech with the historical tradition of the African American church. Like the African satiric performer, like the solo gospel singer calling to a chorus and the preacher calling to a congregation, the orator calls to the audience. In turn, the audience responds, assents, reaffirms, and bears him up with their vocalizations. It makes sense that African American oration would draw on the African American sacred tradition. It is equally reasonable that African American expression in all its many forms drew on an African performance sensibility.[165]

While studying African American culture of the late 1930s, I noticed that the word "jump" began to appear regularly in African American swing tunes in 1937, about the time "jumping" air steps appeared in the Lindy Hop, and the same year the jump shot began to be a force in basketball. "One O'Clock Jump," "Jumping at the Woodside," "The Apple Jump," "The Jeep is Jumping," "Jump for Me," "Up Jumped the Devil" are but a few of the many post-1937 jazz and blues tunes using the word. At a time of great American enthusiasm for speed and flight, jumping was an airborne expression that signified joy but also blackness to many Americans.

Looking further, I discovered that ballrooms regularly booked basketball games before dances or when no dance was scheduled, so that jumping in black basketball, dance, and swing music was happening in many of the same places at the same time. Chicago's Savoy Ballroom had its own team—the Savoy Big Five (who became the Harlem Globetrotters), as did New York's Renaissance Casino, whose team, the Rens, won the 1939 World Championship in professional basketball. In all these places, basketball players were among those dancing after games, which raises the question: who inspired whom to jump?

Whether the cultural exchange flowed from musicians to dancers to basketball players, or from basketball players to dancers to musicians, that there was some sort of connection between music, dance, and sport is undeniable. And as white observers began to imitate and adopt jump tunes, the Lindy Hop and the jump shot as their own, these African American expressions gradually transformed African popular culture, in ways that persist today in rock and roll, popular dance, and of course, basketball.

My jump study suggests that focusing on sites where music, dance, and sport intersect reveals a new vision of African American and American culture, one that stresses relation and interaction, and one that prompts us to ask new questions about the underlying structures of human behavior and cultural expression.[166] By establishing a common ground among different areas of cultural expression, the readings in this volume present a strong foundation for such inquiry.

Readers will notice some holes in this collection. Portia K. Maultsby, Tricia Rose, and Grace Sims Holt note gender differences among gospel and hip hop performers and members of African American congregations, and reading more such work could help us understand the influence of gender and sexual orientation on African American expressions. Gerald Early, Michael Eric Dyson, and Bertram D. Ashe question how class differences, black-white interactions, and audience reception might affect cultural production, issues that deserve further exploration. There are no pieces in this volume on visual art, film, humor, or theater, areas that are under study and merit our attention.

This collection cannot exhaust the field, for it is vast, but these readings present some key moments in the ongoing argument for and historiography of an African American aesthetic. More important, they call to readers and scholars for response.

NOTES

1. Quoted in David W. Stowe, "Uncolored People," *Lingua Franca* 6 (September-October 1996): 71.

2. Johnny Otis, *Upside Your Head! Rhythm and Blues on Central Avenue* (Hanover, N.H.: Wesleyan University Press, 1993), 117.

3. Lawrence Kramer, *Music as Cultural Practice, 1800–1900* (Berkeley: University of California Press, 1990), 6; Gerald Lyn Early, *The Culture of Bruising: Essays on Prizefighting, Literature, and Modern American Culture* (Hopewell, N.J.: Ecco Press, 1994), 154.

4. Gerald Lyn Early, "American Prizefighter," in his *Tuxedo Junction: Essays on American Culture* (New York: Ecco Press, 1989), 184. This chapter is also reprinted on pages 379–387 herein.

5. Early also discusses boxing as a unifying trope in Ellison's *Invisible Man* ("The Black Intellectual and the Sport of Prizefighting," in *Culture of Bruising*).

6. Early, *Culture of Bruising*, 33.

7. Michael Novak, *The Joy of Sports: End Zones, Bases, Baskets, Balls, and the Consecration of the American Spirit* (New York: Basic Books, 1976), 105.

8. Arthur R. Ashe Jr., *A Hard Road to Glory: Basketball* (New York: Amistad, 1988), 24.

9. Nelson George, *Elevating the Game: Black Men and Basketball* (New York: HarperCollins, 1992), xviii.

10. John Edgar Wideman, *Brothers and Keepers* (New York: Vintage Books, 1995 [1984]), 226.

11. I present evidence for this statement in my essay, "Jump for Joy: the Jump Trope in African America, 1937–1941," *Prospects* (1999).

12. Clarence Gaines, telephone interview with author, March 5, 1996.

13. Robert W. Peterson, *Cages to Jump Shots: Pro Basketball's Early Years* (New York: Oxford University Press, 1990), 109.

14. Bill Russell, *Second Wind: The Memoirs of an Opinionated Man* (New York: Random House, 1979), 63–64.

15. Arthur Ashe, quoted in George, *Elevating the Game*, xix.

16. George, *Elevating the Game*, xix.

17. Early, "American Prizefighter," 182; Chris Mead on Joe Louis, cited in Gerald Early, *Tuxedo Junction*, 177.

18. Ibid., 179.

19. John Edgar Wideman, "Michael Jordan Leaps the Great Divide," *Esquire*, November 1990, 144–45. This article is also reprinted on pages 388–406 herein.

20. Ibid., 141.

21. Cornel West, *Race Matters* (Boston: Beacon Press, 1993), 105.

22. Ralph Ellison, "The Charlie Christian Story," in *Shadow and Act* (New York: Random House, 1972), 234.

23. Roger D. Abrahams, *Singing the Master: The Emergence of African American Culture in the Plantation South* (New York: Pantheon, 1992), 104 (emphasis added).

24. Charles Salzberg, *From Set Shot to Slam Dunk: The Glory Days of Basketball in the Words of Those Who Played It* (New York: E. P. Dutton, 1987), 51.

25. Ken Shouler, *The Experts Pick Basketball's Best 50 Players in the Last 50 Years* (New York: Addax, 1998), 60.

26. See Martin Taragano, *Basketball Biographies: 434 U.S. Players, Coaches, and Contributors to the Game, 1891–1990* (Jefferson, N.C.: McFarland & Co., 1991), 190.

27. Doron P. Levin, "Joe Montana, a Study in Good Management," *New York Times*, January 23, 1994, F11.

28. Peter Drucker, *Managing in a Time of Great Change* (New York: Dutton, Truman Talley Books, 1995), 98–101.

29. Shelley Fisher Fishkin, "Interrogating 'Whiteness,' Complicating 'Blackness': Remapping American Culture," *American Quarterly* 47 (September 1995): 428–66.

30. Acknowledging the impact of African aesthetics and philosophy in American culture might require, among other changes, offering courses in African history alongside European history, a step many institutions of higher learning have yet to take.

31. John Edgar Wideman, "Architectonics of Fiction," *Callaloo* 13 (Winter 1990): 43.

32. Meyer Schapiro, "Style," in *Anthropology Today*, ed. A. L. Kroeber (Chicago: University of Chicago Press, 1953), 287; cited in Charles Keil and Steven Feld, *Music Grooves: Essays and Dialogues* (Chicago: University of Chicago Press, 1994), 132.

33. John F. Szwed, "Afro-American Musical Adaptation," in *Afro-American Anthropology: Contemporary Perspectives*, ed. Norman E. Whitten Jr., and John F. Szwed (New York: Free Press, 1970), 220.

34. Gary Tomlinson, "Cultural Dialogics and Jazz: A White Historian Signifies," *Black Music Research Journal* 11 (Fall 1991): 239.

35. Ian Hunter, "Aesthetics and Cultural Studies," in *Cultural Studies*, ed. Lawrence Grossberg, Gary Nelson, and Paul Treichler (New York: Routledge, Chapman and Hall, 1992), 348.

36. Albert Murray, *Stomping the Blues* (New York: McGraw-Hill, 1976), 90; Keil and Feld, *Music Grooves*, 132.

37. In 1926, Newbell Niles Puckett published *Folk Beliefs of the Southern Negro* (New York: Dover, 1969; reprint of 1926 edition), examining African carryovers in the Americas. That same year Erich von Hornbostel, head of the Phonogrammarchiv in Berlin, noted similarities between African and European folksongs in his "American Negro Songs," *International Review of Missions* 15 (1926). Carter G. Woodson in *The African Background Outlined: A Handbook for the Study of the Negro* (New York: Negro Universities Press, 1968; reprint of 1936 edition); W.E.B. Du Bois in *Black Folk, Then and Now: An Essay in the History and Sociology of the Negro Race* (New York: Holt, 1939); Guy Benton Johnson in *Folk Culture on St. Helena Island, South Carolina* (Chapel Hill: University of North Carolina Press, 1930) and, as part of the Federal Writers Project, in his preface to *Drums and Shadows: Survival Studies among the Georgia Coastal Negroes* (Athens: University of Georgia Press, 1940), preceded Melville J. Herskovits's *The Myth of the Negro Past* (Boston: Beacon Press, 1958; reprint of 1941 edition). Following Herskovits was his student Lorenzo Turner's *Africanisms in the Gullah Dialect* (New York: Arno Press, 1969; reprint of 1949 edition). Among anthropologists, Norman E. Whitten and John F. Szwed edited the anthology *Afro-American Anthropology: Contemporary Perspectives* in 1970 (New York: Free Press, 1970); and Sidney W. Mintz and Richard Price wrote *An Anthropological Approach to the Afro-American Past: A Caribbean Perspective* (Philadelphia: Institute for the Study of Human Issues, 1976). Peter Wood in *Black Majority: Negroes in Colonial South Carolina from 1670 through the Stono Rebellion* (New York: Alfred A. Knopf, 1974) and William D. Piersen in *Black Yankees: The Development of an Afro-American Subculture in Eighteenth-Century New England* (Amherst: University of Massachusetts Press, 1988) concentrated on Africanisms in colonial America. Lawrence W. Levine's *Black Culture and Black Consciousness: Afro-American Folk Thought from Slavery to Freedom* (New York: Oxford University Press, 1977); John W. Blassingame's *The Slave Community: Plantation Life in the Antebellum South* (New York: Oxford University Press, 1979); and Sterling Stuckey's *Slave Culture: Nationalist Theory and the Foundations of Black America* (New York: Oxford University Press, 1987) examined African retentions among slave men and women. Several works in the 1970s and 1980s explored African content in American culture, including Winifred K. Vass's *The Bantu Speaking Heritage of the United States* (Los Angeles: UCLA, Center for Afro-American Studies, 1979), Robert Farris Thompson and Joseph Cornet's *The Four Moments of the Sun: Kongo Art in Two Worlds* (Washington, D.C.: National Gallery of Art, 1981) and Thompson's *Flash of the Spirit: African and Afro-American Art and Philosophy* (New York: Random House, 1983). Roger D. Abrahams and John F. Szwed's *After Africa: Extracts from British Travel Accounts and Journals of the Seventeenth, Eighteenth, and Nineteenth Centuries Concerning the Slaves, Their Manners, and Customs in the British West Indies* (New Haven: Yale University Press, 1983) continued the exploration. For work prior to 1970, the introduction to *Afro-American Anthropology*, by editors Norman E. Whitten, Jr. and John F. Szwed, contains a wonderful overview.

38. Herskovits, *Myth of the Negro Past*, 263.

39. Ibid., 292.

40. Sidney W. Mintz and Richard Price, *The Birth of African-American Culture* (Boston: Beacon Press, 1976), 10, 11.

41. John S. Mbiti, *African Religions and Philosophy* (Garden City, N.Y.: Anchor Books, 1970 [1969]), 38.

42. Albert J. Raboteau, *Slave Religion: The "Invisible Institution" in the Antebellum South* (New York: Oxford University Press, 1978), 7.

43. Free Lee Hord (Mzee Lasana Okpara) and Jonathan Scott Lee, eds., *I Am Because We Are: Readings in Black Philosophy* (Amherst: University of Massachusetts Press, 1995), 1.

44. Samuel A. Floyd, Jr., uses the phrase, "Dance, Drum, and Song" to describe the multi-expressive process by which Africans engage the whole person and keep all members of the group involved. *The Power of Black Music: Interpreting Its History from Africa to the United States* (New York: Oxford University Press, 1995), 21.

45. Nathan Irvin Huggins, *Black Odyssey: The Afro-American Ordeal in Slavery* (New York: Pantheon, 1977), 77–8.

46. John Miller Chernoff, *African Rhythm and African Sensibility: Aesthetics and Social Action in African Musical Idioms* (Chicago: University of Chicago Press, 1979), 34. Chernoff's book superseded a previous landmark study, A. M. Jones's two-volume *Studies in African Music* (New York: Oxford University Press, 1959). Although Jones organized his volumes somewhat according to function and by different peoples in Africa, the first contains an entire chapter on the topic of "the homogeneity of African music."

47. Musicologist Peter Van der Merwe defined a similar set of fundamentals, which he phrased slightly differently: note positions versus note length (comparable to Chernoff's rhythmic emphasis and complexity); music and motion (Chernoff's connection of music to the body); speech, song, and instrumental sounds (linking of music and language); end-orientation and end-repetition (two varieties of call-response), and sense of dialogue (call-response). Peter Van der Merwe, *Origins of the Popular Style: The Antecedents of Twentieth-Century Music* (Oxford: Clarendon Press, 1989), 32–39.

48. Chernoff, *African Rhythm*, 35.

49. Ibid., 45, 42.

50. All but Blacking cited in ibid., 50–51. John Blacking, *How Musical Is Man?* (Seattle: University of Washington Press, 1973), 30. Blacking studied the Venda; Chernoff was based in Ghana.

51. Bessie Jones and Bess Lomax Hawes, *Step It Down: Games, Plays, Songs and Stories from the Afro-American Heritage* (Athens: University of Georgia Press, 1972), 20; Keil and Feld, *Music Grooves*, 24.

52. Floyd identifies two types of antiphony: call-and-response and call-and-refrain. *Power of Black Music*, 44. These are techniques Peter Van der Merwe terms end-orientation and end-repetition. *Origins of the Popular Style*, 32–39. Ortiz W. Walton described five varieties of antiphony: instrument-instrument, instrument-voice, instrument-chorus, solo voice–chorus, and vocal solo–instrument. "Contemporary Analysis," in *The Black Aesthetic*, ed. Addison Gayle (Garden City, N.Y.: Doubleday, 1971), 169. Similarly, Walton identifies three forms of polyphony: multi-rhythmic, multi-melodic, and multi-rhythm-multi-melody simultaneously (170).

53. "African musicians create in a balance through which they draw upon the depth of a tradition while they revitalize it and adapt it to new situations." Chernoff, *African Rhythm*, 65.

54. Ibid., 82.

55. Ibid., 58.

56. Ibid., 60.

57. Albert Murray uses this term in *Stomping the Blues*, 90. Discussing basketball star Michael Jordan, Michael Eric Dyson calls this impulse "stylization of the performed self."

58. Chernoff, *African Rhythm*, 82.

59. Anthropologists Sidney Mintz and Richard Price conclude that the urge to innovate and improvise in African American culture is the result of the combination of the "initial cultural heterogeneity" of the transplanted Africans with the "stress on personal style" that resulted from conditions of enslavement. Yet it is perhaps fairer to say that New World conditions enhanced an existing African aesthetic, and that the "expectation of cultural change" Mintz and Price identify as a New World survival skill was in fact an Old World survival. Mintz and Price, *Birth of African American Culture*, 51. Going one step further, Albert Murray believes the origins of the urge to develop an individual style cannot be located specifically in either African America or Africa, since "all human effort . . . is motivated by the need to live in style." Albert Murray, *The Omni-Americans: New Perspectives on Black Experience and American Culture* (New York: Outerbridge and Dienstfrey: 1970), 55.

60. Huggins, *Black Odyssey*, 7.

61. Kwame Anthony Appiah, *In My Father's House: Africa in the Philosophy of Culture* (New York: Oxford University Press, 1992), 76.

62. John Vernon Taylor, *The Primal Vision: Christian Presence amid African Religion* (London: SCM Press, 1975 [1963]), 50. Chernoff calls participation "the most fundamental aesthetic in Africa: without participation there is no meaning." *African Rhythm*, 23.

63. Robert Farris Thompson, "An Aesthetic of the Cool: West African Dance," *African Forum* 2 (1966): 85. (This essay is reprinted on pages 72–86 herein.) In *Flash of the Spirit: African and Afro-American Art and Philosophy* (New York: Random House, 1983), Thompson explains, "Coolness, then, is a part of character, and character objectifies proper custom. To the degree that we live generously and discreetly, exhibiting grace under pressure, our appearance and our acts gradually assume virtual royal power. As we become noble, fully realizing the spark of creative goodness God endowed us with—the shining *ororo* bird of thought and aspiration—we find the confidence to cope with all kinds of situations. *àshe.* This is character. This is mystic coolness" (16).

64. Thompson, "Aesthetic of the Cool," 86.

65. Thompson, "Aesthetic of the Cool," 88.

66. Olly Wilson calls this the "heterogeneous sound ideal" (see pp. 157–171 herein).

67. Thompson, "Aesthetic of the Cool," 91.

68. "Africans unite music and dance but play apart; Europeans separate dance and music but play together." Thompson, "Aesthetic of the Cool," 93.

69. Marshall Stearns and Jean Stearns, *Jazz Dance: The Story of American Vernacular Dance* (New York: Macmillan, 1968), 24; see excerpt in this volume.

70. James Weldon Johnson, *The Books of American Negro Spirituals* (New York: Viking Press, 1951), 15. (This preface is excerpted in this volume, pp. 45–71.)

71. Dena J. Epstein, *Sinful Tunes and Spirituals: Black Folk Music to the Civil War* (Urbana: University of Illinois Press, 1977), 7, 271.

72. Mintz and Price, *Birth of African-American Culture*, chap. 1 and 4.

73. Ibid., 43, 48.

74. Scholars who have given us ample insight into the subject of African origins and or

survivals in African American religion include John Blassingame, Nathan Irvin Huggins, C. Eric Lincoln and Lawrence Mamiya, Lawrence Levine, Eugene Genovese, and Louis Raboteau. I focus on Stuckey in this article because of his convincing tracing of the rise of African American cultural expression to one specific ritual, the ring shout.

75. Stuckey, *Slave Culture*, 11.

76. Samuel A. Floyd, Jr. suggests that spirituals, derived from the musical portion of the ring shouts, fall into two categories, the mournful sorrow songs such as "Nobody Knows the Trouble I've Seen," and jubilees such as "Little David Play on Your Harp." *Power of Black Music*, 41–42.

77. Some scholars believe the word "shout" was used for the circle dance in place of the sinful term "dance," and so long as performers did not lift and cross their legs, the shuffle did not technically constitute a dance. Other scholars, notably L. D. Turner, trace it to the Arabic word "saut," meaning to run and walk in religious ceremony. Stuckey, *Slave Culture*, 16. Descriptions of the ring shout in the early days emphasize the shuffling dance. "This step . . . is something halfway between a shuffle and a dance," according to H. G. Spaulding. Cited in Stearns and Stearns, *Jazz Dance*, 30.

78. In 1850s Philadelphia, where fear of insurrection was slight, slaves were allowed to congregate at fair time for their own "jubilee." There, in a graveyard, ethnically distinct Africans gathered to participate as one group in ring dances. "In that field could be seen at once more than one thousand of both sexes, divided into numerous little squads, dancing, and singing, 'each in their own tongue,' after the customs of their several nations in Africa." Cited in Stuckey, *Slave Culture*, 23.

79. Harold Courlander, *Negro Folk Music, U.S.A.* (New York: Columbia University Press, 1963), 194; Stuckey, *Slave Culture*, 23.

80. Stuckey, *Slave Culture*, 11.

81. C. Eric Lincoln and Lawrence H. Mamiya, *The Black Church in the African American Experience* (Durham: Duke University Press, 1990), 353.

82. Southern, *The Music of Black Americans: A History*, 2d ed. (New York: Norton, 1983), 170–71; quoted in Lincoln and Mamiya, *The Black Church*, 353.

83. Johnson, *Books of American Negro Spirituals*, 33.

84. See Mary Arnold Twining, "I'm Going to Sing and 'Shout' While I Have the Chance": Music, Movement, and Dance on the Sea Islands," and Guy Carawan with Candie Carawan, "Singing and Shouting in Moving Star Hall," both in *Black Music Research Journal* 15 (Spring 1995): 1–16, 17–28.

85. Janet L. Sturman reports regular performances of the Easter Rock in a contemporary northeast Louisiana Baptist parish in her paper, "Afro-Caribbean Resonance in the Sacred 'Rock' Tradition," presented at the 1993 National Conference on Black Music Research.

86. Lincoln and Mamiya, *Black Church*, 365.

87. Dizzy Gillespie with Al Fraser, *To Be or Not . . . to Bop: Memoirs* (New York: DaCapo Press, 1985 [1979]), 31.

88. For a summary of the secular transformations of African musical principles into African American culture, see Floyd, *The Power of Black Music*, 50–57.

89. Southern, *Music of Black Americans*, 42, 49. Southern adds that where a more Catholic culture prevailed, African-style dancing was more likely to emerge in social settings.

90. Abrahams, *Singing the Master*, 45.

91. Cited in John F. Szwed and Morton Marks, "The Afro-American Transformation of European Set Dances and Dance Suites," *Dance Research Journal* 20(1) (Summer 1988): 33.

92. Henry Edward Krehbiel, *Afro-American Folksongs: A Study in Racial and National Music* (New York: G. Schirmer, 1914), ix. For a more detailed overview, see Guthrie P. Ramsey Jr.'s "Cosmopolitan or Provincial?: Ideology in Early Black Music Historiography, 1867–1940," *Black Music Research Journal* 16 (Spring 1996): 11–42.

93. Krehbiel, *Afro-American Folksongs*, 97, 141.

94. Ibid., 91–92.

95. Henry O. Osgood, *So This Is Jazz* (Boston: Little, Brown, & Co., 1926), 11.

96. Maud Cuney-Hare, *Negro Musicians and Their Music* (Washington, D.C.: Associated Publishers, 1936), 34.

97. Ibid., 62, 66.

98. Herskovits, *Myth of the Negro Past*, 262.

99. By contrast, those most familiar with jazz music took a strictly musicological approach, excluding many considerations that later would situate jazz within a cultural context. Winthrop Sargeant in *Jazz: Hot and Hybrid* (New York: Da Capo, 1975 [1938]), 220, declared the use of the flat seventh, the minor scale, a "genuine feel for harmony," and certain "crude harmonic combinations" to be reminiscent of blues music but declined to generalize from these findings. Andre Hodéir went out of his way to point out that African music and American jazz "have fewer points in common than differences." *Jazz: Its Evolution and Essence* (New York: Grove Press, 1956), 40.

100. Marshall Stearns, *The Story of Jazz* (New York: Oxford University Press, 1972 [1958]), 9, 11–12.

101. In *Deep Down in the Jungle: Negro Narrative Folklore from the Streets of Philadelphia* (Hatboro, Pa.: Folklore Associates, 1964), 102, n. 5, Roger Abrahams wonders about this very issue in relation to toasts which, he posits, "may be popular among the Negro because of his predilection, otherwise evinced in calypso, toward improvised pieces of a contest nature," but he declares such hypothesizing to be outside the parameters of his study.

102. Stearns, *Story of Jazz*, 74.

103. Courlander, *Negro Folk Music*, 23. Courlander also noted "moaning and groaning" (25).

104. Gunther Schuller, *Early Jazz: Its Roots and Musical Development* (New York: Oxford University Press, 1968), 16, chap. 1.

105. Imamu Amiri Baraka (as LeRoi Jones), *Blues People: Negro Music in White America* (New York: William Morrow, 1963), 25–26, 31.

106. Ibid., 218.

107. Ibid., 28.

108. Ibid., 28.

109. Dominique-René De Lerma, *Black Music in Our Culture: Curricular Ideas on the Subject, Materials, and Problems* (Kent, Ohio: Kent State University Press, 1970), cited in Olly Wilson, "Black Music As An Art Form," *Black Music Research Journal* 3 (1983): 1.

110. Eileen Southern, *The Music of Black Americans* (New York: W. W. Norton, 1971), 55.

111. Wilson, "Black Music as An Art Form," 3. See also Olly Wilson, "The Significance of the Relationship between Afro-American Music and West African Music," *Black Perspectives in Music* 2 (Spring 1974): 3–22; "The Association of Movement and Music as a Manifestation

of a Black Conceptual Approach to Music-Making," in *More Than Dancing: Essays on Afro-American Music and Musicians*, ed. Irene V. Jackson (Westport, Conn.: Greenwood Press, 1985), 9–24; Olly Wilson, "The Heterogenous Sound Ideal in African American Music," in *New Perspective on Music: Essays in Honor of Eileen Southern*, ed. Josephine Wright with Samuel A. Floyd, Jr. (Warren, Mich.: Harmonie Park Press, 1992), 327–40. (This chapter is reprinted on pp. 157–171 herein.)

112. Imiri Baraka (as LeRoi Jones), *Home: Social Essays* (New York: Morrow, 1966).

113. At a time in the 1980s when the notion of a black aesthetic fell into disfavor, Josef Jarab wrote a critique of such approaches in general and of Jones in particular, declaring that Jones had created a myth of "*white black literature*" and the myth of "*black black music.*" Josef Jarab, "Black Aesthetic: A Cultural or Political Concept," *Callaloo* 25 (Fall 1985): 591.

114. LeRoi Jones and Larry Neal, eds. *Black Fire: An Anthology of Afro-American Writing* (New York: William Morrow, 1968), 653.

115. C. W. E. Bigsby, *The Second Black Renaissance: Essays in Black Literature* (Westport, Conn.: Greenwood Press, 1980), 234.

116. Jones, *Home*, 210–15.

117. Kimberly W. Bentson, "The Aesthetic of Modern Black Drama: From *Mimesis* to *Methexis*," in *The Theater of Black Americans: A Collection of Critical Essays*, ed. Errol Hill (New York: Applause, 1987).

118. I refer to the 1998 National Black Theater Summit at Dartmouth University.

119. For a thorough discussion of vernacularism, see Henry Louis Gates, Jr., and Nellie Y. McKay, "The Vernacular Tradition," introduction to *The Norton Anthology of African American Literature*, ed. Gates and McKay (New York: W.W. Norton, 1997), 1. Gates and McKay define the vernacular as "expression that springs from the creative interactions between the received or learned traditions and that which is locally invented, 'made in America.'" The African American vernacular, according to these authors, consists of forms sacred—songs, prayers, and sermons—as well as secular—work songs, secular hymns and songs, blues, jazz, and stories of many kinds. It also consists of dances, wordless musical performances, stage shows, and visual art forms of many sorts (3).

120. Several studies in anthropology and folklore also began to explore the idea of an African American aesthetic about this same time. Even so, by way of perspective one might remember it was as late as 1970 that Robert Blauner stated in his essay, "The Question of Black Culture," "It is time for social scientists to insist that there are no exceptions to the anthropological law that all groups have a culture. If black Americans are an ethnic group, then they possess an ethnic culture," in *Black America*, ed. John F. Szwed (New York: Basic Books, 1970), 120. It also seems significant that the first essay in the "Black Culture" section of *Black America* was by Ulf Hannerz, entitled "The Notion of Ghetto Culture." Szwed, *Black America*, 99–109. See also Abrahams, *Deep Down in the Jungle*; Roger D. Abrahams, *Positively Black* (Englewood Cliffs, N.J.: 1970); Jones and Hawes, *Step It Down*; Thomas Kochman, *Rappin' and Stylin' Out Communication in Urban Black America* (Urbana: University of Illinois Press, 1972); Lee Rainwater, ed., *Black Experience: Soul* (New Brunswick, N.J.: Transaction Books, 1973). A slightly later but in many ways groundbreaking work in ethnography is Melvin D. Williams, *On the Street Where I Lived* (New York: Holt, Rinehart and Winston, 1981). Williams declined the use of the term "ghetto culture" for "authentic culture."

121. Gayle, *The Black Aesthetic*, xvii–xviii.

122. Ibid., xxiii.

123. Ibid., xxiv. Here Ortiz W. Walton described, in his "Analysis of the African and the Western Aesthetics," several similarities between African and African American music: both employ cries, falsettos, slurs, and trills; instruments in both tend to imitate the human voice; music in both has functional and collective characteristics; improvisation in African American music is even further developed than in African; and both make use of audience participation as a means of unifying the community. Further, Walton noted the importance of antiphony and polyphony in African music and identified antiphony as the basis of improvisional skill and development in African music. Walton was uniquely situated to hear such similarities and to understand them as components of an aesthetic system; a sociologist, he was also a former member of the Boston Symphony, the Buffalo Philharmonic, and principal bassist with the Cairo (U.A.R.) Symphony.

124. Houston A. Baker, Jr., *Blues, Ideology, and Afro-American Literature: A Vernacular Theory* (Chicago: University of Chicago Press, 1984), 5.

125. Ibid., 17–18.

126. Henry Louis Gates, Jr., *The Signifying Monkey: A Theory of African-American Literary Criticism* (New York: Oxford University Press, 1988), 52.

127. Gates pointed the way to this application in *The Signifying Monkey* when he stated that the clarinetist "[Mezz] Mezzrow was one of the first commentators to recognize that Signifyin(g) as a structure of performance could apply equally to verbal texts and musical texts" (69).

128. By this time, other scholars were returning to the notion of cultural aesthetics in interpreting African American music. In her 1985 essay on West African influences on African American music, Portia Maultsby enumerated seven conceptual categories: social functions; community function of musicians; principles of music-making; textual context, organization, and structure; melodic traits; vocal stylistic features; and musical instruments. But her most useful contribution to the gradually coalescing theory of African American expressive culture was her emphasis on the social and community function of music as an agent for promoting group cohesion and mass communication. A 1990 essay extended Maultsby's interest in the social function of African American music to the "physical mode of presentation"—body movements, facial expression, and clothing as means of (1) dialogue with the audience and (2) "total physical involvement through use of the entire body." Maultsby recognized that most of her previous categories were related to one "salient feature of black music": the idea of "music-making as a communal/participatory activity." When Maultsby suggested that such characteristics as "variation in timbre, song interpretation, and presentation style mirror the aesthetic priorities of black people," she reclaimed the idea of the black aesthetic promoted in the 1960s, with the addition of comparative historical research. Portia K. Maultsby, "Africanisms in African-American Music," in *Africanisms in American Culture*, ed. Joseph E. Holloway (Bloomington: Indiana University Press, 1990), 189, 195.

129. Floyd, "Ring Shout!" *Black Music Research Journal* 11 (fall 1991): 26. (This article is reprinted on pp. 135–156 herein.) In a second article, "Troping the Blues: from Spirituals to the Concert Hall," *Black Music Research Journal* 13 (spring 1993): 31–51, Floyd applied "tropology" to music history. Using the "motherless child" trope, Floyd made connections between the spiritual and Gershwin's "Summertime" in *Porgy and Bess*. Floyd's "train" trope

illuminates connections between spirituals, such as "Swing Low, Sweet Chariot," blues songs, and Ellington's train songs ("Daybreak Express," "Happy Go Lucky Local").

130. Floyd, *The Power of Black Music*, 10.

131. Ibid., 8.

132. Gillespie, *To Be or Not . . . to Bop*, 103, 487.

133. Ibid., 58.

134. Correspondence with author, May 14, 1998.

135. Ellison, *Shadow and Act*, 124.

136. Other popular dance styles that seem to have their origin in the American Shimmy or African Shika/Banda are the shake, frug, jerk, and twist.

137. Stearns and Stearns, *Jazz Dance*, 11–12.

138. Stearns and Stearns believe the African American dances that bear the closest resemblance to African dance are the basic African American vernacular (folk) dances: the Strut, Shuffle, Sand, and Grind, and they identify the "most clear-cut survival" of African dance as the Ring Shout, "with its combination of African elements from the counterclockwise movement of the group, through the stiff shoulders and outstretched arm and hand gestures, to the flat-footed Shuffle." *Jazz Dance*, 13. European styles such as the Jig and Clog, "in which the sound of the shoe on the wooden floor is of primary importance," are eliminated or modified in African-influenced American dances. Stearns and Stearns, *Jazz Dance*, 14. Bess Lomax Hawes found the flat-footed shuffle essential to African American games and jumps, even to hand-clapping games, which were accompanied by the flat-foot to "step it down." Jones and Hawes, *Step It Down*, 20.

139. An erect torso is a European characteristic, Stearns speculates, derived from hunting on horseback, while African hunting takes place on the ground, the body bent and crouched. Also indicative of an African dance aesthetic is the extent to which African American dances, like African, are mimetic, particularly of animals, bearing names such as the buzzard lope, eagle rock, crow, turkey trot, and rabbit. Stearns and Stearns, *Jazz Dance*, 15.

140. The third time Elvis Presley appeared on the Ed Sullivan show, in 1957, Sullivan insisted on showing him only from the waist up.

141. Kariamu Welsh Asante, "Commonalities in African Dance: An Aesthetic Foundation," in *African Culture: The Rhythms of Unity*, ed. Molefi Kete Asante and Kariamu Welsh Asante (Trenton, N.J.: Africa World Press, 1990), 73, 78, 77.

142. Brenda Dixon Gottschild, *Digging the Africanist Presence in American Performance: Dance and Other Contexts* (Westport, Conn.: Greenwood Press, 1996), chap. 2.

143. Jaqui Malone, *Steppin' on the Blues: The Visible Rhythms of African American Dance* (Urbana: University of Illinois Press, 1996). There are few full-length studies of African American dance. Harold Courlander devotes a chapter to dance in *Negro Folk Music, U.S.A.*, where he mentions African dance motifs: "shimmy, crawl, shuffle, strut, and jump," taken from African, not European, traditions (202). While an important resource, Lynne Fauley Emery's *Black Dance in the United States from 1619 to 1970* (Palo Alto: National Press Books, 1972) omits discussion of vernacular dance after 1930, reviewing only concert dance after that time.

144. Malone, *Steppin' on the Blues*, 2.

145. Ibid., 2. Later in her book, Malone articulates a slightly different set of "definitive characteristics": rhythm, improvisation, control, angularity, assymetry, and dynamism.

("Keep to the Rhythm and You'll Keep to Life," in ibid., p. 32. This chapter is reprinted herein, pp. 222–238.)

146. Ibid., 10.

147. Ibid., 27.

148. Tricia Rose, "'*All Aboard the Night Train*': Flow, Layering, and Rupture in Post-industrial New York," in her *Black Noise: Rap Music and Black Culture in Contemporary America* (Hanover, N.H.: Wesleyan University Press, 1994), 38. (A portion of this chapter is reprinted herein, pp. 191–221.)

149. Ibid. Rose credits Arthur Jafa for the wording of this framework.

150. Shane White and Graham White, *Stylin': African American Expressive Culture from Its Beginnings to the Zoot Suit* (Ithaca: Cornell University Press, 1998), 128.

151. Ibid., 141.

152. Ibid., 147, 149.

153. Alan Lomax, *The Land Where the Blues Began* (New York: Pantheon, 1993), 137.

154. White and White, *Stylin'*, 261.

155. William D. Piersen, *Black Legacy: America's Hidden Heritage* (Amherst: University of Massachusetts, 1993), 54. (See pp. 348–370 this volume.)

156. Ibid., 63.

157. Jones and Hawes, *Step It Down*, xv; Zora Neale Hurston, *The Sanctified Church: The Folklore Writings of Zora Neale Hurston* (Berkeley: Turtle Island Foundation, 1981), 61.

158. Abrahams, *Deep Down in the Jungle*, 60.

159. Roger D. Abrahams, "Rapping and Capping: Black Talk as Art," in Szwed, *Black America*, 136.

160. Ibid., 135.

161. Ibid., 139–40.

162. Henry H. Mitchell, *Black Preaching* (New York: J. B. Lippincott, 1970), 43–47, 47, 163.

163. Ibid., 98.

164. King transforms the phrase from an introductory statement to a recurring rhetorical summation in what Peter Van der Merwe has identified as the African principles of "end-orientation" and "end-repetition." Van der Merwe, *Origins of the Popular Style*, 38. For an extended analysis of the dialectic of consolation and compensation in King's speech, see David Payne, *Coping with Failure: The Therapeutic Uses of Rhetoric* (Columbia: University of South Carolina Press, 1989), 47–53.

165. Although not directly relevant to my discussion of the African American aesthetic, the effect of African languages on American English is profound; for a brief historical perspective see Nathan Huggins, *Black Odyssey*, 62–68; for a short vocabulary list, see David Dalby "The African Element in American English," in Kochman, *Rappin' and Stylin' Out*, 170–88; for extensive treatment, see J. L. Dillard, *Black English: Its History and Usage in the United States* (New York: Random House, 1972); Grey Gundaker, *Signs of Diaspora, Diaspora of Signs: Literacies, Creolization, and Vernacular Practice in African America* (New York: Oxford University Press, 1998).

166. My essay, "Jump for Joy: The Jump Trope in African America, 1937–1941," appears in *Prospects* (1999).

1
. . . . . .
Music & Dance

From Preface to
The Books of American Negro Spirituals
(1925)

JAMES WELDON JOHNSON

. . . .

Although a prominent writer and political leader, James Weldon Johnson might be most widely remembered today as the co-writer (with his brother J. Rosamond Johnson) of "Lift Every Voice and Sing." Once called the "Negro National Anthem," this piece appears in most contemporary Protestant hymnals. Author of the novel Autobiography of an Ex-Colored Man *(1913), Johnson published three volumes of poetry and an autobiography. From 1920 to 1930, he was the National Secretary of the National Association for the Advancement of Colored People. And during this time he wrote* Black Manhattan *(1930), a cultural history of Harlem, edited* The Book of Negro Poetry *(1922, revised 1931), and collected two volumes of spirituals in* The Books of American Negro Spirituals *(1925, 1926). In the preface to these volumes, Johnson asserts the music's African heritage; even more boldly he claims it as America's "finest distinctive artistic contribution." In addition to detailing several peculiarities of African American rhythms, Johnson attempts one of the first definitions of "swing." Citing the example of the itinerant "Singing" Johnson, James Weldon Johnson shows the importance of improvising in the creation and performance of religious music, and of interactions between the leader and the group. He also points out the important role women have played in African American worship and religious music, as he details the leadership of "Ma" White. Johnson describes the religious "ring shout," through which many African musical practices were preserved. He also emphasizes the importance of quartet singing, which has given rise not only to barbershop quartets but to gospel quartets and through them, much of the harmony in early rock and roll.*

O black and unknown bards of long ago,
How came your lips to touch the sacred fire?
How, in your darkness, did you come to know
The power and beauty of the minstrel's lyre?
Who first from midst his bonds lifted his eyes?
Who first from out the still watch, lone and long,
Feeling the ancient faith of prophets rise
Within his dark-kept soul, burst into song?

Heart of what slave poured out such melody
As "Steal away to Jesus"? On its strains
His spirit must have nightly floated free,
Though still about his hands he felt his chains.
Who heard great "Jordan roll"? Whose starward eye
Saw chariot "swing low"? And who was he
That breathed that comforting, melodic sigh,
"Nobody knows de trouble I see"?

What merely living clod, what captive thing,
Could up toward God through all its darkness grope,
And find within its deadened heart to sing
These songs of sorrow, love and faith, and hope?
How did it catch that subtle undertone,
That note in music heard not with the ears?
How sound the elusive reed so seldom blown,
Which stirs the soul or melts the heart to tears?

Not that great German master in his dream
Of harmonies that thundered amongst the stars
At the creation, ever heard a theme
Nobler than "Go down, Moses." Mark its bars,
How like a mighty trumpet call they stir
The blood. Such are the notes that men have sung
Going to valorous deeds; such tones there were
That helped make history when time was young.

There is a wide, wide wonder in it all,
That from degraded rest and servile toil
The fiery spirit of the seer should call
These simple children of the sun and soil.

O black slave singers, gone, forgot, unfamed,
You—you alone, of all the long, long line
Of those who've sung untaught, unknown, unnamed,
Have stretched out upward, seeking the divine.

You sang not deeds of heroes or of kings;
No chant of bloody war, no exulting pæan
Of arms-won triumphs; but your humble strings
You touched in chord with music empyrean.
You sang far better than you knew; the songs
That for your listeners' hungry hearts sufficed
Still live,—but more than this to you belongs:
You sang a race from wood and stone to Christ.

It was in the above lines, which appeared in the *Century Magazine* nearly twenty years ago, that I tried to voice my estimate and appreciation of the Negro Spirituals and to celebrate the unknown black bards who created them. As the years go by and I understand more about this music and its origin the miracle of its production strikes me with increasing wonder. It would have been a notable achievement if the white people who settled this country, having a common language and heritage, seeking liberty in a new land, faced with the task of conquering untamed nature, and stirred with the hope of building an empire, had created a body of folk music comparable to the Negro Spirituals. But from whom did these songs spring—these songs unsurpassed among the folk songs of the world and, in the poignancy of their beauty, unequalled?

In 1619 a Dutch vessel landed twenty African natives at Jamestown, Virginia. They were quickly bought up by the colonial settlers. This was the beginning of the African slave trade in the American Colonies. To supply this trade Africa was raped of millions of men, women and children.[1] As many as survived the passage were immediately thrown into slavery. These people came from various localities in Africa. They did not all speak the same language. Here they were, suddenly cut off from the moorings of their native culture, scattered without regard to their old tribal relations, having to adjust themselves to a completely alien civilization, having to learn a strange language, and, moreover, held under an increasingly harsh system of slavery; yet it was from these people this mass of noble music sprang; this music which is America's only folk music and, up to this time, the finest distinctive artistic contribution she has to offer the world. It is strange!

I have termed this music noble, and I do so without any qualifications. Take, for example, *Go Down, Moses*; there is not a nobler theme in the whole musical literature of the world. If the Negro had voiced himself in only that one song, it would have been evidence of his nobility of soul. Add to this *Deep River, Stand Still Jordan, Walk Together Children, Roll Jordan Roll, Ride On King Jesus,* and you catch a spirit that is a little more than mere nobility; it is something akin to majestic grandeur. The music of these songs is always noble and their sentiment is always exalted. Never does their philosophy fall below the highest and purest motives of the heart. And this might seem stranger still.

Perhaps there will be no better point than this at which to say that all the true Spirituals possess dignity. It is, of course, pardonable to smile at the naïveté often exhibited in the words, but it should be remembered that in scarcely no instance was anything humorous intended. When it came to the use of words, the maker of the song was struggling as best he could under his limitations in language and, perhaps, also under a misconstruction or misapprehension of the facts in his source of material, generally the Bible. And often, like his more literary poetic brothers, he had to do a good many things to get his rhyme in. But almost always he was in dead earnest. There are doubtless many persons who have heard these songs sung only on the vaudeville or theatrical stage and have laughed uproariously at them because they were presented in humorous vein. Such people have no conception of the Spirituals. They probably thought of them as a new sort of ragtime or minstrel song. These Spirituals cannot be properly appreciated or understood unless they are clothed in their primitive dignity.

No space will here be given to a rehearsal of the familiar or easily accessible facts regarding the origin and development of folk music in general. Nor will any attempt be made at a discussion of the purely technical questions of music involved. A thorough exposition of this latter phase of the subject will be found in H. E. Krehbiel's *Afro-American Folksongs.* There Mr. Krehbiel makes an analysis of the modes, scales and intervals of these songs and a comparative study between them and the same features of other folksongs. Here it is planned, rather, to relate regarding these songs as many facts as possible that will be of interest to the general lover of music and serve to present adequately this collection. Instead of dissecting this music we hope to recreate around it as completely as we can its true atmosphere and place it in a proper setting for those who already love the Spirituals and those who may come to know them.

Although the Spirituals have been overwhelmingly accredited to the Negro as his own, original creation, nevertheless, there have been one or two critics who have denied that they were original either with the Negro or in themselves, and a considerable number of people have eagerly accepted this view. The opinion of these critics is not sound. It is not based upon scientific or historical inquiry. Indeed, it can be traced ultimately to a prejudiced attitude of mind, to an unwillingness to concede the creation of so much pure beauty to a people they wish to feel is absolutely inferior. Once that power is conceded, the idea of absolute inferiority cannot hold. These critics point to certain similarities in structure between the Spirituals and the folk music of other peoples, ignoring the fact that there are such similarities between all folksongs. The Negro Spirituals are as distinct from the folksongs of other peoples as those songs are from each other; and, perhaps, more so. One needs to be only ordinarily familiar with the folk music of the world to see that this is so.

The statement that the Spirituals are imitations made by the Negro of other music that he heard is an absurdity. What music did American Negroes hear to imitate? They certainly had no opportunity to go to Scotland or Russia or Scandinavia and bring back echoes of songs from those lands. Some of them may have heard a few Scotch songs in this country, but it is inconceivable that this great mass of five or six hundred Negro songs could have sprung from such a source. What music then was left for them to imitate? Some have gone so far as to say that they caught snatches of airs from the French Opera at New Orleans; but the songs of the Negroes who fell most directly under that influence are of a type distinct from the Spirituals. It was in localities far removed from New Orleans that the great body of Spirituals were created and sung. There remains then the music which the American Negroes heard their masters sing; chiefly religious music. Now if ignorant Negroes evolved such music as *Deep River, Steal Away to Jesus, Somebody's Knockin' at Yo' Do', I Couldn't Hear Nobody Pray* and *Father Abraham* by listening to their masters sing gospel hymns, it does not detract from the achievement but magnifies it.

Regarding the origin of this music, I myself have referred to the "miracle" of its production. And it is easier to believe the miracle than some of the explanations of it that are offered. Most difficult of all is it to believe that the Negro slaves were indebted to their white masters for the sources of these songs. The white people among whom the slaves lived did not originate anything comparable even to the mere titles of the Spirituals. In truth, the power to frame the poetic phrases that make the titles of so many of the Spirituals betokens the power to create the songs. Consider the sheer magic of:

Swing Low Sweet Chariot
I've Got to Walk My Lonesome Valley
Steal Away to Jesus
Singing With a Sword in My Hand
Rule Death in His Arms
Ride on King Jesus

We Shall Walk Through the Valley in Peace

The Blood Came Twinklin' Down

Deep River

Death's Goin' to Lay His Cold, Icy Hand on Me

and confess that none but an artistically endowed people could have evoked it.

No one has even expressed a doubt that the poetry of the titles and text of the Spirituals is Negro in character and origin, no one else has dared to lay claim to it; why then doubt the music? There is a slight analogy here to the Shakespeare-Bacon controversy. The Baconians in their amazement before the transcendent greatness of the plays declare that Shakespeare could not possibly have written them; he was not scholar enough; he did not know enough Greek; no mere play actor could be gentleman enough to be so familiar with the ways of the court and royalty; no mere play actor could be philosopher enough to know all the hidden springs of human motives and conduct. Then they pick a man who fills these requirements and accounts for the phenomenon of the crowning glory of the English tongue. Lord Francis Bacon, they say, wrote the plays but did not claim them because it was not creditable for a gentleman to be a playwright. However, though it was creditable for a gentleman of the age to be a poet, they do not explain why Lord Bacon did not claim the poems. And it is easy to see that the hand that wrote the poems could write the plays.

Nobody thought of questioning the Negro's title as creator of this music until its beauty and value were demonstrated. The same thing, in a greater degree, has transpired with regard to the Negro as the originator of America's popular medium of musical expression; in fact, to such a degree that it is now completely divorced from all ideas associated with the Negro. Still, for several very good reasons, it will not be easy to do that with the Spirituals.

When the Fisk Jubilee Singers[2] toured Europe they sang in England, Scotland and Germany, spending eight months in the latter country. Their concerts were attended by the most cultured and sophisticated people as well as the general public. In England they sang before Queen Victoria, and in Germany the Emperor was among those who listened to them. Music critics paid special attention to the singers and their songs. The appearance of the Jubilee Singers in Europe constituted both an artistic sensation and a financial success, neither of which results could have been attained had their songs been mere imitations of European folk music or adaptations of European airs.

The Spirituals are purely and solely the creation of the American Negro; that is, as much so as any music can be the pure and sole creation of any particular group. And their production, although seemingly miraculous, can be accounted for naturally. The Negro brought with him from Africa his native musical instinct and talent, and that was no small endowment to begin with.

Many things are now being learned about Africa. It is being learned and recognized that the great majority of Africans are in no sense "savages"; that they possess a civilization and a culture, primitive it is true but in many respects quite adequate; that they possess a folk literature that is varied and rich; that they possess an art that is quick and sound. Among those who know about art it is generally recognized that the modern school of painting and sculpture in Europe and America is almost entirely the result of the direct influence of African art, following the discovery that it was art.[3] Not much is yet known about African music, and, perhaps, for the reason that the conception of music by the Africans is not of the same sort as the conception of music by the people of Western Europe and the United States. Generally speaking, the European concept of music is melody and the African concept is rhythm. Melody has, relatively, small place in African music, and harmony still less; but in rhythms African music is beyond comparison with any other music in the world. Krehbiel, after visiting the Dahomey Village at the World's Fair in Chicago, and witnessing the natives dance to the accompaniment of choral singing and the beating of their drums, wrote of them:

> The players showed the most remarkable rhythmical sense and skill that ever came under my notice. Berlioz, in his supremest effort with his army of drummers, produced nothing to compare in artistic interest with the harmonious drumming of these savages. The fundamental effect was a combination of double and triple time, the former kept by the singers, the latter by the drummers, but it is impossible to convey the idea of the wealth of detail achieved by the drummers by means of exchange of the rhythms, syncopation of both simultaneously, and dynamic devices. Only by making a score of the music could this be done. I attempted to make such a score by enlisting the help of the late John C. Fillmore, experienced in Indian music, but we were thwarted by the players who, evidently divining our purpose when we took out our notebooks, mischievously changed their manner of playing as soon as we touched pencil to paper. I was forced to the conclusion that in their command of the element, which in the musical art of the ancient Greeks stood higher than either melody or harmony, the best composers of today were the veriest tyros compared with these black savages.[4]

The musical genius of the African has not become so generally recognized as his genius in sculpture and design, and yet it has had a wide influence on the music of the world. Friedenthal points out that African Negroes have a share in the creation of one of the best known and most extended musical forms, the

Habanera.[5] This form which is popularly known as the chief characteristic of Spanish music is a combination of Spanish melody and African rhythm. Friedenthal, regarding this combination, says:

> Here stand these two races facing each other, both highly musical but reared in different worlds of music. Little wonder that the Spaniards quickly took advantage of these remarkable rhythms and incorporated them into their own music. . . . The melody of the Habanera came out of Middle or Southern Spain, and the rhythm which accompanies it had its origin in Africa. We therefore have, in a way, the union of Spanish spirit and African technique.[6]

The rhythm of the Habanera reduced to its simplest is:

and is the rhythm characteristic of Spanish and Latin-American music. A considerable portion of Bizet's opera, Carmen, is based on this originally African rhythm.

Further, regarding the musical genius of the Africans, Friedenthal says: "Now the African Negroes possess great musical talent. It must be admitted, though, that in the invention of melodies, they do not come up to the European standard, but the greater is their capacity as inventors of rhythms. The talent exhibited by the Bantus in contriving the most complex rhythms is nothing short of marvelous."[7]

Now, the Negro in America had his native musical endowment to begin with; and the Spirituals possess the fundamental characteristics of African music. They have a striking rhythmic quality, and show a marked similarity to African songs in form and intervallic structure. But the Spirituals, upon the base of the primitive rhythms, go a step in advance of African music through a higher melodic and an added harmonic development. For the Spirituals are not merely melodies. The melodies of many of them, so sweet or strong or even weird, are wonderful, but hardly more wonderful than the harmonies. One has never experienced the full effect of these songs until he has heard their harmonies in the part singing of a large number of Negro voices. I shall say more about this question of harmony later. But what led to this advance by the American Negro beyond his primitive music? Why did he not revive and continue the beating out of complex rhythms on tom toms and drums while he uttered barbaric and martial cries to their accompaniment? It was because at the precise and psychic moment there was blown through or fused into the vestiges of his African music the spirit of Christianity as he knew Christianity.

At the psychic moment there was at hand the precise religion for the condition in which he found himself thrust. Far from his native land and customs, despised by those among whom he lived, experiencing the pang of the separation of loved ones on the auction block, knowing the hard task master, feeling the lash, the Negro seized Christianity, the religion of compensations in the life to come for the ills suffered in the present existence, the religion which implied the hope that in the next world there would be a reversal of conditions, of rich man and poor man, of proud and meek, of master and slave. The result was a body of songs voicing all the cardinal virtues of Christianity—patience—forbearance—love—faith—and hope—through a necessarily modified form of primitive African music. The Negro took complete refuge in Christianity, and the Spirituals were literally forged of sorrow in the heat of religious fervor. They exhibited, moreover, a reversion to the simple principles of primitive, communal Christianity.

The thought that the Negro might have refused or failed to adopt Christianity—and there were several good reasons for such an outcome, one being the vast gulf between the Christianity that was preached to him and the Christianity practiced by those who preached it—leads to some curious speculations. One thing is certain, there would have been no Negro Spirituals. His musical instinct would doubtless have manifested itself; but is it conceivable that he could have created a body of songs in any other form so unique in the musical literature of the world and with such a powerful and universal appeal as the Spirituals? Indeed, the question arises, would he have been able to survive slavery in the way in which he did? It is not possible to estimate the sustaining influence that the story of the trials and tribulations of the Jews as related in the Old Testament exerted upon the Negro. This story at once caught and fired the imaginations of the Negro bards, and they sang, sang their hungry listeners into a firm faith that as God saved Daniel in the lion's den, so would He save them; as God preserved the Hebrew children in the fiery furnace, so would He preserve them; as God delivered Israel out of bondage in Egypt, so would He deliver them. How much this firm faith had to do with the Negro's physical and spiritual survival of two and a half centuries of slavery cannot be known.

Thus it was by sheer spiritual forces that African chants were metamorphosed into the Spirituals; that upon the fundamental throb of African rhythms were reared those reaches of melody that rise above earth and soar into the pure, ethereal blue. And this is the miracle of the creation of the Spirituals.

As is true of all folksongs, there are two theories as to the manner in which the Spirituals were "composed"; whether they were the spontaneous outburst and expression of the group or chiefly the work of individual talented makers. I doubt that either theory is exclusively correct. The Spirituals are true folksongs and originally intended only for group singing. Some of them may be the spontaneous creation of the group, but my opinion is that the far greater part of them is the work of talented individuals influenced by the pressure and reaction of the group. The responses, however, may be more largely the work of the group in action; it is likely that they simply burst forth. It is also true that many of these songs have been modified and varied as they have been sung by different groups in different localities. This process is still going on. Sometimes we find two or more distinct variations of the melody of a song. There are also the interchange and substitution of lines. Yet, it is remarkable that these variations and changes are as few as they are, considering the fact that these songs have been for generations handed down from ear to ear and by word of mouth. Variations in melody are less common than interchange of lines. The committing to memory of all the leading lines constituted quite a feat, for they run high into the hundreds; so sometimes the leader's memory failed him and he would have to improvise or substitute. This substituting accounts for a good deal of the duplication of leading lines.

In the old days there was a definitely recognized order of bards, and to some degree it still persists. These bards gained their recogition by achievement. They were makers of songs and leaders of singing. They had to possess certain qualifications: a gift of melody, a talent for poetry, a strong voice, and a good memory. Here we have a demand for a great many gifts in one individual; yet, they were all necessary. The recognized bard required the ability to make up the appealing tune, to fashion the graphic phrase, to pitch the tune true and lead it clearly, and to remember all the lines. There was, at least, one leader of singing in every congregation but makers of songs were less common. My memory of childhood goes back to a great leader of singing, "Ma" White, and a maker of songs, "Singing" Johnson. "Ma" White was an excellent laundress and a busy woman, but each church meeting found her in her place ready to lead the singing, whenever the formal choir and organ did not usurp her ancient rights. I can still recall her shrill, plaintive voice quavering above the others. Memory distinctly brings back her singing of *We Are Climbing Jacob's Ladder*, *Keep Me From Sinking Down*, and *We Shall Walk Through the Valley in Peace*. Even as a child my joy in hearing her sing these songs was deep and full. She was the recognized leader of spiritual singing in the congregation to which she belonged and she took her duties seriously. One of her duties was to "sing-down" a long-winded or uninteresting speaker at love feasts or experience meetings, and even to cut short a prayer of undue length by raising a song. (And what a gentle method of gaining relief from a tiresome speaker.

Why shouldn't it be generally adopted today?) "Ma" White had a great reputation as a leader of singing, a reputation of which she was proud and jealous. She knew scores of Spirituals, but I do not think she ever "composed" any songs.

On the other hand, singing was "Singing" Johnson's only business. He was not a fixture in any one congregation or community, but went from one church to another, singing his way. I can recall that his periodical visits caused a flutter of excitement akin to that caused by the visit of a famed preacher. These visits always meant the hearing and learning of something new. I recollect how the congregation would hang on his voice for a new song—new, at least to them. They listened through, some of them joining in waveringly. The quicker ears soon caught the melody and words. The whole congregation easily learned the response, which is generally unvarying. They sang at first hesitantly, but seizing the song quickly, made up for hesitation by added gusto in the response. Always the strong voice of the leader corrected errors until the song was perfectly learned. "Singing" Johnson must have derived his support in somewhat the same way as the preachers,—part of a collection, food and lodging. He doubtless spent his leisure time in originating new words and melodies and new lines for old songs. "Singing" Johnson is one of the indelible pictures on my mind. A small but stocky, dark-brown man was he, with one eye, and possessing a clear, strong, high-pitched voice. Not as striking a figure as some of the great Negro preachers I used to see and hear, but at camp meetings, revivals, and on special occasions only slightly less important than any of them. A maker of songs and a wonderful leader of singing. A man who could improvise lines on the moment. A great judge of the appropriate song to sing; and with a delicate sense of when to come to the preacher's support after a climax in the sermon had been reached by breaking in with a line or two of a song that expressed a certain sentiment, often just a single line. "Singing" Johnson always sang with his eyes, or eye, closed, and indicated the tempo by swinging his head and body. When he warmed to his work it was easy to see that he was transported and utterly oblivious to his surroundings.

"Singing" Johnson was of the line of the mightier bards of an earlier day, and he exemplified how they worked and how the Spirituals were "composed." These bards, I believe, made the original inventions of story and song, which in turn were influenced or modified by the group in action.

In form the Spirituals often run strictly parallel with African songs, incremental leading lines and choral iteration. Krehbiel quotes from Denham and Clapperton's *Narrative of Travels in Northern and Central Africa*, the following song by Negro bards of Bornou in praise of their Sultan:

Given flesh to the hyenas at daybreak—
    Oh, the broad spears!
The spear of the Sultan is the broadest—
    Oh, the broad spears!
I behold thee now, I desire to see none other—
    Oh, the broad spears!
My horse is as tall as a high wall—
    Oh, the broad spears!
He will fight ten—he fears nothing!
    Oh, the broad spears!
He has slain ten, the guns are yet behind—
    Oh, the broad spears!
The elephant of the forest brings me what I want—
    Oh, the broad spears!
Like unto thee, so is the Sultan—
    Oh, the broad spears!
Be brave! Be brave, my friends and kinsmen—
    Oh, the broad spears!
God is great! I wax fierce as a beast of prey—
    Oh, the broad spears!
God is great! Today those I wished for are come—
    Oh, the broad spears!

Or take this beautiful song found in one of the Bantu folk-tales. It is the song of an old woman standing at the edge of the river with a babe in her arms, singing to coax back the child's mother, who has been enchanted and taken by the river. The tale is *The Story of Tangalimlibo*, and the song runs as follows:

It is crying, it is crying,
    Sihamba Ngenyanga.
The child of the walker by moonlight,
    Sihamba Ngenyanga.
It was done intentionally by people, whose names cannot be mentioned
    Sihamba Ngenyanga.
They sent her for water during the day,
    Sihamba Ngenyanga.
She tried to dip it with the milk basket, and then it sank,
    Sihamba Ngenyanga.
Tried to dip it with the ladle, and then it sank,
    Sihamba Ngenyanga.

Tried to dip it with the mantle, and then it sank,
   Sihamba Ngenyanga.

   Compare these African songs with the American Spiritual, *Oh, Wasn't Dat a Wide Ribber*:

Oh, de Ribber of Jordan is deep and wide,
   One mo' ribber to cross.
I don't know how to get on de other side,
   One mo' ribber to cross.
Oh, you got Jesus, hold him fast,
   One mo' ribber to cross.
Oh, better love was nebber told,
   One mo' ribber to cross.
'Tis stronger dan an iron band,
   One mo' ribber to cross.
'Tis sweeter dan de honey comb,
   One mo' ribber to cross.
Oh, de good ole chariot passin' by,
   One mo' ribber to cross.
She jarred de earth an' shook de sky,
   One mo' ribber to cross.
I pray, good Lord, I shall be one,
   One mo' ribber to cross.
To get in de chariot an' trabble on,
   One mo' ribber to cross.
We're told dat de fore wheel run by love,
   One mo' ribber to cross.
We're told dat de hind wheel run by faith,
   One mo' ribber to cross.
I hope I'll get dere by an' bye,
   One mo' ribber to cross.
To jine de number in de sky,
   One mo' ribber to cross.
Oh, Jordan's Ribber am chilly an' cold,
   One mo' ribber to cross.
It chills de body, but not de soul,
   One mo' ribber to cross.

   A study of the Spirituals leads to the belief that the earlier ones were built upon the form so common to African songs, leading lines and response. It

From American Negro Spirituals

would be safe, I think, to say that the bulk of the Spirituals are cast in this simple form. Among those following this simple structure, however, are some of the most beautiful of the slave songs. One of these, whose beauty is unsurpassed, is *Swing Low, Sweet Chariot*, which is constructed to be sung in the following manner:

LEADER: Swing low, sweet chariot,
CONGREGATION: Comin' for to carry me home.
LEADER: Swing low, sweet chariot,
CONGREGATION: Comin' for to carry me home.
LEADER: I look over Jordan, what do I see?
CONGREGATION: Comin' for to carry me home.
LEADER: A band of angels comin' after me,
CONGREGATION: Comin' for to carry me home.

LEADER: Swing low, sweet chariot,
        etc., etc., etc.

The solitary voice of the leader is answered by a sound like a rolling sea. The effect produced is strangely moving.

But as the American Negro went a step beyond his original African music in the development of melody and harmony, he also went a step beyond in the development of form. The lead and response are still retained, but the response is developed into a true chorus. In a number of the songs there are leads, a response and a chorus. In this class of songs the chorus becomes the most important part, dominating the whole song and coming first. Such a song is the well known "Steal Away to Jesus." In this song the congregation begins with the chorus, singing it in part harmony:

Steal away, steal away,
Steal away to Jesus.
Steal away, steal away home,
I ain't got long to stay here.

Then the leader alone or the congregation in unison:

My Lord He calls me,
He calls me by the thunder,
The trumpet sounds within-a my soul.

Then the response in part harmony:

I ain't got long to stay here.

Steal away, steal away,
    etc., etc., etc.

This developed form is carried a degree farther in "Go Down Moses." Here the congregation opens with the powerful theme of the chorus, singing it in unison down to the last line, which is harmonized:

Go down, Moses,
'Way down in Egypt land,
Tell ole Pharaoh,
Let my people go.

Then the leader:

Thus saith the Lord, bold Moses said,

And the response:

Let my people go.

Leader:

If not I'll smite your first-born dead.

Response:

Let my people go.

Chorus:

Go down, Moses,
Go down, Moses,
'Way down in Egypt land,
Tell ole Pharaoh,
Let my people go.
    etc., etc., etc.

In a few of the songs this development is carried to a point where the form becomes almost purely choral. Examples of these more complex structures are, *Deep River*, and *Walk Together Children*.

I have said that the European concept of music, generally speaking, is melody and the African concept is rhythm. It is upon this point that most white people have difficulty with Negro music, the difficulty of getting the "swing" of it. White America has pretty well mastered this difficulty; and naturally, because the Negro has been beating these rhythms in its ears for three hundred years. But in Europe, in spite of the vogue of American popular music, based on these rhythms, the best bands are not able to play it satisfactorily. Of course, they play the notes correctly, but any American can at once detect that there is something lacking. The trouble is, they play the notes too correctly; and do not play what is not written down. There are few things more ludicrous—to an American—than the efforts of a European music hall artist to sing a jazz song. It is interesting, if not curious, that among white Americans those who have mastered these rhythms most completely are Jewish-Americans. Indeed, Jewish musicians and composers are they who have carried them to their highest development in written form.

In all authentic American Negro music the rhythms may be divided roughly into two classes—rhythms based on the swinging of head and body and rhythms based on the patting of hands and feet. Again, speaking roughly, the rhythms of the Spirituals fall in the first class and the rhythms of secular music in the second class. The "swing" of the Spirituals is an altogether subtle and elusive thing. It is subtle and elusive because it is in perfect union with the religious ecstasy that manifests itself in the swaying bodies of a whole congregation, swaying as if responding to the baton of some extremely sensitive conductor. So it is very difficult, if not impossible, to sing these songs sitting or standing coldly still, and at the same time capture the spontaneous "swing" which is of their very essence.

Carl Van Vechten writing in *Vanity Fair* about these songs declared it as his opinion that white singers cannot sing them, and that women, with few exceptions, should not attempt to sing them at all. Mr. Van Vechten made this statement in recognition of the element in the Spirituals without which their beauty of melody and harmony is lifeless. His statement also, I take it, has specific reference to the singing of these songs as solos on the concert stage. I agree that white singers are, naturally, prone to go to either of two extremes: to attempt to render a Spiritual as though it were a Brahms song, or to assume a "Negro unctuousness" that is obviously false, and painfully so. I think white singers, concert singers, *can* sing Spirituals—if they *feel* them. But to feel them it is necessary to know the truth about their origin and history, to get in touch with the association of ideas that surround them, and to realize something of what they have meant in the experiences of the people who created them. In a word, the capacity to *feel* these songs while singing them is more important than any amount of mere artistic technique. Singers who take the Spirituals as mere "art" songs and singers who make of them an exhibition of what is merely amusing or exotic are equally doomed to failure, so far as true interpretation is concerned. Mr. Van Vechten's opinion brings up the question of the rendition of these songs as concert solos not only by white but by colored singers. I have seen more than one colored singer floundering either in the "art" or the "exhibition" pit. The truth is, these songs, primarily created and constructed, as they were, for group singing, will always remain a high test for the individual artist. They are not concert material for the mediocre soloist. Through the genius and supreme artistry of Roland Hayes these songs undergo, we may say, a transfiguration. He takes them high above the earth and sheds over them shimmering silver of moonlight and flashes of the sun's gold; and we are transported as he sings. By a seemingly opposite method, through sheer simplicity, without any conscious attempt at artistic effort and by devoted adherence to the primitive traditions, Paul Robeson achieves substantially the same effect. These two singers, apparently so different, have the chief essential in common; they both feel the Spirituals deeply. Mr. Hayes, notwithstanding all his artistry, sings these songs with tears on his cheeks. Both these singers pull at the heart strings and moisten the eyes of their listeners.

We were discussing the "swing" of the Spirituals, and were saying how subtle and elusive a thing it was. It is the more subtle and elusive because there is a still further intricacy in the rhythms. The swaying of the body marks the regular beat or, better, surge, for it is something stronger than a beat, and is more or less, not precisely, strict in time; but the Negro loves nothing better in his music than to play with the fundamental time beat. He will, as it were, take the fundamental beat and pound it out with his left hand, almost monotonously; while with his right hand he juggles it. It should be noted that even in the swaying of head and body the head marks the surge off in shorter waves than does the body. In listening to Negroes sing their own music it is often tantalizing and even exciting to watch a minute fraction of a beat balancing for a slight instant on the bar between two measures, and, when it seems almost too late, drop back into its own proper compartment. There is a close similarity between this singing and the beating of the big drum and the little drums by the African natives. In addition, there are the curious turns and twists and quavers and the intentional striking of certain notes just a shade off the key, with which the Negro loves to embellish his songs. These tendencies constitute a handicap that has baffled many of the recorders of this music. I doubt that it is possible with our present system of notation to make a fixed transcription of these peculiarities that would be absolutely true; for in their very nature they are not susceptible to fixation. Many of the transcriptions that have been made are far from the true manner and spirit of singing the Spirituals. I have gone thus far into the difficulties connected with singing the Spirituals in order that those who are interested in these songs may have a fuller understanding of just what they are. It is not necessary to say that the lack of complete mastery of all these difficulties is not at all fatal to deriving pleasure from singing Spirituals. A group does not have to be able to sing with the fervor and abandon of a Negro congregation to enjoy them. Nor does one have to be a Hayes or a Robeson to give others an idea of their beauty and power.

Going back again, the rhythms of Negro secular music, roughly speaking, fall in the class based on the patting of hands and feet. It can easily be seen that this distinction between the Spirituals and Negro secular music is, in a large way, that of different physical responses to differing sets of emotions. Religious ecstasy fittingly manifests itself in swaying heads and bodies; the emotions that call for hand and foot patting are pleasure, humor, hilarity, love, just the joy of being alive. In this class of his music, as in the Spirituals, the Negro is true to the characteristic of playing with the fundamental beat; if anything, more so. What is largely psychological manifestation in the Spirituals becomes physical response in the secular music. In this music the fundamental beat is chiefly maintained by the patting of one foot, while the hands clap out intricate and varying rhythmic patterns. It should be understood that the foot is not marking straight time, but what Negroes call "stop time," or what the books have no better definition for than "syncopation." The strong accent or down beat is never lost, but is playfully bandied from hand to foot and from foot to hand.

I wish to point out here that the rhapsodical hand clapping connected with singing the Spirituals—except in the "ring shout" songs, of which I shall speak later—is not to be confused with the hand clapping to dance-time music. Recently another Negro dance has swept the country. It was introduced to New York by Messrs. Miller and Lyles in their musical comedy, *Runnin' Wild*. And at present white people everywhere, in the cabarets, on the ball floor and at home count it an accomplishment to be able to "do the Charleston." When Miller and Lyles introduced the dance in their play they did not depend wholly on the orchestra—an extraordinary jazz band—for the accompaniment, but had the major part of the chorus supplement it with hand and foot patting. The effect was electrical and contagious. It was the best demonstration of beating out complex rhythms I have ever witnessed; and, I do not believe New York ever before witnessed anything of just its sort.

It would be interesting to know how many peoples there are other than the Negro in America and Africa, if there are any, who innately beat out these complex and extremely intricate rhythms with their hands and feet. The Spanish people do something of the kind in their castanet dances; but, as has already been shown, this is probably the result of African influence. At any rate, this innate characteristic of the Negro in America is the genesis and foundation of our national popular medium for musical expression.

The temptations for these digressions are almost irresistible. At this point the writer could go far along the line of discussing the origin of Negro secular music and its development until it was finally taken over and made "American popular music." It would be easy also to stray along a parallel line, and note how Negro dances have kept step with Negro secular music, and how from their inglorious beginnings they have advanced until they have been recognized and accepted by the stage and by "society." And this merely to pave the way for another slight digression. And, yet, we can hardly discuss the question of Negro rhythms and "swing" without paying some attention to still another class of songs—the work songs.

With regard to rhythm and "swing" the work songs do not fall into the classification with either the Spirituals or the dance-time songs. The "swing" of these songs is governed by the rhythmic motions made by a gang of men at labor. It may be the motions made in swinging a pick on the road or a hammer on the rock pile, or in loading cotton on the levée. Some of the finest examples of these songs are those originated by the convicts at work in the chain gang. One of these is the poignantly beautiful "Water Boy" frequently sung by Roland Hayes. All the men sing and move together as they swing their picks or rock-breaking hammers. They move like a ballet; not a ballet of cavorting legs and pirouetting feet, but a ballet of bending backs and quivering muscles. It is all in rhythm but a rhythm impossible to set down. There is always a leader and he sets the pace. A phrase is sung while the shining hammers are being lifted. It is cut off suddenly as the hammers begin to descend and gives place to a prolonged grunt which becomes explosive at the impact of the blow. Each phrase of the song is independent, apparently obeying no law of time. After each impact the hammers lie still and there is silence. As they begin to rise again the next phrase of the song is sung; and so on. Just how long the hammers will be allowed to rest cannot be determined; nor, since the movements are not governed by strict time, can any exact explanation be given as to why they all begin to rise simultaneously. There are variations that violate the obvious laws of rhythm, but over it all can be discerned a superior rhythmic law. A fine illustration of what I have been trying to explain was given by Paul Robeson in his rendition of the convict song in "The Emperor Jones."

Brief mention must be made of another class of Negro songs. This is a remnant of songs allied to the Spirituals but which cannot be strictly classified with them. They are the "shout songs." These songs are not true spirituals nor even truly religious; in fact, they are not actually songs. They might be termed quasi-religious or semi-barbaric music. They once were used, and still are in a far less degree, in religious gatherings, but neither musically nor in the manner of their use do they fall in the category of the Spirituals. This term "shout songs" has no reference to the loud, jubilant Spirituals, which are often so termed by writers on Negro music; it has reference to the songs or, better, the chants used to accompany the "ring shout." The "ring shout," in truth, is nothing more or less than the survival of a primitive African dance, which in quite an understandable way attached itself in the early days to the Negro's Christian worship. I can remember seeing this dance many times when I was a boy. A space is cleared by moving the benches, and the men and women arrange themselves, generally alternately, in a ring, their bodies quite close. The music starts and the ring begins to move. Around it goes, at first slowly, then with quickening pace. Around and around it moves on shuffling feet that do not leave the floor, one foot beating with the heel a decided accent in strict two-four time. The music is supplemented by the clapping of hands. As the ring goes around it begins to take on signs of frenzy. The music, starting, perhaps, with a Spiritual, becomes a wild, monotonous chant. The same musical phrase is repeated over and over one, two, three, four, five hours. The words become a repetition of an incoherent cry. The very monotony of sound and motion produces an ecstatic state. Women, screaming, fall to the ground prone and quivering. Men, exhausted, drop out of the shout. But the ring closes up and moves around and around.

I remember, too, that even then the "ring shout" was looked upon as a very questionable form of worship. It was distinctly frowned upon by a great many colored people. Indeed, I do not recall ever seeing a "ring shout" except *after* the regular services. Almost whispered invitations would go around, "Stay after church; there's going to be a 'ring shout.'" The more educated ministers and members, as fast as they were able to brave the primitive element in the churches, placed a ban on the "ring shout." The "shout," however, was never universal. The best information that I have been able to gather indicates that it was most general in the Atlantic and Gulf coastal regions of the south-eastern states. Today it is rarely seen. It has not quite, but has almost disappeared. In parts of Louisiana, and in some parts of the West Indies and South America, or, in other words, where the Negro came under the influence and jurisdiction of the Catholic Church and the Church of England this dance long persisted outside of the church and Christian religion. There it retained its primitive social and ceremonial significance and was practiced with more or less frankness. Two reasons may be advanced to cover these two facts: under the Catholic Church and the Church of England the Negro, practically, never had any place of worship of his own, and, of course, he would never have been allowed to introduce such a practice as the "ring shout," even under a religious guise, into those churches; it is also in a large measure true that the Negro in those localities has never accepted the Christian religion in the sense and degree in which it was accepted by the Negro of the South; there his acceptance was more a matter of outward conformity, and he clung more tenaciously to his African cultural and religious ideas. This survival of an African ceremony has been outlawed in the United States and cannot be seen except in some backward churches of a backward community. But in parts of the West Indies and South America it is still quite frankly practiced as a social function. The Negroes that live along the eastern fringe of Venezuela dance every Saturday. I have often heard their chants and the drums throbbing until far into the night. I was in Haiti several years ago and I learned that the "Saturday night dance," which had been the custom there, too, had been interdicted in the larger cities by the American Occupation authorities. However, the people were still allowed to dance in the rural districts and on holidays. On one national holiday in a small village I saw them dance under a thatched pavilion in the little public square. It was the same thing I had seen in my childhood in a small church in Florida. The formation of the dancers was the same, the shuffling motion was the same, the monotonous, incoherent chant sounded the same, although these folk spoke an unfamiliar language. The only differences I noted were: it was not in a church, there was great gaiety instead of religious frenzy, and the beating drums—real African drums.

I refer again to Mr. Van Vechten's interesting article. In it he said, "Negro folksongs differ from the folksongs of most other races through the fact that they are sung in harmony." I am glad to have this confirmation of my own opinion. I have long thought that the harmonization of the Spirituals by the folk group in singing them was distinctive of them among the folksongs of the world. My speculation was with regard to how many other groups of folksongs there were that were harmonized spontaneously in the singing. The fact that the Spirituals were sung in harmony has always seemed natural to me, because Negroes harmonize instinctively. What about the traditional reputation of Negroes as singers; upon what is it really founded? The common idea is that it is founded upon the quality of their voices. It is not. The voices of Negroes, when untrained, are often overloud, perhaps rather blatant, sometimes even a bit strident; but they are *never discordant*. In harmony they take on an orchestra-like timbre. The popular credit given to Negroes as singers is given, maybe unconsciously, because of their ability to harmonize, and not because of the quality of their voices. When the folks at the "big house" sat on the verandah and heard the singing floating up through the summer night from the "quarters" they were enchanted; and it is likely they did not realize that the enchantment was wrought chiefly through the effect produced by harmonizing and not by the voices as voices.

Pick up four colored boys or young men anywhere and the chances are ninety out of a hundred that you have a quartet. Let one of them sing the melody and the others will naturally find the parts. Indeed, it may be said that all male Negro youth of the United States is divided into quartets. When I was a very small boy one of my greatest pleasures was going to concerts and hearing the crack quartets made up of waiters in the Jacksonville hotels sing. Each of the big Florida resort hotels boasted at least two quartets, a first and a second. When I was fifteen and my brother was thirteen we were singing in a quartet which competed with other quartets. In the days when such a thing as a white barber was unknown in the South, every barber shop had its quartet, and the men spent their leisure time playing on the guitar—not banjo, mind you—and "harmonizing." I have witnessed some of these explorations in the field of harmony and the scenes of hilarity and back-slapping when a new and peculiarly rich chord was discovered. There would be demands for repetitions, and cries of "Hold it! Hold it!" until it was firmly mastered. And well it was for some of these chords were so new and strange for voices that, like Sullivan's *Lost Chord*, they would never have been found again except for the celebrity with which they were recaptured. In this way was born the famous but much abused "barber-shop chord."

It may sound like an extravagant claim, but it is, nevertheless a fact that the "barber-shop chord" is the foundation of the close harmony method adopted by American musicians in making arrangements for male voices. I do not think English musicians have yet used this method of arranging to any great extent. "Barber-shop harmonies" gave a tremendous vogue to male quartet singing, first on the minstrel stage, then in vaudeville; and soon white young men, wherever four or more were gathered together, tried themselves at "harmonizing." The vogue somewhat declined because the old "barber-shop chord" was so overdone that it became almost taboo. But the male quartet is still one of the main features of colored musical shows. These modern quartets avoid the stereotyped chords of twenty, thirty, and forty years ago, but the chief charm of their singing still lies in the closeness of the harmony. No one who heard *Shuffle Along*, can forget the singing of *The Four Harmony Kings*.

Among the early collectors of the Spirituals there was some doubt as to whether they were sung in harmony. This confusion may have been due in part to the fact that in the Spirituals the Negro makes such frequent use of unison harmony. The leading lines are always sung by a single voice or in unison harmony, and many of the refrains or choruses are sung in unison harmony down to the last phrase, and then in part harmony. The chorus of *Go Down Moses* is an example. In *Slave Songs of the United States*, published in 1867, Mr. Allen, one of the editors, in accounting for the fact that only the melodies of the songs in the collection were printed, said in his preface:

JAMES WELDON JOHNSON

There is no singing in parts, as we understand it, and yet no two seem to be singing the same thing; the leading singer starts the words of each verse, often improvising, and others, who 'base' him, as it is called, strike in with the refrain or even join in the solo when the words are familiar. When the 'base' begins the leader often stops, leaving the rest of the words to be guessed at, or it may be they are taken up by one of the other singers. And the 'basers' themselves seem to follow their own whims, beginning where they please, striking an octave above or below (in case they have pitched the tune too high), or hitting some other note that chords, so as to produce the effect of a marvelous complication and variety and yet with the most perfect time and rarely with any discord. And what makes it all the harder to unravel a thread of melody out of this strange network is that, like birds, they seem not infrequently to strike sounds that cannot be precisely represented by the gamut and abound in 'slides' from one note to another and turns and cadences not in articulated notes.

Mr. Allen's opinion that the songs were not harmonized is explained when he says, "There is no singing in parts, as we understand it." And no one can blame him for not attempting to do more than transcribe the melodies. If Mr. Allen were writing today, when America is so familiar with the bizarre Negro harmonies, he would recognize that the Spirituals were harmonized and he would try to transcribe the harmonies. What he heard was the primitive and spontaneous group singing of the Spirituals, and his description of it is, perhaps, as good as can be given. It might also be noted that it is an excellent description of the most modern American form of instrumentation,—a form that most people think of as a brand new invention.

The songs collected in this book have been arranged for solo voice, but in the piano accompaniments the arrangers have sincerely striven to give the characteristic harmonies that would be used in spontaneous group singing. Of course, these harmonies are not fixed. A group or congregation singing spontaneously might never use precisely the same harmonies twice; however, Mr. Rosamond Johnson and Mr. Brown have shown great fidelity to what is characteristic. The ordinary four-part harmonies can, without difficulty, be picked out from the accompaniments to most of the songs, but what the arrangers had principally in mind was to have the instrumentation approach the effect of the singing group in action. . . .*

This book is dedicated to those through whose efforts these songs have been collected, preserved, and given to the world. It is a fitting, if inadequate,

*Pp. 38–46 of the original preface have been omitted.

tribute; for it was wholly within the possibilities for these songs to be virtually lost. The people who created them were not capable of recording them, and the conditions out of which this music sprang and by which it was nourished have almost passed away. Without the direct effort on the part of those to whom I offer this slight tribute, the Spirituals would probably have fallen into disuse and finally disappeared. This probability is increased by the fact that they passed through a period following Emancipation when the front ranks of the colored people themselves would have been willing and even glad to let them die.

The first efforts towards the preservation of this music were made by the pioneer collectors who worked within the decade following the Civil War. These collectors, either through curiosity or as a matter of research, or because they were impressed by the unique beauty of the Spirituals, set down on paper the words and melodies. All of them were more or less successful in getting the melodies down correctly, but none of these pioneers even attempted to set down the anarchic harmonies which they heard. In fact, they had no classification for these sounds or even comprehension of them as harmonies. These pioneers were none of them exceptionally trained, but on this point they were not one whit behind the most advanced thought in American music of their day. Some of these early collectors contented themselves with jotting down simply the melodies and words, and publishing their collections in that form. Others harmonized the melodies. These harmonized arrangements, however, had little or no relation to the original harmonies or the manner of singing them by the group. They were, generally, straight four-part arrangements set down in strict accordance with the standard rules of thorough-bass. Nevertheless, except for the work of these pioneer collectors, done mostly as a labor of love, the number of the Spirituals recorded and preserved would have been only a small fraction of what it is.

The credit for the first introduction of the Spirituals to the American public and the world belongs to Fisk University. It was the famous Fisk Jubilee Singers that first made this country and Europe conscious of the beauty of these songs. The story of the struggles and successes of the Jubilee Singers, as told in the Fisk Collection of the Spirituals, reads like a romance. The first impetus upward was given them in New York under the powerful patronage of Henry Ward Beecher. With far-reaching wisdom Fisk University devoted itself to the careful collection and recording of the Spirituals, and so the work of the earlier collectors was broadened and improved upon. The work of Fisk University was quickly followed up by Hampton; Calhoun School, in Alabama; Atlanta University; Tuskegee Institute, and other schools in the South. These schools have for two generations been nurseries and homes for these songs.

Within the past ten or twelve years thorough musicians have undertaken a study of this music; a scientific study of it as folk music and an evaluation of its sociological as well as its musical importance. Chief among these is H. E. Krehbiel, more than thirty years music critic on the New York Tribune. For many years Mr. Krehbiel made a study of Negro music, and gathered a vast amount of data. In 1914 he published his *Afro-American Folksongs*, which has already been referred to here. Shortly afterwards an excellent and sound book on the subject, *Folk Songs of the American Negro*, was published by Professor John W. Work of Fisk University. Natalie Curtis Burlin issued *The Hampton Series—Negro Folk-Songs*, in four parts containing the results of her investigations and studies at Hampton aided by phonograph records. Maud Cuney Hare of Boston contributed to the sum of historical and scientific knowledge regarding Negro music. A number of foreign musicians and observers, mostly Germans, have written on the same theme.

Today the Spirituals have a vogue. They are beyond the place where the public might hear them only through the quartets of Fisk or Hampton or Atlanta or Tuskegee. Today the public buys the Spirituals, takes them home and plays and sings them. This has been brought about because the songs have been put into a form that makes them available for singers and music lovers. The principal factor in reaching this stage has been H. T. Burleigh, the eminent colored musician and composer. Mr. Burleigh was the pioneer in making arrangements for the Spirituals that widened their appeal and extended their use to singers and the general musical public. Along with Mr. Burleigh and following him was a group of talented colored composers working to the same end: Nathaniel Dett, Carl Diton, J. Rosamond Johnson and N. Clark Smith. The vogue of the Spirituals was added to by the publishing of twenty-four piano arrangements of Spirituals by Coleridge-Taylor. Clarence Cameron White of Boston published a number of arrangements for violin and piano. There were others who aided greatly by organizing choruses and teaching them to sing these songs; foremost among whom were Mrs. Azalia Hackley, Mrs. Daisy Tapley and William C. Elkins. The latest impulse given to the spread of the Spirituals has come within the last year or two through their presentation to the public by colored singers on the concert stage. The superlatively fine rendition of these songs by Roland Hayes, Paul Robeson, Miss Marian Anderson, and Julius Bledsoe has brought them to their highest point of celebrity and placed the classic stamp upon them. Today it is appropriate for any artist, however great, to program one or a group of these Spirituals.

A number of white persons aided in securing the general recognition which the Spirituals now enjoy. Several white musicians have made excellent arrangements for some of these songs. David Mannes, long interested in Negro music, was instrumental together with Mrs. Natalie Curtis Burlin, Mr. Ell-bridge Adams and others in founding a colored music school settlement in the Harlem section of New York City. Clement Wood, the poet, has for several years given lectures on the Spirituals, illustrated by voice and at the piano. Carl Van Vechten, whom I have quoted, has made a study of Negro music and has written a number of articles on the subject. But the present regard in which this Negro music is held is due overwhelmingly to the work of Negro composers, musicians and singers. It was through the work of these Negro artists that the colored people themselves were stirred to a realization of the true value of the Spirituals; and that result is more responsible for the new life which pulses through this music than any other single cause. I have said that these songs passed through a period when the front ranks of the Negro race would have been willing to let them die. Immediately following Emancipation those ranks revolted against everything connected with slavery, and among those things were the Spirituals. It became a sign of not being progressive or educated to sing them. This was a natural reaction, but, nevertheless, a sadly foolish one. It was left for the older generation to keep them alive by singing them at prayer meetings, class meetings, experience meetings and revivals, while the new choir with the organ and books of idiotic anthems held sway on Sundays. At this period gospel hymn-book agents reaped a harvest among colored churches in the South. Today this is all changed. There is hardly a choir among the largest and richest colored churches that does not make a specialty of singing the Spirituals. This reawakening of the Negro to the value and beauty of the Spirituals was the beginning of an entirely new phase of race consciousness. It marked a change in the attitude of the Negro himself toward his own art material; the turning of his gaze inward upon his own cultural resources. Neglect and ashamedness gave place to study and pride. All the other artistic activities of the Negro have been influenced.

There is also a change of attitude going on with regard to the Negro. The country may not yet be conscious of it, for it is only in the beginning. It is, nevertheless, momentous. America is beginning to see the Negro in a new light, or, rather, to see something new in the Negro. It is beginning to see in him the divine spark which may glow merely for the fanning. And so a colored man is soloist for the Boston Symphony Orchestra and the Philharmonic; a colored woman is soloist for the Philadelphia Symphony Orchestra and the Philharmonic; colored singers draw concert goers of the highest class; Negro poets and writers find entrée to all the most important magazines; Negro authors have their books accepted and put out by the leading publishers. And this change of attitude with regard to the Negro which is taking place is directly related to the Negro's change of attitude with regard to himself. It is new, and it is tremendously significant.

The collection here presented is not definitive, but we have striven to make it representative of this whole field of music, to give examples of every variety of Spirituals. There is still enough material new and old for another book like this, and, perhaps, even for another.

In the arrangements, Mr. Rosamond Johnson and Mr. Brown have been true not only to the best traditions of the melodies but also to form. No changes have been made in the form of songs. The only development has been made in harmonizations, and these harmonizations have been kept true in character. And so an old-time Negro singer could sing any of the songs through without encountering any innovations that would interrupt him or throw him off. They have not been cut up or "opera-ated" upon. The arrangers have endeavored above all else to retain their primitive "swing."

This collection is offered with the hope that it will further endear these songs to those who love Spirituals, and will awaken an interest in many others.

NOTES

1. For a history of the slave trade and its horrors, see "The Suppression of the Slave Trade" by W. E. B. Du Bois.

2. The Jubilee Singers of Fisk University first introduced the Spirituals to the public. From 1871 to 1875 they gave many concerts in the United States, and made two tours of Europe. They raised a net sum of more than $150,000 for the University. Jubilee Hall is one of the monuments of their efforts.

3. "Of all the arts of the primitive races, the art of the African Negro savage is the one which has had a positive influence upon the art of our epoch. From its principles of plastic representation a new art movement has evolved. The point of departure and the resting point of our abstract representation are based on the art of that race. It is certain that before the introduction of the plastic principles of Negro art, abstract representations did not exist among Europeans. Negro art has reawakened in us the feeling for the abstract form; it has brought into our art the means to express our purely sensorial feelings in regard to form, or to find new form in our ideas. The abstract representation of modern art is unquestionably the offspring of the Negro Art, which has made us conscious of the subjective state, obliterated by objective education." *African Negro Art—Its Influence on Modern Art*, M. de Zayas.

4. H. E. Krehbiel, *Afro-American Folksongs*. New York, 1914.

5. Alfred Friedenthal, *Stimmen der Volker*. Berlin, 1911.

6. Alfred Friedenthal, *Musik, Tanz und Dichtung bei den Kreolen Amerikas*.

7. Alfred Friedenthal, *Stimmen der Völker*. Berlin, 1911.

An Aesthetic of the Cool

West African Dance (1966)

ROBERT FARRIS THOMPSON

· · · · · · ·

In this landmark essay, Yale professor of art and art history Robert Farris Thompson makes three assertions that have changed the course of African and African American studies. First, he declares West African music and dance to be an integrated nonverbal philosophical articulation. Second, he describes this philosophy as one that values interrelatedness (wholeness) and balance (patience and humility), and third, he states that these philosophical principles translate into a cultural aesthetic of cool. The five traits Thompson finds in West African music and dance are often cited in later studies.

The scope of this article will be restricted to West Africa, for this sector is one of the few in tropical Africa (East Africa is, to a lesser extent, an exception) where a cohesive musical geography, so to speak, has been isolated.[1] For many reasons, of which I shall give but three, the traditional Guinea Coast choreographies deserve study: West African dances are key documents of aesthetic history; they are nonverbal formulations of philosophies of beauty and ethics; and they furnish a means of comprehending a pervasive strand of contemporary American culture.

To take up the last point first, let me say at once that Americans fail to understand the rock-and-roll of their children because of their ignorance of black artistic traditions, which even blue-eyed youngsters seem to have absorbed. In general, American whites still seem to restrict their most genuine singing to the shower, their best dancing to the cabaret or club, and their worship to a weekly remembrance. By contrast, members of Negro sanctified churches sing, worship, and dance in their pews.

Similarly, African traditional cults are *danced faiths*, worship converted into sound and motion, performed in the open air. The alfresco emphasis, in fact, may well explain why with few exceptions—Zimbabwe is one—large-scale religious architecture is absent south of the Sahara.[2] Black religions are instru-

Reprinted from *African Forum* 2 (1966). Used by permission of the author.

ments of moral edification *and* entertainment, excitement *and* decorum;[3] consequently, African devotees blend the sacred with the profane, night after night, day after day. If, while observing an American Negro descendant of this tradition, we are surprised when B. B. King pauses in the middle of his blues to deliver a sermon of the cool,[4] we are admitting an inadequate understanding of the aesthetic history of the Negro. One approach to this history lies in the study of West African dances. The traditional choreographies of tropical Africa constitute, I submit, complex distillations of thinking, comparable to Cartesian philosophy in point of influence and importance.

The equilibrium and poetic structure of traditional dances of the Yoruba in western Nigeria, as well as the frozen facial expressions worn by those who perform these dances, express a philosophy of the cool, an ancient, indigenous ideal: patience and collectedness of mind. Yoruba myths relate tales of disjunction, of the dangerous jarring of elements that had been in balance, of the near-destruction of mankind by breach of trust. In one myth, the Yoruba god of divination locates the mediating principle in cool water; in another, a powerful man named Agirilogbon locates the mediating principle in a cool, healing leaf.[5] There is nothing arbitrary about these myths: They all posit water, certain leaves, and other items as symbols of the coolness that transcends disorder and without which community is impossible. Ask a traditional member of this populous African society, "What is love?" and he may tell you, as one told me, "Coolness."

The last words spoken by Malcolm X were: "Now brothers! Be cool, don't get excited."[6] Was this sheer coincidence? I think it is permissible to sound the idiom of Harlem (which has been appropriated by much of white America) for possible relationships with West African thinking. Perhaps one reason many American Negroes sing a sad song happy and some whites sing it sad is that the Negro is an heir to an aesthetic of the cool and the latter is not. It is cool to sweeten hurt with song and motion; it is hot to concentrate upon the pain.

Marshall McLuhan argues that literacy heats up the eye at the expense of the other senses.[7] When a Yoruba chief explains that men dance to keep the town cool, one might use McLuhan's concepts to analyze the significance of the chief's remark: Dancing returns consciousness to a ratio between the senses— feet touch earth, ears hear drumming, eyes study gesture. Since dance also interrelates the arts themselves, we recognize the urgent need, in speaking of black choreography in Africa, to maintain the ratio between music and dance, and the more we project the findings of ethnomusicologists into the study of West African dance the more we learn. Adeleye, an informal oral critic of traditional dance in the village of Ajilete in western Nigeria, stresses that an excellent dancer "hears" [comprehends] the drum and makes the whole body dance," which succinctly summarizes the involvement Africans relish and the balance between musical and choreographic expression they seek to strike.

Although dance structure may be broadly related to musical structure everywhere in the world, the special African instance of the problem arrests our attention, for we are attempting to discern some broad structural traits of West African dance in relation to dominant West African musical precepts. These seem joint bearers of a dynamic sensibility; both seem to fuse energy and decorum in a manner that confounds the either/or categories of Western thinking.

Another reason for the relationship is that the gross characteristics of African dance have been more or less documented in word descriptions over the years by people who are ignorant of precise movement analysis. Nuances of gesture and dynamics require a painstaking translation of filmed sequences into the objective medium of labanotation, a system of dance notation that has become the archival lingua franca of the modern world of choreography. Although these difficult prescriptions are, happily, being met by Joann Kealiinohomoku at Indiana University and Nadia Chilkovsky Nahumck of the University of Pennsylvania, most of us still depend upon word descriptions—and these are very gross. But to throw them away in favor of an exclusive parlance of notation might well prove as controversial as an exclusive reliance upon written (as opposed to oral) tradition in the writing of African history. The felicitous research of the future will probably involve a cooperation between labanotaters and other observers of African dance, much as African historians have learned to marshall oral and archival data together.

Music and dance, of course, evince some traits peculiar to themselves. Such self-logics, for example, include timbre (as to music) and footwork (as to dance). Except as a metaphor, it would be difficult to portray a formal correspondence between these two phenomena. Yoruba, for example, clearly mark the distinction between music and dance with separate words, respectively *orin* and *ijó*. But we are concentrating on dance music—that is, music which has regular pulsations—since it would be pointless to study the structure of music not specifically intended for the dance, such as certain dirges in Ghana that are metrically free, rhythmically relaxed, and lacking a steady beat.[8]

From the point of view of dance, West Africa is as historically suggestive as it is rich in musicological description. The Guinea Coast lay astride the area of intensive slaving that resulted in the forced transference of the music and dances of the area to the New World. African-influenced dances, where they appear in the Americas, seem to furnish means of testing assertions about the "parent stock." If one believes that West African dances are multimetric in nature, for example, the demonstration that some forms of Afro-Cuban danc-

ROBERT FARRIS THOMPSON

ing are also founded upon the simultaneous use of one or more meters (in addition to the basic time signature of the music) might strengthen the assertion.

Four shared traits of West African music and dance are suggested here, together with a fifth, which, although nonmusical, seems very relevant. These shared characteristics appear to be the following: the dominance of a percussive concept of performance; multiple meter; apart playing and dancing; call-and-response; and, finally, the songs and dances of derision.

The first phrase, which is Alan Merriam's—the dominance of a percussive concept of performance—describes a core element.[9] In the Western classic symphony, two tympani are outnumbered by some forty-three melodic instruments, which is symptomatic of an ascendancy of harmonic and melodic concepts and the relative unimportance of percussive traditions. But in tropical Africa even instruments outside the membranophone and idiophone classes will be played with percussive bias instead of in ways soft and legato. Africans do not traditionally bow fiddles legato, but pluck them energetically, with vigorous attack.[10] So striking is this emphasis upon percussive musical diction (which has to do with aesthetic choices and not the inevitable use of a drum or even hardwood sticks) that I am tempted to designate West Africa as a percussive culture. In fact, heaven itself has been portrayed by a West African poet in terms of percussive display and onomatopoeia:

> Let the calabash
> Entwined with beads
> With blue Aggrey beads
> Resound
> Let the calabash resound
> In tune with the drums
> Mingle with these sounds
> The clang of wood on tin:
> *Kentensekenken*
> *Ken—tse ken ken ken*[11]

In the West African world, it is one of the dancer's aims to make every rhythmic subtlety of the music visible.[12] When the master drummer of the Ijebu Yoruba rises in level of pitch, during a ceremony for the waterspirit named Igodo, the master dancer is said to rise, correspondingly, upon his toes. When a Thundergod drum choir of the Egbado Yoruba plays music expressive of the hot-tempered God of Iron, the master dancer immediately becomes explosive in her gestures to maintain an appropriate balance with the emotional coloring of the percussive patterns being rendered.

Surface appreciation of such procedures may mask the fact that it is West African *dancing* that is percussive, regardless of whether or not it is expressed with a striking of one part of the body against another (the chest whacking with the hands of Dahomean *Kpe*) or with stamping patterns and rattles. Percussive flavoring governs the motion of those parts of the body that carry no weight—the gestures—as well as the steps that do. Unsurprisingly, a good drummer in West Africa is a good dancer, and vice versa, although the degree of specialty and professionalism varies with each individual.

The mnemonic retention of dance steps shares the same verbal basis of drummers who are attempting to impart the memory of a given drum pattern to an apprentice drummer. This verbal basis often consists of drum syllables:[13] They are used when a dancer wishes to speak out the drum or bodily rhythms of a particular dance in order to make clear the duration of the gestures and steps and the contrasts with which a particular movement is built. To return to the master dancer of Ajilete, Nigeria, we note that she pays close attention to the syllables enunciated by the drums, and when she hears the pattern *gẹrẹ gẹrẹ gẹrẹ gẹkan*, she swings her hands across her body during the first six syllables. Each time the last two syllables sound, she draws her hands up to her breasts with a simultaneous inhalation of breath.[14]

Thus, West African dances are *talking dances*, and the point of the conversation is the expression of percussive concepts. This gift reappears in the Negro New World: Marshall and Jean Stearns have informed me that tap dancers sometimes spell out their ideas with syllables, in the West African manner, and I have observed similar instances among New York's Afro-Cuban dancers. Perhaps the absorption of this tradition has sharpened the exceptional mambos of James Evans, one of the finest Negro dancers of New York:

> Over the years Evans has worked out a "semaphoric" mambo that is his own, a means of metrically conversing with his hands. Unlike the handwork in certain Polynesian dances, Evans' is only occasionally pictorial; it is his aim to capture and describe percussion, not specific images, and the extent to which he succeeds is perhaps best summarized by [Hoyt Warner] who once shouted to him "You *caught* that riff."[15]

Warner, a young white mathematician and amateur of mambo, meant that the music indicated a sudden repeated phrase and that Evans had convincingly translated the iteration into motion.

Instead of emphasizing the expression of West African dance (and its derivatives) in terms of taps and rattles, clapping and stamping, it would seem far more penetrating to say that it is West African dancing itself that is percussive.

The vigor and the attack of the idiom can be so subtly elaborated as when Ohori Yoruba open and close their shoulder blades in time to a mental gong.

Multiple meter, the second trait, is a well-documented element of West African music. The phrase means the simultaneous execution of several time signatures, not unlike the sounding of the ¾ of the waltz and the ⁴⁄₄ of jazz at the same time,[16] survivals of which enliven the Negro barrios of the Americas. Polymeter in the West African manner turns up in the urban music of the Spanish-speaking segments of the United States. A pleasing example has been recorded by Mongo Santamaría, wherein two types of drum establish parallel lines of ⁴⁄₄ time with machine-gun celerity while another type of drum lays down a ⁶⁄₈ at a slow tempo.[17]

Multiple meter qualifies much West African dancing as a mirror image. A useful theoretical introduction to the problem was established in 1948 by Richard Alan Waterman:

> The dance of the West African is an essay on the appreciation of musical rhythms. For the performance of a good dancer the drums furnish the inspiration, in response to which the thread of each rhythmic element contributing to the thunderous whole of the percussion *gestalt* is followed in movement without separation from its polyrhythmic context.[18]

Waterman describes a maximum instance. The dancer picks up each rhythm of the polymetric whole with different parts of his body; when he does so, he directly mirrors the metric mosaic. But it is important to note that in many instances West Africans find it convenient to dance to only one rhythm, or to shift from two basic pulsations in their footwork to three (as in a kind of Ewe virtuoso dancing), or to follow three mental pulsations while the gong player actually strikes four. In other words, there are minimum instances of multi-metric dancing to oppose against the full expression described by Waterman.

In this context, the notion of balance is not only a canon of West African dancing but an aesthetic acid test: The weak dancer soon loses his metric bearings in the welter of competing countermeters and is, so to speak, knocked off balance, as if a loser in a bout of Indian wrestling. Multiple meter is, in brief, a communal examination of percussive individuality.

Bertonoff defines multimetric dancing as bodily orchestration:

> The Ewe dances are the most fervent among all the Ghanaian tribes, for in them the body moves as though it were orchestrated. The various limbs and members, head, shoulders, and legs are all moving simultaneously but each in a rhythm of its own. The main movement is carried out at dizzying speed

by the elbows. The motion resembles that of the wings of an injured bird, yet it is as light and easy as the swaying of a fish's fins.[19]

I suspect dancers from different African societies choose different parts of the body for emphasis within the polymetric whole. We know that the rhythmic emphasis of West African music shifts back and forth from meter to meter, and the parts of the dancer's body that reflect these shifts may also constitute major determinants of local styles.

On the northwest "verge" of Ghana, at Lawra, Bertonoff documented a second manifestation of multiple meter. The movement was actually the seated "dance" of the musician playing a xylophone:

> He held a stick in each hand, and the rhythm of the left hand was opposed to that of the right. His head was moving in a third rhythm between the strokes. It seemed to me that the soles of his feet were also on the move and giving the rhythm and counterrhythm an interpretation of their own. During the dance the feet interpret the rhythm according to which the other parts of the body are moving.[20]

The last observation is interesting. Implied is a notion of the dancer monitoring the rhythmic *donnée* of the music with his feet while with other parts of his body he duplicates or comments upon the polymeters of the music. The metric "given" of the music in West Africa is normally the accents of a gong. Significantly, A. M. Jones, who has also briefly studied Ewe dancing, finds that in the *Adzida* club dance ("very popular in Eweland") the foot and hand movements are staggered, though the feet are in phase with the gong. It should be noted, however, that Jones's careful notation shows the bell pattern in 12/8 time, the feet in 3/4; thus, even though the dancer follows the organizing meter of the music with his feet, he has executed a statement at metrical variance from it.

The notion of the feet interpreting the foundation beat of gongs finds an interesting corroboration among the Tiv of central Nigeria. Laura Bohannan reports a confrontation with informants who insisted that she dance at a wedding to prove her solidarity with the relevant family: " 'Teach me then,' I retorted. Duly, she and the other senior women began my instruction: my hands and my feet were to keep time with the gongs, my hips with the first drum, my back and shoulders with the second."[21] Whenever Mrs. Bohannan subsided into an "absent-minded shuffle," indignant old women promptly poked her in the ribs and commanded "Dance." Thus, in at least one Tiv society, the articulation of multiple meter seems to amount to protocol.

Cult and secular dancing among the Negroes of Cuba evinces some multi-

ROBERT FARRIS THOMPSON

metric dancing. Rumbaists, for example, sometimes introduce a passage ⅜ elbow-work at a fast tempo in opposition to the basic ²⁄₄ or ⁴⁄₄ pulsations marked by their footwork. Señor Julito Collazo, an excellent dancer of an entire range of Cuban cult dances, told me that "there have been many times when I was dancing rumba with or against the ²⁄₄ of the music when I varied my steps by adding passages of Cuban-Ibibio style in ⅜ time." Whenever this happened, his steps were immediately at variance with the basic beat.

The third trait is apart playing and dancing. And perhaps the best way to gain an insight into the dissection of experience that affects Western life may be to study the physical movements of the musicians of a classic symphony orchestra. The violin section is seated in ordered rows; and when the violinists are observed in profile, their silhouettes, a repeated pattern of human figures seated stiffly erect, form a kind of step-fret series. At the sign of the conductor's baton, more than a score of violinists take up their instruments and, holding them against their chins, bow-and-finger them in unison; as they do so, their restricted action hovers like a nimbus over the more-or-less motionless body. Action has been restricted, essentially, to the right arm and to the fingers and wrist of the left hand, although the body may sway somewhat.

In dramatic contrast to this remarkable compression of motion, West African musicians move the whole trunk and head, whether seated or standing, in response to the music. West African musicians dance their own music. They play "apart" in the sense that each is often intent upon the production of his own contribution to a polymetric whole. The members of a drum choir of three do not strike the skins of their instruments in unison. At least one—normally the master drummer—creates pleasing clashes with the rhythmic structure of his helpers; he departs from their text, as it were, and improvises illuminations. "Apart playing" defines much of the production of music in West Africa where "synchronous" playing defines much of the music of the West. (But certainly not all: "Classic" compositions come to mind wherein the clarinets may do something different from the violins.) Africans unite music and dance but play apart; Europeans separate dance and music but play together. As A. M. Jones notes: "With Western music deliberate synchrony is the norm from which our music develops; that is why it is possible for one man with a baton to conduct a whole orchestra."[22] Playing apart, on the other hand, grants the West African space in which to maintain his own private or traditional meter and to express his own full corporeal involvement in what he is doing.

A close inspection of dance modes in West Africa will reveal that "apart dancing" is as important a part of choreographic custom as "apart playing." It is one of the more striking traits of sub-Saharan dance,[23] and it is one of the few dance constituents that European outsiders consistently identified in verbal descriptions. F. de Kersaint-Gilly noted in 1922: "In Negro Africa—I have spent time among Bakota and among various societies of West Africa—man and woman never put their arms around each other while dancing, as we generally do in France."[24]

Apart dancing is not correlated with the apart playing of instruments in the sense of absence of body contact. The unity which the musicians and dancers share seems, rather, to constitute a constellation of solo and chorus performances. The master drummer (or drummers) plays alone, intent upon improvisation; the master dancer (or dancers), intent upon following or challenging these improvisations, also dances alone. And the drum chorus and the dancing chorus interact by repetitive patterns, which means that a certain amount of performing together balances the apartness. But the critical fact seems to be this: West Africans perform music and dance apart the better to ensure a dialog between movement and sound.

Dancers of the classic ballet do not touch either, as a rule, but these dancers are governed by a single metrical reference and, moreover, dance together in the sense that all their actions are governed by identical demands of pictorial legibility—which is to say that their *pliés* and *tours en l'air* must project crisply across row upon row of seated spectators. Considering the literary bias of the West, this tendency was inevitable. (Modern dance, in which apart playing and dancing are not uncommon, might be described as a dramatic break with this tendency, comparable with Cézanne's shift from representation to expression; but to what extent African influence and/or independent inventions shaped this revolution cannot be estimated in this article.) Africans seem to dance with full muscular actions so palpably syllabic that one can scarcely fail to comprehend the sense of linguistic community that pervades the whole. To dance with arms enlaced around the partner, in the manner of pre-jazz Western ballrooms, lessens the opportunity to converse. Even when Africans dance together, as in certain performing pairs of Abomey, they are actually operating apart to achieve a playing of hand movements against hips, something not possible were their hands locked in an embrace. Nor could their hands find individual metric inspiration were the members of the percussive choir similarly locked into a single metrical scheme. To recapitulate, West Africans and Afro-Americans dance apart and play apart to liberate their attention, as it were, for continuous conversation between motion and music, instead of specializing in purely musical or choreographic activity.

The fourth trait of West African music and dance is a special form of antiphony, wherein a caller alternates his lines with the regularly timed responses of a chorus; it is the formal structure of indigenous singing,[25] and it is known as call-and-response. The important fact is that the caller frequently overlaps or interrupts the chorus. Antiphony exists the world over, but nowhere else in the world does the overlapping of the phrases of leader and followers so consistently occur. Are there similar patterns in the dance? Yes. J. Van Wing summarized the dances of the important Bakongo peoples of what is now the Democratic Republic of Congo (Kinshasa): "There are always two bodies or two groups of bodies in movement: a solo dancer in front of a group, or an individual before another in a group, or an individual before another in a couple, or two groups placed in front of the other. They perform periodic movements that are like questions and responses."[26]

Similar patterns appear in the world of Spanish Harlem ballrooms, where Puerto Ricans improvise constantly varying steps—dancing apart while their partners maintain a recurrent movement. These men "interrupt" the movement of their women in a call-and-response manner, for they begin a new step or flourish considerably before their partners have finished the execution of their basic movements. In Ushi, an especially musical Ekiti Yoruba village, my wife and I observed a lead dancer improvise patterns that consistently began before a "chorus" had finished its "refrain," which consisted of swinging the ends of their head-ties in concerted rhythm, first to the right, then to the left, over their wrists.

The fifth trait, a nonmusical element, is the moral function of the songs of social allusion and the dances of derision. "In West Africa," Laura Boulton writes, "songs are frequently used as an important moral agent in the community. Songs of satire are very powerful because there is no punishment an African dreads more than being held up to the ridicule of his fellow men."[27] (A wealth of similar examples may be found in Alan P. Merriam's *Anthropology of Music*.) Although we are, of course, referring to *content* rather than to form or style—a different analytic level—we intend to illustrate briefly, in the conclusion, that a relationship between content and style is best displayed by singers' deliberately distorting their voices when singing in traditions noted for moral allusion and inquisition.

The dance of derision, the choreographic correlate of the song of allusion, is a striking trait of much West African dancing. Even in Zululand, outside the purview of West Africa, derision dances are found and have been described by Kaigh as "dances of domestic oddities":

They dance after any event, white or black, which takes their fancy. I have seen danced imitations of myself and party too veracious to be flattering, or even comfortable. After I had lost a steeplechase by being thrown from the horse my boys danced the accident so faithfully that I came away a sadder, if not a wiser clown. The boy who took the part of me was most embarrassingly accurate as to detail.[28]

Pride and pretension are as much a target of the African dancer as they are of the singer of allusion. Surprisingly, the connection between the arts in this regard has not, to my knowledge, been pointed out. The former colonial authorities of what is now the Republic of Zambia were aware of the potentialities of African derision dancing, or so Chapter 120, Section 7, of the former laws of that area implies: "No person may organize or take part in any dance which is calculated to hold up to ridicule or to bring into contempt any person, religion, or duly constituted authority."[29] This apparent characteristic was noted in 1825 by Captain Hugh Clapperton, who witnessed a dance, evidently danced at his expense, at Old Ọyọ, the ancient imperial capital of the Yoruba Peoples.[30]

Dances of derision in the Negro world are legion. Camille Poupeye mentions them in the Bamako area of Mali and calls them "satires in action,"[31] and S. F. Nadel has described one instance at Bida in northern Nigeria. I have observed over the last ten years Puerto Rican dancers mock fatuous or eccentric dancing with cruelly accurate movements in New York City. The dance of derision brings home the fact that Africans and Afro-Americans are interested not only in force and the affirmation of fertility in their controlled energetic dancing, but also with ethics and right living. The man who misbehaves may not only have to "face the music," as in the "signifying songs" of the old-time New Orleans Negroes, but he may also have to face the movement.

To summarize these points with the help of a Yoruba critic: One cultivator—criticizing a dance by members of a society which performs during the installation of the king of the Anago town of Ipokia and during the funerals of its members—said: "This dance is aesthetically pleasing [*ijó nā wù mi dādā*] because the legs and all parts of the body are equal" [*nítorípé ẹsẹ̀ tó ngbe àti gbogbo ara dọ́gba*]. The key word is *dọ́gba*, which means in Yoruba "is symmetrical." The native connoisseur of artistic motion had put his finger on one of the most important canons of West African dance—balance.

The point of one form of Ibo dancing in Nigeria, for example, is to infuse the upper torso and the head with violent vibrations without losing an overall sense of stability. In this case, equilibrium is shown by the relatively motionless extension of the open palms in front of the dancer, almost at arm's length, each palm at an equal distance from the body. And, moreover, despite the ferocity of the "shimmying" of the upper frame, the shuffling feet of the dancer indulge gravity and thus convey balance. When West Africans shuffle—and most of them do in their traditional dancing (although there are dances galore in which dancers, especially men, break the bonds of gravity with special leaps

ROBERT FARRIS THOMPSON

and other gravity-resistant motions)—their bodies are usually bent forward, toward the stabilizing earth. They maintain balance. And balance is cool.

A further case in point: A gifted Egbado Yoruba dancer maintains the whole time she dances a "bound motion" in her head, thus balancing a delicate terracotta sculpture on her head without danger, while simultaneously subjecting her torso and arms to the most confounding expressions of raw energy and force. It is not difficult to find similar instances of control in other African dances. Thundergod devotees, for instance, sometimes dance with a burning fire in a container coolly balanced on the top of their heads. Coolness in the sense of control and symmetry seems a metaphor of the spiritual. And this is not to mention the manifold secular manifestations of this basic tendency—for example, Africans traveling while balancing even ink wells and sheets of paper on their heads or African wrestlers defeating their opponents not by "pinning" them to the ground in the Western manner, but by knocking them off balance.

From this cultural background a philosophy of music and dance seems to emerge. In the case of the dominance of a percussive concept, one is talking about the vigorous involvement of the whole body (the performances of the aged continue to provoke the amazement of Western observers). The vibrations may be subtle but they are diffused throughout the body. This trait might be compared with Yoruba ephebism or the deliberately youthful depiction of the human frame in sculpture.[32]

Old age is rare in West African sculpture. Its depiction seems restricted to situations of satire, psychological warfare, and moral vengeance. The dignity of the Yoruba dancer's facial expression might be profitably compared with the ephebistic (youthful) flawless seal of most Yoruba sculpture. In both cases, in any event, indigenous critics of art may characterize the dignity of the respective expressions as "cool." When Tiv (in northern Nigeria) dance satirically, as in the Ngogh[33] dance making fun of swollen bodies, the flawless seal shatters and faces become twisted with exaggeration and grimaces. But in the aggregate, West Africans dance with a mixture of vigor and decorum.

Multiple meter essentially uses dancers as further voices in a polymetric choir. The conversation is additive, cool in its expressions of community. The balance struck between the meters and the bodily orchestration seems to communicate a soothing wholeness rather than a "hot" specialization. The implications of dialog in apart performing have been discussed. Call-and-response is a means of putting innovation and tradition, invention and imitation, into amicable relationships with one another. In that sense it, too, is cool. Finally, the dance of derision sometimes breaks these rules in order to mime the disorder of those who would break the rules of society.[34] Yoruba moral inquisitors do not really dance; they loom. Their shapes, their cries, their motions are unearthly, meant to startle, meant—quite literally—to frighten the hell out of people.

The dance of derision attests that although most West African dances exist as concrete metaphors of right living, some Africans do cheat, steal, and kill. Terrible events occur in West Africa not because the inhabitants lack moral control (their dances make this clear), but because thus far no society on earth has ever completely satisfied or embodied a definition of ideal behavior.[35]

When Christians go to war (instead of turning the other cheek), they have the effrontery to do so within a system of ethics that imparts the promise of redemption. But when an African, finding his security threatened, kills his neighbor, depressingly large segments of the Western world believe that he does so instinctively, without any moral check whatsoever. But an increasing familiarity with the ideal of the cool, documented by the nonverbal "texts" of the dance, will reveal a fact of moral equality. Should Westerners, white and black alike, forsake comfort and estimate the meaning of the words that are made flesh in the dances of the Guinea Coast, they might find our double standards intolerable. They might even detect logical inconsistencies when they observe that the murder of Greek by Turk, of Turk by Greek, on Cyprus is described as an "historical conflict," but that the murder of Ibo by Hausa, and Hausa by Ibo, in Nigeria is described with horror as a "reversion to savagery."

The time-resistant dances of the cool form a kind of prayer: May humanity be shielded from the consequences of arrogance and the penalties of impatience.

NOTES

It is a pleasure to acknowledge the support of the Ford Foundation, which enabled me, as a Fellow of the Foreign Area Training Program, to study Yoruba sculpture and dance in Nigeria and Dahomey from October 1962, to January 1964. I should also like to thank warmly the Councilium for International Study at Yale for a grant which enabled me to continue these studies in Nigeria during the summer of 1965. The sympathy and advice of Leonard Doob is especially noted in this regard. I have also profited from correspondence with Alan P. Merriam, Chairman of the Department of Anthropology, Indiana University, and with Judith Lynne Hanna, of the Center for Research in Social Systems at the American University. Vincent Scully was kind enough to read portions of a first draft of this paper and made, as did Merriam and Hanna, many relevant criticisms. Finally, I should like to thank John Davis for encouraging this brief study.

1. Alan P. Merriam, "African Music" in *Continuity and Change in African Cultures*, ed. William R. Bascom and Melville J. Herskovits (Chicago: University of Chicago Press, 1959), 76.

2. See Julius Glück, "Afrikanische Architektur," *Tribus* 6 (1956): 65.

3. For example, see Robin Horton's "The Kalabari Ekine Society: A Borderland of Religion and Art," *Africa* (April 1963).

4. Transcribed by Charles Keil in his *Urban Blues* (Chicago: University of Chicago Press, 1966), 98. A slightly variant version may be heard on ABC-Paramount 509, *B. B. King Live at the Regal.*

5. As to a Yoruba myth concerning water as symbol of reconciliation, see the excellent vernacular source *Ijala: Are Ọdẹ*, by Oladipo Yemitan (Ibadan, Nigeria: Ibadan University Press, 1963), 4–6. As to a Yoruba myth concerning leaves, see J. O. George, *Historical Notes on the Yoruba Country* (Lagos, Nigeria, 1895), 62–63. Here the agency of reconciliation was "the leaf of a tree called *Ewe-Alasuwalu*, a leaf that is capable of remodeling a man's evil character. . . . Agirilogbon took it out of the . . . bag of deep mystery, healed all the people, and stopped the calamity."

6. See *Time*, "Death and Transfiguration," March 5, 1965, 23.

7. McLuhn's *Understanding Media: The Extensions of Man* (New York: McGraw-Hill, 1965) is a richly aphoristic text suggestive, by means of a jumpy, electric style, of its subject matter. McLuhan observes that "a hot medium is one that extends one single sense in high definition" (22). He seems to feel that the rise of the concept "cool" (and, symptomatically, he quotes Jack Paar) is caused by the mass media. My own view is historical: I think the philosophy of the cool existed, in one form or another, in Negro-American culture long before the time of the telephone, radio, and television. The fact that American Negroes have been noted for their dancing since the coming of their ancestors to these shores seems to suggest the historical basis of the importance of "not losing one's cool" in their world view. This is in the nature of theory, of course. Much sharpening of issues and further researches are needed.

8. Yet motion in response to the dirge is not uncommon. See J. H. Nketia, *Funeral Dirges of the Akan People* (Achimota, Ghana: 1955), 10.

9. Merriam has enriched our understanding of the interrelationship between percussion music and the dance of tropical Africa. His notions about music clearly inspired my own statement that it is African *dancing* that is percussive, regardless of the presence or absence of percussion. In this regard, it is interesting to look at an observation made shortly after the turn of the century by the Duke of Mecklenburg apropos of Watutsi in his *In the Heart of Africa* (London: Cassell and Co., 1910), 60: "There was no musical accompaniment to the majority of the eleven different kinds of dance which we observed, such as is usual with all the terpsichorean exercises of the Negro people. In spite of this, however, there was no lack of rhythm."

10. Alan P. Merriam, "The African Idiom in Music," *Journal of American Folklore* 75 (April-June 1962): 127.

11. Francis Ernest Kobina Parkes, "African Heaven," in *New World Writing No. 15* (New York: Mentor, 1959), 230–32.

12. Marshall Stearns, "Is Modern Jazz Dance Hopelessly Square?" *Dance*, June 1965, 33.

13. An excellent discussion of the verbal basis of Akan drumming may be found in Nketia's *Drumming in Akan Communities of Ghana* (London: Thomas Nelson and Sons, 1963), 32–50. In addition, an interesting colloquium, "Drumming Syllables in Five Traditions: South India, Colonial North America, Arabic Countries, Japan, and West Africa," held at the New England Chapter Meeting of the American Musicological Society at Boston University on March 5, 1966, furnished fresh insights into similar practices in other parts of the world. For example, in South India, as among Yoruba, syllables ending in nasalization are sustained. And both Yoruba and Colonial North Americans seem to choose the conso-

nant *k* (*que*, actually, in the orthography of the latter instance) to represent heavy beats. Compare, also, the Akan phrase "tiri tiri *kon*" with the American Colonial "ratama*que.*"

14. I am especially beholden to Perk Foss for assisting in many ways the field documentation of Yoruba dancing at Ajilete in April 1966.

15. Robert Farris Thompson, "Portrait of the Pachanga," *Saturday Review*, October 28, 1961, 54.

16. Richard Alan Waterman, "African Influence on the Music of the Americas," in *Acculturation in the Americas*, ed. Sol Tax (Chicago: University of Chicago Press, 1952). This article is a landmark in the literature of Africanist ethnomusicology.

17. Some Afro-Cuban musicians maintain that the secret of their music is an opposition of two pulsations against three. This understates, in my opinion, a rich tradition of multiple meter.

18. Richard Alan Waterman, "Hot Rhythm in Negro Music," *Journal of the American Musicological Society* 1 (Spring 1948): 4.

19. Deborah Bertonoff, *Dance Towards the Earth* (Tel Aviv: Alytiros, 1963), 46.

20. Ibid., 189–90.

21. Laura Bohannan, *Return to Laughter* (Garden City, N.Y.: Doubleday and Co., 1964), 123.

22. A. M. Jones, *Studies in African Music* (London: Oxford University Press, 1959), 1: 193.

23. The phrase "apart dancing" is my own. Marshall Stearns phrases the mode another way: "solo dancing—the universal way of dancing in Africa." See Marshall and Jean Stearns, "Profile of the Lindy," *Show*, October 1963, 112.

24. F. de Kersaint-Gilly, "Notes sur la danse en pays noir," *Bulletin du comité d'études historiques et scientifiques de L'Afrique occidentale française* (January-March 1922): 80.

25. See Alan Merriam, album notes, *Africa South of the Sahara*, Ethnic Folkways FE 4503.

26. J. Van Wing, "Les Danses Bakongo," *Congo: Revue générale de la colonie belge* (July 1937): 122.

27. Laura Boulton, album notes, *African Music*, Ethnic Folkways 8852.

28. Frederick Kaigh, *Witchcraft and Magic of Africa* (London: Richard Lesley and Co., 1947), 26.

29. Quoted in J. Clyde Mitchell, *The Kalela Dance* (Manchester: Rhodes-Livingston Papers, 1956), 12, n. 5.

30. Captain Hugh Clapperton, *Journal of a Second Expedition into the Interior of Africa* (London: John Murray, 1829), 55.

31. Camille Poupeye, *Danses dramatiques en théâtres exotiques* (Brussels: Le Cahiers du Journal des Poètes, 1941), 109.

32. See Robert Farris Thompson, "Yoruba Artistic Criticism," paper read at the Conference on the Artist in Traditional African Society, Lake Tahoe, May 1965.

33. I acknowledge with many thanks a personal communication, dated February 1, 1966, from Charles Keil, who, writing from the field, informed me of the *Ngogh* dance and other items of Tiv traditional choreographies.

34. In a future volume, I shall intensively analyze the problem of the anti-aesthetic in African art, dance, and music.

35. It is convenient for some Westerners to note this basic fact only outside their culture. Thus, in the *New York Times* of October 9, 1966 we read, p. 10E: "Asia where nations preach morality and respect force."

Africa and the West Indies

(1968)

MARSHALL STEARNS & JEAN STEARNS

. . . .

Long after its original publication, the "bible" of American vernacular dance remains Marshall and Jean Stearns's Jazz Dance: The Story of American Vernacular Dance, *from which this selection is taken. Stearns and his wife, Jean, interviewed dancers for over seven years to collect firsthand statements recounting the development of American dance. In this selection, Stearns expands Robert Farris Thompson's observations on African dance to include American and Caribbean forms. Author of* The Story of Jazz *(1956), Marshall Stearns was a professor of English at Hunter College in New York, a founder of the Newport Jazz Festival and of the Institute of Jazz Studies; Jean Stearns collaborated on the research and final publication of* Jazz Dance.

In the early 1950's, during the first years of a summer resort in the Berkshire Mountains called Music Inn, we tried an experiment. Our aim was to entertain—quite informally—a handful of guests in the lounge after dinner, but our host Philip Barber was carried away with his theory of instantaneous talent combustion. "Throw gifted performers together," he said, "get one of them going, and watch them all discover talents which they didn't know they had." With various jazzmen of supposedly separate eras, the idea had worked well.

That evening we had dancers from three different countries: Asadata Dafora from Sierra Leone, West Africa; Geoffrey Holder from Trinidad, West Indies; and Al Minns and Leon James from the Savoy Ballroom, New York City. All of them were alert to their own traditions and articulate, eager to demonstrate their styles.

So we began with the Minns-James repertory of twenty or so Afro-American dances, from "Cakewalk to Cool," asking Dafora and Holder to comment freely. The results were astonishing. One dancer hardly began a step before another exclaimed with delight, jumped to his feet, and executed a related version of his own. The audience found itself sharing the surprise and pleasure of the dancers as they hit upon similarities in their respective traditions. We were soon participating in the shock of recognizing what appeared to be one great tradition.

Certain trends emerged. American dances of predominantly British and European origin, such as the Square Dance, seemed to go back only as far as the West Indies—if at all. The Cakewalk turned up no worthy African counter-part (Minns and James omitted improvised steps), although Holder demon-strated its general relationship to the Bel Air of Trinidad. The basic Mambo, however, was immediately identified with a Congo step from Africa and a Shango step from Trinidad. (The Cuban scholar, Fernando Ortiz, is convinced that *mambo* is a Congo word.)

An American dance, the Shimmy, produced an immediate response from Dafora. "That is only the beginning of the Shika dance of Nigeria," he asserted and illustrated his point by vibrating his shoulders and then gradually shaking down and throughout his entire body. Minns and James were almost grieved: "You're doing our Shake dance!" Whereupon they produced their own ver-sion, throwing in a few grinds and quivers. Both Little Egypt and Elvis Presley, it now appeared, were standing still, and the Twist, Frug, and Jerk were simple-minded substitutes. We learned that the Shake is known as the Banda in Trinidad and the Oleke in West Africa.

Other American dances led to other parallels. The Charleston proved simi-lar to a dance called the King Sailor in Trinidad (the title may have been taken from an American movie) and an Obolo dance of the Ibo tribe in West Africa. Another, Pecking—a neck and shoulder movement which begins with an imi-tation of chickens—was found to be similar to a Yanvallou dance in Trinidad and a Dahomean dance in West Africa. Elements of the Lindy, or Jitterbug, were noted by Holder in a Shango dance, and by Dafora in an Ejor tribal dance.

And thus the evening passed quickly. A rather sensational routine known as Snake Hips (a specialty of loose-jointed Earl Tucker at the Cotton Club in Harlem in the late 1920's), in which the loins are undulated in a very un-European fashion, brought a quick response from Holder: "That's called the Congo in Trinidad." Dafora, who was fiercely proud of his native land, seemed embarrassed, but agreed that it was called the Congo in Africa.

When Minns cut loose with the Fish Tail as a climax to the Snake Hips routine (accompanied by Duke Ellington's recording of "East St. Louis Toodle-Oo"), a movement in which the buttocks weave out, back, and up in a variety of figure eights, both Holder and Dafora were silent. Holder could not seem to place it, but Dafora finally observed with some asperity that although the Fish Tail came from Africa, dancing in the European fashion with one arm around your partner's waist was considered obscene. ("The African dance," writes President Senghor of Senegal, "disdains bodily contact."[1]) He was caught between two cultures and their almost opposite attitudes toward hip movement.

The evening at Music Inn gave us insights that are borne out by other evidence. Like music, the dance is found everywhere in Africa—a "fundamental element in aesthetic expression"[2] in the words of Melville Herskovits—and there seems to be no limit whatsoever to the movements employed.

"Ranging from the walk and all its variations," writes Pearl Primus, "the technique of the African dance embraces the leap, the hop, the skip, the jump, falls of all descriptions, and turns which balance the dancer at the most precarious angles to the ground."[3]

Perhaps the most clear-cut survival of African dance in the United States is the Ring Shout, or Circle Dance, with its combination of African elements from the counterclockwise movement of the group, through the stiff shoulders and outstretched arm and hand gestures, to the flat-footed Shuffle. Not so obvious is the survival of the Cross Over in the Charleston; the Congo hip movements in the Slow Drag, Snake Hips, and other social dances of the Negro folk; the African style of the subtly bouncing Shuffle performed by the dancers in a New Orleans street march; and the African acrobatic dances in the Jitterbug and earlier professional acts. Of course, the original African impulse, so to speak, has often been reinterpreted and diluted.

At the other extreme, several "American" dances have been observed in what was probably their original form in Africa. Take the Charleston, which first destroyed the distinction in the United States between a dance to watch and a dance to perform—everybody seemed to be doing it around 1925. Among the Ashanti, Herskovits recognizes a "perfect example of the Charleston."[4] A. N. Tucker notes "the 'Charleston-like' step which is common to all Barispeakers";[5] and Frederick Kaigh writes, "The children of Africa were doing the Charleston before Julius Caesar had so much as heard of Britain, and they still are."[6]

A few years ago, watching films of West African dancing taken by Professor Lorenzo Turner of Roosevelt University, the present writers saw the Ibibio of Nigeria performing a shimmy to end all shimmies, the Sherbro of Sierra Leone executing an unreasonably fine facsimile of the Snake Hips, and a group of Hausa girls near Kano moving in a fashion closely resembling the Lindy, or Jitterbug.

Again, in her analysis of African dance films, the director of the Philadelphia Dance Academy, Nadia Chilkovsky, found close parallels to American dances such as the Shimmy, Charleston, Pecking, Trucking, Hucklebuck, and Snake Hips, among others.[7] Indeed, most films of African dancing—in and out of Hollywood (fortunately, no director knows how to commercialize the native dances)—are honeycombed with resemblances to American popular dance. The resemblances are strongest, however, to the Afro-American *vernacular*, that is, such basic dances of the Negro folk as the Strut, Shuffle, Sand, and Grind.

The evidence of eyewitnesses is also available. Folklorist Harold Courlander has seen dances in South Africa, Ghana, and Nigeria which were "virtually indistinguishable" from the Cakewalk, Shuffle, and Strut.[8]

The pioneering Negro dancer Thaddeus Drayton, who was born in 1893, remembers meeting an African student named Moleo in Paris during the 1920's. Moleo was putting himself through school by dancing. "He was from German South Africa, and was doing—barefoot—a complicated flash step, which we called Over the Top. We believed that an American Negro, Toots Davis, had invented it, but when I asked Moleo what American had taught him, he laughed and said, 'That step came from my tribe in Africa.' "[9]

"The dance itself," says Herskovits, "has . . . carried over into the New World to a greater degree than almost any other trait of African culture."[10] In fact, it is just possible, as Africanist Robert F. Thompson of Yale University has suggested, that certain basic movements can be associated with certain African tribes.[11] Thus, the Pygmies are famous for their footwork, the Dahomeans for their head and shoulder motions, and the Congolese for their hip and loin movements. We may some day be able to specify the tribal origins of various movements in American popular dance.

As time goes on, the influence of Afro-American dance on American popular dance is increasing. Today the Latin-American dances such as the Rumba, Conga, Samba, Mambo, Cha Cha, Pachanga, and so on, which have been imported from areas where a merging of African and European styles has already taken place, show the greatest African influence, both in quantity and quality. At the same time, these dances are still assimilating elements from such earlier Afro-American dances as the Charleston and Jitterbug. Although the time and speed of blending varies, the very ease of blending suggests a common source.

The matter of style is important. While comparing films of African dancing with social dancing of the twenties and thirties, Chilkovsky, who is an expert at dance notation, found it necessary to formulate a new "signature," that is, a symbol indicating the *style of movement*, to distinguish both African and American dancing from the dancing of the rest of the world.[12] She feels that the styles of African dancing and American popular dancing have become so similar that they differ in the same way from all other dancing.

Similarly, American social dancing—like the jazz to which it is often performed—has taken on an African-like rhythmic complexity. Chilkovsky discovered dance cadences in ⁶⁄₄, or even ⁵⁄₄, for example, executed to musical measures of ²⁄₄ or ⁴⁄₄—a fairly sophisticated rhythmic combination. These intricate steps were performed in ordinary social dancing of the ballroom variety, not in virtuoso jazz and tap dancing which, like the solo of a great jazzman, is much more difficult to notate. "In current rock-and-roll dancing," she observed in 1961, "the African component is even greater."

West Africans "dance with a precision, a verve, an ingenuity that no other race can show,"[13] writes Geoffrey Gorer. It is far too complicated to be described in every detail, but six characteristics of African dance—they are not infallible—can help us identify African influence in the United States. First, because it is danced on the naked earth with bare feet, African dance tends to modify or eliminate such European styles as the Jig and the Clog in which the sound of shoe on wooden floor is of primary importance; the African style is often flat-footed and favors gliding, dragging, or shuffling steps.

Second, African dance is frequently performed from a crouch, knees flexed and body bent at the waist. The custom of holding the body stiffly erect seems to be principally European. (The Flamenco style, it has been suggested, goes back to an imitation of a man on horseback; African dancing to a hunter crouched for the kill.) "The deliberately maintained erectness of the European dancer's spine," writes critic John Martin, "is in marked contrast to the fluidity of the Negro dancer's."[14]

Third, African dance generally imitates animals in realistic detail. Although by no means unique to Africa, animal dances portraying the buzzard, eagle, crow, rabbit, and so on, form a large part of the repertory. (The tales of Uncle Remus form a literary parallel.)

Fourth, African dance also places great importance upon improvisation, satirical and otherwise, allowing freedom for individual expression; this characteristic makes for flexibility and aids the evolution and diffusion of other African characteristics.

Fifth, African dance is centrifugal, exploding outward from the hips. This point is crucial. "The leg moves from the hip instead of from the knee, the arm from the shoulder," writes musicologist Rose Brandel, while the motion of the shoulders and head "often appear as the end result of a motion beginning at the hips."[15] John Martin adds that the "natural concentration of movement in the pelvic region is similarly at odds with European usage."[16]

The same point is made by Nadia Chilkovsky, who declares that African dance and much of American dancing to jazz rhythms "begins with the hips and moves outward, employing the entire body." Starting with the hips tends to make the dancing looser. Brandel notes that these movements are "markedly missing from the Oriental dance world." She might have added that they are almost as markedly missing in Europe, where they are a continuing embarrassment to Western notions of propriety and have often short-circuited any understanding or appreciation of African dance.

Sixth and most significantly, African dance is performed to a propulsive rhythm, which gives it a swinging quality also found—usually to a lesser degree—in the music of jazz and in the best dancing performed to that music. Here again, John Martin refers to the Negroes' "uniquely racial [sic] rhythm."[17]

African dancing gives the impression of "a completely civilized art," wrote Edwin Denby, reviewing the African Dance Festival, staged and danced by Asadata Dafora at Carnegie Hall in 1943, ". . . the lucidity of the style was remarkable—the way the body kept clear to one's eye, the feet distinct from the legs, the legs from the trunk, the shoulders, the arms, the head, each separately defined . . . and when the torso turned or bent it seemed to move from the hips."[18] Eight months earlier, he had written about Dafora: "I thought I recognized as the basis of the style, the dance carriage we know from our own Negro dancing."[19]

A helpful comparison of African elements in Haitian dancing with the dancing of Southeast Asia is made by Harold Courlander.[20] He feels that Indian dancing (which has had a considerable influence on "modern dance") conveys a feeling of poised balance and suspended movement, while African dancing communicates "an attitude of strong frontal assault against natural forces such as gravity, or direct submission to those forces."

"There is almost always a feeling of solidarity between the body and the earth," Courlander adds, concerning African dances in Haiti, "but the total effect is dynamic." For Haitian dancing implies "an intimate understanding of nature," while Indonesian dancing suggests a relationship with the supernatural. Perhaps the reason East Indian dancing tends to be static—in a frequently beautiful sense—while African dancing is dynamic can be found in the accompaniment: Unlike Indian music, African music is often polyrhythmic and propulsive and the dancing swings with it.

An example of what might be termed cultural feedback occurred during the 1940's with the appearance of American-style tap dancing among the Makwaya of Northern Rhodesia. "Choirs" donned shoes and retired to indoor stages, according to the English missionary, the Reverend A. M. Jones, where they put on "an exceedingly clever imitation of Western tap dancing"—inspired by American films.[21] While they gave the effect "of the fast footwork and syncopated accented taps of the conventional white man's practice," Jones insists that it was much more complicated rhythmically, "using a mixture of duple and triple times and staggering the main beats. . . ."

Jones does not realize the complexity of American tap dance. His understanding of the conventional white man's practice is no doubt based on performances in music halls, that is, English vaudeville, and seems to be limited to an old style of tap. Among American tap dancers—and even in ballroom dancing—the typically African blend of "duple and triple times" is a commonplace. Like attracts like. No wonder Africans are intrigued by a style of American dancing which owes so much to Africa.

In the old days, during the voyage from Africa, slaves were forced to dance on shipboard to keep them healthy. Before they reached the United States, however, many had absorbed something of British-European dance. Ships stopped over in the West Indies, leaving the slaves to become acclimatized before taking them to the mainland: The stopover increased the rate of survival, and consequently, the rate of profit. Many of the slaves were purchased then and there, staying on the islands and obtaining their first contact with British and European dances.

At first, because of the initial conquest of the islands by Spain, the blending consisted chiefly of Spanish folk and African tribal dance. But from 1800 on, fashionable dances from the courts and elegant salons of Europe—Spanish, French, and English—became popular and were imitated by the slaves. "Every island of the Caribbean," says the folklorist Lisa Lekis, "has some form of quadrille, reel, jig, or contradance . . . greatly transformed in style and function, but still recognizable."[22]

"At present, the societies are dying out . . . but the dances, *Cocoye*, *Masson*, *Babril*, *el Cata* and *el Juba* are still performed with grace, dignity and elegance," she writes of African cults in Cuba, "using steps and figures of the court of Versailles combined with hip movements of the Congo."[23] The addition of Congo hip movements to the dances of the court of Versailles is rather like serving rum in a teacup.

The Quadrille has been preserved in the Virgin Islands, too, but something new has been added: "The quadrille dances are still regularly performed by organized groups who strut elegantly through the measures of *Lanceros*, *Rigodon*, and *Seven Step*," Lekis notes. "The slow, stately style of the original has been replaced by a rapid shuffling step with hips waving and shoulders jiggling, but the traditional figures are faithfully reproduced."[24] Thus, African shoulder and hip movements—as well as the Shuffle, which became the foundation of several jazz steps—are blended in the European Quadrille.

Similarly, Katherine Dunham, after participating in a Jamaican dance, writes that "gradually it dawned on me that this was a Maroon version of the Quadrille," and as the dance became wilder and wilder, she observed an increase in improvisation with "unveiled hip movements."[25]

It can even happen to a waltz. In Curaçao, Lekis comments, "when seen in informal occasions the waltz loses its decorous manner and the same type of hip movement used in the *Tumba* (an African hip dance) appears."[26]

Conversely, Dunham joined a Koromantee war dance in Jamaica that, she notes, "could easily be compared to an Irish reel."[27]

And of Cuba's Cha Cha Cha, Lekis says that "it combines African style steps with a hopping pattern typical of European schottische dances."[28]

"Africa," said André Malraux at the 1966 Festival of Negro Arts in Dakar, "has transformed dancing throughout the world. . . ."[29] For the merging of African body movements with formal European set dances, aided by the African emphasis upon improvisation, produced a new style of dancing.

Speaking of the blending taking place in the West Indies today, Lekis concludes: "The future of the mixed dance and musical forms is in a sense the future of the Caribbean. It seems inevitable that the blending process now moulding a new race of people will continue. And the final stages of acculturation will produce a new form, not African, not European, but fused from the meeting of two races in the New World."[30] The blending has already produced new forms of dance in the United States—American forms—which evolved years ago in the Afro-American vernacular.

NOTES

1. Leopold Sedar Senghor, "African-Negro Aesthetics," *Diogenes* 16 (winter 1956): 33.

2. Melville J. Herskovits, *The Myth of the Negro Past* (New York: Harper & Brothers, 1941), 76.

3. *Dance* (March 1958): 91.

4. Herskovits, *Myth of the Negro Past*, 146.

5. A. N. Tucker, *Tribal Music and Dancing in the Southern Sudan* (London: Wm. Reeves Ltd., n.d.), 36.

6. Frederick Kaigh, *Witchcraft and Magic in Africa* (London: Richard Lesley & Co. Ltd., 1947), 21.

7. From a lecture at the Philadelphia meeting of the Ethnomusicological Society, 1961.

8. In conversation, New York: 1959.

9. From numerous interviews, New York: 1962–1965.

10. Herskovits, *Myth of the Negro Past*, 76.

11. We are grateful to Professor Thompson for his thoughts on many subjects in the course of numerous lectures, correspondence, and conversations, over the past decade.

12. See supra n. 7.

13. Geoffrey Gorer, *Africa Dances* (London: John Lehmann, 1949), 213.

14. John Martin, *The Dance* (New York: Tudor Publishing Company, 1963), 179.

15. From manuscript for *Grolier Encyclopedia*.

16. Martin, *The Dance*, 179.

17. Ibid., 178.

18. Reprinted in Edwin Denby, *Looking at the Dance* (New York: Pellegrini & Cudahy, 1949), 364.

19. Ibid., 361.

20. Harold Courlander, *The Drum and the Hoe* (Berkeley: University of California Press, 1970), 130.

21. A. M. Jones, *Studies in African Music*, Vol. 1 (London: Oxford University Press, 1959), 256, 274–75.

22. Lisa Lekis, *Dancing Gods* (New York: Scarecrow Press, 1960), 37.

23. Lisa Lekis, *Folk Dances of Latin America* (New York: Scarecrow Press, 1958), 226.

24. Ibid., 277.

25. Katherine Dunham, *Journey to Accompong* (New York: Henry Holt & Co., 1946), 24, 26.

26. Lekis, *Folk Dances of Latin America*, 275.

27. Dunham, *Journey to Accompong*, 135.

28. Lekis, *Folk Dances of Latin America*, 229.

29. "Behind the Mask of Africa," *New York Times Magazine*, May 15, 1966, 30.

30. Lekis, *Folk Dances of Latin America*, 196.

Playing the Blues

(1976)

ALBERT MURRAY

. . . .

*Albert Murray is the author of three novels (*Train Whistle Guitar, *1974;* The Spyglass Tree, *1991;* The Seven League Boots, *1996) and six works of nonfiction. In* The Omni-Americans *(1970) Murray argued for recognition of the aesthetic of improvisation and stylization that has ensured the survival of African American culture and accounts for the distinctiveness of American cultural experience. In this chapter from* Stomping the Blues, *Murray identifies several elements of a distinctive blues "technology of stylization": the vamp, riff, break, chorus, rhythmic nuances of beat and syncopation, and tonal coloration. Murray is an Americanist, not an Africanist; though he compares the tonal coloration of blues and jazz to African talking drums, he does so with considerable American "extension, elaboration, and refinement," including attention to the idiomatic tonalities of down-home life. Murray lives in New York City.*

Sometimes it all begins with the piano player vamping till ready, a vamp being an improvised introduction consisting of anything from the repetition of a chordal progression as a warm-up exercise to an improvised overture. Sometimes the vamp has already begun even before the name of the next number is given. Some singers, for instance, especially those who provide their own accompaniment on piano or guitar, use it as much as background for a running line of chatter, commentary, or mock didacticism as to set the mood and tempo for the next selection. Also, sometimes it is used to maintain the ambiance of the occasion and sometimes to change it.

Then the composition as such, which is made up of verses (optional), choruses (refrains), riffs, and breaks, begins. Some blues compositions such as Handy's *Yellow Dog Blues* have an introductory or verse section which establishes the basis for the choral refrain. Many, like Bessie Smith's *Long Old Road* and Big Joe Turner's *Piney Brown's Blues*, do not, and in practice perhaps more often than not the verse is omitted by singers as well as instrumentalists. But whether there is a vamp and/or a verse section, the main body of a blues composition consists of a series of choruses derived from the traditional three-line-stanza form. There may be as many choruses as the musician is inspired to play, unless there are such predetermined restrictions as recording space, broadcast time, or duration of a standard popular dance tune.

The traditional twelve-bar blues stanza-chorus consists of three lines of four bars each. But there are four bars of music in each line and only two bars (plus one beat) of lyric space:

	1ST BAR	2ND BAR
WORDS	Going to Chicago	Sorry but I can't take you
MUSIC	*1 - 2 - 3 - 4*	*1 - 2 - 3 - 4 - 1*

	3RD BAR	4TH BAR
MUSIC	*2 - 3 - 4*	*1 - 2 - 3 - 4*

	5TH BAR	6TH BAR
WORDS	Going to Chicago	Sorry but I can't take you
MUSIC	*1 - 2 - 3 - 4*	*1 - 2 - 3 - 4 - 1*

	7TH BAR	8TH BAR
MUSIC	*2 - 3 - 4*	*1 - 2 - 3 - 4*

	9TH BAR	10TH BAR
WORDS	S'Nothing in Chicago	That a monkey woman can do
MUSIC	*1 - 2 - 3 - 4*	*1 - 2 - 3 - 4 - 1*

	11TH BAR	12TH BAR
MUSIC	*2 - 3 - 4*	*1 - 2 - 3 - 4*

Which by the way also means that there is always approximately twice as much music in a blues chorus as lyric space—even when it is a vocal chorus and the singer is performing a cappella and has to hum and/or drum his own fills.

Some choruses are refrain stanzas played by an instrumental ensemble, apparently a derivation and extension of the vocal choir. Some are played by a single instrument representing a choir. Originally a chorus, which is derived from the same root as *choreography*, was a dance and by extension a group of dancers (as it still is in musical comedies) and by further extension it also became an ensemble or a band of musicians who played for dancers. In ancient Greek drama it was the group of dancers and chanters who provided the necessary background, so to speak, for the solo performer or protagonist. Hence eventually the passages of the European oratorio which are performed by the choir, whether in unison or in polyphony, as opposed to the solo passages.

In most conventional compositions the chorus or refrain is the part that is repeated by all available voices or instruments. But sometimes musicians refer to the solos as choruses. Duke Ellington, for example, used to announce that the first chorus of his theme song would be played by the pianist (himself); then he would sit down and improvise an extended solo of any number of stanzas. Likewise the singer's solo of a blues arrangement may consist of one or several choruses but is also known as the vocal chorus.

Blues musicians also make extensive use of riff choruses. A blues riff is a brief musical phrase that is repeated, sometimes with very subtle variations, over the length of a stanza as the chordal pattern follows its normal progression. Sometimes the riff chorus is used as background for the lead melody and as choral *response* to the solo *call* line. But many arrangements are structured largely and sometimes almost entirely of riff choruses. In Count Basie's original recording of *One o'Clock Jump* (Decca DXSB-7170) for example, the piano begins with a brief traditional music-hall or vaudeville vamp and a solo and is followed by a tenor-sax solo backed by a trumpet-ensemble riff. Then comes a trombone solo over a reed-ensemble riff; and a second tenor saxophone is backed by the trumpet ensemble playing a different riff; and a trumpet solo is backed by another reed-ensemble riff. Then there is a twelve-bar rhythm chorus punctuated by solo piano riffs; and finally there is a sequence of three more ensemble riff choruses (the trumpets and trombones repeating a call-and-response figure over and over while the reeds play three different unison riffs) as a climax or outchorus.

When they are effective, riffs always seem as spontaneous as if they were improvised in the heat of performance. So much so that riffing is sometimes regarded as being synonymous with improvisation. But such is not always the case by any means. Not only are riffs as much a part of some arrangements and orchestrations as the lead melody, but many consist of nothing more than stock phrases, quotations from some familiar melody, or even clichés that just happen to be popular at the moment. But then in the jam session, which seems to have been the direct source of the Kansas City riff style as featured by Bennie Moten, Count Basie, and Andy Kirk, among others, improvisation includes spontaneous appropriation (or inspired allusion, which sometimes is also a form of signifying) no less than on-the-spot invention. Moreover, as is also the case with the best of the so-called unaltered found objects on exhibition in some of the better avant-garde art galleries, the invention of creative process lies not in the originality of the phrase as such, but in the way it is used in a frame of reference!

Background or accompanimental riffs not only provide a harmonic setting for the solo melody, but sometimes they also function as the ensemble response to the solo call, much the same as the Amen Corner moans and the chants of the general congregation reply to the solo voice of the minister (and the prayer leader) during the Sunday Morning Service. Which is also to say that they may sometimes serve as an exhortation to the soloist. But sometimes what with all the shouting and stomping, it is also somewhat as if the ensembles were either chasing or fleeing, or otherwise contesting the soloist. At other times it is not so much like a contest as like a game of leapfrog.

Nothing is likely to seem more spontaneous than call-and-response passages, especially in live performances, where they almost always seem to grow directly out of the excitement of the moment, as if the musicians were possessed by some secular equivalent of the Holy Ghost. But as is no less the practice in the Sunday Morning Service, the responses are not only stylized (and stylized in terms of a specific idiom, to boot), but are almost always led by those who have a special competence in such devices. After all, no matter how deeply moved a musician may be, whether by personal, social, or even aesthetic circumstances, he must always play notes that fulfill the requirements of the context, a feat which presupposes far more skill and taste than raw emotion.

Obviously, such skill and taste are matters of background, experience, and idiomatic orientation. What they represent is not natural impulse but the refinement of habit, custom, and tradition become second nature, so to speak. Indeed on close inspection, what was assumed to have been unpremeditated art is likely to be largely a matter of conditioned reflex, which is nothing other than the end product of discipline, or in a word, training. In any case practice is as indispensable to blues musicians as to any other kind. As a very great trumpet player, whose soulfulness was never in question, used to say, "Man, if you ain't got the chops for the dots, ain't nothing happening."

That musicians whose sense of incantation and percussion was conditioned by the blues idiom in the first place are likely to handle its peculiarities with greater ease and assurance than outsiders of comparable or even superior conventional skill should surprise no one. But that does not mean, as is so often implied, if not stated outright, that their expression is less a matter of artifice, but rather that they have had more practice with the technical peculiarities involved and have also in the normal course of things acquired what is tantamount to a more refined sensitivity to the inherent nuances.

All of which makes what is only a performance seem like a direct display of natural reflexes, because it obscures the technical effort. But blues performances are based on a mastery of a very specific technology of stylization by one means or another nonetheless. And besides, effective make-believe is the whole point of all the aesthetic technique and all the rehearsals from the outset. Nor does the authenticity of any performance of blues music depend upon the musician being true to his own private feelings. It depends upon his idiomatic ease and consistency.

Another technical device peculiar to blues music is the break, which is a very special kind of ad-lib bridge passage or cadenzalike interlude between two musical phrases that are separated by an interruption or interval in the established cadence. Customarily there may be a sharp shotlike accent and the normal or established flow of the rhythm and the melody stop, much the same as a sentence seems to halt, but only pauses at a colon. Then the gap, usually of not more than four bars, is filled in most often but not always by a solo instrument, whose statement is usually impromptu or improvised even when it is a quotation or a variation from some well-known melody. Then when the regular rhythm is picked up again (while the ensemble, if any, falls back in), it is as if you had been holding your breath.

Louis Armstrong's Hot Seven recording of *Weary Blues* (Columbia Golden Era Series CL 852)—which, by the way, expresses not weariness but a stomping exuberance—contains a number of easily identified breaks. The first follows the opening waillike ensemble chant and is filled by a clarinet. The second follows the first full chorus by the ensemble and is also filled in by the clarinet. The third, fourth, and fifth are filled in by the banjo. The sixth, seventh, and eighth are filled by the tuba; and the ninth by Armstrong himself on trumpet.

In a sense Armstrong's second solo in *Potato Head Blues* (Columbia Golden Era Series CL 852) represents a more elaborate use of the options of the break. It consists of sixteen consecutive two-bar phrases, each filling a break following a heavy beat that functions as the musical equivalent of a colon. Then there is also Duke Ellington's *C-Jam Blues* (RCA Victor LPV 541) in which each of the five solo choruses, beginning with Ray Nance on violin, starts out as a two-bar-break improvisation. Ellington's title *Bugle Breaks* (Jazz Society AA 502) is quite simply a literal reference to the structure of what is one of his versions of *Bugle Call Rag*, which he plays as if mainly to feature four trumpet break-fills plus one by trombone and two by a trumpet ensemble.

Break passages are far more likely to be improvised on the spot than riff figures. But sometimes improvising on the break is also referred to as riffing, as Armstrong does on his recording of *Lazy River* (Columbia Golden Era Series C 854) when he finishes scatting a break and chuckles (not unlike a painter stepping back to admire his own brush stroke): "Boy, if I ain't riffing this evening I hope something."

Many riffs no doubt begin as just such on-the-spot break-fill improvisations as the one Armstrong was so pleased with. Because, as evolution of the so-called head or unwritten arrangement/composition suggests, as soon as the special ones are played they are almost always made a part of the score (written or not) either by the player or somebody else.

Sometimes the riffs replace the original melody, or indeed become the melodic line of an extension that may be a new composition. Duke Ellington's *Crescendo in Blue* and *Diminuendo in Blue* sound like such an extension of *The St. Louis Blues*, and when his arrangement for a vocal version of *The St. Louis Blues* (RCA Victor LPM 306) is heard with the singer out of the range of the microphone as in the recording (Pima 01 and 02) made during a performance at the Chicago Civic Opera, November 11, 1946, then it sounds like still another composition. Similarly, the only scrap of the melody of the original *St. Louis Blues* in the version arranged for Dizzy Gillespie by Budd Johnson (RCA Victor LJM 1009) is Gillespie's trumpet-solo approximation of the vocal lines: "St. Louis woman with her diamond rings / pulls that man around by her apron strings." The rest is mostly riff choruses plus a saxophone solo plus the trumpet playing what amounts to a sort of mini-concerto which, by the way, includes a bop-style break dazzlingly executed by Gillespie—the likes of which was matched only by Charlie Parker.

What with recordings making them available for the most careful study through endless repetition, break passages are also memorized, repeated, imitated, and incorporated into scores. It is not at all unusual for one musician's break to become another's riff chorus—or lead melody. The break with which King Oliver opens his cornet solo in *Snag It* (Decca Jazz Heritage Series DL 79246) seems to have been considered as being in the public domain as soon as other musicians heard it, and has been used as a Buddy Bolden-like clarion call to revelry ever since, not only by other soloists but by arrangers as well. Blues musicians across the nation spent long hours rehearsing and appropriating Armstrong's breaks on *Beau Koo Jack* (Okeh 8680) to name only one, and the same thing happened with Charlie Parker's alto break on *Night in Tunisia* (Baronet Records B 105).

In other words, when Armstrong said what he said on *Lazy River*, he knew very well whereof he spoke. A riff is a musical phrase used as a refrain chorus, background chorus, response chorus, echo chorus, and so on; and a riff tune is one constructed mainly of riff choruses; but the process of riffing (from the verb, *to riff*) refers not only to making riff phrases and playing riff choruses and substituting riffs for melodies as written, but also to improvisation in general. Thus the term *riff session* often refers to a jam session.

Among other fundamental prerequisites for playing (and playing with) blues music are such essentials of rhythmic nuance as beat and syncopation. Keeping the beat or beating time, whether by foot tapping, hand clapping, finger snapping, head rocking, or by means of the bass drum, bass fiddle, tuba, piano pedal, and so on, may seem ever so natural to the uninitiated listener, but it is a matter of very precise musicianship nevertheless. The more precise the musicianship, which is to say, the musical know-how, discipline, and skill, the more natural-seeming the beat—as natural in effect as the human pulse. One of the most precise, distinctive, and highly celebrated rhythm sections in the entire history of blues music was the so-called All American Rhythm Section (Jo Jones, drums; Walter Page, bass; Freddie Greene, guitar; and Count Basie, piano) of the Count Basie Orchestra from the mid-1930s to the late 1940s. And yet the drummer not only seemed to be the most nonchalant person on hand, it was also almost always as if you felt the beat more than you actually heard it, which of course was exactly the way it should be. Sometimes, indeed it was as if Jo Jones only whispered the beat.

At the same time nonchalance was also the ultimate effect created by the flamboyant showmanship of Chick Webb. All of the stamping and sweating of Gene Krupa, a Webb-derived white drummer of the so-called Swing Era, gave the impression that he was putting himself so totally into the act of beating it out that he was possessed (for the time being) by some violent tom-tom-oriented savage force. But with Webb it was as if the breathtaking rolls, light-ninglike breaks and juggler-type stick twirling were designed for the express purpose of making it appear that the drummer was not at all preoccupied with such an elementary matter as timekeeping—or that keeping musical time was so natural that he was ever so free to fool around while doing so.

Yet keeping the appropriate beat is hardly more natural to U.S. Negro musicians than it was for their drum-oriented forebears in ancestral Africa, where musicians were always required to be thoroughly trained and formally certified professionals. To the Africans from whom the dance-beat disposition of U.S. Negroes is derived, rhythm was far more a matter of discipline than of the direct expression of personal feelings. African drummers had to serve a long period of rigidly supervised apprenticeship before being entrusted with such an awesome responsibility as carrying the beat!

Nor is the process of beat, off-beat, or weak-beat accentuation known as syncopation any less a matter of competent musicianship. Used as required by the blues idiom, syncopation seems as natural as the contractions, liaisons, slurs, ellipses, and accents of a normal speaking manner. But the fact that syncopation is necessarily idiomatic means that it is a customary or stylized rather than a natural aspect of expression. Thus it can be refined, elaborated, extended, abstracted, and otherwise played with. It is, as the juxtaposition of any blues recording with any piece of conventional European music will bear out at once, something that blues musicians play with in the sense of making use of it as an indispensable device, as well as in the sense of having fun.

Beat and syncopation are also a matter of taste. But what is taste if not a matter of idiomatic preference? As in the kitchen, taste is a sense of recipe, a sense of the most flavorful proportion of the ingredients. In music it is a sense of nuance that defies notation in the same way as, say, a very fine downhome cook's offhand-seeming use of a pinch of this, a touch of that, and a smidgen of the other, confounds the follower of precisely measured formulas. In both instances the proportions are matters of idiomatic orientation. Thus the preference is also a matter of conditioning which is a result of the most careful training however informal. Indeed, in such cases the more subtle the training, the more likely the outcome to seem like second nature.

Still another fundamental aspect of blues musicianship that is often mistaken as a natural phenomenon is tonal coloration. But once again the quality of voice that notes are given in the actual performance of blues music is, uniquely personal endowments aside, perhaps mainly a matter of idiomatic orientation. Which is to say that it is perhaps mostly a matter of tonal stylization derived from other performers. Before Bessie Smith there was Ma Rainey. Before Louis Armstrong there were King Oliver and Bunk Johnson. Before Duke Ellington there were Jelly Roll Morton, King Oliver, and Armstrong, as well as the Harlem Stride piano players and the Fletcher Henderson orchestra.

That timbre and vibrato are devices that Bessie Smith and Louis Armstrong played with much the same as they played with beat should be so obvious that it need be mentioned only in passing, and no less obscure is the profound influence of Bessie Smith and Louis Armstrong on the tonal coloration of other musicians over the years. But perhaps the most clearcut indication of the blues musician's involvement with tonal coloration is some of the accessory equipment such as wa-wa and Harmon mutes, plungers, and aluminum, felt, and cardboard derbies for brass; an assortment of sticks, brushes, mallets, and various other gadgets for voicing drums; and so on. Duke Ellington's use of timbre and vibrato as orchestral devices, as well as other extensions and refinements, made him the preeminent composer/conductor of blues music.

The tonal nuances of blues music are also a matter of singers playing with their voices as if performing on an instrument, and of instrumentalists using their brasses, woodwinds, strings, keyboards, and percussion as extensions of the human voice. Perhaps reciprocal "voicing" is inherent in the old call-and-response or voice-and-echo pattern as produced by the ratio of instrumental accompaniment space to the lyric space in the basic traditional blues stanza. But, inherent or not, the so-called scat vocal with which the singer plays instrumental music with his voice by using nonsense syllables instead of the words of a lyric is only the most patent form of vocal instrumentation. When Louis Armstrong began singing, it was very much as if he were using his voice to supplement what he had been saying with his trumpet all along—some of which was backtalk for Ma Rainey (as on *Countin' the Blues* [Milestone M 4721] for example) and Bessie Smith (as on *Reckless Blues* and *Sobbing Hearted Blues* [Columbia G 30818]). Nor was the voice of any scat singer ever played more like an instrument than that of Bessie Smith, who, as has been pointed out, could get the same musical effect with the most banal, inconsequential, and indeed *non sequitur* lyrics as with those of the highest poetic quality, which she often misquoted.

On the other hand such was the vocal orientation of Duke Ellington's genius that in addition to achieving the most highly distinctive overall instrumental orchestral sound (made up of instrumental voice extensions), he not only played his orchestra as if it were a single instrument (to an extent that cannot be claimed for any other composer or conductor) but expressed himself on it as if the three-man rhythm section, three trombones, four to six trumpets, five woodwinds (plus occasional strings) were actually the dimensions of one miraculously endowed human voice. As in the tearful hoarseness of the shouting brass ensemble in the call-and-response outchorus of *Perdido* (RCA Victor LPM 1364) for instance; the somewhat worn-out and breathless ensemble woodwinds calling or answering the flippant piano after the drum roll following the stratospheric trumpet solo in *Let the Zoomers Drool* (Fairmont FA 1007); as in the querulous mumbling mixed in with all the stridency of the first trumpet solo of *Hollywood Hangover* (Saga 6926), as in the Armstrong-like gravel tone of the main theme ensemble passages of *Blue Ramble* (Columbia C 31 27).

Such is also the nature of the craft involved in the fusion of incantation and percussion known as blues music that even as they play as if on extensions of human voices, blues musicians proceed at the very same time as if their strings, keyboards, brasses, and woodwinds were also extensions of talking drums, fulfilling the conventional timekeeping function while the designated rhythm section, in addition to filling its traditional role, also functions as an instrumental extension of the human voice, making vocal-type statements along with other instrumental voices.

Of course the conventional tonalities inherent in the very nature of keyboards, strings, brasses, and woodwinds are also utilized as such in the process, just as in the most representational painting where paint is used as paint, brush strokes as brush strokes, while the canvas remains a canvas. Inevitably the idiomatic extensions are based squarely on the fact, or at any rate the supposition, that musicians can do certain things on instruments that cannot be done with the human voice—or with talking drums (which seem to have been used for the same reason in the first place). Nor is there likely to be much doubt that such reedmen, say, as Sidney Bechet, Coleman Hawkins, Lester Young, Johnny Hodges, Charlie Parker, and Harry Carney preferred playing saxophone to being singers—or drummers.

Nevertheless, one way for those whose ears are uninitiated to the idiom to become oriented to blues music is for them to begin by listening as if each blues composition was being played by so many talking drums, some voiced as guitars and banjos, some as pianos, trumpets, trombones, saxophones, clarinets, and so on.

Sometimes, as in *Diminuendo in Blue* and *Crescendo in Blue*, not only do the trumpets and trombones extend the shouting and hey-saying voice of the downhome church choir, but they also take the lead in doing drum work and drum talk at the same time. Nor for the most part are the terms in which any of the brasses or woodwinds speak on Count Basie's *Swinging the Blues*, *Time Out*, and *Panassié Stomp* (Decca DXSB 7170). And what a master drummer among drummers Louis Armstrong becomes with his trumpet and with his voice as well on *Swing that Music* (Decca Jazz Heritage Series DL 79225).

Drum talk is not only what the accompanying guitar, banjo, or piano answers or echoes the folk blues with, and not only what such singers answer and echo themselves with when they hum, beat out or otherwise furnish their own comps, fills, and frills; but it is also most likely to be what all blues singers do even as they play with their voices as if on brasses, keyboards, strings, and woodwinds. But then the use of the break as a fundamental element of blues musicianship already provides an unmistakable clue to how closely blues-idiom statement is geared to the syntax of the drummer. In any case it is a mistake for the uninitiated listener to approach blues music with the assumption that rhythm is only incidental to melody, as it tends to be in European music.

It is not enough, however, to say that blues musicians often play on their horns, their keyboards, and strings as if on drums. Nor is it enough to say that the drums are more African than European in that they keep rhythm and talk at the same time. The rhythmic emphasis of blues music is more obviously African than either the so-called blue note or the call-and-response pattern, but all the same, the actual voices of which all blues instrumentation is an extension speak primarily and definitively as well in the idiomatic accents and tonalities of U.S. Negroes down South. And what is more, not only do they speak about downhome experience, which is to say human experience as perceived by downhome people, but they speak also in the terms, including the onomatopoeia, of downhome phenomena.

So much so that what may once have been West African drum talk has in effect at any rate long since become the locomotive talk of the old steam-driven railroad trains as heard by downhome blackfolk on farms, in work camps, and on the outskirts of southern towns. Not that blues musicians in general are or ever were—or need be—as consciously involved with railroad onomatopoeia as the old-time harmonica players who were Leadbelly's forerunners seem so often to have been. But even so there is more than enough preoccupation with railroad imagery in blues titles, not to mention blues lyrics, to establish the no less mythological than pragmatic role of the old steam-driven locomotive as a fundamental element of immediate significance in the experience and hence the imagination of the so-called black southerners.

Also, as an actual phenomenon of crucial historical significance the old steam-driven railroad train with its heroic beat, its ceremonial bell, and heraldic as well as narrative whistle goes all the way back not only to the legendary times of John Henry and the steel-driving times that were the heyday of nationwide railroad construction, but also to the ante-bellum period of the mostly metaphorical Underground Railroad that the Fugitive Slaves took from the House of Bondage to the Promised Land of Freedom.

The influence of the old smoke-chugging railroad-train engine on the sound of blues music may or may not have been as great as that of the downhome church, but both have been definitive, and sometimes it is hard to say which is the source of what. Item: As used in blues orchestrations one call-and-response sequence may have derived directly from the solo call of the minister and the ensemble response of the congregation in the church service; but another, say as in Louis Armstrong's recording of *Wolverine Blues* (Ace of Hearts AH 7), may well have come from the solo call of the train whistle and the ensemble response of the pumping pistons and rumbling boxcars; and there is a good chance that there are times when a little of both exists in each. Likewise, in church music, cymbals sound as Biblical as tambourines and timbrels, but what they are most likely to suggest when played by blues musicians is the keen percussive explosions of locomotive steam.

Similarly, some of the great variety of bell-like piano sounds that so many blues musicians, piano players in particular, like to play around with may sometimes be stylizations of church bells ringing for Sunday Morning Service, sending tidings, tolling for the dead, and so on; but most often they seem to be train bells. The bell-like piano chorus that Count Basie plays against the steady four/four of the bass fiddle, guitar, and cymbals in *One o'Clock Jump* is far more suggestive of the arrival and departure bell of a train pulling into or out of a station than of church bells of any kind.

And the same is essentially the case with train whistles. The influence of church music on blues music is sometimes very direct indeed. Not only do many blues musicians begin as church musicians, but, as is well known, many blues compositions are only secular adaptations of church tunes. Yet as much church-organ influence as may be heard in numberless blues-ensemble passages, the tonal coloration of most of Count Basie's ensemble passages (as on *9:20 Special* [Epic LN 1117]) sounds much more like a sophisticated extension of the train-whistle stylizations that have long been the stock in trade of so many downhome harmonica players and guitar players than like church hymns, anthems, spirituals, and gospel music.

But then what with all the gospel trains and glory-bound specials and expresses and all the concern about passengers getting on board and on the right track in church music long before blues music as such came into existence, many of the stylizations of locomotive sounds may have come into the tonal vocabulary of blues musicians by way of the church in the first place rather than directly from the everyday world. Thus for one listener Duke Ellington's *Way Low* (Columbia Archives Series C 3L 39) begins with a church moan while for another it sounds like an orchestrated train whistle; both are at least consistent with the idiom.

Nor does the association in either case lead to the implication that blues music is primarily programmatic. It is not. Onomatopoeia is only a point of departure for the idiomatic play and interplay of what is essentially dance-beat-oriented percussion and incantation. Once voiced or played, even the most literal imitation of the sound of the most familiar everyday phenomenon becomes an element of musical stylization and convention. Thus the railroad sounds in such Ellington compositions as *Daybreak Express* (RCA Victor LVP 506), *Happy Go Lucky Local* (Allegro 1591 and Pima DC 01 and 02) and *The Old Circus Train Turn Around Blues* (Verve V 40722) remain unmistakable. But even so, Ellington's unique nuances aside, what all the whistles, steam-driven pistons, bells, and echos add up to is the long-since-traditional sound of blues-idiom dance-hall music. And, except in novelty numbers like Fletcher Henderson's *Alabamy Bound* (Columbia C 4L 19), musicians approach it not as a matter of railroad mimicry, but in terms of form and craft. Indeed, much goes to show that what musicians are always most likely to be mimicking (and sometimes extending and refining and sometimes counterstating) are the sounds of other musicians who have performed the same or similar compositions.

Thus for all the use Duke Ellington had already made of railroad onomatopoeia in his own compositions over the years, what his version of *9:20 Special* (Swing Treasury 105) mimics, elaborates, and extends is not the sound of an actual train but rather the melody, the KC 4/4 beat, the ensemble choruses and solos with which Earle Warren and the Count Basie Orchestra had already stylized the sound of what may have been the original *9:20 Special*—or may have been still another composition derived from other locomotive sounds that nobody now remembers as such. Anyway, what Ellington's own bell-ringing piano fingers play around with are the already abstract bell-like piano choruses of Count Basie, and the same holds for the ensemble passages. The train-whistle-like sonorities are still very much there for those who have ears for that sort of thing, indeed they may be even more obvious, especially in such woodwind passages as follow the first piano bridge. Nevertheless, the musicians are most likely to have approached the whole thing not as another version of a train, a somewhat slower train; but rather as an Ellington takeoff on a Basie jump number, to be played more like a mellow bounce than as an all-out hard-driving stomp.

Such is the stuff of which blues musicianship is made. It is not a matter of having the blues and giving direct personal release to the raw emotion brought on by suffering. It is a matter of mastering the elements of craft required by the idiom. It is a matter of idiomatic orientation and of the refinement of auditory sensibility in terms of idiomatic nuance. It is a far greater matter of convention, and hence tradition, than of impulse.

It is thus also far more a matter of imitation and variation and counterstatement than of originality. It is not so much what blues musicians bring out of themselves on the spur of the moment as what they do with existing conventions. Sometimes they follow them by extending that which they like or accept, and sometimes by counterstating that which they reject. Which is what W. C. Handy did to folk blues at a certain point. Which is what Bessie Smith seems to have done to Ma Rainey's singing style. It is clearly what Louis Armstrong did to what King Oliver and Bunk Johnson had already done to the trumpet style of Buddy Bolden himself. Count Basie extended the Harlem Stride extension of the ragtime piano in the very process of stripping it down for use as an element of Kansas City riff-style orchestration. The unchallenged supremacy of Duke Ellington is not based on pure invention but on the fact that his oeuvre represents the most comprehensive assimilation, counterstatement, and elaboration of most, if not all, of the elements of blues musicianship.

It was not so much what Charlie Parker did on impulse that made him the formidable soloist and influential revolutionary stylist that he was, it was what he did in response to already existing procedures. His own widely quoted account of his evolution provides a concrete example of the dynamics of acceptance, rejection, and counterstatement, as it operates in the process of innovation:

Now, I had been getting bored with the stereotyped changes that were being used all the time at that time, and I kept thinking there's bound to be something else. I could hear it sometimes, but I couldn't play it.

Well, that night I was working over *Cherokee*, and as I did, I found that by using the higher intervals of a chord as a melody line and backing them with appropriately related changes, I could play the things I had been hearing.

Such is the nature of the blues-idiom tradition of stylization that what he played begins by being a most elegant extension of some of the innovations of Buster Smith and Lester Young heard in Kansas City back during the days of his apprenticeship.

As for the ritualistic significance of the essential playfulness involved in blues musicianship, it is in effect the very process of improvisation, elaboration, variation, extension, and refinement (or of just plain fooling around, for that matter) that makes sport of, and hence serves to put the blue demons of gloom and ultimate despair to flight. Much has been made of the personal anguish of Charlie Parker, perhaps even more than has been made of the tribulations of Bessie Smith, and indeed there is always some unmistakable evidence of the blues as such somewhere in all of his music, but they are always at bay somewhere in the background, never in the foreground, for there is probably no species of gloomy demon yet known to man that can tolerate the playful and sometimes insouciant and sometimes raucous elegance of the likes of Charlie Parker performing *Ko-Ko* (Savoy MG 12014), *Parker's Mood* (Savoy MG 12009), *Ornithology* and *Yardbird Suite* (Baronet Records B 105), or *Now is the Time* (Savoy MG 12001) or jamming on *Sweet Georgia Brown* (Milestone MSP 9035). And when the clip gets too fast for most dance couples, as it does on the famous break on *Night in Tunisia*, all they have to do is hold on to each other and listen as Parker makes the notes dance.

Africans, Europeans and
the Making of Music

(1987)

CHRISTOPHER SMALL

. . . .

In the first chapter of his influential book Music of the Common Tongue, *former academic lecturer and composer Christopher Small discusses how relations between Africans and Europeans affected the creation and performance of African American music and dance. Despite the continuous process of modification and accommodation on both sides, Small notes the stability of two distinct and fundamental sets of attitudes that summarize the difference between African and European music and dance as one of emphasis: dynamic social continuity and process on the one hand, and stable, final resolution and product on the other. Small is retired and lives in Spain.*

The first thing we must understand about the Africans who were taken into slavery in the Americas is that they were by no means members of a primitive society. The societies of the Western Sudan, which, at least up to the beginning of the nineteenth century, was the principal source of black slaves, may have been technologically simple by nineteenth-century European standards (at the time of the first large-scale encounters, in the fifteenth and sixteenth centuries, there was little to choose between them, apart from the strategically crucial technologies of shipbuilding and explosives), but, socially, politically, aesthetically and spiritually they had, and still have, much to teach Europeans, those strange creatures whom, according to Okoye, Africans at first derided 'for their horrible looks, red faces, long hair and long heads', and whom they regarded as 'unsightly because they did not possess a black skin, full lips and broad nostrils'.[1]

It is tempting to cite, as evidence for the 'advanced' nature of West African societies, that series of empires which arose in the Western Sudan from the eighth century A.D. onwards, whose names ring in the ears of Europeans like strange music, as alien as the names of planets in an epic of science fiction: Ghana, Mali, Songhai, and Kanem-Bornu. These were immensely wealthy. A fourteenth-century Emperor of Mali, Mansa Musa, who is said to have ruled over the largest domains on earth apart from the Mongol Empire, made his pilgrimage to Mecca in 1324 (Islam spread early into West Africa, but the Africans transformed it, as they did later the Christianity of the missionaries, into a specifically African syncretism that co-existed, and still co-exists, comfortably with the older polytheistic religions); his largesse with gold was so prodigal that the value of the local currency in Cairo was depressed for some twelve years after his visit. The term 'empire' is, however, only a makeshift, for we do not have a term for that kind of political organization in which power, while seemingly vested in a supreme head of state, actually permeated upwards from the smallest social units, from families and clans through a loose confederation, to the Emperor, whose position depended upon the continuing assent of all; government in all essentials took place through the lineage-based community, which was, and seemingly remains today, the basic social unit across the continent. To the western bureaucrat such a community-based system of government will appear proof of primitivity or backwardness; nonetheless I do not intend trying to appease his prejudices by pretending that the decentralized 'empires' of the Western Sudan much resembled their centralized, top-downwards namesakes of Europe.

Instead, one can only point out that, from all accounts, the continent in the centuries before the disruption caused by the slave trade and, later, colonialism, was an orderly and well-governed place. The fourteenth-century Berber traveller Ibn Battuta reported that 'Of all peoples the Negroes are those who most abhor injustice. The Sultan [of Mali] pardons no-one who is guilty of it. There is complete and general safety throughout the land.'[2] That this was a more or less general condition throughout sub-Saharan Africa is confirmed not only by African and Arab travellers but by Europeans also. A Dutch merchant's description of the city of Benin, in what is now Nigeria, was published in Amsterdam in 1668 and includes the following: 'The king's court is square and lies in the right quarter of the town as you approach it from the Cotton Gate. It is as big as the city of Haarlem and is surrounded by a wall like that surrounding the town itself. It is divided into many splendid palaces and comprises beautiful and long square galleries almost as large as the Amsterdam Exchange. These galleries are raised on high pillars covered from top to bottom with cast copper on which are engraved pictures of their war exploits and battles. Each roof is decorated with turrets bearing birds cast in copper with outstretched wings, cleverly made after the living models. The streets of the town are very straight and wide, each over a hundred and twenty feet wide.'[3]

Benin was famous not only for its artistic and architectural achievements but also for the shrewdness and enterprise of its merchants.

Even Henry Morton Stanley, by no means a sympathetic observer of Africa, allowed in 1875 that the King of Uganda was 'a pious Musselman and an intelligent humane king,'[4] while as late as 1906 the anthropologist Leo Frobenius could write of his journey to the Congo: 'And on this flourishing material civilization there was a bloom, like the bloom on a ripe fruit, both tender and lustrous; the gestures, manners and customs of a whole people from the youngest to the eldest, alike in the families of princes and well-to-do and of the slaves, so naturally dignified and refined to the last detail. I know of no northern race who can bear comparison with such a uniform level of education as is to be found among these natives.'[5] Frobenius's further comment is worth noting also: 'Judging from the accounts of navigators from the 15th to the 18th century, there is not a shadow of doubt that Negro Africa of that period, stretching from the south to the edge of the Sahara Deserts, was in the heyday of an uninterrupted efflorescence of the arts, an efflorescence which the European conquistadores callously destroyed as fast as they succeeded in penetrating into the country . . .'[6]

One could continue the list: the great Indian Ocean ports of Kilwa (which Ibn Battuta called 'one of the most beautiful and well-constructed towns in the world'), Mombasa and Mogadishu, centres of intricate networks of trade and cultural exchange that extended as far as Indonesia and even China, which the Portuguese with their superior firepower destroyed in an attempt to take them over; Timbuktu, with its splendid court and army of scholars 'bountifully maintained', wrote the sixteenth-century Spanish traveller Leo Africanus, 'at the king's expense', one of a chain of cities along the southern edge of the Sahara which served as 'ports' for the huge caravans, often twelve thousand strong, that brought European goods across the desert and returned with ivory, salt and gold. The great trading houses of Genoa and Venice knew that they were dealing not with 'primitive' people but with shrewd traders whom they treated with respect and even deference.

But, despite the brilliance of these and other city civilizations, the vast majority of Africans lived, then as now, in village societies, content to work a subsistence economy although, as Davidson says, 'the available evidence suggests that most peoples south of the Sahara had a standard of living far above the minimum subsistence level, and enjoyed a reasonably secure life,'[7] mostly nonliterate (I shall have more to say on literacy later), the basis of social and political life the clan or lineage, the common ancestors. Two characteristics of African social life strike one again and again in commentaries.

The first is an absence of separation between aspects of life which Europeans are inclined to keep apart: the political, the economic, the religious and the aesthetic. Despite an absence of either historical founder or systematic body of doctrine, African religion permeates every aspect of human existence. The Christian theologian Dr. John Mbiti, who insists that indigenous African religion, even when overlaid with Islam or Christianity, is a unity (there are, he says, many branches but only one tree),[8] tells us that no African lacks a knowledge of God as originator, as other than human, or of the ethical responsibility of humanity in the world. A human being can become fully human only in society, and the model for society is the family—not only those presently alive but also those departed, as well as those yet to be born, all of whom are perceived as present in the society of their currently living relatives. Thus, humanness is not confined to the living; love and generosity are due no less to the dead, who in their turn watch over the living community, while those yet unborn have a right to full existence, so that the living have a duty to procreate in order to bring them to that condition.

The reciprocal relationship between individual and community finds expression in a system of rites of passage; nature may bring the child into the world but only the community can make him or her fully human. Hence the importance of naming ceremonies, in which the child dies to its mother but is reborn to the wider community, gaining not just one but many mothers, fathers, uncles, aunts, brothers and sisters, on all of whom falls the responsibility for nurture. Similarly, the rites of puberty and of marriage, procreation and death, each of which is a stage in the integration of the individual into the community, not only of the living but also of the dead and the not yet born, are each at the same time an occasion for the renewal of that community, injecting fresh energy and keeping death and disintegration at bay.

Just as the living individual is the link between the departed and the yet unborn, so he or she is also the link between the physical and the natural worlds, linking God to nature through membership of the natural world (not master over, but priest of, nature) and through the unique human moral and ethical consciousness. Thus all human life and activity take place within a religious framework, and no human act is without religious significance. The arts, too, contribute to this unified consciousness. 'In Africa,' says Davidson, 'tribal sculpture was seldom designed to be enjoyed as "art". Rather, each piece was designed to attract specific religious spirits. An ancestor figure . . . was carved as a home for the spirit of a long-dead chieftain—a spirit which might otherwise roam in anger and harm the village. A beautiful doll was often fashioned to give sanctuary to the spirit of a child not yet born. Without the presence of such spirits, a piece of sculpture has little value. For example, if a wood carving began to crack or rot and was no longer a suitable home for a spirit, another figure was made to replace it, and the first piece, no mater how beautiful, was discarded as worthless.'[9] A major function of the sculptures, the masks and the costumes, no less than of the music and the dance, was their use in rituals affirming and celebrating the power of the lineage and of the common ancestors; thus art and religion together served to reinforce the integrity of the community. Works of art were not kept on display, but were more often than not hidden away until the proper time to bring them out for the particular ritual purpose for which they were designed.

It is this striking temporal, physical and social continuity that has permeated every aspect of African life, in the rituals that embodied their skills and knowledge in agriculture, in the working of metals, in the weaving and dyeing of cloths, the building of houses, the design of villages and towns, the making of musical instruments and the complementary arts of costume, masking, musical performance and dance, themselves thought of as a single unity, the great performance art for which we lack a name (unless it be 'celebration'). All of these have been devoted to one end, which Davidson calls the art of social happiness. 'Few others', he says, 'dealt in the raw material of human nature with more subtlety and ease, or so successfully welded the interests of community and the individual. The Africans practised the art of social happiness, and they practised it brilliantly.'[10] One might say that the intelligence of Africans is devoted to learning how to live well in the world rather than to mastering it, and they do not imagine, as does the scientifically-minded European, that the latter is necessary in order to achieve the former.

None of what has been said need imply that Africa has at any time been an earthly paradise, or that Africans are in any way better, more instinctively moral, artistic, religious, or, especially, 'closer to nature' than any other human people. Not only is much of that vast continent decidedly inhospitable to human life, but also Africans have shared the same tendencies to selfishness, quarrelsomeness and murderousness that characterize the rest of our species. The point is that in that continent human beings evolved ways of coping with these frailties and other kinds of potentially destructive impulses in ways that on the one hand preserved the fabric of society and on the other allowed room for individuals to work out their own development to the limit. Social and individual needs have been thought of not as opposed but as complementary and mutually dependent. It was in the rituals, the music and the dance forms that the society has dramatized and released the tensions within it, without being under any illusion that such releases can ever be achieved once and for all, but in full awareness that they must be negotiated anew by each succeeding generation.

The second characteristic of Africans is adaptability, and the ability to choose eclectically from a variety of sources and to profit from the potential

CHRISTOPHER SMALL

richness of a number of perspectives simultaneously. This can be seen in the way in which Africans seem to be able at one and the same time, and without visible strain, to hold, for example, both polytheistic 'pagan' beliefs and practices and those of either Christianity or Islam, to be at the same time 'traditional' and 'Europeanized' in their daily lives, in ways which often puzzle and even infuriate Europeans; the latter can deal with contradiction only by denying or eliminating one side of it—hence the rejection and even persecution of deviants, both sacred and secular, which has been such a persistent and bloody feature of European history—while Africans seem to be able to live happily with both sides. One might say that while the European lives in a world of 'either/or', the African's is a world of 'both/and'.

Even what Europeans call African 'tribalism', which is represented as an archaic and disruptive force in present-day African states, was in all probability created by the nineteenth-century colonial powers with the collusion of a small number of African rulers and intellectuals. Terence Ranger is of the opinion that in pre-colonial Africa 'there rarely existed the closed corporate consensual system which came to be accepted as characteristic of "traditional" Africa. Almost all studies of nineteenth-century Africa have emphasised that, far from there being a single "tribal" identity, most Africans moved in and out of multiple identities, defining themselves at one moment as subject to this chief, at another moment as a member of that cult, at another moment as part of this clan, and at yet another moment as an initiate in that professional guild. The overlapping networks of association and exchange extended over very wide areas. Thus the boundaries of the "tribal" polity, and the hierarchies of authority within them, did *not* define the conceptual horizons of Africans.' Ranger also quotes another writer who contrasts the 'colonial freezing of political dynamics' with the 'precolonial shifting, fluid imbalance of power and influence.'[11]

That this is not 'primitive' or 'prelogical' behaviour can be seen from the emphasis put on multiplicity in African performing arts; John Miller Chernoff, who himself trained for some years as a drummer in the Ewe tradition of Ghana, makes a strong case for a parallel 'between the aesthetic conception of multiple rhythms in music and the religious conception of multiple forces in the world'. He says, 'African affinity for polymetric musical forms indicates that, in the most fundamental sense, the African sensibility is profoundly pluralistic . . . Just as a participant in an African musical event is unlikely to stay within one rhythmic perspective, so do Africans maintain a flexible and complicated orientation towards themselves and their lives . . . The sensibility we have found in musical expression more accurately appears to represent a method of actively tolerating, interpreting and even using the multiple and fragmented aspects of everyday events to build a richer and more diversified personal experience . . . the adaptability and strength of an African's sense of community and personal identity reside in the aesthetic and ethical sensibility which we have seen cultivated in one of its aspects, music. As such the values of an African musical event represent not an integrity from which we are moving away but rather an integrity which, with understanding, we might approach. It is a felicitous orientation in a world of many forms.'[12]

It is music and dance that have been, and remain, the prime manifestation of the African sensibility and worldview. Robert Farris Thompson goes so far as to say: 'The traditional choreographies of tropical Africa constitute, I submit, complex distillations of thinking, comparable to Cartesian in point of influence and importance.'[13] Music itself, as these statements suggest, hardly exists as a separate art from dance, and in many African languages there is no separate word for it, although there are rich vocabularies for forms, styles, and techniques.

The question, What are the distinguishing features of African music? may seem absurd when we consider the enormous variety of ways in which music is made and listened to in that vast and culturally diverse continent. It can, however, be said that beneath the diversity of technique and instrumentation, of repertory and style, there is a unity of attitude, of approach to the making of music, which can be called African, and which has proved much more persistent in the Americas than any technical features in themselves. It is not surprising that these underlying features can be related to those social attitudes which I have been discussing.

In the first place, music is not set apart in any way from everyday life but is an essential and integral part of it, and plays an important role in all aspects of social interaction and individual self-realization. Music is closely identified with social events and purposes; without music many of those events simply could not take place at all. Just as we noted earlier that various aspects of social life tend not to be kept apart, so we find that the various functions of music making, allied always with dance, flow into one another; the most apparently frivolous of events may well reveal itself as having a serious moral import, while, conversely, the most serious and vital of rituals is extremely enjoyable for the participants. The musician who leads the occasion does so with the realization that he is responsible not only for the sounds he makes but for the whole event; Chernoff goes so far as to say that 'the music is important only in respect to the overall success of a social occasion', and that the African 'does not focus on the music but on the way the social occasion is picked up by the music'.[14] The social importance of music is reflected in the social importance accorded to professional musicians, even where their actual social status is low, and in the high level of tolerance for the deviant behaviour that seems almost

CHRISTOPHER SMALL

to be expected of them. Alan Merriam says that among the Basongye of Zaire, 'the reaction to the facetious suggestion that these ne'er-do-wells be banished was one of extreme seriousness and even real horror . . . The fact of the matter is that without musicians a village is incomplete; people want to sing and dance, and a number of important village activities simply cannot be carried out without musicians. The villagers are unanimous in stating that musicians are extremely important people; without them, life would be intolerable.'[15]

Secondly, rhythm is to the African musician what harmony is to the European—the central organizing principle of the art. In practically all African music making there is a rhythmic polyphony, with at least two different rhythms proceeding in counterpoint with each other, held together only by the existence of a common beat; even the downbeats will quite likely not coincide with different parts. This emphasis on rhythm implies also the existence among Africans of what has been termed a 'metronome sense'—an ability to hear the music in terms of that common beat even when it is not explicitly sounded. It is assumed that musicians, dancers and listeners alike are able to supply it for themselves, making it possible to create rhythmic structures of a complexity and sophistication unknown in European music. This rhythmic sophistication makes up for what Europeans may think of as a lack of melodic development, so that an instrument capable of a very limited range of pitches, even of only one, will be interesting to an African provided he can extract sufficiently interesting rhythms from it. For this reason, sounds of indeterminate pitch are often as much valued in African musical cultures as are precisely pitched sounds; the drum orchestra, in which each instrument is capable of perhaps two or three not very precise pitches only, is a major African ensemble. As one might expect also, percussive sounds are prominent in African music; even the sounds of voices, flutes and stringed instruments may be given a percussive edge, while musicians like to introduce into their instrumental sound a good deal of indefinitely-pitched 'noise', even with such definite-pitch instruments as the xylophone and *mbira*. Their music is rich in buzzes, thuds, bangs and other non-harmonic sounds, of much the same kinds as apparently used to fascinate the medieval ancestors of modern-day Europeans. Chernoff argues strongly that the multiplicity of rhythmic perspectives which is available to musicians, dancers and listeners reflects the multiple orientation of Africans.

Thirdly, it is assumed that everyone is musical, that all are capable of taking part in some capacity in the communal work of music making. Musicking is in fact thought of as being as basic a form of social interaction as talking. This does not mean that everyone is equally gifted or skilled, or that skills are not highly valued; African societies have always supported various kinds of professional and semi-professional musicians, but the music has never been taken over, as has the European classical tradition in our own time, by professional-ism. Musicians are not separated from the rest by their skills, but function as leaders and pacemakers. The balance between leader and followers, between innovation and tradition, between individual and society, is perhaps most strikingly embodied in that ubiquitous feature of African choral singing which is known as call and response, in which solos, often improvised, alternate under strict rhythmic rules with invariant choral responses. But even if not formally involved in the performance, the listeners are never silent and static, but respond with what J. H. K. Nketia calls 'outward, dramatic expression of feeling'. He says: 'Individuals may shout in appreciation when something in the performance strikes them, or indicate at a particular point their satisfac-tion with what they have heard or seen. In addition, their conduct may indi-cate that the performance satisfies or makes manifest a social value, or that it satisfies a moral need.'[16]

Fourthly, improvisation is widespread and richly developed. I shall have more to say about improvisation in a later chapter, but here we should note that it does not mean random or even 'free' playing, even assuming that such things are possible for human beings, but is always carried on within the framework of rules or conventions analogous to those of speech—which may of course be thought of as mainly improvisatory too. Nor does improvisation mean totally new creation on the spot, or rule out the existence of a good deal of pre-existing material; such material is indeed the basis of most improvisa-tion, and it is even true that not much original invention need be involved. A master drummer, for example, will not necessarily wish to invent new patterns of rhythm or melody, but will use existing ones with due regard for the social shape of the occasion for which he is playing, and for the ways in which his fellow-musicians and dancers are performing.

This characteristic, taken with the preceding, means that music making does not depend on the existence of a body of pre-existing pieces; songs may be made up on the spot to suit a specific occasion and be as quickly forgotten once it is over. Everyone is a potential composer, and songs are often made up by taking fragments of existing songs, both words and music (the two may be taken together or separately) and welding them into new shapes. On the other hand, formal composition is by no means unknown, for example among the Chopi of Mozambique, where a composer-music director makes those ex-tended multi-movement works called *mgodo* (plural of *ngodo*) for which the Chopi are famous, for chorus, xylophone orchestra and dancers—but even these *mgodo* are ephemeral, existing for perhaps a year or so before being replaced, movement by movement, with a new work. The old *ngodo* is forgot-ten without regret, even by its composer, as the creative process continues.

CHRISTOPHER SMALL

There are also repertoires of traditional songs which may have been handed down through generations; these are usually associated with the celebration of lineages and ancestral values and serve often to affirm the legitimacy of chiefs and kings. These songs are known and performed mainly by members of a hereditary caste of praise singers known outside Africa by the French term *griots*, whose social function is complex and embraces everything from local historian to social critic and village gossip.

As Nketia says: 'There are restrictive traditions that tend to limit the freedom of performers to make significant changes of their own, such as the court tradition of some societies which demand fidelity to known texts, particularly in historical songs and pieces that legitimize the authority of a reigning chief or his claim to the throne. The latitude for variations as well as for extemporaneous expression gets wider and wider as one moves from such musical types to those which provide a basis for expressions of social values or social interaction. Songs of insult, songs of contest or boasting songs, songs designed in such a way to allow for references relevant to the present moment, all give scope for creativity or for limited improvisation.'[17] A mainly non-literate society, as were most of those of West Africa, was able to remember what it wanted to remember and to forget what it was better to forget, and even the most formal of praise songs would quite likely have undergone changes and adaptations in response to the dynamics of the 'shifting, fluid imbalance of power and influence' of precolonial Africa. In the main, then, fidelity to a received text is not highly valued in African music making.

Lastly, music and dance interpenetrate to an extent that can scarcely be imagined in white society. It is not just a matter of musicians playing while dancers dance, but of musicians dancing as they play and of dancers contributing to the music, and of both responding to one another on equal terms, in doing so contributing to the meaning of the occasion. 'The dance,' says Nketia, 'can be used as a social and artistic medium of communication. It can convey thoughts or matters of personal or social importance through the choice of movements, postures and facial expressions. Through the dance, individuals and social groups can show their reactions to attitudes of hostility or cooperation and friendship held by others towards them. They can offer respect to their superiors, or appreciation and gratitude to well-wishers and benefactors. They can react to the presence of rivals, affirm their status to servants, subjects and others, or express their beliefs through the choice of appropriate dance vocabulary or symbolic gestures.'[18] Likewise, the total bodily involvement of the master drummer as he leads the ensemble, giving the pattern to the other musicians and the dancers, is not merely ornamental but is an essential element of the performance, adding as it does an extra strand to the rhythmic texture, while the sounds made by the dancers as they stamp and leap, often emphasised by bells or sistrums tied around ankles and wrists, are not incidental but integral to the great performance art, which comprises not only music and dance but also masking, costume and drama.

That the continent of Africa is the home of one of the great civilizations of the human race there can be no doubt; and at the heart of that civilization lie music and dance. Nowhere else is the affirmation and the celebration of identity and of right social relationships through music and dance more highly cultivated. Not only tribes and peoples, but religious cults, occupational groups, age groups and the two sexes, all enact in music and dance those rituals which are the embodiment of selfhood, and an acting-out of those myths which shape and give meaning to life. Music and dance give the individual his or her precious sense of uniqueness, of worth, of place in the scheme of things, and mediate relationships, teach responsibilities and show opportunities. That the human values embodied in the great performance art are wide (one is tempted to say, universal) in their appeal is shown not only in the way in which the art proved its value in the social and psychological, as well as the sheer physical, survival of those Africans, and their descendants, who were enslaved in the New World, but also in the way in which it has gone out to become the dominant music and dance in the west in our time. Like all aspects of West African culture brought by the slaves to the Americas, it was profoundly modified both by their ordeal and by the encounter with European culture, but I intend showing that these values, or something very like them, have survived, even when most of the actual technical features of African music have disappeared, and that they continue to exert a life-giving influence, deeply subversive of the official values of industrial society, within that society today.

To conclude this summary of some of the aspects of African culture, which will reveal their relevance in later chapters, it might be useful to remind ourselves of how Europeans have reacted to their encounter with Africa. The two quotations I give below tell us, the first all unawares, and the second with insight, something about the ways in which Europeans persistently project on to Africa, and on to Africans, their own fears and fantasies. The first is from a curious book of African travels by the distinguished Italian novelist Alberto Moravia, in which he says: 'The "Africa sickness" is a spell with a basis of fear, and this fear is the fear of prehistory, that is, of the irrational forces which in Europe man has succeeded in repelling and dominating during many thousands of years, but which here in Africa are, instead, still intrusive and uncontrolled. It is a fear to which the European finally becomes accustomed, partly because he has his roots elsewhere and his personality is sounder and less unstable than that of the African; it is a fear, in fact, that is painfully agreeable.

CHRISTOPHER SMALL

But the fear of the African, who has no historical background, whose personality is flickering as the light of a candle, is a serious fear, a nameless fright, a perpetual, vague terror. Magic is the expression of this prehistoric fear; it is as foul and gloomy and demented as the "Africa sickness" is aphrodisiac, even is disruptive and destructive. The truth is that magic is the other face of the "Africa sickness" '.[19] This extraordinary statement was first published in English, not in 1874, but in 1974.

The second, published in 1979, comes from Patrick Marnham's *Dispatches from Africa*: 'As the North has penetrated Africa, it has proved less and less capable of learning from the experience; we can only instruct. Even the anthropologists, who originally approached their subject in the spirit of pure enquiry, are increasingly willing to place their knowledge at the disposal of governments or international companies whose objectives are less detached. The North justifies its pedagogy by characterizing the African as ignorant, uneducated, or impoverished. At the same time, it has found in Africa "a refuge from the intellect" or an invitation to indulge in stupidity and dishonesty on its own account. It becomes increasingly difficult for us to explain the prolonged frustration of Northern plans in terms of "backwardness" or "isolation". Much of Africa has had close contact with the North for six hundred years and the African characteristics that have survived such long exposure are not going to be eliminated now.

'African resistance to the North takes many forms. But its constant purpose is surely to reject the alien uniformity which the North strives to impose on the unnerving variety of African life. The North finds this variety unnerving because it challenges the necessity for the progress, control, authority and research with which we order our lives. We fear Africa because when we leave it alone, it works'.[20] We might see the history of Afro-American culture, too, and especially its music, as one of constant struggle to resist the uniformity imposed by industrial society, of which slavery was an early manifestation; it is no wonder, then, that those who run the agencies of authority, control and research in western society fear and reject both the bearers of that culture and their music making.

At the time when the first African slaves were imported into the Americas, slavery was a common enough institution, not only in Africa but also in Europe. There had been African slaves in Portugal since the early fifteenth century, long before Columbus, and in West Africa it is by no means extinct, even today. But the slavery practised in Africa bears little resemblance to the ruthless and voracious institution, with its insatiable appetite for human souls and bodies, which evolved in the Americas. An African slave could become a respected member of his master's household, even of his family, perhaps by marriage, and could accumulate wealth in his own right, becoming perhaps the most trusted adviser of a king or aristocrat. Nor was slavery generally hereditary; as Davidson says, 'Captives . . . became vassals, vassals became free men, free men became chiefs.'[21] Even the Arabs, whose system of slavery was in many ways closer to the American, were exhorted by the Koran to manumit slaves, and, again slavery was not hereditary; a child born of slaves could be a full and free member of the household. Those African kings and other rulers who sold prisoners of war and other, to them, surplus subjects to the white adventurers in their huge ships had not the faintest idea of what they were delivering those unfortunates into—a system which equated human beings at best with livestock, to be bought and sold like cattle, not only themselves but their descendants in perpetuity, deprived of any rights through which it might be recognized that they were human. And of course the social and economic ruin brought to West Africa, as one kingdom after another became caught up in the terrible trade, is well documented.

Black slaves were introduced into the economy and the culture of the Americas very early in the history of European colonization; as early as 1503, a mere eleven years after Columbus, the governor of the Caribbean island of Hispaniola, now Haiti and the Dominican Republic, was writing to the Spanish court to complain that African slaves were escaping and preaching insurrection to the Indians, and asking for an end to the importation of Africans. Queen Isabella granted his request, but the shortage of manpower was so acute that within two years the trade had to be resumed. The consequences for the Americas of the slave trade have been beyond calculation; in all, it seems that not less than twelve and perhaps as many as twenty million Africans reached America (how many were taken but did not reach there we shall never know, but mortality on the terrible sea journey, innocuously named the Middle Passage, probably exceeded twenty per cent) during the three and a half centuries of the trade—surely the greatest forced migration of souls in the whole of human history.

It was not until 1619, the year before the *Mayflower* brought the Pilgrim Fathers to Massachusetts, that the first known group of Africans was imported into the British North American colonies; in that year twenty were disembarked from a Dutch vessel at James Town, in the colony, later to be the state, of Virginia. They were designated as indentured servants, a common enough status in those days, rather than as slaves, and it was not for some time that the slave status of Africans and their descendants became legally established in the British colonies; Massachusetts, interestingly in view of its Puritan origins, was the first to make slavery legal, in 1641, with Virginia itself and the other southern colonies not following until 1661. The number of black slaves remained

CHRISTOPHER SMALL

small, a matter of thousands only, until the early eighteenth century, when with development of such labour-intensive cash crops as tobacco, and, later cotton, it burgeoned, creating an insatiable demand for more and more workers, not only on the plantations, but also increasingly in areas that hitherto had been the province of free artisans and craftsmen, as well as in fields such as domestic service, the care of children, stevedoring and animal husbandry. Contrary to popular belief, it was not just the physical strength of the slaves that was exploited but also their skills and knowledge—for example in the working of wood and metal, in tropical farming, of which they might have been expected to have more experience than their masters—and, as we shall see, in music. By 1800 there were in the United States about a million people classified as black; by 1830 the number had increased to three million and in 1860, the year of the last census to be held under slavery, there were about four and a half million blacks, of whom about three quarters were slaves.

I shall leave to a later chapter an account of the patterns of dependence and mutual influence that evolved between the slaves and their masters; it can be said at this point that it was not just a simple matter of the Africans and their descendants being acculturated into a stratum of American society, but rather a complex process of negotiation which affected masters no less than slaves. Let us consider the possible ways in which the enslaved Africans responded initially to the new situation into which they had been so abruptly and traumatically thrust. One thing is clear: the slaves, from the moment when those first Africans were landed at James Town, were never mere passive victims of the system. When they found themselves delivered to the slavers, marched to the sea (tens of thousands perished on that leg of the journey alone) and transported in a terrible voyage under conditions that, in reading of them, still provoke horror and shame, they may have been stripped of all possessions and of the accustomed support of kin, they may often have found no-one to whom they could speak in their own language or who prayed for relief to the same gods, but they were by no means psychologically helpless; those who survived the journey must have been well equipped to survive in the new conditions under which they found themselves. As we have seen, underlying the diversity of language, of ritual and of social customs were deeper shared values, a shared grammar and syntax of social interaction, and, further, those values were not static but dynamic and adaptable; the natural tendency of Africans has been, and remains, to select what they need from a variety of sources, and to use contradictory and disparate elements to construct meaning from their experiences. Nonetheless, it must have been a daunting task, to reconstruct, in the new conditions, structures of value and belief, and their associated social gestures, which would give meaning to the apparently meaningless nightmare into which they had been thrust. Sydney Mintz and Richard Price put the matter well: 'The Africans who reached the New World did not compose, at the moment, *groups*. In fact, in most cases it might be more accurate to view them as *crowds*, and very heterogeneous crowds at that. Without evading the possible importance of some core of common values and the occurrence of situations where a number of slaves of common origin might indeed be aggregated, the fact is that these were not *communities* of people at first, and they could only become communities by processes of cultural exchange. What the slaves undeniably shared at the outset was their enslavement; all—or nearly all—else had to be *created by them*. In order for the slave communities to take shape, normative patterns of behaviour had to be established, and these patterns could only be created on the basis of particular forms of social interaction . . . Thus the organizational task of enslaving Africans in the New World was that of creating institutions, institutions that would prove responsive to the needs of everyday life under the limiting conditions that slavery imposed upon them'.[22] And they add, 'We can probably date the beginnings of any new Afro-American religion from the moment that one person in need received ritual assistance from another who belonged to a different cultural group'.[23]

The struggle for survival, both physical and psychological, must have been unending. One wonders how long it would have taken the Africans to realize that the cruel and irrational world in which they found themselves, and the seemingly arbitrary events which governed their lives (determining whether they stayed with those they knew and loved or were sundered from them, whether they were submitted to a cruel or a lenient master, even whether they lived or died) were in fact governed by a highly rational god whose name was Mammon, whom their masters worshipped above all others and whose rational calculations were, as they remain today, inimical to the needs of human life. In North America and the Caribbean, to satisfy the needs of the rational god, tribes and even families were deliberately broken up to destroy traditional unities and loyalties and discourage insurrection (in Latin America the opposite policy, of keeping ethnic groups together and playing them off one against another, proved in fact more effective). Apart from the fact that labour was incessant and punishment frequent and brutal on the majority of the slave estates, perhaps the worst feature was the sheer hopelessness of the slave's situation, with nothing to look forward to but a lifetime of labour and beatings, with only the remote possibility of escape (but into a hostile society) to keep hope alive, with all possibility of attaining respect and status within a community, a stable family life and the deference due to the old cut off.

But slavery never took over the minds of the slaves to the point where they had no independent life or personality, however cunningly these had to be concealed. Patiently, persistently, generation after generation, they laboured to create for themselves a psychological living space in whatever restricted areas were allowed to them. Despite prohibitions on learning to read and write, they knew who they were, where they were, what their situation was and what was being done to them. Each generation carefully instructed the next in all that could be remembered of the inherited knowledge. Slavery may have taken away the entire material culture, the social and political institutions, but music, dance and oral poetry, folk tales, and above all the essence of the African world view, its spiritual and metaphysical temper, survived. Thomas L. Webber expresses it poetically and precisely: 'The culture of black people under slavery in America can be likened to a deep river. Having as its source a great African well-spring, this ever-moving, ever-changing river had by the 1850s a distinctly American appearance. As it flowed and deepened through its new land it both adapted to the contours of the American landscape and reshaped each bank it touched. It never lost its African undercurrents. For its people it was a healing river. Its waters refreshed them and helped them escape the torturous American environment. To the oppressed slave his culture was like a deep river; to immerse oneself in its water was to commune with one's own cultural identity.'[24]

Of the early music of the black slaves little is known; with a very few exceptions, those whites who left any written record were unable to find in it anything more than a weird and barbarous noise, generally used to accompany what seemed indecent, even lascivious dances. Such perceptive accounts as have come down to us are mainly from the Antilles, where, the blacks being in the majority, more African ways remained than on the North American mainland; nonetheless, they are suggestive of what might have been taking place there also. Thus, one Richard Ligon, an Englishman who may himself have been a professional musician, wrote in 1653 of encountering on Barbados a slave called Macow, 'a very valiant man', according to Ligon, making himself a *balofo*, or African xylophone, which Ligon seems to have thought he had invented for himself; in Martinique in 1694 a French monk saw not only a set of African-style drums but also a four-stringed instrument which was called a *banza*, with a long neck and a body covered with skin. What must have been the same instrument, more or less, was reported also in the English-speaking colonies under the names *banshaw* and *banjil*. The same French monk also reported that some of the slaves on Martinique were proficient on the violin, so that acculturation was clearly under way in both directions by the late seventeenth century.

Of how the process of acculturation began there is practically no record. But if we keep in mind that music and dance were as important as speech to the

Africans as a means of communication and self-definition, then we can deduce something about the process from a similar process of linguistic adaptation that was going on at the same time. The slavers' policy in the British territories of splitting up tribal and linguistic groups would have meant that communication, not only with the masters but also among themselves, was for the slaves a problem of prime importance. There is evidence that the language which formed the initial medium of communication was neither English nor any pure African tongue, but a pidgin (trade language) that had earlier evolved in West Africa for the purpose of trade among the various peoples as well as with Europeans; it would have incorporated elements of a number of African languages as well as of English. In America individual African languages would have fallen rapidly into disuse for want of any extensive speech opportunity, to be supplanted by this pidgin, at first limited to the most practical matters, but gradually taking into itself words and constructions from the one language of which everyone had experience, English, while retaining the simplicity of syntax which marks a pidgin and which characterizes, without any loss of either expressiveness or flexibility, both West Indian and black American speech today. The initial pidgin, in fact, rapidly became a creole, or true language of mixed origin, probably in the space of a generation or two.

Remembering, too, that it was not just brute physical labour that was required of the slaves but also skills and even organizational abilities, from blacksmithing to the nurture of the master's children, it becomes even clearer that, however much the masters might have desired it, there were not two separate societies permanently divided from one another, but only one, of which one segment became increasingly dependent on the other, not just for work on the cash crops, but for practically all the skilled manual work that it needed. This dependence was symbolized by the passing of the creole from the mouths of the slaves into those of the masters and their families, a fact upon which shocked visitors from Europe and from the north often commented.

The new creole would have developed in a somewhat different direction in the slave quarters from the way it did in the big house, owing to the slaves' success in preserving some kind of autonomy when out of the masters' sight; different demeanour and modes of address, especially towards members of the extended family (the vulnerability of families to disruption through sale made the development of extended family ties, often to people who were not blood relatives, an essential source of emotional and social stability), while African or African-style words and expressions, often 'translated' into English, became part of the private language of the blacks simply because a different social and emotional situation required a different vocabulary and usage from that used in the presence of the whites.

CHRISTOPHER SMALL

As far as music was concerned, there would have been fewer outside pressures towards the formation of a creole, since, in the eyes of the masters, music and dance were of little significance in the productive process which was the reason for the slaves' existence, and little attempt was made to control them. Perhaps the most important external pressure was towards the discontinuation of drumming; the masters feared, probably rightly, that the drums would be used as signals for insurrection. Other, less emphatic, ways of marking rhythm had to be found. This had the probable side-effect of hastening the destruction of the old religious rituals, since, as John Storm Roberts puts it, 'when the drums were silent, the old gods came no more.'[25] It is for this reason that drumming is a less central, less autonomous art in North American than in Latin and Caribbean Afro-American music; the art of drumming had virtually to be re-invented in modern times.

Another external pressure towards the absorption of European ways of music making was the reward that could come to the slave from the ability to play a European instrument in the European manner. There is abundant evidence that many slavemasters encouraged their slaves to play, and even supplied them, not only with instruments, but even with instruction, in order that they might provide entertainment and dance music on the often remote plantations; it was a matter of prestige to have slaves who could perform in this way, and skill on fiddle and banjo, as well as on flute, clarinet and even French horn would enhance a slave's saleable value (there is a hint of conspicuous consumption about this, for the slave would have to be withdrawn from productive field or house labour, a luxury which only the wealthier could afford). For the slave himself, or herself, it could be a great advantage since it would mean relief from other duties in fields or house, and even bring a measure of respect and status; the memorable figure of Fiddler in Alex Haley's *Roots* vividly epitomizes such musicians. As Dena Epstein says, 'These obscure musicians at times achieved what would have been professional status if their earnings had remained in their own hands. Many of them earned a reputation for excellence that extended for miles around. Some had homemade instruments, some store-bought ones, but most were encouraged by their masters to play for the dancing of their fellow-slaves as well as for white visitors or dancing parties.'[26] Nothing, in fact, about the Peculiar Institution, with all its inconsistencies and irrationalities, its gross cruelties and occasional mercies, is quite so peculiar as the variable treatment it accorded to slave musicians. One reads advertisements for runaways who had taken with them nothing but their violin, clarinet, flute or even French horn, while descriptions of festivities at Christmas and other seasons include accounts of bands of '3 fiddles, 1 tenor and 1 bass drum, 2 triangles and 2 tambourines', or a band of two violins and a bass,[27] and, most extraordinary of all, Gilbert Chase mentions one Sy Gilliatt, body servant to the Governor of Virginia in the late eighteenth century, who was also official fiddler to the state balls at Williamsburg: 'He wore an embroidered silk coat and vest of faded lilac, silk stockings and shoes with large buckles. He also wore a powdered brown wig, and his manners were said to have been as courtly as his dress'.[28] This, of course, was not much out of line with the servant status of musicians up to the end of the eighteenth century in Europe; Gilliatt's contemporary Josef Haydn might have been seen in similar livery at the Esterhazy court. And in any case it represents once again the increasing dependence of the society of the masters on what the blacks could provide for them.

But there must have been also pressures from inside the slave society itself towards a creole music no less than to a creole language, and for much the same reasons. The linguistically heterogeneous 'crowds' of Africans who left the slave ships must have been equally heterogeneous musically, even if, as we have noted, they were linked by common attitudes and concepts. Given the strength of the urge to make music and to dance which would if anything have been increased by their predicament, there would have been a strong need to find, or to evolve, a common musical, no less than spoken, language. In this fluid situation, the consequence, not only of the absence of a common idiom, but also of their forcible removal from those social situations in which they were accustomed to make music, the adoption of at least some of the idioms of European music which they encountered would have acted as a stabilizing influence, as well as a means of coming to terms with their present plight. And in any case, European concepts of scale and melody, European instruments and even European concepts of harmony, were not so far removed from them that a fairly rapid rapprochement could not take place. And so a creole music would probably have developed in parallel with the creole language, with the European scales modified by less rigid notions of pitch, its foursquare rhythms enlivened by injections of African additive rhythms and polyrhythms, European choral textures by call and response.

I shall leave to a later chapter a detailed discussion of the forms that the slaves' music making took, and look now briefly at the musical inheritance which the white immigrants brought with them to that New World which, unlike the enslaved Africans, they could approach with at least the hope of building a new life. The great majority of those who came to the British colonies were, naturally enough, from the British Isles, and it is their language, their culture and their music that has left the greatest impression on American culture from that time.

Histories of music tell us that the England the first colonists left behind them was in the last days of what has been called the Golden Age of English

CHRISTOPHER SMALL

church polyphony and the madrigal, while the continent of Europe was seeing the first flowering of opera and of Baroque instrumental music. Many of the early colonists, not only those wealthy and aristocratic people who became the major landowners and ruling class in Virginia and the southern colonies, but also the Pilgrim Fathers who came to New England in the 1620s, whose background was from the emerging English middle class, were, as the first governor of the Massachusetts colony said, 'very expert in music'. Despite the abundance of musical skill and knowledge in England, however, neither the elaborate polyphonic church music nor the madrigal, nor, for that matter, the developing instrumental music, was transplanted into the colonies. This was not just a matter of a lack of established communities or of those surplus resources and leisure that are necessary for the growth of a 'cultivated' tradition, though clearly that had much to do with it; it was also actively discouraged by the Puritans of New England, who insisted for their worship on simple settings of the psalms translated into rhyming verse, as often as not in ballad metre, while in the southern colonies only the most perfunctory of attention was paid by the early settlers to religious observance.

Over half of those who came to North America during the colonial period came as indentured servants, having sold themselves into what amounted to slavery for a limited period in return for their passage; we may assume that those who came in this way were members of the lower orders of English society, and that they brought with them their repertory of songs, ballads and dances, as well as the psalms and hymns that were common to all classes. And even they were not necessarily lacking in musical skills and even in literacy, since both were common among all classes in England at that time; as A. L. Lloyd points out, all of the servants whom Samuel Pepys employed during the nine years when he kept his famous Diary in the 1660s were musical performers and sight readers, while playwrights of the time would often in their plays attribute, even to servants and picaresque characters, the ability to read music. 'It would be interesting,' he says, 'to know the rate of musical literacy among the lower classes in the decisive folk song period between 1550 and 1850. We might find that at many moments it was a good deal higher than in the present day.'[29]

Lower and upper classes, then, would seem to have shared a considerable repertory of vocal and instrumental music besides the psalms that they sang together in church, and much of that repertory has remained remarkably unchanged for perhaps three hundred years, or even longer, in the remoter reaches of the United States. In the valleys of the Appalachian Mountains in the early years of this century the English folklorist Cecil Sharp claimed to have found more British ballads and other folksongs than in the whole of England;

many of the British ballads are of considerable antiquity, and have survived many centuries of oral transmission with remarkably little change. The ballad, of course, tells a story, and if that story is to make any sense its internal continuity must be preserved, and the fact that such a large repertory of traditional song is narrative in form tells us something of the inherent nature of the way of making music which the white settlers brought with them.

By contrast with this extensive and long-enduring repertory, practically nothing—a few doubtful examples only—of the actual songs which were brought from Africa by the slaves has survived, despite the fact that first-generation Africans were to be found in America right up to the time of Emancipation. That this is so is clearly due in some measure to the disruption caused by the experience of slavery and the necessary adaptations I discussed earlier, but it points also to a difference in attitude between European, and especially northern European, and African musicians, towards their musical material, a difference which has had a significant effect on the course taken by Afro-American music.

The European folk musician usually thinks of him or herself not as a creator of songs, but as a transmitter. As Henry Glassie says, 'the usual folk singer is no more creative than the usual performer of pop or art song; both share in the Western tradition of the performer as repeater, of the performer as distinct from the audience during performance so that the performance amounts to a presentation requiring authority. He is true to his source, taking pride in the fact that the song is being sung as it was when he learned it. With varying degrees of success he attempts to hold the song steady . . . The commonplace folk performer, his audience and fellow performers do not strive for change; they interact in a system of frequent repetition and reinforcement to prevent it.'[30] This agrees with a comment by Cecil Sharp, that 'the traditional singer regards it as a matter of honour to pass on the tradition as nearly as possible as he received it'.[31] Small changes occur over time, owing to lapses of memory and misunderstandings, but both singer and audience have a strong sense of the identity of a song and feel their responsibility to it, to preserve so far as they can its integrity. People do compose new songs, of course, but it is not a common occurrence; Glassie, in his sensitive and sympathetic study of the composer of the anti-integrationist song *Take That Night Train to Selma*, says that 'creative people like Dorrance Weir are uncommon in European-American communities like his'.[32] He points out also that 'The commercial recordings of the twenties and thirties, which are still [1970] played, have done more than influence Southern Mountain music; they have offered acceptable standard texts and melodies—less efficient than the standard texts and melodies of the art musicians because they continue to involve oral-aural channels—and have rendered the repertoires of contemporary Southern Appalachian singers largely predictable'.[33]

The mention of art musicians reminds us, however, that what we find in the European and Euro-American folk tradition appears to be not very different from the attitudes found in the art, or classical, tradition of European and American music, that is to say, an emphasis on the identity and the integrity of a music-object, an assumption that the power of original creation is rare, a clear-cut distinction between those who perform and those who listen (we notice Glassie's use of the word 'authority' for the performer's relation to his audience), and, where and at such times as it is available, the use of written notation for both words and music, as a means of preservation and transmission—though, as we shall see, it is only in the classical tradition that notation has taken over as the medium through which the very act of creation takes place. That these characteristics are found in some degree within the folk tradition as well, may point to a kind of 'set' which lies deep in the minds of Europeans and which may have to do with the scientific-materialist temper of our culture. We have seen, too, that they are alien to the African temper, and the history of Afro-American music can be seen from one point of view as a succession of accommodations between these two opposing sets of values.

It happened that the first white settlers, in the early seventeenth century, came to America at just the time when the modern tradition of classical music first came into being, with its central concept of music as a drama of the individual soul, and its central expressive technique of tonal harmony as the vehicle for that drama. I have written at length in an earlier book on the meaning of tonal harmony,[34] and do not intend repeating it all here, but some observations on tonal harmony, which, as we shall see, passed in various ways into Afro-American music, need to be made. Tonal harmony is essentially the arranging of chords, usually triads and their derivatives, in temporal succession in such a way as to create meaning, the listener being led forward in time, his expectations frustrated and teased, but ultimately satisfied by the final cadence in the home key. The composer's art lies largely in lacing conventional and predictable chord progressions with surprises, either dramatic or witty, which are caused by the insertion into the sequence of a chord which, while unexpected, can be shown to stand in a logical (that is, syntactical) relationship with those which preceded it. This kind of harmonic drama is used both on a small scale, over a span of seconds, and on a large one, which may be a matter of an hour or more. This kind of large-scale planning is central to classical symphonic and chamber music, with its long-range contrasts, even conflicts, of keys; these are generally fought out to a resolution in the final sections, representing a final solution to the emotional and spiritual conflict in the soul of the protagonist. This final solution is equally devoutly wished for by the audience at a symphony concert, as is shown by the storm of applause which breaks over the heads of the performers the moment they come to the end of their drama. That in African societies such a final solution is not regarded as an option is something I have already discussed; resolutions are temporary only and must be negotiated anew with each new life situation, and in any case, the traditional African societies resorting to head-on conflict to resolve an opposition was not a favoured course of action, but an admission of social failure.

Since the European musician's responsibility is to his drama and to its resolution, he can afford, and indeed needs, to structure his musical performance over a long time-span, whether through the devices of tonal harmony or the narrative progression of a ballad, or indeed an opera, knowing that no matter how the audience responds he is going to finish the performance as planned. The African musician's primary responsibility, on the other hand, is to the occasion and to those taking part in it, and he will adapt his performance to enhance the occasion as it develops. He may well plan what he is going to do, but he will certainly not adopt any technical means that are going to commit him to a course of action regardless of its effect on the listeners or on the occasion.

We may, then, sum up the different attitudes underlying European and African music making in these terms. The European tends to think of music primarily in terms of entities, which are composed by one person and performed to listeners by another. These entities, pieces or songs, which the musician regards as his primary responsibility to reproduce and to hand on as nearly as possible as he received them, are fixed in their over-all identity (some variation within that identity may be possible), and in starting to perform a piece a musician commits himself to finishing it, regardless of the response which it elicits (within limits, of course—the audience may not permit him to finish, although the conduct of conductor and orchestra during the tumultuous 1913 première of Stravinsky's *Rite of Spring* in Paris suggests that it is difficult to stop a really determined musician). It is thus useful for the musician to be able to notate a piece or song, and, to the extent that pieces tend to be treated as permanent objects with an existence over and above any possible performance of them, the tradition as a whole is inclined to be conservative, with new pieces added slowly if at all. Performers and listeners seem to like to play and to hear familiar pieces. The ability to create a new musical entity is thought of as rare, and the ability to perform not very widespread either, while the line between creators and performers, on the one hand, and listeners on the other, is always clear. Composition and performance are separate activities, and the composer dominates the performer as the performer dominates the audience.

The African musician, on the other hand, thinks of music primarily as action, as process, in which all are able to participate. In so far as musical entities exist at all, they are regarded not as sacrosanct, but rather as material for the musicians, whose primary responsibility is to the listeners and to the occasion for which they have come together, to work on. Hence there is as a rule no final form for a piece, rather a constant state of development and change. A new musical entity can come into existence on the instant, and disappear equally instantly once the occasion for it is past. Composition and performance are thus part of a single act which Europeans call improvisation but others call, simply, playing. Notation, if it is used at all, is limited in its utility, since a fully-notated piece defeats the aim of responding to the progress of the occasion. Change is constant and rapid, with new pieces appearing and disappearing with kaleidoscopic speed, though there remains a residuum of pieces and songs that people continue to enjoy playing and singing—but even these will disappear without regret once they have outlived their social usefulness.

When Africans and Europeans encountered one another in the Americas, the first as slaves and the second either as masters or as despised underdogs, in many cases scarcely better off than the slaves, these musical practices underwent profound modification on both sides to give us that kind of music we call Afro-American. It changed, not once and for all, but in a continuous process of accommodation according to the shifting relations of people of African, European and mixed descent, but the two fundamental sets of attitudes have remained remarkably stable and resistant to social, economic and technological change—inevitably, since if music has any meaning at all it must be as the medium through which assumptions about relationships are explored, affirmed and celebrated. Before continuing with the account of the ways in which the two cultures interacted, we need to discuss this more fully.

NOTES

1. Felix N. Okoye, *The American Image of Africa: Myth and Reality* (Buffalo: Black Academy Press, 1971), 72.

2. Quoted in Basil Davidson, *African Kingdom* (New York: Time-Life Books, 1966), 82.

3. Quoted in Dmitry Olderogge and Werner Forman, *Negro Art* (London: Paul Hamlyn, 1969), 43.

4. Quoted in Davidson, *African Kingdom*, 172.

5. Quoted in Nancy Cunard, ed., *Negro: An Anthology* (London: Wishart and Co., 1934), 602.

6. Ibid., 599.

7. Davidson, *African Kingdom*, 21.

8. John Mbiti, "African Religion" (paper delivered at "Africa and the West: The Challenge of African Humanism," Ohio State University, Columbus, May 28, 1982).

9. Davidson, *African Kingdom*, 153.

10. Ibid., 174.

11. Terence Ranger, "The Invention of Tradition in Tropical Africa," in *The Invention of Tradition*, ed. Eric Hobsbawm and Terence Ranger (Cambridge: Cambridge University Press, 1983), 247.

12. John Miller Chernoff, *African Rhythm and African Sensibility* (Chicago: University of Chicago Press, 1979), 155–56.

13. Roger Farris Thompson, "An Aesthetic of the Cool: West African Dance," *African Forum* 2, no. 2 (1966): 86. (See pp. 72–86, this volume.)

14. Chernoff, *African Rhythm*, 67.

15. Alan Merriam, *The Anthropology of Music* (Evanston: Northwestern University Press, 1964), 136.

16. J. H. Kwabena Nketia, *The Music of Africa* (London: Victor Gollancz, 1975), 32.

17. Ibid., 237.

18. Ibid., 207.

19. Alberto Moravia, *Which Tribe Do You Belong To?* trans. A. Davidson (London: Panther, 1976), 17.

20. Patrick Marnham, *Dispatches from Africa* (London: Sphere Books, 1981), xi–xii.

21. Basil Davidson, *Black Mother: Africa and the Slave Trade*, 2d ed. (Harmondsworth: Pelican Books, 1980), 38.

22. Sidney W. Mintz and Richard Price, *An Anthropological Approach to the Caribbean Past: A Caribbean Perspective*, ISHI Occasional Papers in Social Change, no. 2 (Philadelphia: Institute for the Study of Human Issues, 1976), 10.

23. Ibid., 23.

24. Thomas L. Webber, *Deep Like the Rivers: Education in the Slave Quarter Communities, 1831–1865* (New York: Norton, 1978), 60.

25. John Storm Roberts, *Black Music of Two Worlds* (London: Allen Lane, 1973), 39.

26. Dena J. Epstein, *Sinful Tunes and Spirituals: Black Folk Music to the Civil War* (Urbana: University of Illinois Press, 1977), 148.

27. Ibid., 156.

28. Gilbert Chase, *America's Music*, 2d ed. (New York: McGraw-Hill, 1966), 76.

29. A. L. Lloyd, *Folk Song in England* (London: Lawrence and Wishart, 1967), 35.

30. Henry Glassie, " 'Take That Night Train to Selma': An Excursion to the Outskirts of Scholarship," in *Folksongs and Their Makers*, ed. Glassie (Bowling Green: Bowling Green University Popular Press, [1970]), 31.

31. Quoted in Lloyd, *Folk Song*, 18.

32. Glassie, " 'Take That Night Train,' " 30.

33. Ibid., 32.

34. Christopher Small, *Music—Society—Education* (London: John Calder, 1977; New York: Riverrun Press, 1982).

Ring Shout! Literary Studies, Historical Studies, and Black Music Inquiry

(1991)

SAMUEL A. FLOYD, JR.

. . . .

While literary scholars such as Houston Baker and Henry Louis Gates, Jr. turned to the traditions of African American music to discuss African American literature, Samuel A. Floyd, Jr., director of the Center for Black Music Research, was one of the first music scholars to turn to literary models for his analysis. Here Floyd applies Gates's interpretive theory of signifying to musical practices, which he insists are "accompaniments to and ingredients of" black dance. To this interdisciplinary perspective, Floyd adds historian Sterling Stuckey's research on the African-based ring shout. For Floyd, works of music are cultural transactions "fraught with the values of the original contexts from which they spring." As Floyd illuminates relations between music and dance, between ring shouts and contemporary jazz, religious, and classical music, between African American and African music, and among all African American musical practices, he reminds us that the central value supporting African-based aesthetics is that of interrelatedness. Floyd is the author of The Power of Black Music: Interpreting Its History from Africa to the United States *(1995).*

Over the past ten years, black scholars in the field of English literature have identified a black literary tradition and developed critical strategies for studying that tradition from within black culture. And black historians have also been writing black history and American history from a black perspective. In the field of history, their works include Sterling Stuckey's *Slave Culture: Nationalist Theory and the Foundations of Black America* (1987) and Mary Berry's and John Blassingame's *Long Memory: The Black Experience in America* (1982), and in literary criticism, Houston Baker's *Blues, Ideology, and Afro-American Literature: A Vernacular Theory* (1984) and *Modernism and the Harlem Renaissance* (1987) and Henry Louis Gates, Jr.'s *The Signifying Monkey: A Theory*

Reprinted from *Black Music Research Journal* 11 (fall 1991). Used by permission of the author.

of African-American Literary Criticism (1988). By taking an insider's view of black cultural and literary traditions, these books offer insights that cannot be achieved through more conventional means. The success of an Afrocentric perspective in these fields invites black music scholarship to move beyond the standard approaches of musicology and ethnomusicology, by learning from the theoretical insights of black historians and literary scholars and applying that knowledge to the study of black music.

For a glimpse of what existing theories of Afro-American history and letters offer to black music scholars, I will examine the hypothesis of Stuckey and the theory of Gates with musical implications in mind. In doing so, I will use Stuckey and Gates to read black music, Stuckey to read Gates, and Gates to read Stuckey, while recognizing that although literature, history, and music are all different things, certain aspects of black experience may be seen as common to all three.

What I will propose here is a mode of inquiry that is consistent with the nature of black music, that is grounded in black music, and that is more appropriate than other, existing modes for the perception, study, and evaluation of black musical products.

The Ring Shout: The Foundation of Afro-American Music

One of the central tenets of Stuckey's *Slave Culture* is that "the ring shout was the main context in which Africans recognized values common to them—the values of ancestor worship and contact, communication and teaching through storytelling and trickster expressions, and of various other symbolic devices. Those values were remarkable because, while of ancient African provenance, they were fertile seed for the bloom of new forms" (Stuckey 1987, 16).

The shout was an early Negro "holy dance" in which "the circling about in a circle is the prime essential" (Gordon [1979] 1981, 447). From contemporaneous descriptions of the shout we learn that the participants stood in a ring and began to walk around it in a shuffle, with the feet keeping in contact with or close proximity to the floor, and that there were "jerking," "hitching" motions, particularly in the shoulders. These movements were usually accompanied by a spiritual, sung by lead singers, "based" by others in the group (probably with some kind of responsorial device and by hand-clapping and knee-slapping). The "thud" of the basic rhythm was continuous, without pause or hesitation. And the singing that took place in the shout made use of interjections of various kinds, elisions, blue-notes, and call-and-response devices, with the sound of the feet against the floor serving as an accompanying device.[1]

The shout has been identified as an African survival by Courlander (1963). The earliest on record in the United States dates from 1845 (Epstein 1977, 232), but the practice in this country clearly antedates that record. As Epstein (1977), Courlander (1963), and numerous other scholars have shown, all ring shouts had essentially the same elements, with variations manifesting themselves here and there depending on locale and other factors.

From all accounts, the shout was an activity in which music and dance commingled, merged, and fused to become a single distinctive cultural ritual in which the slaves made music and derived their musical styles. Stuckey points particularly to the origin and function of the spirituals in the ring, contending that they should therefore be studied in relation to their ceremonial, slave-ritual context rather than strictly from the standpoint of Christian religious institutions.

Early on, the shout was central to the cultural convergence of African traditions in Afro-America. In New Orleans, for example, the ring became an essential part of the burial ceremonies of Afro-Americans, in which "from the start of the ceremonies in the graveyard, complementary characteristics of a religion, expressed through song, dance, and priestly communication with the ancestors, were organic to Africans in America[;] and their movement in a counterclockwise direction in ancestral ceremonies was a recognizable and vital point of cultural convergence" (Stuckey 1987, 23). What Stuckey does *not* say, but which will be clear to readers familiar with black culture, is that from these burial ceremonies, the ring straightened itself to become the Second Line of jazz funerals, in which the movements of the participants were identical to those of the participants in the ring—even to the point of *individual* counter-clockwise movements by Second Line participants, where the ring was absent because of the necessity of the participants to move to a particular remote destination (the return to the town from the burial ground). And the dirge-to-jazz structure of the jazz funeral parallels the walk-to-shout structure of the ring shout, where "the slow and dignified measure of the 'walk' is followed by a double quick, tripping measure in the 'shout'" (Gordon [1979] 1981, 449). Today, the ring shout has practically disappeared from rural black culture, but remnants of it persist in black churches in solo forms of the dance.

I should point out here that this "straightening" of the ring into the Second Line does not affect the integrity of the shout. Krehbiel tells us, in what can be considered explanation of this contention, that "The 'shout' of the slaves . . . was a march—circular only because that is the only kind of march which will not carry the dancers away from the gathering place" (Krehbiel [1914] 1967, 95). And Courlander reinforces Krehbiel's support as he tells us that the dance is what defines a shout; for, shouting was in reality dancing (Courlander 1963,

195–197), whether, I might add, it is or is not in a ring. It seems, however, that the ritual aspects of the shout are enhanced in the ring, because of symbolic implications that had their origin in Africa.

Stuckey regards the Negro spiritual as central to the ring and foundational to all subsequent Afro-American music-making. He noticed in descriptions of the shout that, in the ring, musical practices from throughout black culture converged in the spiritual. These included elements of the calls, cries, and hollers; call-and-response devices; additive rhythms and polyrhythms; heterophony, pendular thirds, blue notes, bent notes, and elisions; hums, moans, grunts, vocables, and other rhythmic-oral declamations, interjections, and punctuations; off-beat melodic phrasings and parallel intervals and chords; constant repetition of rhythmic and melodic figures and phrases (from which riffs and vamps would be derived); timbral distortions of various kinds; musical individuality within collectivity; game-rivalry; hand-clapping, foot-patting, and approximations thereof; and the metronomic foundational pulse that underlies all Afro-American music.[2] Consequently, since all of the defining elements of black music are present in the ring, Stuckey's formulation can be seen as a frame in which all black-music analysis and interpretation can take place—a formulation that can confirm the importance of the performance practices crucial to black musical expression.

Because the ring shout was a dance in which the sacred and the secular were conflated (Gordon [1979] 1981, 451), I must note here the similar conflation—indeed, near-inseparability—of Afro-American music and dance in black culture, both in the ring and outside it. Indeed, the appreciation of black music and its traits, elements, and practices depends upon our understanding these features (outlined in the previous paragraph) as accompaniments to and ingredients of black dance. For our initial strategies must accept black music as a facilitator and beneficiary of black dance. The shuffling, angular, off-beat, additive, repetitive, and intensive unflagging rhythms of shout and jubilee spirituals, ragtime, and rhythm and blues; the less vigorous but equally insistent and characteristic rhythms of the slower "sorrow songs" and the blues; and the descendants and derivatives of all these genres have been shaped and defined by black dance, within and without the ring, throughout the history of the tradition. In the movements that took place in the ring and in dances such as the breakdown, buck dance, and buzzard lope of early slave culture, through those of the Virginia Essence and the slow drag of the late nineteenth century, on through those of the black bottom, Charleston, and lindy hop of the present century's early years, to the line dances of more recent days can be seen movements that mirror the rhythms of all of the black-music genres. It was in the ring that these terpsichorean and sonic conflations had their origin and

SAMUEL A. FLOYD, JR.

early development and from the ring that they emerged and took many different forms. From their basis in the ring, the sonic practices in these conflations remained singular to the development of all forms of black music. For in moving outside the ring, these musical practices retained the features that made them central to the ring and its expressive values, particularly the elements of call-and-response, the unflagging and off-beat rhythms, and the vocal production techniques.

Throughout the history of black music, its black listeners have also been dancers. Having emerged from the ring, black music, in the words of Albert Murray, "disposes the listeners to bump and bounce, to slow-drag and steady shuffle, to grind, hop, jump, kick, rock, roll, shout, stomp" (Murray 1976, 144). This relationship between black music and black dance has implications for the reading of Gates's hermeneutics, as we shall see. For in his stress on the *material* aspects of black cultural practices, there are significant implications for a cultural-studies approach to inquiry into black music.

On Interpretive Strategies

The inspiration for Gates's hermeneutics, as developed in *The Signifying Monkey*, is Esu-Elegbara (Nigeria), or Legba (Benin), the mythical "classical figure of mediation who is interpreter of black culture," "guardian of the crossroads," "master of style," connector of "the grammar of divination with its rhetorical structures," and trickster, all rolled into one. This figure of African myth possesses many traits: "individuality, satire, parody, irony, magic, indeterminacy, open-endedness, ambiguity, sexuality, chance, uncertainty, disruption and reconciliation, betrayal and loyalty, closure and disclosure, encasement and rupture," and a host of others (Gates 1988, 6). The symbolism of Esu, this guardian and inspirer of the art of interpretation, is profound and has significant metaphors in the black music tradition. Legba (the devil) here appears as guardian of the crossroads and grantor of interpretive skills; as trickster, he is embodied most obviously in the gladiatorial improviser of the jazz tradition.

Esu's Afro-American descendant, for Gates, is the Signifying Monkey of Afro-American vernacular culture. In black America, the Signifying Monkey is a symbol of antimediation, as Gates puts it. The Monkey's use of language in the well-known tales inverts the status of the Lion "by supposedly repeating a series of insults purportedly uttered by the [tale's] Elephant about the Lion's closest relatives (his wife, his mama, and his grandma, too!)" (Gates 1988, 56). These insults proceed through a series of events, with the Monkey emerging triumphant, escaping the Lion's revenge, and living to continue Signifying on later occasions (see Gates 1988; Abrahams [1963] 1970). The tale is filled with sexual innuendo, intimations of abuse and violation, bragging, and put-downs that constitute "versions of day dreams" and "chiastic fantasies of reversal of power relationships" based in vernacular speech, with colloquial, monosyllabic vocabulary and phrasing (Gates 1988, 59, 60). "To signify," Gates tells us, "is to engage in certain rhetorical games" (Gates 1988, 48). "Signification luxuriates in the inclusion of the free play of . . . associative and semantic relations" (Gates 1988, 49). After differentiating the black concept of "Signifyin(g)" from the Standard English meaning of "signifying" and tracing its origins to the Signifying Monkey tales of Afro-American vernacular culture, Gates describes Signifyin(g) as "the black trope of tropes, the figure for black rhetorical figures" (Gates 1988, 51)—a point to which we shall return later. Signifyin(g) is figurative, implicative speech; it is a complex rhetorical device that requires the possession and application of appropriate modes of interpretation and understanding on the part of listeners (something the Lion did not possess). Signifyin(g) is an art, in itself, to which anyone who has the ability has the right—but a right that must be earned through contest and conquest. (Some individual masters of the art of Signifyin(g) have been H. Rap Brown and Muhammad Ali.) As "source and encoded keeper of Signifyin(g)," the Signifying Monkey is Afro-America's functional equivalent to Esu-Elegbara, his Pan-African cousin (Gates 1988, 75).

The Signifying Monkey uses the hermeneutics suggested by the myth of Esu-Elegbara and the Signifying Monkey poems to present a theory of literary inquiry. The theory proposes the "reading" of (i.e. the criticizing of the works of) the black literary tradition by means of the meanings and implications of the myth of Esu and the rhetoric of the Monkey narratives, exploring "the relation of the black vernacular tradition to the Afro-American literary tradition" (Gates 1988, xix). In Gates's theory, Esu-Elegbara is central to interpretation strategies and "stands for discourse upon a text," and "his Pan-African kinsman, the Signifying Monkey, stands for the rhetorical strategies of which each literary text consists"—"the rhetorical principle in Afro-American vernacular discourse" (Gates 1988, 21, 44). Together, this duality, of Esu and the Signifying Monkey, serves as the basis for Gates's theory.

Gates uses the vernacular to examine the formal, assuming that the vernacular contains within it the very critical principles by which it can be read, that "the vernacular informs and becomes the foundation for black formal literature" (Gates 1988, xxii). For Gates, "the vernacular tradition Signifies upon the tradition of letters" (Gates 1988, 22). He assumes that the black tradition has a "fundamental idea of itself, buried or encoded in its primal myths—ambigu-

SAMUEL A. FLOYD, JR.

ous, enigmatic, profoundly figurative, complex rhetorical structures" that can be used for the development of its own critical strategies (Gates 1988, 23).

Gates's theory implies that the musical practices of Stuckey's ring can provide the means for discourse on the musical performances of which they came to be a part. By the same token, they can also serve as Signifiers on and rhetorical strategies of the black music tradition. In vernacular oral culture the black rhetorical tropes subsumed under Signifyin(g) include "marking, loud-talking, testifying, calling out (of one's name), sounding, rapping, playing the dozens, and so on" (Gates 1988, 52). In the same way, in music, calls, cries, hollers, riffs, licks, overlapping antiphony, and the various rhythmic, melodic, and other musical practices of the ring serve as Signifyin(g) *musical* figures and are used as such in musical compositions and performances. These musical figures, as well as others, are used to comment (Signify) on other figures, on the performances themselves, on other performances of the same pieces, and on other and completely different works of music. Moreover, genres also Signify on other genres: ragtime Signifies on European and early Euro-American dance music, including the march; blues on the ballad; the spiritual on the hymn; jazz on blues and ragtime; gospel on the hymn, the spiritual, and the blues; rhythm and blues on blues and jazz; rock 'n' roll on rhythm & blues; soul on rhythm and blues and rock; funk on soul; rap on funk; bebop on swing, ragtime rhythms, and blues. And the Negro spirituals were Signifyin(g) tropes in their day, with the slave community using their texts to Signify on other ideas, through indirection, in the surreptitious communication so necessary in slave culture.

Musical Signifyin(g) is not the same, simply, as the borrowing and restating of pre-existing material, or the performing of variations on pre-existing material, or even the simple reworking of pre-existing material. While it is all of these, what makes it different from simple borrowing, varying, or reworking is its transformation of such material by using it rhetorically or figuratively—through troping, in other words—by trifling with, teasing, or censuring it in some way (Wentworth and Flexman 1960; Major 1970). Signifyin(g) is also a way of demonstrating respect for, goading, or poking fun at a musical style, process, or practice through parody, pastiche, implication, indirection, humor, tone- or word-play, the illusions of speech or narration, and other troping mechanisms. As Gates (1988, 48, 49) puts it, "To Signify . . . is to engage in certain rhetorical games . . . through the free play of associative rhetorical and semantic relations." It "luxuriates . . . in free play." Signifyin(g) shows, among other things, either reverence or irreverence toward previously stated musical statements and values.

A twelve-bar blues in which a two-measure instrumental "response" answers a two-measure sung "call" is a classic example of Signifyin(g): here, the instrument performs a kind of sonic mimesis, creating the illusion of speech or narrative conversation. And when performers of gospel music begin a new phrase while the other musicians are only completing the old one, they may be Signifyin(g) on what is occurring and what is to come through implication and anticipation. The implication is that "I'm already there"; when soloists hang back, hesitating for a moment to claim their rightful place in the flow of things, they're saying "but I wasn't, really." This kind of Signifyin(g) is a way of being in both places at the same time.

Signifyin(g) is an essential element of the "Toast" of Afro-American culture. These "long oral epic poems," with their "complex metrical arrangements," varying meters, and swing, whose tellers are "entitled to make [their] own modifications or additions," recall jazz improvisation (Labov et al. [1979] 1981, 331; Mitchell-Kernan [1979] 1981, 341). And jazz improvisations *are* toasts—metaphoric renditions of the troping and Signifyin(g) strategies of Afro-American oral toasts (which include "The Signifying Monkey," "The Titanic," "Stackolee," "Squad Twenty-Two," "The Great MacDaddy," and others). The theatrical recitations of these narrative poems by black toast-tellers, which can be heard on street corners, in barbershops, and in pool halls throughout Afro-America, allow great freedom within the restrictions of their form and are characterized by ironic comment; oppositional balance, e.g., "Hand full of chives, pocket full of herbs" (Abrahams [1963] 1970, 99); quick, fluid, and dramatic rendition; situational and textural variation; and what Abrahams calls "*tropisms*, those elements toward which the performers of the group are attracted" (Abrahams [1963] 1970, 174). Toasts make use variously of all of the six techniques and strategies of black talk, as identified by Kochman: "running it down, rapping and capping, shucking and jiving, gripping and copping a plea, signifying, and playing or sounding" (quoted in Baker 1972, 114). Contests are based around these toasts and are akin to—perhaps led to—the cutting contests that were so prevalent in early jazz and ragtime music. Such Afro-American musical contests metaphorically trope these characteristically Afro-American toasting contests, reflecting the mutability of the expressive structures and strategies that exist in various aspects of Afro-American culture.

To recapitulate, the Signifiers we observed in the ring—call-and-response, blue notes and elisions, pendular thirds, etc.—became part of the black-idiom-informed musical genres that emerged from the shout, so that all Afro-American musical products become models to be revised through a continuing Signifyin(g) process, as also do some European genres. It is through this musical troping and Signifyin(g) that the more profound meanings of black music are expressed and communicated. As Gates (1988, 81) tells us, "the ensuing alteration or deviation of meaning makes Signifyin(g) the black trope for all other tropes, the trope of tropes, the figure of figures. Signifyin(g) *is* troping." And when used in works composed for the concert hall, it informs that music with Afro-American vernacular meanings, as is evident in works by black composers such as William Grant Still, Florence Price, William Dawson, and T. J. Anderson, and in some works by white composers such as Aaron Copland, Morton Gould, Charles Ives, and others.

A word should be said here about the concept of "swing" in Afro-American music, for it is an essential element and a most elusive quality of black music. Most commentators ignore it or assume that to try to explain it is futile; others provide overly elaborate explanations of it (Schuller 1986, 5; 1989, 222–25). From the perspective of the interpretive strategies I am proposing here, however, swing is a natural and perfectly explicable product or by-product of the tropings of black music. When sound-events Signify on the time-line, against the flow of its pulse, making the pulse itself lilt freely—swing has been effected. This troping of the time-line by the placement of events against its flow creates the slight resistances that result in the lilt that, while common to all black music, is most pronounced, evident, and persistent in jazz, where this driving, rhythmic persistence in a relaxed atmosphere is typical. Swing is an essential *quality* of black music. Swing is a dance-related legacy of the ring shout. And the effectiveness of the Signifyin(g) tropes of black music can be measured in part by the extent to which they create and contribute to it. The power of swing is such that even in the absence of motivic and thematic ideas, its presence creates a sense of eventful continuity in a work of music.

The relationship of Signifyin(g) to the presence and relationship of dance to music in the ring must be considered. Gates makes the point that Signifyin(g), by redirecting attention from the signified to the signifier, places the stress of the experience on the *materiality* of the signifier: "the importance of the Signifying Monkey poems is their repeated stress on the sheer materiality, and the willful play, of the signifier itself" (Gates 1988, 59). There is a strong relationship between Gates's point and the physical presence of the body in the ring shout (clapping, shuffling, jerking of the shoulders, etc.) and in subsequent music/dance derivatives of black music. Such dance movements are material signifiers in the music/dance experience, joining the Signifyin(g) musical tropes, discussed above, as material elements that should be the focus of our perceptual and analytical attention. For in Signifyin(g), the materiality of the signifier becomes "the dominant mode of discourse" (Gates 1988, 58). It is this materiality and its solid cultural grounding that prove the impropriety and futility of applying to black music, as aesthetic determinant, the European notion of transcendant, abstract beauty (which leads to formalist analysis and criticism in which "good intonation," "ensemble blend and balance," "proper harmonic progressions," "precise attacks," and other such concerns take precedence over the content of what is expressed and communicated), and that therefore suggest, or *demand*, a cultural-studies approach to black music—that is, the ring shout itself contains within it the very basis for inquiry from within the tradition. For it is in this way that black culture understands itself.

In sum, I believe that the frame of the ring, the interpretive strategies of Esu-Elegbara, and the Signifyin(g) figures derived from the Monkey tales can coalesce to form the background for a mode of musical inquiry that can expand black music scholarship's intellectual reach. The critical approach introduced below is based on two assumptions: that inquiry into the music of black Americans, including all genres from spirituals to Afro-influenced, Europe-oriented concert works, should engage perceptions, beliefs, and assumptions from within Afro-American culture, and that the expressive values of the ring provide the best means of achieving that goal. The test of this approach will lie in its power to produce culturally and musically meaningful evaluation and criticism.

On Criticism of the Music

Gates and Stuckey in their work have identified black vernacular traditions that can be effectively examined for their analytical and interpretive implications. And Gates, together with others, has identified a canon—a tradition—of black literature. Through their works, these scholars and those from other disciplines invite us to "step outside the white hermeneutical circle into the black" (Gates 1988, 258) and to invent other modes of inquiry that reveal the distinctive qualities of the black music tradition.

Explanations of musical works and performances as realizations of "ideal form," achievements of "organic unity," or as functional artifacts are insufficient for black music inquiry because they all separate the works from their cultural and aesthetic foundations. And conventional musical analysis is in itself inadequate for the demands of black music scholarship and criticism. In its concern for recognizing previously sanctioned and favored harmonic progressions, melodic contours, rhythmic conventions, formal structures and their implications and deviations (recognitions that merely stand and substitute for musical evaluation and judgment), traditional musicology has given little attention to the development of judgmental criteria and has ignored

SAMUEL A. FLOYD, JR.

fundamental cultural concerns, having found both areas of concern to be subjective and speculative, and the latter to be "social, not musical." Therefore, it is imperative that music scholarship develop criteria for the aesthetic evaluation of works and for the fundamental cultural concerns of every repertory.

The key to effective criticism lies in understanding the tropings and Signifyin(g)s of black music-making, for such practices *are* criticism—perceptive and evaluative acts and expressions of approval and disapproval, validation and invalidation through the respectful, ironic, satirizing imitation, manipulation, extension, and elaboration of previously created and presented tropes and new ideas. For our purposes, therefore, criticism may be seen as the act of discovering, distinguishing, and explaining cultural and musical value in works of black music through the identification of the elements that captivate our attention and mediate our perceptions and reactions. Attention to this task implies the responsibility of explaining how well or, indeed, *whether* composers and performers have *succeeded* in capturing and mediating our perception.

As culture-based and culture-wise observers respond to poorly done oral-verbal Signifyin(g) with such disapproving comments as "That's phoney" and "That's lame" (Mitchell-Kernan [1979] 1981, 324) and to well-done Signifyin(g) with positive comments and expressions—recognizing the effectiveness of the intended witty put-downs and other poetic constructions of oral Signifyin(g) artists—such observers of black music-making respond similarly to musical Signifyin(g) tropes. Whether in verbal or musical arts, this responding customarily often takes place *during* rather than after performances, creating as a counterpoint to them a variety of call-and-response events. In this way, the black-music experience is, to a large degree, self-criticizing and self-validating, with criticism taking place as the experience progresses. Comments such as "Oh yeah," "Say it," "He's cookin'," and "That's bad" (in response to Signifyin(g) musical events) show approval of those events and, as Murray would say, their extensions, elaborations, and refinements. Musical Signifyin(g) by the performers elicits response and interaction from a knowledgeable and sensitive audience, which participates by responding either vigorously or calmly to the performance. The musical "toasting" that is improvisation is particularly noted by black-music audiences. To paraphrase Mitchell-Kernan ([1979] 1981, 325), a Signifyin(g) act that surpasses another in an excellent performance is particularly treasured, while incompetent performances are "likely to involve confusion, annoyance, boredom, and . . . indifference" (Murray 1973, 87). Those who know the culture know when the notes and the rhythms do not fit the context and when the idiomatic orientation is wrong. So must critics. If they are to be taken seriously within the tradition they are criticizing, they must recognize their duty "to increase the accessibility of aesthetic presentation. . . . [It is] primarily a matter of coming to terms with such special peculiarities as may be involved in a given process of stylization" (Murray 1976, 196).

(The self-criticizing process operates spontaneously where performers sing and play in contact with their cultural base. But it cannot function the same way when, for example, blues, jazz, or gospel music are performed for audiences whose behavior is governed by the customs of the European concert hall.)

All of this implies that Signifyin(g) tropes must be decoded before they can be appreciated and explained (Mitchell-Kernan [1979] 1981, 327). Indeed, decoding and explaining are what I have tried to do below in my analyses of the Morton and Still pieces. Such decodings and explanations are the stuff of interpretation, and they will vary somewhat from critic to critic. Therefore, we must not eschew differing interpretations of a particular work; but we can insist that they result in warrantably assertible statements of value-perception.

"Call-Response": The Musical Trope of Tropes

The musical practices present in the ring are all musical tropes[3] that can be subsumed under the master musical trope of Call-Response,[4] a concept embracing all the other musical tropes (as the black literary concept of Signifyin(g) embraces the rhetorical tropes of the dozens, rapping, loud-talking, etc.).[5] The term Call-Response is used here to convey the dialogical, conversational character of black music. Its processes include the Signifyin(g), troping practices of the early calls, cries, whoops, and hollers of early Afro-American culture, which themselves were tropes from which evolved—through extension, elaboration, and refinement—varieties of the subtropes: call-and-response, elision, multimeter, pendular and blue thirds, and all the rest, including interlocking rhythms, monosyllabic melodic expressions, instrumental imitations of vocal qualities, parlando, and other processes that have a kind of implicative musical, as well as semantic, value.

The lyrics of a work of black music obviously have semantic value—value whose meaning can easily be understood by informed auditors. And for those familiar with black musical culture, the semantic value of instrumental music is equally evident. Such non-verbal semantic value is explained by Albert Murray in *The Hero and the Blues*, where he contends that the musician is concerned with "achieving a *telling effect*" (emphasis mine, Murray 1973, 10). Murray describes how the solo instruments in Ellington's band, for example, state, assert, allege, quest, request, and imply, while others mock, concur, groan, "or signify misgivings and even suspicions" (Murray 1973, 86). But this semantic meaning, this telling effect, is not external to the music. In one sense, at least, Murray's "telling effect" is synonymous with Gates's "semantic relations" (see Gates 1988, 48); and both concepts can account for and intellectualize what black vernacular musicians feel and assume as they nonchalantly claim that when they play they are "telling a story." Another aspect of semantic value is the exhortative potential of such instrumental music: the tropes, Signifyin(g)s, and other constructions can exhort soloists to create ever more exciting improvisations and riffs, these exhortations carrying the semantic values of urging, beseeching, and daring. What is being asserted, implied, mocked, exhorted—indeed, Signified—here are the musical tropes of Call-Response: tropes that carry with them the values, sensibilities, and cultural derivatives of the ring.

Call-Response—this master trope, this musical trope of tropes—functions in black music as Signifyin(g) functions in black literature and can therefore be said to Signify. It implies the presence within it of Signifyin(g) figures (Calls) and Signifyin(g) revisions (Responses, in various guises) that can be one or the other, depending on their context. For example, when pendular thirds are used in an original melodic statement, they may constitute a "Call"; when they are used to comment upon, or "trope," a pre-existing use of such thirds, they can be said to constitute a "Response," or Signifyin(g) revision. This concept of Call-Response, although suggested by Gates's rhetorical trope of Signifyin(g), is implied by and derived from the musical processes of Stuckey's ring, as described on pages 137–138 above; it is subject to the hermeneutical strategies of Gates's Esu.

The theory implied here assumes that works of music are not just objects, but cultural transactions between human beings and organized sound—transactions that take place in specific idiomatic cultural contexts, that are fraught with the values of the original contexts from which they spring, that require some translation by auditors in pursuit of the understanding and aesthetic substance they can offer. With this in mind, I turn now to the application of this approach to two recorded performances, building in the first instance on Gunther Schuller's analysis of Jelly Roll Morton's "Black Bottom Stomp" and then on Orin Moe's provocative analysis of William Grant Still's *Afro-American Symphony*.

"Black Bottom Stomp"

The performers in "Black Bottom Stomp" are Morton, piano; George Mitchell, trumpet; Kid Ory, trombone; Omer Simeon, clarinet; Johnny St. Cyr, banjo;

John Lindsay, bass; and Andrew Hillaire, drums. Together they form the typical New Orleans ensemble: trumpet, clarinet, and trombone fronting a rhythm section. The recording was made on September 15, 1926, as Victor 20221. For my analysis here, I used the Smithsonian Institution's reissue in the *Smithsonian Collection of Classic Jazz* set. Gunther Schuller's analysis, illustrated on a chart in his *Early Jazz* (1968), divides the performance into thirteen "structural divisions" in which he notes the instrumentation and number of bars in each and points out other matters of structural interest such as "breaks," "stop-time" events, and modulations (Schuller 1968, 157). Schuller's narrative reveals "at least four different themes and one variant," "a brilliantly stomping Trio," the usual key relationships and chord progressions, the appearances of solos, varieties of rhythm, metric fragments, and use of instruments (Schuller 1968, 155–61). Schuller's analysis, as usual, is perceptive, revealing, and informative. I would like now to expand upon it from the perspective established in the preceding pages.

In "Black Bottom Stomp" the "exuberance and vitality," the "unique forward momentum," and what constitutes those "Morton ingredients," all mentioned but not explained by Schuller, are the very derivations from the ring that are basic to Afro-American music. The performance is governed by the Call-Response principle, relying upon the Signifyin(g) elisions, responses to calls, improvisations (in fact or in style), continuous rhythmic drive, and timbral and pitch distortions that I have identified as retentions from the ring. At every point, "Black Bottom Stomp" Signifies on black dance rhythms. Underlying it all is the time-line concept of African music: as rhythmic foundation for the entire piece, but kept in the background for the most part and sometimes only implied, there is a continuous rhythm that subdivides Morton's two beats per bar into an underlying rhythm of eight pulses. This continuous, implied, and sometimes-sounded pulse serves the function of a time-line over which the foreground two-beat metric pattern has been placed, and it serves as the reference pulse for the two-beat and four-beat metric structures and the cross-rhythms and additive rhythms that occur throughout the performance. The clarinet and the banjo frequently emphasize this time-line with added volume, thereby bringing it into the foreground as a Signifyin(g) trope, as in, especially B^2 and B^5, respectively, but also throughout the performance. At B^2 the clarinet revises and emphasizes the "stomp" rhythm introduced in A^3, as well as the time-line, with cross-rhythms derived from African performance practices; in B^5 the banjo does the same. This is accomplished by these instruments' filling in the quarter-note values and the eighth-note rest of the A^3 pattern with repeated eighth notes in which the accents expected on beat three of each measure are anticipated by a half beat. It is against and around

SAMUEL A. FLOYD, JR.

the time-line that all other rhythmic organization and activity take place. The four-beat rhythm that occurs in B^1, B^3, and B^5, the breaks that occur in B^1 and B^7 and the stop-time of B^4, the accented cross-rhythm of the drummer in B^2 and B^6, the "stomp" rhythm highlighted in A^3 (clarinet) and B^7, and the after-beats on the tom-toms in B^7 all signify on and serve as enhancements of the time-line. The activity in B^5 that Schuller calls "partly 4-beat" is particularly effective, and the breaks serve effectively as goal-delay devices that Signify on the goal-directedness of the piece's melodic, harmonic, and rhythmic structures.

It is within this rhythmic and structural frame that improvisation takes place—improvisation that Signifies on (1) the structure of the piece itself, (2) the current Signifyin(g)s of the other players in the group, and (3) the players' own and others' Signifyin(g)s in previous performances. These Signifyin(g)s take place at the same time the performers are placing within the frame and including within their improvisations timbral and melodic derivations from the ring—the trombone's smears (elisions) in A^1, the trombone's Signifyin(g) smear on the clarinet's note in B^1, the muted trumpet with its elided phrase endings in B^4, the cymbal break in B^5, the trombone smears (cries) and the new tom-tom timbre in B^7. Highlighting the entire structure is the string of solos that occur between B^1 and B^5 and then the out-chorus (B^7). Like Martin Williams (1963) and unlike Schuller, I hear the exchange between the trumpet and the full band in A^2 as a call-and-response structure, albeit composed (the calls change, the response remains the same), as I do the exchanges in the modulatory interlude following A^3—revising tropes that extend and elaborate, or update, the call-and-response device, which operates on many different structural levels. I also hear the trombone's held-notes in the out-chorus (B^7) as evocative "shouts" that Signify black religious shouting and its counterpart expression in secular life—calls, cries, and hollers—and I hear Morton's solo in B^3 as Signifyin(g) on ragtime, which itself Signifies on the foot-patting, hand-clapping after-beats of the shout (with a "pretty" and embroidered version of the style) and on the stomp rhythm by playing on the time-line while introducing a four-beat rhythm (i.e., the bass player or drummer plays on every beat instead of every other one). The banjo's strummed solo (B^5) does not repeat the melody that preceded it but Signifies on it and on the accompanying harmony. And the out-chorus Signifies on all that has gone before it. The entire performance, of course, Signifies on the stomp rhythm first heard in A^3, a troping that validates the title of the piece.

Throughout the performance, the breaks, riffs, four-beat tropings, and trombone smears serve as exhortations to the soloists, exciting and inciting them to create more inspired solos, as for example, in B^1 (four-beat), B^2 (additive accents), B^4 (stop-time and turn-around), B^6 (four-beat and additive accents), and B^7 (trombone smears and break). And the performance swings—exhibiting that essential quality of products of the ring—with the normal tropings of the time-line throughout the performance. This quality is pronounced at points where off-beats, back-beats, cross-rhythms, and four-beat rhythms occur—sometimes subtle, sometimes pronounced—such as in the interlude; at B^1, B^4, and B^5, where the bass and the drums trope the time-line and the banjo's phrasings; and in the last three measures of B^3. The back-beats of the out-chorus (B^7) are particularly effective in this regard. Related to this quality is the constant filling of the musical space by the banjo as it tropes the time-line by sounding all its notes, when the other instruments lay out, except in stop-time passages, as at A^3. Swing is particularly pronounced in the sections for full band, where several instruments trope the time-line together, in different ways, and at different points.

The elisions (smears), call-and-response devices, meter changes, accented cross-rhythms, after-beats, breaks, stop-time tropes—indeed, all the shuckin' and jivin' Signifyin(g) figures in the piece (particularly those of the clarinet and piano)—are rhetorical Call-Response figures that Signify on the musical values and expressions of the ring and its musical derivations; each improvisation Signifies on Morton's melodies and on the inventions of some of the other musicians; and the structure of the piece Signifies, most immediately, on ragtime and, though perhaps indirectly, on European social dance music (which, by the way, includes the compositions of the black composer Frank Johnson who, a century earlier, also improvised on and added inventions to the form with rhetorical tropes, as in his *Voice Quadrilles* and some of his marches).

"Black Bottom Stomp" is fraught with the referentiality that Gates describes as "semantic value," exemplifying (1) how performers contribute to the success of a performance with musical statements, assertions, allegations, questings, requestings, implications, mockings, and concurrences that result in the "telling effect" Murray has described and (2) what black performers mean when they say that they "tell a story" when they improvise.

Much more could be said about this piece along similar lines, but my goal in discussing it has been simply to suggest that, heard in this way, the Morton band's performance of "Black Bottom Stomp" is fraught with funded meanings from the Afro-American musical tradition, and its grounding in the ring is unmistakably evident. The expression and communication of the performance, in other words, is fully and deeply rooted in black culture. Like the descendants of Esu—the tricksters of Afro-American culture—its performers combine the ritual teasing and critical insinuations of Signifyin(g) with self-empowering wit, cunning, and guile.

SAMUEL A. FLOYD, JR.

Afro-American Symphony

Orin Moe—like Schuller, not an Afro-American (as are Stuckey, Gates, and Murray) but sensitive to both the cultural and musical values of both the European and Afro-American traditions—shows an understanding of the dual lineage of black music in two articles: "William Grant Still: *Songs of Separation*" (1980) and "A Question of Value: Black Concert Music and Criticism" (1986). Moe's work is superb, as far as it goes, and as with Schuller's analysis, I want to use it as the basis for my own inquiry.

In "A Question of Value: Black Concert Music and Criticism," Moe discusses William Grant Still's *Afro-American Symphony* as a "long blues meditation," a "blues-dominated symphony rather than symphonically dominated blues" in which "the black materials fundamentally alter the inherited shape of the symphony" as the composer "bends the forms to control much of the musical flow." Moe hears Still's intended four movements as five—"two faster outer movements, with two slow movements surrounding a central scherzo," sections "one, three, and five . . . unmistakably black in inspiration," "two and four . . . predominantly American." Moe finds Still emphasizing "flow and sectionalization, the variation structure of the blues over the architectonic structure of the symphony" (Moe 1986, 62–64). Moe's brief analysis is revealing and provocative. It is also a good starting point for more detailed investigation and interpretation from the perspective of our new mode of inquiry.

Afro-American Symphony begins with the Afro-American trope of the blues. Following a brief, six-measure introduction in $\frac{4}{4}$ time, a twelve-bar blues is presented as the first theme of the sonata form under which it is structurally subsumed. The first chorus is accompanied by a three-note/two-note riff in the horns and trombones, the second by a steady "walking" rhythm in the strings and riffing figures in the woodwinds in call-and-response dialogue with the clarinet's melody. This is followed by a modulating transition passage that Signifies on figures from the two blues choruses by their loving and approving repetition and revision first through upward transpositions then by turning the repetitions downward again; this transition leads to a second theme area of thirty-two measures, with the second eight measures, and more, being Signifyin(g) revisions created by melodic embellishments and timbral variations. The latter Signifies on the Afro-American spiritual and possesses many of the characteristics and qualities of that genre, including call-and-response between oboe and flutes/clarinets. This is followed by a brief but vigorous and unusual "development" section that Signifies on the second theme and its figures—actually a song-like section in which the themes—unlike those of development sections in the traditional European symphony—remain intact. Then the second theme recurs in revised form in a different key, with a different instrumentation and accompaniment Signifyin(g) on itself and on the activity that took place in the development section. A four-bar vamp with a two-note riff signals the return of the first theme in muted trumpets, this time over a Signifyin(g) walking accompaniment in the strings and Signifyin(g) comments by the bassoon, horns, and woodwinds. The section features muted trumpets; and accompanying the blues theme are two-note riffs in the French horns and Signifyin(g) figures in the strings and woodwinds. In the truncated second chorus we hear overlapping call-and-response between the clarinet, which carries the theme, and the answering flutes, over a "walking" accompaniment in the strings. A brief troping coda, featuring lower woodwinds and Signifyin(g) on the blues theme, brings the movement to a close.

The second movement begins with a six-measure introduction that tropes fragments from the blues theme of the first movement. A primary theme of eight measures is stated twice, followed by extensions and elaborations of it in a brief transition that leads to a second theme—a Signifyin(g) revision of the blues theme of the first movement. This second theme, four measures long, is repeated and then is itself extensively elaborated. The first theme is then Signified upon with extensions and elaborations and then is restated. As Moe suggests, this movement is more American, or European, than Afro-American in character, showing little of the troping and Signifyin(g) of the black cultural tradition (in spite of the blue notes and modal tinges and the timpani's suggestions of dance-beats). But this does not reflect on the value of the movement; it simply means that the application of Call-Response criteria to formulations based in the Western European tradition is as invalid as the reverse application. Such application trivializes our criteria, just as the methods of traditional musicology, when applied to Afro-American music, have tended to seem trivial and ineffective to those familiar with black culture.

The third movement, a scherzo in ²⁄₄, tropes Afro-American secular dance and dance music, employing the banjo—an African retention—playing idiomatic, Call-Response back-beats as accompaniment to the movement's single melody. (What Haas [1975, 30] hears as a second theme I hear as a variation of the initial statement.) In the rhythmically free introduction, the rhythmic and intervallic structure of the theme is foreshadowed successively by the lower winds, horns, trombones, strings, and trumpets. Then enters the complete melody, recalling the shout spiritual, with its banjo accompaniment. Call-and-response figures occur throughout the movement, particularly in transition and development passages. The back-beats of the banjo (a Call-Response instrument *par excellence*) and the cross-rhythms that result from the syncopations in the melody trope the underlying time-line of sixteen pulses per measure, creating a swinging environment that is a Signifyin(g) revision of the third movement of the classical symphony of Western European lineage.

The work's fourth movement—slow, in triple meter—opens with a brand new theme, which is followed first by an extended elaboration of itself and then by a second theme that Signifies on the blues theme of the first movement. The latter theme then receives extensions and elaborations that lead to a variation of the movement's first theme. These appearances of the themes and their variations occur at several different speeds and key centers, Signifyin(g) on tempo and tonal stability. What Moe hears as a fifth movement and others hear as further variation (Haas 1975, 38), I hear as an extended troping coda that Signifies on the work as a whole, summing up the composer's Signifyin(g) revisions of the romantic symphony and Afro-American folk song. Melodic rhetorical tropes in the form of the falling and pendular thirds that characterize Afro-American melodic expression are prominent throughout the complete movement; muted trumpets Signify on classical trumpet timbre and on the black expressive practice of timbral distortion.

Murray's "telling effect" is strongly evident in the *Afro-American Symphony*, particularly in the first and fourth movements—two of Moe's "Afro-American" sections—and the third movement suggests dance, *is* a dance movement, with its flirtatious, stomping, and shouting implications; but even here, the melody is a "telling" one, carrying significant semantic value in its call-and-response construction, statements, and assertions. In the first and fourth movements, the semantic value of the statements, assertions, and allegations made in the expositions are transformed in the development sections of those movements into Murray's suspicions, misgivings, questings, and requestings, together resulting in extended dialogical, rhetorical tropes.

This analysis of Still's *Afro-American Symphony* confirms, I believe, the contention that there can be—and in this case there is—a significant relationship between the black vernacular tradition and that of black concert music, and that the use of the vernacular to examine the formal is a productive and revealing approach to musical analysis and interpretation.

Summary and Conclusions

"Analysis" is an activity that emerged and matured as a way of examining chiefly European works of music, and it can shed some light on works from the Afro-American tradition also, as evidenced by Schuller's treatment of "Black Bottom Stomp." But there are many elements of African-American music that it will not uncover. For those, an Afrocentric approach is indispensable—an approach that must be based on the following elements: (1) a system of referencing, here called Signifyin(g), drawn from Afro-American folk music; (2) a tendency to make performances occasions in which the audience participates, in reaction to what performers do, which leads in turn to (3) a framework of continuous self-criticism that accompanies performance in its indigenous cultural context; (4) an emphasis on competitive values that keep performers on their mettle; and (5) the complete intertwining of black music and dance. All these elements combine to create, foster, and define what I have called here Call-Response.

Perhaps continuing application of this theory, together with its refinement and additional research, will tell us more about its efficacy and its limits. But my preliminary analyses suggest that the mode of inquiry introduced here can be applied successfully to music as diverse as Bessie Smith's "Empty Bed Blues," Thomas A. Dorsey's "Precious Lord, Take My Hand," Olly Wilson's *Akwan*, and T. J. Anderson's *Variations on a Theme by M. B. Tolson*.

The relationship of black music and dance is evident in the very existence and character of "Black Bottom Stomp," which is unadulterated Signifyin(g) black dance music, and in the expressions of the *Afro-American Symphony*, where the themes have been modeled on blues and spiritual melodies and where the rhythmic character of the music could support dancing, particularly the slow drag of turn-of-the-century black culture. Our awareness of this interdependence, which had its genesis in the ring, will enhance our understanding of the nature and character of the music and its Signifyin(g) revisions. And our critical interpretations should take into account this relationship, as I have tried to do in the cases of the Morton and Still pieces.

The approach offered here is intended to address directly these issues in a way that will allow students of the music to recognize, explain, and judge the drama of the progression, juxtaposition, and Signification of the idiomatic tropes of black music-making. Perhaps this beginning will lead to increasing refinement of this mode of inquiry, with the expectation that it will increasingly illuminate black music as a much more complex and richly textured art than has been made clear by more traditional and inappropriate analytical procedures.

NOTES

1. Some of the best descriptions of the shout can be found in Gordon ([1979] 1981), Epstein (1977), and Courlander (1963); and there are numerous descriptions in the WPA Slave Narratives.

2. Certainly, antiphonal, heterophonic, and motivic devices, as well as unflagging rhythm

SAMUEL A. FLOYD, JR.

and other such processes, are used in European music. Nevertheless, it is the idiomatic nature and character of these devices and the idiomatic way in which they function in Afro-American music that validate them as definers of the black music tradition. For one of the most recent and perhaps the most thorough discussion of the devices as they have been treated by scholars over the decades, see Reisser (1982).

3. The term "trope," originally a literary expression, "denotes any rhetorical or figurative device" (Cuddon 1979, 725); it was later used to refer to "a newly composed [literary] addition . . . to one of the antiphonal chants," usually as a preface to or interpolation to a chant (Grout and Palisca 1980, 52–53). The term is used here in its original meaning, but it is applied in this instance to a purely musical device and thus is distantly related to the trope of the Middle Ages known as "sequence." Musical troping, as I have used the term here, is more properly understood as a rhetorical or figurative music device—a Signifyin(g) musical event.

4. Call-Response must not be confused with call-and-response. The latter is a musical *device*, but Call-Response is meant here to name a musical principle, a dialogical musical rhetoric under which are subsumed all the music tropological devices, including call-and-response.

5. I am grateful to Bruce Tucker for putting me onto this idea early in the development of my ideas, when he stated to me that something like the Afro-American musical process of call-and-response, metaphorically speaking, might be considered as the musical trope of tropes. Call-and-response seemed to be too limited a concept to embody all of the black musical tropes, but Bruce's statement carried the necessity of a dialogic and descriptive terminology for this all-important, all-encompassing concept. So, in trying to remain as close as possible to the spirit of Bruce's statement and to the dialogic nature of the music, I coined the term Call-Response.

DISCOGRAPHY

Jelly Roll Morton's Red Hot Peppers, Black bottom stomp. RCA Victor 1649. (Available in the *Smithsonian Collection of Classic Jazz*.)

Still, William Grant. *Afro-American symphony*. London Symphony Orchestra. Columbia M-32782. *Black Composers Series*. (Available from The College Music Society.)

WORKS CITED

Abrahams, Roger. [1963] 1970. *Deep down in the jungle: Negro narrative folklore from the streets of Philadelphia*. Hawthorne, N.Y.: Aldine Publishing Company.

Baker, Houston. 1972. *Long black song: Essays in black American literature and culture*. Charlottesville: University Press of Virginia.

———. 1984. *Blues, ideology, and Afro-American literature: A vernacular theory*. Chicago: University of Chicago Press.

———. 1987. *Modernism and the Harlem Renaissance*. Chicago: University of Chicago Press.

Berry, Mary Frances, and John Blassingame. 1982. *Long memory: The black experience in America*. New York: Oxford University Press.

Courlander, Harold. 1963. *Negro folk music, U.S.A.* New York: Columbia University Press.

Cuddon, J. A. 1979. *A dictionary of literary terms*. Rev. ed. New York: Penguin Books.

Epstein, Dena J. 1977. *Sinful tunes and spirituals: Black folk music to the Civil War*. Urbana: University of Illinois Press.

Floyd, Samuel A., Jr., and Marsha J. Reisser. 1984. The sources and resources of classic ragtime music. *Black Music Research Journal* 4:22–59.

Gates, Henry Louis, Jr. 1988. *The signifying monkey: A theory of African-American literary criticism.* New York: Oxford University Press.

Gordon, Robert Winslow. [1979] 1981. Negro "shouts" from Georgia. In *Mother wit from the laughing barrel: Readings in the interpretation of Afro-American folklore*, Alan Dundes, ed. New York: Garland.

Grout, Donald J., and Claude Palisca. 1980. *A history of Western music.* 3d ed. New York: W. W. Norton.

Haas, Robert Bartlett, ed., with Paul Harold Slatery, Verna Arvey, William Grant Still, and Louis and Annette Kaufman. 1975. *William Grant Still and the fusion of cultures in American music.* Los Angeles: Black Sparrow Press.

Krehbiel, Henry Edward. [1914] 1967. *Afro-American folksongs: A study in racial and national music.* New York: Frederick Unger.

Labov, William, Paul Cohen, Clarence Robbins, and John Lewis. [1979] 1981. Toasts. In *Mother wit from the laughing barrel: Readings in the interpretation of Afro-American folklore*, Alan Dundes, ed. New York: Garland.

Major, Clarence. 1970. *Dictionary of Afro-American slang.* New York: International Publishers.

Mitchell-Kernan, Claudia. [1979] 1981. Signifying. In *Mother wit from the laughing barrel: Readings in the interpretation of Afro-American folklore*, Alan Dundes, ed. New York: Garland.

Moe, Orin. 1980. William Grant Still: *Songs of separation. Black Music Research Journal* 1:18–36.

———. 1986. A question of value: Black concert music and criticism. *Black Music Research Journal* 6:57–66.

Murray, Albert. 1973. *The hero and the blues.* Columbia: University of Missouri Press.

———. 1976. *Stomping the blues.* New York: McGraw-Hill.

Reisser, Marsha J. 1982. Compositional techniques and Afro-American musical traits in selected published works by Howard Swanson. Ph.D. diss., University of Wisconsin.

Schuller, Gunther. 1968. *Early jazz: Its roots and musical development.* New York: Oxford University Press.

———. 1986. *Musings: The musical worlds of Gunther Schuller.* New York: Oxford University Press.

———. 1989. *The swing era: The development of jazz, 1930–1945.* New York: Oxford University Press.

Stuckey, Sterling. 1987. Slave culture: Nationalist theory and the foundations of black America. New York: Oxford University Press.

Wentworth, Harold, and Stuart Berg Flexman, comps. and eds. 1960. *Dictionary of American slang.* New York: Thomas Y. Crowell.

Williams, Martin. 1963. *Jelly Roll Morton.* Kings of Jazz series. New York: A. S. Barnes & Co.

The Heterogeneous Sound Ideal
in African-American Music

(1992)

OLLY WILSON

. . . .

Composer and professor of music at the University of California at Berkeley, Olly Wilson has written widely about African predilections in African American music, based on extensive travel in Africa. He continues his formulation of the African American musical aesthetic with this essay on the preference for timbral contrast. For Wilson, aesthetic practices reflect cultural values, and in attention to timbral nuances he sees a cultural tradition of relatedness and respect for the individual within the group. Talking drums are shown to capture the tonal levels of African speech. And by the same token, singing, dancing, and playing are not just interrelated parts of the performance process but embody connections at a deep, structural level. The heterogeneous sound ideal also suggests an African and African American respect for the integrity of the individual within the group. Wilson conceives of the African sound ideal as a mosaic in which separate elements combine to form a whole, but the whole is not a unified blend of sound. Wilson begins and ends his essay with a discussion of swing, an elusive concept to which the heterogeneous sound ideal opens a few doors.

In 1932, Duke Ellington enriched the repertory of jazz and enlivened popular parlance by creating a new piece of music that contained the following classic line: "It don't mean a thing if it ain't got that swing." Not only was this couplet another marvelous gem of Duke's inimitable verbal wit, but it captured with classic simplicity a basic truth about the musical tradition in which Edward Kennedy Ellington worked. That is, it was at once both an example of and a commentary about the values of that tradition. Duke, of course, was commenting on the music generally referred to as jazz, but he could have been referring to the blues, ragtime, African-American spirituals, or worksongs. In

Reprinted from *New Perspectives on Music: Essays in Honor of Eileen Southern*, edited by Jessie Ann Owens and Anthony M. Cummings, Detroit Monographs in Musicology/Studies in Music, No. 18 (Warren, Mich.: Harmonie Park Press, 1992), 327–38. Used by permission of the publisher.

any of these cases, the phrase would have been equally appropriate. "It don't mean a thing if it ain't got that swing" tells us something of fundamental importance about basic values within the African-American music tradition. The statement speaks of an essential quality of the music.

For several decades, scholars have attempted to define the peculiar qualities of African-American music. Most listeners who have experienced various types of this music sense that the musical subtypes are related. Similarly, listeners familiar with sub-Saharan African music are aware, again on empirical grounds, that the music, while clearly distinct, has obvious similarities to African-American music. Moreover, the significant role of music in sub-Saharan African cosmology, coupled with the obvious historical-cultural connection of peoples of African descent throughout the world, suggests that all peoples within this diaspora share common modes of musical practice. This is true of any large group of human beings with similar historical, cultural, and ethnic ties. For example, musicologists may still speak intelligently of broad general qualities that characterize western European music, notwithstanding the importance of cultural distinctions within a large population mass sharing a geographically defined region.

The effort to define the peculiar qualities of African-American music is made difficult by the fact that the music of black Americans exists within a larger, multicultural social context, like that of all ethnic groups within the United States. Thus, African-American music has both influenced and been influenced in several ways by non-black musical traditions. Therefore, it is difficult to pinpoint precisely the essential qualities that make this music a part of a larger African or black American music tradition. In spite of this fact:

> ... the empirical evidence overwhelmingly supports the notion that there is indeed a distinct set of musical qualities which are an expression of the collective cultural values of peoples of African descent. This musical tradition has many branches which reflect variations in basic cultural patterns over time, as well as diversity within a specific time frame. However, all of these branches share, to a greater or lesser extent, a group of qualities which, taken together, comprise the essence of the black musical tradition. The branches of this tradition, though influenced in different ways and degrees by other musical traditions, share a "critical mass" of these common qualities. It is the common sharing of qualities which comprises and defines the musical tradition.[1]

In a 1974 article, I proposed an approach to the problem of definition of that broader musical tradition. The substance of that approach is that the essence of the black musical tradition consists of:

. . . shared conceptual approaches to music making, and hence is not basically quantitative but qualitative. Therefore, the particular forms of black music which evolved in America are specific realizations of this shared conceptual framework which reflect the peculiarities of the American black experience. As such, the essence of their Africanness is not a static body of something which can be depleted but rather a conceptual approach, the manifestations of which are infinite. The common core of this Africanness consists of the way of doing something, not simply something that is done.[2]

An in-depth discussion of all the specific conceptual approaches to the process of music making that constantly interact with one another and collectively form the essence of the black music tradition is beyond the purview of this paper. However, it may be helpful to describe briefly several of these predilections for conceiving music. Among them are:

1. The tendency to approach the organization of rhythm based on the principle of rhythmic and implied metrical contrast—a tendency to create musical events in which rhythmic clash or disagreement of accents is the ideal, and cross-rhythm and metrical ambiguity are the accepted, expected norm. (It is this conceptual approach that accounts for the quality of "swing" that Duke Ellington celebrated, which is the result of the "clash" or contrast that occurs on either a rhythmic or metrical level.)
2. The tendency to approach singing or the playing of any instrument in a percussive manner—a manner in which qualitative stress accents are frequently used.
3. The tendency to create musical forms in which antiphonal, responsorial, or call-and-response musical structures abound. These responsorial structures frequently exist simultaneously on a number of different architectonic levels.
4. The tendency to create a high density of musical events within a relatively short musical time frame—a tendency to fill up all the musical space.
5. The tendency to incorporate physical body motion as an integral part of the music making process.[3]

An analysis of any genre of black music will reveal the existence of demonstrable musical characteristics that consistently reflect the presence of these underlying conceptual approaches. It is precisely the pervasive existence of these qualities that gives the music its distinctive character.

In this paper, I shall discuss another component of that core of underlying conceptions that define African and African-American music. I call this basic conception "the heterogeneous sound ideal." By this term, I mean that there exists a common approach to music making in which a kaleidoscopic range of dramatically contrasting qualities of sound (timbre) is sought after in both vocal and instrumental music. The desirable musical sound texture is one that contains a combination of diverse timbres. This fundamental bias for contrast of color—heterogeneity of sound rather than similarity of color or homogeneity of sound—is reflected in musical practice in at least two ways.

First, it is reflected in the nature of the "sound" texture of musical ensembles. By sound texture, I mean the relationship of the resultant qualities of sound produced when several instruments perform simultaneously. When a string quartet plays, for example, the resultant composite texture may be described as timbrally homogeneous inasmuch as all component instruments (first and second violins, viola, violoncello) produce timbres that are similar to one another. It is sometimes very difficult for the average listener to determine which instrument is playing a particular pitch because of the fact that all four instruments share overlapping musical ranges and timbral qualities. They blend in a timbrally homogeneous manner. On the other hand, when a drum, metal bell, and a flute play together, it is easy to discern which instrument performs within the texture at any moment because each instrument possesses a distinct, contrasting quality of sound. The resultant composite texture may be described as timbrally heterogeneous in this case; the blend it produces is of a different nature than that of the string quartet.

Secondly, the heterogeneous sound ideal is reflected in the common usage of a wide range of timbres within a single line. This is particularly true when the single line is the principal point of musical interest as, for example, in an unaccompanied part for voice or instrument, or the solo line of an accompanied piece. Practically every scholar who has analyzed African and African-American music has noted the presence of a myriad of vocal sounds used in performance (moans, groans, yells, screams, shouts, shifts in sonority), a seemingly inexhaustible repertory of vocal injections used to intensify musical expression. This common practice of using vocal shadings—from the subtle to the extreme—is a manifestation of the heterogeneous sound ideal. This same ideal is present, moreover, in instrumental music. Within that tradition, the single-line instrumental soloist is expected to explore a wide range of timbral variations, so much so that some observers have spoken of the tradition of making the instrument simulate vocal technique, or "talk" or "speak." In this instance, both instrumental and vocal performance are informed by the same basic concept—the heterogeneous sound ideal.

The heterogeneous sound ideal also explains the customary usage of a broad continuum of vocal sounds, ranging from speech to song. This practice may be due in part to the fact that most African languages are tonal languages and, hence, use tonal levels as a means of defining a specific word. Two words with the same syllables and rhythm may have entirely different meanings if spoken at different pitch levels. In Yoruba, for example, the syllables o̩ and ko̩ may have at least three different meanings, depending upon the tonal level of the syllables:[4]

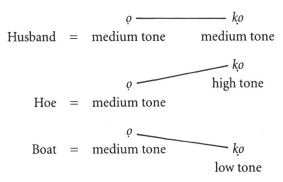

The simulation of the rhythm and tonal levels of speech on uniquely constructed drums enables Yoruban drummers to imitate some speech and hence develop a repertory of "musical speech." These drums are called talking drums.

Linguistic sensitivity to tonal levels accounts perhaps for the common African and African-American practice of moving easily from a speaking to a singing mode within a musical context. On a more complex level, music and language are interrelated in other significant ways. For example, drum patterns are usually verbalized as a memory or mnemonic device. African drummers use non-semantic syllables to reproduce an aural pattern that is analogous to a drum pattern they wish to convey to another person. This verbalization of drum patterns is used as a means of recalling musical patterns or teaching patterns to novices. Nketia advises, for example, that:

> In drumming, nonsense syllables are chosen to convey the aural impression of one or more series of successive drum beats, or, conversely, to indicate to drummers the sound sequences that are required. They are, therefore, a means of speaking rhythms.[5]

In addition, the pre-existing repertory of drum patterns used by master drummers in many African cultures is based on musical patterns derived from selected genres of oral poetry. The underlying basic rhythmic patterns associated with much of this repertory are derived directly from a body of verbal text and are recognizable as such to some or all members of a particular ethnic group. The musical performance, then, is often literally a statement of a particular poetic form.[6]

Having established this general background, I wish to examine two musical practices in African and African-American music that illustrate the function of the heterogeneous sound ideal. By examining the preference for this concept in these musical concepts, we may gain insight into its importance.

The first performance practice pertains to the organization of musical ensembles. Though musical ensembles in African cultures follow a variety of different formats, a general principle appears to govern the division of a musical ensemble into at least two functional groups. The first is one that I refer to as the "fixed rhythmic group," so called because its instruments maintain a fixed rhythmic pulsation throughout the duration of the composition with little variation. This group has a time-keeping or metronomic function; it is frequently manifest in a relatively complex rhythmic form and serves, according to Nketia, as the "time line."[7] The second is the "variable rhythmic group," so named because the rhythms performed by these instruments change.

A configuration of at least two different strata of rhythm consequently is created, and the function of each is enhanced by a contrast of timbre. Typically, the "time-line" stratum is performed by either a metallic instrument (double or single bell), rattle, sticks, some other idiophone and/or handclaps. In some elaborate ensembles a combination of bells, rattle, handclaps, and high-pitched drum form the fixed rhythmic group. What is important here is that the timbre of the fixed rhythmic group is usually highly distinct. The variable group also is associated usually with one or more contrasting tone qualities that further clarify the musical structure. The central point here is that the structure of the ensemble reflects the working of the heterogeneous sound ideal, in this instance operating in conjunction with the principle of rhythmic contrast. The independence of each rhythmic stratum is highlighted by its timbral distinction. What results is a composite musical texture whose components collectively form a mosaic of varying tone colors. This is part of the music's unique charm.

Nketia describes this aspect of African music as follows:

> In multilinear organization, the use of instruments of different pitches and timbres enables each one to be distinctly heard. It enables their cross rhythms to stand out clearly in front of little "tunes." Hence, although rhythm is the primary focus in drumming, some attention is paid to pitch level, for the aesthetic appeal of drumming lies in the organization of the rhythmic and melodic elements.[8]

What Nketia refers to as "little tunes," I call mosaics of tone color and pitch. In both instances, the resultant composite pattern is what is perceived and valued. The operation of the heterogeneous sound ideal is obviously of vital importance here.

Sub-Saharan African instrumental music clearly illustrates the heterogeneous sound ideal. The most vivid examples result from the timbral mosaic created by the interaction between lead voice, chorus, rattle, metallic gong, hand clapping, various wind or string instruments, and drums, which exist in greater or lesser degrees of complexity in almost all African ensemble music. Though this sound ideal finds its most elaborate expression in the music of West Africa—particularly in the large ensembles of the Ewe of Ghana,[9] the one-string harp ensembles of the Senufo of the Ivory Coast,[10] or the bowed string and rattle ensembles of various peoples of the Savannah region—it is also present in the xylophone and *mbira* ensembles of East Africa, as well as in the stamping gourd ensembles of South Africa.

Another manifestation of the heterogeneous sound ideal is found in vocal music. For example, the extraordinary unaccompanied singing of the Dorze of Ethiopia is characterized not only by polyphonic and canonic textures, but also by the use of a wide range of vocal timbres that help define its stratified musical structure.[11] Similarly, the striking vocal technique of the Sidamo (also of Ethiopia), with resultant "roar-like" timbres that are created within the context of varied individual and choral sonorities,[12] or the brilliant combination of the voice and *hindewhu* (a whistle-like instrument) of the Ba-Benzele Pygmies of Central Africa are all reflections of the heterogeneous sound ideal. Thus, the preponderance of timbral differentiation in sub-Saharan Africa's instrumental music, vocal-ensemble music, and solo music underscores a cultural predilection for timbral contrast.

The following music example illustrates the unique vocal-ensemble technique of the Ba-Benzele Pygmies of Central Africa, who create a single musical line through a combination of the voice and *hindewhu* that results in an exciting pitch-timbral mosaic as a by-product of the projection of a single, rhythmically interesting line.

The heterogeneous sound ideal is clearly operative also in African-American music. An examination of writings by early chroniclers of black music-making during colonial times as well as observers of twentieth-century practices make it evident that this underlying conceptual approach has survived in North America for several centuries. Eileen Southern quotes, for example, in *The Music of Black Americans* the following excerpt from an eighteenth-century informant's description of black 'Lection Day festivities held in Newport, Rhode Island:

> Every voice in its highest key, in all the various languages of Africa, mixed with broken and ludicrous English, filled the air, accompanied with the music of the fiddle, tambourine, banjo and drum.[13]

EX. 1   *Hindewhu,* from *An Anthology of African Music,* vol. 3: *Music of the Ba-Benzele Pygmies* (UNESCO recording BM30L2303). Transcribed by Olly Wilson.

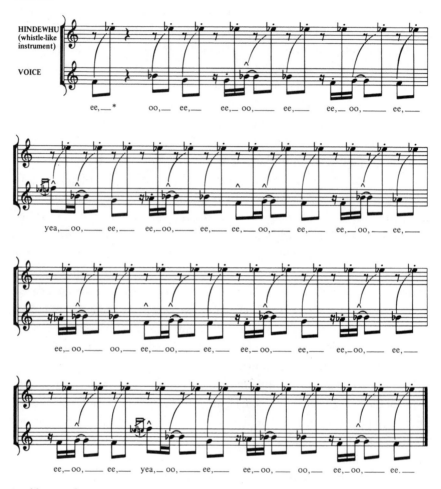

* *ee*-like sound

What is interesting about this quote is that the described performance practices reveal several important things. First, when the chronicler describes the situation as one in which "Every voice [is] in the highest key in all the various languages of Africa, mixed with broken and ludicrous English," he reveals that he can discern individual voices within a composite vocal chorus. He assumes that this is ludicrous because it is uncommon in his cultural experience. He does not understand that an ensemble of contrasting timbres is highly desirable from an African aesthetic viewpoint. This quote then indicates to the contemporary student of black music history that the values associated with the heterogeneous sound ideal were very much intact during the colonial period. Secondly, this quote identifies instruments commonly used to accompany singing in African-American music during the eighteenth and nineteenth centuries. It is noteworthy that the fiddle, tambourine, banjo, and drums blend in a heterogeneous manner. Furthermore, it is also significant that these instruments (with the exception of drums) are associated with the minstrel band that whites created in imitation of black plantation performing practices. Instruments associated with secular African-American ensemble music throughout the eighteenth and nineteenth centuries (fiddle, tambourine, bones, and various drums) are instruments that were doubtlessly selected and/or conceived because they created a heterogeneous sound texture. Chronicles and iconographic evidence (paintings, etchings, engravings) that describe or illustrate black American music of this period clearly document this fact.[14] The frequency with which one encounters the fiddle, banjo, tambourine, and an idiophone of some type of black plantation music is very high, so much so that the fiddler became an archetypical figure in plantation society.

The second performance practice that I wish to focus upon in this paper is the African-American singing tradition. Writings about black American vocal music in the eighteenth and nineteenth century describe performance practices that commonly feature a wide range of vocal nuances. The contemporary vocal style that comes closest is perhaps the lined-out "Watts hymn" (also referred to as the "long-meter hymn") or lined-out psalm, which is an unaccompanied responsorial style of choral singing generally associated today with prayer meetings in traditional African-American churches. This style of singing dates back to the eighteenth century (or earlier) and clearly reflects the continuity of the heterogeneous sound ideal in black music. Most of the descriptions of this style of sacred song discuss the common usage of a diversity of vocal nuances, a musical texture in which individual voices are discerned within a mass of sound, and the prevalence of an unmetrical rhythm in which each individual choral member's response varies in tempo, melodic contour, and vocal nuances that range from speech to song.[15]

The tradition of African-American solo song that most vividly preserves the heterogeneous sound ideal is the "holler," "cry," or "moan." These textless, single-line interjections illustrate with expressive brilliance the significance of timbral nuance in black music. The hollers, cries, and calls that have been documented from the eighteenth and nineteenth centuries comprise a folk song repertory that contributed in significant measure to the evolvement of the blues in the late nineteenth century.[16]

The recording of the song "Black Woman" by Rich Amerson (see Ex. 2) combines elements of the holler or call (e.g., a repertory of vocal nuances, glis-

"Black Woman," sung by Rich Amerson, *Negro Folk Music of Alabama,* vol. 1: *Secular Ethnic* (Folkways Records P417). Transcribed by Olly Wilson.

Well, I say come here black wo-man___ a-hum, don't you hear me

crying, oh_ Lor-dy_____ a-hum,_ I said run here black wo-man___

I want you to sit on_ black da-dy's_ knee, Lord_____ a-hum, ___

I know your house feels lone-some, ___ a-don't you a-hear me whoopin' oh_ Lor-dy_

Don't your house feel lone-some when your vic-to-ro-la's gone? Lord help my cry-

- ing, don't your house feel lone-some__ ma-ma when your vic-to-ro-la's gone?

I said my house feels lone-some__ I know you hear me crying, oh,_ Lor-dy_

a-hum, ah when I look in my kit-chen__ ma-ma,

and I went all through my__ din'room_ a-hum, I__

woke up this morn - ing,___ I find my bis-cuit roll-er done_ gone. _____

*[♪ ♪ = ♪]

sandos, falsetto, repetition of pitches and pitch contours, unmetrical rhythm) with a text that expresses sentiments commonly found in the blues. This song (and similar holler-like songs like it) is performed by an unaccompanied singer, and represents perhaps a genre of music that preceded the blues. Particularly noteworthy is Amerson's use of the non-lexical intensifier *a hum* (sung on the same two pitches), which functions as a short contrasting musical refrain or anchor to the more florid musical lines associated with the text.

In analyzing historical developments in jazz, it is important to note how fundamental African-American conceptions about the nature of music impact on specific historical choices. For example the practice of marching and music making existed in African cultures prior to the forced migration of Africans to the New World, and the tradition of African festivals, which was characteristic of many sub-Saharan ethnic groups, involved parades of various sectors of society (warriors, nobility, priests), accompanied by drums (which were carried), various other instruments, and ensemble singing.[17] This martial music reflected all of the common characteristics of African music, including the heterogeneous sound ideal. It is equally important to note that the tradition of African festivals (complete with parades and instrumental music) was continued in the United States among early Africans during the eighteenth and nineteenth centuries.[18]

Thus, the prior existence of a marching tradition in Africa which found continuity in continental America underscores the notion of cultural syncretism as a principle that shaped cultural adaptation of peoples of African descent in the New World. Because colonial Anglo-American culture contained some musical practices that were congruent with pre-existing African cultural patterns, African-Americans were attracted to these specific practices and reinterpreted them from an African or African-American point of view.[19]

It is my hypothesis that blacks were attracted to European marching bands not only because the process of music making and marching was consistent with African concepts of the association of physical body motion with music, but also because European marching band music tended to focus upon timbral contrast between various sections. In that tradition, cornets and trumpets tended to provide the principal melodic line in a middle register; clarinets and flutes played an embellished obligato melody at a higher register; and the low brass played countermelodies. The resultant texture contained a great deal of timbral contrast. Hence, blacks were attracted to this European musical tradition, participated in it, and adapted and transformed it to conform more completely to their own conceptual approaches. I believe this is why there has been a long tradition of the involvement of blacks in marching bands throughout American history. This had an important effect upon the development of ragtime and jazz.

In early jazz, the presence of the heterogeneous sound ideal is very strong as a basic concept that affected surface features of the music. The basic New Orleans jazz band clearly was organized into two groups: a) the fixed variable group, consisting of piano, banjo, bass or tuba, and drums, and b) the variable rhythmic group of front-line instruments, most commonly composed of cornet, clarinet, and trombone. The timbral independence of these instruments is clear. The practice of collective improvisation, whereby all three front-line instruments improvised simultaneously, created a musical texture that highlighted the timbral mosaic-like quality of the ensemble. This development was highly significant because it created a new paradigm—a distinctly African-American means of realizing a fundamentally African idea. This paradigm, in turn, then spawned its own modifications.

Preference for a specific quality in jazz required new solutions to achieve the desired end. As big bands evolved in the 1920s, for example, it became impossible for there to be simultaneous individual improvisation among instruments of contrasting timbres. Arranger Don Redman (of the Fletcher Henderson Band) eventually developed the solution of grouping instruments together by timbre, adding additional instruments to each instrumental group in order to create music that highlighted the contrast between groups. This ingenious solution enabled more instruments to participate, yet preserved the basic principle of timbral contrast.

Further developments in jazz reflect a continued observance of the heterogeneous sound ideal. There have been historical movements when a particular performer and/or composer focused more intently upon this aspect of the tradition. For example, the continuity of the heterogeneous sound ideal has been reflected through the innovative performances with mutes of trombonist "Tricky Sam" Nanton and trumpeter "Bubber" Miley in Duke Ellington's early bands, which focused much of their improvisation upon subtle nuances of sonority, much to the delight of audiences. Other manifestations included the so-called "growling and talking brass" of the early Ellington bands; Duke Ellington's own imaginative orchestrations, which created new heterogeneous blends, as in *Mood Indigo*; the striking manner in which the Count Basie Band and other southwestern bands used timbral nuances to illuminate the dynamic interplay of alternating riffs between sections; the dramatic asymmetrical phrasings, extreme shifts in range and timbre, and rhythmic vitality of innovations by Charlie Parker and Dizzy Gillespie with bebop; the subtlety and elegance of Miles Davis's muted ballads of the 1950s; the intense wailing and dynamism of the explosive, wide-ranging musical excursions of John Coltrane.

It is in the domain of twentieth-century African-American vocal music, however, that one finds the most highly developed, imaginative realization of the heterogeneous sound ideal. One observes, for instance, that this underlying concept is of much importance both within the secular dimension of blues, rhythm and blues, and soul, as well as in the sacred dimension of gospel music, which have historically interacted constantly with and profoundly influenced each other. In studying the blues and gospel music, several researchers (e.g., Horace Boyer, Pearl Williams-Jones, Charles Keil, Tony Heilbut, Mellonee Burnim) have discussed the ritualistic quality of the performance situation— i.e., a situation in which all participants are aware of what will transpire but are unaware of how a particular performer will realize the predetermined plan. Within the gospel and blues traditions, people familiar with these art forms know that the expected goal is a point in the performance when the expressive power of the performer is so overwhelming that it demands a spontaneous response from the audience. That moment of collective catharsis is extremely important in reinforcing a sense of cultural solidarity. According to Burnim,

> When the expectations of the Black congregation or audience are met, performer and audience merge; they become one. The personalized interpretation of a given gospel selection generates a sense of ethnic collectivity and spiritual unity.[20]

Within the black performance tradition, there is a communion of participants, not isolation between performer and audience.

The means by which contemporary twentieth-century black singers achieve the goal of the heterogeneous sound ideal is primarily through their judicious use of timbral and rhythmic nuances. An imaginative performer will have developed the sensitivity to know precisely when to utilize an extraordinary range of vocal timbres in order to achieve his or her purpose. Performers James Brown, Aretha Franklin, Al Green, Rev. James Cleveland, and Stevie Wonder, like their predecessors Louis Armstrong, Mahalia Jackson, and Billie Holiday, are noted not only for voices that have highly distinctive timbres but also for their musical sensitivity and use of timbral nuances in expressively powerful ways at precisely the right moment.

Mellonee Burnim observes, for example, that

> The performer must express emotion, but he or she must also prepare the audience properly for musical and emotional climaxes by alternating peak phrases with periods of relaxation. Herein lies the basis for extreme and often sudden dynamic vocal contrasts and the juxtaposition of different vocal textures so characteristic of gospel music.[21]

She further quotes a church member's critique of a gospel singer:

> See, I was watching for a pattern; I watched how she had a raspy sound; then she went into a real smooth, melodic type thing. Then she went right back into it, so I was trying to see if she was going to do it this time. I was waiting for her, and she said "Yap!" and got real percussive with it, you know. So I was just laughing.[22]

Though space has not permitted a complete discussion of all the ways in which the heterogeneous sound ideal is reflected in all genres of black music, I hope the preceding discussion has demonstrated the significance of this concept as a shaping force in the history of African-American music.

In conclusion, I want to return to the opening point I made about Duke Ellington's composition. When Ellington followed the line "It don't mean a thing if it ain't got that swing" with the line "do-wah, do-wah, do-wah, do-wah, do-wah, do-wah," he illustrated the principle of swing by setting up the implied metrical contrast that I discussed earlier and by tying this metrical contrast to a contrast in timbre. The line was not *do-ooo, do-ooo,* etc.; but *do-wáh, do-wáh,* which accents the affect of timbral contrast working in conjunction with a cross rhythm. This is a perfect example of the operation of the heterogeneous sound ideal. If you recognize the musical difference between these two examples, you understand this principle.

NOTES

1. Olly Wilson, "Black Music as an Art Form," *Black Music Research Journal* 3 (1983): 2.

2. Olly Wilson, "The Significance of the Relationship between Afro-American Music and West African Music," *Black Perspective in Music* 2 (1) (Spring 1974): 20.

3. John Blacking, *How Musical Is Man?* (Seattle: University of Washington Press, 1973), 27; J. H. Kwabena Nketia, *Music of Africa* (New York: W. W. Norton, 1974), 206; Olly Wilson, "The Association of Movement and Music as a Manifestation of a Black Conceptual Approach to Music Making," in *More than Dancing: Essays on Afro-American Music and Musicians,* ed. Irene V. Jackson (Westport, Conn.: Greenwood Press, 1985), 10–13.

4. The syllable ǫ is pronounced like *aw* in English.

5. J. H. Kwabena Nketia, *Drumming in Akan Communities of Ghana* ([Edinburgh]: Published on behalf of the University of Ghana by T. Nelson, [ca. 1963]), 33.

6. Ibid. Nketia devotes a chapter, entitled "The Verbal Basis of Drumming," to this topic.

7. J. H. Kwabena Nketia, *Music of Africa* (New York: W. W. Norton, 1974), 131.

8. Ibid., 137–38.

9. *Africa South of the Sahara* (Folkways Records FE 4503). While any one of the thirty-eight excerpts on this album will reflect the heterogeneous sound ideal, no. 30, entitled "Music of the Ewe People," illustrates a timbral mosaic created by dynamic interaction between the lead voice, chorus, rattle, bell, hand clapping, and a consort of interlocking drums that is very striking.

10. "Fodonon," *Anthology of African Music,* vol. 8: *Music of the Senufo* (UNESCO record-

ing BM30L2308), band no. 2. This recording features two men's voices alternating in an elaborate, vocally-infected melody against the accompaniment of a fixed rhythmic group composed of nine one-string harps with sympathetic vibrators and three large calabash rattles. The result is a highly diverse timbral texture that supports the structural rhythmic contrast.

11. Cf. the music of the Dorze, *Ethiopie polyphonies et techniques vocales* (Ocora OCR44), side A, track 1. The Dorze, who are a Cushitic-speaking ethnic group living in the high mountain region of south central Ethiopia (west of Lake Abaya), have an extraordinary style that is not only polyphonic and canonic—something western musicologists until recently had thought existed only in western Europe—but also employ a wide range of vocal timbres. The choral singing in this example is unaccompanied. The music maintains its stratified timbrally defined structure.

12. Ibid., side B, track 1.

13. Quoted in Eileen Southern, *Music of Black Americans*, 2nd ed. (New York: W. W. Norton, 1983), 54.

14. Eileen Southern and Josephine Wright, comps., *African-American Traditions in Song, Sermon, Tale, and Dance, 1600s–1920: An Annotated Bibliography of Literature, Collections, and Artworks* (Westport, Conn.: Greenwood Press, 1990).

15. See Ben Bailey, "The Lined-Hymn Tradition in Black Mississippi Churches," *Black Perspective in Music* 6 (1) (spring 1978): 3–18.

16. Southern, *Music of Black Americans*, 156, 323–33; also Willis Laurence James, "The Romance of the Negro Folk Cry in America," *Phylon* 16 (1950): 15–30, reprinted in *Mother Wit from the Laughing Barrel: Readings in the Interpretation of Afro-American Folklore*, ed. Alan Dundes (Englewood Cliffs, N.J.: Prentice-Hall, 1973), 340–44.

17. Thomas Edward Bowdich, *Mission from Cape Coast Castle to Ashantee* (London: John Murray, 1819), 31–40, 358–69, 449–52; excerpts reprinted in 2d ed. of *Readings in Black American Music*, ed. Eileen Southern (New York: W.W. Norton, 1983), 8–26.

18. Southern, *Music of Black Americans*, 53–57.

19. Melville J. Herskovits, *Myth of the Negro Past*, 2d ed. (Boston: Beacon Press, 1958).

20. Mellonee V. Burnim, "The Black Gospel Music Tradition: A Complex of Ideology, Aesthetic, and Behavior," in *More than Dancing*, ed. Irene V. Jackson (Westport, Conn.: Greenwood Press, 1985), 157.

21. Ibid.

22. Ibid., 158.

The Impact of Gospel Music
on the Secular Music Industry

(1992)

PORTIA K. MAULTSBY

. . . .

A professor of Afro-American studies and adjunct professor of music and ethnomusicology at Indiana University, Portia Maultsby discusses the aesthetics of gospel music as part of a performance style that reflects black life in America. The vocal stylings and timbral variations of gospel singers echo those of gospel preachers and join "infectious rhythms, melismatic melodies, complex harmonies, call-response structures" to define an approach to music-making that permeates both sacred and secular African American music. Maultsby shows how radio helped to promote gospel music commercially, expanding its audience and increasing the demand for gospel music on record. She notes that many question whether gospel music will one day cease to belong to the church. Yet she also documents the cycling of musical practices through gospel and popular music forms, underscoring the inseparability of the sacred and secular in an Africanist aesthetic.

I've had a lot of offers to stop singing gospel and take up singing jazz and blues, but blues and jazz just aren't me.—Albertina Walker

Many of the past gospel hits of the [Staple Singers] crossed over into the pop charts, which is just another indication of the common roots from which black music sprang.—"Special Edition"

Crossing over from gospel to pop wasn't hard because it was just a matter of changing words.—Lou Rawls

Since the 1930s, Black gospel music has loomed from its status as the exclusive property of storefront African American churches to become a dynamic and viable force in the commercial music industry. It became an economic commodity in secular contexts when its performers were broadcast over network and independent radio stations; recorded by independent record companies; and showcased in large concert halls, coliseums, theaters, jazz festivals, and nightclubs. The exposure and acceptance of gospel music outside the sanctuaries of Black churches simultaneously expanded its consumer market and led to its appropriation by purveyors of secular idioms. The infectious rhythms, melismatic melodies, complex harmonies, call-response structures, and compelling character of this music permeate the vinyl of various popular music styles. Even the gospel message could not be contained within the walls of the Black church as former gospel singers rerecorded gospel songs under rhythm and blues, soul, and pop labels. While serving as a catalyst for new popular music styles, gospel music propelled the growth of a post–World War II, multibillion-dollar secular music industry. This essay will examine the commercialization of gospel music and its transformation into popular song.

The Commercialization of Gospel Music

In a 1979 article on contemporary gospel music, scholar-performer Horace Clarence Boyer posed a question that continues to be debated among African American church congregations: "Is it possible that one day gospel music will no longer belong to the church?" (Boyer 197a, 6). Eight years later, *Billboard* published a report on the status of gospel music that indirectly addressed the issue: "Perhaps the biggest news in gospel music this year [1987] is the stunning growth and wider acceptance of black gospel music. No longer an esoteric cultural phenomenon, it is now presented in many styles and is quickly becoming another popular form of black music without losing any of its message" ("Black Gospel: Rocketing to Higher Prominence" 1987, G–6). While this commentary accurately assesses the growth of a non-Christian and cross-cultural consumer market for Black gospel music, it totally misinterprets the continued existence of gospel as both a religious and a cultural phenomenon.

Over the last seventy years, gospel music has evolved from the improvised singing of congregations and from the traditional styles of Thomas A. Dorsey, William Herbert Brewster, Lucie Campbell, and Roberta Martin to the contemporary sounds of quartets, choirs, small groups, and ensembles. The coexistence and popularity of these diverse gospel styles among African American Christians and non-Christians suggest that gospel continues to be a vital form of expression in the African American community. In a study on gospel music, ethnomusicologist Mellonee Burnim concluded that "Gospel is not just a musical exercise; it is a process of esoteric sharing and affirmation. It is more than the beat; it is more than the movement; it even embodies much more than text, harmonies or instrumental accompaniment. All of these factors and others intertwine to produce a genre which represents a uniquely Black perspective, one which manifests itself in a cogent, dynamic cultural philosophy or world view" (Burnim 1988, 112). Gospel music therefore is a complex form that embodies the religious, cultural, historical, and social dimensions of Black life in America. The current misinterpretation about the religious and cultural significance of this tradition emanates from the exploitation of gospel music as an economic commodity.

Gospel music has been expropriated and used by the music industry to generate new consumer markets, giving rise to new functions and performing contexts. Repackaged and promoted as entertainment to a cross-cultural and non-Christian audience in nontraditional arenas, the spiritual message and cultural aesthetic of gospel were subordinated to the money-making interest of the music industry.

From the 1930s through the 1960s, performances of gospel music were held primarily at religious events in churches and in public venues for African American audiences. During this time, media exposure ranged from fifteen- and twenty-minute broadcasts on general-market radio to one to three hours of daily programs on Black-formatted radio stations. Over the last two decades, gospel music experienced an explosion on many levels. Its audiences have become multiracial in composition. It is broadcast on full-time gospel-formatted stations and on religious television programs. Its performers are featured in music festivals, with symphony orchestras, and on recordings of popular music; major concerts are jointly sponsored by record companies and national advertisers. Additionally, gospel recordings, once available only in African American "mom and pop" record shops and at performance sites, are now found in mainstream retail outfits.

Many of these trends were precipitated by the crossover appeal of the gospel song "Oh Happy Day," recorded in 1968 by the Edwin Hawkins Singers. When Hawkins recorded his gospel arrangement of the hymn "Oh Happy Day," he unwittingly opened the doors for the commercial exploitation of gospel music. The song, laced with elements from contemporary Black popular styles, was programmed as gospel and soul music on Black-oriented radio and as pop on Top 40 stations. A graduate student at the time, I remember hearing the remarks of an African American DJ when he introduced the song on WVON, a soul music radio station in Chicago: "Here's a new song climbing the charts. I don't know what to call it. It sounds like gospel and it sounds like soul. Whatever it is, the beat has a groove. I like it and I'm gonna play it." The message, aesthetic, danceable beat, and contemporary sound of "Oh Happy Day" made it accessible to a diverse audience.

Through mass-media exposure, gospel music slowly penetrated every artery of American life, linking the sacred and secular domains of the African American community, breathing life into new secular forms, and bringing flair and distinction to the American stage of entertainment.

Gospel Music in Secular Contexts

LOCAL COMMUNITIES AND PUBLIC VENUES

The seeds for the commercialization of gospel music were planted in the 1930s when its performers were showcased in a variety of nonreligious settings. Gospel quartets were the first to garner a secular following by performing at local community events, on radio broadcasts, and on commercial records. Evolving out of jubilee quartets in the 1930s, they expanded their repertoire of Negro spirituals to include secular songs and a new body of religious music known as gospel. By the 1940s, the songs of pioneering gospel composers Thomas A. Dorsey, Theodore Frye, William Herbert Brewster, Kenneth Morris, Lucie E. Campbell, and Roberta Martin had become standard repertoire in jubilee-gospel quartet performances. Members of quartets occupied a unique position in African American community life, functioning as both evangelists and entertainers for activities sponsored by Black churches, schools, and social clubs, and by white businesses (Seroff 1980). Kerill Rubman, in his study of gospel music, comments on the widespread popularity of these quartets: "Factory and construction workers, porters, and other employees sang in company or union-affiliated quartets, performing at picnics, parties, dances, and other business or community events. Family members formed quartets. Negro colleges continued to sponsor such groups, and Baptist and Methodist churches often formed male quartets to sing sacred music at worship services and evening programs" (Lornell 1988, 18). Some local quartets developed regional and national reputations that led to a change in their status. As regional "stars" in the 1930s, they toured while maintaining full-time jobs, but by the mid-1940s, several were touring the country as full-time professional musicians (Lornell 1988, 64–78).

Gospel quartets initially performed for Black audiences. But as the gospel sound spread through radio broadcasts in the 1920s, gospel music found its way into public venues traditionally reserved for America's white bourgeoisie. Jazz critic and record producer John Hammond organized a musical extravaganza, "From Spirituals to Swing," that featured performances of blues, jazz, spirituals, and gospel music. Staged in 1938 in Carnegie Hall, Hammond selected Mitchell's Christian Singers and Sister Rosetta Tharpe to render spirituals and gospel songs, respectively. According to Hammond, "Except for one fleeting appearance at the Cotton Club, she [Tharpe] had never sung anywhere except in Negro churches. She was a surprise smash; knocked the people out. Her singing showed an affinity between gospel and jazz that all fans could recognize and appreciate" (Hammond and Townsend 1981, 203). The success of this concert and favorable reviews by music critics resulted in the staging of a second "Spirituals to Swing" concert in 1939 that featured the Golden Gate Jubilee Quartet (Hammond and Townsend 1981, 231).

During the 1950s, Hammond seized other opportunities to expose gospel singing to white America. Serving on the board of the Newport Jazz Festival, he was determined to obliterate musical and racial segregation from the nation's social fabric. To this end, Mahalia Jackson was invited to perform at the Festival. According to Hammond, "[Mahalia] gave the Festival a great boost of respectability in 1956 by her unprecedented appearance and glorious singing at a Sunday morning service in Newport's unassailably white Trinity Episcopal Church" (Hammond and Townsend 1981, 339). One year later, Clara Ward and the Ward Singers appeared on the stage of the Newport Jazz Festival, and, in 1958, Mahalia Jackson was featured again.

The cross-cultural appeal of gospel and its growing popularity across religious and social boundaries in African American communities were observed by enterprising individuals who quickly seized the opportunity to cash in on its message, musical sound, and cultural aesthetic. Facilitated by promotional strategies of the secular music industry, gospel music emerged as big business. In the 1950s, many singers became full-time performers, appearing in major concert halls, large theaters, auditoriums, and stadiums before audiences averaging twenty-five thousand or more throughout the United States and in Europe. Some performers witnessed their income rise from church free-will offerings of unpredictable amounts to actual performance fees of two to five thousand dollars. Music critic Richard Gehman noted in 1958 that "gospel singers have forged their art into a business now grossing, in the estimate of New York promoter Joe Bostic, around $15 million annually" (Gehman 1958, 113). These performances, supported by radio broadcasts and record sales, firmly entrenched gospel music in the secular fabric of Black community life. Succinctly stated by Horace Clarence Boyer, "The Black American who had never discovered gospel music, or who had simply decided to deny it for whatever reason, began to support it—not in the church, but in places outside the church" (Boyer 1979a, 9). Walter Grady, promoter for Malaco Records, which specializes in gospel and blues, further elaborates, "Most [Black] non-church goers and non-Christians can be responsive [to gospel] because of their upbringing. Once, all of us were kids and you heard gospel in the home every Sunday and maybe blues two days a week [on the radio]. . . . When you were brought up on gospel it's very hard to get away from it" (Maultsby 1990a).

For whatever reason—its spiritual message, musical sound, or cultural aesthetic—gospel music had a magnetic effect on people, especially Black people. The music industry, in recognizing the power of this music, explored various strategies to market gospel as an entertainment commodity. One approach was to showcase gospel singers in nightclubs and theaters traditionally reserved for performances of jazz, blues, and rhythm and blues music. Sister Rosetta Tharpe appears to be the first gospel singer to sing in such nontraditional public arenas. Singing and playing the electric guitar with Lucky Millinder's band in the late 1930s and 1940s, she performed Thomas Dorsey's "Hide Me in Thy Bosom" under the title "Rock Me," which she recorded in 939 with Millinder's band (MCA 1357).

Prompted by John Hammond, during the early 1940s, the Golden Gate Jubilee Quartet and the Dixie Hummingbirds joined Tharpe as singers of gospel music performing in nightclubs (Tallmadge 1974, 14; Salvo and Salvo 1974, 62). Such performances, however, were rare among gospel performers, since the Black church considered this activity blasphemous and, therefore, inappropriate (Hentoff 1963, 46). Even so, gospel music resurfaced in nightclubs during the following decades.

In the mid-1950s and early 1960s, Clara Ward and Della Reese, who performed at various times with Mahalia Jackson, the Clara Ward Singers, and the Roberta Martin Singers, were among the few gospel singers (including Bessie Griffin, the Dixie Hummingbirds, the Nathaniel Lewis Singers, and Howard Saunders) who accepted offers to perform in nightclubs and theaters. Surrounded by criticism from gospel performers, ministers, and the Black community, both Ward and Reese defended their position. Ward maintained that her mission was to evangelize rather than to entertain: "Although perhaps there are many people who would not share my feelings on the subject, I now feel that God intended for his message to be heard in song not solely by those who attend churches, but also by the outsiders who in many cases never attend a house of worship. For that reason the Ward Singers and I have taken our gospel singing into the Apollo Theater in New York . . . [and into clubs in Las Vegas]" (Ward 1956, 16). Della Reese, to the contrary, declared that her performances with the Meditation Singers at New York's Copacabana served only an entertainment purpose: "We are not presented as holy singers; we are there to show that gospel is interesting music. We don't perform in night clubs to save souls." She also acknowledged that financial considerations played a role in her decision to perform gospel in nightclubs: "I like a comfortable apartment, a healthy bank account and some good solid real estate" ("Gospel to Pop to Gospel" 1962, 107, 110).

Despite lucrative offers for nightclub appearances, many gospel singers refused. Mahalia Jackson declared, "It's not the place for my kind of singing" (Gehman 1958, 114), and James Cleveland, in agreement, revealed, "I don't feel I can do much good in a club. I don't feel that the atmosphere is conducive, and I don't feel that the reason for bringing me there is the reason for which I am singing" (Lucas 1972, 21). Rejections from established gospel singers and the objections of African American ministers and members of the African American community, however, did not dissuade enterprising club owners from exploring alternative marketing strategies. A new twist to an old concept was the establishment of "gospel nightclubs." The May 18, 1963 and May 24, 1963 issues of *Billboard* and *Time*, respectively, reported that one such club called Sweet Chariot opened in Manhattan. Although the targeted clientele was America's white teenagers, marketing techniques proved insulting, demeaning, and contradictory to the mores of Black people. Restrooms were labeled *Brothers* and *Sisters*, and waitresses dressed as angels served alcoholic beverages during performances of gospel music. Curious patrons nevertheless filled the club to capacity, prompting the owner to announce plans to open similar clubs in Chicago, San Francisco, and Los Angeles (Hentoff 1963, 46).

Within two years, declining clientele and continued criticism from the African American community influenced the closing of some of these clubs, but not before Columbia Records recorded and repackaged gospel as a "popular" music genre. Convinced that this "new" music would rebound sagging record sales, a Columbia executive proclaimed, "It's the greatest new groove since rock 'n' roll. In a month or two, it'll be all over the charts" ("Gospel Singers: Pop up, Sweet Chariot" 1963, 48). Although Columbia's recordings did not make the charts (see Williams 1963 for a review of the recordings), its executive accurately assessed the future impact of gospel music on the pop music field. Aided by radio, gospel redefined the sound, beat, and stylings of popular music.

GOSPEL MUSIC ON RADIO

Radio became the major source of entertainment in the 1920s. Even though its programming was targeted at middle-class white America, the gospel singing of Sanctified and Baptist storefront congregations traveled the airwaves through the Sunday morning broadcast of church services. By the late 1930s, live performances of gospel quartets, including the Southernaires, the Golden Gate Jubilee

Quartet, Mitchell's Christian Singers, the Fairfield Four, the Swan Silvertones, and the Selah Jubilee Singers, had become integral to many formats. These fifteen- and twenty-minute daily or weekly broadcasts proliferated during the 1940s and 1950s in response to the growth of postwar urban African American populations (Lornell 1988, 22–26; Spaulding 1981, 101–8).

Controlling a multibillion-dollar economy, African Americans became a major consumer group at a time when the white radio audience was declining. The advent and growing popularity of television redefined the position of radio as the primary entertainment medium. Struggling to survive, radio stations experimented with programming in search of new audiences. Many expanded their Black programming, while others revamped their formats to become full-time Black-oriented stations. For example, in 1943 "only four stations throughout the country were programming specifically for blacks, [but] ten years later, 260 stations were attracting national and local sponsors to their broadcasts" (MacDonald 1979, 366). By 1961, over 310 stations "devoted some portion of their programming to black interests, about 70 of which geared at least 10 hours of air time, each week, in this area. Slightly more than half of those 70 aimed all their programming at the black [sic] community. [At the close of the decade], at least 65 outlets were geared entirely to black [sic] audiences" (Garnett 1970).

The proliferation of Black programming formats increased the exposure of gospel music. Jack Gibson, a DJ on Chicago's WJJD (a general-market station) from 1947 to 1949, recalled that gospel programs aired daily "for about an hour, 9:00–10:00 A.M. Everybody's gone to work and the woman left at home wants to settle down before she starts into housework. So she would listen to the gospel music" (Maultsby 1979).

As gospel music's audience grew by leaps and bounds during the 1950s, so did its programming on stations with an all-Black format. Birmingham's WEDR and Houston's KYOK, for example, featured two gospel music programs daily for two and three hours, respectively. On Sunday, both stations broadcast Black church services and live performances of gospel music (Maultsby 1990b, 1990c). This programming format also characterized gospel music broadcasts through-out the 1960s. The April 1962 programming schedule of Atlanta's WERD, the nation's first Black-owned and -operated radio station, for example, lists two daily gospel music programs. The first one, "Gospel Gems," aired from 6:15 to 7:30 A.M., and "The Gospel Train" from 3:05 to 4:05 P.M., the latter replaced by "Old Ship of Zion" on Saturdays and broadcast from 4:30 P.M. until the station went off the air at sunset. Sunday's format was entirely religious—church services and a variety of religious music programs.

Most radio stations targeted at African American communities were low powered (two hundred fifty to ten thousand watts) and licensed to broadcast from sunrise to sunset. Nashville's WLAC was an exception. It was a fifty-thousand-watt CBS affiliate station whose power catapulted its evening Black music programs to several regions in the United States, Canada, the Caribbean islands, and, via shortwave radio, to New Zealand, Europe, and North Africa. Before these programs were launched in 1946, the station served as the radio home from 1939 to 1951 for the gospel quartet the Fairfield Four. This group enjoyed wide exposure through their fifteen-minute morning broadcast, which was recorded and syndicated to other stations (Landes 1987, 68). When WLAC instituted its evening programs of Black music, gospel was included only in the advertising of "record specials" offered through mail-order outlets that sponsored the programs. This arrangement juxtaposed gospel with rhythm and blues and blues records, blurring the lines between sacred and secular and making gospel music available to both religious and nonreligious audiences.

Black-formatted stations began competing with general-market radio for national advertisers in the late 1960s and early 1970s. Scrambling to increase market ratings by diversifying their listening audience, these stations either rescheduled their daily broadcast of gospel music to 5:00–7:00 A.M. or discontinued the programs altogether. Black religious services and gospel music nevertheless continued to dominate Sunday programming (Maultsby 1990c). When most Black-oriented stations abated their gospel music programs, WLAC ironically instituted its first gospel show since 1951, when the Fairfield Four went off the air. WLAC's DJ William "Hoss" Allen launched and hosted a four-hour gospel program in 1971, known as "Early Morning Gospel Time," that aired 1:00–5:00 A.M. daily. Recalling the show's rise from its humble beginnings, Allen commented, "I knew so many record companies that had gospel and didn't know what to do with it. They had no exposure. So I called four record companies and sold them two hours and forty-five minutes [of advertising time]. That's how the gospel [program] started. It got bigger, bigger and bigger until it was just as big as the blues had been, because nobody was playing gospel for four hours at a time anywhere, every night, five hours on the weekend. Well, it became the biggest gospel show in the country" (Maultsby 1984a). Allen's listening audience was diverse, including night-shift employees, truck drivers, "dyed-in-the-wool gospel fans, . . . a lot of shut-ins and people who have trouble sleeping and are just laying in bed all day and they lay awake all night" (Landes 1987, 75).

Radio was instrumental in expanding the listening audience for both gospel and rhythm and blues. The early practice of juxtaposing the two forms exposed their affinity. Among the churchgoing gospel fans who once distanced themselves from "sinful" music, some demonstrated tolerance, while others became consumers of rhythm and blues without relinquishing their loyalty to gospel music. Similarly, many "sinners" came to appreciate gospel music, identifying with its aesthetic and even its spiritual message. The experiences of Walter Grady, a record promoter and former record retailer, graphically illustrate this point: "I've even seen situations when I owned a record store where 'winos' would come in with a six-pack of beer under one arm and a bottle of wine in one hand, buy two blues records and two gospel records which means they were going to a party but they still were going to give a few minutes of listening to God's music which was gospel music" (Maultsby 1990a).

Throughout the 1970s, gospel music took a back seat to the hegemonic programming of Black popular music. During this decade, Black-formatted radio stations concentrated on improving market ratings, attracting crossover audiences, and courting national advertisers. But in the 1980s, gospel music resurfaced as a viable commercial product, giving rise to several full-time gospel-formatted stations. The expanding consumer market for gospel music generated by radio and live performances created a demand for gospel records.

GOSPEL MUSIC ON RECORD

During the developing years (late 1940s–50s) of full-time, Black-oriented radio stations, DJs were challenged with the task of finding records to play. The unprecedented demand for Black music exceeded the supply. Mail-order record ships that sponsored Black music radio programs frequently ran out of stock. Retailers, in an effort to replenish their supply, went "all over the country trying to buy Black records and there weren't a whole lot" (Maultsby 1984a). This shortage was triggered by government restrictions on the use of shellac during the second World War, the 1942–44 ban on recording stemming from a musicians' strike, and the small number of record companies specializing in Black music.

The first recordings of Black religious music were issued during the first decade of the twentieth century. Beginning in the 1920s, major and independent companies marketed the music of African American preachers and their congregations and jubilee quartets under the label of "race music" (Oliver 1984). Religious music represented one-third of the five hundred race records issued in 1927 and about one-fourth of those released during each of the next three years (Dixon and Godrich 1970, 57). The Depression years severely curtailed the recording of race music. Many companies folded, and the few that remained in business limited their involvement in gospel music to reissuing previously recorded material and recording jubilee-gospel quartets and such established performers as Mahalia Jackson and Rosetta Tharpe.

The recording industry resumed full-scale production after the war years, but many of the companies that once specialized in race music chose to abandon the field. The demand for Black music nevertheless persisted. Responding to this demand, local entrepreneurs formed independent record companies and became the primary producers of postwar Black music. Some of these companies, including Savoy, Apollo, Specialty, Peacock, Nashboro, and Vee-Jay, developed an impressive catalogue of gospel music that supported the programming efforts of radio. Although major companies largely ignored gospel music during the first four decades after the war, they joined the gospel bandwagon in the 1980s. Aware of the cross-cultural popularity of this music and its pervasive influence on popular styles, they teamed up with independent companies to record and distribute gospel music. Radio, in turn, became a promotional tool for these companies and the growing number of gospel music promoters. Forming a national network, record companies, radio stations, retail outlets, and promoters brought unprecedented exposure to gospel music. The demand for the gospel sound and its beat led to the appropriation of this music by purveyors of popular styles.

THE TRANSFORMATION OF GOSPEL INTO POPULAR SONG

Paralleling the rise of gospel music was the growth of a teenage consumer market for popular music. African American teenagers, who served their musical apprenticeship performing in church choirs and in professional gospel groups, were lured into the more lucrative field of popular music. Gospel singer Albertina Walker contends that even though gospel music became "big business," it was "a good money-making business for everybody except the singer" (Banks 1974a, 74). Gospel singer-minister Reverend Cleophus Robinson noted that crooked managers, promoters, and record companies exploited "the art and its artists for the money, then put very little money back into the art to strengthen it and make it more popular" (Banks 1974b, 65). Rather than reinvest in the form, the industry capitalized on the popularity of the gospel sound, offering gospel singers money and other perks to switch to blues, jazz, and rhythm and blues. Savoy Records, for example, offered Clara Ward ten thousand dollars to become a blues singer ("Clara Ward . . . Gospel Singer" 1953, 38). She and others declined such offers, but some defected and transformed gospel into various popular music styles—rhythm and blues, soul, funk, and other contemporary forms. Beginning in 1949, *Billboard* used the term *rhythm and blues* to identify all post–World War II forms of Black popular music. In 1969, this term was changed to *soul*. Through the 1970s, soul music was transformed into funk and disco.

Among the first gospel singers to establish successful careers as rhythm and blues artists were soloists Sister Rosetta Tharpe and Dinah Washington and

PORTIA K. MAULTSBY

quartets including the Delta Rhythm Boys (formerly the Hampton Institute Quartet); the Larks (formerly the Selah Jubilee Singers); a gospel group led by Billy Ward and renamed the Dominoes; and the Isley Brothers. They and others found the transition from gospel to rhythm and blues to be "just a matter of changing the words," as Lou Rawls notes (Shearer 1983). All of the components—sound construct, interpretative devices, and performance style—that define the gospel tradition are found in its secular counterparts.

Rhythm and blues vocal groups had a religious sound, according to Diz Russell, a vocalist with the Orioles, because they imitated instruments in a manner popularized by gospel-jubilee quartets, and they duplicated the "straight-up" harmonies heard in church. This harmonic structure places the bass on the bottom to accentuate the chord. Russell adds, "A floating tenor, which comes in and out, carries the chord up and down. The baritone remains in the middle of the chord and sings a straight part" (Maultsby 1984b). Through their immersion in African American church culture at a very young age, emerging musicians not only learn fundamental musical concepts but also master aesthetic principles essential to Black music performance.

Soul-disco performer Candi Staton, for example, recalls her first performance at a Baptist church at age five and the responses of the congregation: "I sang and those people started shouting, really getting involved in what I was doing and that frightened me more than my singing because I didn't know why they were shouting. I didn't understand the feelings that they felt" (Shearer 1981). Having a similar experience singing a solo in an AME church choir at age eight, disco performer Donna Summer reminisces, "the people started crying and it scared me that I could touch people and they were moved by something that I had that was intangible. It gave me an incredible sense of power" (Shearer 1982).

Staton and Summer were too young to comprehend why people "shouted" and "cried," but a review of a concert by soul singer Aretha Franklin provides an explanation while revealing the affinity between performances of gospel and Black popular styles:

> At every show I wondered what it was—that very special thing she was always able to get going with an audience. Sometimes there were 16,000 people in a sports arena and Aretha would be working on stage, doing *Dr. Feelgood* [sic] and then *Spirit in the Dark* [sic], and it seemed that all 16,000 people would become involved in a kind of spiritual thing with her, sort of like what must have happened on the Day of Pentecost, and those people— all kinds: dudes, sisters in Afros and those in blonde wigs, even church-looking people—would start moving with the music, and as Aretha took

them higher and higher some of them would scream and jump up on their seats, and even men like 50 and 60 years old would run down to the stage and try to touch her. (Sanders 1971, 126)

Aretha's performance transformed the concert hall into a type of spiritual celebration—one similar to that of an African American worship service in which the preacher and gospel singers engage in verbal and physical exchanges with the congregation. Gospel music scholar and performer Pearl Williams-Jones accurately observes that "in seeking to communicate the gospel message, there is little difference between the gospel singer and the gospel preacher in the approach to his subject. The same techniques are used by the preacher and the singer—the singer perhaps being considered the lyrical extension of the rhythmically rhetorical style of the preacher" (Williams-Jones 1975, 381).

Aretha revealed to music critic Phyl Garland that her vocal style was influenced by the preaching techniques employed by her father (Garland 1969, 199). This singer-preacher link is described by Aretha's brother, the Reverend Cecil Franklin:

You listen to her and it's just like being in church. She does with her voice exactly what a preacher does with his when he *moans* to a congregation. That moan strikes a responsive chord in the congregation and somebody answers you back with their own moan, which means I know what you're moaning about because I feel the same way. So you have something sort of like a thread spinning out and touching and tieing [*sic*] everybody together in a shared experience just like the getting happy and shouting together in church. (Sanders 1971, 126)

As Aretha moans a meaningful message to her audience,

She leans her head back, forehead gleaming with perspiration, features twisted by her intensity, and her voice—plangent and supple—pierces the hall:

> Oh, baby, what you done to me . . .
> You make me feel, you make me feel,
> You make me feel like a natural woman.

"Tell it like it is," her listeners exhort, on their feet, clapping and cheering. ("Lady Soul: Singing It Like It Is" 1968, 62)

Aretha's masterful display of vocal dexterity and her down-home, foot-stomping, intense and demonstrative performance style continue a tradition popularized in the 1950s by Big Maybelle, Big Mama Thornton, James Brown, Little Richard, Jackie Wilson, and the Dominoes. In the 1960s, this style defined performances of the Isley Brothers, Wilson Pickett, Gene Chandler, Otis Redding, and Sam and Dave. While this performance style prevails in rhythm and blues and its derivative forms, it represents only one dimension of the gospel sound in Black popular music.

The gospel sound encompasses many vocal styles and timbres. It ranges from the lyrical, semiclassical, and tempered style of Roberta Martin, Alex Bradford, Inez Andrews, and Sara Jordan Powell to the percussive and shouting approach of Sallie Martin, Archie Brownlee, Albertina Walker, Clara Ward, and Norsalus McKissick. Many singers, including Mahalia Jackson, Marion Williams, and the Barrett Sisters, employ components from both styles in their performances. This range of stylistic possibilities has brought variety to the Black popular tradition.

The vocal style of many rhythm and blues and soul singers, for instance, is more lyrical and tempered than that of Aretha. Among the exponents of this style are the Orioles, Little Anthony and the Imperials, the Impressions, Roy Hamilton, Sam Cooke, Jerry Butler, Brook Benton, Smokey Robinson, O. C. Smith, Isaac Hayes, Dinah Washington, Dionne Warwick, the Jones Girls, and Deniece Williams. The church roots of their lyrical and tempered style and the way it differs from the percussive and foot-stomping approach of Aretha Franklin and others are explained by Shirley Jones of the Jones Girls: "Our sound was developed primarily by singing in church with our mother. Even though we are [former] gospel singers, we are not the foot-stomping, down-home gospel type singers. We are more the subdued side of it. Very soft voices . . ." (Maultsby 1983a). Deniece Williams also acknowledges that, despite her upbringing in the Church of God in Christ, her style is not "the same deliverance as Aretha or Mahalia Jackson, [but] you feel it. I've had a lot of people say [when] you sing it, I feel it. I think that feeling comes from those experiences of church and gospel music and spirituality which play a big role in my life" (Maultsby 1983b).

The "feeling" experienced by Williams's audiences results from her subtle use of aesthetic principles associated with gospel music. Regardless of vocal style employed, singers of popular idioms use a wide range of aesthetic devices in interpreting songs: melismas, slides, bends, moans, shouts, grunts, hollers, screams, melodic and textual repetition, extreme registers, call-response structures, and so on. Dinah Washington, a protégée of Roberta Martin, was a master in the subtle manipulation of timbre, shading, time, pitch, and text. Her trademark sound echoes the vocal control, timing ("lagging behind the beat"), and phrasing of Roberta Martin. Dinah's style was imitated by a host of singers, including Lavern Baker, Etta James, Nancy Wilson, Dionne Warwick, and Diana Ross.

Vocal techniques, timbres, and delivery style were not the only components of gospel appropriated by rhythm and blues. Gospel rhythms and instrumental stylings, which originated in secular contexts, became integral to this sound. David "Panama" Francis, studio drummer for many Black artists, brought a rhythmic excitement to post–World War II popular forms when he incorporated the rhythms of the Holiness church into several rhythm and blues recordings. In Screaming Jay Hawkins's "I Put a Spell on You" (1956) and Lavern Baker's "See See Rider" (1962), for example, he employed $^{12}/_8$ meter (known as common meter in the Church of God in Christ) and the triplet note pattern associated with this meter (Maultsby 1983c). These structures as well as the rhythms that accompany the "shout" (religious dance) provide the rhythmic foundation for many contemporary popular songs.

Ray Charles was another performer who drew from his church roots for musical inspiration. His performances employ every cultural aesthetic known to the Black folk church, including the movements of its congregants. Francis, who played drums on Charles's "Drown in My Own Tears" (1956), explains how he used brushes rather than sticks to capture the nuances of these movements in this song:

> Ray was the one who told me to play with brushes like in the church and with a gospel feeling. All I played was straight quarter notes with brushes. If you remember, in the church, that was the way the mothers used to keep the babies quiet on their knees when they were singing; all they did was lift their foot and then drop it—just a straight $^4/_4$. . . . And they'd be patting the baby and it would go right back to sleep. And that's what I was playing on the drums in "Drown in My Own Tears." Ray Charles suggested it and showed me how to do it, too. (Maultsby 1983c)

Ray Charles also incorporated the structures and instrumental stylings of gospel music in his songs. When he repackaged the well-known gospel version of the spiritual "This Little Light of Mine" as "This Little Girl of Mine," in 1955, he retained the underlying repeated eight-bar structure. In doing so, Charles broadened the musical parameters of rhythm and blues beyond its traditional twelve-bar blues structure.

In subsequent recordings, including "Drown in My Own Tears" (1956), "Right Right Time" (1959), and "What'd I Say" (1959), Charles employed the gospel piano style of Roberta Martin in conjunction with his gospel-rooted vocals. Martin, in developing a distinctive performance style, elevated the role of the piano from that of background for vocals to one of "an integral and integrating force in the performance, supplying accompaniment, rhythm, and effects. Her style is characterized by improvisatory fills, a rhythmic bass line and colorful and complex chord structures" (Williams-Jones 1982, 15). In the 1960s, the Roberta Martin piano style, the rhythms of the Black folk church, and the harmonic structures and vocal stylings of gospel music transformed rhythm and blues into a new popular idiom known as soul music.

The spirit and energy of soul music were so powerful that this style penetrated all arteries of the African American community and spilled over into those of mainstream America. In 1969, James Brown, a pioneer with Ray Charles in the development of soul music, "became the first black man in the 30-year history of *Cash Box* to be cited as the male vocalist on single pop records. For the uninitiated, 'pop' means sales to the whole record-buying public, not simply in the predominantly Negro rhythm 'n' blues market" (Barry 1969, 56). Brown's influence was so great that many white singers, including the Righteous Brothers, Joe Cocker, Tom Jones, and Elvis Presley, imitated his style, giving rise to the concept of "blue-eyed soul singers."

James Brown, proclaimed the "godfather of soul," along with his female counterpart, Aretha Franklin, the "queen of soul," made gospel music and its delivery style a permanent fixture in American popular music. Horace Clarence Boyer, quoted in *U.S. News & World Report*, observed that "gospel became a style of performance into which you could put any message" ("Gospel Music Rolls out of the Church, onto the Charts" 1986, 56). In other words, gospel music became more than a musical genre; it was an idiomatic style that wielded tremendous influence not only on Black popular idioms but on the entire American popular tradition. The musical trends of the 1970s and 1980s support this axiom.

When funk and other urban forms evolved from soul music during the mid-1970s and 1980s, they retained the energy, rhythms, textures, and stylings of gospel music. The funk style developed by Larry Graham of Graham Central Station, for example, employs many of the features associated with the 1950s gospel sound. In the 1977 song "Release Yourself" (Warner Bros. BS 2814), the texture produced by mixed voices, the high-energy and percussive vocal style, the instrumental stylings of the organ and piano, and the beat of the tambourine recreate the fervor of the Roberta Martin Singers and the singing of Black folk churches.

Many components of gospel music have been incorporated into popular music, where they have intermingled with new techniques and expressions and then recycled back into gospel. This cyclical process has expanded the foundation of gospel and popular forms, generating new styles in both traditions. It therefore calls into question the artificial boundaries that historically have separated religious and secular styles, their performers, and their audiences. Whereas many singers once were compelled to choose between gospel and popular, they now freely move between and juxtapose both traditions on a single album. Deniece Williams, Ashford & Simpson, Al Green, and Candi Staton are singers who consistently include gospel songs on their albums of popular music. Williams explains her commitment to gospel: "I'd grown up singing in the choir and I'd always wanted to record a gospel song. . . . I told CBS I wanted to record a gospel album someday. They said, 'Yeah, sure, sure,' but never thought I was serious. I don't think CBS thought I'd go on to record a gospel song on every album after that [1976], either, but I did" (Gospel music column 1987). In 1986, when Williams's contract was up for renewal at CBS, she was granted permission to record a gospel album for Sparrow Records. The album, *So Glad I Know* (Sparrow SP 61121), not only received two Grammys but also appeared on four music charts: inspirational, gospel, pop, and Black music. Following Williams's lead, many singers in the popular idiom have begun to include gospel songs on their albums. The rap song "Pray" by M. C. Hammer (Capitol CDP 7928572) is an example of this trend among the 1990s generation of Black performers.

The 1980s witnessed the move of gospel music into the pop and rock corners of the music industry as its performers were featured as background singers on popular recordings. In 1984, the British group Foreigner recorded its "I Want to Know What Love Is" on *Agent Provocateur* (Atlantic A281999) using a gospel choir. When Foreigner toured America, it employed the services of local gospel choirs in every major city. The Winans have proven to be on the cutting edge of gospel music, pioneering new but controversial trends with each album (Gospel music column 1988). Perhaps the most controversial has been the use of established vocalists, instrumentalists, and producers from various popular idioms. For example, the 1987 album *Decisions* (Qwest 925510-1) features Anita Baker in the crossover hit "Aint' No Need to Worry." The Winans' first single, "It's Time" from *Return* (Qwest 261612), is a gospel rap produced by Teddy Riley, the force behind the success of Bobby Brown, Keith Sweat, and David Peaston. Other nongospel musicians included on the album are Stevie Wonder and Kenny G.

If other artists follow the direction of the Winans and Deniece Williams, the 1990s indeed will witness a continued wedging together of the sacred and secular spheres of Black community life. As contemporary gospel groups attempt to reach the youth and non-Christian market, and as religious record labels adopt "secular" promotion methods, the question posed in 1979—"Is it possible that one day gospel music will no longer belong to the church?"—will continue to be pondered.

WORKS CITED

Banks, Lacy. 1974a. "Albertina the Mirror." *Black Stars* (August): 68–74.

———. 1974b. "The Double-Barreled Gospel of Rev. Cleophus Robinson." *Black Stars* (April): 64–69.

Barry, Thomas. 1969. "The Importance of Being Mr. James Brown." *Look* (February 18): 56–62.

"Black Gospel: Rocketing to Higher Prominence." 1987. *Billboard* (October 10): G–6.

Boyer, Horace Clarence. 1979a. "Contemporary Gospel." *The Black Perspective in Music* 7 (Spring): 5–11, 22–58.

Burnim, Mellonee. 1988. "Functional Dimensions of Gospel Music Performance." *Western Journal of Black Studies* (Summer): 112–20.

"Clara Ward . . . Gospel Singer." 1953. *Our World* (December): 38–41.

Dixon, Robert M. W., and John Goodrich. 1970. *Recording the Blues.* New York: Stein and Day.

Garland, Phyl. 1969. *The Sound of Soul.* Chicago: Henry Regnery Company.

Garnett, Bernard E. 1970. "How Soulful Is 'Soul' Radio?" Unpublished paper produced for Race Relations Information Center, Nashville.

Gehman, Richard. 1958. "God's Singing Messengers." *Coronet* (July): 113–16.

Gospel music column. 1987. *Billboard* (August).

Gospel music column. 1988. *Billboard* (July).

"Gospel Music Rolls out of the Church, onto the Charts." 1986. *U.S. News & World Report* (August): 56.

"Gospel to Pop to Gospel." 1962. *Ebony* (July): 107–12.

"Gospel Singers: Pop up, Sweet Chariot." 1963. *Time* (May): 48.

Hammond, John, and Irving Townsend. 1981. *John Hammond on Record.* New York: Penguin Books.

Hentoff, Nat. 1963. "Gospel Gimmick." *The Reporter* (August): 46–47.

"Lady Soul: Singing It Like It Is." 1968. *Time* (June): 62–66.

Landes, John. 1987. "WLAC, the Hossman, and Their Influence on Black Gospel." *Black Music Research Journal* 7:67–81.

Lornell, Kip. 1988. *"Happy in the Service of the Lord": Afro-American Gospel Quartets in Memphis.* Urbana: University of Illinois Press.

Lucas, Bob. 1972. "Gospel Superstar." *Sepia* (May): 21–26.

MacDonald, J. Fred. 1979. *Don't Touch That Dial!* Chicago: Nelson-Hall.

Maultsby, Portia. 1979. Interview with Jack Gibson, Orlando, February 28.

———. 1983a. Interview with Shirley Jones, Los Angeles, March 9.

———. 1983b. Interview with Deniece Williams, Los Angeles, April 22.

———. 1983c. Interview with David "Panama" Francis, Orlando, December 31.

———. 1984a. Interview with Hoss Allen, Nashville, September 7.

———. 1984b. Interview with Albert "Diz" Russell, Washington, DC, September 27.

———. 1990a. Interview with Walter Grady, Atlanta, August 17.

———. 1990b. Interview with Eddie Castleberry, Atlanta, August 17.

———. 1990c. Interview with George Nelson, Atlanta, August 17.

Oliver, Paul. 1984. *Songsters and Saints: Vocal Traditions on Race Records.* New York: Cambridge University Press.

Salvo, Patrick, and Barbara Salvo. 1974. "45 Years of Gospel Music." *Sepia* (April): 60–64.

Sanders, Charles. 1971. "Aretha." *Ebony* (December): 124–34.

Seroff, Doug. 1980. Record album notes for *Birmingham Quartet Anthology* (Clanka Lanka Records CL 144, 001–14, 002).

Seward, Theodore F. 1872. *Jubilee Songs: As Sung By the Jubilee Singers of Fisk University.* New York: Taylor and Barwood.

Shearer, Karen. 1981. Interview with Candi Staton on radio program "Special Edition," Westwood One, Culver City, California, October 10.

———. 1982. Interview with Donna Summer, Westwood One, Culver City, California, June 21.

———. 1983. Interview with Lou Rawls, Westwood One, Culver City, California, April 12.

Spaulding, Norman. 1981. "History of Black Oriented Radio in Chicago 1929–1963." Ph.D. diss., University of Illinois.

Tallmadge, William H. 1974. Record album notes for *Jubilee to Gospel: A Selection of Commercially Recorded Black Religious Music, 1921–1953* (JEMF–108).

Ward, Clara. 1956. "How a Visit to the Holy Land Changed My Life." *Color* (May): 15–17.

Williams-Jones, Pearl. 1975. "Afro-American Gospel: A Crystallization of the Black Aesthetic." *Ethnomusicology* 19 (September): 373–84.

———. 1982. "Roberta Martin: Spirit of an Era." In *Roberta Martin and the Roberta Martin Singers: The Legacy and the Music,* ed. Bernice Johnson Reagon and Linn Shapiro, 12–21. Washington, DC: Smithsonian Institution, National Museum of American History, Program in African American Culture.

Flow, Layering, and Rupture in Postindustrial New York

(1994)

TRICIA ROSE

. . . .

An associate professor of history and African studies at New York University, Tricia Rose describes stylistic continuities among rapping, breakdancing, and graffiti-writing as manifestations of "flow, layering, and rupture." Yet she also notes continuities between hip hop and traditional African American forms. Although she does not use the term "signifying," the competitive interacton between dancers and between DJs, the satirical and confrontational nature of hip hop clothing styles, and the way rappers signify on a multitude of situations have deep roots in African American aesthetics. The ring within which breakdancers execute their solos appears throughout the African Diaspora, and Rose's discussion of the Diasporic antecedents of hip hop culture confirms the African origins of influences that have profoundly shaped American popular culture.

> Got a bum education, double-digit inflation
> Can't take the train to the job, there's a strike at the station
> Don't push me cause I'm close to the edge
> I'm tryin' not to lose my head
> It's like a jungle sometimes it makes me wonder
> How I keep from going under.
> —Grandmaster Flash and the Furious Five, "The Message"

Hip hop culture emerged as a source for youth of alternative identity formation and social status in a community whose older local support institutions had been all but demolished along with large sectors of its built environment.

Alternative local identities were forged in fashions and language, street names, and most important, in establishing neighborhood crews or posses. Many hip hop fans, artists, musicians, and dancers continue to belong to an elaborate system of crews or posses. The crew, a local source of identity, group affiliation, and support system appears repeatedly in all of my interviews and virtually all rap lyrics and cassette dedications, music video performances, and media interviews with artists. Identity in hip hop is deeply rooted in the specific, the local experience, and one's attachment to and status in a local group or alternative family. These crews are new kinds of families forged with intercultural bonds that, like the social formation of gangs, provide insulation and support in a complex and unyielding environment and may serve as the basis for new social movements. The postindustrial city, which provided the context for creative development among hip hop's earliest innovators, shaped their cultural terrain, access to space, materials, and education. While graffiti artists' work was significantly aided by advances in spray paint technology, they used the urban transit system as their canvas. Rappers and DJs disseminated their work by copying it on tape-dubbing equipment and playing it on powerful, portable "ghetto blasters." At a time when budget cuts in school music programs drastically reduced access to traditional forms of instrumentation and composition, inner-city youths increasingly relied on recorded sound. Breakdancers used their bodies to mimic "transformers" and other futuristic robots in symbolic street battles. Early Puerto Rican, Afro-Caribbean, and black American hip hop artists transformed obsolete vocational skills from marginal occupations into the raw materials for creativity and resistance. Many of them were "trained" for jobs in fields that were shrinking or that no longer exist. Puerto Rican graffiti writer Futura graduated from a trade school specializing in the printing industry. However, as most of the jobs for which he was being trained had already been computerized, he found himself working at McDonald's after graduation. Similarly, African-American DJ Red Alert (who also has family from the Caribbean) reviewed blueprints for a drafting company until computer automation rendered his job obsolete. Jamaican DJ Kool Herc attended Alfred E. Smith auto mechanic trade school, and African-American Grandmaster Flash learned how to repair electronic equipment at Samuel Gompers vocational High School. (One could say Flash "fixed them alright.") Salt and Pepa (both with family roots in the West Indies) worked as phone telemarketing representatives at Sears while considering nursing school. Puerto Rican breakdancer Crazy Legs began breakdancing largely because his single mother couldn't afford Little League baseball fees.[1] All of these artists found themselves positioned with few resources in marginal economic circumstances, but each of them found ways to become famous as an entertainer by appropriating the most advanced technologies and emerging cultural forms. Hip hop artists used the tools of obsolete industrial technology to traverse contemporary crossroads of lack and desire in urban Afrodiasporic communities.

Stylistic continuities were sustained by internal cross-fertilization between rapping, breakdancing, and graffiti writing. Some graffiti writers, such as black American Phase 2, Haitian Jean-Michel Basquiat, Futura, and black American Fab Five Freddy produced rap records. Other writers drew murals that celebrated favorite rap songs (e.g., Futura's mural "The Breaks" was a whole car mural that paid homage to Kurtis Blows's rap of the same name). Breakdancers, DJs, and rappers wore graffiti-painted jackets and tee-shirts. DJ Kool Herc was a graffiti writer and dancer first before he began playing records. Hip hop events featured breakdancers, rappers, and DJs as triple-bill entertainment. Graffiti writers drew murals for DJ's stage platforms and designed posters and flyers to advertise hip hop events. Breakdancer Crazy Legs, founding member of the Rock Steady Crew, describes the communal atmosphere between writers, rappers, and breakes in the formative years of hip hop: "Summing it up, basically going to a jam back then was (about) watching people drink, (break) dance, compare graffiti art in their black books. These jams were thrown by the (hip hop) D.J. . . . it was about piecing while a jam was going on."[2] Of course, sharing ideas and styles is not always a peaceful process. Hip hop is very competitive and confrontational; these traits are both resistance to and preparation for a hostile world that denies and denigrates young people of color. Breakdancers often fought other breakdance crews out of jealousy; writers sometimes destroyed murals and rappers and DJ battles could break out in fights. Hip hop remains a never-ending battle for status, prestige, and group adoration, always in formation, always contested, and never fully achieved. Competitions among and cross-fertilization between breaking, graffiti writing, and rap music was fueled by shared local experiences and social position and similarities in approaches to sound, motion, communication, and style among hip hop's Afrodiasporic communities.

As in many African and Afrodiasporic cultural forms, hip hop's prolific self-naming is a form of reinvention and self-definition.[3] Rappers, DJs, graffiti artists, and breakdancers all take on hip hop names and identities that speak to their role, personal characteristics, expertise, or "claim to fame." DJ names often fuse technology with mastery and style: DJ Cut Creator, Jazzy Jeff, Spindarella, Terminator X Assault Technician, Wiz, and Grandmaster Flash. Many rappers have nicknames that suggest street smarts, coolness, power, and supremacy: L.L. Cool J. (Ladies Love Cool James), Kool Moe Dee, Queen Latifah, Dougie Fresh (and the Get Fresh Crew), D-Nice, Hurricane Gloria, Guru, MC Lyte, EPMD (Eric and Parrish Making Dollars), Ice-T, Ice Cube, Kid-N-Play,

Boss, Eazy E, King Sun, and Sir Mix-a-Lot. Some names serve as self-mocking tags; others critique society, such as, Too Short, The Fat Boys, S1Ws (Security of the First World), The Lench Mob, NWA (Niggas with Attitude), and Special Ed. The hip hop identities for such breakdancers as Crazy Legs, Wiggles, Frosty Freeze, Boogaloo Shrimp, and Headspin highlight their status as experts known for special moves. Taking on new names and identities offers "prestige from below" in the face of limited access to legitimate forms of status attainment.

In addition to the centrality of naming, identity, and group affiliation, rappers, DJs, graffiti writers, and breakdancers claim turf and gain local status by developing new styles. As Hebdige's study on punk illustrates, style can be used as a gesture of refusal or as a form of oblique challenge to structures of domination.[4] Hip hop artists use style as a form of identity formation that plays on class distinctions and hierarchies by using commodities to claim the cultural terrain. Clothing and consumption rituals testify to the power of consumption as a means of cultural expression. Hip hop fashion is an especially rich example of this sort of appropriation and critique via style. Exceptionally large "chunk" gold and diamond jewelry (usually fake) mocks, yet affirms, the gold fetish in Western trade; fake Gucci and other designer emblems cup up and patch-stitched to jackets, pants, hats, wallets, and sneakers in custom shops, work as a form of sartorial warfare (especially when fake Gucci-covered b-boys and b-girls brush past Fifth Avenue ladies adorned by the "real thing"). Hip hop's late 1980s fashion rage—the large plastic (alarm?) clock worn around the neck over leisure/sweat suits—suggested a number of contradictory tensions between work, time, and leisure.[5] Early 1990s trends—super-oversized pants and urban warrior outer apparel, "hoodies," "snooties," "tims," and "triple fat" goose down coats, make clear the severity of the urban storms to be weathered and the saturation of disposable goods in the crafting of cultural expressions.[6] As an alternative means of status formation, hip hop style forges local identities for teenagers who understand their limited access to traditional avenues of social status attainment. Fab Five Freddy, an early rapper and graffiti writer, explains the link between style and identity in hip hop and its significance for gaining local status: "You make a new style. That's what life on the street is all about. What's at stake is honor and position on the street. That's what makes it so important, that's what makes it feel so good—that pressure on you to be the best. Or to try to be the best. To develop a new style nobody can deal with."[7] Styles "nobody can deal with" in graffiti, breaking, and rap music not only boost status, but also they articulate several shared approaches to sound and motion found in the Afrodiaspora. As Arthur Jafa has pointed out, stylistic continuities between breaking, graffiti style, rapping, and musical construction seem to center around three concepts: *flow*, *layering*, and *ruptures in line.*[8] In hip hop, visual, physical, musical, and lyrical lines are set in motion, broken abruptly with sharp angular breaks, yet they sustain motion and energy through fluidity and flow. In graffiti, long-winding, sweeping, and curving letters are broken and camouflaged by sudden breaks in line. Sharp, angular, broken letters are written in extreme italics, suggesting forward or backward motion. Letters are double and triple shadowed in such a way as to il-lustrate energy forces radiating from the center—suggesting circular motion—yet, the scripted words move horizontally.

Breakdancing moves highlight flow, layering, and ruptures in line. Popping and locking are moves in which the joints are snapped abruptly into angular positions. And, yet, these snapping movements take place one joint after the previous one—creating a semiliquid effect that moves the energy toward the fingertip or toe. In fact, two dancers may pass the popping energy force back and forth between each other via finger to finger contact, setting off a new wave. In this pattern, the line is both a series of angular breaks and yet sustains energy and motion through flow. Breakers double each other's moves, like line shadowing or layering in graffiti, intertwine their bodies into elaborate shapes, transforming the body into a new entity (like camouflage in graffiti's wild style), and then, one body part at a time reverts to a relaxed state. Abrupt, fractured yet graceful footwork leaves the eye one step behind the motion, creating a time-lapse effect that not only mimics graffiti's use of line shadowing but also creates spatial links between the moves that gives the foot series flow and fluidity.[9]

The music and vocal rapping in rap music also privileges flow, layering, and ruptures in line. Rappers speak of flow explicitly in lyrics, referring to an ability to move easily and powerfully through complex lyrics as well as of the flow in the music.[10] The flow and motion of the initial bass or drum line in rap music is abruptly ruptured by scratching (a process that highlights as it breaks the flow of the base rhythm), or the rhythmic flow is interrupted by other musical passages. Rappers stutter and alternatively race through passages, al-ways moving within the beat or in response to it, often using the music as a partner in rhyme. These verbal moves highlight lyrical flow and points of rupture. Rappers layer meaning by using the same word to signify a variety of actions and objects; they call out to the DJ to "lay down a beat," which is expected to be interrupted, ruptured. DJs layer sounds literally one on top of the other, creating a dialogue between sampled sounds and words.

What is the significance of flow, layering, and rupture as demonstrated on the body and in hip hop's lyrical, musical, and visual works? Interpreting these concepts theoretically, one can argue that they create and sustain rhythmic motion, continuity, and circularity via flow; accumulate, reinforce, and embellish this continuity through layering; and manage threats to these narratives by building in ruptures that highlight the continuity as it momentarily challenges it. These effects at the level of style and aesthetics suggest affirmative ways in which profound social dislocation and rupture can be managed and perhaps contested in the cultural arena. Let us imagine these hip hop principles as a blueprint for social resistance and affirmation: create sustaining narratives, accumulate them, layer, embellish, and transform them. However, be also prepared for rupture, find pleasure in it, in fact, *plan on* social rupture. When these ruptures occur, use them in creative ways that will prepare you for a future in which survival will demand a sudden shift in ground tactics.

Although accumulation, flow, circularity, and planned ruptures exist across a wide range of Afrodiasporic cultural forms, they do not take place outside of capitalist commercial constraints. Hip hop's explicit focus on consumption has frequently been mischaracterized as a movement *into* the commodity market (e.g., hip hop is no longer "authentically" black, if it is for sale). Instead, hip hop's moment(s) of incorporation are a shift in the already existing relationship hip hop has always had to the commodity system. For example, the hip hop DJ produces, amplifies, and revises already recorded sounds, rappers use high-end microphones, and it would be naive to think that breakers, rappers, DJs and writers were never interested in monetary compensation for their work. Graffiti murals, breakdancing moves, and rap lyrics often appropriated and sometimes critiqued verbal and visual elements and physical movements from popular commercial culture, especially television, comic books, and karate movies. If anything, black style through hip hop has contributed to the continued Afro-Americanization of contemporary commercial culture. The contexts for creation in hip hop were never fully outside or in opposition to commodities; they involved struggles over public space and access to commodified materials, equipment, and products of economic viability. It is a common misperception among hip hop artists and cultural critics that during the early days, hip hop was motivated by pleasure rather than profit, as if the two were incompatible. The problem was not that they were uniformly uninterested in profit; rather, many of the earliest practitioners were unaware that they could profit from their pleasure. Once this link was made, hip hop artists began marketing themselves wholeheartedly. Just as graffiti writers hitched a ride on the subways and used its power to distribute their tags, rappers "hijacked" the market for their own purposes, riding the currents that were already out there, not just for wealth but for empowerment, and to assert their own identities. During the late 1970s and early 1980s, the market for hip hop was still based inside New York's black and Hispanic communities. So, although there is an element of truth to this common perception, what is more important about the shift in hip hop's orientation is not its movement from precommodity to commodity but the shift in control over the scope and direction of the profit-making process, out of the hands of local black and Hispanic entrepreneurs and into the hands of larger white-owned, multinational businesses.

Hebdige's work on the British punk movement identifies this shift as the moment of incorporation or recuperation by dominant culture and perceives it to be a critical element in the dynamics of the struggle over the meaning(s) of popular expression. "The process of recuperation," Hebdige argues, "takes two characteristic forms . . . one of conversion of subcultural signs (dress, music, etc.) into mass-produced objects and the 'labelling' and redefinition of deviant behavior by dominant groups—the police, media and judiciary." Hebdige astutely points out, however, that communication in a subordinate cultural form, even prior to the point of recuperation, usually takes place via commodities, "even if the meanings attached to those commodities are purposefully distorted or overthrown." And so, he concludes, "it is very difficult to sustain any absolute distinction between commercial exploitation on the one hand and creativity and originality on the other."[11]

Hebdige's observations regarding the process of incorporation and the tension between commercial exploitation and creativity as articulated in British punk is quite relevant to hip hop. Hip hop has always been articulated via commodities and engaged in the revision of meanings attached to them. Clearly, hip hop signs and meanings are converted, and behaviors are relabeled by dominant institutions. As the relatively brief history of hip hop that follows illustrates, graffiti, rap, and breakdancing were fundamentally transformed as they moved into new relations with dominant cultural institutions.[12] In 1994, rap music is one of the most heavily traded popular commodities in the market, yet it still defies total corporate control over the music, its local use and incorporation at the level of stable or exposed meanings.

Expanding on the formulation advanced by Lipsitz and others at the outset, in the brief history of hip hop that follows I attempt to demonstrate the necessary tension between the historical specificity of hip hop's emergence and the points of continuity between hip hop and several black forms and practices. It is also an overview of the early stages of hip hop and its relationship to popular cultural symbols and products and its revisions of black cultural practices. This necessarily includes hip hop's direct and sustained contact with dominant cultural institutions in the early to mid-1980s and the ways in which these practices emerge in relation to larger social conditions and relationships, including the systematic marginalization of women cultural producers. In each practice, gender power relations problematized and constrained the role of women hip hop artists, and dominant cultural institutions shaped hip hop's transformations.

Graffiti

Although graffiti as a social movement (i.e., writing names, symbols, and images on public facades) first emerged in New York during the late 1960s, it is not until almost a decade later that it began to develop elaborate styles and widespread visibility. Even though the vast majority of graffiti writers are black and Hispanic, the writer credited with inspiring the movement, Taki 183, is a Greek teenager named Demetrius who lived in the Washington Heights section of Manhattan. While working as a messenger, traveling by subway to all five boroughs of the city, Taki wrote his name all over the subway cars and stations. In 1971, a staff writer at the *New York Times* located Taki and published a story about his tagging that apparently "struck a responsive chord" among his peers. Martha Cooper and Henry Chalfant describe the effect Taki's notoriety had on his peers:

> Kids were impressed by the public notoriety of a name appearing all over the city (and) realized that the pride they felt in seeing their name up in the neighborhood could expand a hundredfold if it traveled beyond the narrow confines of the block. The competition for fame began in earnest as hundreds of youngsters, emulating Taki 183, began to tag trains and public buildings all over town. "Getting up" became a vocation. Kids whose names appeared the most frequently or in the most inaccessible places became folk heroes.[13]

By the mid-1970s, graffiti took on new focus and complexity. No longer a matter of simple tagging, graffiti began to develop elaborate individual styles, themes, formats, and techniques, most of which were designed to increase visibility, individual identity, and status. Themes in the larger works included hip hop slang, characterizations of b-boys, rap lyrics, and hip hop fashion. Using logos and images borrowed from television, comic books, and cartoons, stylistic signatures, and increasingly difficult executions, writers expanded graffiti's palette. Bubble letters, angular machine letters, and the indecipherable wild style were used on larger spaces and with more colors and patterns. These stylistic developments were aided by advances in marker and spray paint technology; better spraying nozzles, marking fibers, paint adhesion, and texture enhanced the range of expression in graffiti writing.[14] Small-scale tagging developed into the top to bottom, a format that covered a section of a train car from the roof to the floor. This was followed by the top to bottom whole car and multiple car "pieces," an abbreviation for graffiti masterpieces.

The execution of a piece is the culmination of a great deal of time, labor, and risk. Writers work out elaborate designs and patterns in notebooks, test new markers and brands of spray paints and colors well in advance. Obtaining access to the subway cars for extended periods requires detailed knowledge of the train schedules and breaking into the train yards where out of service trains are stored. Writers stake out train yards for extended periods, memorizing the train schedule and wait for new trains to leave the paint shop. A freshly painted train would be followed all day and when it reached its designated storage yard (the "lay-up") at night, writers were ready to "bomb" it.

Writers climbed walls, went through holes in fences, vaulted high gates, and "ran the boards" (walked along the board that covers the electrified third rail) to gain access to the trains. Once inside the yards, the risks increased. Craig Castleman explains:

> Trains frequently are moved in the yards, and an unwary writer could be hit by one. Trains stored in lay-ups are hazardous painting sites because in-service trains pass by them closely on either side, and the writer has to climb under the parked train or run to the far side of the tracks to escape being hit. Movement through tunnels is dangerous because the catwalks are high and narrow, it is dark and there are numerous open grates, abutments, and low hanging signs and light fixtures that threaten even the slowest moving writer.[15]

Some writers who have been seriously injured continued to write. In an exceptional case, master writer Kase 2 lost his arm in a yard accident and continued to execute highly respected multicar pieces.

Train facades are central to graffiti style for a number of reasons. First, graffiti murals depend on size, color, and constant movement for their visual impact. Although handball courts and other flat and stationary surfaces are suitable, they cannot replace the dynamic reception of subway facades. Unlike handball courts and building surfaces, trains pass through diverse neighborhoods, allowing communication between various black and Hispanic communities throughout the five boroughs and the larger New York population and disseminating graffiti writers' public performance. Second, graffiti artists are guerilla outlaws who thrive on risk as a facet of one's skill—the element of surprise and eluding authority among writers, the fact that it is sometimes considered criminal to purchase the permanent markers, spray paints, and other supplies necessary to write. Subway cars are stored in well-protected but dangerous yards that heighten the degree of difficulty in execution. An especially difficult and creative concept, coloration and style are all the more appreciated when they are executed under duress. Well-executed train work is a sign of mastering the expression.

Although (master) pieces are usually executed individually, writers belong to and work in crews. Group identity and individual development are equally central to graffiti writers' practices. These crews meet regularly and work on ideas, share knowledge, and plan trips to the train yards and other desired locations together. Crew members, among other things, compete with other crews (and each other), photograph each other's work for study, protect each other, and trade book outlines for paint supplies. Pieces are often signed individually and then identified by crew. Craig Castleman identified hundreds of crews; prominent ones include: Three Yard Boys (3YB), The Burners (TB), The Spanish Five (TSF), Wild Styles, Destroy All Trains (DAT) and the Mad Transit Artists (MTA).[16]

Female graffiti writers participated alongside male writers rather than in separate groups or crews. In addition to risks associated with execution in yards and elsewhere, women writers had to combat sexism from their male peers. Two prominent female writers, Lady Pink, an Hispanic American born in Ecuador, and Lady Heart, an African-American born in Queens, understood that their three o'clock in the morning trips to the train yards involved risking their safety as well as their reputations. In some cases, male graffiti writers spread rumors about female writers' sexual promiscuity to discourage female participation and discredit female writers' executions. So, unlike male writers, female writers had to protect their artistic reputations by protecting their sexual reputation. Lady Heart believes that, although it was sometimes an effective strategy, fear of family reprisals and the physical risks in train yards were much greater deterrents against female participation.[17]

Although both male and female writers chose to paint pieces involving social criticism and developed elaborate tags and characterizations, female writers often chose different colors and selected images that highlighted their female status as a means to greater recognizability. Many female writers used bright pinks, less black, more landscapes and flower scenes around the tags, and fewer "death and destruction" cartoon characters. However, female writers sustained the stylistic approaches to line, motion, and rupture. In this way, color selection and subject matter were forms of gender-based individualization inside the parameters of the expression that were not unlike male writer Dondi's use of a character in comic book artist Vaughn Bode's work, or graffiti writer Seen's use of Smurf characters.[18]

Although city officials had always rejected graffiti as a form of juvenile delinquency, antigraffiti discourse and policy took a dramatic turn in the mid-to late 1970s. No longer merely "an infuriating type of juvenile delinquency," as it was defined by municipal leaders in the late 1960s and early 1970s, the graffiti problem was reconstructed as a central reason for the decline in quality of life in a fiscally fragile and rusting New York. By the mid 1970s, graffiti emerged as a central example of the extent of urban decay and heightened already existing fears over a loss of control of the urban landscape. If the city could not stop these young outlaws from writing all over trains and walls, some political leaders feared, then what could the city manage?[19] Reconstructed as symbols of civic disorder, graffiti writers were understood as a psychic as well as material toll on New York, solidifying its image as a lawless, downtrodden urban jungle.

As the *New York Times* and municipal representatives searched for newer and more aggressive strategies to stamp out graffiti writing and symbolically reestablish control, graffiti writers were expanding and refining the form. In the mid-1970s, elaborate train facade murals and multicar pieces arrived on platforms most mornings. A simple name tag had developed into multiple train car skylines, Christmas greetings, abstract drawings likened to cubist art, romantic expressions, and political slogans all drawn with illustrations in dozens of colors, shades, styles, and elaborate lettering.

In 1977 the Transit Authority made an extensive effort to regain control. At the center of this effort was a new chemical many believed spelled disaster for graffiti writers: the buff. Although the buff did not end graffiti writing, it discouraged many writers and dramatically limited the life of the murals on the train facades. Steve Hager describes the chemical process and its effects:

> Many writers dropped out in 1977, when the Transit Authority erected its "final solution" to the graffiti problem in a Coney Island train yard. At an annual cost of $400,000, the T.A. began operating a giant car wash that sprayed vast amounts of petroleum hydroxide on the sides of graffitied trains. The solvent spray was followed by a vigorous buffing. At first the writers called it "the Orange Crush," after Agent Orange, a defoliant used in Vietnam. Later it was simply known as "the buff." Fumes emanating from the cleaning station were so deadly that a nearby school closed after students complained of respiratory problems. . . . Even T.A. workers admitted that they couldn't stand downwind from the station without getting nauseous. Meanwhile the solvent was seeping into the underfloorings of the trains, causing considerable corrosion and damage to electrical parts.[20]

"The buff" was followed by $24 million worth of system-wide fencing that included barbed wire fences, ribbon wire (which ensnares and shreds the body or object that attempts to cross it), and for a brief stint, attack dogs.[21] By the early 1980s, the T.A. had regained control of the subway facades by preventing most of the work from reaching the public *intact*. Yet, this did not spell the end of graffiti art. Kase 2, Lee Quinones, Futura 2000, Rammelzee, Lady Pink, Dondi, Lady Heart, Seen, Zephyr, and many other writers continued to write. The buff did not erase the graffiti, it just discolored it, rendering the subway cars truly defaced and a profoundly depressing symbol of a city at war to silence its already discarded youths. Writing continued, albeit less often and new locations for graffiti and new means of dissemination developed.

The level of municipal hostility exhibited toward graffiti art was matched only by the SoHo art scene's embrace of it. Early interest in graffiti art among gallery owners and collectors in the mid 1970s was short-lived and inconsistent. However, in the late 1970s, new interest was sparked, in part as a result of the promotional efforts of Fab Five Freddy, who now appears as a rap host on MTV. Appearing in an article in the Scenes column in the *Village Voice* in February 1979, Fab Five Freddy offered graffiti mural services at $5 a square foot. Using his art school training and fluidity with art school language, Freddy became a broker for graffiti. Making a number of critical contacts between the "legitimate art world" and graffiti writers, Freddy led the way for future exhibits at the Fun Gallery, Bronx gallery Fashion Moda, and the Times Square Show throughout the early 1980s, coupled with the efforts of artists, collectors, and gallery owners (e.g., Stephan Eins, Sam Esses, Henry Chalfant, and Patti Astor) gave graffiti momentary institutional clout and provided mostly unemployed graffiti artists financial remuneration for their talents. Clearly, the downtown art scene, in providing the graffiti artists with fleeting legitimacy, was most interested in making an investment in their own "cutting-edge image." Few writers would make a living as gallery artists for long, and almost all writers were paraded about as the latest "naturally talented" street natives.[22] Once the art world had satisfied its craving for street art, writers continued to work, albeit not as much on the subways.

Graffiti is no longer a widely visible street form, a fact that has led to the assumption that the form is no longer practiced. However, recent research by Joe Austin demonstrates that graffiti writers continue to write, using strategies for display and performance that work around social constraints. According to Austin, writers paint murals, videotape and photograph them, and distribute the tapes and photos through graffiti fan magazines all over the country. Via videotape and fanzines, train murals are documented before they are painted over or deformed by "the buff," allowing the process of writing on the train surface to be shared.[23] Although many writers are still outlaws, their status as such is no longer a major source of public embarrassment for city officials. In fact, Transit Authority publicity campaigns in 1992 and 1993, such as "subtalk," refer to their victory against graffiti as a sign of their role in the city's supposed improving health, all the while continuing to scrub and paint hundreds of train cars before they go into service to sustain these illusions. Although SoHo seems uninterested in graffiti art, business and community centers in the Barrio, Harlem, the Bronx, and Brooklyn still commission graffiti art for logos, building facades, and graffiti art is represented on tee-shirts, rap artists' clothing, and music video set designs.

Breakdancing

In the mid-1970s, dancing to disco music was a seamless and fluid affair. Disco dances, such as the Hustle, emphasized the continuity and circularity of the beat and worked to mask the breaks between steps. In disco music, the primary role of the DJ was to merge one song's conclusion into the next song's introduction as smoothly as possible, eliminating or masking the breaks between songs. At the height of disco's popularity, a new style of dance and musical pastische emerged that used disco music to focus on the break points, to highlight and extend the breaks in and between songs. At these break points in the DJ's performance, the dancers would *breakdance*, executing moves that imitated the rupture in rhythmic continuity as it was highlighted in the musical break.[24]

Described as a "competitive, acrobatic and pantomimic dance with outrageous physical contortions, spins and backflips [which are] wedded to a fluid syncopated circling body rock," breakdancing is the physical manifestation of hip hop style.[25] Breaking, originally referring only to a particular group of dance moves executed during the break beat in a DJ's rap mixes, has since come to include a number of related movements and dances (e.g., electric boogie and up-rock) that take place at various points in the music.[26]

As the dance steps and routines developed, breaking began to center on the freeze, an improvised pose or movement that ruptured, or "broke the beat." Usually practiced in a circle formation, breaking involved the entry into the circle, the footwork, which was highlighted by the freeze, and the exit. Nelson George offers an insightful and rich description of the dance:

Each person's turn in the ring was very brief—ten to thirty seconds—but packed with action and meaning. It began with an entry, a hesitating walk that allowed him to get in step with the music for several beats and take his place "on stage." Next the dancer "got down" to the floor to do the footwork, a rapid, slashing, circular scan of the floor by sneakered feet, in which the hands support the body's weight while the head and torso revolve at a slower speed, a kind of syncopated sunken pirouette, also known as the helicopter. Acrobatic transitions such as head spins, hand spins, shoulder spins, flips and the swipe—a flip of the weight from hands to feet that also involves a twist in the body's direction—served as bridges between the footwork and the freeze. The final element was the exit, a spring back to verticality or a special movement that returned the dancer to the outside of the circle.[27]

To stop the time was only one part of the freeze. In the freeze, the dancer also took on an alternative identity and served as a challenge to competitors. Dancers would freeze-pose as animals, super heroes, business men, GQ models, elderly or injured people and as female pin-up models. The freeze pose embodied an element of surprise that served as a challenge to the next dancer to outdo the previous pose. As a moment of boasting or sounding on the dancers' competitors, freeze poses might include presenting one's behind to an opponent, holding one's nose or grabbing one's genitals to suggest bad odor or sexual domination.[28]

Breaking was practiced in hallways on concrete and sometime with cardboard pads. Streets were preferred practice spaces for a couple of reasons. Indoor community spaces in economically oppressed areas are rare, and those that are available are not usually big enough to accommodate large groups performing acrobatic dances. In addition, some indoor spaces had other drawbacks. One of the breakers with whom I spoke pointed out that the Police Athletic League, which did have gymnasium-size space, was avoided because it was used as a means of community surveillance for the police. Whenever local police were looking for a suspect, kids hanging out in the PAL were questioned.

Breakdancers practiced and performed in crews that dominated certain neighborhoods. During competitions, if one crew's boasting or sounding won over the crowd completely, the embarrassment it caused the other crew usually resulted in fighting. Bad blood between crews often remained long after the competition and dancers had to be careful in their travels around New York. Crazy Legs, known for inventing the "W" move as well as a special backspin, explained that during the Rock Steady Crew's heyday, they had to fight other crews just about every weekend.[29]

Although the Rock Steady Crew, a mostly Puerto Rican group, always had female breakers, such was not the case with all predominantly male breakdancing crews. Rock Steady's Daisy Castro, aka "Baby Love," attributes this absence to lack of exposure, social support, and male discouragement.[30] Female breakdance crews, such as the Dynamic Dolls, breakers such as Janet, aka "Headspin," Suzy Q, Rock Steady's Yvette, Chunky and Pappy were always part of the breakdance scene. Yet, few women regularly performed the break-specific moves, such as the headspin or the hand-glide; they were more likely to be seen executing the popping, locking, and electric boogie moves.

Although this absence has in some cases to do with relative ease of execution of specific moves for female bodies, most girls were heavily discouraged from performing break moves because they were perceived by some male peers as "unsafe" or "unfeminine." Female breakdancers sometimes executed moves in conventionally feminine ways, to highlight individuality and perhaps to deflect male criticism. Again, women who performed these moves were often considered masculine and undesirable or sexually "available." Although these sexist attitudes regarding the acceptable limits of female physical expression are widespread, they are not absolute. In my interview with Crazy Legs and Wiggles, two Rock Steady Crew dancers, Crazy Legs had no objections to any female dancers executing any moves, whereas Wiggles would "respect" a female breaker but was not as comfortable with females exhibiting the level of physical exertion breaking required.[31]

Breaking combines themes and physical moves found in contemporary popular culture with moves and styles commonly found in Afrodiaspora dances. Breakdancing shares "families of resemblance" with a number of African-American dances. It shares moves and combinations with the lindy-hop, the Charleston, the cakewalk, the jitterbug, the flashdancing in Harlem in the 1940s, double dutch, and black fraternity and sorority stepping. Breaking has also frequently been associated with the Afro-Brazilian martial arts dance Capoiera, particularly for the striking similarities between their spinning and cartwheel-like moves. Yet, breakers also borrow and revise popularized Asian martial arts moves by watching "karate" movies in Times Square. Recent hip hop dance moves, such as the Popeye, the Cabbage Patch, or the Moonwalk, imitate and are named after popular cultural images and characters. Sociologist Herman Gray, referring to another hip hop dance, the Running Man, points out that it may also mime the common experience of young black men being chased by the police. The "lockitup" is a Newark, New Jersey–based dance inspired by carjacking, an armed form of auto theft. According to Marcus Reeves, its moves are said to "act out the procedures of 'poppin' (stealing) a car. While the dancer mimics the car theft ritual, the crowd urges him or her on with chants of 'lockitup!'"[32]

Much like graffiti, breakdancing developed a contradictory relationship to dominant culture. In January 1980, one of the first published articles on breakdancing covered a group of breakdancers who were detained by the police for fighting and causing a disturbance in a Washington Heights area subway station. Once the police were convinced that it was, in fact, "just a dance," the breakers were let go. As unsanctioned public dance and public occupation of space, particularly by black and Puerto Rican youths, breakdancing continued to draw the attention of the police. Over the following five years, articles in the *New York Times, Washington Post*, and the *Los Angeles Times* continued to cite examples of the police arresting breakdancers for "disturbing the peace" and "attracting undesirable crowds" in the malls.[33]

At the same time, breakdancing became the latest popular dance craze in the United States, Europe, and Japan. Not only were breakdance crews forming, but dance schools began hiring breakdancers to teach breakdancing lessons, geared to "hip" middle-class whites.[34] Like SoHo's response to graffiti, breakdancers were hired by popular downtown dance clubs for private parties to provide entertainment for their leisured clientele. Crazy Legs recollects this period of notoriety and exploitation and his reaction to it:

> We got ripped off by so many people. When it came down to Roxy's, they gave me a 50-person guest list every week, but I realize now that they were making crazy dollars. Packed. We weren't making no money. But the bottom line was, they were giving me and Bam (Afrika Bambaataa) and all these other people such a great guest list because all these white people were coming in. . . . We were pretty much on display, and we didn't even know it. We just thought it was great because we was like "Wow, now we got a great floor to dance on, and go party, and we have juice, and we have ghetto status and things like that . . ." Now I realize we were on display. People were paying $8 and $7 whatever it cost . . . to watch us. And we weren't getting anything from the door.[35]

By 1986, when commercial outlets seemed to have exhausted breakdancing as a "fad," breakdancers as mainstream press copy all but disappeared. Yet, the form is still heavily practiced, particularly alongside rap artists and other dance music genres. Dancers in hip hop clubs still perform in circles, inventing steps in response to rap's rhythms. Although rappers' dances are no longer named *breakers*, the moves are extensions of and revisions of breakers' stock moves and with approaches to motion, line, and rupture that refer to and affirm the stylistic approaches of graffiti writers, rap DJs, and the early breakers. The Public Broadcasting System's 1991 dance special "Everybody Dance Now!" demonstrated the stylistic continuities between the moves executed by early breakers and more recent rock, soul, and dance performers such as Janet and Michael Jackson, Madonna, C&C Music Factory, New Kids on the Block, New Edition, The Fly Girls on Fox Television's Comedy Show *In Living Color*, and MC Hammer—illustrating the centrality of hip hop dance style in contemporary popular entertainment.

TRICIA ROSE

Rap Music

Rapping, the last element to emerge in hip hop, has become its most prominent facet. In the earliest stages, DJs were the central figures in hip hop; they supplied the break beats for breakdancers and the soundtrack for graffiti crew socializing. Early DJs would connect their turntables and speakers to any available electrical source, including street lights, turning public parks and streets into impromptu parties and community centers.

Although makeshift stereo outfits in public settings are not unique to rap, two innovations that have been credited to Jamaican immigrant DJ Kool Herc separated rap music from other popular musics and set the stage for further innovation. Kool Herc was known for his massive stereo system speakers (which he named the Herculords) and his practice of extending obscure instrumental breaks that created an endless collage of peak dance beats named b-beats or break-beats. This collage of break-beats stood in sharp contrast to Eurodisco's unbroken dance beat that dominated the dance scene in the mid- to late 1970s. Kool Herc's range of sampled b-beats was as diverse as contemporary rap music, drawing on, among others, New Orleans jazz, Isaac Hayes, Bob James, and Rare Earth. Within a few years, Afrika Bambaataa, DJ and founder of the Zulu Nation, would also use beats from European disco bands such as Kraftwerk, rock, and soul in his performances. I emphasize the significance of rap's earliest DJs' use of rock, because popular press on rap music has often referred to Run DMC's use of samples from rock band Aerosmith's "Walk This Way" in 1986 as a crossover strategy and a departure from earlier sample selections among rap DJs. The bulk of the press coverage on Run DMC regarding their "forays into rock" also suggested that by using rock music, rap was maturing (e.g., moving beyond the "ghetto") and expanding its repertoire. To the contrary, the success of Run DMC's "Walk This Way" brought these strategies of intertextuality into the commercial spotlight and into the hands of white teen consumers. Not only had rock samples always been reimbedded in rap music, but also Run DMC recorded live rock guitar on *King of Rock* several years earlier.[36] Beats selected by hip hop producers and DJs have always come from and continue to come from an extraordinary range of musics. As Prince Be Softly of P.M. Dawn says, "my music is based in hip-hop, but I pull everything from dance-hall to country to rock together. I can take a Led Zeppelin drum loop, put a Lou Donaldson horn on it, add a Joni Mitchell guitar, then get a Crosby Stills and Nash vocal riff."[37]

Kool Herc's Herculords, modeled after the Jamaican sound systems that produced dub and dance-hall music, were more powerful than the average DJ's speakers and were surprisingly free of distortion, even when played outdoors.[38]

They produced powerful bass frequencies and also played clear treble tones. Herc's break-beats, played on the Herculords, inspired breakdancers' freestyle moves and sparked a new generation of hip hop DJs. While working the turntables, Kool Herc also began reciting prison-style rhymes (much like those found on The Last Poets' *Hustler's Convention*), using an echo chamber for added effect. Herc's rhymes also drew heavily from the style of black radio personalities, the latest and most significant being DJ Hollywood, a mid-1970s disco DJ who had developed a substantial word-of-mouth following around the club scene in New York and eventually in other cities via homemade cassettes.

Like the graffiti and breakdance crews, DJs battled for territories. Four main Bronx DJs emerged: Kook Herc's territory was the west Bronx, Afrika Bambaataa dominated the Bronx River East, DJ Breakout's territory was the northernmost section of the Bronx, and Grandmaster Flash controlled the southern and central sections.[39] These territories were established by local DJ battles, club gigs, and the circulation of live performance tapes. DJs' performances, recorded by the DJ himself and audience members, were copied, traded, and played on large portable stereo cassette players (or "ghetto blasters"), disseminating the DJ's sounds. These tapes traveled far beyond the Bronx; Black and Puerto Rican army recruits sold and traded these tapes in military stations around the country and around the world.[40]

Grandmaster Flash is credited with perfecting and making famous the third critical rap music innovation: scratching. Although Grand Wizard Theodore (only 13 years old at the time) is considered its inventor, Theodore did not sustain a substantial enough following to advance and perfect scratching. Scratching is a turntable technique that involves playing the record back and forth with your hand by scratching the needle against and then with the groove. Using two turntables, one record is scratched in rhythm or against the rhythm of another record while the second record played. This innovation extended Kool Herc's use of the turntables as talking instruments, and exposed the cultural rather than structural parameters of accepted turntable use.

Flash also developed the backspin and extended Kool Herc's use of break beats.[41] Backspinning allows the DJ to "repeat phrases and beats from a record by rapidly spinning it backwards." Employing exquisite timing, these phrases could be repeated in varying rhythmic patterns, creating the effect of a record skipping irregularly or a controlled stutter effect, building intense crowd anticipation. Break beats were particularly good for building new compositions. Making the transition to recordings and anticipating the range of sounds and complexity of collage now associated with sampling technology, Flash's 1981 "The Adventures of Grandmaster Flash on the Wheels of Steel" lays the groundwork for the explosive and swirling effects created by Public Enemy producers, the Bomb Squad, seven years later. In an attempt to create the virtuosity of Flash's techniques and the vast range of his carefully selected samples, I have included a lengthy and poetic description of his performance of the "The Adventures of Grandmaster Flash on the Wheels of Steel." Nelson George describes the Grandmaster's wizardry:

> It begins with "you say one for the trouble," the opening phrase of Spoonie Gee's "Monster Jam," broken down to "you say" repeated seven times, setting the tone for a record that uses the music and vocals of Queen's "Another One Bites the Dust," the Sugar Hill Gang's "8th Wonder," and Chic's "Good Times" as musical pawns that Flash manipulates at whim. He repeats "Flash is bad" from Blondie's "Rapture" three times, turning singer Deborah Harry's dispassion into total adoration. While playing "Another One Bites the Dust," Flash places a record on the second turntable, then shoves the needle and the record against each other. The result is a rumbling, gruff imitation of the song's bass line. As the guitar feedback on "Dust" builds, so does Flash's rumble, until we're grooving on "Good Times." Next, "Freedom" explodes between pauses in Chic's "Good Times" bass line. His bass thumps, and then the Furious Five chant, "Grandmaster cuts faster." Bass. "Grandmaster." Basss. "Cut." Bass. "Cuts . . . cuts . . . faster." But the cold crusher comes toward the end when, during "8th Wonder" Flash places a wheezing sound of needle on vinyl in the spaces separating a series of claps.[42]

Using multiple samples as dialogue, commentary, percussive rhythms, and counterpoint, Flash achieved a level of musical collage and climax with two turntables that remains difficult to attain on advanced sampling equipment ten years later.

The new style of DJ performance attracted large excited crowds, but it also began to draw the crowd's attention away from dancing and toward watching the DJ perform.[43] It is at this point that rappers were added to the DJs' shows to redirect the crowd's attention. Flash asked two friends, Cowboy and Melle Mel (both would later become lead rappers along with Kid Creole for Flash and the Furious Five) to perform some boasts during one of his shows. Soon thereafter, Flash began to attach an open mike to his equipment inspiring spontaneous audience member participation. Steve Hager's description of their intertextuality, fluidity, and rhythmic complexity indicates a wide range of verbal skills not generally associated with early rappers: "Relying on an inventive use of slang, the percussive effect of short words, and unexpected internal rhymes, Mel and Creole began composing elaborate rap routines, intricately weaving their voices through a musical track mixed by Flash. They would trade solos, chant, and sing harmony. It was a vocal style that effectively merged the aggressive rhythms of James Brown with the language and imagery of *Hustler's Convention*."[44] Many early rappers were inspired by the intensity of Melle Mel's voice and his conviction. Kid, from rap group Kid-N-Play, attributed some of this intensity to the fact that Mel was rapping for a living rather than a hobby: "For Melle Mel, rapping was his job. Melle Mel made a living rapping each weekend at a party or whatever. So he's rapping to survive. As such, his subject matter is gonna reflect that. I go on record as saying Melle Mel is king of all rappers. He's the reason I became a rapper and I think he's the reason a lot of people became rappers. That's how pervasive his influence was."[45] Melle Mel's gritty dark voice was immortalized on Flash and Furious Five's 1982 "The Message," voted best pop song of 1982. The power of rappers' voices and their role as storytellers ensured that rapping would become the central expression in hip hop culture.

The rappers who could fix the crowd's attention had impressive verbal dexterity and performance skills. They spoke with authority, conviction, confidence, and power, shouting playful ditties reminiscent of 1950s black radio disc jockeys. The most frequent style of rap was a variation on the toast, a boastful, bragging form of oral storytelling sometimes explicitly political and often aggressive, violent, and sexist in content. Musical and oral predecessors to rap music encompass a variety of vernacular artists including the Last Poets, a group of late 1960s to early 1970s black militant storytellers whose poetry was accompanied by conga drum rhythms, poet and singer Gil Scott Heron, Malcolm X, the Black Panthers, the 1950s radio jocks, particularly Douglas "Jocko" Henderson, soul rapper Millie Jackson, the classic Blues women, and countless other performers. "Blaxploitation" films such as Melvin Van Peebles' *Sweet Sweetback's Baadasssss Song*, Donald Goines's gangsta fiction, and "pimp narratives" that explore the ins and outs of ghetto red-light districts are also especially important in rap. Regardless of thematics, pleasure and mastery in toasting and rapping are matters of control over the language, the capacity to outdo competition, the craft of the story, mastery of rhythm, and the ability to rivet the crowd's attention.[46]

Rap relies heavily on oral performance, but it is equally dependent on technology and its effects on the sound and quality of vocal reproduction. A rapper's delivery is dependent on the use and mastery of technology. The iconic focus of the rapper is the microphone; rappers are dependent on advanced technology to amplify their voices, so that they can be heard over the massive beats that surround the lyrics. Eric B. & Rakim's "Microphone Fiend" describes the centrality of the microphone in rap performance:

I was a microphone fiend before I became a teen.
I melted microphones instead of cones of ice cream
Music-oriented so when hip hop was originated
Fitted like pieces of puzzles, complicated.[47]

As rapping moved center stage, rappers and DJs began to form neighborhood crews who hosted block parties, school dances, and social clubs. Like breakdance crew competitions, rappers and DJs battled for local supremacy in intense verbal and musical duels. These early duels were not merely a matter of encouraging crowd reaction with simple ditties such as "Yell, ho!" and "Somebody Scream." (Although these ditties have important sentimental value.) These parties and competitions lasted for several hours and required that the performers had a well-stocked arsenal of rhymes and stories, physical stamina, and expertise. Local independent record producers realized that these battles began to draw consistently huge crowds and approached the rappers and DJs about producing records. While a number of small releases were under way, Sylvia Robinson of Sugar Hill records created the Sugar Hill Gang whose 1979 debut single "Rapper's Delight" brought rap into the commercial spotlight. By early 1980, "Rapper's Delight" had sold several million copies and rose to the top of the pop charts.[48]

"Rapper's Delight" changed everything; most important, it solidified rap's commercial status. DJs had been charging fees for parties and relying on records and equipment for performance, but the commercial potential at which "Rapper's Delight" only hinted significantly raised the economic stakes. Like rock 'n' roll's transition into mainstream commercial markets, rap was fueled by small independent labels and a system of exploitation in which artists had no choice but to submit to draconian contracts that turned almost all creative rights and profits over to the record company if they wanted their music to be widely available. Black-owned and white-owned labels alike paid small flat fees to rappers, demanded rigid and lengthy production contracts (such as five completed records in seven years), made unreasonable demands, and received almost all of the money. Salt from the female rap group Salt 'N' Pepa said that before they signed with Next Plateau Records they were paid $20 apiece per show. When she challenged her manager about their arrangement he threatened her and eventually beat her up for asking too many business questions.[49]

"Rapper's Delight" has also been cited by rappers from all over the country as their first encounter with hip hop's sound and style. In fact, the commercial success of "Rapper's Delight" had the contradictory effect of sustaining and spawning new facets of rap music in New York and elsewhere and at the same time reorienting rap toward more elaborate and restraining commercial needs and expectations. Within the next three years Kurtis Blow's "The Breaks," Spoonie Gee's "Love Rap," The Treacherous Three's "Feel The Heartbeat," Afrika Bambaataa and the Soul Sonic Force's "Planet Rock," Sequence's "Funk You Up," and Grandmaster Flash and the Furious Five's "The Message" were commercially marketed and successful rap singles that made and continue to make more money for Sugar Hill records and other small labels than they do for the artists.[50]

Although Salt 'N' Pepa have been cited as the first major female rappers, some of the earliest rap groups, such as the Funky Four Plus One More had female members, and there were a few all-female groups, such as Sequence. In keeping with young women's experiences in graffiti and breaking, strong social sanctions against their participation limited female ranks. Those who pushed through found that "answer records" (rap battles between the sexes records) were the most likely to get airplay and club response. The first "queen of rap," Roxanne Shante, wrote and recorded a scathing rap in response to UTFO's "Roxanne Roxanne," a rap that accused a girl named Roxanne of being conceited for spurning sexual advances made by UTFO. Roxanne Shante's "Roxanne's Revenge" was a caustic and frustrated response that struck a responsive chord among b-girls and b-boys.[51] Rapped in a sassy high-pitched girl's voice (Shante was 13 years old at the time), Shante told UTFO: "Like corn on the cob you're always trying to rob / You need to be out there lookin' for a job." And the chorus: "Why you have make a record 'bout me? The R/O/X/A/N/N/E?" has become a classic line in hip hop.[52]

Although black and Latino women have been a small but integral presence in graffiti, rapping, and breaking, with the exception of Sha Rock, who was one of the innovators of the beat box, they have been virtually absent from the area of music production. Although there have been female DJs and producers, such as Jazzy Joyce, Gail 'sky' King, and Spindarella, they are not major players in the use of sampling technology nor have they made a significant impact in rap music production and engineering. There are several factors that I believe have contributed to this. First, women in general are not encouraged in and often actively discouraged from learning about and using mechanical equipment. This takes place informally in socialization and formally in gender-segregated vocational tracking in public school curriculum. Given rap music's early reliance on stereo equipment, participating in rap music production requires mechanical and technical skills that women are much less likely to have developed.

Second, because rap music's approaches to sound reproduction developed

212   TRICIA ROSE

informally, the primary means for gathering information is shared local knowledge. As Red Alert explained to me, his pre–hip hop interest and familiarity with electronic equipment were sustained by access to his neighbor Otis who owned elaborate stereo equipment configurations. Red Alert says that he spent almost all of his free time at Otis's house, listening, learning, and asking questions. For social, sexual, and cultural reasons young women would be much less likely to be permitted or feel comfortable spending such extended time in a male neighbor's home.

Even under less intimate circumstances, young women were not especially welcome in male social spaces where technological knowledge is shared. Today's studios are extremely male-dominated spaces where technological discourse merges with a culture of male bonding that inordinately problematizes female apprenticeship. Both of these factors have had a serious impact on the contributions of women in contemporary rap music production. Keep in mind, though, that the exclusion of women from musical production in rap is not to be understood as specific to rap or contemporary music, it is instead the continuation of the pervasive marginalization of women from music throughout European and American history.

One of the ways around these deterrents is to create female-centered studio spaces. I have always imagined that rap's most financially successful female rappers would build a rap music production studio that hired and trained female technicians and interns, a space in which young women of color would have the kind of cultural and social access to technology and musical equipment that has, for the most part, been a male dominion. It would also quickly become a profitable and creative space for a wide range of musicians committed to supporting women's musical creativity and forging new collaborative environments.

Unlike breakdancing and graffiti, rap music had and continues to have a much more expansive institutional context within which to operate. Music is more easily commodified than graffiti, and music can be consumed away from the performance context. This is not to suggest that rap's incorporation has been less contradictory or complicated. Quite to the contrary; because of rap music's commercial power, the sanctions against as well as the defenses for rap have been more intense, and thus resistance has been more contradictory.

Throughout the late 1980s, rap music's commercial status increased dramatically, rappers began exploring more themes with greater intertextual references and complexity, and hip hop crews from urban ghettos in several major cities began telling stories that spoke not only of the specifics of life in Houston's fifth ward for example but also of the general bridges between the fifth ward and Miami's Overtown or Boston's Roxbury. In the same time period, Run DMC's mid- to late 1980s popularity among white teens prompted the *New York Times* to declare that rap had finally reached the mainstream.[53] At the same time, Eric B. & Rakim, Public Enemy, KRS One, L.L. Cool J, MC Lyte and De La Soul also emerged as major figures in rap's directional shifts.[54]

During the late 1980s Los Angeles rappers from Compton and Watts, two areas severely paralyzed by the postindustrial economic redistribution, developed a West Coast style of rap that narrates experiences and fantasies specific to life as a poor, young, black male subject in Los Angeles. Ice Cube, Dr. Dre, Ice-T, Ezy-E, Compton's Most Wanted, W.C. and the MAAD Circle, Snoop Doggy Dogg, South Central Cartel, and others have defined the gangsta rap style. The Los Angeles school of gangsta rap has spawned other regionally specific hardcore rappers, such as New Jersey's Naughty by Nature, Bronx-based Tim Dog, Onyx and Redman, and a new group of female gangsta rappers, such as Boss (two black women from Detroit), New York-based Puerto Rican rapper Hurrican Gloria, and Nikki D.

Mexican, Cuban, and other Spanish-speaking rappers, such as Kid Frost, Mellow Man Ace and El General, began developing bilingual raps and made lyrical bridges between Chicano and black styles. Such groups as Los Angeles-based Cypress Hill, which has black and Hispanic members, serve as an explicit bridge between black and Hispanic communities that builds on long-standing hybrids produced by blacks and Puerto Ricans in New York. Since 1990, in addition to gangsta raps, sexual boasting, Afrocentric and protest raps, rap music features groups that explore the southern black experience, that specialize in the explicit recontextualization of jazz samples, live instrumentation in rap performance and recording, introspective raps, raps that combine acoustic folk guitar with rap's traditional dance beats and even New Age/Soul rap fusions.[55]

These transformations and hybrids reflect the initial spirit of rap and hip hop as an experimental and collective space where contemporary issues and ancestral forces are worked through simultaneously. Hybrids in rap's subject matter, not unlike its use of musical collage, and the influx of new regional, and ethnic styles have not yet displaced the three points of stylistic continuity to which I referred much earlier: approaches to flow, ruptures in line and layering can still be found in the vast majority of rap's lyrical and music construction. The same is true of the critiques of the postindustrial urban America context and the cultural and social conditions that it has produced. Today, the South Bronx and South Central are poorer and more economically marginalized than they were ten years ago.

Hip hop emerges from complex cultural exchanges and larger social and political conditions of disillusionment and alienation. Graffiti and rap were especially aggressive public displays of counterpresence and voice. Each asserted the right to write[56]—to inscribe one's identity on an environment that seemed Teflon-resistant to its young people of color; an environment that made legitimate avenues for material and social participation inaccessible. In this context, hip hop produced a number of double effects. First, themes in rap and graffiti articulated free play and unchecked public displays; yet, the settings for these expressions always suggested existing confinement.[57] Second, like the consciousness-raising sessions in the early stages of the women's rights movement and black power movement of the 1960s and 1970s, hip hop produced internal and external dialogues that affirmed the experiences and identities of the participants and at the same time offered critiques of larger society that were directed to both the hip hop community and society in general.

Out of a broader discursive climate in which the perspectives and experiences of younger Hispanic, Afro-Caribbeans, and African-Americans had been provided little social space, hip hop developed as part of a cross-cultural communication network. Trains carried graffiti tags through the five boroughs; flyers posted in black and Hispanic neighborhoods brought teenagers from all over New York to parks and clubs in the Bronx and eventually to events throughout the metropolitan area. And, characteristic of communication in the age of high-tech telecommunications, stories with cultural and narrative resonance continued to spread at a rapid pace. It was not long before similarly marginalized black and Hispanic communities in other cities picked up on the tenor and energy in New York hip hop. Within a decade, Los Angeles County (especially Compton), Oakland, Detroit, Chicago, Houston, Atlanta, Miami, Newark and Trenton, Roxbury, and Philadelphia have developed local hip hop scenes that link various regional postindustrial urban experiences of alienation, unemployment, police harassment, social and economic isolation to their local and specific experience via hip hop's language, style, and attitude.[58] Regional differentiation in hip hop has been solidifying and will continue to do so. In some cases these differences are established by references to local streets and events, neighborhoods and leisure activities; in other cases regional differences can be discerned by their preferences for dance steps, clothing, musical samples, and vocal accents. Like Chicago and Mississippi blues, these emerging regional identities in hip hop affirm the specificity and local character of cultural forms, as well as the larger forces that define hip hop and Afrodiasporic cultures. In every region, hip hop articulates a sense of entitlement and takes pleasure in aggressive insubordination.

Few answers to questions as broadly defined as "what motivated the emergence of hip hop" could comprehensively account for all the factors that contribute to the multiple, related, and sometimes coincidental events that bring cultural forms into being. Keeping this in mind, this exploration has been organized around limited aspects of the relationship between cultural forms and the contexts within which they emerge. More specifically, it has attended to the ways in which artistic practice is shaped by cultural traditions, related current and previous practice, *and* by the ways in which practice is shaped by technology, economic forces, and race, gender, and class relations. These relationships between form, context, and cultural priority demonstrate that hip hop shares a number of traits with, and yet revises, long-standing Afrodiasporic practices; that male dominance in hip hop is, in part, a by-product of sexism and the active process of women's marginalization in cultural production; that hip hop's form is fundamentally linked to technological changes and social, urban space parameters; that hip hop's anger is produced by contemporary racism, gender, and class oppression; and finally, that a great deal of pleasure in hip hop is derived from subverting these forces and affirming Afrodiasporic histories and identities.

Developing a style nobody can deal with—a style that cannot be easily understood or erased, a style that has the reflexivity to create counterdominant narratives against a mobile and shifting enemy—may be one of the most effective ways to fortify communities of resistance and *simultaneously* reserve the right to communal pleasure. With few economic assets and abundant cultural and aesthetic resources, Afrodiasporic youth have designated the street as the arena for competition, and style as the prestige-awarding event. In the postindustrial urban context of dwindling low-income housing, a trickle of meaningless jobs for young people, mounting police brutality, and increasingly draconian depictions of young inner city residents, hip hop style *is* black urban renewal.

NOTES

1. Rose interviews with all artists named except Futura, whose printing trade school experience was cited in Steve Hager, *Hip Hop: The Illustrated History of Breakdancing, Rap Music, and Graffiti* (New York: St. Martin's Press, 1984), 24.

2. Rose interview with Crazy Legs, November 6, 1991. *Piecing* means drawing a mural or masterpiece.

3. See Henry Louis Gates, Jr., *The Signifying Monkey: A Theory of African-American Literary Criticism* (New York: Oxford University Press, 1988), 55, 87. Gates's suggestion that naming be "drawn upon as a metaphor for black intertextuality" is especially useful in hip hop, where naming and intertextuality are critical strategies for creative production.

4. Dick Hebdige, *Subculture: The Meaning of Style* (London: Routledge, 1979), 17–19, 84–89.

5. For an interesting discussion of time, the clock, and nationalism in hip hop, see Jeffrey L. Decker, "The State of Rap: Time and Place in Hip Hop Nationalism," *Social Text* 34 (1993): 53–84.

6. *Hoodies* are hooded jackets or shirts, *snooties* are skull caps, and *tims* are short for Timberland brand boots.

7. Cited in Nelson George et al., eds., *Fresh: Hip Hop Don't Stop* (New York: Random House, 1985), 111.

8. Although I had isolated some general points of aesthetic continuity between hip hop's forms, I did not identify these three crucial organizing terms. I am grateful to Arthur Jafa, black filmmaker, artist, and cultural critic, who shared and discussed the logic of these defining characteristics with me in conversation. He is not, of course, responsible for any inadequacies in my use of them here.

9. For a brilliant example of these moves among recent hip hop dances, see "Reckin' Shop in Brooklyn," directed by Diane Martel (Epoch Films, 1992). Thanks to A. J. for bringing this documentary film to my attention.

10. Some examples of explicit attention to flow are exhibited in Queen Latifah's *Ladies First*: "Some think that we can't flow, stereotypes they go to go"; Big Daddy's *Raw*: "Intro I start to go, my rhymes will flow so"; in Digital Underground's *Sons of the P* (*Son's of the Flow*): "Release your mind and let your instincts flow, release your mind and let the funk flow."

11. Hebdige, *Subculture*, 94–95.

12. Ibid. Published in 1979, *Subculture* concludes at the point of dominant British culture's initial attempts at incorporating punk. The remaining chapters in this project focus on the moments after the first stabs at incorporation and more specifically attend to the various thematic, creative, and discursive responses to these ongoing processes. In this way, the following chapters examine the points of incorporation and responses that come after the initial moment of incorporation into which Hebdige's study is devoted.

13. Martha Cooper and Henry Chalfant, *Subway Art* (New York: Holt, Rinehart & Winston, 1984), 14. Other accounts of the early years in New York graffiti consider Taki one of several early taggers, along with Chew 127, Frank 207, and Julio 204. Taki was the first to receive media notoriety.

14. The expansion of graffiti art was significantly aided by technological advances in permanent markers and spray paint formulas. In both tools, product improvement allowed writers to apply colors more smoothly, with greater precision and technique. Furthermore, technique is not limited to these formal advances; writers used these advances in new ways to make them respond to artistic impulses. For example, according to Cooper and Chalfant, writers customized these new products, fitting "nozzles from household products on spray-cans to vary the width of the spray." See Cooper and Chalfant, *Subway Art*, 14, 33.

15. Craig Castleman, *Getting Up: Subway Graffiti in New York* (Cambridge: MIT Press, 1982), 50. Other academic profiles and histories of graffiti include: Nancy Guevara, "Women Writin' Rappin' Breakin'," in Mike Davis et al., eds., *The Year Left 2: An American Socialist Yearbook* (London: Verso, 1987); Atlanta and Alexander, "Wild Style: Graffiti Painting" in Angela McRobbie, ed., *Zoot Suits and Second-Hand Dresses: An Anthology of Fashion and Music* (Boston: Unwin Hyman, 1988), 156–68. Notable film and video histories include *Style Wars*, produced by Tony Silver and Henry Chalfant, directed by Tony Silver (1983), and *Wild Style*, produced and directed by Charlie Ahern.

16. Castleman, *Getting Up*, 114.

17. Guevara, "Women Writin'," 161–75. It is important to point out that Castleman's research suggests that there have probably been much larger numbers of female writers than we are aware of, because women writers often used male names as tags. In his work on

graffiti writing gangs in the early 1970s, a male writer/gang member claimed that upward of twenty-five women were a part of the writing crews for the Ex-Vandals, and many of them used boys' names for tags. See Castleman, *Getting Up*, 100–101.

18. Guevara refers to the differences between female and male writers as stylistic differences, when in fact I think the differences are better described as gender-based strategies for individualization that are articulated at the level of style but do not deviate from the larger stylistic parameters and approaches to line, motion, and rupture that I have discussed. Furthermore, the same categories of "stylistic" differences (e.g., colors and themes) that Guevara notes between males and females can be identified among male writers.

19. See Nathan Glazer, "On Subway Graffiti in New York," *The Public Interest* (winter 1979): 11–33. In this article, Glazer argues that the significance of the graffiti "problem" was in fact its symbolic power. According to Joe Austin and Craig Castleman, Glazer's "out of control" rhetoric was instrumental in solidifying the image of graffiti writers as the source of New York's civic disorder and tarnished image, effectively displacing the more substantial and complex factors for New York's decline onto an unidentified band of black and Hispanic marauders. This move justified treating graffiti writers as dangerous criminals who threatened social order and contributed to the social tenor that resulted in the fatal beating of graffiti writer Michael Stuart at the hands of the transit police in 1982.

20. Hager, *Hip Hop*, 60.

21. For an extended description of TA expenditures and an insightful reading of the institutional discourse that surrounded the war on graffiti, see Joe Austin, "A Symbol That We Have Lost Control: Authority, Public Identity, and Graffiti Writing," unpublished paper in possession of the author at the University of Minnesota, Department of American Studies. See also, Castleman, *Getting Up*, esp. chapters 7, 8, 9. Although Castleman offers substantial data, he unfortunately does not offer sufficient critique or analysis either of the graffiti itself or of the institutional discourse that surrounds it.

22. Jean Michel Basquiat was one of the only graffiti artists to make a successful transition into the "legitimate art world" and was quite celebrated until his drug-related death in 1985. He has been noted particularly for his ability to play on white gallery owners' stereotypes of him as a wild, animallike talent—using the myth of black bestiality as a means of manipulation. Another artist who was able to remain in the art world, Rammelzee, continues to draw and develop performance art in the United States, Europe, and Japan. Both of these writers also produced rap records.

23. This aspect of the contemporary graffiti scene emerged in discussions following the presentation of his paper, "A Symbol That We Have Lost Control," which was delivered at the 1991 American Studies Association meeting.

24. The break is a point in a song or performance where the rhythmic patterns established by the bass, drums, and guitar are isolated from the harmonic and melodic elements and extended. In jazz, the break refers to the soloist's improvised bridge between stanzas.

25. George et al., *Fresh*, 79.

26. Electric boogie is a robotic, mimelike dance that began in California and was most popular there and in parts of the South. The Lockers, a Los Angeles–based dance troupe (that evolved from the Soul Train dancers) used many electric boogie moves, in more fluid patterns. Up-rock is a very acrobatic, confrontational, and insulting gesture or move that is specifically directed at an opponent.

27. George et al., *Fresh*, 90.

TRICIA ROSE

28. Ibid., 96.

29. Interview with Crazy Legs and Wiggles, November 6, 1991. The fact that fights were and remain common in and around hip hop is important, because it stands in contrast to one of the central media depictions of hip hop as a form that redirected gang-related energies into peaceful creative outlets. In fact, the "celebratory" media discourse regarding hip hop relied on this myth to justify its celebration. Although it is quite possible that breaking, rapping, and graffiti writing absorbed time that might have otherwise been spent fighting or stealing, fighting and stealing remain common.

30. Guevara, "Women Writin'," 171.

31. Rose interview with Crazy Legs and Wiggles, November 6, 1991.

32. This connection was made in Gray's unpublished paper presented at the 1990 American Studies Association meeting; Marcus Reeves, "Ear to the Street," *The Source* (March 1993): 18. For discussions on black dance and movement see Robert Farris Thompson, "Kongo Influences on African-American Artistic Culture," in *Africanisms in American Culture*, ed. Joseph E. Holloway (Bloomington: University of Indiana Press, 1990), 148–84, and "Hip Hop 101," *Rolling Stone*, March 27, 1986, 95–100; Elizabeth C. Fine, "Stepping, Saluting, Cracking and Freaking: The Cultural Politics of Afro-American Step Shows," *The Drama Review* 35(2) (summer 1991): 39–59; and Katrina Hazzard, *Jookin'* (Philadelphia: Temple University Press, 1991).

33. Sally Banes, "Breaking Is Hard to Do," *Village Voice*, April 22–28, 1981, 31–33; Wesley G. Hughes, "Putting the Breaks on Break Dancing?," *Los Angeles Times*, March 5, 1984, pt. 2, 1; "C'mon Gimme a Break," *Newsweek*, May 14, 1984, 28; Laura Castaneda, "Annapolis Banishes Breakdancers from City Dock," *Washington Post*, August 3, 1984, C13.

34. Cathleen McGuigan et al., "Breaking Out: America Goes Dancing," *Newsweek*, July 2, 1984, 46–52. This cover story is an exploration into the discovery of breaking among middle-class Americans, particularly the "urban chic" who frequent posh clubs. These clubs may let in breakers for "color" but will not generally permit their black and Latino peers. See advertisements for breakdance workshops, *Village Voice*, December 4, 1984, 100.

35. Interview with Crazy Legs and Wiggles, 6 November 1991.

36. See Peter Watrous, "It's Official: Rap Music Is in the Mainstream," *New York Times*, May 16, 1988, C11; After expressing frustration over the coverage of "Walk This Way" as a crossover strategy, Run describes his motivation: "I made that record because I used to rap over it when I was twelve. There were lots of hip-hoppers rapping over rock when I was a kid." Ed Kierch, "Beating the Rap," *Rolling Stone*, December 4, 1986, 59–104.

37. Cited in Jon Young, "P.M. Dawn Sample Reality," *Musician* (June 1993): 23.

38. According to Hager, the Herculords were two Shure brand speaker columns aided by a Macintosh amplifier. Hager, *Hip Hop*, 33. It is also interesting to note that, even though the equipment and Herc's style were heavily influenced by Jamaican sound systems and dub, Herc claims that he could not get the crowd to respond to Jamaican music. This is one of the many interesting points of diasporic hybridity in which the influences move bidirectionally.

39. MTV, *Rapumentary* (1990).

40. Interview with Red Alert, May 8, 1990.

41. Not long after his rise to local fame, Kool Herc was stabbed multiple times during one of his shows. After this incident, he dropped out of the hip hop scene.

42. George et al., *Fresh*, 6–7. I explore the technical and artistic practices in rap music production in Chapter 3.

43. According to Flash and Red Alert, a still crowd seemed to be more prone to fighting and confrontations.

44. Hager, *Hip Hop*, 48. *Hustler's Convention* is the 1973 album written and performed by Jalal Uridin, leader of the black militant ex-convicts, The Last Poets. *Hustler's Convention* (and the related blaxploitation genres of the late 1960s and early 1970s) are clear predecessors to contemporary gangsta rap's thematic and stylistic preference for violence, drugs, sex, and sexism. The critical formal difference is rap's emphasis on danceable beats and its musical complexity.

45. Interview with Kid, from Kid-N-Play, January 11, 1990.

46. Rap's roots in black oral practices are extensive, and research on black oral practices is equally so. Some major texts that explore the history of black oral practices are listed here: Houston Baker, *Long Black Song: Essays in Black American Literature and Culture* (London: University Press of Virginia, 1972, 1990); Gates, *The Signifying Monkey*; Dennis Wepman, Ronald Newman, and Murry Binderman, *The Life The Lore and Folk Poetry of the Black Hustler* (Philadelphia: University of Philadelphia Press, 1976); Alan Dundes, ed., *Mother Wit from the Laughing Barrel: Readings in the Interpretation of Afro-American Folklore* (New York: Garland, 1981); Daniel Crowley, *African Folklore in the New World* (Austin: University of Texas Press, 1977); Lawrence Levine, *Black Culture and Black Consciousness: Afro-American Folk Thought from Slavery to Freedom* (New York: Oxford University Press, 1977); Roger D. Abrahams, *Deep Down in the Jungle: Negro Narrative Folklore from the Streets of Philadelphia* (Chicago: Aldine, 1970); Geneva Smitherman, *Talkin' and Testifyin': The Language of Black America* (Boston: Houghton Mifflin, 1977).

47. Eric B. & Rakim, "Microphone Fiend," in *Follow the Leader* (Uni Records, 1988). In Chapter 3 I explore the relationship between technology and orality in rap in much greater depth.

48. There is a great deal of controversy regarding the Sugar Hill Gang's sudden, albeit short-lived success. According to a number of rappers and DJs from this period, the three members of Sugar Hill Gang were not local performers. One of the members, Hank, was a doorman/bouncer at a rap club in New York and had access to bootleg tapes that he played back in northern New Jersey, an area that at this point had no local rap scene. Sylvia Robinson heard one of Hank's tapes and approached him about recording a rap single. According to Hager's *Hip Hop*, Hank borrowed Grandmaster Caz's rhyme book and used his rhymes in "Rapper's Delight." Kool Moe Dee, Red Alert, and others explained to me that when they heard the record, they were shocked. Not only had they never heard of the Sugar Hill Gang, but they could not believe that a rap record (even one that they thought was so elemental) could become commercially successful.

49. Rose interview with Salt, May 22, 1990.

50. "Rapper's Delight" sold over two million copies in the United States, and "The Breaks" sold over 500,000 copies. These record sales were primarily the result of word of mouth and hip hop club play.

51. Shante's single "Roxanne's Revenge" (Pop Art Records, 1984) sold over two million copies.

52. Women rappers are the subject of Chapter 5, in which their contributions and an analysis of rap's sexual politics are explored in greater depth.

53. Watrous, "It's Official."

54. The purpose of this chapter is not to give a chronological history of all the develop-

ments in hip hop. As stated, I have focused on the context for creativity and hip hop's links to Afrodiasporic styles and practices. For more background on hip hop artists and commercial developments, see Havelock Nelson and Michael A. Gonzales, *Bring the Noise: A Guide to Rap Music and Hip Hop Culture* (New York: Crown, 1991); Joseph D. Eurie and James G. Spady, *Nation Conscious Rap: The Hip Hop Version* (New York: PC International, 1991); David Toop, *Rap Attack 2* (Boston: Consortium Press, 1992); Bill Adler, *Tougher Than Leather: Run DMC* (New York: Penguin, 1987); Bill Adler, *Rap: Portraits and Lyrics of a Generation of Black Rockers* (New York: St. Martin's Press, 1991). For a sobering look at how independent labels (where almost all rappers contracts are negotiated) have been maneuvered into a subcontractor's position in relation to the large music companies, see Frederic Dannen, *Hit Men: Powerbrokers and Fast Money inside the Music Business* (New York: Random House, 1990), especially chapter 17.

55. For examples, see Gang Starr, *Step in the Arena* (Chrysalis, 1990); Guru, *Jazzamatazz* (Chrysalis, 1993); MTV, *Rap Unplugged* (Spring 1991); Basehead, *Play with Toys* (Image, 1992); Disposable Heroes of Hiphoprisy, *Disposable Heroes of Hiphoprisy* (Island, 1992); P.M. Dawn, *Of the Heart, Of the Soul and Of the Cross* (Island, 1991); and Me Phi Me, *One* (RCA, 1992); Arrested Development, *3 Years, 5 Months and 2 Days in the Life Of* (Chrysalis, 1992).

56. See Duncan Smith, "The Truth of Graffiti," *Art & Text* 17 (April 1985): 85–95.

57. For example, Kurtis Blow's "The Breaks" (1980) was both about the seeming inevitability and hardships of unemployment and mounting financial debt and the sheer pleasure of "breaking it up and down," of dancing and breaking free of social and psychological constrictions. Regardless of subject matter, elaborate graffiti tags on train facades always suggested that the power and presence of the image was possible only if the writer had escaped capture.

58. See Bob Mack, "Hip-Hop Map of America," *Spin*, June 1990.

"Keep to the Rhythm and You'll Keep to Life"

Meaning and Life in African American Vernacular Dance (1966)

JACQUI MALONE

. . . .

An associate professor of drama, theater, and dance at Queens College, Flushing, New York, and a former dancer, Jacqui Malone defines "vernacular dance" as that "performed to the rhythms of African American music: dance that makes those rhythms visible." Malone identifies six definitive traits of African American vernacular dance, but she also discusses multidimensionality *and* style *as distinctive features of African American artistic expression. That is, Malone describes dance as one part of an integrated "way of life."*

> Listen Ocol, my old friend
> The ways of your ancestors
> Are good,
> Their customs are solid
> And not hollow
> They are not thin, not easily breakable
> They cannot be blown away
> By the winds
> Because their roots reach deep into the soil.
> —Okot p'Bitek, *Song of Lawino, Song of Ocol*

To us life with its rhythms and cycles is dance and dance is life.
—A. M. Opoku, "Thoughts from the School of Music and Drama"

Through art we celebrate life. As Albert Murray says, "Our highest qualities come from art; that's how we know who we are, what we want, what we want to do."[1] The attainment of wholeness, rather than the amassing of power, is what ultimately makes people happy, and the goal of art is to help achieve that wholeness by providing humanity with basic "equipment for living."[2] Among African Americans that equipment is partially rooted in a vital and dynamic cultural style.

African American vernacular dance, like jazz music, mirrors the values and worldview of its creators. Even in the face of tremendous adversity, it evinces an affirmation and celebration of life. Furthermore, African American dance serves some of the same purposes as traditional dances in western and central African cultures: on both continents black dance is a source of energy, joy, and inspiration; a spiritual antidote to oppression; and a way to lighten work, teach social values, and strengthen institutions. It also teaches the unity of mind and body and regenerates mental and physical power. The role of dance as a regenerative force is echoed in the words of Bessie Jones of the Georgia Sea Islands: "We'd sing different songs, and then we'd dance a while to rest ourselves."[3]

Much has been written about the role of music and folklore among black people in the United States, but the meaning and the pervasiveness of dance have been sorely neglected despite the fact that dance touches almost every aspect of African American life. As Melville Herskovits tells us, "The dance itself has in characteristic form carried over into the New World to a greater degree than almost any other trait of African culture[s]." Since the publication of Herskovits's groundbreaking work, *The Myth of the Negro Past*, the identification of African continuances in African American culture has been a source of much debate among American studies scholars. Fortunately, the discourse has evolved beyond a search for specific elements to the recognition of shared cultural processes of creativity, based on the notion that "art moves within people" and that cultural continuity is never completely broken.[4] The composer and scholar Olly Wilson suggests that African and African American music and dance share similar "ways of doing things, although the specific qualities of the something that is done varies with time and place and is also influenced by a number of elements outside the tradition."[5] Recognition of the strong relationship between the dances of traditional African cultures and the dances of black Americans is now a commonplace among students and scholars of American history, music, and dance.

Although visual source materials are not available to trace with accuracy the evolution of African American dances in the United States during the seventeenth, eighteenth, and nineteenth centuries, certain movement patterns, gestures, attitudes, and stylizations present in the body language of contemporary black Americans are assertive proof of African influences. African Americans "refine all movement in the direction of dance-beat elegance. Their work movements become dance movements and so do their play movements; and so, indeed, do all the movements they use every day, including the way they walk, stand, turn, wave, shake hands, reach, or make any gesture at all."[6]

Because movement behavior has a tendency to be conservative, the stylistic features of movement and dance represent a significant area of "historical inertia."[7] Hence, the dance movements and body language embedded in the muscle memory of captives from western and central Africa provided a deep and enduring wellspring of creativity for black Americans.

Five percent of the approximately twelve million slaves taken from Africa were transported to North America. Colonial populations, especially in the South, had heavy concentrations of Africans. By 1720, South Carolina, the port of entry for most slaves, was dominated by western Africans. There were twelve thousand black inhabitants and nine thousand Europeans. Seventy percent of the slaves brought to Charleston between 1735 and 1740 were transported from Angola; and at the onset of the American Revolution, South Carolina was over 50 percent black. During North America's peak years of importation, 1741 to 1810, slaves were exported in large numbers from central Africa's Bantu-speaking areas.[8]

Peter Wood has written insightfully about the presence of Africans in colonial South Carolina. His findings reveal that "the Bakongo culture of the Congo River area was well represented in South Carolina's early black majority." The Bakongo are descendants of an ancient classical civilization, Kongo, that included modern Bas-Zaïre and neighboring lands in modern Cabinda, Gabon, Congo-Brazzaville, and northern Angola. During the Atlantic slave trade,

> thousands of persons were abducted from this culturally rich area. And as opposed to a prevalent view of Africans—as belonging to different "tribes," speaking different "dialects," thrown together in the holds of slave ships, and hopelessly alienated, one from the other—Africans from Kongo and Angola shared fundamental beliefs and languages. When they met on the plantations and in the cities of the western hemisphere, they fostered their heritage. Kongo civilization and art were not obliterated in the New World: they resurfaced in the coming together here and there, of numerous slaves from Kongo and Angola.[9]

In the kingdom of the Kongo, dancing was rarely done for pleasure alone; it usually functioned within ritual dramas. The sacred implications of dancing made it a primary part of initiation ceremonies; indeed, all other important Kongo rites involved dance because spiritual power itself could not be summoned without the influence of designated ceremonial dances. Kongo-Angolan culture "has inspired the whole planet to dance," writes C. Daniel Dawson. "In the Americas everyone practices some aspects of these Central African traditions in their daily lives, but without recognizing these activities as having a Kongo-Angola origin. For example, rumba, tango and samba, to name just three dances, are viewed in their respective countries as national dances. In reality, these dances should be understood as Central African movement forms shared with the world through their countries." Pelvic thrusts and circular pelvic movements known as the "Congo grind" in American jazz dance parlance probably have a Kongo-Angola origin.[10]

Bantu-speaking peoples constituted the largest culturally related group brought to North America: 41 percent of those arriving between 1701 and 1810. During that same period, western Africans comprised 59 percent of the newly arrived slaves, but their languages were less related. New Orleans, in particular, was a stronghold of Kongo-Angolan culture.[11]

From that culture came music, literature, art, drama, religion, philosophy, social morality, and speech. ("Bantu speech has a proven ability to move into a culture, to absorb it, and to change its language.")[12] Many western and central African adaptations have become thoroughly woven into the fabric of American culture, while their origins have been unwittingly or deliberately obscured.

Resilience toward new experience is a deeply ingrained tradition in many African societies. The Africanist Georges Balandier makes this observation about Kongo culture: "In the Kongo a way of life managed to survive where towns fell in ruins and powers collapsed. This way of life made it possible to make a new start without being disloyal to tradition, without forgetting a style of existence which remained a precious possession inherited from the ancestors. The setting and the institutions might change; the Mukongo slowly altered the habits that governed his daily life. Innovations did not worry him, as long as they did not disturb the ancient fabric of his days." Among western African peoples it was not unusual for the conquerors and the conquered to adopt each other's gods.[13]

The ability to disregard outer form yet retain inner values led to the persistent reworking of African musics and dances even in new and difficult settings. The attitude of people in traditional African cultures toward what is new and foreign endowed North American slaves with a psychological resilience that proved to be their mainstay in facing difficulties in their new lands. The historian Lawrence W. Levine maintains that "culture is not a fixed condition but a process: the product of interaction between the past and the present. Its toughness and resiliency are determined not by a culture's ability to withstand change, which indeed may be a sign of stagnation not life, but by its ability to react creatively and responsively to the realities of a new situation." [14]

Murray calls black Americans' cultural mechanism for surviving the adverse circumstances in the United States a "riff-style life style." "We swing because we survived by being flexible and resilient." Murray adds, "riff-style flexibility and an open disposition towards the vernacular underlie the incomparable endurance of black soulfulness or humanity." [15]

Much of what looks like mere entertainment to someone unfamiliar with black idiomatic expression has spiritual significance for persons grounded in African American culture. Although their rituals do not necessarily have the specific religious meanings of rites that were practiced by their ancestors, black Americans nonetheless *ritualize their lives.* [16]

Murray, who has written extensively about the ritual significance of the public jazz dance or the "Saturday night function," sees the dance hall as a temple where rituals of purification, affirmation, and celebration are held. It is a place where the "blues idiom" dancer disperses hard times or adversity as she or he *stomps the blues.* At the Saturday night function, the music and the dance serve as a potent counterstatement to blue moods; and the dancer's response to the music is actually a lesson in how to live. "The blues-idiom dancer like the solo instrumentalist turns disjunctures into continuities [and] is not disconcerted by intrusions, lapses, shifts in rhythm, intensification of tempo, for instance; but is inspired by them to higher and richer levels of improvisation." "What the customary blues-idiom dance movement reflects is a disposition to encounter obstacle after obstacle as a matter of course." Dance-beat improvisation is "so much a part of many people's equipment for living that they hardly ever think about it as such anymore." [17]

Most black Americans learn vernacular dance within the context of their culture. Children are taught to hear and feel the beat at very young age, and they grow up listening and moving to music. It is not uncommon to witness very young children performing the most current social dances. Traditional African American children's games revolve around dance, and its influence can be seen in almost all physical activities. Song and dance are an integral part of storytelling, for example. Cheerleading becomes dance, double-dutch rope jumping becomes dance, and so do the agile exertions of teenage athletes. [18]

Play serves as training for performance. It teaches us the rules of the game and of a culture. Through interaction, we learn fair play. That is, we learn the ethics of a culture and we learn to identify good play, which is similar to learning how to recognize good performance. The determining factors have to do with personal creativity, styling, and aesthetics. Thus play becomes performance. [19]

In an essay entitled "Remembering Richard Wright," Ralph Ellison comments that although Wright possessed the confidence of a jazz man, he knew little about jazz and "didn't even know how to dance. Which is to say that he didn't possess the full range of Afro-American culture."[20] Black youth and adults generally don't take classes to learn social dance—their academies are dance halls, house parties, social clubs, and the streets. In fact, formal dance studios are usually years behind the real source of America's major social dances: the black community. The tap dancer Charles "Honi" Coles concurs: "In my neighborhood in Philadelphia, the only form of recreation was dancing. Everyone I knew could dance. We used to dance on street corners at night, and then we'd start going to the various neighborhood houses and amateur contests. . . . I [didn't] know anyone who went to school to learn show business or dancing. You learned it . . . as you were exposed to it." Training in this context is a matter of conditioning. It is informal, but it is training nevertheless. Because the training is so subtle, the outcome often seems like second nature.[21]

Black idiomatic dancers have always found the European tradition of dance manuals and dancing masters inadequate for their approach to creating and learning movement, just as jazz musicians have found the European musical notation system not totally adequate for their purposes. European dances lack the freedom of expression that is inherent in vernacular dance. The rigidly codified dances that were studied so systematically by planters in colonial America served as a point of departure for North American slaves, who took what they could use from the dance traditions of Europeans, but retained their own African-derived style, steps, and rhythmical sense.

A tendency to "dance the song" in traditional African cultures was preserved in the secular and sacred expression of U.S. slaves. Spirituals were always sung with some degree of body motion. A black plantation preacher testifies: "The way in which we worshipped is almost indescribable. The singing was accompanied by a certain ecstasy of motion, clapping of hands, tossing of heads, which would continue without cessation about half an hour; one would lead off in a kind of recitative style, others joining in the chorus. The old house partook of the ecstasy; it rang with their jubilant shouts, and shook in all its joints." To thoroughly understand these slave songs one must imagine them as performed. For they were not just sung at worship services and in the field but they were also danced in the ring shout. A band of shouters dramatized the lyrics through movement. The elements involved in performing the African American ring shout, as practiced during slavery, represented dramatic continuances of western and central African expressive culture.[22]

U.S. slave literature is replete with descriptions of black performance style and the adaptation of that style to religion and work. Chroniclers frequently comment on the vitality and dynamism of the participants, although they routinely mistake survival strategy and cultural orientation for shallow merriment and contentment.[23]

The use of the body in religious expression is still highly valued by twentieth-century gospel singers. Mahalia Jackson wrote, "I want my hands . . . my feet . . . my whole body to say all that is in me. I say, 'Don't let the devil steal the beat from the Lord! The Lord doesn't like us to act dead. If you feel it, tap your feet a little—dance to the glory of the Lord." Thomas A. Dorsey had this to say: "Don't let the movement go out of the music. Black music calls for movement! It calls for feeling. Don't let it get away." Dorsey's attitude points to one of the most distinctive features of African American artistic expression: multidimensionality.[24]

Black people attend musical events with the expectation that the performers will appeal to their visual and aural senses. One attends a social event to hear the gutsy scream of James Brown and to witness his smooth dance moves; to see the precision stepping of black sororities and fraternities and to hear their polyrhythms, chants, and songs of allusion; to listen to the halftime music of the FAMU Marching 100 and to watch the high-stepping drum majors and musicians strut their stuff. Sidney Bechet comments on the multidimensionality of a New Orleans second-line parade: "The Marshall, he'd be a man that really could strut. . . . He'd keep time to the music, but all along he'd keep a strutting and moving so you'd never know what he was going to be doing next. Naturally, the music, it makes you strut, but it's *him* too, the way he's strutting, it gets you. It's what you want from a parade: you want to *see* it as well as hear it. And all those fancy steps he'd have—oh that was really something! . . . It would have your eyes just the same as your ears for waiting."[25]

African American musicians, dancers, and singers all testify to the spiritual dimension of their art. Many tap dancers describe tap as a "way of life." The tenor saxophonist Lester Young was totally consumed by his musical gift: "Just all music, all day and all night music. Just any kind of music you play for me, I melt with all of it."[26]

A distinctive and characteristic style is manifest in the artistic expression of black dancers, singers, and musicians. Style is an attitude, a mechanism for sizing up the world, and a mode of survival. "Behind each artist," writes Ellison, "there stands a traditional sense of style, a sense of the felt tension indicative of expressive completeness; a mode of humanizing reality and of evoking a feeling of being at home in the world." What then is the background for the strong emphasis on self-presentation among African American dancers, musicians, and singers?[27]

Because the Bakongo were constantly aware of the image they presented to others, personal appearance and other factors in self-presentation were extremely important. "The concern for elegance was dominant." The art of dressmaking and weaving was associated with royalty, and nobles of the court were always elegantly attired and richly adorned. Women of rank wore rings and heavy copper bracelets and neck bands.[28] Among the Akan of Ghana, coiffure and dress signified status. "The divine Ghana or King, according to Arab chroniclers, held court in splendid robes with gold ornaments, his horses' hooves were worked in gold, ivory and silver, and his retinue carried shields and swords embossed with gold." Yoruban art is heavily influenced by male and female hairstyles, dress, jewelry, body scarification, and painting. Some type of body art was practiced by most traditional societies; it was the Nuba's only visual art and was related to their wrestling, fighting, and dancing. The strong impulse to adorn can be identified in numerous African cultures.[29]

Slave literature shows that the importance ascribed to self-presentation and style was preserved in the Americas. Whenever possible, slaves created special attire for parties, festivals, and Sunday activities. The relationship between dress and dance is articulated in the 1789 autobiography of Gustavus Vassa, a former slave: "I laid out above eight pounds of my money for a suit of superfine clothes to dance in at my freedom, which I hoped was then at hand."[30] From the minstrel stage through traveling shows, musical theater, vaudeville, cabarets, and beyond, African American performing artists have attached great significance to personal style and dress.

The king of "strutting," George Walker, of the famous turn-of-the-century team Williams and Walker, was noted for his flashy haberdashery off and on stage.[31] Charles "Honi" Coles, who performed regularly from the thirties through the fifties, says that dancers were always very aware of the correctness and elegant arrangement of their stage clothing: "If you wore a walking outfit, it was correct down to the last detail."[32] Josephine Baker routinely required three dressing rooms, one near the stage for dressing, one for socializing, and one for housing her glamorous costumes. During a single performance she changed at least six to eight times.[33] The Cotton Club chorus line dancers were known as extremely sharp dressers: "They had about twelve dancing girls and eight show girls, and they were all beautiful chicks. They used to dress so well! On Sunday nights, when celebrities filled the joint, they would rush out of the dressing room after the show in all their finery. Every time they went by, the stars and the rich people would be saying, 'My, who is *that?*'"[34]

Many musicians developed classic styles in dress and deportment. The stride pianist Willie "the Lion" Smith elaborates: "You had to be real sharp in the way you dressed, the manner in which you approached the piano, and in the originality of your ideas. . . . Today we call it showmanship, but back then it was called 'attitude.' " "I had my own attitude and way of working at the piano. My way was to get a cigar clenched between my teeth, my derby tilted back, knees crossed, and my back arched at a sharp angle against the back of the chair. I'd cuss at the keyboard and then caress it with endearing words."[35] According to James P. Johnson, Smith's "every move was a picture." Johnson was also impressed by the attitude of the legendary Jelly Roll Morton:

> I've seen Jelly Roll Morton, who had a great attitude, approach a piano. He would take his overcoat off. It had a special lining that would catch everybody's eye. So he would turn it inside out and, instead of folding it, he would lay it lengthwise along the top of the upright piano. He would do this very slowly, very carefully and very solemnly as if the coat was worth a fortune and had to be handled very tenderly. Then he'd take a big silk handkerchief, shake it out to show it off properly, and dust off the stool. He'd sit down then, hit his special chord (every tickler had his special trademark chord, like a signal), and he'd be gone![36]

Louis Armstrong, Lester Young, and Duke Ellington were national style setters not just in music but also in dress, demeanor, language, and movement. The trumpeter Rex Stewart was one of many ardent Armstrong admirers: "Then Louis Armstrong hit town! I went mad with the rest of the town. I tried to walk like him, talk like him, eat like him, sleep like him. I even bought a pair of big policeman shoes like he used to wear and stood outside his apartment waiting for him to come out so I could look at him."[37]

Many classic blues singers developed reputations for their individual styles. Dance movements, gestures, and dress were no less important than their actual singing. In the mid-twenties, Gertrude "Ma" Rainey's dramatic entrances shook up Thomas Dorsey:

> Ma Rainey's act came on as a last number or at the end of the show. I shall never forget the excited feeling when the orchestra in the pit struck up her opening theme, music which I had written especially for the show. The curtain rose slowly and those soft lights on the band as we picked up the introduction to Ma's first song. We looked and felt like a million. Ma was hidden in a big box-like affair built like an old Victrola of long ago. This stood on the other side of the stage. A girl would come out and put a big record on it. Then the bank picked up the Moonshine Blues. Ma would sing a few bars inside the Victrola. Then she would open the door and step out into the spotlight with her glittering gown that weighed twenty pounds and wearing a necklace of five, ten and twenty dollar gold-pieces. The house went wild. It was as if the show had started all over again. Ma had the

audience in the palm of her hand. Her diamonds flashed like sparks of fire falling from her fingers. . . . When Ma had sung her last number and the grand finale, we took seven [curtain] calls.[38]

The blues singer Alberta Hunter was sometimes photographed in her "King Tut" pose: "one hand on hip, the other against her forehead, her . . . nose in profile, her curvy hips hugged by a sleek long dress." During performances she typically dangled a long bright scarf that was attached to her ring: "I like to be different. . . . If I had on a black dress, I'd get a gorgeous red or yellow one, something that would be a contrast. I'd just handle it unconsciously but with flair. Jiving."[39]

Nowhere is African American style more manifest than in dance. The six definitive characteristics of African American vernacular dance are *rhythm, improvisation, control, angularity, asymmetry,* and *dynamism.*

The importance of rhythm to human existence is an ongoing theme in the writings of Katherine Dunham. She understood as early as the 1950s that the breaking of *rhythm* in an individual or society results in disintegration, malaise, and energy diffusion. It is the key to human potentials for social and personal integration. Rhythm, asserts Léopold Senghor, is "the architecture of being, the inner dynamic that gives it form, the pure expression of the life force. Rhythm is the vibratory shock, the force which, through our sense, grips us at the root of our being. It is expressed through corporeal and sensual means; through lines, surfaces, colours, and volumes in architecture, sculpture or painting; through accents in poetry and music, through movements in the dance. . . . In the degree to which rhythm is sensuously embodied, it illuminates the spirit."[40]

African American vernacular dance is characterized by propulsive rhythm. Coming from dance-beat-oriented cultures, black Americans demand a steady beat in their dance music. Although the beat can be embellished, the basic rhythm provides the dancer with dramatic exits and entrances. The jazz dancer James Berry comments: "The rhythmic motion on the beat with the music has something. You feel free to do what you want and you can't get lost, because you can always come in, you can dance with abandon but still you are encased within the beat. That is the heart of dancing."[41]

Improvisation, an additive process, is a way of experimenting with new ideas; that mind-set is Africa's most important contribution to the Western Hemisphere. One offshoot of that mind-set is the tendency toward elasticity of form in African American art. When Duke Ellington asked a candidate for his orchestra if he could read music, his reply was: "Yeah, I can read, but I don't let it interfere with my blowing!" That point of view is prevalent among jazz musicians, who thrive on improvisation. "True jazz is an art of individual assertion within and against the group. Each true jazz moment (as distinct from the uninspired commercial performance) springs from a contest in which each artist challenges all the rest; each solo flight, or improvisation, represents (like the successive canvases of a painter) a definition of his identity: as individual, as member of the collectivity and as a link in the chain of tradition."[42]

Improvisation, for the black idiomatic dancer, functions in much the same way. It is one of the key elements in the creation of vernacular dance. From the turn-of-the-century cakewalk through the Charleston of the twenties and the lindy of the thirties and forties, black dancers inserted an improvisational "break" that allowed couples to separate at various points so that they could have maximum freedom of movement. According to Thompson, "breaking the beat or breaking the pattern in Kongo is something one does to break on into the world of the ancestors, in the possession state, precisely the rationale of drum-breaks (casée) in Haiti." From the "breakdown" of colonial slave frolics to the break dancing of the twentieth century, the improvisational interlude has remained a cornerstone of African American dance in the United States. Indeed, throughout the Kongo-influenced communities of the African diaspora, there are many styles of " 'breaking' to the earth." For example, the "Break Out" or "Break Away" is the main section in Jamaican Jonkonnu performances, during which several dancers execute solos simultaneously.[43]

All African American social dances allow for some degree of improvisation, even in the performance of such relatively controlled line dances as the Madison and the stroll of the fifties. In this dance tradition, the idea of executing any dance exactly like someone else is usually not valued. When vocal groups perform choreographed dance movements, the audience expects each singer to bring his or her own personality to the overall movement style, thereby creating diversity within unity. Contrary to popular opinion, black idiomatic dancers always improvise with intent—they compose on the spot—with the success of the improvisations depending on the mastery of the nuances and the elements of craft called for by the idiom.

Within the context of vernacular dance performance, the "aesthetic of the cool" functions to help create an appearance of control and idiomatic effortlessness. What vernacular dance celebrates is a "unique combination of spontaneity, improvisation, and control." According to Murray, blues-idiom dance movement has nothing to do with sensual abandonment. "Being always a matter of elegance [it] is necessarily a matter of getting oneself together." Like all good dances, practitioners of this style do not throw their bodies around; they do not cut completely loose. When the musical break comes, it is not a matter of "letting it all hang out," but a matter of proceeding in terms of "a very specific technology of stylization."[44] A loss of control and a loss of coolness places one *squarely* outside of the tradition.

Angularity is a prominent feature of African American body language, dress, and performance. Thompson has identified several Bakongo angulated gestures and body postures that show up in sports, musical performances, religious expressions, and day-to-day conversations of African Americans. Black nonverbal communication is rife with angles. We see them in female and male stances, walking styles, and greetings. In *Jazz Masters of the 30s*, Rex Stewart contends that the "insouciant challenge" of Louis Armstrong's personal style was conveyed to the world by "his loping walk [and] the cap on his head tilted at an angle, which back home meant: 'Look out! I'm a bad cat—don't mess with me!'" Zora Neale Hurston identified this characteristic as early as the 1930s: "After adornment the next most striking manifestation of the Negro is Angularity. Everything that he touches becomes angular. In all African sculpture and doctrine of any sort we find the same thing. Anyone watching Negro dancers will be struck by the same phenomenon. Every posture is another angle. Pleasing, yes. But an effect achieved by the very means which a European strives to avoid."[45]

Hurston also identified asymmetry as a significant feature of African arts and black American literature and dance:

It is the lack of symmetry which makes Negro dancing so difficult for white dancers to learn. The abrupt and unexpected changes. The frequent changes of key and time are evidences of this quality in music (Note the St. Louis Blues). The dancing of the justly famous Bo-Jangles and Snake Hips are excellent examples. The presence of rhythm and lack of symmetry are paradoxical, but there they are. Both are present to a marked degree. There is always rhythm, but it is the rhythm of segments. Each unit has a rhythm of its own, but when the whole is assembled it is lacking in symmetry. But easily workable to a Negro who is accustomed to the break in going from one part to another, so that he adjusts himself to the new tempo.[46]

The participatory nature of black performance automatically ensures a certain degree of dynamism because the demands of the audience for dynamic invention and virtuosity prevent the performer from delivering static reproductions of familiar patterns or imitations of someone else's hard-earned style.

When performers demonstrate their knowledge of the black musical aesthetic, the responses of audiences can become so audible that they momentarily drown out the performer. The verbal responses of audiences are accompanied by hand-clapping; foot-stomping; head, shoulder, hand, and arm movement; and spontaneous dance. This type of audience participation is important to performers; it encourages them to explore the full range of aesthetic possibilities, and it is the single criterion by which black artists determine whether they are meeting the aesthetic expectations of the audience.[47]

The folklorist Gerald Davis calls this phenomenon of African American performance "circularity": a dynamic system of influences and responses whose components include performers, audiences, and their traditions. Davis's model begins with an ideal form—a preacher's sermon, for example—and ends with a realized form that is shaped by all three components of the circular interchange. Davis's study concentrates on sermons but he also observes circularity in certain musical forms, selected expressions of material culture, and—quite significantly for our purposes—in some types of dance.[48]

The African American aesthetic encourages exploration and freedom in composition. Originality and individuality are not just admired, they are expected. But creativity must be balanced between the artist's conception of what is good and the audience's idea of what is good. The point is to add to the tradition and extend it without straying too far from it. The circle in black social dance is a forum for improvising and "getting down" but the good dancer does not go outside the mode established by the supporting group. "DO YOUR OWN THING," explains the playwright Paul Carter Harrison, "is an invitation to bring YOUR OWN THING into a complementary relationship with the mode, so that we all might benefit from its power." When a dancer enters the magic circle it is a way of renewing the group's most hallowed values.[49]

Among African Americans, the power generated by rhythmical movement has been apparent for centuries in forms of work, play, performance, and sacred expression. Rhythmical movement as a unifying mechanism and a profound spiritual expression is poetically voiced in an excerpt from Ellison's short story "Juneteenth." The speaker, Reverend Hickman, addresses a crowd at an Emancipation Day celebration:

Keep to the rhythm and you'll keep to life. God's time is long; and all short-haul horses shall be like horses on a merry-go-round. Keep, keep, keep to the rhythm and you won't get weary. Keep to the rhythm and you won't get lost. . . . They had us bound but we had our kind of time, Rev. Bliss. They were on a merry-go-round that they couldn't control but we learned to beat time from the seasons. . . . They couldn't divide us now. Because anywhere they dragged us we throbbed in time together. If we got a chance to sing, we sang the same song. If we got a chance to dance, we beat back hard times and tribulations with a clap of our hands and the beat of our feet, and it was the same dance. . . . When we make the beat of our rhythm to shape our day the whole land says, Amen! . . . There's been a heap of Juneteenths before this one and I tell you there'll be a heap more before we're truly free! Yes! But keep to the rhythm, just keep to the rhythm and keep to the way.[50]

NOTES

1. Albert Murray, lecture, Center for Afro-American Studies, Wesleyan University, Middletown, Conn., Spring 1985.

2. Kenneth Burke, *The Philosophy of Literary Form: Studies in Symbolic Action* (Baton Rouge: Louisiana State University Press, 1941; reprint, New York: Vintage Books, 1957), 253–62.

3. Bessie Jones and Bess Lomax Hawes, *Step It Down: Games, Plays, Songs, and Stories from the Afro-American Heritage* (New York: Harper and Row, 1972; reprint, Athens: University of Georgia Press, 1987), 124.

4. Melville J. Herskovits, *The Myth of the Negro Past* (Boston: Becaon, 1958 [1941]), 76; John Michael Vlach, *The Afro-American Tradition in Decorative Arts* (Cleveland: Cleveland Museum of Art, 1978), 120, quotation from 148; Charles Joyner, *Down by the Riverside: A South Carolina Slave Community* (Urbana: University of Illinois Press, 1984), 237.

5. Olly Wilson, "The Influence of Jazz on the History and Development of Concert Music," in *New Perspectives on Jazz*, ed. David N. Baker (Washington, D.C.: Smithsonian Institution Press, 1990), 29; see also Wilson, "The Significance of Relationship between Afro-American Music and West African Music," *Black Perspective in Music* 2, no. 1 (spring 1974), 3–22; Olly Wilson, "The Association of Movement and Music as a Manifestation of a Black Conceptual Approach to Music-Making," in *More Than Dancing: Essays on Afro-American Music and Musicians*, ed. Irene V. Jackson (Westport, Conn.: Greenwood Press, 1985), 9–23.

6. Albert Murray, *Stomping the Blues* (New York: McGraw-Hill, 1976; reprint, New York: Vintage, 1982), 189. "Playing the Blues," a chapter from this volume, is printed on pages 96–109 herein.

7. Gerhard Kubik, *Angolan Traits in Black Music, Games, and Dances of Brazil: A Study of African Cultural Extensions Overseas*, Estudos de Anthropologia Cultural no. 10 (Lisboa: Centro de Estudos de Anthropologia Cultural, 1979), 20.

8. Wood, " 'Gimme de Kneebone Bent': African Body Language and the Evolution of American Dance Forms," in *The Black Tradition in American Modern Dance*, ed. Gerald E. Myers (American Dance Festival, 1988), 7; Peter H. Wood, *Black Majority: Negroes in Colonial South Carolina from 1670 through the Stone Rebellion* (New York: Alfred A. Knopf, 1974; reprint, New York: W. W. Norton, 1975), 145, 335; Winifred Kellersberger Vass, *The Bantu Speaking Heritage of the United States* (Los Angeles: Center for Afro-American Studies, University of California, 1979), 12.

9. Wood, " 'Gimme de Kneebone Bent,' " 7; Robert Farris Thompson, *Flash of the Spirit: African and Afro-American Art and Philosophy* (New York: Random House, 1983), 103, quotation from 104.

10. C. Daniel Dawson, ed., *Dancing between Two Worlds: Kongo-Angola Culture and the Americas* (New York: Ragged Edge, 1991), iii; Georges Balandier, *Daily Life in the Kingdom of*

the Kongo: From the Sixteenth to the Eighteenth Century (New York: World, 1969), 233; Gerhard Kubik, Angolan Traits in Black Music, Games and Dances of Brazil: A Study of Cultural Extensions Overseas (Lisbon: Junta de Investigacoes Clentificas do Ultramor, 1979), 20.

11. Winifred Vass, The Bantu Speaking Heritage of the United States (Los Angeles: Center for Afro-American Studies, University of California, 1979), 3; Robert Farris Thompson and Joseph Cornet, The Four Moments of the Sun: Kongo Art in Two Worlds (Washington, D.C.: National Gallery of Art, 1981), 149; Philip D. Curtin, The Atlantic Slave Trade: A Census (Madison: University of Wisconsin Press, 1969), 222.

12. Vass, Bantu, 3.

13. Balandier, Daily Life, 153; Herskovits, Myth, 141, 297–98.

14. Lawrence W. Levine, Black Culture and Black Consciousness: Afro-American Folk Thought from Slavery to Freedom (New York: Oxford University Press, 1978), 5; Herskovits, Myth, 297–98.

15. Quotations from Albert Murray, The Omni-Americans (New York: McGraw-Hill, 1976), 184; Albert Murray, interview with author, New York, N.Y., May 8, 1993, and Murray, Omni-Americans, 185.

16. Robert Farris Thompson, lecture, New York University, New York, N.Y., spring 1991.

17. Quotations from Murray, Omni-Americans, 59, and Murray, Stomping the Blues, 254, 16.

18. I know this to be true because I grew up in a southern segregated environment where I was immersed in African American culture.

19. Gerald L. Davis, The Performed Word (Anthropology Film Center Foundation, 1982).

20. Ralph Ellison, "Remembering Richard Wright," in Going to the Territory (New York: Random House, 1986), 208.

21. Charles "Honi" Coles quoted in Jack Schiffman, Harlem Heyday: A Pictorial History of Modern Black Show Business and the Apollo Theater (Buffalo: Prometheus Books, 1984), 164–65; Murray, Stomping the Blues, 108 (reprinted in this volume).

22. James L. Smith, Autobiography of James L. Smith (Norwich, Conn., 1881), 27, quoted in John W. Blassingame, The Slave Community: Plantation Life in the Antebellum South, revised and enlarged (New York: Oxford University Press, 1979), 134; Herskovits, Myth, 265; Albert J. Raboteau, Slave Religion: The "Invisible Institution" in the Antebellum South (New York: Oxford University Press, 1980), 245; see also Sterling Stuckey, Slave Culture: Nationalist Theory and the Foundation of Black America (New York: Oxford University Press, 1988), 3–97.

23. See Eileen Southern, The Music of Black Americans, 2d ed. (New York: W. W. Norton, 1983), and Dena Epstein, Sinful Tunes and Spirituals: Black Folk Music to the Civil War (Urbana: University of Illinois Press, 1981).

24. Mahalia Jackson with Evan McLeod Wylie, Movin' on Up (New York: Hawthorn Books, 1966), 66; Thomas A. Dorsey, "Gospel Music," in Reflections on Afro-American Music, ed. Dominique-René de Lerma (Kent, Ohio: Kent State University Press, 1973), 190–91, quoted in Levine, Black Culture, 184.

25. Quotation from Sidney Bechet, Treat It Gentle (London: Cassell, 1960; reprint, New York: Da Capo Press, 1978), 66; Lazarus E. N. Ekwueme, "African-Music Retentions in the New World," Black Perspectives in Music 2(2) (Fall 1974): 137–39.

26. Douglas Henry Daniels, "Lester Young: Master of Jive," American Music 3(3) (Fall 1985): 317.

27. Ralph Ellison, *Shadow and Act* (New York: Random House, 1964; reprint, New York: Vintage Books, 1972), xvii; Murray, *Omni-Americans*, 54–55.

28. Balandier, *Daily Life*, 166–69, quotation from 169.

29. Gillon, *Short History*, 236, 152, 156, 34, quotation from 87. See Angela Fisher, *Africa Adorned* (New York: Harry N. Abrams, 1984).

30. Gustavus Vassa quoted in Arna Bontemps, ed., *Great Slave Narratives* (Boston: Beacon, 1969), 100.

31. Richard Newman, "The Brightest Star: Aida Overton Walker in the Age of Ragtime and Cakewalk," ms., 5.

32. Honi Coles, "The Dance," in *The Apollo Theater Story* (New York: Apollo Operations, 1966), 9.

33. Phyllis Ashinger, "Dress and Adornment of African American Entertainers," in *African American Dress and Adornment: A Cultural Perspective*, ed. Barbara M. Starke, Lillian O. Holloman, and Barbara K. Nordquist (Dubuque, Iowa: Kendall/Hunt, 1990), 179–87.

34. Duke Ellington, *Music Is My Mistress* (Garden City, N.J.: Doubleday, 1973; reprint, New York: Da Capo Press, 1976), 81.

35. Willie "the Lion" Smith with George Hoefer, *Music on My Mind: The Memoirs of an American Pianist* (New York: Doubleday, 1964; reprint, New York: Da Capo Press, 1978), 52–53, 155.

36. Tom Davin, "Conversation with James P. Johnson," in *Jazz Panorama: From the Pages of the Jazz Review*, ed. Martin Williams (New York: Crowell-Collier, 1962; reprint, New York: Da Capo Press, 1979), 56, 59–60.

37. Rex Stewart quoted in Nat Shapiro and Nat Hentoff, eds., *Hear Me Talkin' to Ya: The Story of Jazz as Told by the Men Who Made It* (New York: Rinehart, 1955; reprint, New York: Dover, 1966), 206.

38. Thomas Dorsey quoted in Sandra R. Lieb, *Mother of the Blues: A Study of Ma Rainey* (Amherst: University of Massachusetts Press, 1981), 28–30.

39. Frank C. Taylor with Gerald Cook, *Alberta Hunter: A Celebration in Blues* (New York: McGraw-Hill, 1987), 84, 41.

40. Léopold Sédar Senghor, "L'esprit de la civilisation ou les lois de la culture négro-africaine," *Présence Africaine* (Paris) 8–10 (1956): 60, quoted in Janheinz Jahn, *Muntu: African Culture and the Western World* (New York: Grove Press, 1961; reprint, New York: Grove Weidenfeld, 1990), 164. Millicent Hodson, "How She Began Her Beguine: Dunham's Dance Legacy," in *Kaiso!: Katherine Dunham, An Anthology of Writings*, ed. Vèvè A. Clark and Margaret B. Wilkerson (Berkeley: CCEW Women's Center, Institute for the Study of Social Change, University of California, 1978), 197–98.

41. James Berry with Mura Dehn, "Jazz Profound," *Dance Scope* 11(1) (fall–winter 1976–77): 24.

42. Duke Ellington quoted in Stanley Dance, *The World of Earl Hines* (New York: Scribner, 1977; reprint, New York: Da Capo Press, 1983), 3; Ellison, *Shadow and Act*, 234; Vlach, *Afro-American Tradition*, 150.

43. Robert Farris Thompson, "Coming Down the Body Line: Kongo Atlantic Gestures and Sports," in *Dancing between Two Worlds: Kongo-Angola Culture and the Americas*, ed. C. Daniel Dawson (New York: Ragged Edge, 1991), 8; Judith Bettelheim, "Jonkonnu and Other Christmas Masquerades," in *Caribbean Festival Arts*, ed. John W. Nunley and Judith Bettelheim (Seattle: University of Washington Press, 1988), 64.

44. Murray, *Stomping the Blues*, 50, 90, 126.

45. Rex Stewart, *Jazz Masters of the 30s* (New York: Macmillan, 1972; reprint, New York: Da Capo Press, 1982), 40; Zora Neale Hurston, "Characteristics of Negro Expression," in Nancy Cunard, *Negro*, 54 (this essay is reprinted herein, pp. 293–308); Robert Farris Thompson, "Kongo Influences on African-American Artistic Culture," in *Africanisms in American Culture*, ed. Joseph E. Holloway (Bloomington: Indiana University Press, 1990), 157–64; see also Benjamin G. Cooke, "Nonverbal Communication among Afro-Americans: An Initial Classification," in *Rappin' and Stylin' Out: Communication in Urban Black America*, ed. Thomas Kochman (Urbana: University of Illinois Press, 1972), 32–64.

46. Hurston, "Characteristics," 55.

47. Quotation from Portia Maultsby, "Africanisms in African American Music," in *Africanisms in American Culture*, ed. Joseph E. Holloway (Bloomington: Indiana University Press, 1990), 195; Gerald L. Davis, *I Got the Word in Me and I Can Sing It, You Know: A Study of the Performed African-American Sermon* (Philadelphia: University of Pennsylvania Press, 1985), 26–27.

48. G. Davis, *I Got the Word*, 26–31.

49. Paul Carter Harrison, *The Drama of Nommo: Black Theater in the African Continuum* (New York: Grove Press, 1972), 72–73; John Michael Vlach, "Afro-American Aesthetic," in *Encyclopedia of Southern Culture*, ed. Charles Reagan Wilson and William Ferris (Chapel Hill: University of North Carolina Press, 1989), 457–58; Stuckey, *Slave Culture*, 88.

50. Ralph Ellison, "Juneteenth," *Quarterly Review of Literature* 13(3–4) (1965): 274–76.

Lester Young and
the Birth of Cool

(1998)

JOEL DINERSTEIN

. . . .

American studies scholar Joel Dinerstein designed and teaches a course at the University of Texas at Austin on the history of being cool in America. In this essay from The Cool Mask *(forthcoming) he shows how the African American concept of cool synthesizes African and Anglo-European ideas, describing African American cool as both an expressive style and a kind of public composure. For African Americans, cool resolves the conflict between competing needs to mask and to express the self, a paradox exacerbated by historical exigencies of life in the United States. For Dinerstein, the jazz musician Lester Young modeled a strategy of self-presentation that became the dominant emotional style of African American jazz musicians and several generations of African American men.*

Miles Davis's 1957 collection *The Birth of the Cool* tends to serve as a lightning rod for discussions of "cool" in jazz and African American culture.[1] A spate of jazz recordings, however, testify to the importance of being "cool"—of maintaining emotional self-control—during World War II as a strategy for dealing with dashed hopes of social equality. The messages of Erskine Hawkins's hit, "Keep Cool, Fool" (1941) and Count Basie's "Stay Cool" (1946) and the cerebral quality of Charlie Parker's "Cool Blues" (1946) testify to a new valuation of public composure and disparagement of the outward emotional display long associated with stereotypes of blacks, from Uncle Tom to the happy-go-lucky "southern darky." Contemporary American usage of the word "cool" has its roots in the jazz culture of the early 1940s, and the legendary tenor saxophonist Lester Young probably used it first to refer to a state of mind.[2] When Young said, "I'm cool" or "that's cool," he meant "I'm calm," "I'm OK with that," or just "I'm keeping it together in here." The jazz musician and scholar Ben Sidran rightly noted that this cool ethic reflected "actionality turned inward" and was "effected at substantial cost and suffering."[3]

According to Gunther Schuller, Lester Young was "*the* most influential artist after [Louis] Armstrong and before Charlie Parker," the creator of the "cool" saxophone style and the father of the "cool school" of jazz with which Miles Davis later became associated. Yet he is little known outside the jazz world because his groundbreaking 1930s recordings were made with the Count Basie Orchestra and Billie Holiday. Young was the "genius soloist" on the classic 1930s Basie band recordings and the saxophone complement (the second voice, really) to Billie Holiday's best vocal performances.[4] Young was Holiday's favorite musician, and they bestowed the nicknames on each other that stuck for life: she dubbed him "Pres" because he was "the president of all saxophone players," and Young dubbed her "Lady Day."

Young burst into recorded jazz history in 1936 with a revolutionary, vibrato-less tenor sound: fast, floating, airy, clean, light. It was so completely opposed to the then-dominant model of tenor playing, Coleman Hawkins's rhapsodic, powerful, "macho" tone, that it confused most black jazz musicians.[5] Young's combination of lightning speed, blues feeling, rhythmic balance, precise articulation, and inexhaustible melodic ideas made him, in retrospect, something like the Michael Jordan of jazz. Dizzy Gillespie called it a "cool, flowing style" to emphasize Young's long, fluid phrases, strategic use of silence and space, and rhythmic mastery. Young's sound and style represented a musical synthesis of early jazz history: from his childhood on the New Orleans streets and adolescence on the black vaudeville circuit to his responsiveness to white Chicagoan influences such as Jimmy Dorsey and Bix Beiderbecke; from his mastery of the blues and his classical virtuosity to his involvement in "the big music workshop" of early 1930s Kansas City.[6] Young influenced hundreds of white and black musicians between 1937 and 1944. After suffering traumatic experiences at a southern army base in World War II, however, he withdrew into a quiet, gin-soaked nonconformity.

Between 1945 and his death in 1959, Young's strategies of self-insulation were as influential on younger jazz musicians as his music.[7] Young's renowned use of hip slang influenced jazz culture, black cultural pride, white Beat Generation writers, and (through them) the counterculture of the 1960s. His prodigious consumption of marijuana and alcohol, his humor, his trademark porkpie hat, and his silent, expressive sadness generated so much jazz lore that he remains a model of the hip jazz musician of the period (for example, as the character Dale Turner in the movie 'Round Midnight [1986] and Edgar Poole in John Clellon Holmes's novel, The Horn [1958]). He made more than $50,000 a year during this period yet self-consciously drank himself to death in a small room in the Alvin Hotel on Fifty-second Street, neither proud nor ashamed of either his substance abuse or his sadness.[8] Between his continued dedication to expressing his inner pain artistically, and the blank facial expression he wore to resist the white "gaze," Young embodied two aspects of cool that seem contradictory: expressiveness in music and emotional self-control.

There were four core African American cool concepts alive at the birth of cool, all of which still influence contemporary ideas of cool. Cool the first: to control your emotions and wear a mask in the face of hostile, provocative outside forces. Cool the second: to maintain a relaxed attitude in performance of any kind. Cool the third: to develop a unique, individual style (or sound) that communicates something of your inner spirit. Cool the fourth: to be emotionally expressive within an artistic frame of restraint (as in jazz or basketball). (Cool is also the word used to express aesthetic approval of such a performance ["cool!"].) Cool can be seen as an ideal state of balance, a calm but engaged state of mind between the emotional poles of "hot" (excited, aggressive, intense, hostile) and "cold" (unfeeling, efficient, mechanistic)—in other words, a "relaxed intensity."

Nelson George reflects that for young urban black men in the mid-1940s, "cool came to define a certain sartorial elegance, smooth charm, and self-possession that . . . suggested a dude that controlled not only himself but his environment." Lester Young was a musical genius with a legendary sense of humor who influenced hundreds of musicians during the most dynamic years of the black migration, a time when American race relations were undergoing a radical shift. Young's whole life was self-consciously dedicated to being original—in his music, in his mannerisms, in his style of detachment—as if being original was the vital force of human life itself. He was often described as " 'cool'—calm, imperturbable, unhurried, and balanced in his playing and personal demeanor."[9] Although Young died nearly forty years ago, longtime rhythm and blues bandleader Johnny Otis claimed in 1993 that he "is the one figure who stands above the entire field of music as the guiding spirit of African American artistry."[10] In this essay I will explore the West African, Anglo-American, African American, and popular culture roots of cool, and show how Young's synthesis of these materials gave birth to cool.

From Blackface Minstrels to Jazz Artists

Even among jazz musicians, Lester Young was thought of as a visitor from another planet. A shy, reserved, and gentle man, he was a fierce musical competitor but one who otherwise recoiled from interpersonal conflict. When insulted, he pulled out a small whisk broom and brushed off his shoulder; when a bigot appeared on the scene, he said softly, "I feel a draft"; he rang a little bell when a fellow musician made a mistake on the bandstand. As Young's Basie bandmate, the guitarist Freddie Green, reflected: "Most of the things he came up with were . . . things you'd never heard before. . . . He was a very original man."[11] His trademarks were a slow, relaxed step no one could hurry and the flat, black porkpie hat he had custom-made from a Victorian women's magazine. He seems to be one major source for the essential jazz idea that it is more important to "tell a story" in a solo than to be virtuosic; his sage advice was, "Ya gotta be original, man."

After 1940, Young spoke a nearly impenetrable hip slang, which more than one fellow musician claimed it took him several months to understand.[12] To express desire for something, he said "big eyes for that" (or "no eyes" if he disapproved), an expression still used among jazz musicians; he called police-men "Bing and Bob," an old girlfriend "a wayback," and white jazz musicians "gray boys"; he addressed fellow musicians as "Lady" plus their last name (Lady Basie, Lady Tate, Lady Day) and stuck many of them with permanent nicknames.[13] His vocal inflections were so expressive that a New York clergy-man called it "his personal poetry," noting that "[n]o one . . . but Prez could say [the word] 'mother-fucker' like music, bending the tones until it was a blues."[14] He was that rare jazz musician whose use of hip slang "corre-spond[ed] with the popular magazine and radio concept of a jazz musician's jargon . . . 'dig,' 'cool' and 'hip' are key words with him."[15] When jazz scholar and producer Ross Russell called Lester Young "the greatest bohemian and hipster in the jazz community," he meant Young was an anti-authoritarian, peace-loving, jive-talking nonconformist long before those qualities were ac-ceptable in the average American man (black *or* white).[16]

Two strains of the African American historical experience converged in the 1930s that helped create the conditions for the emergence of cool: first, a new impatience among blacks with the historical need to mask their feelings in front of whites; second, the fight for recognition of individual self-expression. As blacks moved north and west and became part of the national social fabric, a new sense of possibility arose along with economic success and this freedom of movement. The two most important cultural forms of what Cornel West calls "New World African modernity" were "a dynamic language and mobile music"; big-band swing and "hipster jive" became the portable expressions of American society's "perennial outsiders."[17] Black jazz musicians helped stimu-late cultural pride and became national culture heroes. In validating black vernacular culture, they helped "nurture the undercurrent of protest in the black community between the 1930s and 1970s."[18] But until the early 1930s, these changes were bubbling beneath the surface only.

Ironically, the confluence of black masked behavior and African American

JOEL DINERSTEIN

artistic expression first took place when blacks replaced whites as entertainers in the business of blackface minstrelsy in the 1870s. African Americans created a professional class of singers, dancers, musicians, and comedians "under the cork," minstrelsy being one of the only paths to success open to them in the late nineteenth century. Blues composer and businessman W. C. Handy claimed "the minstrel show was one of the greatest outlets for talented musicians and artists."[19] Minstrel performers forever shaped American popular comedy through character sketches, slapstick comedy, rhythmic dance (cakewalk, tap, flash), and syncopated music.[20] Kansas City bandleader and arranger Jesse Stone grew up in his family's minstrel band, and he perceived a musical continuity between rhythm and blues and "the flavor of things I had heard when I was a kid."[21] But there was a serious social cost: white Americans believed African Americans were actually like the stereotype black characters portrayed on the idyllic southern plantation of the minstrel show: the smiling "Sambo," the slow-witted, shuffling southern darky (Jim Crow), the northern urban dandy (Zip Coon), the black buck, Uncle Tom, Mammy, old Uncle and old Auntie.[22] These were, in Kenneth Burke's words, the "frames of acceptance" within which whites saw blacks. The social contradictions created by this overlap of performative skill, rhythmic genius, and smiling pretense still confound race relations. Minstrelsy's most enduring legacy may have been "the grinning black mask . . . embedded in American consciousness," but the power of African American cultural expression was such that a great blackfaced performer inspired perhaps the earliest definition of black cool by a white observer, poet and physician William Carlos Williams.[23]

In an essay entitled "Advent of the Slaves" (1925), Williams perceived a certain "quality" among his working-class African American neighbors in Paterson, New Jersey: "There is a solidity, a racial irreducible minimum, which gives them *poise in a world where they have no authority.*"[24] It's hard to imagine a better first definition of cool. This poise was manifested locally in the homespun existential philosophy of the poet's neighbors, and publicly in the comedian Bert Williams's performance of his signature song "Nobody." Bert Williams was the most famous African American entertainer of the century's first two decades, and the first to draw large white audiences. As half of the famous vaudeville duo Williams and Walker, he helped tone down the wilder minstrel-derived antics into a "cooler [style that] more realistically mirrored actual black behavior."[25] "Nobody" was an ode sung by a downtrodden man in tattered clothes who claimed "nobody did nothin' for him," and Bert Williams made of it a meditation on the basic rights of food, shelter, companionship, and love, managing to "express the existential desire to be treated as a person." The song was a huge hit. William Carlos Williams expressed wonder at Bert

Williams's ability to bring dignity to "saying *nothing*, dancing *nothing*... [*to*] '*NOBODY*,'" and then in the way he amplified his message in dance: "waggin', wavin', weavin', shakin' ... bein' nothin'—with gravity, with tenderness." The poet saw beneath the mask to the "affirmation" of human existence at the heart of all African American rituals of music and dance, the goal of imparting a sense of "somebodiness."[26]

Ralph Ellison maintained that early blackface minstrelsy was a popular masking ritual that allowed for a "play upon possibility"; it allowed white men to act silly and irrational, and to express joy through movement, without sacrificing their public face and role responsibilities.[27] Underneath the burnt cork, in an escape from the work ethic, Christian ideals of saintly behavior, and Republican virtue, white minstrels displayed a more tolerant humanness for their working-class and immigrant audiences. Minstrelsy provided therapeutic relief from a society whose then-heroic model required a combination of rational thinking, virtuous public behavior, and repressed emotion—what Ronald Takaki has termed an emotional "iron cage."[28] Although the content of the shows often depicted African Americans as happy-go-lucky slaves, fit only for the hard work and dependence of plantation life, clearly whites who put on blackface were bestowing a twisted compliment on the African American cultural elements they mocked in the sense that "imitation is the sincerest form of flattery." Eric Lott calls this conflicted admiration of African American music, dance, humor, and movement "love and theft." Ellison stated simply that "in ... America humanity masked its face with blackness."[29]

Why is this phenomenon related to cool? First, because the demise of minstrelsy and the beginnings of jazz overlap in the first three decades of the century; second, because white audiences brought old minstrel-derived "frames of acceptance" to their experience of the new urban music and its musicians.[30] Louis Armstrong did not have to "black up," yet he wore the smiling mask of the happy-go-lucky darky on stage throughout his life. His mainstream success was probably dependent upon allowing whites to hold on to their ideas of white supremacy while enjoying his music as purely entertainment. As Gerald Early puts it: "Did the whites love Armstrong for his undeniably powerful musicality or because he was a one-man revival of minstrelsy without blackface? ... Could his genius be contained only by having it entrapped in a halo of intolerable nostalgia, of degrading sentiment about darkies on the southern campground?"[31]

Jazz musicians helped destroy these plantation-derived images, but it was a slow process because the business of American popular entertainment had for so long been *southern* business.[32] The very names of 1920s jazz bands and venues tell the story of southern stereotypes come north: every city had a

Cotton Club or a Plantation Club, a Kentucky Club or a Club Alabam; bands drew specifically on mythic southern images (McKinney's Cotton Pickers, the Dixie Syncopators, the Chocolate Dandies). Plantation themes also served as the content for much of the world-famous entertainment at Harlem's Cotton Club. "The whole set was like a sleepy-time down South during slavery," band-leader Cab Calloway later reflected, "[and] the idea was to make whites who came feel like they were being catered to and entertained by black slaves."[33] The bands of Duke Ellington and Calloway set national standards of jazz *and* jive, of new African American economic success within plantation-derived frames of acceptance. Most Americans believed in the African American "types" co-invented by northern minstrels and southern slaveowners to emphasize black inferiority, and perpetuated both by pseudo-scientific theories of racial hier-archy and Hollywood images.[34]

Hiding one's feelings under the grinning black mask was a survival skill of great importance to all black males up through World War II; a black man could get lynched for pretending to be on equal terms with a white man under almost any circumstances. Drummer Panama Francis remembered a man who used to come see his band every week in his Florida hometown and every week put a hole in his bass drum. The man always gave him five dollars to fix it, but the drummer hated the ritual humiliation. "I used to get so mad, but I had to smile because back in those days, you had better smile, so I smiled; but I didn't like it too well."[35] At the time, black sociologist Charles S. Johnson called emotional masking "accommodation" to white expectations; in the vernacular it was known as "Tomming."[36]

Even the most successful African American bandleaders needed to create a "readable" public front. Cab Calloway played the joyful, out-of-control, ener-getic wild man: "I was . . . energy personified."[37] Duke Ellington played the debonair, gentlemanly dandy on stage; in a *Downbeat* profile extolling his genius, the editor astutely noted that "he will not even talk to a white woman without his manager . . . know[ing] too well the inflammatory moods of a dominant race."[38] Jimmie Lunceford's crack band of former college students flipped their instruments in the air and tap-danced in sections as part of their act.[39] The classically trained bandleader George Morrison still played the old "darky lament" of "Shine" for white audiences when he sensed any hostility—an act he deemed "black diplomacy."[40] These bandleaders all took pride in what was then called "showmanship"—and they had fun on stage—but these nonmusical gestures enabled white audiences to deemphasize the skill and intelligence of jazz as art. Swing bandleaders were "heads of a business organi-zation and public figures concerned with the artistic, emotional, and symbolic function[s] of a band and its music." These men were grossing as much as

$10,000 a week in the 1930s, yet had to appeal to white expectations, had to provide the old symbolic associations.[41]

"Tomming" was the racial order of the era. African American bandleaders who totally eschewed showmanship for musical artistry in the early 1940s—for example, Teddy Wilson and Benny Carter—never "hit" with the public. They did not provide the wild energy and therapeutic escape from guilt and the work ethic that white audiences looked for in black entertainers. "Benny's band never caught on too well," according to saxophonist Howard Johnson. "At that time they wanted black musicians to 'get hot,' and nearly all bands had gimmicks of one kind or another. They were entertainers more than musicians, and we were not entertainers." Teddy Wilson's bassist Al Hall claimed, "Everybody kept saying we sounded too white." George Simon, the white editor of the jazz magazine *Metronome* noted, " 'Polite' black bands were hard to sell in those days."[42] Certainly many successful white bandleaders had an identifiable gimmick or theme song, but audiences did not demand that they ingratiate themselves as inferiors.

Lester Leaps In

It was left to a swing band's star soloist—a performer who did not have to engage with the audience—to start a quiet, nonviolent revolt against Tomming. Lester Young was born and raised in Mississippi and New Orleans at a time when to speak out against racial injustice would have meant economic death, at the very least. Between the ages of ten and nineteen, he was a key member of his father's family band, the Billy Young Band, a staple attraction on the black vaudeville circuit (the Theater Owners Booking Association, or TOBA) in the 1920s. Young was proud to have grown up in "travelin' carnivals [and] minstrel shows," but he hated the South and spoke with pride about avoiding it as an adult: "Only time I went through the South was with Basie."[43] Young made his only public statement about racism at the age of fifty, two months before his death—in France, significantly—and focused on the mask as the symbol of black male limitation. "They want everybody who is a Negro to be a Uncle Tom or Uncle Remus or Uncle Sam, and I can't make it."[44] Young here clearly identified the frames (or masks) of acceptance by which he was most often seen: as the smiling, servile southern servant who always agreed with white men (Uncle Tom); as the desexualized old man who distributed folk wisdom (Uncle Remus); as the regular-guy soldier who disowned his cultural heritage (Uncle Sam).

Willis Young, Lester's father, was a school principal and trumpeter. He formed a carnival band and left the New Orleans area in the violent summer of 1919, when race riots broke out all over the country and lynchings increased for the first time in several years. The senior Young believed the music business held the greatest opportunities for blacks at the time; Lee Young (Lester's brother) remembers his father saying, "My son will never be a porter; my daughter will never be a maid. You're going to learn to play music."[45] The Billy Young Family Band toured throughout the Midwest, South and Southwest, playing carnivals, state fairs, minstrel shows, and theaters. The band was popular enough—and good enough—to have carried three future jazz giants for short periods: Ben Webster, Cootie Williams, and John Lewis, all of whom attested to Billy Young's ability as a musician and teacher.

With his father as the front man during his formative years, Lester focused on music and became the band's musical star. His siblings and cousins smiled, danced, and did acrobatic flips while playing, but Young grew to hate the "Uncle Tomming that went on," and his idea of jiving was just to play the saxophone upside down. Young was a disciplined musical apprentice; he ran scales, practiced six to seven hours a day along with the records of classical saxophone virtuoso Rudy Wiedoft, and synthesized Louis Armstrong's powerful expressiveness with the cleaner white jazz styles of Bix Beiderbecke, Jimmy Dorsey, and his "idol," Frankie Trumbauer. The senior Young knew Lester was gifted musically and sometimes rode him pretty hard—for example, when he forced him to learn to read music. When his father beat him, Lester ran away for short periods—he never could endure emotional discord—but he always returned, and did not express any resentment toward his father in later life.[46]

A telling example of generational change among African American men is that Lester Young's declaration of independence from his father dovetailed with his rejection of southern "accommodation." In January 1928, the family band got ready for a series of Texas dates and Lester refused to go: "I told him [his father] how it would be down there, and that we could have some fine jobs back through Nebraska, Kansas and Iowa, but he didn't have eyes for that."[47] He said later, "I was just ready to be grown is all." Young stayed behind with two other bandmates in Salina, Kansas, and joined up with the local territory band, Art Bronson's Bostonians, for a year. He barnstormed for the next four years, first touring with New Orleans legend King Oliver for a season, then settling in Minneapolis where the grapevine spread his reputation. In 1930, bassist and bandleader Walter Page offered him a spot in the legendary Oklahoma City Blue Devils, a territory band whose nucleus later formed the foundation of Count Basie's band in Kansas City in 1935.[48] Young freelanced with the Blue Devils, the Bostonians, and several Kansas City bands before joining Basie in 1934. Young was well known enough among black musicians by 1934 that when he temporarily replaced Coleman Hawkins in the Fletcher Henderson band, two leading black newspapers referred to him as "one of the most celebrated tenor sax players in the music world."[49]

Young's refusal to "accommodate" to whites was representative of a new breed of jazz musicians, just as his cool style and nonchalant demeanor were responses to the "hot" jazz of the 1920s. Until bebop, jazz was widely known as "hot music," a reference to the music's faster, syncopated rhythms, its improvisation, and its ability to stir up emotional and physical response. During the "Jazz Age" of the 1920s, the featured soloist was in fact called the "hot man." There weren't yet many musicians who could improvise well, and the hot man's drive and originality propelled the jazz band to moments of peak excitement and emotional release. Clarinetist Mezz Mezzrow claimed musicians first introduced the word "swing" because the "unhip public" had taken over the word "hot" and would stand by the bandstand and yell at musicians, "Come on man, get hot! Get hot!"[50] Young would help change the idea of the hot man to the cool man.

During the swing era, the structure of Tomming began to shift. Increasing visibility of African American cultural heroes (Joe Louis, Jessie Owens, Ethel Waters), the success of big-band swing music, the relative freedom of northern and western cities, the new economic and political power blacks felt after leaving the South—all contributed to what I call the "swing hopes" that social equality was around the corner. Historian Lewis Erenberg calls big-band swing "the music of the black migration," and claims the musicians were walking advertisements for urban (and urbane) northern promise.[51] Cab Calloway's bassist, Milt Hinton, said the bandleader often reminded them that their job was to "uplift" people in the South and "elevate the black customer."[52] Musicians validated African American vernacular culture by displaying its attitudes, heroes, dances, phrases, foods, and sounds in song: Ellington's "Harlem Air Shaft," Calloway's "Pickin' Cabbage" and "Chili Con Conga," Basie's "Stompin' at the Savoy," Lunceford's "What's Your Story, Morning Glory?" Looking back from the 1970s, both Cab Calloway and Earl Hines referred to their big bands as the first "Freedom Riders" who went behind enemy lines to help change racist assumptions and inscribe a new set of urban, sophisticated images on African Americans.[53]

The most colorful memoir of the social and cultural leadership of big-band swing musicians is *The Autobiography of Malcolm X*; nearly a quarter of the book revolves around Malcolm X's transformation from rural hick to hip city slicker between 1937 and 1943. The arenas of change were the great ballrooms where jazz heroes and dynamic dancers, speaking hip slang and sporting flamboyant clothes and hairstyles, took that nightly ride to a less limited future on the brash, loud, chugging, confident, big-band night train. Ralph Ellison reflected back on the sound and sight of Ellington's band in 1930s Oklahoma: "Where in the white community . . . could there have been found . . . examples such as these? Who were so worldly, who so elegant, who so mockingly creative? Who so skilled at their given trade and who treated the social limitations placed in their paths with greater disdain?" Black jazz musicians were the epitome of 1930s urban sophistication.[54]

Lester Young's contribution to these swing hopes was to help develop new self-presentation strategies for the individual musician—without drawing on the minstrel legacy of "the darky entertainer" or fading into the collective sheen and sound of the big bands. At the time, most big band musicians wore tuxedos or uniforms on stage, and exercised their sartorial tastes offstage; Young wanted to stand out onstage. His first stylistic trademark was his completely original way of holding a saxophone, up and out to the side at a 45-degree angle.[55] At the start of a solo, he looked about to "paddle a canoe"; once he really got going, it became "almost horizontal."[56] He held it high in the air and blew musical worlds into the sky: fast, rhythmic flights of musical consciousness. It drove audiences wild.

Ralph Ellison caught the saxophonist's dramatic synthesis of sight and sound in 1929 when Lester Young was an unknown twenty-year-old kid in the great territory band, the Blue Devils:

> [an] intense young musician . . . who, with his heavy white sweater, blue stocking cap and up-and-out-thrust silver saxophone left absolutely no reed player and few young players of any instrument unstirred by the wild, excitingly original flights of his imagination. . . . Lester Young . . . with his battered horn upset the entire Negro section of town . . . [We tried] to absorb and transform the Youngian style.[57]

At twenty, Young stood out with a stocking cap and sweater, perhaps adapted from the popular collegiate look of the 1920s. (All dance bands played colleges regularly.) Fourteen years later, Young was a world-famous hipster, and a white soldier experienced some of the same "upset" seeing him perform with the Al Sears band at a USO show at a Texas air force base: "Lester was working with a fine group of Negro musicians . . . [but] when he stepped out in front with his pork-pie hat and dark glasses (no USO monkey suit for him), he blew the crackers, the hayseeds, and even we studiedly casual easterners right out of our seat."[58]

Young made the saxophone into a new weapon, an instrument of speed and flight; standing still, he sounded like he was taking off. Americans were obsessed with aviation in the 1930s: Charles Lindbergh flew solo across the Atlantic right before the decade started and Superman first appeared in the skies over Metropolis toward the end. Young belongs in their company: he flew across the middle ground, a man riding atop a big-band train. One jazz scholar has suggested that the jazzman's horn had an iconic sexual value as a phallic symbol at a time when any assertion of African American male sexuality was a matter of life or death. Perhaps holding up your "horn"—also known as an "ax"—mediated a joyful celebration of individual black male creative energy: physical, sensual, sexual, intellectual.[59] That Young brought the horn down in front of him during the mid-1940s underscores the sexual symbolism. The Beat novelist Jack Kerouac, ever on the lookout for models of masculinity, judged Young's mood over time from how he held the saxophone, from his glory days "holding his horn high," to "when he let his horn half fall down," through the time "when all our horns came down."[60]

Young's soaring saxophone style was "cool" because he generated excitement without getting excited; he stayed cool. He dazzled listeners' minds with rhythmic surprise and melodic ideas, not technique or flash. As his Basie bandmate Harry Edison described his solos: "He didn't put a whole lot of notes in a solo. He put the right note in the right place at the right time. . . . His timing was perfect."[61] The cool message came through Young's rhythmic control—surefooted solos in which he cut lightly across the shouting brass and crisp rhythms, maintaining his own personal beat even while being shouted at by three trombones and a drummer. The cool message came through Young's fast, smooth, floating tone, a rebellion against the heavy, powerful style of the tenor's primogenitor, Coleman Hawkins.[62] Young's friend and Basie alto saxophonist Earle Warren wondered even in 1980, "A thing I've never been able to figure out . . . is why so many black players followed Lester *and* so many white ones did." Young had synthesized what were then seen as black strengths (speed, rhythmic depth, emotional feeling) with the strengths of white musicians (purity of tone, precise attack, "clean" phrasing).[63]

Young's second contribution to individual self-expression on the bandstand was the strategic use of sunglasses. Young was the first jazz musician to wear sunglasses on stage (indoors and outdoors).[64] Long before Charlie Parker and Miles Davis became famous for turning their backs on the audience, Young recognized the use of shades as a mask to deflect the gaze of others without causing conflict, and to create an air of mystery. In July 1938, he wore something resembling wraparound plastic shades on the stage of the Swing Jamboree at Randall's Island in New York City, a concert featuring twenty-six bands that drew 25,000 young people.[65] He looked calm and aloof amid a noisy, joyous, outdoor throng; the Basie band seemed excited but Young was detached and dispassionate. Sunglasses became a key element of the stylistic rebellion of black jazz musicians in the postwar era, perhaps the primary symbol of the cool mask.

Third, Young introduced the idea of "relaxation" into jazz soloing and combined a revolutionary use of silence, space, and accent into the structure of a solo (his cool, flowing style).[66] For example, on Count Basie's "Doggin' Around" (1939), Young starts his solo by holding one note for the whole bar, slides into a long, fluid line for six bars, then lays out for four beats.[67] Count Basie's rhythm section was a key element in Young's ability to soar. Universally considered "the greatest percussion combination in the history of jazz," the depth of its groove freed the soloists from having to accentuate the beat. The big band was often a fast, loud, chugging, shouting machine, but Basie's band created an easy, relaxed swing beat—call it a *cool groove*—that revolutionized big-band swing.[68] Young sometimes soared over the rhythm, but more often set up exciting cross-rhythms and musical tension with his phrasing; according to Wilfrid Mellers, Basie's band brought creative conflict into swing music.[69] Drummer Jo Jones insisted that just keeping the reins on the band took all his energy: "I didn't need to worry about [competing with drummers] Gene Krupa or Buddy Rich, I was catching hell sitting up there, trying to play in Basie's band."[70] The implicit challenge of playing in Basie's band was to maintain one's individuality in the face of a powerful collective rhythmic drive. Here then is the first contribution of big-band swing to African American cool: a cultural form that publicly displayed the fight for individual self-expression within a larger unit.[71]

Young spent his happiest and most productive years (1934–1940) with the Basie band, first in Kansas City and later in New York. Before living in Kansas City, Young did not curse or drink or smoke pot or speak that "funny language."[72] He seemed an inwardly focused dreamer, a musical artist for whom "the grinning black mask" had no meaning. Kansas City, however, was the Las Vegas of the Midwest in the early 1930s, a wide-open town where the clubs never closed and Prohibition was not recognized as law. Mayor Tom Pendergast's corrupt political machine was run in service to the big farmers, cattle ranchers, and oilmen of the region. "If you want to see some sin, forget about Paris and go to Kansas City," an Omaha journalist wrote at the time.[73] It was a lively city with steady work, a strong African American community, and so much music cooking in the street that "people walked in time" said Jo Jones, . . . "in swing-time." The Basie band worked seven nights a week, from 9 P.M. to 5 A.M., and Young loved every minute of it: "I'd sit up all night and wait to go to work."[74] Then he would make the round of local jam sessions, and jam until noon or one o'clock. Impresario John Hammond wrote of Young in 1936: "He is the kind of guy who just likes to make music, with the result that he is always

to be found jamming in some unlikely joint." Legendary trumpeter Roy Eldridge reflected that Young "was *always* a cat who loved to play."[75]

Kansas City jam sessions resonated with both western frontier aesthetics
and African American humor. Musicians in what were known as "the territory
bands" thought of their artistry "in terms of self-reliant individualism . . .
[in terms of] performances associated with violent contests and gunfights."[76]
Trumpeter Buck Clayton remembers his experience when he first came from
California to join the Basie band in Kansas City, and word got out that he
would be at the Sunset Club that night:

> [A]fter a few minutes about two more trumpet players came in and started
> jamming . . . I figured we'd all have a ball. Then about half an hour later in
> came about three more trumpet players. . . . Then, as the evening went on,
> more and more trumpet players came into blow. To me, it seemed as if they
> were coming from all directions.[77]

When the tenor saxophone's reigning king, Coleman Hawkins, came through
with the Fletcher Henderson band in 1934, he got "hung up" at the Cherry
Blossom all night, battling the tenor saxophonists Ben Webster, Lester Young,
and Herschel Evans—all mostly unknown at the time—in perhaps the most
famous jam session in jazz history. At four in the morning, Ben Webster
begged the pianist Mary Lou Williams to get out of bed: "Get up, pussycat,
we're jammin' and all the pianists are tired out now. Hawkins has got his shirt
off and is still blowing."[78] Following that session, Hawkins ruined his car's
engine making the Henderson band's next gig in St. Louis.

Lee Young, Lester's brother and a fine jazz drummer himself, saw this
gunslinging attitude as the motivation for Lester's jam-session prowling: "Anyone who picked up a saxophone, you know, Lester wanted some of it . . . he
really wanted to see who was the better man. It would be just like a prize fighter
or a wrestler." Young was a jam-session legend, renowned for his competitive
zeal and his fertile imagination. Billie Holiday bragged that Young could blow
fifteen choruses in a row, "each one prettier than the last." "It took him several
choruses to get started," commented the less partisan Kansas City jazz pianist
Mary Lou Williams, "then, brother, what a horn."[79] Perhaps Young spent so
much time in jam sessions because it was the only public forum in American
life where black and white adult men exchanged ideas in a relaxed atmosphere.[80] At jam sessions, African American men could display excellence
unmasked—in their own faces—and receive respect from peers (both black
and white) in a relaxed-but-competitive African American ritual. The Count
Basie Orchestra brought this kind of gunslinging attitude to New York City
when John Hammond brought them east in 1936.[81]

JOEL DINERSTEIN

From the moment the band came to New York until Young was drafted into the army in 1944, he enjoyed the universal admiration of jazz musicians. Although he was erratically employed after quitting the band in 1940, he was a brand-name player. Record reviewers referred to other saxophonists as "Lester Youngish"; arch-rival Coleman Hawkins named him number one among tenor saxophonists for originality and flow of musical ideas; Benny Goodman had Young sit in with his band for a recording session, insulting his regular tenor player.[82] Up-and-coming tenors like Dexter Gordon and the young John Coltrane favored Young's sound over that of Hawkins.[83] Trumpeter Joe Newman saw Young at Alabama State College and was awed by his "flamboyant style . . . I mean it was smooth, it was easy, and it flowed so freely that it excited me."[84]

In 1943, Young starred in the best jazz film of the period, *Jammin' the Blues*. *Life* magazine photographer Gjon Mili directed the Academy Award–nominated ten-minute short, and made jazz icons of Young's porkpie hat, his floating, expressive tone, his relaxed, aloof manner, and his blank, pained facial expression.[85] When Harlem jam-session enthusiast Jack Kerouac wrote that Lester Young had "put it all together for his generation just as Armstrong had for his," he meant Young had combined a new sound and self-presentation style to produce one of the nation's greatest artistic voices of the World War II era.

White (Anglo) Cool and Black (West African) Cool

In Anglo-American culture, the adjective "cool" reflects the ability to repress one's emotions to think more clearly and to effect a more "objective" intellectual analysis. The archetypal cool characters of American popular culture—the private detective of film noir (Bogart), the western gunslinger (John Wayne, Clint Eastwood, the Lone Ranger), the existential motorcycle wanderer—are untamable, self-sufficient male loners who create and live by private codes of ethics; they exist as "free radicals" on the fringes of society and cultivate a calm impudence regarding social norms. In the vernacular they were called "cool characters"—nonconformist, unpredictable, mysterious, adept at violence. There is an unbroken line from the Enlightenment philosophical ideal of living in "the middle state" between heaven and earth to the classic composure of the English gentleman and the stereotypical British reserve of fictional models such as Sherlock Holmes and James Bond.[86] Anglo-American cool characters are existential loners valued for the ability to repress emotion and resist temptation (women, money) in exchange for an unimpeachable reputation for straight talk and the self-satisfaction of seeking the "Truth."

Among many West African peoples—especially the Yoruba, whose cultural legacy is strongest in the Americas—"coolness" has associations with smoothness, balance, silence, and order.[87] Robert Farris Thompson first noticed the importance of "cool" across the African diaspora—in West Africa, the Caribbean, and the United States. Thompson found thirty-five West African languages with conceptions of what Yorubans call "mystic coolness" (or *itutu*), a philosophical concept with associations such as "discretion, healing, rebirth, newness, purity." There are many similarities between West African cool and Anglo-American cool: emotional control, the calm face, a demeanor "composed, collected, unruffled, nonchalant, imperturbable, detached" (especially in time of stress). There is, however, no West African equivalent of the European idea of "icy determination" or "cold efficiency." In addition, the West African "mask of coolness" is admired in the midst of pleasure as well as stress, and has the connotation of healing. In West Africa, a cool action can "cool the heart," or "make a country safe." Coolness is also associated with silence: to "cool one's mouth" (keep a "cool tongue") is to keep strategically silent (i.e., "cool it"). A common meaning of cool is to "restore order."[88]

In public rituals of music and dance, coolness is a *force* of community—of maintaining the social order. A cool West African performer stimulates the participation of others and thus *generates* community. For example, a master drummer directs the generation of continuous, building rhythms to create a solid foundation for the contributions of dancers; he shows coolness by contrasting the propulsive rhythms he creates with steady, calm execution in motion. A dancer might do the reverse, and use accelerated steps to work against slow, steady drumming. Both provide a model of coping with dynamic forces with grace, expressiveness, and composure.[89] As a West African, then, to be cool is to participate actively in an event while maintaining a detached attitude. The symbol of one's coolness is the relaxed, smiling face.

American anthropologist John Miller Chernoff apprenticed for years with a West African master drummer named Ibrahim Abdulai, a Dagomba man who described cool as a kind of spiritual calm displayed in performance: "[The word] 'baalim' is not 'cool' in the way that water or the weather is cool, but rather it means 'slow' or 'gentle.' . . . The one who has learned well, he plays with understanding, and *he has added his sense* and cooled his heart" (emphasis added). The pun of sense/cents is useful. To add "your two cents" is an American capitalist metaphor of participation and it means to give your opinion. In Dagomba musical ritual, you add musical "sense" to the rhythmic discussion. Ibrahim declared that only the old men play coolly; they understand the essence of being "generous" with their rhythms, whereas the young men are too busy "taking big steps and shaking their bodies when they dance"—in other words, *hot*-dogging. He contrasted the diffusion of sound to coarse, thudding, heavy "beating," and pointed out that when a drummer is uncool, he is relieved from his job: "Sometimes when we are playing hard and then come to make everything cool, and the one who knows only force is beating, we just hold his hand and collect his stick so that he won't play again."[90]

Coolness is thus an aesthetic attitude *of participation* effected through an individual's ability to contribute his or her own rhythms to a larger communal event. At a West African musical event, everyone is expected to lend energy—and their individual styles—to the larger "beat." West African cool is less about striving for the middle state than about partaking of both extremes—the "sweet" and the "pain"—in public ritual without losing control. Cool balances the duality of hot and cold, of propulsive rhythms and smooth execution, of call and response. Just as colors opposite each other on the color wheel (say, blue and orange) bring out the most intense dynamics in each other, to "cool one's head" is first to heat it up—as when eating hot, spicy foods in the summer—so as to detoxify the built-up stress. Coolness concerns balancing opposites, *with* style and *without* being average or conformist.

For a West African dancer, the analogy to cool, gentle drumming is the ability to maintain "facial serenity." A dancer often keeps time to three or more rhythms, using different parts of the body to dialogue with different rhythms. When a dancer smiles through this hard work, she celebrates the rhythms and her own vitality by implying that these graceful motions, this dialogue with the drums, is effortless, easy, no sweat, a piece of cake. The "mask of coolness" shows serenity of mind *and* mastery of the body: the cool performer thus shares with the community the joy of one's body, the pleasure one gets in contributing beauty and greace to an event, the skill in producing a distinctive rhythm that links up with other rhythms.[91] The objective is to display a relaxed sense of control, to turn difficult physical acts into smooth, fluid, easy motion. This idea of "relaxation" does not exist in the Anglo-American "cool" model.

The salient difference between West African and Anglo-American ideas of cool rests in the relationship of individual action to the community. Anglo-American cool figures "save" the community from external threats (criminals, governmental corruption, social stratification) but do not participate in the community; West African–derived cool performers generate community by drawing the crowd into the performance and challenging others to equal their performance. The goal of a drummer's or dancer's maintenance of rhythms is to add depth and texture to the event—an event maintained collectively through the "beat." The display of physical mastery—of being "cool in motion"—calls forth competitors to share the honor and glory of recognized excellence.

Perhaps American jam sessions were the kind of public ritual in which West African coolness was admired and called forth. No one was paid to play and yet everyone was expected to contribute, often until they wore themselves out. In other words, this *African American* musical event provided an opportunity to express "excellence" of personal character in relation to other participants. As Kansas City pianist Mary Lou Williams explained about jam sessions, "My whole thing is to needle the man [musician] to play their best for anybody who is soloing because if he plays a good solo then I have inspiration to play."[92] This kind of competition was as common among African American dancers as among musicians.

The legacy of West African coolness to African American cool centers on the transition from community ritual performance to American popular entertainment, and it reflects three non-European strategies. First, playing "hot" or "cool" is a West African idea, as Thompson notes. "It is cool to sweeten hurt with song and motion; it is hot to concentrate on the pain." Second, in the dialogue between the drummers and dancers, the boundary between performer and audience dissolves. Third, "relaxed, effortless grace" in a musical or dance performance is a valued achievement.

Jazz musicians seemingly had no direct access to the hot and cool modes of West African performance beyond an untraceable continuity in Mississippi Delta and New Orleans culture; for example, there is no indication that Lester Young thought of his style as cool playing in an African mode. Yet this quality still exists today within traditional jazz values. In the recent book *What Jazz Is*, a young jazz musician emphasizes the importance of striving for "relaxed intensity," explaining that when he would coast, his teacher would drive him harder, yet when he became too "hot," he was told he was "too intense."[93]

The contrast between propulsive rhythms and gentle execution is the essence of Lester Young's cool musical revolution in the big-band era. Pianist Oscar Peterson claimed Young could "cool" any song and any rhythm section. "Lester . . . had this remarkable ability to transmit beauty from within himself to the rhythm section . . . [He would] play some lines that were so relaxed that, even at a swift tempo, the rhythm section would relax." Two cardinal qualities of all African music are "propulsive rhythms" and the "clash of rhythms."[94] Unlike swing tempo, which was called the "push-beat," or playing "on top of the beat" (one dancer called it the "kicking-your-ass" beat), the Basie band played slightly behind the beat.[95] Young was the best solo exemplar of this style. Using long, flowing phrases punctuated by held notes and short honks, Young took his relaxed time during his solos as if to wait and see where the band was headed, setting off the collective rhythmic drive by coming up behind its power. Many scholars have pointed out that his solos set up cross-rhythms within the call-and-response of the big band sections. But while adding his "sense" to the big-band message, Young always kept in mind a Romantic-derived artistic concept of self-expression: "musicians wishing to say something really vital must learn to express their feelings with a minimum of outside influence."[96] Jazz composer Johnny Carisi described how a typical Young solo provoked participation from other musicians: "Just when you think he had done it [was finished], he would, like, back off a little bit, he would goof and then descend on you again, only more so than before, [and] get everybody crazy, man."[97]

At jam sessions Young may have acted as a western gunslinger, but as a swing band musician, he saw his role as something akin to a West African master drummer.[98] Young claimed he "missed the dancers" of the swing era, and specifically the dialogue of dancers and musicians. "I wish jazz were played more often for dancing," he reflected in 1956. "I have a lot of fun playing for dances because I like to dance, too. The rhythm of the dancers comes back to you when you're playing. When you're playing for dancing, it all adds up to playing the right tempo. After three or four tempos, you find the tempo they like. What they like changes from dance date to dance date."[99] Young and the band found their musical cues by judging the "tempo" of each evening and each audience. At a time when many musicians and critics were trying to make jazz into a concert form, and saw dancing as *the* main symbol of commercialism, Young was proud of his function—his "job"—to increase the level of participation of the dancers.

Young is, of course, not the only carrier of West African cool aesthetics into American popular culture between the wars. For example, there was an enormous reciprocal development between jazz and African American vernacular dance. As early as 1925, "jazz drummers were getting ideas from tap dancers," and many swing-era drummers *were* originally tap dancers.[100] In the 1920s, jazz musicians and chorus-line dancers in floor shows caught one another's rhythms, leading to a more sophisticated and elastic groove. The lindy hoppers at the Savoy Ballroom would stand in front of the band and beat out the rhythm they wanted the band to play, an action common in West Africa (and in rural black America) and uncommon elsewhere in American society.[101] Most pre-bebop jazz musicians were good dancers and proud of it. As the pianist and composer James P. Johnson reflected, "All of us used to be proud of our dancing—Louis Armstrong, for instance, was considered the finest dancer among the musicians. It made for attitude and stance when you walked into a place and it made you strong with the gals."[102]

Another factor in the dissemination of West African cool aesthetics in American society during the swing era was the emergence of the modern trap-set drummer. Drummer-leaders such as Gene Krupa, Chick Webb, Jo Jones, and Buddy Rich came to have responsibilities more akin to the master drummers of West Africa than to the classical percussionist. In the 1920s, the drummer was thought of as a "time-keeper," not even a musician; in classical music, only the conductor controls the performance.[103] In a big band, jazz musicians needed a more solid rhythmic foundation—a clearer set of cues—both to ground the more complex sound and to support their solos. In a sense, the role of the dancers in a West African ritual had been replaced by the interaction between the rhythm section and the melody instruments. As the pioneering black folklorist Willis Lawrence James wrote in 1945, "The rhythmic feeling of the players, which would otherwise find expression in the dance, is expressed through the instruments."[104]

As the classical composer Igor Stravinsky observed about jazz, "the percussion and bass . . . function as a central-heating system. They must keep the temperature 'cool,' [or] not cool."[105] Since the drummer commands the most potentially dynamic sonic forces, it becomes his job to manage the band's dynamics. Duke Ellington's drummer, Sonny Greer, explained how this worked in a live performance: "A guy, naturally, playing a solo, he gets over-energetic and he has a tendency to turn loose. You've got to hold it. Right away he wants to take it up to the sky. But no, we have to hold him down."[106] Legendary drummer Chick Webb called swing tempo "the push beat," because he "pushed" each individual soloist according to his needs: held him down or kicked him into gear. Count Basie said plainly: "The drummer is the boss of the band, not the bandleader. If the drummer's not right, nothing's happening."[107]

Jazz drumming has roots in military drumming, brass bands, minstrel bands, circus bands, and the pit-drumming for silent movies. But the role of the jazz drummer came of age in the swing era and the primary influences on the music were "African percussive techniques."[108] Significantly, the now-standard trap set emerged between the world wars: the bass-drum pedal, the hi-hat, and brushes were invented; Chinese cymbals and the African-derived tom-toms were added. The modern drummer arrived at the head of a drum battery that combined the functions of four African drummers into one percussion point man.[109]

That the term "cool" arose in this period seems like either a remarkable historical accident, a semantic mystery, or an indication that African-American oral tradition carries more Africanisms than has been suspected. Yet as important as was Young's adaptation of West African cool into African American sound and style, his adaptation of the Anglo-American pose of repressing emotion was an even more important symbol of the post-war cool of African American males.

JOEL DINERSTEIN

Being cool (that is, toward white people) reflected the disappointment of African Americans in the progress toward social equality during World War II. Cool was "an attitude that really existed," according to Amiri Baraka, who defines it this way: "To be cool was . . . to be calm, even unimpressed, by what horror the world might daily propose . . . [such as] the deadlily predictable mind of white America."[110] In the early 1940s, examples abounded. Labor leader A. Philip Randolph had to threaten a march on Washington before President Franklin Roosevelt would open up federal defense jobs to African Americans by executive order in 1941. Race riots broke out in several major cities in the summer of 1943 as whites rejected the presence of African Americans in their neighborhoods and in the workplace. The internment of Japanese Americans was a scary, foreboding precedent of racial judgment and disfranchisement. Harlem's famous Savoy Ballroom—a national symbol of social equality—was temporarily padlocked for the summer of 1943 on the patently false charge that black hostesses were selling sex to white servicemen. Black soldiers endured virulent racism from their own (white American) officers, served in separate units and were generally assigned as mess attendants.[111]

African Americans recognized the irony of fighting in Jim Crow regiments against an enemy, Nazi Germany, that believed in white supremacy when they faced their own version of race war at home. As a young black college graduate put it in a 1943 Chester Himes novel, "As long as the Army is Jim Crowed, a Negro who fights in it is fighting against himself."[112] The editors of the influential black weekly, *The Pittsburgh Courier*, called for a two-front patriotism known as the "Double-V campaign": victory against fascism abroad and racism at home.[113] It was necessary to hide one's feelings behind "a bullet-proof vest known as cool," Ralph Ellison reflected, which was less a matter of Hemingway's heroic "grace under pressure . . . than of good common sense."[114]

Lester Young suffered in a personal microcosm of America's domestic race war. Drafted in September of 1944 by an undercover agent who followed the Basie band in a zoot suit, he was denied a musical assignment at a base band by a middle-class African American bandleader who thought he lacked proper musical education.[115] His inability to submit to discipline drew the attention and hostility of his commanding officer, who soon found marijuana and barbiturates in his trunk. Young was court-martialed in a Kafkaesque trial in which he calmly admitted his long-term drug use and proudly claimed he had never harmed a man; he was sentenced to nearly a year in solitary at Fort Gordon, Georgia, where he was often beaten. He occasionally got a break from the solitude because the members of the all-white big band at that base wanted

Young to practice with them. Every day, a white trumpeter would pick him up from the African American side of the camp, and both had to play-act their southern caste-roles. The trumpeter would say, "Come on, nigger," and Young would answer "Yessir, boss." Young rarely discussed his army experience. He wrote one song to commemorate it ("D.B. Blues" or "Detention Barracks Blues") and in a 1948 interview said simply: "[It was a] nightmare, man, one mad nightmare. They sent me down South, Georgia. That was enough to make me blow my top. It was a drag."[116]

When Young returned to playing in 1945, many writers and musicians commented on his blank face, his weary stride, and the lack of joy in his playing. Young "numbed his feelings . . . with much alcohol and some marijuana and hid behind a disguise—his long . . . face, expressionless as a mummy's—that he seldom removed even among the few people he trusted."[117] Many writers and musicians of the time pinpointed the musical end of Young's legendary career as his induction into the army, and discussed his post-war life as a version of the tragic artist myth.[118] This myth of Young's dissipation has been overstated, as many recordings of 1946–47 show, but he was a less consistent player after the war, and his playing often lacked the old *joie de vivre*.[119]

Still, young jazz musicians—both black and white—consistently called Young "a beautiful man," and commented on his good humor, his gentle humanness, his "balanced mind."[120] Young's silence helped him keep his sanity; more than a few young musicians declared him to be the sanest, most human man in their experience. Many white writers observed that Young avoided the company of whites, and wondered aloud why he didn't play the way he used to.[121] Young always told them, in effect, "that was then, this is now"; it was not his job to be who he was in 1939, but rather to ask, "what are you going to play today?" Though Young treated white jazz musicians warmly, he did keep most other whites at arm's length and at a masked remove. By keeping a blank face and rejecting a "get-along" attitude, Young refused to play up to white expectations in public encounters. Young's solitary resistance reflected a larger movement among African American writers and musicians to reject the old racial order of accommodation and Tomming.

Between 1938 and 1952, four major African American male writers and musicians used their art to rebel against accommodation by symbolically executing the figure of Uncle Tom. In Richard Wright's first collection of short stories, *Uncle Tom's Children* (1938), every male protagonist (literally, every son of Uncle Tom) either shoots a white man or refuses the orders of a white man. In 1941, Duke Ellington and a team of Hollywood writers put together a theatrical revue called "Jump for Joy," whose objective was to "take Uncle Tom out of the theatre [and] eliminate the stereotyped image that had been exploited by Hollywood and Broadway."[122] In Chester Himes's 1943 story, "Heaven Has Changed," a soldier fighting overseas in World War II dreams he is back in a southern cotton field, where he stumbles upon a funeral procession of old sharecroppers who tell him simply, "Ol' Uncle Tom is dead." And the first spoken lines in Ralph Ellison's *Invisible Man* (1952) comprise a deathbed confession by the protagonist's grandfather, who explains that Tomming was actually a sophisticated form of rebellion. "Our [African American] life is a war," he exclaims, and implores his grandson to keep up the grinning and shuffling: "overcome 'em with yeses, undermine 'em with grins, agree 'em to death and destruction, let 'em swoller you till they vomit or bust wide open." Ellison later wrote that this scene was "a rejection of *a current code . . .* a denial become metaphysical."[123]

The nameless, faceless central character of *Invisible Man* symbolizes the larger black migration of the time—the South come north—and Ellison evoked the tense temporary balance between swing hopes of equality and the survival skill needed to act inferior before whites. Invisible Man comes up north with the hope that social equality is within reach, and finally rejects all the limited, preconceived conceptions of African American possibility. He finds that all black men in the novel wear masks in front of whites with authority; Invisible Man watches with disgust as even the president of his black college "compose[s] his face into a bland mask" before meeting with the school's white trustee.

Like Lester Young, Invisible Man was the symbol of a generation that refused to live by accommodation. Yet the novel ends with him living underground; without the old plantation stereotypes, there is no new "face" for him to wear.[124] Invisible Man has but one clue as to the new "mask" of self-preservation: before he goes underground, he observes a new quiet style among young black men on the street—the serious, introspective silent mask Young helped provide.

It was as though I'd never seen their like before: Walking slowly, their shoulders swaying, their legs swinging from their hips in trousers that ballooned upward from cuffs fitting snug about their ankles; their coats long and hip-tight. . . . These fellows whose bodies seemed—what had one of my teachers said to me?—'You're like one of these African sculptures'. . . .

They seemed to move like dancers in some kind of funeral ceremony, swaying, going forward, *their black faces secret . . .* the heavy heel-plated shoes making a rhythmical tapping as they moved . . . they were men outside of historical time. . . . *Men of transition whose faces were immobile.*[125]

They were new to Harlem, these cool boys in their zoot suits, long coats, quiet, blank faces, rhythmic strides, "speak[ing] a jived-up transitional language full of country glamour." Nelson George believes this new style was a direct consequence of the black migration as "many Southern boys now wise to the concrete jungle started to move with a fluid, no-sweat attitude everybody called 'cool' . . . [C]ool was clearly an African-urban thing."[126] The new response to the white gaze of superiority was to drop the grinning black mask—the symbol that everything was all right—and cool the face. In a novel based on the rejection of masks, the cool mask provides the only new strategy of self-preservation.

Just as black male writers killed off Uncle Tom, bebop musicians such as trumpeter Dizzy Gillespie targeted Louis Armstrong's "plantation image" for execution. Gillespie honored Armstrong's trumpet playing but never his stage persona: "Handkerchief over his head, grinning in the face of white racism, I never hesitated to say I didn't like it." Gillespie, who admitted the need for a new public style, affected a pose of nonchalance. His hip, ironic style became the prototype of beatnik chic: beret, black-rimmed glasses, goatee, hip slang.[127] Both Miles Davis and Charlie Parker became legends for literally turning their backs on audiences,[128] and other bebop musicians kept a cool silence on stage as befits classical musicians (artists) while playing the "willfully harsh, anti-assimilationist sound of be-bop."[129] By refusing the role of "entertainer," bebop musicians displayed a *cool remove* from mainstream American assumptions, rebelling simultaneously against both masked modes of behavior and the society's disrespect of jazz. According to Orrin Keepnews, a white jazz producer of the time, the bebop rebellion was "brought to the surface by the ferment of the war years . . . [and] reflected a protest against the position of the Negro [and] against the position of the Negro entertainer."[130]

Lester Young was an elder statesman at the famous jam sessions at Minton's and Monroe's Uptown House where bebop was created, and was a familiar musical presence to all the bebop pioneers (Gillespie, Parker, Kenny Clarke, Thelonious Monk). In his 1979 autobiography, when Dizzy Gillespie calls the roll of musicians he has outlived and wants to pay tribute to, the only pre-bebop (and non-bebop) musician he names is Lester Young.[131]

Lester Young was the musical and stylistic bridge between Louis Armstrong's sambo act and Charlie Parker's audience-defying artistry. Parker's musical mentor was alto saxophonist Buster Smith, but he grew up watching and worshiping Young from the wings of the Reno Club in Kansas City, and often said he "attended Lester Young University." Parker took Young's first records with him on a six-month gig in the Ozark Mountains, and memorized each solo note for note. Young once told him the challenge of music was to use your whole body to create a personal sound, "to shape the air."[132] "I was crazy about Lester," Parker once claimed. "He played so clean and beautiful. But . . . our ideas ran on differently."[133] A 1943 photograph of Earl Hines's big band provides iconographic evidence of Parker's adaptation of Young's nonconformist stage stance: he sits at the end of the front row, sunglasses on, legs splayed, seemingly detached, as if leaning away from the saxophone section.[134] It is Parker—more than any other bebop musician—who used Young's hip slang to avoid conversation with those fans and writers who idolized him, turning core hipster terms like "cool," "heavy," "dig," "solid," and "crazy" into one-word ideograms.[135] Amiri Baraka celebrated Young's language play in "Pres Spoke in a Language":

> in the teeming whole of us he lived
> tooting on his sideways horn
> translating frankie trumbauer into
> Bird's feathers
> Tranes sinewy tracks
> the slickster walking through the crowd
> surviving on a terrifying wit
> its the jungle the jungle the jungle
> we living in[136]

Bebop musicians were largely responsible for disseminating the word and concept of "cool," but they came to it through Lester Young.

Young's most influential heir was Miles Davis. "Man, playing with Prez was something," Davis wrote in his autobiography. "I learned a lot from the way he played the saxophone . . . [and] I tried to transpose some of his saxophone licks over to my trumpet." Davis was influenced by Young's "real, fast, hip, slick, Oklahoma style" and his combination of rhythmic flexibility with a "cool sonority." Davis liked the way Young "flood[ed] the tone," and the way he approached each and every note, rather than running up and down scales. Pianist Sadik Hakim, who often toured with Young in the mid-1940s, said that Davis always came to see the band when it came through his hometown of St. Louis. "He'd sit in and he really dug Prez at the time and . . . much of his style, if you listen to him closely, was from Prez. He took many of the things Prez did and transferred them to his style, which we know as the cool style."[137] Davis's first session as leader of the Charlie Parker Quintet in May 1947 rebelled against bebop's virtuosity, and was instead smooth, fluid, relaxed, and laid-back. As one biographer noted, "the liquid spirit of Lester Young hangs over the music."[138]

Davis's self-presentation featured a fierce reserve that said, "You don't wanna know—or ask." His music, like Young's, was accessible and admired by white fans, musicians, and writers; yet Davis symbolized the cool, aloof, sometimes hostile African American jazz musician of the 1950s. He turned his back on audiences, and often walked off stage to smoke a cigarette while the band continued. Davis's well-dressed stage presence, his disregard for both artistic and social convention, his mix of personal mystery and artistic mastery, his tough, don't-fuck-with-me stance kept white jazz fans at a safe distance and suggested a churning inner complexity. Nightclub owner Max Gordon once asked why Davis didn't announce his songs or talk with the audience: "I'm a musician, I ain't no comedian," Miles answered. "The white man always wants you to smile, always wants the black man to bow. I don't smile and I don't bow. OK? I'm here to play music. I'm a musician." Lester Young's strategic withdrawal set the stage for musicians like Miles Davis and Charles Mingus to give voice to their anger; although a few perceptive writers saw the hurt underneath the swagger, clearly Uncle Toms were no longer welcome on the jazz scene.[139]

At its most functional, "to keep your cool" has always meant not to "blow your top," phrases that suggest the potential for violence. For Young to have spoken out about racism as directly as Miles Davis (who grew up the son of a middle-class dentist in St. Louis) would have been suicide in the deep south of the nineteen-teens. Jazz has in fact always been chock-full of language that sublimated violence into musical combat: the horn was an "ax" (long before guitars were); musicians "cut" and "carved" each other at "cutting contests" and "carving sessions"; white people were called "ofays" (pig latin for "foe"). As Duke Ellington once noted, "[m]usic has always had to say what we couldn't otherwise say." Young instead poured his complex ideas into long, flowing, well-structured solos, "loose in space, transform[ing] his life every night into what it ought to be." He imagined a better world and put it in his sound, a dreamy romanticism with enough rhythmic power and blues feeling to generate a "special intensity . . . with cool understatement."[140]

Like many jazz musicians, Young believed his "sound," not the notes or songs he played, told the world who he was. Your "sound" was you, it was your literal voice—and the maintenance of that sound was effected at considerable artistic and emotional effort. Young had something of an identity crisis when many musicians adapted his melodic ideas and cool, fragile tone (including the entire "four brothers" saxophone section of the Woody Herman band in the late 1940s). He often wondered aloud, "What am I to play? Should I copy them?" Tenor saxophonist Stan Getz—then one of the best and most successful jazz musicians in the country—often came up to Young's hotel room and asked him how he created certain sounds on his old records. Young enjoyed the attention but was saddened by it. "The trouble with most musicians today is that they are copycats," he said in 1948.[141]

JOEL DINERSTEIN

The "love and theft" of Young's sound was one factor in his physical deterioration through alcoholism; others included a perceived lack of recognition and simply the nomadic musician's life. Young drank up to two quarts of gin a day on and off from the late 1940s until his death in 1959, and often forgot to eat. He was seen by white writers as "slow and unsteady of movement, detached from reality [and] sealed off in a private world," and framed as a victim of a racist society. Although he married a second time in 1946 and enjoyed short periods of domestic stability in the early 1950s with his wife Mary, he was not a successful (or attentive) family man. After long stretches on the road, Young stayed in small hotels in midtown Manhattan, where he was often found by friends looking out the window, listening to his favorite "pretty music": Frank Sinatra, Doris Day, Jo Stafford. Former jazz critic and producer Nat Hentoff reflected that he had "never seen anyone who was more alone wherever he was."[142]

But the younger musicians (black and white) who played with Young in the 1950s saw a different "Pres," one they revered as a mentor, a poet, a spiritual figure, and something of a philosopher, especially on the fate and destiny of African-Americans. "The . . . principles he taught me are: the philosophy of the spirituals, the musician as a philosopher and a scientist, that we [African-Americans] have made a major contribution to this country and [that] we are Americans," drummer Willie Jones typically reported of Young; "Prez opened my eyes." Such statements suggest the effort (and success) with which Young insulated himself from white people after his army experience. Ex-Basie band drummer Jo Jones declared in 1973 that for all his contacts with black civil rights and political leaders, "there has never been nobody from Marcus Garvey up, that ever loved the black man like Lester Young, nobody!"[143]

As jazz musician and scholar Ben Sidran wrote in 1969, cool was "actionality turned inward"; Young wasn't simply the bruised romantic victim of a racist society but had a rich underground life in which he fought battles by other means. As Young said in his last interview before his death: "[I]t's the same way all over, you dig? It's fight for your life, that's all. Until death do we part." Cool is, in one sense, composed violence.[144]

If Lester Young was not the actual model for the ending of *Invisible Man*, he was certainly a real-life counterpart of Ellison's character. Young was an original kind of American rebel who, despite his gentleness, remained a walking indictment of the society that denied the recognition of his accomplishments. A famous 1947 study of American hostility toward jazz concluded that the reaction to a new cultural form depends upon the "prestige of the donors," and that anti-jazz sentiments were based on the low status of African Americans. "The jazz musician is an 'invisible man,'" the sociologist Charles Nanry wrote, "contributing mightily to American cultural life yet usually rewarded with facelessness and anonymity."[145] The jazz world alone recognized Young's accomplishments, and a year before his death, he moved into the Alvin Hotel on Fifty-second Street, "to look down on Broadway and look at Birdland [the jazz club]," according to drummer Willie Jones. Sick with alcoholism and malnutrition, Young was assisted in the move by Miles Davis, Max Roach, Sonny Rollins, and Jo Jones. A major musical innovator of the cultural form by which Americans signified "freedom" during World War II, the slow-walking, pot-smoking, monkishly dressed, gentle alcoholic Lester Young wore a silent face and asked for no attention. He simply played his sadness every night, just as Billie Holiday sang in her cracked voice until the very end, and who knows, but at the lower frequencies, he spoke for the dashed swing hopes of social equality?

The Legacy of Black Cool

William Irwin Thompson, an important American historian and philosopher, points to jazz as the catalyst for a major African American cultural shift in the 1940s: "Jazz was . . . essentially the expression of the underdog going through a *cultural transformation* in which the 'hot' agricultural slave became the 'cool' urban artist."[146] In the post-war period, the musical mode of cool came to mean "relaxed, cerebral, sophisticated'—that is, emotional power and intensity restrained in favor of musical complexity. Young created this musical approach, and brought a lyrical, bluesily romantic, introspective approach to jazz that Miles Davis and Charlie Parker adapted and took in different directions.[147] The word and concept of cool disseminated into American society quickly: it was regularly mocked in the media in the late 1940s; by the early 1950s, "playing it cool" was a common "hip phrase" and a staple of sociological literature; in 1957, the song "Cool" was one of the showpieces of the movie and play *West Side Story*.

The "cool mask" was a blank facial wall, suggesting resistance to mainstream social norms and an inner complexity few Americans ever suspected of their black "entertainers." Cool can be seen as a three-front cultural civil war against mainstream society (both white and black): (1) a person wore a cool "front" (or mask) as invisible armor to hold off the prejudice, irrationality, and hostility of the society—"you didn't leave home without it," as one writer recently reflected;[148] (2) "cool" stands as an umbrella term for a set of non-European aesthetic values that provided a base for the display of artistic excellence, ultimately traceable to West African sociocultural functions of music

JOEL DINERSTEIN

and dance; (3) cool heralded the necessary creation of a personal sound and style in a society that rarely saw African Americans as individuals.

The philosophical objective of African American cool was—is—to combine expressive style with public composure. Jazz cool reflected a medium between West African cool and Anglo-American cool: the intelligent expression of one's human experience in the world at a given moment. Listening to the beautifully sad ballads of Lester Young's last years, one hears a record of his daily experience and the emotional costs of his attempt to share them. Albert Murray compared Young's later sound to the "somewhat painful but nonetheless charismatic parade-ground strut of the campaign-weary soldier who had been there one more time and made it back in spite of hell and high water." The cornetist and composer Thad Jones, who roomed with Young on a 1957 tour, said, "You could feel the pain in the man, I could, but he was still one of the most humorous. . . . In the midst of all of the pain of it, he was able to laugh at it." Johnny Otis likewise heard both sadness and affirmation, "a melancholy power and a lament . . . but [also] a joyous celebration of life, the human spirit, and sexuality."[149]

Duke Ellington called jazz "freedom of expression music," and its universal symbol is probably a black man playing a tenor saxophone.[150] One jazz scholar terms this image "the first truly nonmechanical metaphor for the twentieth century."[151] It is certainly one of the first global icons of what Kenneth Burke once termed "man-as-communicant": a human being communicating his or her emotional experience *in the moment* without losing control.[152] It is an image that owes as much to Lester Young's life and art as to anyone.

I am suggesting that "cool"—or the birth of cool, anyway—was a synthesis of West African aesthetic attitudes and Anglo-American ideas of self-mastery, braided and historically embedded in the African American struggle for social equality in the United States. In valuing musical communication over technical skill, Lester Young expressed his "somebodiness" without blowing his public cool. In the process Young helped dignify a stance and a pose—a cooled face—that his jazz heirs have used to signify spiritual self-mastery and to resist American self-congratulation. The cool mask was a public face that displaced the smiling accommodation of Tomming, and displayed instead *"poise in a world where one had no authority."*

NOTES

1. Richard Williams, "The Conception of the Cool," in *The Miles Davis Companion*, ed. Gary Carner (New York: Schirmer, 1996), 93–97; Bill Kirchner, "Miles Davis and the Birth of the Cool: A Question of Influence," in *A Miles Davis Reader*, ed. Kirchner (Washington, D.C.: Smithsonian Institution Press, 1997), 38–46.

2. For two claims that Young coined the contemporary American usage of the word "cool," see Joachim Berendt, *The New Jazz Book* (New York: Lawrence Hill, 1975), 79, and Leonard Feather, "Pres Digs Every Kind of Music," in *A Lester Young Reader*, ed. Lewis Porter (Washington, D.C.: Smithsonian Institution Press, 1991), 149. For a short Anglo-American etymology of "cool," see J. E. Lighter, "Way Past Cool," *Atlantic Monthly*, December 1994, 148.

3. Ben Sidran, *Black Talk* (New York: Da Capo, 1980 [1969]), 112.

4. Gunther Schuller, *The Swing Era* (New York: Oxford University Press, 1988), 547; Sidran, *Black Talk*, 93.

5. Young was hounded from Fletcher Henderson's band by fellow musicians in 1934 for having too "thin" a tone. The first time Count Basie heard Young, he thought his tone the "weirdest" he had ever heard, and "wasn't even sure he liked it." Bassist Walter Page heard the speed first: "Who's that fast saxophone?" he asked. Cited in Nathan Pearson, *Goin' to Kansas City* (Urbana: University of Illinois Press, 1987), 200–204.

6. African Americans often honor an important artistic synthesis with the term "cool." See Donnell Alexander, "Are Black People Cooler Than White People?" *Might*, July-August 1997, 44–53. A short discussion of the Kansas City "workshop" can be found in Albert Murray, *Stomping the Blues* (New York: Da Capo, 1976), 149–78.

7. The varied contemporary meanings of cool can all be found within jazz culture of the late 1940s. See Robert S. Gold, *Jazz Lexicon* (New York: Knopf, 1964), 65–68.

8. Young stated openly at an army court-martial hearing that these substances were necessary for a musician to cope with life on the road. Quoted in Frank Buchmann-Moller, *You Just Fight for Your Life: The Story of Lester Young* (New York: Praeger, 1990), 123–24.

9. Nelson George, *Elevating the Game* (New York: Fireside, 1992), 62; Douglas Henry Daniels, "Goodbye Pork Pie Hat: Lester Young As a Spiritual Figure," *Annual Review of Jazz Studies* (1988): 172.

10. Johnny Otis, *Upside Your Head: Rhythm and Blues from Central Avenue* (Hanover: Wesleyan University Press, 1993), 78.

11. Quoted in Buchmann-Moller, *You Just Fight*, 84. Another typical reflection comes from Texas blues pianist Sammy Price. "I don't ever remember having met a person that was as unique. He was just a cute man . . . sweet, high, nice, polite, kind, but mean as hell [when he wanted to be]." Dan Morganstern interview with Sammy Price, Jazz Oral History Project (New Brunswick, N.J.: Institute of Jazz Studies, Rutgers University, 1980): 57–58 (hereafter, "IJS" will be used to refer to interviews in this collection).

12. Sadik Hakim, "Reflections of an Era: My Experiences with Bird and Prez," unpublished pamphlet, vertical file, IJS, n.d.

13. Douglas Henry Daniels, "Lester Young: Master of Jive," *American Music* 3 (fall 1985), 313–27; Whitney Balliett, *American Musicians: Fifty-six Portraits in Jazz* (New York: Oxford University Press, 1986), 234–40; Berendt, *New Jazz Book*, 76–83.

14. Cited in Lewis Porter, *Lester Young* (Boston: Twayne, 1985), 2.

15. Leonard Feather in Porter, *Lester Young Reader*, 142.

16. Ross Russell, *Jazz Style in Kansas City and the Southwest* (New York: Da Capo, 1997 [1971]), 159.

17. Cornel West, *Keeping Faith* (New York: Routledge, 1994), xii–xiv.

18. John Blassingame and Mary Frances Berry, *Long Memory* (New York: Oxford University Press, 1982), 368. The best analysis of the influence of swing-era musicians on 1930s

African American culture is Ben Sidran's chapter entitled "The Evolution of the Black Underground, 1930–1947," 78–115; see also Lewis Erenberg, "News from the Great Wide World: Duke Ellington, Count Basie and Black Popular Music, 1927–1943," *Prospects* 18 (1993): 483–506, and Gunther Schuller, *The Swing Era*, 1–6.

19. W. C. Handy, *Father of the Blues* (New York: Da Capo, 1969 [1941]), 62, 30–54.

20. Mel Watkins, *On the Real Side* (New York: Touchstone, 1994), 80–133; Thomas L. Riis, *Just before Jazz: Black Musical Theater in New York between 1890–1915* (Washington, D.C.: Smithsonian Institution Press, 1989), 4–7; W. T. Lhamon, *Raising Cain: Blackface Performance from Jim Crow to Hip Hop* (Cambridge: Harvard University Press, 1998).

21. Chris Goddard interview with Jesse Stone, New York, 1981, IJS: II:131.

22. Robert Toll, *Blacking Up: The Minstrel Show in Nineteenth-Century America* (New York: Oxford University Press, 1974), 75–79; Eric Lott, *Love and Theft* (New York: Oxford University Press, 1993), 23, 222.

23. Toll, *Blacking Up*, 274.

24. William Carlos Williams, *In the American Grain* (New York: New Directions, 1956 [1925]), 209 (emphasis added).

25. Watkins, *On the Real Side*, 160.

26. Williams, *American Grain*, 208–11; Eric Ledell Smith, *Bert Williams: A Biography of the Pioneer Black Comedian* (Jefferson, N.C.: McFarland & Co., 1992), 81–82, 228; Ann Charters, *Nobody: The Story of Bert Williams* (New York: MacMillan, 1970), 102, 107. On affirmation, see Murray, *Stomping the Blues*, 21–42, and Ralph Ellison, *Shadow and Act* (New York: Vintage, 1972 [1964]), 189; on "somebodiness," see James Cone, *The Spirituals and the Blues: An Interpretation* (Maryknoll, N.Y.: Orbis Books, 1972), 16.

27. Ralph Ellison, *Going to the Territory* (New York: Vintage, 1986), 163–68, and *Shadow and Act*, 45–59.

28. Ronald Takaki, *Iron Cages* (New York: Oxford University Press, 1991), 1–12. The construction of whiteness as an American ethnic identity led to the projection onto blacks of those traits that fell outside the ideal of Republican virtue (e.g., passion, childish joy, emotional expression, immediate gratification). One source of the nation's complex relationship to black skin and black masks is the Revolutionary period, when proud Englishmen traded in their European identities for as-yet-unknown American ones. "Far from English civilization, they had to remind themselves constantly what it meant to be civilized—Christian, rational, sexually controlled, and white." See also David Roediger, *The Wages of Whiteness* (London: Verso, 1991), 3–15; Edmund Morgan, *American Slavery, American Freedom* (New York: W.W. Norton, 1974), 328–37.

29. Lott, *Love and Theft*, 23–29; Ellison, *Shadow and Act*, 44; see also Lhamon, *Raising Cain*, 7, 139–40.

30. Kenneth Burke's term "frames of acceptance" is useful since it privileges the visual mode (how blacks were seen) over the rhetorical (how blacks were discussed). Kenneth Burke, *Attitudes towards History* (Boston: Beacon Press, 1961 [1937]), 20–22.

31. Gerald Early, *Tuxedo Junction* (New York: Ecco, 1989), 279.

32. Bebop musicians completed the job that swing-era musicians had started. See Eric Lott, "Double-V, Double-Time: Bebop's Politics of Style," in *Jazz among the Discourses*, ed. Krin Gabbard (Durham, N.C.: Duke University Press, 1995), 243–55.

33. Quoted in Tom Scanlan, *The Joy of Jazz: The Swing Era 1935–1947* (Golden, Colo.: Fulcrum Publishing, 1996), 68; see also James Haskins, *The Cotton Club* (New York: Hippo-

crene Publishers, 1977) and Kathy J. Ogren, *The Jazz Revolution* (New York: Oxford University Press, 1989), 76.

34. Early movies fastened on such stereotypes as "[the tom], the coon, the tragic mulatto, the mammy, and the brutal black buck. . . . to entertain by stressing Negro inferiority." Donald Bogle, *Toms, Coons, Mulattoes, Mammies & Bucks* (New York: Continuum, 1994), 3–4.

35. Milt Hinton interview with Panama Francis, New York, 1980, IJS: IV: 7–9.

36. Charles S. Johnson, *Patterns of Negro Segregation* (New York: Harper & Brothers, 1943), 244; see also Dizzy Gillespie with Al Fraser, *To Be or Not . . . to Bop* (New York: Doubleday & Co., 1979), 295–97.

37. Cab Calloway and Bryant Rollins, *Of Minnie the Moocher & Me* (New York: Crowell, 1976), 184.

38. Carl Cons, "A Black Genius in a White Man's World," *Downbeat*, July 1936, 6.

39. Jacqui Malone, *Steppin' on the Blues* (Urbana: University of Illinois Press, 1996), 108.

40. Otis, *Upside Your Head*, 77. A long interview with George Morrison appears in Gunther Schuller's *Early Jazz* (New York: Oxford University Press, 1968), 359–72.

41. Morroe Berger, Edward Berger, and James Patrick, *Benny Carter: A Life in American Music* (Metuchen, N.J.: The Scarecrow Press and the Institute of Jazz Studies, Rutgers University, 1982), 238.

42. Quotes from George T. Simon, *The Big Bands* (New York: Schirmer, 1981), 115–16, 483–84; Berger, Berger, and Patrick, *Benny Carter*, 105–106.

43. See Young's statements about his early life in Allan Morrison, "You Got to Be Original," and Pat Harris, "Pres Talks about Himself," both in Porter, *Lester Young Reader*, 132, 138. At the age of 14, Young was called upon to smuggle a gun to a band member who was being chased by a lynch mob; Buchmann-Moller, *You Just Fight*, 9. See also John McDonough, liner notes, *The Giants of Jazz: Lester Young* (Alexandria, Va.: Time-Life Records, 1980). This three-record boxed set includes a pamphlet featuring McDonough's well-researched oral history of Young's life.

44. Francois Postif, "Interview with Lester Young," in Porter, *Lester Young Reader*, 181.

45. Lee Young quoted in Buchmann-Moller, *You Just Fight*, 12; McDonough, *Giants of Jazz*, 7–8. Many African American swing bandleaders were middle-class college graduates who found conventional career paths closed to them. Hsio Wen Shih, "The Spread of Jazz and the Big Bands," in Nat Hentoff and Albert J. McCarthy, *Jazz* (New York: Da Capo, 1959), 177–79.

46. Buchmann-Moller, *You Just Fight*, 8–9 and 18–20.

47. Pat Harris, "Pres Talks about Himself," 138.

48. Luc Delannoy, *Pres: The Story of Lester Young* (Fayetteville: University of Arkansas Press, 1993), 25–37; Buchmann-Moller, *You Just Fight*, 27–40; Porter, *Lester Young*, 6–9; Russell, *Jazz Style*, 151–52.

49. Both the *Chicago Defender* and the *New York Amsterdam News* reported Young's new assignment in their April 14, 1934 issues. Citations reprinted in Walker C. Allen, *Hendersonia* (Highland Park, N.J., 1973), 294–95.

50. Mezz Mezzrow with Bernard Wolfe, *Really the Blues* (New York: Citadel Press, 1990 [1946]), 140–42; Berger, Berger, and Patrick, *Benny Carter*, 105–106.

51. Erenberg, "News from the Great Wide World," 483–503.

52. Interview with the author, August 19, 1997, Jamaica, New York.

53. Stanley Dance, *The World of Earl Hines* (New York: Da Capo, 1977), 81; David W. Stowe uses the term "soldiers of music" in *Swing Changes: Big-Band Jazz in New Deal America* (New York: Harvard University Press, 1994), 10–13.

54. Malcolm X with Alex Haley, *The Autobiography of Malcolm X* (New York: Grove, 1966), 35–136; Ellison, *Going to the Territory*, 220; Douglas Henry Daniels, "Schooling Malcolm: Malcom Little and Black Culture during the Golden Age of Jazz," *Steppingstones* (winter 1983): 45–60.

55. Russell, *Jazz Style*, 152–53; Buchmann-Moller, *You Just Fight*, 33.

56. Balliett, *American Musicians*, 234–35.

57. Ellison, *Shadow and Act*, 236–37.

58. Buchmann-Moller, *You Just Fight*, 109.

59. Krin Gabbard, "Signifyin(g) the Phallus: Mo' Better Blues and Representations of the Jazz Trumpet," in *Representing Jazz*, ed. Krin Gabbard (Durham, N.C.: Duke University Press, 1995), 104–30.

60. Jack Kerouac, *Visions of Cody* (New York: McGraw-Hill, 1972), 391–96. Kerouac's hero-worship of Lester Young is analyzed in W. T. Lhamon, *Deliberate Speed* (Washington, D.C.: Smithsonian Institution Press, 1991), 166–67, 177–78.

61. Quoted in Buchmann-Moller, *You Just Fight*, 115.

62. For the best short discussion of Young's musical style and achievement, see Schuller, *The Swing Era*, 547–62; for a longer technical analysis of Young's solos, see Porter, *Lester Young*, 38–98, and the essays in Porter, *Lester Young Reader*, 197–305.

63. Earle Warren quoted in McDonough, *Giants of Jazz*, 13; see also the discussion of Young's synthesis in Bennie Green, *The Reluctant Art* (New York: Da Capo, 1962), 91–118.

64. Photos dating back to 1937 show Young wearing sunglasses on stage, predating all other jazz musicians. See Buchmann-Moller, *You Just Fight*, 119, and Delannoy, *Pres*, 105–106.

65. Paramount News, "Jitterbugs Jive at Swingeroo," newsreel, 1938, Ernie Smith Collection 491.230, Smithsonian Institution Archives Center, Washington, D.C. See also "All Day Swing Carnival Draws 25,000," *Metronome*, July 1938, 9.

66. "Lester . . . augured the slow changeover from hot jazz to cool jazz." Leonard Feather in Porter, *Lester Young Reader*, 144–45.

67. This analysis is drawn from Martin Williams in the liner notes of *The Smithsonian Collection of Classic Jazz* (Smithsonian/Columbia Special Products P6 118910973); see also Buchmann-Moller, *You Just Fight*, 43–44, and bassist Gene Ramey's comment in Delannoy, *Pres*, 45.

68. Schuller, *Swing Era*, 222–62; Simon, *Big Bands*, 79–87.

69. Wilfrid Mellers, *Music in a New Found Land* (New York: Oxford University Press, 1987 [1964]), 312–14.

70. Quoted in Stanley Dance, *The World of Count Basie* (New York: Da Capo, 1980), 53–54.

71. The pianist Dave Brubeck thought this relationship of individual to community crucial to jazz, "a fusion of African group consciousness with the Renaissance concept of individualism." Dave Brubeck, "Jazz Perspective" in *Reading Jazz*, ed. David Meltzer (San Francisco: Mercury House, 1993), 206.

72. Eddie Barefield, quoted in McDonough, *Giants of Jazz*, 13.

73. Cited in Frank Driggs, *Black Beauty, White Heat* (New York: Da Capo, 1982), 148; on social aspects of Kansas City, see Russell, *Jazz Style*, 3–24.

74. Young quoted in Porter, *Lester Young Reader*, 138–39.

75. John Hammond, "Kansas City a Hotbed for Fine Swing Musicians," *Downbeat*, September 1936, 1, 9. Roy Eldridge quoted in liner notes, *The Kansas City Six with Lester Young: A Complete Session*, Commodore XFL 15352 (1961 [1944]). For testimonies of Young's improvisatory prowess in jam sessions, see Count Basie with Albert Murray, *Good Morning Blues* (New York: Random House, 1985), 147–48, and Delannoy, *Pres*, 44–47. For the importance of the jam session in Kansas City, see Ellison, *Shadow and Act*, 208–11.

76. David W. Stowe, "Jazz in the West: Cultural Frontier and Region during the Swing Era," *Western Historical Quarterly* 23(1) (February 1992): 53–74. During the 1920s and 1930s, the territory bands provided the most dynamic new musical elements of big-band swing: a more freewheeling sense of improvisation, a focus on "head" arrangements, and a blues-based hard-swinging drive. For a more thorough account of territory bands, see Thomas J. Hennessey, *From Jazz to Swing: African-American Jazz Musicians and Their Music, 1890–1935* (Detroit: Wayne State University Press, 1994), 103–21; Schuller, *Swing Era*, 770–805; Murray, *Stomping*, 166–70.

77. Buck Clayton, *Buck Clayton's Jazz World* (London: Macmillan, 1986), 89–90; Buchmann-Moller, *You Just Fight*, 45–48.

78. This famous jam session is described by various sources in Nat Hentoff and Nat Shapiro, *Hear Me Talkin' To Ya* (New York: Da Capo, 1955), 291–93, and in Buchmann-Moller, *You Just Fight*, 45–48. In a 1939 jam session, Hawkins battled Young in New York. Hawkins felt so sure of victory he walked off the bandstand; Young refused to concede and "walked out right behind him and was playing his horn right behind Hawk as Hawk was going to his car in the street." Bill Kirchner interview with Cozy Cole, April 1980, IJS: 22–24.

79. Lee Young with Patricia Willard, "The Young Family Band," in Porter, *Lester Young Reader*, 20; Billie Holiday with William Dufty, *Lady Sings the Blues* (New York: Doubleday, 1956), 56–57; Mary Lou Williams quoted in Hentoff and Shapiro, *Talkin'*, 309; Buchmann-Moller, *You Just Fight*, 75.

80. The few white musicians and fans who attended Kansas City jam sessions spoke of the communal spirit at the clubs, and an easy acceptance of their presence. See, for example, Milt Hinton interview with Cliff Leeman, n.d., IJS: 30–42.

81. A bartender at Monroe's Uptown House in Harlem remembered, "Lester Young and Ben Webster use to tie up in battle like dogs in the road. They'd fight on those saxophones until they were tired out, then they'd put in long-distance calls to their mothers . . . and tell them about it." Quoted in Ellison, *Shadow and Act*, 210. Kerouac quoted in Lhamon, *Deliberate Speed*, 166–67.

82. Gordon Wright, "DISCussions," *Metronome*, March 1940, 46. Wright notes Young twice in the same review. Of a Ziggy Elman recording, he writes, "[I] wish that Jerry Jerome would be his natural self instead of trying to imitate Lester Young"; of a Harlan Leonard record, "the Lester Youngish tenor and rhythm section aren't too exciting." In a 1941 magazine survey, Hawkins rated Young fourth best of all saxophonists; cited in John Chilton, *The Song of the Hawk: The Life and Recordings of Coleman Hawkins* (Ann Arbor: University of Michigan Press, 1993), 191. For Goodman anecdote, see James Lincoln Collier, *Benny Goodman and the Swing Era* (New York: Oxford University Press, 1989), 203, 223.

83. See Dexter Gordon's comments in Russell, *Jazz Style*, 154. Gordon based his stellar performance as Dale Turner in *'Round Midnight* on his memories of Young's last years.

84. Quoted in Ira Gitler, *Swing to Bop* (New York: Oxford University Press, 1986), 39.

85. For a discussion of the film's reception and its revolutionary presentation of African American musicians on film, see Arthur Knight, "The Sight of Jazz," in Gabbard, *Representing Jazz*, 11–53, and Buchmann-Moller, *You Just Fight*, 113–15.

86. A short discussion of "the middle state" can be found in David Nye, *American Technological Sublime* (Cambridge: MIT Press, 1994), xiii–xiv. As early as 1764, Immanuel Kant described the English as "cool," "steady," "reasonable," and "indifferent" in his essay "On National Characteristics." Duke Ellington praised Londoners as "the most civilized [people] in the world," lauding English tolerance for human imperfection, emphasis on self-discipline, and their remarkable "sense of *balance.*" Considering how important "balance" was to Ellington—"my aim in life is to obtain *balance*," he wrote—this observation constitutes a significant compliment. Duke Ellington, *Music Is My Mistress* (New York: Da Capo, 1973), 139–40, 379.

87. Robert Farris Thompson, "An Aesthetic of the Cool," *African Arts* 7 (1) (Fall 1973): 40–43, 64–67, 89. For analysis of the Yoruba legacy on the Americas, see Robert Farris Thompson, *Flash of the Spirit* (New York: Vintage, 1984), 1–97; Andrew Apter, "Herskovits's Heritage: Rethinking Syncretism in the African Diaspora," *Diaspora* 1 (3) (1991): 235–60.

88. This discussion of West African cool relies on the following sources: Robert Farris Thompson, "An Aesthetic of the Cool: West African Dance," *African Forum* 2(2) (Fall 1966): 85–102 (reprinted in this volume); R. F. Thompson, *Flash of the Spirit*, 9–16; R. F. Thompson, *African Art in Motion* (Los Angeles: University of California Press, 1974), 1–44; John Miller Chernoff, *African Rhythm and African Sensibility* (Chicago: University of Chicago Press, 1979), 30–115; John Collins, *West African Pop Roots* (Philadelphia: Temple University Press, 1992), 1–15. The Collins book contains a useful discussion on how Africans view "hot and cool rhythms."

89. Cultural values are affirmed, shared, and transmitted in African musical functions. John Blacking, *How Musical Is Man?* (Seattle: University of Washington Press, 1973).

90. Chernoff, *African Rhythm*, 105–11; see also Ayo Bankole, Judith Bush, and Sadek H. Samaan, "The Yoruba Master Drummer," *African Arts* 8(2) (Winter 1975): 48–56, 77–78. Master drummers are the conductors of African tribal music: they control the texture of the musical event through the beat, making sure it is deep and steady, but always changing.

91. In West African societies, "couples" do not dance; a dancer needs her whole body to communicate with other dancers and musicians.

92. John S. Wilson interview with Mary Lou Williams, New York, June 1973, IJS: 119.

93. Johnny King, *What Jazz Is* (New York: Walker & Co., 1997), 24–26.

94. Oscar Peterson quoted in Buchmann-Moller, *You Just Fight*, 162. See A. M. Jones, *Studies in African Music* (London: Oxford University Press, 1959), 1–55; John Storm Roberts, *Black Music of Two Worlds* (New York: Praeger, 1972), 1–16.

95. Burt Korall, *Drummin' Men* (New York: Schirmer, 1990), 29; see also Norma Miller with Evette Jensen, *Swingin' at the Savoy: The Memoir of a Jazz Dancer* (Philadelphia: Temple University Press, 1996), 69.

96. Young quoted in Porter, *Lester Young Reader*, 132; Green, *Reluctant Art*, 99–108.

97. Johnny Carisi quoted in Gitler, *Swing to Bop*, 39–40.

98. Douglas Henry Daniels has explored Young's humor, musical approach, philosophy, and spirituality from the vantage point of someone raised in a West-African derived oral tradition. See Daniels, "Goodbye Pork Pie Hat," 161–77.

99. Quoted in Porter, *Lester Young Reader*, 161–62. The idea of finding out what an audience wants—and then giving it to them—I find only in African American musicians.

100. Marshall and Jean Stearns, *Jazz Dance* (New York: Da Capo, 1994 [1968]), 140. Tap-dancing drummers included Jo Jones, Buddy Rich, Cozy Cole, and Louis Bellson. See interview with Cozy Cole, IJS: II:27.

101. Malone, *Steppin'*, 91–110. In the Broadway show *Runnin' Wild* (1923), the chorus boys danced the Charleston to only hand-clapping and foot-stamping, "the way it had been danced for many years in the South." Stearns and Stearns, *Jazz Dance*, 134; see also Norma Miller, *Swingin'*, 102.

102. Tom Davin, "Conversation with James P. Johnson," in *Jazz Panorama*, ed. Martin T. Williams (New York: Crowell-Collier, 1962), 56–57.

103. Korall, *Drummin' Men*, 50–51; Mezzrow, *Really the Blues*, 142–47. Mezz Mezzrow explained clearly how white Chicagoan drummers—Gene Krupa, Davey Tough, Ben Pollack—learned from black drummers that keeping a steady beat involved more than just playing straight time, but was instead "a sequence of different sounds accented at the right intervals."

104. Willis Lawrence James, *Stars in de Elements: A Study of Negro Folk Music* (Durham, N.C.: Duke University Press, 1995 [1945]), 456.

105. Stravinsky quoted in Meltzer, *Reading Jazz*, 252.

106. Stanley Crouch interview with William "Sonny" Greer, New York 1977, IJS: IV: 15–6.

107. Korall, *Drummin' Men*, 29–30; Basie quoted in Stanley Dance, *The World of Count Basie* (New York: Da Capo, 1980), 14.

108. Theodore Dennis Brown, "A History and Analysis of Jazz Drumming to 1942," Ph.D. diss., University of Michigan, 1976: 1–42 (on African influences), 102–33 (on the trap set), 424–48 (on Chick Webb).

109. Cosmo Anthony Barbaro, "A Comparative Study of West African Drum Ensemble and the African-American Drum Set," Ph.D. diss., University of Pittsburgh, 1993: 62. By discussing the emergence of a master drummer in a culture that had none, the existence of a body of joyfully assertive and rhythmically sophisticated dancers, and the difference between English and West African cool aesthetics, I hope to open up a larger discussion of the importance of African aesthetics in both black and American culture.

110. Amiri Baraka (as LeRoi Jones), *Blues People* (New York: William Morrow, 1963), 111–12; Ellison, *Going to the Territory*, 166–67.

111. Manning Marable, *Black American Politics: From the Washington Marches to Jesse Jackson* (London: Verso, 1985), 74–87; Charles S. Johnson, *To Stem This Tide* (Boston: The Pilgrim Press, 1943), 109; Nat Brandt, *Harlem at War* (Syracuse University Press, 1996); Russell Gold, "Guilty of Syncopation, Joy, and Animation: The Closing of Harlem's Savoy Ballroom," *Studies in Dance History* 5(1) (Spring 1994): 50–64.

112. Chester Himes, *If He Hollers Let Him Go* (New York: Thunder's Mouth Press, 1986 [1943]), 121.

113. For the relationship between jazz musicians and the Double-V campaign, see Lott, "Double-V," 245–50.

114. Ellison, *Going to the Territory*, 166–67. "Coolness kept our values warm, and racial hostility stoked our fires of inspiration," 167.

115. Young's army experience is discussed in detail in Buchmann-Moller, *You Just Fight*, 117–30, Delannoy, *Pres*, 134–48, and McDonough, *Giants of Jazz*, 25–27.

116. Quoted in Porter, *Lester Young Reader*, 135.

117. See McDonough, *Giants of Jazz*, 5; Bill Coss, "Lester Young," in Porter, *Lester Young Reader*, 154.

118. The Basie trumpeter Harry Edison said, "The army just took all his spirit"; Buchmann-Moller, *You Just Fight*, 129. Young's close friend Gene Ramey believed he lost some of his technical skill from the beatings he received; see Ramey interview, IJS, V:37–41. In the late 1940s, European writers expressed disbelief that this was the legendary Lester Young; see Delannoy, *Pres*, 140–55, and Ross Russell, *Bird Lives* (London: Quartet, 1972), 327.

119. See Lewis Porter, liner notes, *Sarah Vaughan/Lester Young: One Night Stand*, Blue Note CD, 1997 [1947]; see also Porter, *Lester Young*, 102–103.

120. See Daniels, "Goodbye Pork Pie Hat"; Buchmann-Moller, *You Just Fight*, 174–77 and 181–84; Bobby Scott, "The House in the Heart," in Porter, *Lester Young Reader*, 99–118.

121. Porter, *Lester Young*, 27.

122. Ellington referred to it as a "social significance show," and originally the show was to open with Uncle Tom on his death bed. Ellington, *Music*, 175.

123. Ellison, *Shadow and Act*, 56 (emphasis added); Chester Himes, *If He Hollers Let Him Go* (London: Pluto, 1986 [1945]); Ralph Ellison, *Invisible Man* (New York: Vintage International, 1980 [1952]).

124. See Joel Dinerstein, "The Cool Mask: The Evolution of an African-American Male Survival Strategy, 1934–1945," M.A. thesis, University of Texas, May 1995.

125. Ellison, *Invisible Man*, 439–44 (emphasis added). Invisible Man spots the cool boys at a pivotal moment regarding his faith in racial progress, having just witnessed the arrest and subsequent murder of his friend, Tod Clifton. Clifton had turned and punched a policeman for shoving him, an act designated by Invisible Man as "plung[ing] outside of history." The policeman shoots Clifton dead for stepping out of the racial order.

126. George, *Elevating the Game*, 62.

127. Gillespie, *To Be or Not*, 295–96. Struggling for the right to self-definiton and freedom from both white assumptions and outmoded southern self-defense strategies, bebop musicians rebelled against show business traditions and the clichés of swing. Neil Leonard, *Jazz: Myth and Religion* (New York: Oxford University Press, 1987), 16–18; Berger, Berger, and Patrick, *Benny Carter*, 18.

128. Sidran, *Black Talk*, 112–13; Ellison, *Shadow and Act*, 226–27.

129. Amiri Baraka, cited in Lott, "Double-V," 248.

130. Orrin Keepnews, *The View from Within* (New York: Oxford University Press, 1988), 39.

131. Gillespie, *To Be or Not*, 116–17, 185, 241, 502. Young was briefly the tenor saxophonist in Gillespie's first bebop band (October–December 1943), but his father's death compelled him to travel to California. He was replaced by Don Byas. Buchmann-Moller, *You Just Fight*, 110, 112. See also Dempsey Travis, *An Autobiography of Black Jazz* (Chicago: Urban Research Institute, 1983), 341.

132. Al Young, "We Jazz June/We Die Soon: Jazz Film Thoughts," in *On Music*, eds. Daniel Halpern and Jeanne Wilmot Carter (Hopewell, N.J.: Ecco, 1994), 123; Russell, *Bird Lives*, 68, 89–95.

133. Parker quoted in Hentoff and Shapiro, *Talkin'*, 355; Schuller, *Swing Era*, 794–96.

134. Photo in Russell, *Kansas City Style*, 198–99.

135. Ellison, *Shadow and Act*, 221–32; Sidran, *Black Talk*, 110–12.

136. Amiri Baraka, *Transbluesency: The Selected Poems of Amira Baraka/LeRoi Jones, 1961–1995* (New York: Marsilio, 1995), 171–72.

137. Miles Davis with Quincy Troupe, *Miles: The Autobiography* (New York: Simon and Schuster, 1989), 44–45, 99; Hakim quoted in Jack Chambers, *Milestones I: The Music and Times of Miles Davis to 1960* (University of Toronto Press, 1983), 16; see also Andre Hodeir, *Jazz: Its Evolution and Essence* (New York: Grove Press, 1956), 116–36, especially his definition of the "cool sonority" in jazz.

138. Ian Carr, *Miles Davis: A Critical Biography* (London: Quartet, 1982), 26.

139. Max Gordon, "Miles—A Portrait," in Garner, *Miles Davis Companion*, 93–97; see also Chris Albertson, "The Unmasking of Miles Davis," in *Miles Davis Reader*, 190–97.

140. Evan Hunter, "Streets of Gold" (excerpt) in Meltzer, *Reading Jazz*, 196–97; Russell, *Bird Lives*, 43; Nat Hentoff, *Boston Boy* (New York: Knopf, 1986), 125–26; Murray, *Stomping the Blues*, 89.

141. Tate-Young conversation related in Buchmann-Moller, *You Just Fight*, 210. Bassist Gene Ramey, a longtime close friend of Young, remembers Getz and other white musicians "would come around to his room every night" at the Alvin Hotel, to "sit around and listen to his old records and have him explain to them [how he created certain sounds]." Young would often beg Ramey not to leave: " 'Stay here,' Ramey recalls Young saying, 'maybe we can get these guys to leave.' " See Stanley Dance interview with Gene Ramey, IJS, V:37–41. For an excellent discussion of how Young's ideas were diffused into jazz in the 1950s, see Green, *Reluctant Art*, 113–18; see also Donald L. Maggin, *Stan Getz: A Life in Jazz* (New York: William Morrow, 1996), 38–43.

142. Buchmann-Moller, *You Just Fight*, 137–39, 201–212; Hentoff, 126.

143. Daniels, "Goodbye Pork-Pie Hat"; Willie Jones quoted in Buchmann-Moller, *You Just Fight*, 212; Milt Hilton interview with Jo Jones, January 1973, IJS, 92.

144. Postif, "Interview with Lester Young," in Porter, *Lester Young Reader*, 181; Sidran, *Black Talk*, 111.

145. Morroe Berger, "Jazz: Resistance to the Diffusion of a Culture Pattern," in *American Music*, ed. Charles Nanry (New Brunswick, N.J.: Transaction, 1972), 11–43; Nanry's "invisible man" connection comes from his introduction, 6.

146. William Irwin Thompson, *The American Replacement of Nature* (New York: Doubleday, 1991), 51 (emphasis added).

147. Schuller, *Swing Era*, 547.

148. Thad Mumford, "Where Is the Class of '96," *New York Times*, May 5, 1996, sec. 5, 25.

149. Murray, *Stomping*, 162–63; Thad Jones quoted in Porter, *Lester Young Reader*, 125; Otis, *Upside Your Head*, 78.

150. Ellington, *Music*, 421.

151. John Szwed, "Foreword," in Clyde E. B. Bernhardt, *I Remember: Eighty Years of Black Entertainment, Big Bands, and the Blues* (Philadelphia: University of Pennsylvania Press, 1986), ix.

152. Burke, *Attitudes*, 262.

On the Jazz Musician's Love/Hate Relationship with the Audience

(1998)

BERTRAM D. ASHE

. . . .

An assistant professor of English at the College of the Holy Cross, Bertram D. Ashe discusses how the intersection of an African American cool style with a black vernacular tradition and multi-racial audiences complicates audience-performer relations. In the vernacular tradition, performers play not "to" but "with" an audience, drawing on the call-response patterns that characterize the black aesthetic. Ashe notes that the vernacular tradition is not racial but cultural, and class can be as important a marker as race in determining audience expectations. Differing cultural backgrounds create, in Ashe's words, "competing realities," distinct sets of expectations that can shape a musical performance. Ashe presented this paper at a Cyrus Chestnut Trio concert in Worcester, Massachusetts, January 16, 1998.

One Sunday afternoon when [Charles] Mingus was leading a group at the Village Vanguard, the audience was particularly noisy and inattentive. A couple of tables of patrons right in front of the bandstand seemed completely oblivious to the music. Their animated conversation was distracting to the musicians and made it difficult for the patrons sitting farther back to hear. Indignantly, Mingus hauled his bass up to the microphone and made a few scathing remarks about the noise, but the offending patrons were so wrapped up in their conversation that they heard none of Mingus's diatribe.

"Okay," said Mingus, "We're not going to fight you any more. On this next number, we'll take turns. We'll play four bars, and then you-all *talk* four bars. Okay?"

He stomped off a tune, and after the opening chorus Mingus played a four-bar break and waved the band out. The loud conversation at the front tables continued. The musicians carefully counted out four measures during the hubbub and then the band took the next four, with the solo tenor playing as loudly as possible. Another four for the oblivious talkers, another for the band. As the rest of the audience laughed, Mingus continued grimly with his announced format until the end of the number. The talkers never knew they had been featured, but they joined the applause at the end (Crow 1990, 316–17).

Involuntarily, those "front tables" were participating in what's known as the African American "vernacular tradition." Henry Louis Gates, Jr. defines the "vernacular" as "the church songs, blues, ballads, sermons, and stories . . . that are part of the oral, not primarily the literate (or written down) tradition of black expression" (Gates and McKay 1997, 1). What distinguishes this body of work is its in-group status: "it is not, generally speaking, produced for circulation beyond the black group itself" (ibid. 1). Listen to this description of the vernacular and see if it doesn't sound familiar: "call/response patterns of many kinds; group creation; and a percussive, often dance-beat orientation not only in musical forms but in the rhythm of a tale or rhyme. . . . [I]mprovisation is a highly prized aspect of vernacular performance" (ibid. 4). This thumbnail sketch of the vernacular could serve as a rough description of jazz itself.

The "jazz itself" I'm concerned with here is the interplay between jazz musician and audience. Although the jazz-record-buying consumer is a vital part of the jazz public, I'm specifically concerned with jazz performance here and most interested in jazz-as-vernacular in terms of the way audiences are figured in the vernacular tradition. An examination of three distinctly different readings of the jazz performance of Charlie Parker and his contemporaries reveals competing realities between the expectations of performing jazz musicians and some of their audiences.

What's important to realize is that, in a sense, there *is* no audience as such— at least in the Western conception of the term. When Gates describes "group creation" as an integral part of the vernacular, he's talking about the way an audience's spontaneous reaction to the performer makes the audience itself a part of the performance. The way a congregation or audience "responds" to the "call" of the preacher or performer—in an oral, demonstrative fashion— essentially breaks down the Western barrier between performer and audience, making the church service or the musical performance an inclusive, communal, communicative event.[1]

Perhaps the best examples of the vernacular tradition might be the responses of "Yes, Lord," or "Um-hmm" to the call of the pastor during sermons at certain African American church services. Or the way the audience on, say, "Showtime at the Apollo" appears to be as much a part of the show as whoever's on stage. Or the way some audience members at a jazz or blues club will often laugh out loud with pleasure at recognizing a surprise musical quotation from a standard, or shout phrases like, "Play that horn!" in response to a clever solo. These scenes are examples of the vernacular tradition at work, a survival of the ancient African oral tradition.[2]

What's interesting about jazz, though, is that almost from its inception, it was confronted with a sizable white audience, an audience that didn't grow up immersed in the vernacular tradition. Jazz musicians performed at two types of concerts: those that were in black clubs and those that were not in black clubs. I'm going to call the latter "non-vernacular" events.[3] The reason I don't refer to them as majority white concerts is that the vernacular tradition can be practiced by whites who've been acculturated into the black vernacular tradition, and, certainly, not all blacks have been acculturated into the vernacular tradition. The black vernacular is not a racial so much as a cultural phenomenon.

But the vernacular tradition is a reality, even if it's only a strategy at jazz concerts played to non-vernacular audiences. Branford Marsalis, in this excerpt from an appearance in 1997 on a Boston-area radio show called "The Connection," talks about an ingenious way he incorporated an audience member into his performance at Sculler's, a Boston jazz club, on January 30 of that year:

> In one of the songs last night there was a lady pulling out a mint from her bag. And I said, "You got one for me?"—in the middle of the song. She was taken aback by it because she thought I was teasing her. But what she really didn't understand ([as] she was passing the mints off to her friends) [was that] as the song went along it actually became a part of the song for me. Almost like . . . the paper was crinkling with such consistency . . . like, those cellophane wrappers? like on cough drops? It was with such consistency that it had the effect of a percussionist playing *chimes*—that crinkle, crinkle, crinkle. So when she stopped I actually looked at her and said, you know, "You shouldn't've stopped!"—which confused her even more. It had actually become a part of the song for me. And the fact that it had become a part of the song made me laugh about, like, the great realities of jazz. It was a very funny moment. And I think she may have thought we were laughing *at* her, because she doesn't really understand we were laughing with her, that we were going along with her. ("The Connection" 1997)

An artist who saw himself or herself as separate and distinct—if not elevated—from an audience might have been offended or put off by such seeming rudeness. Marsalis, acting from a vernacular viewpoint, saw her as part of the show. Or as he stressed during the interview, "What makes jazz different from other musics is that it is conceived in the present tense—and everything that occurs in the environment has a direct outcome in the song."

Accordingly, my favorite live jazz recording is Miles Davis's *Live at the Plugged Nickel 1965* boxed set, mostly for the way that a folksy black audience in attendance at the Plugged Nickel in December 1965 becomes a part of the performance in ways that are, by turns, touching, humorous, and exasperating (the vernacular tradition including the risk that any and all of the above are possible). A good example occurs during the second set on the first day of the club date.

We hear Davis begin "When I Fall in Love," and, as usual, he leaves a whole lot of space in his phrasing. An audience member presently fills up that space with a "call" by suggesting some notes that Davis could play once he continues, and, incredibly, Davis's "response" is to actually play the notes the patron suggests—instantly and expertly making him a momentary music director. We hear Davis repeat the man's vocalizations, and then the music continues. But in the audience there is a moment of quiet, a pause during which, I imagine, the startled audience member, after realizing Davis has actually played his suggested phrase, probably makes some sort of self-congratulatory gesture, confirming his contribution; because after the pause you can hear the audience laugh at the gesture and at what has just happened. Now, this is Miles Davis, in 1965: supposedly, he's the "Sorcerer," the scowling, raspy Prince of Darkness, well known for his chilly on-stage demeanor. But here he good-naturedly nods to the "group creation" aspect of the vernacular tradition, easily and effortlessly expanding the stage to include the audience.

As we saw with the opening Mingus example, however, group creation extended to the audience is not always a shared experience. In an exchange later in the same song, Ron Carter's bass solo is, well, "informed" by an overly enthusiastic listener. Traditionally, the bass is a valuable part of the quintet's rhythm section, and also the softest of the five instruments. Playing an acoustic bass solo in a jazz club is risky, since there must be quiet in order to hear the notes. During "When I Fall in Love," Carter gamely attempts to solo as a deep-voiced, possibly inebriated man claps intrusively and speaks loudly to Davis—as if to presume an intimate friendship as he congratulates him on his just-completed solo. The man then rambles on during Carter's solo, briefly discussing, apparently with no one in particular, the bassist Ray Brown's possible retirement before offering the name "Paul Chambers," as if the notes that Carter is playing remind him of another popular bassist of the time. It is a pitiably short solo; Davis's trumpet soon returns, seemingly ending Carter's efforts mid-solo, and the song continues apace.

It is yet another instance of group creation, although it is of the sort that is probably not welcomed by jazz musicians, and the reality of the possibility of this sort of "exchange" adds another layer to the love/hate relationship the jazz musician has with the audience, this episode having taken place fully within the vernacular tradition. Bob Blumenthal of the Boston *Globe*, who wrote the liner notes for Davis's boxed set, uses stronger language than mine in describing the patron: "Carter begins to solo as our ringside nuisance name-drops Ray Brown, Oscar Peterson and Paul Chambers. [Davis] quickly rescues his bassist from further indignity."

So on some fundamental level, the jazz musician's love/hate relationship with the audience isn't only confined to the tension between musicians and non-vernacular audiences. The problem of pleasing a sometimes difficult and demanding vernacular audience is, as we see here, in many ways just as complex as playing to an audience that doesn't possess the African American vernacular legacy. But even with those inherent difficulties, these Miles Davis examples are drawn from a cultural experience that is, to use Frederick Douglass's term, "within the circle" (Douglass 1982, 57). Branford's previous example, moreover, was taken from a contemporary, mixed-race club date, confirming that a jazz musician can take a conscious vernacular approach even in non-vernacular circumstances. Often, however, jazz musicians play to quiet houses for non-vernacular concerts or club dates, concerts where the largest concession to the vernacular tradition is applause after each solo (at some venues a hit-or-miss proposition) and after the song.

So the question is this: what happens when only the onstage half is actively participating in the supposed group creation of what is, in theory, a vernacular event? In a sense, when jazz as vernacular performance is played to a non-vernacular audience, a set of competing realities between musician and audience is likely to result. Ideally, the jazz musician inhabits the vernacular persona of the accessible musical storyteller for an eager, lively, participatory audience. But the American cultural reality that views blacks in a racialist way sometimes interferes with the jazz musician's concept of himself as a vernacular performer. As a result, non-vernacular audiences can create a tension between the black performer's self-conception as "entertainer" versus his or her self-conception as "artist."

Around the time bebop became popular in the 1940s, some black jazz musicians began to de-emphasize some of the vernacular roots of the jazz performance aesthetic and began to pose solely as "artists." Ralph Ellison, in a 1962 article on Charlie Parker called "On Bird, Birdwatching, and Jazz," has this to say about jazz performance during Parker's heyday:

The thrust toward respectability exhibited by the Negro jazzmen of Parker's generation drew much of its immediate fire from their understandable rejection of the traditional entertainer's role—a heritage from the minstrel tradition—exemplified by such an outstanding creative musician as Louis Armstrong. But when they fastened the epithet "Uncle Tom" upon Armstrong's music they confused artistic quality with questions of personal conduct, a confusion which would ultimately reduce their own music to the mere matter of race. By rejecting Armstrong they thought to rid themselves of the entertainer's role. And by way of getting rid of the role, they demanded, in the name of their racial identity, a purity of status which by definition is impossible for the performing artist.

The result was a grim comedy of racial manners, with the musicians employing a calculated surliness and rudeness . . . and the white audiences were shocked at first but learned quickly to accept such treatment as evidence of "artistic" temperament. Then comes a comic reversal. Today the white audience expects the rudeness as part of the entertainment. If it fails to appear, the audience is disappointed. For the jazzmen it has become a proposition of the more you win, the more you lose. (Ellison 1995b, 259–60)

Ellison speaks to the political nature of jazz performance, the jazz musician's urge to define a stage presence while playing *to* (rather than with) a non-vernacular audience. Contrasting with Ellison's account of jazz performance in Parker's day is that of Amiri Baraka, at the time a black nationalist poet and playwright, who described Parker's own performance motive and aesthetic through a character in his 1964 play *Dutchman*:

Charlie Parker? Charlie Parker. All the hip white boys scream for Bird. And Bird saying, "Up your ass, feeble-minded ofay! Up your ass." And they sit there talking about the tortured genius of Charlie Parker. Bird would've played not a note of music if he just walked up to East Sixty-seventh and killed the first ten white people he saw. Not a note! (Baraka 1997, 1897)[4]

The problem here is that Baraka (then LeRoi Jones) has his character see the motive for black cultural expression as beginning and ending with white folk. The black-performer-to-black-audience vernacular performance ideal is, seemingly, thrown out the window in a concession to black rage. You just can't have a valid vernacular performance on the one hand and then on the other say that the *only* reason Parker is playing music is to metaphorically murder white people.

And yet, as Ellison's earlier commentary makes clear, some white jazz listeners of the era expected and enjoyed studied alienation from black jazz musicians (Miles Davis, especially, was legendary for giving audiences what Ellison says they wanted). If nothing else, this stage presence, read by many white patrons as barely controlled hostility, was, for them, a validation of the jazz musician's status as alienated "artists" in the Western tradition. We can see the same sort of identity politics being played out in the nineties, in a far less hostile manner, as audiences revel in the serious, studious demeanor and dapper Armani suits of the current jazz generation. The stage presence and attire of these "young lions" validates them as "artists" the same way studied indifference did a generation ago.

Indeed, as a result of the lack of obvious tension between contemporary jazz musicians and their audiences, it may appear that since the sixties musicians such as Branford Marsalis have negotiated that dangerous American cultural terrain between "entertainer" and "artist" and emerged whole. Marsalis, in the "Connection" interview, talked about how when his group came on the scene they were less "deferential" and "studious" than their peers. They started "telling jokes to each other and laughing" when they came on stage, and then they'd start playing. This approach to the jazz performance aesthetic, as Marsalis says, threw "a wrench in the mortar . . . because the visual idea that a lot of people have about what it is that we do and the actual application were completely different. Some of the . . . reviews early in my career would say that our show was 'silly,' because they couldn't really hear the content of what we were playing so they needed the visual assistance." Ultimately, Marsalis concludes, "I just believed in it enough to continue to do what I was doing and I believed that in the long run a couple of the writers would catch on to what we were doing musically, a couple of the musicians would catch on and then the people would just follow along. And that's pretty much the way it's gone" ("The Connection" 1997).

I certainly believe Marsalis is being sincere here, but as cultural commentary his conclusion is a little too easy, a little too neat. To complicate things a bit, here is what Marsalis said just five years earlier, in 1992, from his video called "The Music Tells You":

> I think a lot of the older guys—like Charlie Parker and those cats— thought that for all of the racist, social injustice that was going on at the time, I think they really, really truly thought that if they could come up with this great music, come up with this bad shit, that it would tip the scales in their favor and white America would embrace them as true intellectuals and say, "Yeah, you guys aren't all, you know, apes and incapable of thought and all that shit." When it didn't happen, I think it just took them—out. I think the difference between them and us is that we know that that shit's not

gonna happen. And I accept that, you know? I'm not playing this music for social justice, I'm not playing this music for equality, or none of that shit. The reason I play music is because I love this music. I mean, all the social ramifications. . . . ("The Music Tells You" 1992)

At this point, Marsalis is, indeed, validating the difference between bebop artists of the post-war era and his own, post–Civil Rights Movement era. But he widens and alters his commentary in his next breath:

> You go to Europe—I remember a French dude told me once, "Doesn't it make you feel good to play jazz because you can vent out all of your hatred for the white man." I said, "Man, how European of you to feel that anything that a Negro contributes would have some direct correlation to *you*." And that took him aback a little bit. The nerve—the *nerve* of him to think for a second that when I'm creating the most . . . unbelievably complicated music in the history of the world I'm thinking about *his* trite ass—you know what I mean?
>
> And that's the kind of stuff that Charlie Parker and them had to face every day. I mean, when they were calling jazz "fake" music, calling it "vacant." They invented the music and they paid the price with their lives, they paid the price with their lives. ("The Music Tells You" 1992)

Here Marsalis implicitly opposes Baraka's interpretation as Eurocentric. Baraka sees Parker as a black nationalist who, far from seeking white empathy, actually despises his white clientele. But if Baraka views him as metaphorically murdering white people, Marsalis sees Parker's performance and that of his contemporaries as a plea for inclusion in American society—as a means to integration. Yet Marsalis then stresses that he will have no part of such a purpose, that he is merely playing his own music and nothing more. But if nothing else, his illustrating example—and the way he sees the French journalist's question as being exactly "the kind of stuff that Charlie Parker and them had to face every day"—suggests that the matter is not nearly as settled for Marsalis as he would have us believe in his previous interview quotation; that, in fact, competing realities remain when it comes to the way jazz is performed and the way it is perceived today.

Charlie Parker is, then, in an Ellisonian sense, "invisible."[5] This invisibility—a by-product of the competing realities inherent in jazz performance for non-vernacular audiences—is at the core of what I call the jazz musician's love/hate relationship with audience. In a sense, there's a "game within a game" being played here, a struggle for autonomy and agency (if not, literally, "visibility") when the jazz musician is onstage, even during a seemingly benign performance. Ultimately, the performing jazz musician hopes for and expects an appreciative, enthusiastic audience, one that will "respond" to his "call" in a way that enacts the vernacular tradition; the audience, on the other hand, has certain expectations that will validate their own point of view as to proper jazz performance decorum. Somewhere in between we find the performance itself.

The question, then, for both the jazz musician and the jazz audience member, is this: *what do we see* when we're watching a jazz performance? There is a distinct difference between going to see a jazz concert and listening to a jazz recording made in the studio, and the difference goes beyond jazz as music "conceived in the present tense"—although that is a crucial component as well. The fact is, an onstage jazz musician not only performs the music but also "performs" the role of "jazz musician." In a sense, it's theater, although that theatrical aspect is, certainly, subordinate to the music. The jazz musician's performance of the role of jazz musician informs the way we hear the music—as Marsalis points out above, the performance aesthetic inevitably acts as visual context for the music.

Here's an illustration: After a public presentation of a previous version of this article, I chatted briefly with a white woman who told me that she had seen a Miles Davis performance at Great Woods in Massachusetts during the seventies, when he played with his back to the audience. According to this woman, much of the audience, also white, left the concert "in outrage" as a result of Miles's onstage antics. But the woman happened to attend the concert with a blind man—and she said he had loved the show. He literally couldn't see what much of the audience was so upset about; he couldn't contextualize Davis's music the way his sighted fellow concertgoers could. Such anecdotal evidence suggests that Marsalis is correct when he talks about jazz audiences needing visual assistance in order to hear the music.[6]

Of course, the public performance of all musics includes extramusical, political considerations. Rock music is about rebellion, about the angry young man (and, increasingly, the angry young woman), and the stage demeanor of the musicians reflects this preoccupation. Similarly, rap is angry urban music, and rappers grimly prowl the stage, holding the microphone "like a grudge," as Rakim puts it. Classical musicians, on the other hand, have a performance aesthetic that reflects the history of the music, its relation to Western culture, and its self-perceived status as established, if not Establishment music. So where does jazz fit in? Historically it has claims on the same rebellious stance as rock and rap, and yet it has also grown into being called America's classical music as well. So just what constitutes an "authentic" jazz performance?

This question is so vexing that even the musicians themselves don't agree on the answer. Branford Marsalis has said he would never stoop to pop-music crowd-pleasers like saying "Clap your hands everybody" while he was playing jazz. But at the same time, the *New York Times Magazine* describes the end of a 1994 Christian McBride performance at the Village Vanguard this way:

> The set closes with . . . "Gettin' to It" . . . McBride's funk-jazz tribute to James Brown. In [an earlier,] Carrboro, [North Carolina concert,] McBride actually did [a] microphone-stand twirling routine, just like Brown, which he's practiced since he was a kid. Tonight, he has the audience clapping in time, exhorting them with "Help me out now!" but, this being the Vanguard, the temple of jazz, the mike stand stays put. (Hooper 1995, 37)

The implication here is that McBride is showing admirable restraint in not twirling the mike-stand; and yet in Marsalis's view, merely having the "audience clapping in time"—let alone yelling, "Help me out now!"—is violating the dictates of traditional jazz performance.[7] To complicate matters even more, McBride said in passing in that same *New York Times Magazine* article, "Someone got on me for smiling too much on stage. I say get out of my face, I'm having fun. I'm not going to frown because it looks hipper in your eyes" (ibid.).

It seems to me the questions about the jazz performance aesthetic, as well as the numerous and competing ways Charlie Parker and his contemporaries were "read," speak to jazz performance as a viable cultural site for exploration. After all, the jazz performer is a political text in that he or she serves as a contribution to African-American culture, as well as a representation of African-American culture to whites, and to other blacks (particularly in terms of class differences among African Americans). When a jazz musician performs, he or she is making a cultural statement that links him or her to a long-standing tradition; and yet also commenting on and widening the parameters of that tradition as he or she balances between the tradition of performers like Duke Ellington and Count Basie and the stage persona of someone like James Brown.

Perhaps Baraka described the sociocultural realities of jazz best in his poem "In Walked Bud": "The African in the West / with European harmonies" (Baraka 1991). What Baraka's line implies is that, in a sense, the competing realities laid out here (vernacular performance vs. non-vernacular audience; nationalist statement vs. integrationist statement; status as entertainer vs. status as artist; playing an African-based art form vs. the Western musical and performance aesthetic) create the tension that makes jazz what it is. The inherent tension between these realities aids and abuts the creation of the music itself; the constant need to define and redefine, to engage in vernacular play as a means to communicate with audiences, whether they're vernacular audiences or not, is all part of the way, as Marsalis puts it, "everything that occurs in the environment has a direct outcome in the song." If we expand the term "environment" beyond Marsalis's original intention to include the entire experience of the "African in the West," these competing realities form the basis for the combustible nature of jazz music itself. In a sense, then, the tension of that love/hate relationship the jazz musician has with the audience is a vital part of the very tradition of jazz itself.

This is why jazz is, essentially, a "blues" music. As Ellison insists, the blues is "a major expression of an attitude toward life ... and man's ability to deal with chaos" (Ellison 1995b, 287). In this case, the "chaos" is the sociocultural, perceptual whirlwind in which performing jazz musicians find themselves. It was not only the case with those of Parker's era; on some level, with varying degrees of awareness, all jazz musicians playing onstage publicly play out the attempt to free themselves from the constrictions of the repeated interpretations (including, to be fair, the one you're reading) of what they're doing. It is in part this very struggle for freedom that provides the music with the crackling intensity it needs to sustain itself. The onstage performance of jazz is the exhibition of this struggle in its purest form.

The jazz musician's struggle for autonomy, as difficult as it might be for him or her to perform a role as "jazz musician," may be a necessary aspect for the viable performance of the music itself. Indeed, the next time you're watching some live jazz, I invite you to examine yourselves in terms of what your expectations are as you sit and watch and/or actively listen and participate. Examine the criteria that you (perhaps unconsciously) use to evaluate a jazz musician's extramusical performance. The next time you see a jazz performance, pay attention not only to the music, but to the issues and expectations surrounding the way the musicians perform the music. It will reveal an additional dimension to what will, hopefully, be a wonderful "performance."

NOTES

The author would like to thank Eve Shelnutt as well as the wonderful students at the ALL School in Worcester, Massachusetts. Their curiosity and provocative questions greatly informed a revision of this article.

1. Undoubtedly, jazz is a Western creation. It is a mix of African polyrhythms and European melodic structure, with a vernacular improvisational tradition at its core. And by all means, I acknowledge the African American foundation to American culture. As a friend of mine so aptly put it, "We can't cede Western culture to white folk." But while musically jazz is a blend of influences developed in the West, I believe the public performance of jazz owes far more to the African-inspired vernacular tradition than to the Western performance aesthetic.

2. A character in David Bradley's novel *The Chaneysville Incident* talks about the lived experience of the vernacular tradition: "The Africanisms—the anthropologists aptly call

them 'survivals'—exist in all of us, independent of our knowledge or our volition. Those of us who have learned about them can recognize them in our own behavior; those of us who were raised in certain conditions that reinforce the behavior can see it in everything we do. Those of us who know less about Africa than did the European slavers nevertheless tell tales that echo African tales, sing songs that call on African patterns; nobody may know that the form is called 'call and response,' but that's the way you sing a song" (Bradley 1981, 213).

3. It is important to note that the music itself is a form of vernacular performance—call-and-response patterns constantly occur in the music, as well as (and in the form of) the ongoing vernacular communication of the music's call. When I use the term "non-vernacular event," I'm referring to the lack of response from some majority white audiences—not to the lack of vernacular aspects of the music itself.

4. I am mixing genres here, to make my point. For as David Lionel Smith writes in "What Is Black Culture?" "Obviously, Clay's speech is a dramatic moment in a play, not an essay in cultural criticism. On the other hand, there is no dramatic necessity that his tirade be expressed as a sweeping claim about black cultural history, complete with biographical illustrations. In effect, Baraka uses the dramatic moment as a platform on which cultural criticism struts about in the guise of spontaneous emotion" (Smith 1997, 184).

5. Early in Ralph Ellison's *Invisible Man*, the title character says:

I am a man of substance, of flesh and bone, fiber and liquids—and I might even be said to possess a mind. I am invisible, understand, simply because people refuse to see me. Like the bodiless head you see sometimes in circus sideshows, it is as though I have been surrounded by mirrors of hard, distorting glass. When they approach me they see only my surroundings, themselves, or figments of their imagination—indeed, everything and anything except me. (Ellison 1989, 3)

6. For the record, Davis, in *Miles: The Autobiography*, says this about the matter:

I could communicate with the band just by giving them a certain look. . . . I listen constantly and if anything is just a little off, I hear it right away and try to correct it on the spot while the music is happening. That's what I'm doing when I have my back turned to the audience—I can't be concerned with talking and bullshitting with the audience while I'm playing because the music is talking to them when everything's right. If the audience is hip and alert, they know when the music is right and happening. When that's the case, you just let things groove and enjoy what's going on. (Davis 1989, 356)

Not only do his comments allude to competing realities, but he also implicitly agrees with Marsalis's "the music tells you" position when he insists that "the music is talking to them"—not his visual presentation. Miles's preference for a "hip and alert" audience suggests he is aware of audience variation.

7. Indeed, at the close of *Bloomington*, Branford Marsalis's live 1991 album, he cheerfully bids the audience goodnight by saying, "Hope we didn't confuse you too much!"—as if it were a given that his audience was confused, and he just hoped they weren't *too* confused. Although he was likely referring specifically to the music the band had just played, his post-concert announcement suggests that he, like Davis, is all too aware of the chasm between artistic possibilities and audience expectations. It also suggests that Marsalis embraces the competing realities as a way to enhance his performance, unlike jazz musicians such as McBride and Joshua Redman, who try to bridge that gap by borrowing music and performance aspects from different (albeit sometimes black) musical genres.

Baraka, Amiri. 1997. "Dutchman." From *The Norton Anthology of African American Literature.* Ed. Henry Louis Gates, Jr. and Nellie Y. McKay. New York: W.W Norton.

———. "In Walked Bud." 1991. *JazzSpeak: A Word Collection.* New Alliance Records, NAR CD 054.

Bradley, David. 1981. *The Chaneysville Incident.* New York: Harper and Row.

Crow, Bill. 1990. *Jazz Anecdotes.* New York: Oxford University Press.

Davis, Miles with Quincy Thorpe. 1989. *Miles: The Autobiography.* New York: Simon and Schuster.

Douglass, Frederick. 1982 [1845]. *Narrative of the Life of Frederick Douglass, An American Slave, Written by Himself.* New York: Penguin Books.

Ellison, Ralph. 1989 [1952]. *Invisible Man.* New York: Vintage Books.

———. 1995a. "Blues People." *The Collected Essays of Ralph Ellison.* Ed. John F. Callahan. New York: The Modern Library.

———. 1995b. "On Bird, Birdwatching, and Jazz." *The Collected Essays of Ralph Ellison.* Ed. John F. Callahan. New York: The Modern Library.

Gates, Henry Louis Jr. and Nellie Y. McKay. 1997. "The Vernacular Tradition." From *The Norton Anthology of African American Literature*, ed. Henry Louis Gates, Jr. and Nellie Y. McKay. New York: W.W. Norton.

Hooper, Joseph. 1995. "Christian McBride: Godson of Soul." *New York Times Magazine*, June, 34–37.

Smith, David Lionel. 1997. "What Is Black Culture?" *The House That Race Built: Black Americans, U.S. Terrain.* Ed. Wahneema Lubiano. New York: Pantheon Books.

2

. . . . . .

Signifyin(g)

Characteristics of Negro Expression

(1933)

ZORA NEALE HURSTON

. . . .

At a time when African American intellectuals were focused on racial uplift and the "New Negro" of the urban North, novelist and folklorist Zora Neale Hurston bucked the trend by documenting the vernacular culture of the rural South. In this brief set of observations, originally published in Nancy Cunard's Negro: An Anthology, *Hurston offers several startling points of departure for further study. Her description of African American dance as "dynamic suggestion," her observation of African Americans' capacity for reinterpretation and mimicry, and her caustic critique of the way popular white entertainers (including Mae West) adopted African American styles are as prescient as they are enduring. Hurston's lists of African American contributions to American English and her comments on dialect stand up to more recent linguistic studies. With regard to folklore and the verbal art of signifying, Hurston's suggestion that the trickster-hero of West Africa lives on in African American verbal arts has proved particularly perceptive.*

Drama

The Negro's universal mimicry is not so much a thing in itself as an evidence of something that permeates his entire self. And that thing is drama.

His very words are action words. His interpretation of the English language is in terms of pictures. One act described in terms of another. Hence the rich metaphor and simile.

The metaphor is of course very primitive. It is easier to illustrate than it is to explain because action came before speech. Let us make a parallel. Language is like money. In primitive communities actual goods, however bulky, are bartered for what one wants. This finally evolves into coin, the coin being not real wealth but a symbol of wealth. Still later, even coin is abandoned for legal tender, and still later cheques for certain usages.

Reprinted from *Negro: An Anthology*, ed. Nancy Cunard.

Every phase of Negro life is highly dramatized. No matter how joyful or how sad the case there is sufficient poise for drama. Everything is acted out. Unconsciously for the most part of course. There is an impromptu ceremony always ready for every hour of life. No little moment passes unadorned.

Now the people with highly developed languages have words for detached ideas. That is legal tender. "That-which-we-squat-on" has become "chair." "Groan-causer" has evolved into "spear" and so on. Some individuals even conceive of the equivalent of cheque words, like "ideation" and "pleonastic." Perhaps we might say that *Paradise Lost* and *Sartor Resartus* are written in cheque words.

The primitive man exchanges descriptive words. His terms are all close fitting. Frequently the Negro, even with detached words in his vocabulary—not evolved in him but transplanted on his tongue by contact—must add action to it to make it do. So we have "chop-axe," "sitting-chair," "cook-pot" and the like because the speaker has in his mind the picture of the object in use. Action. Everything illustrated. So we can say the white man thinks in a written language and the Negro thinks in hieroglyphics.

A bit of Negro drama familiar to all is the frequent meeting of two opponents who threaten to do atrocious murder one upon the other.

Who has not observed a robust young Negro chap posing upon a street corner, possessed of nothing but his clothing, his strength, and his youth? Does he bear himself like a pauper? No, Louis XIV could be no more insolent in his assurance. His eyes say plainly "Female, halt!" His posture exults "Ah, female, I am the eternal male, the giver of life. Behold in my hot flesh all the delights of this world. Salute me, I am strength." All this with a languid posture, there is no mistaking his meaning.

A Negro girl strolls past the corner lounger. Her whole body panging* and posing. A slight shoulder movement that calls attention to her bust, that is all of a dare. A hippy undulation below the waist that is a sheaf of promises tied with conscious power. She is acting out "I'm a darned sweet woman and you know it."

These little plays by strolling players are acted out daily in a dozen streets in a thousand cities, and no one ever mistakes the meaning.

Will to Adorn

The will to adorn is the second most notable characteristic in Negro expression. Perhaps his idea of ornament does not attempt to meet conventional standards, but it satisfies the soul of its creator.

---

*From "pang."

In this respect the American Negro has done wonders to the English language. This is true, but it is equally true that he has made over a great part of the tongue to his liking and has his revision accepted by the ruling class. No one listening to a Southern white man talk could deny this. Not only has he softened and toned down strongly consonated words like "aren't" to "ain't" and the like, he has made new force words out of old feeble elements. Examples of this are "ham-shanked," "battle-hammed," "double-teen," "bodaciously," "muffle-jawed."

But the Negro's greatest contribution to the language is: (1) the use of metaphor and simile; (2) the use of the double descriptive; (3) the use of verbal nouns.

1. METAPHOR AND SIMILE

One at a time, like lawyers going
    to heaven.
You sho is propaganda.
Sobbing hearted.
I'll beat you till: (a) rope like okra,
    (b) slack like lime, (c) smell like
    onions.
Fatal for naked.
Kyting along.
That's a rope.
Cloakers—deceivers.
Regular as pig-tracks.
Mule blood—black molasses.
Syndicating—gossiping.
Flambeaux—cheap cafe (lighted by flambeaux).
To put yo'self on de ladder.

2. THE DOUBLE DESCRIPTIVE

High-tall.
Little-tee-ninchy (tiny).
Low-down.

Top-superior.
Sham-polish.
Lady-people.
Kill-dead.
Hot-boiling.

Characteristics of Negro Expression

Chop-axe.

Sitting-chairs.

De watch wall.

Speedy-hurry.

More great and more better.

3. VERBAL NOUNS

She features somebody I know.

Funeralize.

Sense me into it.

Puts the shamery on him.

'Taint everybody you kin confidence.

I wouldn't friend with her.

Jooking—playing piano or guitar as
  it is done in Jook-houses (houses of
  ill-fame).

Uglying away.

I wouldn't scorn my name all up on you.

Bookooing (beaucoup) around—showing off.

NOUNS FROM VERBS

Won't stand a broke.

She won't take a listen.

He won't stand straightening.

That is such a compliment.

That's a lynch.

The stark, trimmed phrases of the Occident seem too bare for the voluptuous child of the sun, hence the adornment. It arises out of the same impulse as the wearing of jewelry and the making of sculpture—the urge to adorn.

On the walls of the homes of the average Negro one always finds a glut of gaudy calendars, wall pockets and advertising lithographs. The sophisticated white man or Negro would tolerate none of these, even if they bore a likeness to the Mona Lisa. No commercial art for decoration. Neither the calendar nor the advertisement spoils the picture for this lowly man. He sees the beauty in spite of the declaration of the Portland Cement Works or the butcher's announcement. I saw in Mobile a room in which there was an over-stuffed mohair living-room suite, an imitation mahogany bed and chifferobe, a console victrola. The walls were gaily papered with Sunday supplements of the

Mobile Register. There were seven calendars and three wall pockets. One of them was decorated with a lace doily. The mantel-shelf was covered with a scarf of deep home-made lace, looped up with a huge bow of pink crepe paper. Over the door was a huge lithograph showing the Treaty of Versailles being signed with a Waterman fountain pen.

It was grotesque, yes. But it indicated a desire for beauty. And decorating a decoration, as in the case of the doily on the gaudy wall pocket, did not seem out of place to the hostess. The feeling back of such an act is that there can never be enough of beauty, let alone too much. Perhaps she is right. We each have our standards of art, and thus we are all interested parties and so unfit to pass judgment upon the art concepts of others.

Whatever the Negro does of his own volition he embellishes. His religious service is for the greater part excellent prose poetry. Both prayers and sermons are tooled and polished until they are true works of art. The supplication is forgotten in the frenzy of creation. The prayer of the white man is considered humorous in its bleakness. The beauty of the Old Testament does not exceed that of a Negro prayer.

Angularity

After adornment the next most striking manifestation of the Negro is Angularity. Everything that he touches becomes angular. In all African sculpture and doctrine of any sort we find the same thing.

Anyone watching Negro dancers will be struck by the same phenomenon. Every posture is another angle. Pleasing, yes. But an effect achieved by the very means by which a European strives to avoid.

The pictures on the walls are hung at deep angles. Furniture is always set at an angle. I have instances of a piece of furniture in the *middle* of a wall being set with one end nearer the wall than the other to avoid the simple straight line.

Asymmetry

Asymmetry is a definite feature of Negro art. I have no samples of true Negro painting unless we count the African shields, but the sculpture and carvings are full of this beauty and lack of symmetry. It is present in the literature, both prose and verse. I offer an example of this quality in verse from Langston Hughes:

I ain't gonna mistreat ma good gal any more,
I'm just gonna kill her next time she makes me sore.

I treats her kind but she don't do me right,
She fights and quarrels most every night.

I can't have no woman's got such low-down ways
Cause de blue gum woman aint de style now'days.

I brought her from the South and she's goin on back,
Else I'll use her head for a carpet tack.

It is the lack of symmetry which makes Negro dancing so difficult for white dancers to learn. The abrupt and unexpected changes. The frequent change of key and time are evidences of this quality in music. (Note the St. Louis Blues).

The dancing of the justly famous Bo-Jangles and Snake Hips are excellent examples.

The presence of rhythm and lack of symmetry are paradoxical, but there they are. Both are present to a marked degree. There is always rhythm, but it is the rhythm of segments. Each unit has a rhythm of its own, but when the whole is assembled it is lacking in symmetry. But easily workable to a Negro who is accustomed to the break in going from one part to another, so that he adjusts himself to the new tempo.

Dancing

Negro dancing is dynamic suggestion. No matter how violent it may appear to the beholder, every posture gives the impression that the dancer will do much more. For example, the performer flexes one knee sharply, assumes a ferocious face mask, thrusts the upper part of the body forward with clenched fists, elbows taut as in hard running or grasping a thrusting blade. That is all. But the spectator himself adds the picture of ferocious assault, hears the drums and finds himself keeping time with the music and tensing himself for the struggle. It is compelling insinuation. That is the very reason the spectator is held so rapt. He is participating in the performance himself—carrying out the suggestions of the performer.

The difference in the two arts is: the white dancer attempts to express fully; the Negro is restrained, but succeeds in gripping the beholder by forcing him to finish the action the performer suggests. Since no art can ever express all the variations conceivable, the Negro must be considered the greater artist, his dancing is realistic suggestion, and that is about all a great artist can do.

Negro Folklore

Negro folklore is not a thing of the past. It is still in the making. Its great variety shows the adaptability of the black man: nothing is too old or too new, domestic or foreign, high or low, for his use. God and the Devil are paired, and are treated no more reverently than Rockefeller and Ford. Both of these men are prominent in folklore. Ford being particularly strong, and they talk and act like good-natured stevedores or mill-hands. Ole Massa is sometimes a smart man and often a fool. The automobile is ranged alongside of the oxcart. The angels and the apostles walk and talk like section hands. And through it all walks Jack, the greatest culture hero of the South; Jack beats them all—even the Devil, who is often smarter than God.

CULTURE HEROES

The Devil is next after Jack as a culture hero. He can outsmart everyone but Jack. God is absolutely no match for him. He is good-natured and full of humour. The sort of person one may count on to help out in any difficulty.

Peter the Apostle is third in importance. One need not look far for the explanation. The Negro is not a Christian really. The primitive gods are not deities of too subtle inner reflection; they are hard-working bodies who serve their devotees just as laboriously as the suppliant serves them. Gods of physical violence, stopping at nothing to serve their followers. Now of all the apostles, Peter is the most active. When the other ten fell back trembling in the garden, Peter wielded the blade on the posse. Peter first and foremost in all action. The gods of no peoples have been philosophic until the people themselves have approached that state.

The rabbit, the bear, the lion, the buzzard, the fox are culture heroes from the animal world. The rabbit is far in the lead of all the others and is blood brother to Jack. In short, the trickster-hero of West Africa has been transplanted to America.

John Henry is a culture hero in song, but no more so than Stacker Lee, Smokey Joe or Bad Lazarus. There are many, many Negroes who have never heard of any of these song heroes, but none who do not know John (Jack) and the rabbit.

Why de Porpoise's Tail is on Crosswise

Now, I want to tell you 'bout de porpoise. God had done made de world and everything. He set de moon and de stars in de sky. He got de fishes of de sea, and de fowls of de air completed. He made de sun and hung it up. Then He made a nice gold track for it to run on. Then He said, "Now, Sun, I got everything made but Time. That's up to you. I want you to start out and go round de world on dis track just as fast as you kin make it. And de time it takes you to go and come, I'm going to call day and night." De Sun went zoomin' on cross de elements. Now, de porpoise was hanging round there and heard God what he told de Sun, so he decided he'd take dat trip round de world hisself. He looked up and saw de Sun kytin' along, so he lit out too, him and dat Sun!

So de porpoise beat de Sun round de world by one hour and three minutes. So God said, "Aw naw, this aint gointer do! I didn't mean for nothin' to be faster than de Sun!" So God run dat porpoise for three days before he runs him down and caught him, and took his tail off and put it crossways to slow him up. Still he's de fastest thing in de water. And dat's why de porpoise got his tail on crossways.

Rockefeller and Ford

Once John D. Rockefeller and Henry Ford was woofing at each other. Rockefeller told Henry Ford he could build a solid gold road round the world. Henry Ford told him if he would he would look at it and see if he liked it, and if he did he would buy it and put one of his tin lizzies on it.

Originality

It has been said so often that the Negro is lacking in originality that it has almost become a gospel. Outward signs seem to bear this out. But if one looks closely its falsity is immediately evident.

It is obvious that to get back to original sources is much too difficult for any group to claim very much as a certainty. What we really mean by originality is the modification of ideas. The most ardent admirer of the great Shakespeare cannot claim first source even for him. It is his treatment of the borrowed material.

So if we look at it squarely, the Negro is a very original being. While he lives and moves in the midst of a white civilization, everything that he touches is reinterpreted for his own use. He has modified the language, mode of food preparation, practice of medicine, and most certainly the religion of his new country, just as he adapted to suit himself the Sheik haircut made famous by Rudolph Valentino.

Everyone is familiar with the Negro's modification of the whites' musical instruments, so that his interpretation has been adopted by the white man himself and then re-interpreted. In so many words, Paul Whiteman is giving an imitation of a Negro orchestra making use of white-invented musical instruments in a Negro way. Thus has arisen a new art in the civilized world, and thus has our so-called civilization come. The exchange and re-exchange of ideas between groups.

Imitation

The Negro, the world over, is famous as a mimic. But this in no way damages his standing as an original. Mimicry is an art in itself. If it is not, then all art must fall by the same blow that strikes it down. When sculpture, painting, dancing, literature neither reflect nor suggest anything in nature or human experience we turn away with a dull wonder in our hearts at why the thing was done. Moreover, the contention that the Negro imitates from a feeling of inferiority is incorrect. He mimics for the love of it. The group of Negroes who slavishly imitate is small. The average Negro glories in his ways. The highly educated Negro the same. The self-despisement lies in a middle class who scorns to do or be anything Negro. "That's just like a Nigger" is the most terrible rebuke one can lay upon this kind. He wears drab clothing, sits through a boresome church service, pretends to have no interest in the community, holds beauty contests, and otherwise apes all the mediocrities of the white brother. The truly cultured Negro scorns him, and the Negro "farthest down" is too busy "spreading his junk" in his own way to see or care. He likes his own things best. Even the group who are not Negroes but belong to the "sixth race," buy such records as "Shake dat thing" and "Tight lak dat." They really enjoy hearing a good bible-beater preach, but wild horses could drag no such admission from them. Their ready-made expression is: "We done got away from all that now." Some refuse to countenance Negro music on the grounds that it is niggerism, and for that reason should be done away with. Roland Hayes was thoroughly denounced for singing spirituals until he was accepted by white audiences. Langston Hughes is not considered a poet by this group because he writes of the man in the ditch, who is more numerous and real among us than any other.

But, this group aside, let us say that the art of mimicry is better developed in the Negro than in other racial groups. He does it as the mocking-bird does it, for the love of it, and not because he wishes to be like the one imitated. I saw a group of small Negro boys imitating a cat defecating and the subsequent toilet of the cat. It was very realistic, and they enjoyed it as much as if they had been imitating a coronation ceremony. The dances are full of imitations of various animals. The buzzard lope, walking the dog, the pig's hind legs, holding the mule, elephant squat, pigeon's wing, falling off the log, seabord (imitation of an engine starting), and the like.

Absence of the Concept of Privacy

It is said that Negroes keep nothing secret, that they have no reserve. This ought not to seem strange when one considers that we are an outdoor people accustomed to communal life. Add this to all-permeating drama and you have the explanation.

There is no privacy in an African village. Loves, fights, possessions are, to misquote Woodrow Wilson, "Open disagreements openly arrived at." The community is given the benefit of a good fight as well as a good wedding. An audience is a necessary part of any drama. We merely go with nature rather than against it.

Discord is more natural than accord. If we accept the doctrine of the survival of the fittest there are more fighting honors than there are honors for other achievements. Humanity places premiums on all things necessary to its well-being, and a valiant and good fighter is valuable in any community. So why hide the light under a bushel? Moreover, intimidation is a recognized part of warfare the world over, and threats certainly must be listed under that head. So that a great threatener must certainly be considered an aid to the fighting machine. So then if a man or woman is a facile hurler of threats, why should he or she not show their wares to the community? Hence, the holding of all quarrels and fights in the open. One relieves one's pent-up anger and at the same time earns laurels in intimidation. Besides, one does the community a service. There is nothing so exhilarating as watching well-matched opponents go into action. The entire world likes action, for that matter. Hence prize-fighters become millionaires.

Likewise love-making is a biological necessity the world over and an art among Negroes. So that a man or woman who is proficient sees no reason why the fact should not be moot. He swaggers. She struts hippily about. Songs are built on the power to charm beneath the bed-clothes. Here again we have individuals striving to excel in what the community considers an art. Then if all of his world is seeking a great lover, why should he not speak right out loud?

It is all in a view-point. Love-making and fighting in all their branches are high arts, other things are arts among groups where they brag about their proficiency just as brazenly as we do about these things that others consider matters for conversation behind closed doors. At any rate, the white man is despised by Negroes as a very poor fighter individually, and a very poor lover. One Negro, speaking of white men, said, "White folks is alright when dey gits in de bank and on de law bench, but dey sho' kin lie about wimmen folks."

I pressed him to explain. "Well you see, white mens makes out they marries wimmen to look at they eyes, and they know they gits em for just what us gits em for. 'Nothing thing, white mens say they goes clear round de world and wins all de wimmen folks way from they men folks. Dat's a lie too. They don't win nothin, they buys em. Now de way I figgers it, if a woman don't want me enough to be wid me, 'thout I got to pay her, she kin rock right on, but these here white men don't know what to do wid a woman when they gits her—dat's how come they gives they wimmen so much. They got to. Us wimmen works jus as hard as us does an come home an sleep wid us every night. They own wouldn't do it and its de mens fault. Dese white men done fooled theyself bout dese wimmen.

"Now me, I keeps me some wimmens all de time. Dat's whut dey wuz put here for—us mens to use. Dat's right now, Miss. Y'll wuz put here so us mens could have some pleasure. Course I don't run round like heap uh men folks. But if my ole lady go way from me and stay more'n two weeks, I got to git me somebody, ain't I?"

The Jook

Jook is the word for a Negro pleasure house. It may mean a bawdy house. It may mean the house set apart on public works where the men and women dance, drink and gamble. Often it is a combination of all these.

In past generations the music was furnished by "boxes," another word for guitars. One guitar was enough for a dance; to have two was considered excellent. Where two were playing one man played the lead and the other seconded him. The first player was "picking" and the second was "framming," that is, playing chords while the lead carried the melody by dexterous finger work. Sometimes a third player was added, and he played a tom-tom effect on the low strings. Believe it or not, this is excellent dance music.

Pianos soon came to take the place of boxes, and now player-pianos and victrolas are in all of the Jooks.

Musically speaking, the Jook is the most important place in America. For in its smelly, shoddy confines has been born the secular music known as blues, and on blues has been founded jazz. The singing and playing in the true Negro style is called "jooking."

The songs grow by incremental repetition as they travel from mouth to mouth and from Jook to Jook for years before they reach outside ears. Hence the great variety of subject-matter in each song.

The Negro dances circulated over the world were also conceived inside the Jooks. They too made the round of Jooks and public works before going into the outside world.

In this respect it is interesting to mention the Black Bottom. I have read several false accounts of its origin and name. One writer claimed that it got its name from the black sticky mud on the bottom of the Mississippi River. Other equally absurd statements gummed the press. Now the dance really originated in the Jook section of Nashville, Tennessee, around Fourth Avenue. This is a tough neighborhood known as Black Bottom—hence the name.

The Charleston is perhaps forty years old and was danced up and down the Atlantic seaboard from North Carolina to Key West, Florida.

The Negro social dance is slow and sensuous. The idea in the Jook is to gain sensation, and not so much exercise. So that just enough foot movement is added to keep the dancers on the floor. A tremendous sex stimulation is gained from this. But who is trying to avoid it? The man, the woman, the time and place have met. Rather, little intimate names are indulged in to heap fire on fire.

These too have spread to all the world.

The Negro theatre, as built up by the Negro, is based on Jook situations, with women, gambling, fighting and drinking. Shows like "Dixie to Broadway" are only Negro in cast, and could just as well have come from pre-Soviet Russia.

Another interesting thing—Negro shows before being tampered with did not specialize in octoroon chorus girls. The girl who could hoist a Jook song from her belly and lam it against the front door of the theatre was the lead, even if she were as black as the hinges of hell. The question was "Can she jook?" She must also have a good belly wobble, and her hips must, to quote a popular work song, "Shake like jelly all over and be so broad, Lawd, Lawd, and be so broad." So that the bleached chorus is the result of a white demand and not the Negro's.

The woman in the Jook may be nappy headed and black, but if she is a good lover she gets there just the same. A favorite Jook song of the past has this to say:

Singer: It aint good looks dat takes you through dis world.
Audience: What is it, good mama?
Singer: Elgin* movements in your hips. Twenty years guarantee.

And it always brought down the house too.

Oh de white gal rides in a Cadillac,
De yaller girl rides de same,
Black gal rides in a rusty Ford
But she gits dere just de same.

The sort of women her men idealize is the type put forth in the theatre. The art-creating Negro prefers a not too thin woman who can shake like jelly all over as she dances and sings, and that is the type he put forth on the stage. She has been banished by the white producer and the Negro who takes his cue from the white.

Of course a black woman is never the wife of the upper class Negro in the North. This state of affairs does not obtain in the South, however. I have noted numerous cases where the wife was considerably darker than the husband. People of some substance, too.

This scornful attitude towards black women receives mouth sanction by the mud-sills.

Even on the works and in the Jooks the black man sings disparagingly of black women. They say that she is evil. That she sleeps with her fists doubled up and ready for action. All over they are making a little drama of waking up a yaller* wife and a black one.

A man is lying beside his yaller wife and wakes her up. She says to him, "Darling, do you know what I was dreaming when you woke me up?" He says, "No honey, what was you dreaming?" She says, "I dreamt I had done cooked you a big fine dinner and we was setting down to eat out de same plate and I was setting on yo' lap jus huggin you and kissin you and you was so sweet."

Wake up a black woman, and before you kin git any sense into her she be done up and lammed you over the head four or five times. When you git her quiet she'll say, "Nigger, know whut I was dreamin when you woke me up?"

*Elegant (?). [from the Elgin Watch, Ed.]
*Yaller (yellow), light mulatto

You say, "No honey, what was you dreamin?" She says, "I dreamt you shook yo' rusty fist under my nose and I split yo' head open wid a axe."

But in spite of disparaging fictitious drama, in real life the black girl is drawing on his account at the commissary. Down in the Cypress Swamp as he swings his axe he chants:

> Dat ole black gal, she keeps on grumblin,
> New pair shoes, new pair shoes,
> I'm goint to buy her shoes and stockings
> Slippers too, slippers too.

Then adds aside: "Blacker de berry, sweeter de juice."

To be sure the black gal is still in power, men are still cutting and shooting their way to her pillow. To the queen of the Jook!

Speaking of the influence of the Jook, I noted that Mae West in "Sex" had much more flavor of the turpentine quarters than she did of the white bawd. I know that the piece she played on the piano is a very old Jook composition. Honey let yo' drawers hang low" had been played and sung in every Jook in the South for at least thirty-five years. It has always puzzled me why she thought it likely to be played in a Canadian bawdy house.

Speaking of the use of Negro material by white performers, it is astonishing that so many are trying it, and I have never seen one yet entirely realistic. They often have all the elements of the song, dance, or expression, but they are misplaced or distorted by the accent falling on the wrong element. Everyone seems to think that the Negro is easily imitated when nothing is further from the truth. Without exception I wonder why the black-face comedians *are* black-face; it is a puzzle—good comedians, but darn poor niggers. Gershwin and the other "Negro" rhapsodists come under this same axe. Just about as Negro as caviar or Ann Pennington's athletic Black Bottom. When the Negroes who knew the Black Bottom in its cradle saw the Broadway version they asked each other, "Is you learnt dat *new* Black Bottom yet?" Proof that it was not *their* dance.

And God only knows what the world has suffered from the white damsels who try to sing Blues.

The Negroes themselves have sinned also in this respect. In spite of the goings up and down on the earth, from the original Fisk Jubilee Singers down to the present, there has been no genuine presentation of Negro songs to white audiences. The spirituals that have been sung around the world are Negroid to be sure, but so full of musicians' tricks that Negro congregations are highly entertained when they hear their old songs so changed. They never use the new style songs, and these are never heard unless perchance some daughter or son has been off to college and returns with one of the old songs with its face lifted, so to speak.

I am of the opinion that this trick style of delivery was originated by the Fisk Singers; Tuskegee and Hampton followed suit and have helped spread this misconception of Negro spirituals. This Glee Club style has gone on so long and become so fixed among concert singers that it is considered quite authentic. But I say again, that not one concert singer in the world is singing the songs as the Negro songmakers sing them.

If anyone wishes to prove the truth of this let him step into some unfashionable Negro church and hear for himself.

To those who want to institute the Negro theatre, let me say it is already established. It is lacking in wealth, so it is not seen in the high places. A creature with a white head and Negro feet struts the Metropolitan boards. The real Negro theatre is in the Jooks and the cabarets. Self-conscious individuals may turn away the eye and say, "Let us search elsewhere for our dramatic art." Let 'em search. They certainly won't find it. Butter Beans and Susie, Bo-Jangles and Snake Hips are the only performers of the real Negro school it has ever been my pleasure to behold in New York.

Dialect

If we are to believe the majority of writers of Negro dialect and the burnt-cork artists, Negro speech is a weird thing, full of "ams" and "Ises." Fortunately, we don't have to believe them. We may go directly to the Negro and let him speak for himself.

I know that I run the risk of being damned as an infidel for declaring that nowhere can be found the Negro who asks "am it?" nor yet his brother who announces "Ise uh gwinter." He exists only for a certain type of writers and performers.

Very few Negroes, educated or not, use a clear clipped "I." It verges more or less upon "Ah." I think the lip form is responsible for this to a great extent. By experiment the reader will find that a sharp "i" is very much easier with a thin taut lip than with a full soft lip. Like tightening violin strings.

If one listens closely one will note that a word is slurred in one position in the sentence but clearly pronounced in another. This is particularly true of the pronouns. A pronoun as a subject is likely to be clearly enunciated, but slurred as an object. For example: "You better not let me ketch yuh."

There is a tendency in some localities to add the "h" to "it" and pronounce it "hit." Probably a vestige of Old English. In some localities "if" is "ef."

In story telling "so" is universally the connective. It is used even as an introductory word, at the very beginning of a story. In religious expression "and" is used. The trend in stories is to state conclusions; in religion, to enumerate.

I am mentioning only the most general rules in dialect because there are so many quirks that belong only to certain localities that nothing less than a volume would be adequate.

Signifying, Loud-Talking
and Marking

(1972)

CLAUDIA MITCHELL-KERNAN

. . . .

Now a dean of graduate programs at the University of California at Los Angeles, anthropologist Claudia Mitchell-Kernan discusses three variations of verbal art, all of which she considers forms of metaphorical communication. All three cleverly convey messages indirectly, and all depend for their effectiveness on culturally shared knowledge. The third form Mitchell-Kernan discusses, marking, is a form of the mimicry Zora Neale Hurston notes in her essay, and of the satire William D. Piersen discusses in his.

Signifying—Introduction

A number of individuals interested in black verbal behavior have devoted attention to the way of talking which is known in many black communities as "signifying." Signifying can be a tactic employed in verbal dueling which is engaged in as an end in itself; it is signifying in this context which has been the subject of most previous analysis. Signifying, however, also refers to a way of encoding messages or meanings which involves, in most cases, an element of indirection. This kind of signifying might best be viewed as an alternative message form, selected for its artistic merit, and may occur embedded in a variety of discourse. Such signifying is not focal to the linguistic interaction in the sense that it does not define the entire speech event. While the primacy of either of these uses of the term is difficult to establish, the latter deserves attention due to its neglect in the literature.

According to Abrahams, signifying

can mean any number of things; in the case of the toast, "The Signifying Monkey and the Lion," it certainly refers to the monkey's ability to talk with great innuendo, to carp, cajole, needle and lie. It can mean in other instances the propensity to talk around a subject, never quite coming to the point. It can mean "making fun" of a person or situation. Also it can denote speaking with the hands and eyes, and in this respect encompasses a whole complex of expressions and gestures. Thus, it is signifying to make fun of the police by parodying his motions behind his back, it is signifying to ask for a piece of cake by saying, "My brother needs a piece of that cake." It is, in other words, many facets of the smartalecky attitude.[1]

While the present researcher never obtained consensus from informants in their definition of signifying, most informants felt that some element of indirection was criterial to signifying; many would label the parodying of the policeman's motions "marking" and the request for cake "shucking," in the examples above.

Kochman differentiates two forms of signifying and classifies them in terms of their functions:

When the function of signifying is *directive* the *tactic* employed is indirection, i.e., the signifier reports or repeats what someone else has said about the listener; the "report" is couched in plausible language designed to compel belief and arouse feelings of anger and hostility. There is also the implication that if the listener fails to do anything about it—what has to be done is usually quite clear—his status will be seriously compromised. . . . When the function of signifying is to arouse feelings of embarrassment, shame, frustration, or futility, to diminish someone's status, the tactic employed is direct in the form of a taunt.[2]

Informants in the present sample referred to the direct taunts which Kochman suggests are the formal features of signifying when its function is to arouse emotions in the absence of directive intent as "sounding" or "woofing." Differences in usage may in part reflect regional variation. More important, however, they may correspond to internal social-structural differentiation, particularly of sex and age. Verbal dueling receives its greatest elaboration among young males, and the routines of dueling are commonly highly stylized. As a consequence, we may expect to find that usage differs in this context in contrast to other speech events where signifying may be employed. One informant suggested that only when direct insults were attributed to a third party could they be considered signifying. When I was a child in the Chicago area, my age group treated signifying and sounding as contrasting tactics. Signifying at that time was a fairly standard tactic which was employed in sounding (as a verbal insult game). That is, the speech event sounding could involve either direct insults (sounds) or indirect insults (signifying), but they were mutually exclusive tactics. Closely related was the activity of playing the dozens, which then involved broadening the target of the insults to include derogatory remarks about the family of the addressee, particularly his mother. In playing the dozens, one could either sound on the addressee's ancestors or signify about them. Sounding and playing the dozens categorically involve verbal insult; signifying does not. It may be that what these folk categories have in common has obscured what are felt by many to be crucial differences and, moreover, functions which are more diverse than have been assumed.

The standard English concept of signifying seems etymologically related to the use of this term within the black community. An audience, for example, may be advised to signify "yes" by standing or to signify its disapproval of permissive education by saying "aye." It is also possible to say that an individual signified his poverty by wearing rags. In the first instance we explicitly state the relationship between the meaning and the act, informing the audience that in this context the action or word will be an adequate and acceptable means of expressing approval. In the second instance the relationship between rags and poverty is implicit and stems from conventional associations. It is in this latter sense that standard English usage and black usage have most in common.

The black concept of signifying incorporates essentially a folk notion that dictionary entries for words are not always sufficient for interpreting meanings or messages, or that meaning goes beyond such interpretations. Complimentary remarks may be delivered in a left-handed fashion. A particular utterance may be an insult in one context and not another. What pretends to be informative may intend to be persuasive. The hearer is thus constrained to attend to all potential meaning-carrying symbolic systems in speech events—the total universe of discourse. The context embeddedness of meaning is attested to by both our reliance on the given context and, most important, by our inclination to construct additional context from our background knowledge of the world. Facial expressions and tone of voice serve to orient us to one kind of interpretation rather than another. Situational context helps us to narrow meaning. Personal background knowledge about the speaker points us in different directions. Expectations based on role or status criteria enter into the sorting process. In fact, we seem to process all manner of information against a background of assumptions and expectations.

More Formal Features of Signifying

Labeling a particular utterance "signifying" involves the recognition and attribution of some implicit content or function which is potentially obscured by the surface content or function. The obscurity may lie in the relative difficulty it poses for interpreting (1) the meaning or message the speaker is adjudged as intending to convey; (2) the addressee—the person or persons to whom the message is directed; (3) the goal orientation or intent of the speaker. A precondition for the application of "signifying" to some speech act is the assumption that the meaning decoded was consciously and purposely formulated at the encoding stage. In reference to function the same condition must hold.

Some Examples of Signifying
with Accompanying Explanations

The present section will be devoted to the presentation of a series of examples of speech acts which are labeled signifying in the community in queston. The examples will be followed by interpretations which are intended to clarify the messages and meanings which are being conveyed in each case.

(1) *The interlocutors here are Barbara (an informant), Mary (one of her friends), and the researcher. The conversation takes place in Barbara's home; the episode begins as I am about to leave.*

BARBARA: What are you going to do Saturday? Will you be over here?

R: I don't know.

BARBARA: Well, if you're not going to be doing anything, come by. I'm going to cook some chitlins. (*rather jokingly*) Or are you one of those Negroes who don't eat chitlins?

MARY: (*Interjecting indignantly*): That's all I hear lately—soul food, soul food. If you say you don't eat it you get accused of being saditty [affected, considering oneself superior]. (*matter of factly*) Well, I ate enough black-eyed peas and neckbones during the depression that I can't get too excited over it. I eat prime rib and T-bone because I like to, not because I'm trying to be white. (*sincerely*) Negroes are constantly trying to find some way to discriminate against each other. If they could once get it in their heads that we are all in this together maybe we could get somewhere in this battle against the man. (*Mary leaves.*)

BARBARA: Well, I wasn't signifying at her, but like I always say, if the shoe fits, wear it.

While the manifest topic of Barbara's question was food, Mary's response indicates that this is not a conversation about the relative merits of having one thing or another for dinner. Briefly, Barbara was, in the metaphors of the culture, implying that Mary and/or I were assimilationists.

First of all, let us deal with the message itself, which is somewhat analogous to an allegory in that the significance or meaning of the words must be derived from known symbolic values. An outsider or nonmember (perhaps not at this date) might find it difficult to grasp the significance of eating chitlins or not eating chitlins. Barbara's "one of those Negroes that" places the hearer in a category of persons which, in turn, suggests that the members of that category may share other features (in this case, negatively evaluated ones) and indicates something more significant than mere dietary preference.

Chitlins are considered a delicacy by many black people, and eating chitlins is often viewed as a traditional dietary habit of black people. Changes in such habits are viewed as gratuitous aping of whites and are considered to imply derogation of these customs. The same sort of sentiment often attaches to other behaviors, such as changes in church affiliation of upward-mobile blacks. Thus not eating or liking chitlins may be indicative of assimilationist attitudes, which in turn imply a rejection of one's black brothers and sisters. It is perhaps no longer necessary to mention that assimilation is a far from neutral term, intraculturally. Blacks have traditionally shown ambivalence toward the abandonment of ethnic heritage. Many strong attitudes attached to certain kinds of cultural behavior seem to reflect a fear of cultural extermination.

It is not clear at the outset to whom the accusation of being an assimilationist was aimed. Ostensibly, Barbara addressed her remarks to me. Yet Mary seems to indicate that she felt herself to be the real addressee in this instance. The signifier may employ the tactic of obscuring his addressee as part of his strategy. In the following case the remark is, on the surface, directed toward no one in particular.

(2) "I saw a woman the other day in a pair of stretch pants, she must have weighed 300 pounds. If she knew how she looked she would burn those things."

Such a remark may have particular significance to the 235-pound member of the audience who is frequently seen about town in stretch pants. She is likely to interpret this remark as directed at her, with the intent of providing her with the information that she looks singularly unattractive so attired.

The technique is fairly straightforward; the speaker simply selects a topic which is selectively relevant to his audience. A speaker who has a captive audience (such as a minister) may be accused of signifying by virtue of his text being too timely and selectively apropos to segments of his audience.

It might be proposed that Mary intervened in the hope of rescuing me from a dilemma by asserting the absence of any necessary relationships between dietary habits and assimilationist attitudes. However, Barbara's further remarks lend credence to the original hypothesis and suggest that Mary was correct in thinking that she was the target of the insinuation.

> BARBARA: I guess she was saying all that for your benefit. At least, I hope she wasn't trying to fool me. If she weren't so worried about keeping up with her saditty friends, she would eat less T-bone steak and buy some shoes for her kids once in a while.

Although Mary never explicitly accuses Barbara of signifying, her response seems tantamount to such an accusation, as is evidenced by Barbara's denial. Mary's indignation registers quite accurately the spirit in which some signifying is taken. This brings us to another feature of signifying: the message often carries some negative import for the addressee. Mary's response deserves note; her retaliation also involves signifying. While talking about obstacles to brotherhood, she intimates that behavior such as that engaged in by Barbara is typical of artificially induced sources of schism which are in essence superficial in their focus—and which, in turn, might be viewed as a comment on the character of the individual who introduces divisiveness on such trivial grounds.

Barbara insulted Mary, her motive perhaps being to injure her feelings or lower her self-esteem. An informant asked to interpret this interchange went further in imputing motives by suggesting possible reasons for Barbara's behavior; he said that the answer was buried in the past. Perhaps Barbara was repaying Mary for some insult of the past—settling a score, as it were. He suggested that Barbara's goal was to raise her own self-esteem by asserting superiority of a sort over Mary. Moreover, he said that this kind of interchange was probably symptomatic of the relationship between the two women and that one could expect to find them jockeying for position on any number of issues. "Barbara was trying to *rank* Mary," to put her down by typing her. This individual seemed to be defining the function of signifying as the establishment of dominance in this case.

Terry Southern narrates an excellent example of this allegorical kind of signifying message-form in the anthology *Red Dirt Marijuana*. Here we find two brothers signifying at each other in an altercation leading to a razor duel in which both men are killed. One of the brothers, C.K., tells the following story:

(3) C.K.: There was these two boys from Fort Worth, they was over Paris,
France, and with the Army, and they was standin' on the corner
without much in partic'lar to do when a couple of *o-fay* chicks
come strollin' by, you know what I mean, a couple of nice French
gals—and they was very nice indeed with the exception that one
of them appeared to be considerable *older* than the other one,
like she might be the great grandmother of the other one or
somethin' like that, you see. So these boys was diggin' these chicks
and one of them say: "Man, let's make a move, I believe we do
awright there!" And the other one say: "Well, now, similar
thought occurred to me as well, but . . . er . . . uh . . . how is we
goin decide who takes the grandmother? I don't want no old
bitch like that!" So the other one say: "How we decide? Why man,
I goin take the grandmother! I the one see these chicks first, and I
gets to take my choice!" So the other one say: "Well, now you
talking! You gets the grandmother, and I gets the young one—
that's fine! But tell me this, boy,—how comes you wants the
old lady, instead of the fine young gal?" So the other one say,
"Why don't you know? Ain't you with it? She been *white* . . .
LON-GER!"

BIG NAIL: You ain't change much, is you boy?

This story was not told for its pure entertainment value. C.K.'s message to
Big Nail was that the fellow who preferred the grandmother was his allegorical
counterpart. This alleged social type is the target of some ethnic humor and
has been explored particularly by Cleaver in *Soul on Ice*. Such an allegation
would be considered a deep insult by many.

The preceding messages are indirect not because they are cryptic (i.e.,
difficult to decode), but because they somehow force the hearer to take additional steps. To understand the significance of not eating chitlins or a yen for a
grandmotherly white woman, one must voyage to the social world and discover the characteristics of these social types and cultural values and attitudes
toward them.

The indirect message may take any number of forms, however, as in the
following example.

(4) *The relevant background information lacking in this interchange is that
the husband is a member of the class of individuals who do not wear suits
to work.*

WIFE: Where are you going?

HUSBAND: I'm going to work.

WIFE: [You're wearing] a suit, tie and white shirt? You didn't tell me you got a promotion.

The wife, in this case, is examining the truth value of her husband's assertion (A) "I'm going to work" by stating the obvious truth that (B) he is wearing a suit. Implicit is the inappropriateness of this dress as measured against shared background knowledge. In order to account for this discrepancy, she advances the hypothesis (C) that he has received a promotion and is now a member of the class of people who wear suits to work. (B) is obviously true, and if (C) is not true then (A) must be false. Having no reason to suspect that (C) is true, she is signifying that he is *not* going to work; moreover, he is lying about his destination.

Now the wife could have chosen a more straightforward way of finding an acceptable reason for her husband's unusual attire. She might have asked, for example, "Why are you wearing a suit?" And he could have pleaded some unusual circumstances. Her choice to entrap him suggests that she was not really seeking information but more than likely already had some answers in mind. While it seems reasonable to conclude that an accusation of lying is implicit in the interchange, and one would guess that the wife's intent is equally apparent to the husband, this accusation is never made explicit. This brings us to some latent advantages of indirect messages, especially those with negative import for the receiver. Such messages, because of their form—they contain both explicit and implicit content—structure interpretation in such a way that the parties have the option of avoiding a real confrontation.[3] Alternately, they provoke confrontations without at the same time unequivocally exposing the speaker's intent. The advantage in either case is for the speaker, because it gives him control of the situation at the receiver's expense. The speaker, because of the purposeful ambiguity of his original remark, reserves the right to subsequently insist on the harmless interpretation rather than the provocative one. When the situation is such that there is no ambiguity in determining the addressee, the addressee faces the possibility that, if he attempts to confront the speaker, the latter will deny the message or intent imputed, leaving him in the embarrassing predicament of appearing contentious.

Picture the secretary who has become uneasy about the tendency of her knee to come in contact with the hand of her middle-aged boss. She finally decides to confront him and indignantly informs him that she is not that kind of girl. He responds by feigning hurt innocence, "How could you accuse me of such a thing?" If his innocence is genuine, her misconstrual of the significance of these occasions of body contact possibly comments on her character more

CLAUDIA MITCHELL-KERNAN

than his. She has no way of being certain, and she feels foolish. Now a secretary skilled in the art of signifying could have avoided the possibility of "having the tables turned" by saying, "Oh, excuse me, Mr. Smith, I didn't mean to get my knee in your way." He would have surely understood her message if he were guilty, and a confrontation would have been avoided. If he were innocent, the remark would have probably been of no consequence.

When there is some ambiguity with reference to the addressee, as in the first example, the hearer must expose himself as the target before the confrontation can take place. The speaker still has the option of retreating and the opportunity (while feigning innocence) to jibe, "Well, if the shoe fits, wear it."

The individual who has a well-known reputation for this kind of signifying is felt to be sly and, sometimes, not man or woman enough to come out and say what he/she means.

Signifying does not, however, always have negative valuations attached to it; it is clearly thought of as a kind of art—a clever way of conveying messages. In fact, it does not lose its artistic merit even when it is malicious. It takes some skill to construct messages with multi-level meanings, and it sometimes takes equal expertise to unravel the puzzle presented in all of its many implications. Just as in certain circles the clever punster derives satisfaction and is rewarded by his hearers for constructing a multi-sided pun, the signifier is also rewarded for his cleverness.

The next example was reported by an informant to illustrate the absence of negative import as a criterial feature of signifying.

(5) *After I had my little boy, I swore I was not having any more babies. I thought four kids was a nice-sized family. But it didn't turn out that way. I was a little bit disgusted and didn't tell anybody when I discovered I was pregnant. My sister came over one day; I had started to show by that time.*
   ROCHELLE: Girl, you sure do need to join the Metrecal for lunch bunch.
   GRACE: (*noncommitally*) Yea, I guess I am putting on a little weight.
   ROCHELLE: Now look here, girl, we both standing here soaking wet and you still trying to tell me it ain't raining.

Grace found the incident highly amusing. She reports the incident to illustrate Rochelle's clever use of words, the latter's intent being simply to let her know in a humorous way that she was aware of her pregnancy. "She was teasing—being funny." Such messages may include content which might be construed as mildly insulting, except that they are treated by the interlocutors as joking behavior.

(6) What a lovely coat; they sure don't make coats like that anymore. (*Glossed: Your coat is out of style.*)

(7) You must be going to the Ritz this afternoon. (*Glossed: You're looking tacky.*)

(8) *The following interchange took place in a public park. Three young men in their early twenties sat down with the researcher, one of whom initiated a conversation in this way:*

I: Mama, you sho is fine.

R: That ain't no way to talk to your mother.

(*Laughter.*)

I: You married?

R: Um hm.

I: Is your husband married?

(*Laughter.*)

R: Very.

(*The conversation continues with the same young man doing most of the talking. He questions me about what I am doing and I tell him about my research project. After a couple of minutes of discussing "rapping," I returns to his original style.*)

I: Baby, you a real scholar. I can tell you want to learn. Now if you'll just cooperate a li'l bit, I'll show you what a good teacher I am. But first we got to get into my area of expertise.

R: I may be wrong but seems to me we already in your area of expertise.

(*Laughter.*)

I: You ain't so bad yourself, girl. I ain't heard you stutter yet. You a li'l fixated on your subject though. I want to help a sweet thang like you all I can. I figure all that book learning you got must mean you been neglecting other areas of your education.

II: Talk that talk! (*Gloss: Olé!*)

R: Why don't you let me point out where I can best use your help.

I: Are you sure you in the best position to know?

(*Laughter.*)

I: I'mo leave you alone, girl. Ask me what you want to know. Tempus fugit, baby.

The folk label for the kind of talking engaged in by I is "rapping," defined by Kochman as "a fluent and lively way of talking characterized by a high degree of personal style," which may be used when its function is referential or directive—to get something from someone or get someone to do something. The interchange is laced with innuendo—signifying because it alludes to and implies things which are never made explicit.

The utterance which initiated the conversation was intended from all indications as a compliment and was accepted as such. The manner in which it was framed is rather stylized and jocularly effusive; it makes the speaker's remarks less bold and presumptuous and is permissive of a response which can acknowledge the compliment in a similar and jokingly impersonal fashion. The most salient purpose of the compliment was to initiate a conversation with a strange woman. The response served to indicate to the speaker that he was free to continue. Probably any response (or none at all) would not have terminated his attempt to engage the hearer, but the present one signaled to the speaker that it was appropriate to continue in his original style. The factor of the audience is crucial, because it obliges the speaker to continue attempting to engage the addressee once he has begun. The speaker at all points has a surface addressee, but the linguistic and nonlinguistic responses of the other two young men indicate that they are very aware of being integral participants in this interchange. The question "Is your husband married?" is meant to suggest to the hearer, who seeks to turn down the speaker's advance by pleading marital ties, that such bonds should not be treated as inhibitory except when one's husband has by his behavior shown similar inhibition.

The speaker adjusts his rap to appeal to the scholarly leanings of his addressee, who responds by suggesting that he is presently engaging in his area of virtuosity. I responds to this left-handed compliment by pointing out that the researcher is engaging in this same kind of speech behavior and is apparently an experienced player of the game—"I ain't heard you stutter yet"—as evidenced by her unfaltering responses. At the same time he notes the narrowness of the speaker's interests and states the evidence leading him to the conclusion that there must be gaps in her knowledge. He benevolently offers his aid. His maneuvers are offensive and calculated to produce defensive responses. His repeated offers of aid are intended ironically. A member of the audience interjects, "Talk that talk!" This phrase is frequently used to signal approval of some speaker's virtuosity in using language skillfully and colorfully, language which is appropriate and effective to the social context. The content of the message is highly directive, but the speaker indicates by many paralinguistic cues (particularly a highly stylized leer) that he does not expect to be taken seriously; he is parodying a tête à tête and not attempting to engage the hearer in anything other than conversation. He is merely demonstrating his ability to use persuasive language. He is playing a game, and he expects his addressee and audience to recognize it as such. He signals that the game is over by saying, "I'mo leave you alone" and redirecting the conversation. The juxtaposition of the lexical items, which typically are not paired, is meant to evoke more humor by the dissonant note it strikes.

Another tactic of the signifier is to allude to something which somehow has humor value or negative import for the hearer in a casual fashion—information-dropping.

(9) Thelma, these kids look more and more like their fathers every day. (*Signifying about the fact that the children do not all have the same father.*)

(10) What time is it? (*May in certain contexts be taken to mean, "It's time for you to go." It will be said that the person was signifying that it's time to go home.*)

(11) Who was that fox [pretty girl] I saw you with last night? Sure wish you'd introduce me to her. (*Signifying: I saw you with a woman who was not your wife. If said in the presence of the addressee's wife, this kind of signifying is felt to have a highly malicious intent, because it drops information which is likely to involve negative consequences for the addressee.*)

(12) I: Man, when you gon pay me my five dollars?
II: Soon as I get it.
I (*To audience*): Anybody want to buy a five-dollar nigger? I got one to sell.
II: Man, if I gave you your five dollars, you wouldn't have nothing to signify about.
I: Nigger, long as you don't change, I'll always have me a subject.

Signifying as a Form of Verbal Art

Not all attempts at signifying are as artful as those illustrated above. That these attempts are poor art rather than nonart is clear from comments with which some of them are met. For example, needless and extreme circumlocution is considered poor art. In this connection, Labov has similar comments about sounding.[4] He cites peer-group members as reacting to some sounds with such metalinguistic responses as "That's phony," and "That's lame." Signifying may be met with similar critical remarks. Such failures, incidentally, are as interesting as the successes, for they provide clues as to the rules by violating one or more of them, while at the same time meeting other criteria.

One of the defining characteristics of signifying is its indirect intent or metaphorical reference. This indirection appears to be almost purely stylistic.

It may sometimes have the function of being euphemistic or diplomatic, but its art characteristics remain in the forefront even in such cases. Without the element of indirection, a speech act would not be considered signifying.

Indirection means here that the correct semantic (referential) interpretation or signification of the utterance cannot be arrived at by a consideration of the dictionary meaning of the lexical items involved and the syntactic rules for their combination alone. The apparent significance of the message differs from its real significance. The apparent meaning of the sentence "signifies" its actual meaning.

Meaning conveyed is not apparent meaning. Apparent meaning serves as a key which directs hearers to some shared knowledge, attitudes, and values or signals that reference must be processed metaphorically. The words spoken may actually refer to this shared knowledge by contradicting it or by giving what is known to be an impossible explanation of some obvious fact. The indirection, then, depends for its decoding upon shared knowledge of the participants, and this shared knowledge operates on two levels.

It must be employed, first of all, by the participants in a speech act in the recognition that signifying is occurring and that the dictionary-syntactical meaning of the utterance is to be ignored. Second, this shared knowledge must be employed in the reinterpretation of the utterance. A speaker's artistic talent is judged upon the cleverness used in directing the attention of the hearer and audience to this shared knowledge.

Topic may have something to do with the artistic merit of an act of signifying. Although practically any topic may be signified about, some topics are more likely to make the overall act of signifying more appreciated. Sex is one such topic. For example, an individual offering an explanation for a friend's recent grade-slump quipped, "He can't forget what happened to him underneath the apple tree," implying that the young man was preoccupied with sex at this point in his life and that the preoccupation stemmed from the relative novelty of the experience. A topic which is suggested by ongoing conversation is appreciated more than one which is peripheral. Finally, an act of signifying which tops a preceding one, in a verbal dueling sense, is especially appreciated.

Kochman cites such an example in the context of a discussion of rapping: "A man coming from the bathroom forgot to zip his pants. An unescorted party of women kept watching him and laughing among themselves. The man's friends hip [inform] him to what's going on. He approaches one woman— 'Hey, baby, did you see that big Cadillac with the full tires, ready to roll in action just for you?' She answers, 'No, mother-fucker, but I saw a little gray Volkswagen with two flat tires.'"[5]

Verbal dueling is clearly occurring; the first act of signifying is an indirect and humorous way of referring to shared knowledge—the women have been laughing at the man's predicament. It is indirect in that it doesn't mention what is obviously being referred to. The speaker has cleverly capitalized on a potentially embarrassing situation by taking the offensive and at the same time displaying his verbal skill. He emphasizes the sexual aspect of the situation with a metaphor that implies power and class. He is, however, as Kochman says, "capped." The woman wins the verbal duel by replying with an act of signifying which builds on the previous one. The reply is indirect, sexual, and appropriate to the sitution. In addition, it employs the same kind of metaphor and is, therefore, very effective.

The use of "mother-fucker" is a rather common term of address in such acts of verbal dueling. The term "nigger" is also common in such contexts. For example: "Nigger, it was a monkey one time wasn't satisfied till his ass was grass," and "Nigger, I'm gon be like white on rice on your ass."

These two examples are illustrative of a number of points of good signify-ing. Both depend on a good deal of shared cultural knowledge for their correct semantic interpretation. It is the intricacy of the allusion to shared knowledge that makes for the success of these speech acts. The first refers to the toast, "The Signifying Monkey." The monkey signified at the lion until he got himself in trouble. A knowledge of this toast is necessary for an interpretation of the message. "Until his ass was grass" can only be understood in the light of its common use in the speech of members of the culture—meaning, until he was beaten up—occurring in such forms as "His ass was grass and I was the lawnmower." What this example means is something like: You have been sig-nifying at me and like the monkey, you are treading on dangerously thin ice. If you don't stop, I am likely to become angry and beat you!

"Nigger, I'm gon be like white on rice on your ass," is doubly clever. A com-mon way of threatening to beat someone up is to say, "I'm gonna be all over your ass." And how is white on rice? All over it. Metaphors such as these may lose their effectiveness over time due to over-use. They lose value as clever wit.

The use of "nigger" in these examples is of interest. It is often coupled with the use of code features which are farthest removed from standard English. That is, the code utilizes many linguistic markers which differentiate black speech from standard English or white speech. More such markers than might ordinarily appear in the language of the speaker are frequently used. Inter-estingly, the use of "nigger" with other black English markers has the effect of "smiling when you say that." The use of standard English with "nigger," in the words of an informant, is "the wrong tone of voice" and may be taken as abusive.

It would seem that the use of these terms and this style of language serve the

CLAUDIA MITCHELL-KERNAN

same function. They both serve to emphasize that black English is being used, and that what is being engaged in is a black speech act. This serves a function other than simply emphasizing group solidarity; it signals to the hearer that this is an instance of black verbal art and should be interpreted in terms of the subcultural rules for interpreting such speech acts.

Such features serve to define the style being used, indicating its tone and describing the setting and participants as being appropriate to the use of such an artistic style. Further, such features indicate that it should be recognized that a verbal duel is occurring and that what is said is meant in a joking, perhaps also threatening, manner. A slight switch in code may carry implications for other components in the speech act. Because verbal dueling treads a fine line between play and real aggression, it is a kind of linguistic activity which requires strict adherence to sociolinguistic rules. To correctly decode the message, a hearer must be finely tuned to values which he observes in relation to all other components of the speech act. To do so he must rely on his conscious or unconscious knowledge of the sociolinguistic rules attached to this usage. Meaning, often assumed by linguists to be signaled entirely through code features, is actually dependent upon a consideration of other components of a speech act.[6] A remark taken in the spirit of verbal dueling may, for example, be interpreted as insult by virtue of what on the surface seems to be merely a minor change in personnel or a minor change in topic. Crucially, paralinguistic features must be made to appropriately conform to the rules. Changing in posture, speech rate, tone of voice, facial expression, etc., may signal a change in meaning. The audience must also be sensitive to these cues. A change in meaning may signal that members of the audience must shift their responses and that metalinguistic comments may no longer be appropriate.

It is this focus in black culture—the necessity of applying sociolinguistic rules, in addition to the frequent appeal to shared background knowledge for correct semantic interpretation—that accounts for some of the unique character and flavor of black speech. There is an elaboration of the ability to carefully and skillfully manipulate other components of the speech act in relation to code to signal meaning, rather than using poor syntactic and lexical elaboration.[7]

Loud-talking

The term "loud-talking" is applied to a speaker's utterance which by virtue of its volume permits hearers other than the addressee, and is objectionable because of this. Loud-talking requires an audience and can only occur in a situation where there are potential hearers other than the interlocutors. It may take the form of a statement, question, or imperative, or a response to any of these, and may be delivered at low, normal, or high volume, requiring only overhearing.

What to say, what not to say, and what should be said privately are decisions commonly made on the basis of the semantic content of the message; one is expected to exhibit sensitivity and an awareness of the appropriate in this regard. The loud-talker breaches norms of discretion; his strategy is to use the factor of audience to achieve some desired effect on his addressee. Loud-talking often has the effect of unequivocally signaling the intent of the speaker from the perspective of the addressee. That is to say, it assures that intent will be imputed beyond the surface function of the utterance, which might be to seek information, make a request, make an observation, or furnish a reply to any of these.

The presence of an audience (overhearers) may act as a deciding factor in the addressee's interpretation of whether, for example, some utterance is an expression of compassion and sympathy or a "catty" remark. "I'm sorry to hear that you and Bill are separated" may be taken in the former spirit when the addressee is the only potential hearer, but when an audience is present, such a remark may be felt to be mean and malicious. It is as if the audience factor causes the addressee to reject the harmless interpretation of intent while, at the same time, rendering more opprobrious the real intent because it intensifies its effect. Loud-talking serves as a key to the interpretation of ends.

An accusation of loud-talking carries the implication that the speaker (loud-talker) has, by his remarks, trod on some taboo area. It may be taboo solely due to the presence of an audience, or it may be reproachable under any circumstances—in which case the audience factor compounds the effrontery. The remark is tactless because it divulges some information the addressee does not wish to have made public or comments in some negative way about the speaker or his private affairs, causing him discomfort and embarrassment.

Except in the context of joking behavior, it is defined as a hostile and aggressive speech act which violates social conventions where shared expectations are taken for granted. Thus, when it occurs, it is assumed to be deliberate and with malice aforethought. When an individual has been the victim of loud-talking, his aggravation derives from, and is intensified by, the fact that he has been made vulnerable through exposure. The fact that the remark has functioned to expose in some way serves to define it as offending and, in addition, magnifies the offense. Although its effect may be shattering on the addressee, this tactic frequently serves to insure some form of retaliation as a face-saving device, no matter how passive and noninterfering the audience.

Whispered communications often signal to an addressee that the speaker does not wish to be overheard. When an addressee permits his response to be overheard, making it possible for those present to infer the content of the remark which the speaker has signaled should be kept private, he is loud-talking his interlocutor. Such a response may occur not as a provocation but as a sanction to censure the original remark, which perhaps has been felt to be impertinent. When an audience hears a huffy "I don't know" or an indignant "None of your business," it is usually clear that some offense (prying, in this case) has been committed and is being censured. Such a sanction carries the further implication that the transgression was so great as to require no diplomacy, creating an aura of justified indignation.

In a classroom situation, a student upon completing an assignment had begun reading a novel when he noticed that a neighbor had turned his paper over and was copying his answers. He turned to the young lady and at a volume sufficiently loud to enable all those present to overhear said, "What are you doing, girl?" The young lady retorted angrily, "You didn't have to loud-talk me," attempting to imply that he too had violated a norm. The circumstances were such that the speaker could have avoided both having his work copied and exposing the transgressor with a minimum of effort. It was, therefore, apparent that his desire to censure and expose his addressee at least equaled his desire to protect his work. The result was that everyone in the class got a laugh at the young lady's expense.

Loud-talking may be used, for example, when an individual is the focus of undesired attention. If polite and discreet requests to cease the annoyance have been ineffectual, the victim may resort to a retort or reply which will not only make known to all present that he is being pestered, but also the issue involved.

An informant reported that, after having been the repeated focus of the unwanted and offensive attention of a middle-aged man, she no longer felt any necessity to be polite and responded to an advance in a voice audible to others present, saying, "Mr. Williams, you are old enough to be my father. You ought to be ashamed of yourself." This served not only to communicate to the audience (which had probably perceived Mr. Williams's intent) that he was being unsuccessful, but to make his effrontery public, which assured an end to the annoyance.

To loud-talk is to assume an antagonistic posture toward the addressee. When it is used to censure, it reveals not only that the loud-talker has been aggrieved in some way; it also indicates, by virtue of making the delict public, that the speaker is not concerned about the possibility of permanently antagonizing his addressee. It is therefore revealing of the speaker's attitude toward the addressee. Although such a breach is not irreversible, one would not ordinarily loud-talk an individual one liked. Whether it occurs as a provocation or sanction, it frequently serves to sever friendly relations if they were held theretofore.

When a speaker uses the presence of an audience to add persuasive pressure, it may also be said that he is loud-talking. This may occur when a speaker is trying to direct an addressee to do something that he is not disposed to doing, but the reasonableness of the request, for example, may put the hearer in a somewhat bad light if he refuses. The factor of audience adds persuasive pressure because it compounds the loss of face engendered by the refusal.

Loud-talking may occur in a context to expose the failure of the addressee to fulfill some obligation. A young man of seventeen years recounted an event where this form of loud-talking generated a violent confrontation in which he shot a peer, leading to his subsequent detention for several years. Although he does not describe his initiation of the encounter as loud-talking, it appears that his addressee did just that. Larry reported that he had loaned several dollars to a young man whom he did not know well at the request of a mutual friend. On the occasion that he next saw the fellow, several months later, he requested repayment. There was a rather large audience present, including several young girls who were accompanying the debtor. Larry apparently made no attempt to be circumspect, saying, "When you gon give me my money, man?" This accusation of being beholden in the context served to raise Larry's status at the expense of loss of face on his addressee's part. Larry notes that at this point the fellow began loud-talking him, "showing off for a bunch of girls." The response elicited was a stream of verbal abuse and epithets causing loss of face for our protagonist and, unfortunately, escalating the conflict. The alleged debtor made a gesture toward his pocket; Larry reacted by drawing a pistol and shooting him twice. Altercations between males are not uncommon when an individual has been made to lose face via loud-talking, although the former may be atypical in its degree of physical violence.

Labov mentions the term "louding" in the context of verbal interaction between teenagers, describing it as a style where loud comments are made by a speaker about or to some individual in order to exert social pressure on the subject. This use seems very much related to the one described here.

An accusation of loud-talking symbolizes that some norm of social interaction has been violated, a norm relating to discretion which must be observed with regard to the content of messages. The boundaries with regard to what is permissible and what is taboo vary according to the social situation, topic, participants, and characteristics of the group. The addressee may, depending on the interplay of these components, define the speech act as rude, in poor taste, or (in the extreme) real provocation. The kinds of sanctions which are likely to be employed relate also to the factors of the speech event. Except in the context of joking, a teenage boy may feel that the loss of face resulting from loud-talking requires physical engagement, if he can find no suitable verbal response. An adult might respond to loud-talking with a retort in kind or merely with a cold rebuff.

A speech act may be defined as both signifying and loud-talking (see Example 12 in the section on signifying) if the audience is being used to achieve an end. When some norm operates to exclude signifying or loud-talking, a simple accusation of engaging in these behaviors may be sufficient censure for the individual violating the norm and, to some degree, puts the offending party in a position of losing face.

Marking

A common black narrative tactic in the folktale genre and in accounts of actual events is the individuation of character through the use of direct quotation. When a narrator, in addition to reproducing the words of individual actors, affects the voice and mannerisms of the speaker, he is using the style referred to as "marking."[8] "Marking" is essentially a mode of characterization. The marker attempts to report not only what was said, but the way it was said, in order to offer implicit comment on the speaker's background, personality, or intent. Rather than introducing personality or character traits in some summary form, such information is conveyed by reproducing or sometimes inserting aspects of speech ranging from phonological features to particular content which carry expressive value. The above dictionary-entry meaning in the message of the marker is signaled and revealed by his reproduction of such things as phonological or grammatical peculiarities, his preservation of mispronounced words or provincial idioms, dialectal pronunciation, and, most particularly, paralinguistic mimicry.

The marker's choice to reproduce such features may reflect only his desire to characterize the speaker. It frequently signifies, however, that the characterization itself is relevant for further processing the meaning of the speaker's words. If, for example, some expressive feature has been taken as a symbol of the speaker's membership in a particular group, his credibility may come into question on these grounds alone.

The marker attempts to replay a scene for his hearers. He may seek to give the implications of the speaker's remarks, to indicate whether the emotions and affect displayed by the speaker were genuine or feigned—in short, to give his audience the full benefit of all the information he was able to process by virtue of expressive or context cues imparted by the speaker. His performance may be more in the nature of parody and caricature than true imitation. But the features selected to overplay are those which are associated with membership in some class. His ability to get his message across, in fact, relies on folk notions of the covariance of linguistic and nonlinguistic categories, combined, of course, with whatever special skills he possesses for creating imagery.

The kind of context most likely to elicit marking is one in which the marker assumes his hearers are sufficiently like himself to be able to interpret this metaphoric communication. Since there is, more likely than not, something unflattering about the characterization, and the element of ridicule is so salient, the relationship between a marker and his audience is likely to be one of familiarity and intimacy and mutual positive effect.

An informant quoted a neighbor to give me an appreciation of her dislike for the woman. She quoted the following comment from Pearl in a style carefully articulated in order to depict her as "putting on the dog," parodying gestures which gave the impression that Pearl is preposterously affected: "You know my family owns their own home and I'm just living here temporarily because it is more beneficial to collect the rent from my own home and rent a less expensive apartment." "That's the kind of person she is," my informant added, feeling no need for further explanation. This is, incidentally, a caricature of a social type which is frequently the object of scorn and derision. This quote was delivered at a pitch considerably higher than was usual for the informant, and the words were enunciated carefully so as to avoid loss of sounds and elision characteristics of fluid speech. What was implied was not that the phonological patterns mimicked are to be associated with affectation in a one-one relationship, but that they symbolize affectation here. The marker was essentially giving implicit recognition to the fact that major disturbances in fluency are indices of "monitored" speech. The presence of the features are grounds for the inference that the speaker is engaged in impression management, which is contextually inappropriate. Individuals who are characterized as "trying to talk proper" are frequently marked in a tone of voice which is rather falsetto.

A marker wishing to convey a particular impression of a speaker may choose to deliver a quotation in a style which is felt to best suit what he feels lies underneath impression management or what is obscured by the speaker's effective manipulation of language. In the following example, the marker departs radically from the style of the speaker for purposes of disambiguation. The individuals here, with the exception of S_1, had recently attended the convention of a large corporation and had been part of a group which had been meeting prior to the convention to develop some strategy for putting pressure on the corporation to hire more blacks in executive positions. They had planned to bring the matter up in a general meeting of delegates, but before they had an opportunity to do so a black company man spoke before the entire body. S_2 said, "After he spoke our whole strategy was undermined, there was no way to get around his impact on the whites."

s_1: What did he say?

s_2 (*drawling*): He said, "Ah'm so-o-o happy to be here today. First of all, ah want to thank all you good white folks for creatin so many opportunities for us niggers and ya'll can be sho that as soon as we can git ourselves qualified we gon be filin our applications. Ya'll done what we been waiting for a long time. Ya'll done give a colored man a good job with the company."

s_1: Did he really say that?

s_3: Um hm, yes he said it. Girl, where have you been? (*Put down by intimating S_1 was being literal.*)

s_1: Yeah, I understand, but what did he really say?

s_4: He said, "This is a moment of great personal pride for me. My very presence here is a tribute to the civil rights movement. We now have ample evidence of the good faith of the company and we must now begin to prepare ourselves to handle more responsible positions. This is a major step forward on the part of the company. The next step is up to us." In other words, he just said what S_2 said he said. He sold us out by accepting that kind of tokenism.

S_2 attempted to characterize the speaker as an Uncle Tom by using exaggerated, stereotyped southern speech coupled with content that was compromising and denigrating. It would certainly be an overstatement to conclude that southern regional speech is taken by anyone as a sign of being an "Uncle Tom," but there is a historical association with the model of this stereotype being southern.

The characterization of individuals according to the way they speak is of course not peculiar to black people, although the implicit association of particular ways of speaking with specific social types may be more elaborated than elsewhere.

The parodying of southern regional black speech may sometimes serve as a device for characterizing a speaker as uneducated or unintelligent, and sometimes it is used to underscore the guilelessness of the speaker.

The marker encodes his subjective reactions to the speaker and is concerned with the *expressive* function of speech more than with its *referential* function.

Because marking relies on linguistic expression for the communication of messages, it is revealing of attitudes and values relating to language. It frequently conveys many subtleties and can be a significant source of information about conscious and unconscious attitudes toward language. An individual, on occasion, may mark a non-black using exaggerated black English, with emphasis clearly on communicating that the subject was uneducated and used nonstandard usages. Perhaps more than anything, marking exhibits a finely tuned linguistic awareness in some areas and a good deal of verbal virtuosity in being able to reproduce aspects of speech which are useful in this kind of metaphorical communication.

NOTES

1. Roger D. Abrahams, *Deep Down in the Jungle: Negro Narrative Folklore from the Streets of Philadelphia* (Hatboro, Pa.: Folklore Associates, 1964), 54, n. 8.

2. Thomas Kochman, " 'Rapping' in the Black Ghetto," *Trans-action* (February 1969): 26–34.

3. Cf. Roger Brown, *Words and Things* (Glencoe, Ill.: The Free Press, 1958), for a similar discussion.

4. William Labov et al., *A Study of the Nonstandard English of Negro and Puerto Rican Speakers in New York City*, Cooperative Research Project #3288, vol. 2; see also Labov article in *Rappin' and Stylin' Out: Communication in Urban Black America*, ed. Thomas Kochman (Urbana: University of Illinois Press, 1972), 290–91.

5. Kochman, " 'Rapping,' " 27, and essay in his *Rappin' and Stylin' Out*.

6. John J. Gumperz, "Linguistic and Social Interaction in Two Communities," in *The Ethnography of Communication*, ed. John J. Gumperz and Dell Hymes, special publication of *American Anthropologist* 66 (6), pt. 2: 196.

7. Ibid.

8. Clearly related to "mocking."

Stylin' Outta the Black Pulpit

(1972)

GRACE SIMS HOLT

. . . .

Daughter of a Baptist minister, communications professor Grace Sims Holt begins her essay by reminding readers of the ways in which African American preaching styles signified on those of white ministers by transforming them. Holt declares Baptist ritual and ceremony the "matrix out of which black communication style has evolved." Call-and-response between preacher and congregation, the tonal mosaic formed by congregational responses, and tonal and timbral variations of the preachers are parts of the communication style Holt describes and attributes to black religious traditions in this country and in Africa.

Long before there was a college degree in the race, there were great black preachers, there were great black saints, and there were great black churches. The man systematically killed your language, killed your culture, tried to kill your soul, tried to blot you out—but somewhere along the way he gave us Christianity, and gave it to us to enslave us. But it freed us—because we understood things about it, and we *made it work in ways for us that it never worked for him.*

—Reverend Calvin Marshall, *Time*, April 6, 1970

Roots

The black church occupies a unique place in American society. It was born out of the necessity of immoral slave-holders attempting to justify their own conduct within the stringent mandates of Puritanism. The black church became the bastard child of white immorality, teaching the ultimate absurdity: the slave and the master both worshiping the identical benevolent God.

From the white slave-owner's perspective the early black church served a dual purpose. First, the slaves had to be made content with their status; this condition was partially accomplished by having blacks' thoughts directed toward attaining humanity upon entry into the pearly gates of heaven. Second, the master's devotion to his Christian God had to be satisfied to speed *his* entry into heaven. The blacks, denied access to other forms of institutional development, took the white man's religion and from within the black church developed routines and variations of form, substance, and ritual to satisfy black psychological needs.

A primary function of the church was to nourish and maintain the souls of black folk by equating them with the essence of humanness. Religion was molded into an adaptive mode of resistance to the dehumanizing oppression, degradation, and suffering of slavery. The black church developed as the institution which counteracted such forces by promoting self-worth and dignity, a viable identity, and by providing help in overcoming fear. It did this by using the power of the Holy Spirit to transform black suffering and equate it with the suffering of Jesus. The religious aspect was always correlated with the common denominator of oppression. By enumerating perversions of the Christian ethic by white society in an emotional manner, the preacher hoped to alleviate the inhumane conditions under which blacks labored.

Similarity of problems (e.g., poverty, travail) was tied to release and redemption by the Lord. A slave seeking release from an overseer's whip could call on the Lord to help him and give him relief. This religious form of hallucination provided the basis of hope that allowed him to get through another week, when emotional release could again be provided.

White slave-owners perceived that the religion and the church served the function of containment and mollification. Religion undoubtedly served an important function as an outlet for frustration and for implanting the concept that no matter how tough things might be at present, in heaven everybody was going to enjoy the fruits of utopia. Yet it was also clear that the afterlife concept was intended to be sustaining rather than inviting (no sane people have been known to commit genocide or suicide to promote a quicker entry into heaven), and therefore much more had to be provided to make the slave reality bearable.

If the primary function of the church was to develop a will to survive, its ancillary functions were aimed at making survival endurable. It was through these secondary functions that the church became the matrix out of which black society was to be cohesive—by developing the social contacts necessary to provide intercourse between isolated plantations, by providing an outlet for musical and linguistic expression, and above all by concealing from the dominating eye of the master the activities of his slaves, regardless of their form or content. It was in this latter cast that a language code emerged to facilitate in-group communication and conceal black aspirations from the dominant white society. The black church thus also served the need to be devious in a white world.

Even today, a white person visiting a rural or ghetto church might find it difficult if not impossible to decipher or interpret the "code" talk of the preacher. What developed as a necessary mode of communication has become an integral part of the language system of blacks, though the necessity is not as great as it was in the beginning. This communication behavior is more preva-lent in the nonreligious society of today's blacks, whose communication is specifically designed to baffle any white within hearing distance of the conver-sation. These codes are also used by blacks to say to one another that "I'm *really* a brother," and much satisfaction is gained from the fact that by using this device white society may be "put down" in the presence of whites, without their having the faintest notion that they are the objects of ridicule.

Rites, Roles, and Strategies

THE SERVICE

The black church (if such diversity can be characterized as *a* church) has a ritual nearly as rigid and unvarying as that used by the Catholic and High Lutheran services. The service begins with the singing of hymns, some of which would be familiar to virtually all church-going whites, and some of which bear more relationship to African syncopation than to the solemn mass of the white church. The preacher usually begins his message in a low key, stating what the topic of the worship is to be. A moral virtue liberally borrowed from puritan-ism is common. A favorite theme is man's unworthiness to enter the kingdom of God. Then, like Beethoven building a masterpiece, the preacher begins the variations on the theme. The vices of man—cruelty, avarice, destructiveness, inhumanity, licentiousness, and sexual misconduct—flow from his mouth as easily as Catholic liturgy emanates from the pope. The congregation is warned of the consequences of practicing these vices and is authoritatively assured that the guilty ones cannot possibly enter the kingdom of God. The congregation gives verbal recognition by responding vigorously when these vices are paraded before their consciences. The more vividly worldly sins are painted, the more emotional are the responses.

The preacher relates his knowledge of local happenings to the sin context, ex-horting his audience, which shares his local knowledge, to redeem themselves of their sins. The ritual begins with the preacher "stylin' out," which the audience eagerly awaits. ("Stylin' out" means he's going to perform certain acts, say certain things with flourish and finesse.) The virtuosity of the preacher is called to task, for he must get his message across (e.g., why one shouldn't "sin"), without offending the members of the congregation whose sins are being talked about. The preacher has to supplicate without alienating the "sinner." The preacher's beginning is slow-moving (funky) to get the audience physically involved. The preacher walks, body swaying from side to side, slightly bent, from one side of the pulpit to the other, or from one end of the platform to the other. He waits until he gets to one side, stands up straight, and makes a statement about sin. If a husband "ain't acting right," if he's running around with another woman, or gambling, and not bringing his money home to his wife and children, the preacher must "get on his case" with a strong use of melody and rhythm.

PREACHER: Husbands gettin' money and ain't comin' home wit it . . . Hunh?

AUDIENCE (*Usually female response here. Men will begin to fidget, shift arm positions, stare straight ahead, lean forward slightly, or lower the head*): Yes? Let's go, alright now!

PREACHER: Gettin' Hogs (*Cadillacs*), booze, etc. Can I get a witness? Ya'll know what I mean?

AUDIENCE: You know it is. You got a witness. Oh yes! Yes, Jesus.

PREACHER: Dressin' it up when the children don't have shoes to wear and decent clothes.

AUDIENCE (*Females will react with anger and glee in responding*): Keep goin', go on, you tellin' it, Preach! Lord, yes!

PREACHER: Don't you think they got a *right* to what you earn?

AUDIENCE: Yeah, Preach, take yo time now, awright, awright now!

At this point the preacher walks to the other side of the pulpit or platform and makes another statement. He may at this point have a handkerchief in one hand and at intervals wipe his face as he builds the utterances in pitch, intensity, and volume. The white handkerchief signals the congregation that he's going to say something of importance and they'd better pay close attention. The spanking white handkerchief may be in the back pocket, tucked up a sleeve, folded and placed on the pulpit or in the Bible. The preacher reaches for it with a certain style, shakes it out with one flip of the wrist, and wipes the sweat from his brow or froth from his mouth.

PREACHER: Don't you think they got a *right* to—

AUDIENCE (*louder*): Yeah!

PREACHER: Don't you think they got a *right* to yo love? Y'all wit me?

AUDIENCE (*shouts*): Yeah! Eeesy! Awright now! Tell it, tell it right, Come on! He's on the road now. Preach!

The intensity and volume of audience response signals the preacher that he is getting across, that he's telling the truth, that the audience is enjoying what he says and appreciates how he says it. In this example the intimacy of the subject is tricky, and the preacher must maneuver the straying males into response if he is to be perceived as successful in his message. Thus, even though it is clear for whom the core of that message is intended (the preacher has "put the hurt on" the males), he must also "get on" the wives and effect a reconciliation as the climax of that message. Both males and females may be guilty of the same sin, and the message must be embroidered to include the role of the female. The next ritualistic step usually goes something like this:

PREACHER: Wives playin' round. Just about as bad as the husbands. . . . Hunh?

AUDIENCE (*male responses come strong and loud*): Tell the truth!

PREACHER: Talkin' bout I love you and not having no dinner ready when the man comes home from a hard day's work, and *he* got to wait. Let the church say A-men.

AUDIENCE: A-men! (*May be repeated several times with varying degrees of intensity.*)

The preacher then goes on to enumerate various "sins" of the wives to partially expiate the heavy male guilt, to indicate how the female contributes to the first sin, and to indicate a solution for both parties. The preacher talks about female sins with numerous variations on the theme, which leads into a charge of the woman's responsibilities.

PREACHER: To make the man do right—what would *God* have you do? Let the church answer A-men.

AUDIENCE: A-men.

PREACHER: To make the man do right you got to do yo part. Do I hear a witness?

AUDIENCE: Tell the truth! Tell it! Talk!

PREACHER: You got to get up early in the morning when your eyes still heavy and you limbs still weary.

AUDIENCE: Come on now. Tell it right. Tell it like it is.

PREACHER: You got to smile over tears, you got to make the man feel good like a *man*—when he's been kicked and tossed like a dog and a feather. You got to soothe his brow, tend his comfort, and *let him see* you love. You ain't got to talk 'bout yourself all the time.

Stylin' Outta the Black Pulpit

AUDIENCE: Come on now!

PREACHER: And you got to smile—radiant, like the stars of heaven.

AUDIENCE: We hear ya; Go ahead! Go brother! I hear you.

PREACHER: You got to love . . . hunh? (*Meaning "Am I right," or "You ain't listening to me."*)

You got to persevere . . . hunh?

You got to give yo' all . . . hunh?

You got to be long suffering . . . hunh?

You got to *do* right!

The preacher has invoked the charge of forbearance, mutual responsibility, and hope for the future: "And things will be better by and by!" or "There'll be a new and brigher day." Then he must challenge the congregation to try to live up to the invocation.

"Will you do it? Will you *try*?" The preacher may quote scripture at this point in support of the anticipated effort, or he may break into a line of a moving song to accomplish the same purpose. Thus not only is the self-purification theme prevalent, but the strategies for self-purification or ridding oneself of sin and its temptations are also indicated. An aroused preacher and an emotional flock together make religious music, music never contemplated by John Calvin. What a white witness could never conceive is that the man who can never enter the kingdom of God is the *white* man. The flock understands this with crystal clarity, and it is this clarity which is the emotional furnace feeding the flames of fever, providing the orchestral accompaniment to this "Black Mass." How else could it be? The propertyless slave or black (take your choice) was incapable of being guilty of the sins of greed, avarice, gluttony, callousness, brutality, and hypocrisy. The emotion aroused was not so much *for* God as it was stimulated *by* a chronicle of the sins of The Man. It is in this manner that the sobriquet The Man became the synonym for "white" in black English. A white heaven was virtually abolished by definition since, also by definition, very few whites could meet the admission standards.

The verbal exchange between preacher and audience throughout the service is accompanied by a variety of counterpoint. When the preacher makes his charges of sin he may shout or whisper, point a finger, lean on the pulpit, pause, or look long and hard at the audience, letting the words sink in for effect. At this point, after a dead silence, some woman usually lets out a single piercing scream. The other women moan, groan, sway, wave fans, handkerchiefs, and hands at the preacher in total communion of the female wronged, while responding vocally. Men hang their heads lower in shame or raise them in determination to "do better." The preacher may use the pointed finger or hand at any time in the delivery to represent the feeling, which the black audience understands, to say the congregation *knows* that what he says is true, backed by the scripture. The white handkerchief, wiping the face, pausing to get a drink of water, and changing to a shaking voice all signal to the audience that the preacher is really going to get down and preach; the spirits of the audience lift. Attention, if wandering, is abruptly recaptured. Anticipation mounts for how and what the preacher will do next and is a signal to the audience to get ready to respond. The verbal responses may be accompanied by patting the feet several times in staccato fashion, one-foot stomps, hand-clapping, low moaning, and delighted laughter.

The preacher may roll his eyes heavenward, as though to invoke divine sanction; he may scowl, beat on the pulpit, or change facial expressions to pantomime the emotion he is talking about.

Ranging over a wide continuum of behavior, the preacher must constantly evaluate the feedback from the congregation and revise and create new, additional, or already frozen responses to that feedback in a continuing build-up to the climax of the sermon. At some point style becomes part of the substance, too, as the preacher combines past, present, and future in his sermon.

Because of the nature of the creation of black society, many congregations have a dual composition. Educated upper-class or middle-class blacks (I deny the existence of a bona fide black middle class) and those of lesser intellectual attainments are integrated in the church structure, a common meeting-ground for all blacks. The minister inheriting such diversity will preach two sermons, one devoted to reason and intellect for his more affluent and sophisticated parishioners, appealing to reason and morals, a sermon more philosophical than religious in its focus. After getting warmed up with reason, he then proceeds to symbolically take off his frock (often physically doing so), and "gets with it," embracing all the myths, superstitions, and irrational assumptions of fundamentalist religion. Abe Jackson and Jesse Jackson, for example, use black preaching style to bridge black class lines, to capitalize on a sense of community by reminding the audience of past breaches, broken promises, and access denied. *All* blacks are linked in a community of historic suffering which allows the preacher to switch his image for dual audiences. The preacher knows and capitalizes on the ability of black intelligentsia to relate to and appreciate his ability to manipulate (perhaps momentarily) the real, though submerged, feelings of the audience around black oppression.

THE PREACHER

The role of the black preacher was defined and rooted in the very circum-stances that founded the existence of the black church. If, as noted above, the slave-owners permitted the church to exist in order to satisfy the Puritan-Protestant worldly mission to Christianize all members of the order of *Homo sapiens*, including subspecies, and were psychologically shrewd enough to perceive, if not to understand, that the primitive slave (at least that human facet of the beast) needed the sustenance of his own kind to remain psychologically healthy enough to do the master's work, then they also recognized their inability to accomplish these ends themselves. This task was delegated to the black preacher, who in reality was conceived by the master to be his agent in the conspiracy to make the slave contented enough to work, to deter his humanly murderous instincts toward the master, and to accept his miserable existence in the hope of living in streets of gold after death. Lacking insight into the slave mentality, the slave-owner could not communicate with the slave directly or outline detailed instructions to the agent-preacher. Given, therefore, this relative autonomy and broad discretion, and hidden from the eye of the owner, the preacher developed a forum that was in fact a sanctuary, a platform and a captive audience, which among other things was used to bring some cohesiveness into the slave milieu. The historical fact that the black preacher became the only leader permitted in black society has consequences that persist in today's racial conflicts, the implications of which need to be dealt with in another paper. A moment's reflection by the reader now, however, will note the lack of a truly national black leader who has not been a preacher.

Stylin' Out

Whatever other functions fell to the minister in the early black church, it was clear that the most important one was to create the form of hallucination that would provide the basis of hope which would allow one to endure another week, at which time emotional release could again be provided. It was in the capacity to arouse an emotional response that these ministers became true artists; none lacking this talent can survive in the black church. The rich, descriptive, allegorical phrases in black English are paraded before the congregation, and the response of the church is emotionally charged with sisters fainting, sweating, groaning, and simulating a mass orgasm. The service itself is as formal, rigid, and stylized as a Catholic mass, but unlike the mass—which is designed to be remote, mystical, solemn—the *raison d'etre* here is emotion. The frustrations of living the black life are vented in paying homage to the white God (more recently, black God). It was from such a tradition that such latter-day "Soul Jerkers" as the Reverend Clay Evans have come.

The "Soul Jerker" is renowned for his ability to move the congregation to shouting, whooping, hollering, and "falling out" (fainting) when he preaches. He is the most flamboyant preacher of all, with high style and a good, strong, singing voice. If he has a gravel voice, it is considered an additional asset.

The service usually begins with deacons or deaconesses singing old hymns reminiscent of slave dirges ("I'm Gonna Wade in the Water" is one I distinctly remember from my childhood). The message of sorrow in lamentation and intonation resembles little of the formal liturgy of white churches. A capella or accompanied by piano or organ, an assemblage of the church's official hierarchy begins the slow procession to the appointed places at the front of the church, just like slaves in chains. The emotional tone is set for cohesiveness and the ritual of expected response to an anticipated situation, act, and expression. After scripture and prayer the Soul Jerker swings very quickly into his liturgy. This type of ritual is so highly structured and familiar as a medium of emotional response that it doesn't take long for the congregation to begin "rejoicing." Joy, happiness, and ecstasy are actualized in shouting by the women. A woman will suddenly begin to get rigid: her head and face become trancelike, her arms and feet begin to move, her body twists and convolutes according to the way the Spirit moves. The woman may sit or stand upright where she is as she screams or shouts her joy. She may get up and move out in the aisles, feet moving in an ecstatic rhythm as she bends and sways, twists and moves her arms. She may shout all over the church. She is unhampered in her movements by the congregation. Members or ushers will often move to protect a member who is so carried away that she is in danger of hurting herself.

The male church member usually just sits there enjoying himself, watching the women get happy. Occasionally, a male may get carried away and shout— but usually he does not do so, for his masculinity may be questioned. He may react with tears, verbal responses, clenching the fist, patting the feet, rolling the eyes to look at a neighbor in agreement, nodding the head, or assisting a "fallen" female.

But the women, as the backbone of the church, are *expected* to react vigorously to the preacher. The more vigorous the reaction, the more a woman is moved by the Spirit. Some of the rejoicing is very reminiscent of African dances, especially when the shouting becomes frenzied. Many members may be rejoicing simultaneously. Those who do not shout rejoice in any of the ways previously discussed. Often, if the preacher is really good, the whole church is rejoicing and shouting, the preacher included; he urges the crowd on with praise and encouragement. During this time, if the Spirit moves, anyone may get up and testify to the power, joy, and release of the Holy Spirit. It's a way of praising the Lord in song, testimony, and dance. The love of God as a symbol of humanity gives those treated inhumanely a reason for being. The goodness of God, to be realized through man, is exemplified in "rejoicing" together. The preacher's ability to arouse an erotic response is an index of his success and vitality. The preacher evaluates his own power and becomes more aware of its usage and effect as he develops and polishes his personal style and delivery in manipulating the listeners. An example follows.

Preacher	Responses of congregation at various intervals
Early one morning!	Yeah!
	He's on the road now!
	Talk! Tell it!
Early one morning!	Come on now!
Early one morning!	Lord have mercy!
I walked through the valley—You hear me? You hear what I said? I said I've been through the valley.	Preach it brother! Yessih, Yessuh!
You followin' me?	A-men! Preach, preach!
Lord you know it's not right.	Tell the truth. Lord have mercy!
Look what they doin' to us *down* here.	
We know there's higher ground and you said "come on up."	Thas right! "Come on up!"
Come on up to higher ground.	"To higher ground."
You won't forsake us. There's a brighter day ahead! You said—	Yes Lord! Yes he said
You said you'd lift this burden from my shoulders.	Lift this burden!
We goin' to come on up to high ground.	Yes Lord! High ground—

The preacher indicates it's time to stop by signaling the choir to sing. He may also verbalize (e.g., "I'm go wrap up now!"). If, however, the audience is reluctant to stop the message, he will hear a shout, "Preach on! You got to tell it all!" "Go on and preach!" or "Keep on keepin' on!" The preacher may respond by continuing to peach a while longer before swinging into the next part of the ritual; or he may simply end the sermon anyway.

GRACE SIMS HOLT

People in the congregation who are not members of that particular church or who have not "been saved by Jesus" are entreated to come and join the church. The preacher states the invitation as he steps down to the floor of the congregation, hands extended in welcome. "Jesus is waiting. Won't you come? He needs you. He will help you. Won't you come?" The deacons (and sometimes the church mother) stand in a semicircle, arms folded front or back. The preacher is free to move anyplace within the semicircle to increase his effectiveness. Music provides a soft, enticing background. The preacher may continue to issue as many calls as he deems advisable. He has to be expert at reading the body cues of any sinners who may be tempted but are wavering and can't make the final big decision to plunge down the aisle. The congregation is watching these potential candidates and expects the preacher to turn on his most persuasive powers to get them into the fold. The preacher is allowed great verbal latitude and as much time as he thinks he needs to accomplish this task. Since this part of the ritual is not formalized, it presents the greatest challenge to his communicative virtuosity. If he fails, he is judged harshly. If he succeeds, he enhances his stature. If the congregation observes that no potential candidates exist at that time, the preacher's reputation is not damaged. The evangelist or revivalist, as the visiting preacher, is most skilled at getting sinners to join. He usually has a week of revival meetings with mighty sermons. He is expected to provide highly intense emotional communion and release which result in bringing many sinners into the bosom of the church. When sinners are moved to come, from the efforts of the preacher and the prayerful urging of the congregation, they are asked to sit on the mourners' bench, and they are welcomed by handshakes all around. Official processing to the church roll, and duties to be assumed, occur at a later date.

When the invitation and joining are over, the whole audience joins in singing "Halleluyah, Tis Done" or some other favorite. The song is one of distilled joy that another soul is saved by the grace of God.

It is traditional to have prayer at this point. Numerous forms are available from a wide repertoire of prayers. The preacher chooses the prayer best suited to a given event in the ritualistic process; the deacon may also assume this responsibility.

The Reverend C. L. Franklin begins a prayer with: "Can I get somebody to pray with me right now—Great God!"

The Reverend R. B. Thurmond moans, followed by a hushed rendition of

"Great God—" and finishes the prayer with a moan and, "And that will be enough."

Reverend Daniel Harris uses a more extensive prayer.

PREACHER (*moans*): Good God—a mighty (*Moans.*) One day the sun will refuse to shine. (*Moans ————*) Sooooon, soon one morning, soon-uh one morning, I said, soon-uh one morning death is a-comin'.

CONGREGATION: Come on Rev.!

PREACHER: Pray wit' me. Lord have mercy on me. O-o-o-h Lord, the chariot of God will swing low, the wheels of justice will turn.

CONGREGATION: Let the wheels turn.

PREACHER: Let the church say A-men, 'cause one day I was way down yonder by myself and I couldn't hear nobody pray. (*Congregation moans and hums softly.*)

PREACHER: We need good church members to pray, and tell God how these dark clouds are hanging above our heads and how deep the valley is, and how high the mountain is. Tell God about the rough roads you got to walk. But thank God, the journey's started. A-men. Let the church say A-men.

CONGREGATION: A-men.

THE MONEY RITUAL (ALSO CALLED COLLECTING THE MONEY, TAKING THE COLLECTION, OR PASSING THE PLATE/BASKET)

Without missing a beat, the choir begins the offertory song. The preacher or head deacon extends the invitation to contribute while the people are still aroused. The preacher often preaches a short post-sermon about the beauty of having a church, a place to meet and enjoy oneself worshiping God. The preacher will take his glasses off (if he wears them), wipe his brow again, reach into his pocket to "put the first dollar in," come back down from the pulpit, and hand it to the church mother—*always* to the church mother. After the collection the church is blessed and dismissed until another Sunday.

Another device used is the "build-up" approach to finance. The build-up of the audience is designed to stimulate giving money to the church. The preacher, as Jesse Jackson illustrates, also calls on select people in the audience to "lead off the taking of the collection." Usually these leaders are financially better off than most or have some status or influence in the community. Put on the spot, they must "lead off" with a most generous contribution. The preacher cajoles the audience to continue giving generously as the congregation either parades down the aisles to the offertory table (a fast-disappearing practice) or the offertory baskets or plates are passed. A running stream of chatter and encouragement, even to the point of sometimes embarrassing a reluctant giver, is kept up by the preacher. Soft choir music usually accompanies this ritual. Every effort is expended to amass as much money for the church as possible. The congregation is highly appreciative of the pastor's remarks during this time. The offering is finally blessed with a short prayer.

The discussion up to this point has attempted to sketch the Baptist ritual and ceremony, with its call and response patterns reminiscent of African drum ceremonies, as an illustration of the matrix out of which black communication style has evolved. It is clear, for example, that the black ministerial figure (pastor, preacher, reverend, or leader) does not deliver a message *to* his audience; he involves the audience in the message. Expressive communication (emotion, feeling) is mandatory for both speaker and receiver. Both move without shame to the syncopation of movement, are sensitive to the shifting nuances, and call on the church for guidance whenever and wherever the spirit moves. The preaching style displays virtuosity in both effect and affect, using devices filled with emotion and a sense of the dramatic. From this communication cradle have come such Spellbinders (as opposed to Soul Jerkers) as Father Divine, Martin Luther King, Jr., Calvin Marshall, Adam Clayton Powell, Tom Skinner, Samuel Williams, Rabbi Divine, Jesse Jackson, Frank Sims, and Abe Jackson.

"Movin' Out"—Church Communication Styles in Secular Contexts

As has been shown above, how to deal with The Man, maintain black identity, and improve the conditions of existence for black people have long been functions of the church. To these functions a new and pressing one has been added: to aid in the acquisition of power to achieve economic goals.

In organizing black people around this objective, ministers like Tom Skinner of the east coast and Jesse Jackson of the midwest illustrate the use of manipulative, expressive, black modes in blending evangelistic fervor with pragmatic goals. Tom Skinner is especially appealing to the young when his evangelistic style compares David and Goliath with blacks and "whitey." He relates what David accomplished with what blacks can do when God is on their side. Skinner "hustles" his past gang-leader role to young ghetto blacks as proof of blacks' ability to play David and Goliath. "Hustling" in this context is the promotion of black pride, awareness, dignity, identity, and power.

Jesse Jackson uses his spellbinding abilities in the deliberate manipulation of symbols to change attitudes and beliefs. Jackson engenders awareness and hustles a sense of pride and power with "I Am Somebody." Being black requires an absolute commitment to an illusionary view of reality (that rats *don't* exist) with equal commitment to hope for the future (that rats *won't* exist). Jackson's "hustling time" clearly serves religious purposes, but it is a good deal more social and economic than religious. With an awareness of his power to verbally transfigure disillusionment and despair into powers of survival, Jackson shouts, "I Am Somebody" and black audiences respond, "I Am Somebody." Blacks know full well that when the rats stop biting they'll know they're somebody, but the power and magic of the word as antecedent for the action are so strong it is for the moment believed. In "true believing," blacks' actions are thereby influenced to help make the words reality. Claude Lewis reports from an Operation Breadbasket meeting in 1968 the following excerpts which illustrate Jackson's expert manipulation of black communicative patterns and functions.

> "I am what I am and I am proud."
> "We seek not the privilege to integrate, but rather the *power* to negotiate."
> "Money is the next most righteous thing in the Kingdom other than subjects."
> "David sought not a church but a kingdom. Go take the land, then make the decisions. I know my Father's house from the hog trough."

And while he preaches he asks for response:

> "We black people ought to reappraise our relationship to American white people and redefine our relationship with our colored brothers elsewhere. . . . Can I get a witness?" And the entire congregation becomes his witness with a resounding "Yes brother" and "Tell it like it is."

He moves his audience, he excites them, he pushes them, he inspires and manipulates them.

> "To have the symbols of freedom and no power is to be denied the substance of freedom."
> "Now we deserve the job or an income."
> "Stay on the case," a black woman shouted.
> "Tell it like it is brother," an old black man yelled out.
> "We've got to keep on pushing."
> "I'm constantly reminded of Martin's favorite prayer that goes like this: 'Lord, we ain't what we ought to be, and we ain't what we want to be, we ain't what we gonna be, but thank God, we ain't what we was.'"

Crises within the black community are also frequently handled within a church or church-like setting. For example, recently in Chicago a South Side church was burned; its pastor, the Reverend Curtis Burrell, had declared war on Chicago street gangs. The Reverend Jesse Jackson was invited to preach the next Sunday's sermon. In order to ensure maximum attendance and participation in the creation of the event, he announced through the press that he was going to preach a "Dry Bones" sermon. The mention of "Dry Bones" was a signal to the black community that an overriding and urgent social issue was going to be discussed; since the "Dry Bones" sermon is a ritual within the black church—many variations of the sermon exist which have become quite formalized through time—interest and speculation was high over how Jackson would develop the sermon relative to the current social conflict.

Traditionally, the "Dry Bones" sermon has functioned as a unifying force within the black community; it was designed especially to bridge class lines and overcome divisive factionalism. Whatever structural and stylistic variations existed among preachers in their handling of the sermon, one theme has been invariant—namely, that conflicts within the black community arise out of the conditions under which black people are forced to live and that such conflicts produce divisions which aid and abet The Man in his efforts to keep black people down. Therefore, one of the chief goals of the preacher through the use of the "Dry Bones" sermon is to supplant inhuman white authority with religious black authority where white authority is declared unjust and un-Christian and the authority of the black church is declared the only just authority for black people. Listeners are inspired, impressed, and challenged to aspire to the loftier means and ends, to move from the "Dry Bones valley" of degradation and internal social conflict to the "garden humanity" of the mountain. Aware of this tradition, most Chicago blacks knew or anticipated that Jackson would use the sermon to talk about the local conflict between blacks. The mere mention of "Dry Bones" produced maximum attendance and participation that Sunday. (Since Burrell's church was burned, the service occurred in a makeshift, open, sidewalk church.)

What follows are some quotes from Jackson's sermon:

Who is it that does not mind the people here burning up, destroying each other so they can get this property back? . . .

Who is it that burns the houses, that the people are movin' out of, not puttin' people back in 'em, so they can use it for airport property?

Who is it wants . . . Lake Meadows and Prairie Shores?

Repeated refrain: God made the garden.

Man made the valley.

The valley just makes you tired.

You just get tired of seein' the blue lights turn aroun'.

You get tired of seein' people stand in line to use the bathroom.
You just get tired of men being treated like boys.
You just get tired of women being treated like girls.
You just get tired, and wanna leave the valley. And however you can get out you leave.
I get tired of *criticism.* But there's something within.
I get tired of *the lies.* But there's something within.
I get tired of *exploitation.* But there's something within.
I get tired of *oppression.* But there's something within.

As each successive line of the pattern is enumerated, the voice rises ever higher and becomes increasingly emphatic. The congregation usually responds with corresponding intensity after each line if the preacher is effective. When the audience does not respond, it signals the speaker that he is not moving the listeners. He may then try some other motivational device from his repertoire with more success.

See, if you just walkin' up and down the streets of the ghetto, you get frustrated talkin' bout the *effect* and you *never* get to the cause. *The effect is,* an illiterate and semi-literate people. *The effect is,* babies dying. *The effect is,* fathers fighting sons, *and* mothers fighting daughters, *and* confusion in the household *and,* burning the church *and,* glorifying the corner. . . .

The communication devices illustrated function in Operation Breadbasket meetings, a semi-religious context. Jesse Jackson is the speaker.

Man making money *can be crude,* but his making nuff money to send his child to college.
Man *can be crude,* but if he's makin' enough money, he can get a house.
Can be crude, if he's makin' nuff money, he can get a car. Can fly an airplane, can go to the doctor, does not have to be on welfare.

Wherever you're listening, pull out a quarter and a dime. Twenty-five-cent piece and a dime. Y'all too. *Quarter and a dime.* I'm not really a teacher, but I can if I have to. Necessity is the mother of invention I told y'all. All the "war on poverty" people up there pullin' out these—I didn't say a ten dollar bill or a $25.00 bill, I say *a quarter money and a dime.*

We are in Chicago a little better than 25% of the population. That what this quarter is. We live on less than 10% of the land. Follow me now! Now what you must do is to try to *fit the quarter on the dime.*
AUDIENCE: Tell it! Right on Jesse!

JESSE: Try to fit it. Figure out how you can do it. One a ya'll smart nough to figure it out just when I'm telling it. You got a position on how you *put the quarter on the dime?* Hear what I said? You can't stick all black folks up on top of each other. You got to *fit on it.* I didn't say stick it on the dime. (AUDIENCE: *Right!*) That's what the —— are trying to do. They're tryin' to *stick us on the dime.* Now turn it over so you can look at the dime. These people that are on the dime *live* in the ghetto. . . . It ain't no accident that 30,000 people per square mile live in the black community, and 3,000 per square mile live in the white community. Which means that in the white community you got more land than people, and the premium is on the people and not on the land. And in a black community you got more people than property and therefore the premium is on the property and not on the man. In the white community you defend white folks. In the black community you defend property. No accident. Listen!!

AUDIENCE: Awright!

JESSE: Listen!

AUDIENCE: Awright!

JESSE: Think about the *people who can't get on the dime.*

Besides the use of other stylistic devices already mentioned, note how Jackson makes effective use of *repetition* as a communication device, which serves to emphasize and drive home to the congregation an important point. By means of repetition, Jackson ensures that the cruciality of *what* he is saying is not lost in the emotionalism of the audience. Black speakers generally are keenly aware of the need to offset any emotionalism that might interfere with information processing. For example, at another Operation Breadbasket meeting, on introducing another speaker, Jackson prepares his audience to receive and relate to a different tempo and rhythm from that of the preacher: "Brothers and sisters, I want you to greet warmly at this time, not a preacher. You won't hear no—them things me and Bob and Calvin and Ed 'n' 'em go through where we start dippin' and goin' on, cause Holy Ghost a start us movin'. Information be makin' him stand still, so you got to *hear* him. Just be hearing what's on his mind."

In summary, communication in the black church is highly dependent on the style and skill of the preacher interacting with the affective responses of involved audiences. This "turn-on" ability in terms of communication style is a cohesive force incorporating a large body of blacks. Black preaching style mixes moralism and idealism with pragmatism, promotes institutionalized authority, bridges generations, and relies on and extends the general effect that is basic to the black experience.

A Resistance Too Civilized to Notice

(1993)

WILLIAM D. PIERSEN

. . . .

At the time of his death in 1996, William D. Piersen was a professor of history at Fisk University. Satire is not exclusive to African or African American culture, but Piersen documents a long history of the satirizing force among Africanist peoples. He traces the effective uses of satire among African Americans to African communities, where satire helped air public opinion and was used to release frustration, providing a kind of safety valve or communal psychological medicine. The allusion, metaphor, subtlety, and wry indirection of satirical songs and dances link them to the signifying verbal arts Holt describes. And because satire "cools the soul," we see it as part of Robert Farris Thompson's "aesthetic of the cool." Piersen also suggests some traits of African-based satire: rhyming, improvisation, parody, and combining verbal satire and songs with dance and movement.

Just as African Americans used African-style oral narratives to develop a communal understanding of the enslavement process and its meanings, so too they maintained patterns of aggressive humor which had been used in Africa to defuse hostility and check antisocial behavior. Across the Americas the shortcomings and abuses of the powerful were lampooned in song just as they had been in Africa. Of course, in America, it was whites in general and oppressive masters in particular that became the favorite targets of this satire.

Too often in the history of American slavery we assume acts of effective resistance are best defined by organized violence because rebellion and revolution are thought by American culture to be the highest, most worthy, most manly forms of protest. But such a vision is far too narrow for African-American studies since traditional African cultures held different values based on differing forms of political science. Indeed, in some ways it might be said that the institutions of traditional African politics were sometimes simply too civilized to be understood by Western categorization.

Most African political systems, for example, did not recognize the right to violent revolution. Instead, African political and social systems depended on a series of built-in control mechanisms designed to head off problems before they became irreconcilable. These social controls usually involved public criticism of abuses of power or deviant behavior and were expressed overtly in institutionalized forms of satiric commentary. Therefore, when African Americans attempted similar controls, it should not immediately suggest a secondary strategem developed by those too weak for more violent tactics, for African Americans came out of a tradition too sophisticated to regard violence as the primary mode of social and political reconciliation.

Thus it was that, through derisive and satirical songs performed directly before the eyes and ears of their socially dominant targets, black bondsmen were able to release some of their own anger and frustration while redirecting white behavior toward lines more in accord with African-American expectations.[1] The sophistication of this form of resistance is the more remarkable because the whites being held over the satiric grill could not help smacking their lips over the satire even while being roasted with the message. However, this manner of resistance proved too subtle and too civil for our own cruder, more violence-laden culture to recognize, and so satiric song has been generally overlooked as an important countervailing institution. A more African perspective, on the other hand, would permit us to understand that the black bondsmen intended their musical satire as a basic and primary weapon in their arsenal of resistance against oppression.

African Uses of Satire

In Africa social associations, work groups, master singers, and individual villagers all traditionally wielded satirical songs against abuses by neighbors, relatives, great men, and rulers. As the traveler Richard Burton explained, "The [West African] people are fond of singing, and compose extempore, whilst playing, dancing, or working—the African can do nothing without a chant,—short songs, often highly satirical and much relished by the listeners."[2] The songs were especially useful in fostering social harmony because they permitted socially approved criticism without fostering unpleasant and dangerous personal, face-to-face confrontations. Since these satiric songs carried the propriety of custom and good manners, private slights were not allowed to fester, nor were the great and powerful permitted to remain immune from the complaints of the weak; instead, grievances and frustrations could be aired before the bar of public opinion where they could be controlled and dealt with by social pressure and communal wisdom.

Africans used such satire to reduce both social and personal stress; in fact, it was a kind of communal psychological medicine, as a high priest of the Ashanti explained to R. S. Rattray:

> You know that every one has a *sunsum* [soul] that may get hurt or knocked about or become sick, and so make the body ill. Very often, although there may be other causes, e.g. witchcraft, ill health is caused by the evil and hate that another has in his head against you. Again, you too may have hatred in your head against another, because of something that person has done to you, and that, too, causes your *sunsum* to fret and become sick. Our forbears knew this to be the case, and so they ordained a time, once every year, when every man and woman, free man and slave, should have freedom to speak out just what was in their head, to tell their neighbors just what they thought of them, and of their actions, and not only their neighbors, but also the king or chief. When a man has spoken freely thus, he will feel his *sunsum* cool and quieted, and the *sunsum* of the other person against whom he has now openly spoken will be quieted also. The King of Ashanti may have killed your children, and you hate him. This has made him ill, and you ill, too; when you are allowed to say before his face what you think, you both benefit. That was why the King of Ashanti in ancient times, when he fell sick, would send for the Queen of Nkoranza to insult him, even though the time for the ceremony had not yet come round. It made him live longer and did him good.[3]

Suggestively, in terms of the African-American experience, Africans used precisely this kind of satire to resist European colonialism. The satiric form of the criticism, as Leroy Vail and Landeg White discovered, legitimized the content: "This 'free expression' is in many African societies not only tolerated but openly welcomed as a major channel of communication between the powerless and the powerful, the client and the patron, the ruled and the ruler."[4]

A victim of African public ridicule was obliged to grin and bear the mocking allusions in somewhat the same manner that in Western society a man is expected to be able to take a joke at his expense whereas he would be justified in avenging an insult. As an informant explained about a song directed against the field manager of a Mozambican sugar estate, "You could swear at him [in the song] and he just smiled." To say the same things outside the song "would be just insulting him . . . , just provoking him," but sung criticism permitted no retaliation—"there will be no case."[5]

Some African societies limited most of their political satire to holiday festivals or special situations, but satiric songs of more personal gossip and recrimination were a part of daily life. Such satire was especially refined by the bardic *griots* who were renowned for their praise songs but equally feared for the sharp, deflating barbs of their wit.

Throughout much of Africa, songs used for social control traditionally made fun of the pompous and condemned those who neglected their duties or were cruel and overbearing. "One can well imagine," explained Hugh Tracey in his study of Chopi musicians, "the forcefulness of the reprimand conveyed to a wrong doer when he finds his misdeeds sung . . . before all the people of a village, or the blow to the pride of an overweening petty official who has to grin and bear it while the young men jeer to music at his pretentiousness."[6] What better sanction, he wondered, against those who outrage the ethics of a community than to know they will be pilloried by the barbs of a master singer and the general laughter of the public. In such songs, cleverly veiled but pointed references to the sources of social injustice were broadcast throughout the marketplace to the widespread enjoyment and satisfaction of the public.[7]

Among the Ashanti such satire was directly institutionalized in the traditional *Apo* rites and similar ceremonies, where ridicule of authority was especially sanctioned and encouraged for a limited period.[8] During such occasions a ruler would be reminded of his vulnerability to social criticism:

> All is well to-day
> We know that a Brong man eats rats,
> But we never knew that one of royal blood eats rats.
> But to-day we have seen our master, Ansah, eating rats.
> To-day all is well and we may say so, say so, say so.
> At other times we may not say so, say so, say so.[9]

Such satiric traditions also characterized the Africa of the slaving era. William Bosman, for example, observed just such an annual festival at Axim on the Gold Coast at the beginning of the eighteenth century, where, he reported, for eight days perfect liberty of lampooning was allowed; indeed, he said, "scandal is so highly exalted, that they may freely sing of all the faults, villainies, and frauds of their superiors as well as inferiors, without punishment, or so much as the least interruption; and the only way to stop their mouths is to ply them lustily with drink, which alters their tone immediately, and turns their satirical ballads into commendatory songs on the good qualities of him who hath so nobly treated them."[10]

The satire was not only political. John Atkins noted in 1721 that as part of the diversion of evening entertainments the inhabitants of Sierra Leone would gather in an open part of town to form "all round in a circle laughing, and with uncouth notes, blame or praise somebody in the company."[11] Africans used satiric song to burlesque domestic quarrels and neighborly disputes as well as to hew villagers to the line of proper social conduct. As Brodie Cruickshank observed from the Gold Coast in the nineteenth century, such songs were often improvised by singers who were "very expert in adapting the subjects of [their] songs to current events, and [who] indulge in mocking ridicule, in biting sarcasm, in fulsome flattery, or in just praise of men and things, according as circumstances seem to demand." As Cruickshank explained, "This habit of publishing the praise, or shame of individuals in spontaneous song, exercises no little influence upon conduct."[12] Africans, like all men, were susceptible to flattery and in dread of public ridicule. And as the press is feared and courted in modern America, so too were the improvisational singers who served as the organs of public opinion in traditional African society.

In Africa as in Afro-America, work songs were a favorite vehicle for satire. For this reason visitors to Sierra Leone in the eighteenth and nineteenth centuries found the songs of native boatmen particularly entertaining. To the stroke of the oars a lead singer among the rowers would boom out an impromptu couplet, and his crew would respond in a general chorus. The songs boasted the exploits of the rowers and lampooned females of their acquaintance; they also broadcast the news of the coast and added gossipy satires of current events. Sometimes the sarcasm of the crew was more pointedly directed at their employers or the important men of their society. As Thomas Winterbottom observed in the 1790s, the songs were often "of a satirical cast lashing the vices of the neighboring head men."[13] Though it may have been safer to criticize neighboring leaders, the allusions were of unmistakably wider application. Subtlety and wry indirection were the requirements of African verbal wit, and the demonstration of verbal skill demanded satire by allusion. The rowers were not afraid to be more direct in their comments; as Winterbottom noted, the impromptu songs of the boatmen "frequently describe the passengers in a strain of praise or of the most pointed ridicule."[14]

Satire functioned in African society as an important way of releasing frustrations that would otherwise have been repressed. The satiric functions of the "amusing spirits" of the Poro society of Sierra Leone, the topical satire of the Egungun cult, and the humorous pantomime of the Ogo society of the Yoruba and Igbo peoples of Nigeria all show marked similarity to African-American examples.[15] Likewise, the satiric commentary of secret society maskers in Sierra Leone and Hausa praise-singers in northern Nigeria parallel African-American holiday songs used by slaves to win gifts from a master. The songs of both areas display a quality of social blackmail, since the persons honored by the attentions of the singers had to come up with a gift to avoid being publicly mimed or ridiculed. Yet, because great generosity to the spirits or praise-singers was the expected behavior, the gifts were regarded not as a response to extortion but, rather, as a worthwhile display of the victim's social prestige, which the singers naturally reciprocated with fitting songs of praise.[16]

Work-song texts from a coffee and quinine plantation in the Kiv area of the then Belgian Congo are particularly suggestive in showing the transition from praise to satire that also characterized New World plantation work songs. Young Bashi women directed their songs at the owner of their plantation, who was also serving as interpreter of the texts. He had recently stopped giving rations of salt and oil because he had raised wages. The singers began by praising the plantation and its owner until in the fourth song the question of the salt and oil rations was raised. By the fifth and final song the women were threatening to take jobs elsewhere if the rations were not reinstated. The songs informed the owner of a discontent that he had not realized existed among his workers. The young women had not complained directly, but through the medium and progression of their songs they had been able politely but pointedly to express their unhappiness.[17]

Whites had been favorite targets of African satire and mimicry since early Portuguese and French missionaries on the slave coast found themselves and their services mocked in local frolics led by their best catechism pupils.[18] In the same way, Thomas Edward Bowdich and his junior officers found their alien idiosyncrasies a source of contemptuous amusement to the Ashanti war captains who were pledging their loyalty to the king before setting out to battle the Fantees: "Each captain made the oath impressive in his own peculiar manner; some seriously, some by ridicule, at our expense, and that of the Fantees, pointing at our heads and ears, and endeavouring to intimidate us by the most insolent action and gesture." The king's troop of small boys also considered the white men figures to be mocked, Bowdich reports, and "used to entertain themselves with mimicking our common expressions and our actions, which they did inimitably."[19]

European traders fared just as badly, for they too were universal targets of local humor. Brodie Cruickshank noted that on the Gold Coast any passing white man was soon caricatured by the improvisational talents of local songsters: "They would quickly seize some peculiarity of his character whether good or bad, and celebrated it aloud, amidst the unrestrained merriment of the bystanders."[20] A. B. Ellis explained the same situation later in the nineteenth century, noting that "it is not uncommon for singers to note the peculiarities of persons who pass, and improvise at their expense. This is particularly the case when the strangers are European, as the latter do not . . . understand Tshi, and the singers can allow themselves greater latitude than would be the case if their remarks were understood."[21]

Almost everything the white man did was funny to his African observers, as Captain Hugh Clapperton discovered while visiting the Yoruba in 1826 when a special series of plays was given in honor of his arrival. The third act featured a "white devil" which, Clapperton reports, "went through the motions of taking snuff, and rubbing its hands; when it walked, it was with the most awkward gait, treading as the most tender-footed white man would do in walking bare-foot, for the first time over new frozen ground. The spectators often appealed to us, as to the excellence of the performance. . . . I pretended to be fully as pleased with this caricature of a white man as they could be, and certainly the actor burlesqued the part to admiration."[22]

In 1827 René Caillié found himself a special favorite of the Mandingo women of Tieme: "They ridiculed my gestures and my words, and went about the village mimicking me and repeating what I had said. . . . My sore foot was the object of their ridicule, and the difficulty I experienced in walking excited their immoderate laughter."[23] Similarly, in the 1860s Richard Burton found his note-taking to be an object of mime and satire by the jesters of Dahomey.[24] Such traditions continued into colonialism when companies recording tunes sung by African laborers in European ports discovered that the songs sold well in West Africa precisely for their biting satire of white society.[25]

Satiric Resistance in the Americas

Given the use of satiric song in Africa, it should not be surprising that through-out the New World during the slave era African-American bondsmen also displayed a genius for improvising songs lampooning the foibles of their masters and advertising harsh or unfair treatment for the general censure of so-ciety. Bryan Edwards observed that blacks in the eighteenth-century West Indies adopted a special genre of improvised ballad for their "Merry meetings and midnight festivals," where they gave "full scope to a talent for ridicule and derision, . . . exercised not only against each other, but also, not infrequently, at the expense of their owner or employers."[26] James Phillippo noted at the beginning of the nineteenth century that in Jamaica such songs "had usually a ludicrous reference to the white people, and were generally suggested by some recent occurrence."[27] As Richard R. Madden explained in 1835, the African-American facility for extemporaneous song-making and sarcastic mimicry was extraordinary: "They are naturally shrewd and quick observers, fond of imitation, and wonderfully successful in practicing it. I think they have the best perception of the ridiculous of any people I ever met."[28]

On the British island of Saint Christopher, Clement Caines recorded that "the Negroes dress every occurence in rhyme, and give it a metre, rude indeed, but well adapted to the purposes of raillery or sarcasm." Caines had personal experience of the matter when he discovered he himself had been the subject of a young slave girl who had been "singing her master" all over his estate for failing to give her a promised coin. Apparently, she kept it up until Caines's wife gave her a hearing.[29]

Sometimes the satire was as cruel as it was humorous; one of the most interesting examples was recorded in British Jamaica at the beginning of the nineteenth century. Robert Renny reports that Europeans arriving at the dock in Port Royal were met by a boatful of black women selling fresh fruits and singing what seems to me the strangest advertising jingle on record:

> New-come buckra [white man],
>   He get sick,
> He take fever,
>   He be die.
>   He be die.
> New-come buckra,
>   He get sick.[30]

Since fever was a real and terrifying danger for newly arrived Europeans, the song was sharply pointed indeed. Mocking arriving Europeans was also a favorite pastime in mid-nineteenth-century Rio de Janeiro where, according to the German traveler Ernst von Bibra, blacks welcomed incoming vessels by sticking out their tongues and yelling curses and obscenities.[31]

Jamaican slaves used satiric song to commemorate the infamous conduct of a local master who threw his critically ill slaves into a gully to die after stripping them of their belongings. One of the slaves recovered and fled to Kingston where he was later discovered by his master, who immediately reclaimed him. But when the full story came out, it was the master who was driven from Kingston, with the event becoming the inspiration for what became a well-known song:

> Take him to the Gulley! Take him to the Gulley!
>   But bringee back the frock and board.—
> Oh! Massa, Massa! me no deadee yet!—
> Take him to the Gulley! Take him to the Gulley!
>   Carry him along.[32]

Similar satires were found on the French islands where, as Jean Baptiste Dutertre noted in the seventeenth century, the Africans were "satirists who reveal even the slightest faults of our Frenchmen [who] cannot do the least reprehensible thing without [the blacks] making it the subject of amusement among themselves. In their worksongs, they repeat all their masters or overseers have done to them, good or bad."[33] Father Jean Baptiste Labat had observed the same characteristics on his travels. The blacks, he reported, were "satirical to excess, and few people apply themselves with greater success to knowing the defects of people and above all of the whites, to mock among themselves."[34]

As in Africa, African-American ridicule and censure gained force through musical presentation. Much like proverbs set to music, improvisational lampoons of the moment were transformed into pieces of traditional folk wisdom and entertainment, enjoyed and remembered in good part for the melodies connected to them. As Lafcadio Hearn noted in late-nineteenth-century Martinique, "vile as may be the motive, the satire, the malice, these chants are preserved for generations by the singular beauty of the air, and the victim of a carnival song need never hope that his failings or his wrong will be forgotten; it will be sung long after he is in his grave."[35]

In Spanish Cuba, J. G. F. Wurdemann observed that such songs were often combined with dancing, and he reported that "in their native dialects [the slaves] ridicule their owners before their faces enjoying with much glee their happy ignorance of the burden of their songs."[36]

But generally it does not seem to have mattered if the victims of the songs understood that they were being burlesqued. In fact, Edward Long reported from eighteenth-century Jamaica that having a nearby overseer listen to the derision directed at him "only serves to add poignancy to their satire, and heightens the fun."[37] Thus, on the Haitian island of La Gonave, when the leading citizen landowner—a mulatto named Constant Polynice—hosted a Congo dance, a guest lampooned him with a song:

> Polynice the tax collector
> Rides at night on his white horse.
> We will drive him away with stones,
> And a misfortune will strike him.

Despite the lyrics, Polynice was generally well liked, and he apparently accepted the song without malice, smiling as if he would have been hurt not to have been so honored.[38]

Slave gangs often used their work songs to comment on their own foibles as well as those of their masters, overseers, and slave drivers—sometimes, as in

WILLIAM D. PIERSEN

Brazil, it was in the riddle form of a *jongo* under the direction of a master singer who would disguise his allusions where necessary with African words and by transforming his targets metaphorically into animals or trees.[39]

At other times the New World satires became openly insurrectionary. In 1805 Trinidad a Mr. de Gannes de la Chancellerie was bathing in the river that ran through his plantation when twelve black women, balancing plantain baskets on their heads, came by on the path. Swaying their hips to the rhythm of the chac-chac pods they carried, the chorus of women offered up what was to him a bloodcurdling threat:

> Pain c'est viande beque [Bread is white man's flesh]
> Vin c'est sang beque [Wine is white man's blood]
>   San Domingo! [a reference to the recent revolt]
> Nous va boire sang beque [We will drink white blood]
>   San Domingo!

After other Trinidadian whites heard the same or similar songs foreshadowing an impending slave revolt, an inquiry was begun that resulted in both executions and severe punishments for the accused rebel leaders.[40]

Mrs. A. C. Carmichael heard another type of insubordinate "funny song" on the same island in the early 1830s, which ridiculed the whites' inability to stop the fires set by Maroons in the hillside sugarcane:

> Fire in de mountain
> Nobody for out him [No one will put it out]
> Take me daddy's bo tick [dandy stick]
> And make a monkey out him
> Poor John! Nobody for out him. [Poor John Bull][41]

In North America, too, slaves used a variety of forms of satiric resistance. Among themselves, bondsmen especially enjoyed parodying their owners in both mime and music. A South Carolina white was scandalized when he secretly beheld a Saturday night country dance of the blacks near Charleston in 1772. "The entertainment," he reported, "was opened by the men copying (or taking off) the manners of their masters, and the women those of their mistresses, and relating some highly curious anecdotes, to the inexpressible diversion of that company."[42] South Carolina slaves continued to parody their masters well into the nineteenth century. A "street girl" from Beaufort explained in the 1840s that "us slaves watched the white folks' parties when the guests danced a minuet and then paraded in a grand march. . . . Then we'd do it, too, but we used to mock 'em, every step. Sometimes the white folks noticed it but they seemed to like it. I guess they thought we couldn't dance any better."[43]

Whites usually seemed flattered by what they interpreted as "awkward" attempts by black society to duplicate their manners. Typical of white obtuseness was the report of Peter Marsden in the 1780s that Jamaican slaves during Christmas holidays danced "minuets with the mulattoes and other brown women, imitating the motion and steps of the English but with a degree of affectation that renders the whole truly laughable and ridiculous."[44] Several decades later another Jamaican, James Stewart, once again overlooked the obvious: "Scenes were exhibited in which his Lordship, with several other distinguished characters, were personated by negroes in full costume, [but] . . . they had lost sight of one grand requisite to complete the resemblance, viz.—ease of manner, and consequently their deportment [was] strangely at variance with that of their originals, rendering such mimic actions truly amusing."[45]

If masters refused to realize there was more than one dimension to such slave foolishness, the black audience knew better. As Shepard Edmunds explained when describing Tennessee slaves doing a cakewalk, "The slaves both young and old would dress up in hand-me-down finery to do a high-kicking, prancing walk-around. They did a take-off on the high manners of the white folks in the 'big house,' but their masters, who gathered around to watch the fun, missed the point."[46]

In late-eighteenth-century New England, black election day celebrations were marked by a grand parade and training of troops by the newly elected black leaders. Whites always found ludicrous the consummate dignity of the black officials; it seemed even more ridiculous when the black troops would take the command "Fire and fall off" literally—tumbling from their horses onto the common field. Such parodies were considered fun, and it was reported that masters did not interfere until "the utmost verge of decency had been reached, good-naturedly submitting to the hard hits leveled against themselves, and possibly profiting a little by some shrewd allusion."[47] Similar satiric parodies were found in South Carolina where in 1843 William Cullen Bryant described a mock military parade by the blacks as "a sort of burlesque of our militia trainings, in which the words of command and the evolutions were extremely ludicrous," and corresponding satiric parades were also common in Haiti during Mardi Gras celebrations.[48]

The "foolishness" of the slaves in their pastimes reflects the traditional wisdom of the jester that satire is safer and more effective when veiled as coming from a clown. Charles William Day noted how, during carnival in nineteenth-century Trinidad, black celebrants lampooned the slave condition to the general enjoyment of black and white.[49] But James Phillippo observed how Jamaican blacks used this self-parody and feigned ignorance to their own advantage: "The lowest and most unintelligent of the tribes are Mungolas.

WILLIAM D. PIERSEN

Their stupidity, however, has often been more feigned than real; thus, when attracting the gaze of the multitudes at their annual carnivals by their grotesque appearance and ridiculous gambols, they have often been known to indulge in the keenest satire and merriment at their own expense, repeating in chorus, 'Buckra tink Mungola nigger fool make him tan so.' "[50]

A satire of a master did not seem so dangerous when it followed on the heels of a self-parody of the slave condition or a series of praise songs flattering the master's vanity. Consider the progression of a Louisiana slave song:

> Negro cannot walk without corn in his pocket,
>> It is to steal chickens.
> Mulatto cannot walk without rope in his pocket,
>> It is to steal horses.
> White man cannot walk without money in his pocket,
>> It is to steal girls.[51]

The preceding song is also interesting because it approached the topic of the white man's access to black women, an access that black men were often powerless to prevent. That whites could use their wealth and power to "steal girls" must have been a source of constant irritation, if not humiliation, for black men who were allowed neither equal opportunities of their own nor even normal social defenses for their women. One way to strike back and to release frustration was through satiric song.

Consider an example of this genre recorded during a John Canoe festival in early-nineteenth-century Kingston, Jamaica; again, an African-like song progression satirizes white male attitudes about sex and race. To the tune of "Guinea Corn" the John Canoe performer sang and tumbled before a white man in his audience to bring forth humorously the theme of the inevitable conversion of white men to the superiority of women of color.

> But Massa Buccra have white love,
> Soft and silken like one dove.
> To brown girl—him barely shivel—
> To black girl—oh, Lord, de Devil!
> But when him once two tree year here,
> Him tink white lady wery great boder;
> De coloured peoples, never fear,
> Ah him lob him de morest nor any oder.
> But top—one time bad fever catch him,
> Colour'd peoples kindly watch him—
> In sick room, nurse voice like music—

From him hand taste sweet de physic.
So always come—in two tree year,
And so wid you, massa—never fear
Brown girl for cook—for wife—for nurse;
Buccra lady—poo—no wort a curse.[52]

"Get away, you scandalous scoundrel," Michael Scott reports himself as having responded to this comic challenge. The song had clearly been offered in jest, and not without a touch of flattery about the sexual opportunities open to the white massa. But also embedded in the lyrics were sly innuendoes about the deadly fevers when whites would lie helplessly dependent on their servants, and a reverse kind of sexual argument that white wandering resulted because no man would reasonably choose a white woman over a woman of color. If that were true, then the unequal access by men of different races to each other's women seemed less unsettling; also if that were true, black men faced competition not so much because they were weak but because their women were so much more desirable.

A far more personal and more pointed song on the same theme comes from Saint Kitts, where a slave singer named Cubenna recalls in a kind of calypso air how his master sent him off on an overnight journey to the capital carrying a note to Doctor Thompson. Cubenna, however, met the doctor on the road and was told he could return home at once; the doctor would send an answer the next day. The overjoyed slave ran home to be with his wife:

Heart been so glad now. Ey-ey-a-a-eye
Ya mee do run, man, ya mee dig, man . . .
I run na mi house, man!
I call 'pon mi wife, man!
I push-um [the door]—I shove um:
[S]he won't gie no hanswer;

I wake um at las', man,
I tell um 'bout someting,
Someting de waalk de [there]
He walk to mi chamber.
[S]he tell me: 'he b'lieve say de Jumbee [spirit].
    Ey-ey-a-a-eye etc.

I look for me bow'tick [heavy walking stick]
Ya mi da lick wi' [which I beat with]
I lick 'way 'pon Jumbee,

WILLIAM D. PIERSEN

Jumbee de bawl de'—Ey-ey-a-a-eye.
He jump na de back-door;

I meet Uncle Quacoo,
I tell um 'bout Jumbee;
Jumbee bin waalk de',
He waalk de wi' shoe on!

He tell me, since be bin barn now,
He never bin hearee,
Jumbee could waalk de, and walk wi' de shoe on.
He tell me, he b'lieve say: "Da, Massa!"
	Ey-ey-a-a-eye.

Massa go killa me—oh![53]

Here the difficult topic of a white master's access to a black man's woman is confronted directly. On the surface the black man has been cuckolded by his devious master and played for a fool by his unfaithful wife, but Cubenna clearly gets his revenge by beating upon the massa who his wife claims is only a noisy spirit. It must be noted, however, that the singer is also a realist who understands that such revenge would inevitably have its own costs. Here in a satiric song aired before the general public a black singer humorously tried to come to terms with a problem that struck to the very core of black male life.

Since in satire the slaves were able to use their own weakness to advantage, the satiric resistance of bondsmen in the Americas was seldom repressed. Blacks used an African-style improvisation that permitted them to move toward either praise or ridicule, flattery or criticism, so as to influence the behavior of those in power. As Nicholas Cresswell reported in 1774, the blacks of Nanjemoy, Maryland, sang to their banjos a "very droll music indeed. In their songs they generally relate the usage they have received from their masters or mistresses in a very satirical style and manner."[54] William Faux noted this same propensity a half-century later in 1819 while listening to the work songs of a chorus of galley slaves in Charleston but saw where the songs were heading: "The verse was their own, and abounding in praise or satire, intended for kind or unkind masters."[55]

This ability to transform songs of praise into songs of recrimination was especially important in using improvisational tunes to countervail a master's domination or to win a reward. Black oarsmen in eighteenth-century Louisiana were no different from the Krumen of eighteenth-century Sierra Leone or the oarsmen of nineteenth-century Charleston in alternating praise with sarcasm to create a self-fulfilling prophecy:

> Sing lads; our master bids us sing
> For master cry out loud and strong
> The water with long oar strike
> Sing, lads, and let us haste along. . . .
>
> See! See! The town! Hurrah! Hurrah!
> Master returns in pleasant mood.
> He's going to treat his boys all 'round.
> Hurrah! Hurrah for master good.[56]

The hint that a good master treats his slaves could hardly be missed, for as John Lambert explained about a similar "nonsense" rowing song he heard on the Savannah River in the early nineteenth century, "I however remarked that brandy was very frequently mentioned, and it was understood as a hint to the passengers to give [the slave rowers] a dram."[57]

When patriarchal southern masters permitted their servants an entertainment, as at Christmas or corn-shucking time, they would often indulge their bondspeople's desire to sing for them. And, as with similar entertainments in Africa, the singers required a treat for their efforts. Sometimes the slaves went from plantation to plantation, like the John Canoers of North Carolina and Jamaica, singing satiric frolic and praise songs before demanding small rewards.[58] A master who failed to offer the expected treat would be derided by a song like the following:

> Poor massa, so dey say;
> Down in de heel, so dey say;
> Got no money, so dey say;
> Not one shillin, so dey say;
> Got A'mighty bless you, so dey say.[59]

At other times, the subject of recompense was approached indirectly but still through a use of humor. As Robert Shepherd recalled, the slaves at a corn shucking sang, "Oh! My head, my poor head. Oh! My poor head is affected!" But as Shepherd explained, "Dere weren't nothing wrong with our heads. Dat was just our way of lettin' our overseer know us wanted some liquor. Purty soon he would come 'round with a big horn of whiskey, and dat made de poor head well, but it weren't long before it got worse again, and den us got another horn of whiskey."[60] Sometimes a master might forget (or try to evade) what

WILLIAM D. PIERSEN

was expected of him; but he would be quickly reminded of his failure by a pointed improvised verse in the ongoing corn song:

> Young Tim Barnet no great thing,
>> Oh! Jenny gone away!
> Never say, come take a dram.
>> Oh! Jenny gone away!
> Master gi's us plenty meat,
>> Oh! Jenny gone away!
> Might apt to fo'git de drink.
>> Oh! Jenny gone away![61]

Later, as the victorious team in a corn shucking carried the master or overseer around on their shoulders, they crowned him with a garland of praise songs, but a perceptive master might have noticed even then that some of the leaves were the poison ivy of sarcasm:

> Oh, Mr. Reid iz er mighty fine man,—
> Er mighty fine man indeed;
> He plants all de taters,
> He plows all de corn,
> He weighs all de cotton,
> An' blows de dinner horn;
> Mr. Reid iz er mighty fine man.[62]

Slaves with relatively decent masters encouraged their kindness by emphasizing their masters' best traits through flattering songs of praise; but always there was the implicit threat to turn this praise around. As one slave sang,

> Massa's nigger am slick and fat,
>> Oh! Oh! Oh!
> Shine jes like a new beaver hat,
>> Oh! Oh! Oh! . . .
> Jones' niggers am lean an po'
>> Oh! Oh! Oh!
> Don't know whether they git 'nough ter eat or no,
>> Oh! Oh! Oh![63]

Few masters could resist comments on fellow whites (even knowing they should not have been permitted) when they came as part of such gratifying praise. But neither should they have missed the implications about the public censure of slave owners who neglected the needs of their bondsmen. Slaves might report the derelictions of ol' Massa Jones when they had a master nearer to home in mind, just as Africans in Sierra Leone couched their criticisms in complaints about neighboring headmen and the blacks of Trinidad disguised theirs in the process of ridiculing the governments of neighboring islands.[64]

Masters, of course, loved the songs of praise and blocked out the impropriety of slaves judging their owners when the comments seemed positive. Consider, for example, the black oarsmen who sang of the physical attractions of their white mistress, Fanny Kemble; she loved every romantic minute of it:

> There is one privilege which I enjoy here which I think few Cockneyesses have ever had experience of, that of hearing my own extemporaneous praises chanted bard-fashion by our Negroes. . . . Rowing yesterday evening through a beautiful moonrise, my two sable boatmen entertained themselves and me with alternate strophe and antistrophe of poetical description of my personal attractions, in which my "wire waist" recurred repeatedly, to my intense amusement . . . ; and I suppose that the fine round natural proportions of the uncompressed waists of the sable beauties of these regions appear less symmetrical to eyes accustomed to them than our stay-cased figures.[65]

Whether the bondsmen were using the moonlight to croon smoothly of Ms. Kemble's many charms or were softly making fun of her corseted figure that was far too narrow by African tastes, what was happening was that black men were openly commenting on the physical attractions of a white woman, moreover, on the physical attractions of the woman who was Massa's wife.

Of course, not all slave owners got off easily with songs of praise or veiled allusions. Frederick Douglass records that bitter derision also appeared. It was clear enough in a frolic song he recorded when the slaves sang:

> We raise de wheat,
> Dey gib us de corn;
>
> We bake de bread,
> Dey gib us de crust;
>
> We sif de meal,
> Dey gib us de huss;
>
> We peel de meat,
> Dey gib us de skin;
>
> And dat's de way,
> Dey take us in;

Dey skim de pot
Dey gib us de liquor,
And say dat's good enough for nigger.[66]

Even a well-thought-of master had to be careful of his behavior or face ridicule. When Ned Lipscomb, described by one of his slaves as "de best massa in de whole country," ran off to avoid Sherman's army during the Civil War, his slaves fitted him into a song then making the rounds, which began:

White folks, have you seed old massa
Up the road, with he mustache on?
He pick up he hat and he leave real sudden
And I believe he's up and gone.

Old massa run away
And us darkies stay at home.
It must be now dat Kingdom's comin'
And de year of Jubilee.[67]

During the same era, Thomas Wentworth Higginson, a white officer greatly respected by his black troops, discovered their remarkable propensity for satire; though they did not lampoon him, they did satirize white enlisted men who were to receive higher wages than corresponding black troops: "My presence apparently checked the performance of another verse, beginning, 'De buckra 'list for money,' apparently in reference to the controversy about the pay question, then just beginning, and to the more mercenary and less noble aims they attributed to the white soldiers."[68]

Thus it was that throughout the era of slavery African Americans across the New World used satiric songs to resist white oppression. When, under the interdictions of bondage, blacks found themselves unable to develop formal methods of social regulation, they fought back with the informal controls that in Africa had accompanied public satire, praise, and ridicule. By cleverly intermixing criticism of their masters with flattery, and by combining their praise and criticism with corresponding lampoons of black behavior, African-American bondsmen desensitized the seeming impropriety of black slaves satirizing the society of their white owners. Thus, in their songs slaves were able cleverly to voice many of their grievances before their masters and openly vent their frustrations and disdain as well.

By commenting on the virtues and foibles of white society, the slaves were sometimes able to improve their own situations, for few masters preferred the barbs of ridicule to the enticements of praise and flattery. That it did not work better on European Americans is unfortunate but understandable since the whites lacked well-developed similar institutions of their own; nonetheless, such satire still worked more effectively in most cases than desperate acts of violence or running away—both of which usually only resulted in severe punishments and hardened attitudes. Moreover, the songs were emotionally healing to the singers themselves. If slavery could not be overcome, it could be withstood. The soul would survive.

We have long known that slaves adept at dissembling behavior relished "puttin' on Ole Massa," as it was known, but clearly there was more to African wit than the clever lie and more to African-American resistance than flight or suicidal violence. In the satire of song and pantomime slaves not only put Ole Massa on, they put him down as well, and put him down directly, in public, to his face.

NOTES

1. Some of the arguments and examples in this chapter were first published in *Research in African Literatures* 7(2) (1977): 166–80, and republished in Daniel J. Crowley, ed., *African Folklore in the New World* (Austin, Tex., 1977), 20–34.

2. Richard F. Burton, *Wanderings in West Africa from Liverpool to Fernando Po*, 2 vols. (London, 1863), 2:169.

3. R. S. Rattray, *Ashanti*, 2 vols. (1923; rpt. ed., Oxford, 1969), 1:153.

4. Leroy Vail and Landeg White, "Forms of Resistance: Songs and Perceptions of Power in Colonial Mozambique," *American Historical Review* 88 (4) (October 1983): 888.

5. Ibid., 887–88.

6. Hugh Tracey, *Chopi Musicians: Their Music, Poetry, and Instruments* (New York, 1948), 3.

7. Melville J. Herskovits, *The New World Negro* (Bloomington, Ind., 1969), 138.

8. Rattray, *Ashanti*, 1:151–71.

9. Ibid.

10. William Bosman, *A New and Accurate Description of the Coast of Guinea* (1705; rpt. ed., London, 1967), 158. See also John Barbot, "A Description of the Coasts of North and South Guinea, and of Etheopia Inferior, Vulgarly Angola," in *A Collection of Voyages and Travels*, eds. Awnsham Churchill and John Churchill, 6 vols. (London, 1746), 5:317.

11. John Atkins, *A Voyage to Guinea, Brazil, and the West Indies* (1735; rpt. ed., London, 1970), 53.

12. Brodie Cruickshank, *Eighteen Years on the Gold Coast of Guinea*, 2 vols. (London, 1853), 2:265–66.

13. Thomas Winterbottom, *An Account of the Native African in the Neighborhood of Sierra Leone*, 2 vols. (1803; rpt. ed., London, 1969), 1:112. A similar description can be found in Horatio Bridge, *Journal of an African Cruiser* (New York, 1853), 16–17.

14. Winterbottom, *Account of the Native African*, 1:112.

15. Kenneth Little, *The Mende of Sierra Leone* (New York, 1967), 246–51; Oludare Olajubu, "Iwi Egungun Chants: An Introduction," in *Forms of Folklore in Africa*, ed. Bernth

Lindfors (Austin, Tex., 1977), 159; and Phoebe Ottenberg, "The Afikpo Ibo of Nigeria," in *Peoples and Cultures of Africa*, ed. James L. Gibbs, Jr. (New York, 1966), 14–15, 34.

16. Little, *The Mende*, 251; and M. G. Smith, "The Social Functions and Meaning of Hausa Praise-Singing," in *Peoples and Cultures of Africa*, ed. Elliot P. Skinner (Garden City, N.Y., 1973), 561.

17. Alan P. Merriam, "Song Texts of the Bashi," *Zaire* 8 (1954): 41; similarly, see the examples provided from the Tiv area of northern Nigeria in Elenore Smith Bowen, *Return to Laughter* (New York, 1964), 64.

18. James Pope-Hennessy, *Sins of the Fathers* (New York, 1969), 167.

19. T. Edward Bowdich, *Mission from Cape Coast Castle to Ashantee* (1819; rpt. ed., London, 1966), 59, 292. Similarly, for a more modern example, see Bowen, *Return to Laughter*, 291–92.

20. Cruickshank, *Eighteen Years on the Gold Coast*, 2:266.

21. Alfred B. Ellis, *The Tshi-Speaking Peoples of the Gold Coast of West Africa* (London, 1887), 328.

22. Hugh Clapperton, *Journal of a Second Expedition into the Interior of Africa* (1829; rpt. ed., London, 1966), 55. There continue to be Egungun maskers who specialize in lampooning the white man; see Olajubu, "Iwi Egungun Chants," 156. The tradition probably began with satirical take-offs of other African peoples such as are still practiced by the Egungun; see Margaret Thompson Drewal and Henry John Drewal, "More Power than Each Other: An Egbado Classification of Egungun," *African Arts* 11(3) (April 1978): 35–36.

23. René Caillié, *Journal d'un voyage à Temboctou et à Jenne dans l'Afrique Centrale* (Paris, 1830), as quoted in Christopher Hibbert, *Africa Explored: Europeans in the Dark Continent, 1769–1889* (New York, 1984), 169.

24. Richard F. Burton, *A Mission to Gelele, King of Dahome* (1964, rpt. ed., New York, 1966), 130. See also his *Wanderings in West Africa*, 2:291: "Africans are uncommonly keen in perceiving and in caricaturing any ridicule."

25. Herskovits, *New World Negro*, 139.

26. Bryan Edwards, *The History, Civil and Commercial, of the British Colonies in the West Indies*, 3 vols. (London, 1793–1801), 2:103.

27. James M. Phillippo, *Jamaica: In Past and Present State* (Philadelphia, 1843), 75.

28. Richard R. Madden, *A Twelvemonth's Residence in the West Indies during the Transition from Slavery to Apprenticeship*, 2 vols. (Philadelphia, 1835), 1:107, 2:passim.

29. Clement Caines, *The History of the General Council and General Assembly of the Leeward Islands . . .* (Saint Christopher, 1804), 110–11. The custom of "singing" someone, or being "put on the banjo" as it was sometimes called, seems closely related to the African-American custom of blacks "talking to themselves" loudly in public about personal grievances. "The negro is very fond of talking to himself or herself, or at least of publishing in the streets his private opinions on his own private affairs for the benefit of the public at large . . . to 'put it to you' whether he has been fairly dealt with. The women are particularly prone to this"; Charles William Day, *Five Years' Residence in the West Indies*, 2 vols. (London, 1852), 1:23. See also "Sketches in the West Indies," *Dublin University Magazine* 56 (November 1860), 613; Rev. J. S. Scoles, *Sketches of African and Indian Life in British Guiana* (Demerara, 1885), 48; and the *Virginia Gazette*, March 7, 1777, runaway advertisement for an African woman described as "remarkable for talking to herself," in *Runaway Slave Advertisements*, comp., Lathan A. Windley, 3 vols. (Westport, Conn., 1983), 1:180.

30. Robert Renny, *An History of Jamaica* (London, 1807), 241.

31. Ernst von Bibra, *Reise in Sudamerika* (Mannheim, 1854), 109–10.

32. Matthew G. Lewis, *Journal of a West India Proprietor, 1815–1817* (London, 1834), 322.

33. Jean Baptiste Dutertre, *Historie générale des Antilles habitées par les François*, 2 vols. (Paris, 1671), 2:497. It was the same for black work songs in Jamaica in the early twentieth century; see Walter Jekyll, *Jamaican Song and Story* (1907; rpt. ed., New York, 1966), 188.

34. Jean Baptiste Labat, *Nouveau voyage aux îles de l'Amérique* (La Haye, 1724), 57–58.

35. Lafcadio Hearn, *Two Years in the French West Indies* (1890; rpt. ed., Boston, 1922), 250–51. Melville Herskovits has also commented on the satire in Brazilian carnival songs; see *New World Negro*, 22.

36. J. G. F. Wurdemann, *Notes on Cuba* (Boston, 1844), 84. Satire was also connected to the calenda dance in the French West Indies; see M. L. E. Moreau de Saint-Méry, *Description . . . de la partie française de l'Ile Saint-Domingue*, 2 vols. (1797; rpt. ed., Paris, 1958), 1:44.

37. Edward Long, *The History of Jamaica*, 2 vols. (London, 1774), 2:423.

38. William Seabrook, *The Magic Island* (New York, 1929), 225–26. For an example of a white judge in New Orleans who was lampooned for the kind of dance he hosted, see George Washington Cable, "The Dance in Place Congo," in *The Negro and His Folklore*, ed., Bruce Jackson (Austin, Tex., 1967), 207.

39. Melville J. Herskovits, *Life in a Haitian Valley* (New York, 1937), 26; and Stanley J. Stein, *Vassouras: A Brazilian Coffee County, 1850–1900* (Cambridge, Mass., 1957), 206–207.

40. Quoted in V. S. Naipaul, *The Loss of El Dorado* (New York, 1984), 293–94, 297.

41. Mrs. A. C. Carmichael, *Domestic Matters and Social Conditions of the . . . West Indies*, 2 vols. (London, 1833), 2:301; or see Lewis, *Journal*, 288, for the insurrectionary song of the "King of the Eboes."

42. *South Carolina Gazette*, September 17, 1772, as quoted in Peter H. Wood, *Black Majority: Negroes in Colonial South Carolina from 1670 through the Stono Rebellion* (New York, 1974), 342.

43. Quoted in Marshall Stearns and Jean Stearns, *Jazz Dance* (New York, 1968), 22.

44. Peter Marsden, *An Account of the Island of Jamaica* (Newcastle, 1788), as quoted in *After Africa: Extracts from British Travel Accounts and Journals*, ed. Roger D. Abrahams and John F. Szwed (New Haven, 1983), 230.

45. James Stewart, *A View of the Past and Present State of the Island of Jamaica* (London, 1808), 266, as quoted in John W. Nunley and Judith Bettelheim, *Caribbean Festival Arts* (Seattle, 1988), 45.

46. Quoted in Rudi Blesh and Harriet Janis, *They All Played Ragtime* (New York, 1971), 96.

47. James R. Newhall, *History of Lynn, Essex County, Massachusetts* (Lynn, 1883), 49; see also William D. Piersen, *Black Yankees: The Development of an Afro-American Subculture in Eighteenth-Century New England* (Amherst, 1988), 137–38. Compare this to the similar report from Jamaica of Cynric R. Williams, *A Tour through the Island of Jamaica* (London, 1826), as quoted in Abrahams and Szwed, *After Africa*, 250: "The slaves sang satirical philippics against their master, communicating a little free advice now and then; but they never lost sight of decorum."

48. William Cullen Bryant, *The Life and Works of William Cullen Bryant*, ed. Parke Godwin, 6 vols. (New York, 1884), 6:26, and Harold Courlander, *The Drum and the Hoe* (Berkeley, 1960), 136.

49. Day, *Five Years' Residence*, 2:314.

50. Phillippo, *Jamaica*, 80.

51. Lyle Saxon, *Gumbo Ya-Ya* (Cambridge, Mass., 1945), 430.

52. Michael Scott, *Tom Cringle's Log* (1829–33; rpt. ed., London, 1969), 241–45, as quoted in Abrahams and Szwed, *After Africa*, 238. Roger Buckley notes that it was customary throughout the West Indies for European men to be nursed by mulatto women, who also often served as their mistresses; see Roger Norman Buckley, ed., *The Haitian Journal of Lieutenant Howard, York Hussars, 1796–1798* (Knoxville, 1985), 181.

53. Day, *Five Years' Residence*, 2:121–22. Another variant of this genre is probably represented in the poem "Buddy Quow" (recorded in a Gullah-Jamaican dialect around the turn of the nineteenth century) in which Buddy's woman, Quasheba, gives birth to a mulatto child. See Donald R. Kloe, "Buddy Quow: An Anonymous Poem in Gullah-Jamaican Dialect Written circa 1800," *Southern Folklore Quarterly* 38 (2) (June 1974): 82–85, 87–88.

54. Nicholas Cresswell, *The Journal of Nicholas Cresswell* (New York, 1924), 18–19.

55. William Faux, *Memorial Days in America, Being a Journal of a Tour* (London, 1823), 195.

56. George Washington Cable, "Creole Slave Songs," in Jackson, *The Negro and His Folklore*, 239; similarly, see Trelawny Wentworth, *The West India Sketch Book*, 2 vols. (London, 1834), 2:240, 242; C. Schlichthorst, *O Rio de Janeiro como e, 1824–1826*, as quoted in Mary C. Karasch, *Slave Life in Rio de Janeiro, 1808–1850* (Princeton, 1987), 239; or Winterbottom, *Account of the Native African*, 1:112. Several good examples of satiric boat songs are noted in Dena J. Epstein, *Sinful Tunes and Spirituals* (Urbana, Ill., 1977), 168–69.

57. John Lambert, *Travels through Canada, and the United States of North America, in the Years 1806, 1807, & 1808*, 2 vols. (London, 1816), 2:254.

58. See, for example, Kenneth M. Stampp, *The Peculiar Institution* (New York, 1963), 386; Lewis, *Journal*, 56; and for a similar Haitian example, see Courlander, *Drum and Hoe*, 107.

59. Harriet A. Jacobs, *Incidents in the Life of a Slave Girl* (Boston, 1861), 180–81.

60. Quoted in Norman R. Yetman, ed., *Life under the "Peculiar Institution"* (New York, 1970), 267.

61. James S. Lamar, *Recollections of Pioneer Days in Georgia* (n.p., 1928), as quoted in Roger D. Abrahams, *Singing the Master: The Emergence of African American Culture in the Plantation South* (New York, 1992), 210.

62. Mary Ross Banks, *Bright Days on the Old Plantation* (Boston, 1882), 131.

63. Booker T. Washington, *The Story of the Negro*, 2 vols. (1904; rpt. ed., New York, 1940), 1:160.

64. Winterbottom, *Account of the Native African*, 1:112; and Melville J. Herskovits, *Trinidad Village* (New York, 1964), 278.

65. Frances Anne Kemble, *Journal of a Residence on a Georgia Plantation in 1838–1839* (1863; rpt. ed., New York, 1961), 141.

66. Frederick Douglass, *The Life and Times of Frederick Douglass* (Hartford, 1881), 181; similarly, see Saxon, *Gumbo Ya-Ya*, 450. On this topic in general, see Roger D. Abrahams, "Afro-American Worksongs on Land and Sea," in *By Land and Sea: Studies in the Folklore of Work and Leisure Honoring Horace P. Beck on His Sixty-fifth Birthday*, ed. Roger D. Abrahams, Kenneth S. Goldstein, and Wayland Hand (Hatboro, Pa., 1985), 1–9.

67. Quoted in Yetman, *Life under the "Peculiar Institution,"* 113. The song appears to have been a well-known black folk song; other versions are noted in Abrahams, "Afro-American

Worksongs," 149, and in *Bullwhip Days: The Slaves Remember*, ed. James Mellon (New York, 1988), 340.

68. Thomas Wentworth Higginson, *Army Life of a Black Regiment* (1869; rpt. ed., New York, 1984), 212, 238; the noisy complaints of the black troops eventually led Higginson to take an active part in calling for the repeal of the unjust pay differential between white and black soldiers.

WILLIAM D. PIERSEN

3

. . . . . .

Sports and Public Display
of the Body

The Black and White Truth about Basketball

(1975)

JEFF GREENFIELD

. . . .

Journalist Jeff Greenfield wrote this essay about different cultural styles in basketball for Esquire *in 1975. While it is possible to see some of his conclusions as perpetuation of stereotypes, Greenfield notes a number of traits that appear in many other discussions of an African American aesthetic. The quality of deception is present in signifying and satire; it is also one that Michael Eric Dyson mentions as a key to understanding the style of Michael Jordan. Greenfield points out the pleasure of the unexpected, which John Edgar Wideman calls "improvisation," Michael Jordan "surprise," and Dyson "spontaneity." Greenfield says black playground basketball features "speed, mobility, quickness, acceleration," all factors that Arthur Ashe included in his description of the black basketball style that emerged in the 1940s. Developing a unique "calling card" or a trademark move in basketball parallels the development of personal styles in jazz, which Olly Wilson describes in his theory of "heterogeneous sound ideal." The black basketball style is a form of "electric self-expression," according to Greenfield, and yet integral to this style is virtuoso performance that shows no strain. Greenfield's exemplar of this cool quality is George Gervin, whose expressionless face and effortless finger rolls gave him the nickname "The Iceman."*

The dominance of black athletes over professional basketball is beyond dispute. Two thirds of the players are black, and the number would be greater were it not for the continuing practice of picking white bench warmers for the sake of balance. The Most Valuable Player award of the National Basketball Association has gone to blacks for twenty-three of the last twenty-five years. The NBA was the first pro sports league of any stature to hire a black coach (Bill Russell of the Celtics) and the first black general manager (Wayne Embry of the Bucks). What discrimination remains—lack of opportunity for lucrative benefits such as speaking engagements and product endorsements—has more to do with society than with basketball.

This dominance reflects a natural inheritance; basketball is a pastime of the urban poor. The current generation of black athletes are heirs to a tradition half a century old: in a neighborhood without the money for bats, gloves, hockey sticks, tennis rackets, or shoulder pads, basketball is accessible. "Once it was the game of the Irish and Italian Catholics in Rockaway and the Jews on Fordham Road in the Bronx," writes David Wolf in his brilliant book, *Foul!* "It was recreation, status, and a way out." But now the ethnic names are changed; instead of Red Holzmans, Red Auerbachs, and McGuire brothers, there are Julius Ervings and Darryl Dawkins and Kareem Abdul-Jabbars. And professional basketball is a sport with a national television contract and million-dollar salaries.

But the mark on basketball of today's players can be measured by more than money or visibility. It is a question of style. For there is a clear difference between "black" and "white" styles of play that is as clear as the difference between 155th Street at Eighth Avenue and Crystal City, Missouri. Most simply (remembering we are talking about culture, not chromosomes), "black" basketball is the use of superb athletic skill to adapt to the limits of space imposed by the game. "White" ball is the pulverization of that space by sheer intensity.

It takes a conscious effort to realize how constricted the space is on a basketball court. Place a regulation court (ninety-four by fifty feet) on a football field, and it will reach from the back of the end zone to the twenty-one-yard line; its width will cover less than a third of the field. On a baseball diamond, a basketball court will reach from home plate to just beyond first base. Compared to its principal indoor rival, ice hockey, basketball covers about one-fourth the playing area. And during the normal flow of the game, most of the action takes place on about the third of the court nearest the basket. It is in this dollhouse space that ten men, each of them half a foot taller than the average man, come together to battle each other.

There is, thus, no room; basketball is a struggle for the edge: the half step with which to cut around the defender for a lay-up, the half second of freedom with which to release a jump shot, the instant a head turns allowing a pass to a team-mate breaking for the basket. It is an arena for the subtlest of skills: the head fake, the shoulder fake, the shift of body weight to the right and the sudden cut to the left. Deception is crucial to success; and to young men who have learned early and painfully that life is a battle for survival, basketball is one of the few games in which the weapon of deception is a legitimate rule and not the source of trouble.

If there is, then, the need to compete in a crowd, to battle for the edge, then the surest strategy is to develop the *unexpected*; to develop a shot that is simply and fundamentally different from the usual methods of putting the ball in the basket. Drive to the hoop, but go under it and come up the other side; hold the ball at waist level and shoot from there instead of bringing the ball up to eye level; leap into the air and fall away from the basket instead of toward it. All these tactics take maximum advantage of the crowding on a court; they also stamp uniqueness on young men who may feel it nowhere else.

"For many young men in the slums," David Wolf writes, "the school yard is the only place they can feel true pride in what they do, where they can move free of inhibitions and where they can, by being spectacular, rise for the moment against the drabness and anonymity of their lives. Thus, when a player develops extraordinary 'school yard' moves and shots . . . [they] become his measure as a man."

So the moves that begin as tactics for scoring soon become calling cards. You don't just lay the ball in for an uncontested basket; you take the ball in both hands, leap as high as you can, and slam the ball through the hoop. When you jump in the air, fake a shot, bring the ball back to your body, and throw up a shot, all without coming back down, you have proven your worth in uncontestable fashion.

This liquid grace is an integral part of "black" ball, almost exclusively the province of the playground player. Some white stars like Bob Cousy, Billy Cunningham, Doug Collins, and Paul Westphal had it: the body control, the moves to the basket, the free-ranging mobility. They also had the surface case that is integral to the "black" style; an incorportion of the ethic of mean streets—to "make it" is not just to have wealth, but to have it without strain. Whatever the muscles and organs are doing, the face of the "black" star almost never shows it. George Gervin of the San Antonio Spurs can drive to the basket with two men on him, pull up, turn around, and hit a basket without the least flicker of emotion. The Knicks' former great Walt Frazier, flamboyant in dress, cars, and companions, displayed nothing but a quickly raised fist after scoring a particularly important basket. (Interestingly, the black coaches in the NBA exhibit far less emotion on the bench than their white counterparts; All Attles and K. C. Jones are statuelike compared with Jack Ramsey or Dick Motta or Kevin Loughery.)

If there is a single trait that characterizes "black" ball it is leaping agility. Bob Cousy, ex-Celtic great and former pro coach, says that "when coaches get together, one is sure to say, 'I've got the one black kid in the country who can't jump.' When coaches see a white boy who can jump or who moves with extraordinary quickness, they say, 'He should have been born black, he's that good.' "

Don Nelson, former Celtic and coach of the Milwaukee Bucks, recalls that in 1970, Dave Cowens, then a relatively unknown Florida State graduate, prepared for his rookie season by playing in the Rucker League, an outdoor Harlem competition that pits pros against playground stars and college kids. So ferocious was Cowens' leaping power, Nelson says, that "when the summer was over, everyone wanted to know who the white son of a bitch was who could jump so high." That's another way to overcome a crowd around the basket—just go over it.

Speed, mobility, quickness, acceleration, "the moves"—all of these are catch-phrases that surround the "black" playground style of play. So does the most racially tinged of attributes, "rhythm." Yet rhythm is what the black stars themselves talk about; feeling the flow of the game, finding the tempo of the dribble, the step, the shot. It is an instinctive quality, one that has led to difficulty between systematic coaches and free-form players. "Cats from the street have their own rhythm when they play," said college dropout Bill Spivey, onetime New York high-school star. "It's not a matter of somebody setting you up and you shooting. You *feel* the shot. When a coach holds you back, you lose the feel and it isn't fun anymore."

Connie Hawkins, the legendary Brooklyn playground star, said of Laker coach Bill Sharman's methodical style of teaching, "He's systematic to the point where it begins to be a little too much. It's such an action-reaction type of game that when you have to do everything the same way, I think you lose something."

There is another kind of basketball that has grown up in America. It is not played on asphalt playgrounds with a crowd of kids competing for the court; it is played on macadam driveways by one boy with a ball and a backboard nailed over the garage; it is played in Midwestern gyms and on Southern dirt courts. It is a mechanical, precise development of skills (when Don Nelson was an Iowa farm boy his incentive to make his shots was that an errant rebound would land in the middle of chicken droppings), without frills, without flow, but with effectiveness. It is "white" basketball: jagged, sweaty, stumbling, intense. A "black" player overcomes an obstacle with finesse and body control; a "white" player reacts by outrunning or outpowering the obstacle.

By this definition, the Boston Celtics are a classically "white" team. The Celtics almost never use a player with dazzling moves; that would probably make Red Auerbach swallow his cigar. Instead, the Celtics wear you down with execution, with constant running, wth the same play run again and again. The rebound triggers the fast break, with everyone racing downcourt; the ball goes to Larry Bird, who pulls up and takes the jump shot, or who fakes the shot and passes off to the man following, the "trailer," who has the momentum to go inside for a relatively easy shot.

Perhaps the most classically "white" position is that of the quick forward, one without great moves to the basket, without highly developed shots, without the height and mobility for rebounding effectiveness. What does he do? He runs. He runs from the opening jump to the last horn. He runs up and down the court, from base line to base line, back and forth under the basket, looking for the opening, for the pass, for the chance to take a quick step and the high-percentage shot. To watch San Antonio's Mark Olberding, a player without speed or moves, is to wonder what he is doing in the NBA—until you see him swing free and throw up a shot that, without demanding any apparent skill, somehow goes in the basket more frequently than the shots of any of his teammates. To watch Kurt Rambis of the Los Angeles Lakers, an ungainly collection of arms, legs, and elbows, thumping up and down the court at half-speed is to wonder whether the NBA has begun a hire-the-handicapped program—until you see Rambis muscling aside an opponent to grab a rebound, or watch him trail the fast-break to steer an errant shot into the basket. And to have watched Boston Celtic immortal John Havlicek is to have seen "white" ball at its best.

Havlicek stands in dramatic contrast to Julius Erving of the Philadelphia 76ers. Erving has the capacity to make legends come true; leaping from the foul line and slam-dunking the ball on his way down; going up for a lay-up, pulling the ball to his body and throwing under and up the other side of the rim, defying gravity and probability with moves and jumps. Havlicek looked like the living embodiment of his small-town Ohio background. He would bring the ball downcourt, weaving left, then right, looking for the path. He would swing the ball to a teammate, cut behind a pick, take the pass and release the shot in a flicker of time. It looked plain, unvarnished. But there are not half a dozen players in the league who can see such possibilities for a free shot, then get that shot off as quickly and efficiently as Havlicek.

To former pro Jim McMillian, a black with "white" attributes, himself a quick forward, "it's a matter of environment." Julius Erving grew up in a different environment from Havlicek—John came from a very small town in Ohio. There everything was done the easy way, the shortest distance between two points. It's nothing fancy, very few times will he go one-on-one; he hits the lay-up, hits the jump shot, makes the free throw, and after the game you look up and you say, 'How did he hurt us that much?' "

"White" ball, then, is the basketball of patience and method. "Black" ball is the basketball of electric self-expression. One player has all the time in the world to perfect his skills, the other a need to prove himself. These are slippery categories, because a poor boy who is black can play "white" and a white boy of middle-class parents can play "black." Jamaal Wilkes and Paul Westphal are athletes who seem to defy these categories. And what makes basketball the most intriguing of sports is how these styles do not necessarily clash; how the punishing intensity of "white" players and the dazzling moves of the "blacks" can fit together, a fusion of cultures that seems more and more difficult in the world beyond the out-of-bounds line.

The Hero of the Blues

(1989)

GERALD EARLY

. . . .

In this review of Chris Mead's biography Champion: Joe Louis, Black Hero in White America, *Gerald Early points to some of the complexities in America's relation to "greatest, the most expansive and mythical blues hero in twentieth-century Amerca." As Early notes, the figure of Louis brings up uncomfortable questions about the "commercialization of the [black] body." Yet as a blues hero Louis transcended complications of race, class, gender, and commerce to provide black and white America with a "heroic stylization in which personal meaning and the symbolic ritual of triumph and defeat can be played out." Early is a professor of English and African and Afro-American studies at Washington University in St. Louis and a noted essayist.*

> In art both agony and ecstasy are matters of stylization.
> —Albert Murray, *The Hero and the Blues*

To outlive one's greatness is an especial destiny of the champion athlete whose period of greatness is so intense because it is so brief and so contextual, a fling during a godly and incredibly beautiful youth. Joe Louis surely outdistanced his greatness, about as completely as a runner in the middle of a long race has left behind the starting block. When he died in 1981 at the age of sixty-six, he seemed even more used up than his age would have indicated. He seemed the way everyone always imagines great athletes and especially great boxers to be in their dotage. He was particularly to be pitied because he had gone crazy in his last years, an occurrence that most of the public mistakenly thought came about as a result of his time in the ring. It was, as one Louis biographer, Barney Nagler, implied, and as most medical experts believed, a case of heredity. His father had gone mad when Louis was a child and died in a segregated asylum shortly after Louis became a headline fighter.

At the time of his death, of course, Louis had not fought a memorable fight in nearly two generations; the last was at the end of his prime in the late forties; and it was difficult for younger sports fans, especially young black ones who cared nothing for nostalgia and love, instead desiring only the newest currency in the improvisations of style and moves, to picture the old man with the receding hairline and paunchy belly who was predicting George Foreman would destroy Ali in Zaire as anything more than a tired old man. This was a new generation that admired Ali and was not even born when Louis was an active fighter. Every time Louis predicted Ali would lose, which he did fairly often and quite without malice, never wishing for Ali to lose, the men on the stoops would say, "Joe talkin' crazy again. He ain't never called a fight right in his whole motherfarmin' life"; or, "If Joe say the other guy gonna win, then all my money goes on Ali." It was hard for those of us of the generation of civil rights marches, black power, and the Eastern approaches of exotic names and religions to believe our fathers and grandfathers who told us he was not only the greatest fighter in America but the most famous black man in history at that time.

As a pop cultural symbol, he had been thoroughly revised by that great showman, Muhammad Ali. But try as he might, Ali, who was in truth always trying to slay the father figure of Louis, could never quite obscure him. Louis was, as in the Zaire drama, always in the background, and his fame and ability and downfall were the measuring rods for Ali and for Ali's public, both black and white. Could Ali match Louis's thirteen-year reign? Could he match Louis's knockout record? Would he wind up broke like Louis? Louis's long shadow resulted partly because his period of success was unusually long for an athlete, particularly a champion boxer. He was more the king of an era than any fighter before him including Jack Dempsey, Jack Johnson, and John L. Sullivan, who each held the heavyweight title long enough during their respective reigns actually to be considered the maestro of an epoch in American social history. In fact, except for Ali, no fighter after him has ever been able to match the magnitude of his myth and his longevity. No fighter has ever been able to match his consistency, not even Ali or Larry Holmes. In his prime, Louis had a methodical excellence that bordered on being uncanny, slightly bizarre and eerie in its disciplined power. It is true, doubtless, that most of his opponents were inferior fighters, but then what heavyweight champion has made a career of greatness fighting anyone other than stiffs and bums for the most part? His opponents, on the whole, were better than Dempsey's and Johnson's challengers during their championship periods and were probably the equal of

Ali's, whose only prime first-class foes were Joe Frazier (his nemesis and alter ego), George Foreman, and Ken Norton. It is, alas, hard to find big men who fight well. But Louis was and is our most mythical athlete, our most beloved athlete, which means, in the end, he was luckier than most fighters who are usually loved by the public in only a kind of amused or cast-off way. Louis became, as Chris Mead points out in his generally fine biography, "a symbol of national unity," something that no black had ever achieved before or has ever accomplished since. And certainly no prizefighter ever has. Even Jess Willard, the great white hope who defeated Jack Johnson in Havana in 1915 and returned the title to "the white race," was never a symbol of any kind of unity, racial or national. He was simply both an essence and a sign of the white male's pathological preoccupation with white supremacy, nothing more. In fact, Willard was not even liked much by the white public and, within a year of winning the title, was humiliated by Harry Houdini in front of an audience in California and hooted from the theater. It is hard to imagine this ever happening to Louis, for whom Jim Crow customs bowed down and white folk made entranceways. But Louis's heroism has been misunderstood by the public that insisted, in Louis's later years, that he must be a victim, that it must be recognized that he was used, that he was the prototypical pawn in the white man's game. It has become for both blacks and whites necessary to see him in this way largely to assuage their very different but undeniably real senses of guilt about his last years. The whites say we should not have let this happen to an American hero. The blacks say we should not have let this happen to a black hero. It is a horribly misguided reduction of the man and the divinity of his stature. And it reveals more about our collective unease about prizefighting and the meaning of black male heroism in popular culture than it does anything about the concern over Louis's fate, which did not seem to have made him nearly as unhappy as it did a distressed American public. Those vestiges of Victorianism that linger like a remnant in our cultural subconsciousness make it impossible to accept a prizefighter as a bona fide hero unless we can qualify it in some way, such as making him a victim. But we do not wish to make him a victim of America's social or political structures but rather, in a vague sort of social protest, a victim of his origins, of some sort of trap from which the impoverished, no matter how wealthy they become in their endeavors, can never escape. There is the possibility that Louis may have been used by his managers, his promoters, his government, by a white public that represented an alien and sometimes hostile culture. But perhaps in the end Louis was not used more than any hero is used by the society that creates him and needs him. There was always a great sense of both irritating condescension and deep, touching innocence in America's relationship with Joe Louis. One fact is perfectly clear, despite everything else: Louis was the greatest, the most expansive and mythical blues hero in twentieth-century America, nothing less.

One of the great features of Chris Mead's biography of Joe Louis, published in the fall of 1985, is that, unlike the five previous major Louis biographies, Edward Van Every's *Joe Louis, Man and Superfighter* (1936), Margary Miller's *Joe Louis: American* (1945), Barney Nagler's *The Brown Bomber* (1972), A. O. Edmonds's *Joe Louis* (1973), and Gerald Astor's *". . . And a Credit to His Race": The Hard Life and Times of Joseph Louis Barrow* (1974), Mead comes closest to understanding Louis as a blues hero, to understanding his life as if it were the utterance of one simple yet crucial phrase: How I got over. In a very vital sense, no one was more determined not to lose than Joe Louis. Yet his victory was not one of achievement but rather of process: "how I got over," a phrase used by both black preachers and black hustlers, the autobiographical summing up of both the sacred life and the profane life. "How I got over" is the sign of the underground victory, the rebel victory that is not simply enduring one's adversities but outslicking them. Mead's greater understanding in this regard occurs in part because he places Louis within the context of Afro-American culture, shows Louis to be a product of it. No other biographer had ever done what now appears such a natural and necessary thing to do. The result in Mead's work is that the reader sees Louis more as the complex meshing of two distinct cultural attitudes, a meshing that is not always balanced and does not always work well. But one comes to see Louis as more than a kind of stereotypical put-upon and distressed black American male. For instance, as Mead writes about Louis's last years as a greeter for a Las Vegas casino:

> He was happy in Las Vegas and did not think of his circumstances as pathetic. He was not the type of person who worried about justifying his life in terms of achievement, who measured his self-worth in terms of a regular job and money in the bank. Even if he had, his success in boxing would have been more than enough. He had far outstripped the most grandiose dreams of any boy growing up in the Detroit ghetto during the Depression. Nor would Louis have ever thought that there was anything wrong with working for a casino. He accepted the world as he found it.

This explains why Louis was such close friends with Sonny Liston when Liston moved out to Las Vegas in the sixties, despite the difference in their ages. Or perhaps because of it. Louis was the father Liston never had. They were both black male delinquents who now found themselves strolling along the ways of the glittering American wasteland of garish entertainment. They understood each other well because they knew the fates they would have suffered had they not become boxers, the fates of working-class men, black and white, who lived anywhere: a life of crime or a life of ordinary manual labor, the life of the urban serf. They both refused to be condemned to those lives of utter degradation when they discovered that people were willing to pay to see them fight in a prize ring. There they found a degradation that was almost quaint in its hypocrisy, and they themselves became nearly quixotic cynics, the type of people whose favorite word is "bullshit" and who are more inclined to watch the world warily than to comment on anything that happens in it. Of course, the black bourgeoisie rejected Louis at first, rejecting the idea of having the "genius" of the Negro race represented by a mere prizefighter in much the same way that whites rejected him at first as representative of American manhood and masculinity. Whites came around because Louis seemed inoffensive; he even became "the man who named the war" when, during a speech for the Navy Relief Society on March 10, 1942, he said, "We're on God's side." As Mead notes, those words became among "the most famous . . . to emerge from all the overblown oratory during World War II." The black bourgeoisie came to accept him for the same reason that the black masses did: he was beating up white folk in the ring. (Louis had only one black opponent during his championship reign until he fought Jersey Joe Walcott shortly before his retirement.) And blacks, starved for any kind of heroism, felt their frustrations about their status in American society released every time Louis punched out a white fighter. A generation later, neither blacks nor whites were willing to accept Sonny Liston. "God help us!" blacks said when Liston entered the ring. "He's a jailbird!" said the whites. But Louis and Liston were the same men: poor, big, dumb country boys up North who went into prizefighting because they had nothing to lose. Each could have had the other's fate.

Mead touches upon a very vital point, a point we must understand if we are to appreciate exactly the kind of hero Joe Louis was. For a prizefighter to wind up working in a casino is not an unusual or shameful destiny; anybody who is knowledgeable about the history of boxing is aware that, since the days of the English Regency, it was the standard ambition of every ex-pug to wind up owning a tavern. As Alan Lloyd writes in *The Great Prizefight*, Tom Sayers, the British openweight champion of the 1850s, "dreamed of becoming a prizefighting publican" because all he could see around him were taverns owned and operated by fighters. If Louis wound up in a den of liquor and gambling, it was after all the money from such dens that supported him during his career. The relationship between the boxer and the underworld or netherworld of respectable society has always been a close one for two reasons. First, since the days of the bareknuckle brawls of Jack Broughton in the eighteenth century, prizefighters have always been the socially outcast men of bourgeois society. Who else but such a man would be willing to take the risks involved in the gouging, spiking, wrestling, and endlessly endured punishment that bare-knuckle fighting was? It had to be someone who had nothing to lose and everything to gain by going into the endeavor on a professional level. And always those men with nothing to lose in our society have been the outcast, the criminal. It has always been a sure sign of not belonging to the order of things when one has nothing to lose. As former heavyweight champion Floyd Patterson wrote, "How else can Negroes like [Cassius] Clay and myself, born in the south, poor, and with little education, make so much money?" Or as Sonny Liston observed, "Most colored boys who go into boxing are poor, and boxing offers them a chance to make money, to get somewhere." It was not so unusual that Liston and Patterson, two very different men, indeed, should agree upon this point. The boxer knows what the game is about. But as much as the poor male may need boxing, the bourgeois society needs the boxer and the entire ritual of degradation in the prize ring, not only to give these potentially dangerous men something "safe" with which to occupy their time, but also to give us a framework in which we can admire them while feeling superior to and removed from them. The miracle that Louis wrought was that he was the only boxer in history who has ever been described as possessing dignity. Without doing anything in particular except beating fighters and enlisting in the armed services during wartime, Louis made the sensibility of the poor boy a respectable ethos in American culture. "He is truly one of us," we said.

The second reason the fighter is attached to the underworld is that fighters have always been poor boys, used to being socially outcast and around the socially outcast: to being disreputable, to fighting in clubs and saloons. Logically, after retirement, despite whatever notice he may have received from the bourgeois world, he would want to return to the world not of his origins, but the world that most appreciated his success and esteemed his talents; for the autobiographical utterance of the old heads on the corner, the prostitute, the confidence man, and the gambler is also "how I got over." As James Brown, former prizefighter and, despite his associations with rock and roll, the greatest bluesman of the last twenty years, is wont to sing, "You got to use what you got to get just what you want." The world that the prizefighter comes from is one that understands the hypocrisy surrounding the commercialization of the body in a bourgeois, Calvinist-tinged culture.

There are other impressive features of Mead's work: how he places the presence of Louis within the scheme of American popular culture:

> Louis was the first black American to achieve lasting fame and popularity in the twentieth century. When he began to box professionally in 1934, there were no blacks who occupied positions of public prominence, no blacks

who commanded attention from whites. Historians recognize W. E. B. DuBois and A. Phillip Randolph as the most important black leaders of the 1930s; white Americans of that era would have been hard pressed to recognize their names, still less their faces.

Also, Mead's social and cultural analysis of sports writing is quite fine; this is an area of literary criticism that is long overdue in its emergence. Mead's reading of these pieces provides us with an important interpretation of Louis through the eyes of those scribes of popular tastes and makers of popular heroes, and an interesting psychological examination of the men themselves. (The discussions of Grantland Rice and Paul Gallico are especially intriguing.) We can see through the shift in the sports columns on Louis throughout the years of his reign not only how the mythology of his heroism was constructed, but also how deeply complex it was. His account of the second Schmeling-Louis fight, the most symbolic and probably the most important sporting event in American social history, it is the best available. (Although I must add here that the blow-by-blow descriptions of this and other important Louis fights are a bit tedious and still fail, despite their detail, to give at least this reader a real sense of the fight. Unlike baseball, a fight cannot meaningfully be described merely by plotting its action.)

But Mead's book is, in the end, puzzling. Despite the grand historical scaffolding and the lush care for certain types of critical detail and interpretation, the work never really becomes a biography. Louis remains uncaptured and, to a certain degree, unknown by book's end. We learn little of Louis's southern origins or the experiences he had as a youth growing up in the ghetto of Detroit during the Depression. Virtually nothing of his personal life is revealed. His marriages are recounted very sketchily and his love affairs with such women as Lena Horne and Sonja Henie are not even mentioned. This sort of stuff is not just gossip (although gossip has its critical uses in biography and psychology) but necessary detail in understanding the man as a psychological and emotional being. Mead also does not provide very much insight about Louis's relationships with other men, particularly other black fighters. He does not mention Louis's friendship with Liston at all, and this seems to me a serious omission, for much about the inner workings of both men could have been revealed by a rigorous examination of their friendship. Louis was a pallbearer at Liston's funeral (Liston died of an apparent drug overdose in 1970), and he seemed to have been deeply shaken by Liston's death and somewhat disoriented at the funeral. Also, much more should have been provided on Louis's own drug addiction and his mental illness. Both problems plagued him from the 1950s on. Mead does a good job discussing Louis's anxiety-of-influence relationship with Jack Johnson, but a much lesser job of considering Louis's example as a psychological barrier or a source of inspiration for the black champs who followed him, particularly Floyd Patterson, Sonny Liston, who openly admitted his undying admiration for Louis, and Muhammad Ali, whose response to Louis as father figure seems in some respects the most bitter and the most touching. Some of these details concerning Louis's southern origins, his marriages, his drug addiction, and his mental illness can be found in fuller and more compelling accounts in the Nagler and Astor biographies. So despite the tremendous amount of information of a historical and cultural kind that Mead's book provides, it will not supersede the existing Louis books. Perhaps in all fairness, Mead did not intend his book to do that. In which case, we still await the necessary psychoanalytic biography of Louis, the equivalent of Erik Erikson's *Young Man Luther* or Dr. Bernard Meyer's *Houdini: A Mind in Chains*. After all, what do we really know about the psychological makeup of any champion boxer? For instance, consider the similarities between Louis and Sonny Liston, both country boys who wound up migrating to big cities, both estranged from their fathers, both nearly illiterate until well into their adulthood, both too big to be in their class at school, and both winding up with ties to organized crime. Perhaps the next Louis biography should start with these details and make something of them.

We still need to try to answer the epistemological questions: What is a prizefighter? How does our culture know him? How does our culture make him? Albert Murray's observations about the matador in his *The Hero and the Blues* are, I think, applicable to our appreciation and definition of the prizefighter:

> Not only is the matador a volunteer who seeks out, confronts, and dispatches that which is deadly; he is also an adventurer who runs risks, takes chances, and exposes himself with such graceful disdain for his own limitations and safety that the tenacity of his courage is indistinguishable from the beauty of his personal style and manner.

The prizefighter, like the matador, provides his culture with a heroic stylization in which personal meaning and the symbolic ritual of triumph and defeat can be played out. He is, more so than any other athlete, the hero and devil of absolute anarchy and of absolute absurdity. And to answer the epistemological questions is of paramount importance for us as Americans when we realize one dimly recognized fact: The three black persons who have exercised the greatest influence upon our social reality and our mythical selves have all been men and have all been prizefighters: Joe Louis, Jack Johnson, and Muhammad Ali. How shocking it is to think that the victims of our order should be the beautiful princes of our disorder.

Finally, I would like to quote from an article about Cassius Clay ghost-written for Joe Louis in a 1967 issue of *The Ring*. Toward the end, Louis tells this little story:

> Once I happened to walk along when Clay was hollering "I am the Greatest!" to some fellows outside the Theresa Hotel in Harlem. When he saw me, Clay came over and shouted to the crowd: "This is Joe Louis. *WE* is the Greatest!"
>
> That was nice. Cassius Clay is a nice boy and a smart fighter.

Fathers and sons. Sons and fathers. It is a very good story. In fact, it is one of the best short stories in all of American prizefighting. Like Queequeg and Ishmael, the pagan and the reformed Calvinist, the cynic and the mad Muslim go off together arm in arm, at last. The prize ring has always been the most profound of all of America's realized fantasies.

Michael Jordan Leaps
the Great Divide

(1990)

JOHN EDGAR WIDEMAN

. . . .

A novelist and professor of English at the University of Massachusetts, John Edgar Wideman is also a former all-Ivy basketball player and a Rhodes scholar. At the University of Pennsylvania he served as assistant basketball coach and is in the Philadelphia Big Five Basketball Hall of Fame. In his essay on Michael Jordan, Wideman writes that a great artist transforms our world by teaching us "to perceive reality differently." Wideman claims that Jordan changes our perception of what is humanly possible through improvisation, spontaneity, and the "African-American way of playing basketball." Jordan himself says the secret of the "Afro-American game" he's been playing his whole career is the ability "to create . . . in the situation." Zora Neale Hurston wrote that when individuals "excel in what the community considers an art," they "do the community a service." As one of the great artists of our century, Jordan reflects glory on the community and raises interesting questions about what determines and defines community in America. Americans who want to be like Mike want to feel, in Jesse Jackson's words, that they are somebody, or in Jordan's words, that "they're part of the game." More specifically, they want to feel part of Jordan's ever expanding community.

This old woman told me she went to visit this old retired bullfighter who raised bulls for the ring. She had told him about this record that had been made by a black American musician, and he didn't believe that a foreigner, an American—and especially a black American—could make such a record. He sat there and listened to it. After it was finished, he rose from his chair and put on his bullfighting equipment and outfit, went out and fought one of his bulls for the first time since he had retired, and killed the bull. When she asked him why he had done it, he said he had been so moved by the music that he just had to fight the bull.
—Miles Davis with Quincy Troupe, *Miles: The Autobiography*

When it's played the way it's spozed to be played, basketball happens in the air, the pure air; flying, floating, elevated above the floor, levitating the way oppressed peoples of this earth imagine themselves in their dreams, as I do in my lifelong fantasies of escape and power, finally, at last, once and for all, free. For glimpses of this ideal future game we should thank, among others, Elgin Baylor, Connie Hawkins, David Thompson, Helicopter Knowings, and of course, Julius Erving, Dr. J. Some venerate Larry Bird for reminding us how close a man can come to a perfect gravity-free game and still keep his head, his feet firmly planted on terra firma. Or love Magic Johnson for confounding boundaries, conjuring new space, passing lanes, fast-break and break-down lanes neither above the court nor exactly on it, but somehow whittling and expanding simultaneously the territory in which the game is enacted. But really, as we envision soaring and swooping, extending, refining the combat zone of basketball into a fourth, outer, other dimension, the dreamy ozone of flight without wings, of going up and not coming down till we're good and ready, then it's Michael Jordan we must recognize as the truest prophet of what might be possible.

A great artist transforms our world, removes scales from our eyes, plugs from our ears, gloves from our fingertips, teaches us to perceive reality differently. Proust said of his countryman and contemporary, the late-nineteenth-century Impressionist Auguste Renoir: "Before Renoir painted there were no Renoir women in Paris, now you see them everywhere." Tex Winters, a veteran Chicago Bulls coach, a traditionalist who came up preaching the conventional wisdom that a lay-up is the highest-percentage shot, enjoys Michael Jordan's dunks, but, says MJ, "Every time I make one, he says, 'So whatever happened to the simple lay-up?' 'I don't know, Tex, this is how I've been playing my whole career.' You know, this stuff here and this stuff here [the hands are rocking, cradling, stuffing an imaginary ball] is like a lay-up to me. You know I've been doing that and that's the creativity of the game now. But it drives him nuts . . . and he says, 'Well, why don't you draw the foul?' I say I never have. The defense alters many of my shots, so I create. I've always been able to create in those situations, and I guess that's the Afro-American game I have, that's just natural to me. And even though it may not be the traditional game that Americans have been taught, it works for me. Why not?"

The lady is gaudy as Carnival. Magenta, sky-blue, lime, scarlet, orange swirl in the dress that balloons between her sashed waist and bare knees. Somebody's grandmother, gift-wrapped and wobbly on Madison Street, toreadoring through four lanes of traffic converging on Chicago Stadium. Out for a party. Taxi driver says this is where they stand at night. Whore women, he calls them, a disgusted judgmental swipe in his voice, which until now has been a mellow tour-guide patter, pointing out the Sears Tower, Ditka's, asking me how tall is Michael Jordan. The tallest in basketball? Laughing at his memory of a photo of Manute Bol beside Muggsy Bogues. Claiming to have seen Michael Jordan at Shelter, a West Side club late on Wednesday, the night of Game Four after the Bulls beat Detroit last spring to even the best-of-seven NBA championship semifinal at two games apiece. Yes, with two other fellas. Tall like him. Lots of people asking him to sign his name. Autographs, you know. A slightly chopped, guttural, Middle-Eastern-flavored Chicagoese, patched together in the two and a half years he's resided in the States. "I came here as student. My family sent me three thousand dinars a year, and I could have apartment, pay my bills, drive a car. Then hard times at home. Dinar worth much less in dollars. Four people, all of them, must work a month to earn one thousand dinars. No school now. I must work now. American wife and new baby, man."

The driver's from Jordan, but the joke doesn't strike me until I'm mumbling out the cab in front of Chicago Stadium. JORDAN, the country. Appearing in the same column, just above JORDAN, MICHAEL, in *Readers' Guide to Periodical Literature*, where I researched Michael Jordan's career. Usually more entries in each volume under JORDAN, MICHAEL, than any other JORDAN.

The other passenger sharing a cab from O'Hare to downtown Chicago is a young German from Hamburg, in the city with about one hundred thousand fellow conventioneers for the Consumer Electronics Show. It's while he's calculating exchange rates to answer the driver's question about the cost of a Mercedes in Germany that the lady stumbles backward from the curb into the street, blocking strings of cars pulled up at a light. She pirouettes. Curtsies. The puffy dress of many colors glows brighter, wilder against grays and browns of ravaged cityscape. Partially demolished or burnt-out or abandoned warehouses and storefronts line both sides of Madison. Interspersed between buildings are jerry-rigged parking lots where you'd leave your car overnight only if you had a serious grudge against it. I think of a mouth rotten with decay, gaps where teeth have fallen out. Competing for the rush of ballgame traffic, squads of shills and barkers hip-hop into the stalled traffic, shucking and jiving with anyone who'll pay attention. One looms at the window of our cab, sandwiched in, a hand-lettered sign tapping the windshield, begging us to park in his oasis, until the woman impeding our progress decides to attempt the curb again and mounts it this time, Minnie Mouse high heels firmly planted as she gives the honking cars a flounce of Technicolor behind and a high-fived middle finger.

The woman's black, and so are most of the faces on Madison as we cruise toward the stadium in a tide of cars carrying white faces. Closer, still plenty of black faces mix into the crowd—vendors, scalpers, guys in sneakers and silky sweat suits doing whatever they're out there doing, but when the cab stops and deposits me into a thin crust of dark people who aren't going in, I cut through quickly to join the mob of whites who are.

I forget I am supposed to stop at the press trailer for my credentials but slip inside the building without showing a pass or a ticket because mass confusion reigns at the gate. Then I discover why people are buzzing and shoving, why the gate crew is overwhelmed and defeated: Jesse Jackson. Even if it belongs to Michael Jordan this evening, Chicago's still Jackson's town too. And everyone wants to touch or be touched by this man who is instantly recognized, not only here in Chicago but all over the world. Casually dressed tonight, black slacks, matching black short-sleeved shirt that displays his powerful shoulders and arms. He could be a ballplayer. A running back, a tight end. But the eyes, the bearing are a quarterback's. Head high, he scans the whole field, checks out many things at once, smiles, and presses the flesh of the one he's greeting but stays alert to the bigger picture. When a hassled ticket-taker stares suspiciously at me, I nod toward Jesse, as if to say, I'm with him, he's the reason I'm here, and that's enough to chase the red-faced gatekeeper's scrutiny to easier prey. This minute exchange, insignificant as it may be, raises my spirits. Not because Jesse Jackson's presence enabled me to get away with anything—after all, I'm legit, certified, qualified to enter the arena—but because the respect, the recognizability he's earned reflects on me, empowers me, subtly alters others' perceptions of who I am, what I can do. When I hug the Reverend Jesse Jackson I try to impart a little of my appreciation to the broad shoulders I grip. By just being out there, being heard and seen, by standing for something—for instance, an African-American man's right, duty, and ability to aim for the stars— he's saved us all a lot of grief, bought us, black men, white, the entire rainbow of sexes and colors, more time to get our sorry act together. *Thank you* is what I always feel the need to say when I encounter the deep light of his smile.

Your town, man.

Brother Wideman, what are you doing here?

Writing about Michael Jordan.

We don't get any further. Somebody else needs a piece of him, a word, a touch from our Blarney stone, our Somebody.

In Michael's house the PA system is cranked to a sirenlike, earsplitting pitch, many decibels higher than a humane health code should permit. The Luvabulls, Chicago's aerobicized version of the Dallas Cowboy Cheerleaders, shake that fine, sculpted booty to pump up the fans. Very basic here. Primal-scream time. The incredible uproar enters your pores, your blood, your brain. Your nervous system becomes an extension of the overwhelming assault upon it. In simplest terms, you're ready for total war, transformed into a weapon poised to be unleashed upon the enemy.

From my third-row-end-zone folding chair, depth perception is nil. The game is played on a flat, two-dimensional screen. Under the opposite basket the players appear as they would crowded into the wrong end of a telescope.

Then, as the ball moves toward the near goal, action explodes, a zoom lens hurtles bodies at you larger, more intense than life. Middle ground doesn't exist. You're surprised when a ref holds up both arms to indicate a three-point goal scored from beyond the twenty-three-foot line. But your inability to gauge the distance of jump shots or measure the swift, subtle penetration, step by step, yard by yard as guards dribble between their legs, behind the back, spinning, dipping, shouldering, teasing their way upcourt, is compensated for by your power to watch the glacial increments achieved by big men muscling each other for position under your basket, the intimacy of those instants when the ball is in the air at your end of the court and just about everybody on both teams seems driven to converge into a space not larger than two telephone booths. Then it's grapple, grunt, and groan only forty feet away. You can read the effort, the fear, the focus in a player's eyes. For a few seconds you're on the court, sweating, absorbing the impact, the crash of big bodies into one another, wood buckling underfoot, someone's elbow in your ribs, shouts in your ear, the wheezes, sighs, curses, hearing a language spoken here and nowhere else except when people are fighting or making love.

MJ: What do I like about basketball? *Hmmm.* That's a good question. I started when I was twelve. And I enjoyed it to the point that I started to do things other people couldn't do. And that intrigued me more. Now I still enjoy it because of the excitement I get from fans, from the people, and still having the same ability to do things that other people can't do but want to do and they can do only through you. They watch you do it, then they think that they can do it. Or maybe they know it's something they can't do and ironically, that's why they feel good watching me. That drives me. I'm able to do something that no one else can do.

And I love competition. I've earned respect thanks to basketball. And I'm not here just to hand it to the next person. Day in and day out I see people take on that challenge, to take what I have earned. Joe Dumars, for one—I mean, I respect him, don't get me wrong. It's his job. I've got something that people want. The ability to gain respect for my basketball skills. And I don't ever want to give it away. Whenever the time comes when I'm not able to do that, then I'll just back away from the game.

JW: We've always been given credit for our athletic skill, our bodies. You've been blessed with exceptional physical gifts, and all your mastery of the game gets lost in the rush. But I believe your mind, the way you conceive the game, plays as large a role as your physical abilities. As much as any other player I've seen, you seem to play the game with your mind.

MJ: The mental aspect of the game came when I got into college. After winning the national championship at North Carolina in 1982, I knew I had the ability to play on that level, but there were a lot of players who had that ability. What distinguishes certain players from others is the mental aspect. You've got to approach the game strong, in a mental sense. So from my sophomore year on, I took it as a challenge to try and outthink the defense, outthink the next player. He might have similar skills, but if I can be very strong mentally and really determined mentally, I can rise above most opponents. As you know, I went through college ball with Coach Dean Smith, and he's a very good psychological-type coach. He doesn't yell at you. He says one line and you think within yourself and know that you've done something wrong. . . . When I face a challenger, I've got to watch him, watch what he loves to do, watch things that I've done that haven't worked. . . . How can I come up with some weapon, some other surprises to overpower them?

JW: You don't just use someone on your team to work two-on-two. Your plan seems to involve all ten players on the court. A chesslike plan for all four quarters.

MJ: I think I have a good habit of evaluating situations on the floor, offensively, defensively, teammate or opponent. And somehow filling in the right puzzle pieces to click. To get myself in a certain mode or mood to open a game or get a roll going. For instance, the last game we lost to Detroit in the playoffs last spring: We're down twenty, eighteen, twenty-two points at the half. Came back to eleven or ten down. I became a point guard. Somehow I sensed it, sensed no one else wanted to do it or no one else was going to do it until I did it. You could see once I started pushing, started doing these things, everybody else seemed like they got a little bit higher, the game started to go higher, and that pushes my game a little higher, higher, higher. I kept pulling them up, trying to get them to a level where we could win.

Then, you know, I got tired, I had to sit out and rest. Let Detroit come all the way back. It hurts a little bit, but then again I feel good about the fact that I mean so much to those guys, in a sense that if I don't play, if I don't do certain things, then they're not going to play well. It's like when people say it's a one-man gang in Chicago. I take it as a compliment, but then it's unfair that I would have to do all that.

I can dictate what I want to do in the course of the game. I can say to my friends, Well, I'll score twelve points in the first quarter . . . then I can relax in the second quarter and score maybe six, eight. Not take as many shots, but in the second half I can go fifteen, sixteen, quick. That's how much confidence I have in my ability to dictate how many points I can score and be effective and give the team an opportunity to win.

I don't mind taking a beating or scoring just a few points in the first half, because I feel the second half I'm going to have the mental advantage. My man is going to relax. He feels he's got an advantage, he's got me controlled, that means he's going to let down his guard just a little bit. If I can get past that guard one time I feel that I've got the confidence to break him down.

On the same night in July that Michael Jordan slipped on a damp outdoor court at his basketball camp on the Elmhurst College campus, jamming his wrist and elbow, on a court in a park called Mill River in North Amherst, Massachusetts, my elbow cracked against something hard that was moving fast, so when I talked with Michael Jordan the next morning in Elmhurst, Illinois, on the outskirts of Chicago, my elbow was sore and puffy, his wrapped and packed in ice.

We'd won two straight in our pickup, playground run, pretty ordinary, local, tacky hoop that's fine if you're inside the game, but nothing to merit a spectator's attention. Ten on the court, nine or ten on the sidelines hanging out or waiting to take on the winners, a small band of witnesses, then, for something extraordinary that happened next. On a breakaway dribble Sekou beats everybody to the hoop except two opponents who hadn't bothered to run back to their offensive end. It was that kind of game, spurts of hustle, lunch breaks while somebody else did the work. Sekou solo, racing for the hoop, two defenders converging to cut him off, slapping at the ball, bodying him into a vise to stop his momentum. What happens next is almost too quick to follow. Sekou picks up his dribble about eight feet from the basket, turns his back to the goal, to the two guys who are clamping him, as if, outnumbered, he's looking downcourt for help. A quick feint, shoulders and head dipped one way, and then he brings the ball across his body, slamming it hard against the asphalt, *blam*, in the space his fake has cleared. Ball bounds higher than the basket and for an instant I think he's trying a trick shot, bouncing the ball into the basket, a jive shot that's missing badly as the ball zooms way over the rim toward the far side of the backboard. While I'm thinking this and thinking Sekou's getting outrageous, throwing up a silly, wasteful, selfish shot even for the playground, even in a game he can dominate because he's by far the best athlete, while I'm thinking this and feeling a little pissed off at his hotdogging and ball hogging, the ball's still in the air, and Sekou spins and rises, a pivot off his back foot so he's facing the hoop, one short step gathering himself, one long stride carrying him around the frozen defenders and then another step in the air, rising till he catches the rock in flight and crams it one-handed down, *down* through the iron.

Hoop, poles, and backboard shudder. A moment of stunned silence, then the joint erupts. Nobody can believe what they've seen. The two players guarding Sekou kind of slink off. But it wasn't about turning people into chumps or making anybody feel bad. It was Sekou's glory. Glory reflected instantly on all of us because he was one of us out there in the game and he'd suddenly lifted the game to a higher plane. We were all larger and better. Hell, none of us could rise like Sekou, but he carried us up there with him. He needed us now to amen and goddamn and high-five and time-out. Time out, stop this shit right here. Nate, the griot, style-point judge, and resident master of ceremonies, begins to perform his job of putting into words what everybody's thinking. *Time out.* We all wander onto the court, to the basket that's still vibrating, including the two guys Sekou had rocked. Sekou is hugged, patted, praised. Skin smacks skin, slaps skin. Did you see that? Did you see that? I ain't never seen nothing like that. Damn, Sekou. Where'd you learn that shit? Learned it sitting right here. Right here when I was coming up. My boy Patrick. Puerto Rican dude, you know Patrick. He used to do it. Hey man, Patrick could play but Patrick didn't have no serious rise like that, man. Right. He'd bounce it, go get it, shoot it off the board. Seen him do it more than once. Sitting right here on this bench I seen him do it. Yeah, well, cool, I can believe it. But man that shit you did. One hand and shit . . . damn . . . damn, Sekou.

I almost told Michael Jordan about Sekou's move. Asked Michael if he'd ever attempted it, seen it done. Maybe, I thought, someday when I'm watching the Bulls on the tube Michael will do a Sekou for a national audience and I won't exactly take credit, but deep inside I'll be saying, Uh-huh, uh-huh. Because we all need it, the sense of connection, the feeling we can be better than we are, even if better only through someone else, an agent, a representative, Mother Teresa, Mandela, one of us ourselves taken to a higher power, altered for a moment, alive in another's body and mind. One reason we need games, sports, the heroes they produce. To rise. To fly.

I didn't have to tell Michael Jordan Sekou's story. MJ earns a living by performing nearly on a regular basis similar magical feats for an audience of millions across the globe. I told him instead about my elbow. Tuesday night had been a bad night for elbows all over North America. Commiserating, solicitous about his injury, but also hopelessly vain, proud of mine, as if our sore elbows matched us, blood brothers meeting at last, a whole lifetime of news, gossip, and stuff to catch up on. Since we couldn't very well engage in that one-on-one game I'd been fantasizing, not with him handicapped by a fat elbow, we might as well get on with the interview I'd been seeking since the end of the NBA playoffs. Relax and get it on in this borrowed office at Elmhurst, my tape recorder on the desk between us, Michael Jordan settled back in a borrowed swivel chair, alert, accommodating. Mellow, remarkably fresh after a protracted autograph session, signing one item apiece for each of the 350 or so campers who'd been sitting transfixed in a circle around him earlier that morning as he shared some of his glory with them in a luminous exchange that masked itself as a simple lesson in basketball basics from Michael Jordan.

JW: Your style of play comes from the playground, comes from tradition, the African-American way of playing basketball.

MJ: Can't teach it.

JW: When I was coming up, if a coach yelled "playground move" at you it meant there was something wrong with it, which also meant in a funny way there was something wrong with the playground, and since the playground was a black world, there was something wrong with you, a black player out there doing something your way rather than their way.

MJ: I've been doing it my way. When you come out of high school, you have natural, raw ability. No one coaches it, I mean, maybe nowadays, but when I was coming out of high school, it was all natural ability. The jumping, quickness. When I went to North Carolina, it was a different phase of my life. Knowledge of basketball from Naismith on . . . rebounds, defense, free-throw shooting, techniques. Then, when I got to the pros, what people saw was the raw talent I'd worked on myself for eleven, twelve years *and* the knowledge I'd learned at the University of North Carolina. Unity of both. That's what makes up Michael Jordan's all-around basketball skills.

JW: It seems to me we have to keep asserting the factors that make us unique. We can't let coaches or myths about body types take credit for achievements that are a synthesis of our intelligence, physical gifts, our tradition of playing the game a special way.

MJ: We were born to play like we do.

JW: Players like you and Magic have transformed the game. Made it more of a player's game, returned it closer to its African-American roots on the playground.

MJ: You know, when you think about it, passing like Magic's is as natural, as freewheeling, as creative as you can be. You can call it playground if you want, but the guy is great. And certainly he's transcended the old idea of point guard.

You never saw a six-eight, six-nine point guard before he came around. No coach would ever put a six-eight guy back there.

JW: If you were big, you were told to go rebound, especially if you were big and black.

MJ: Rebound. Go do a jump lay-up, be a center, a forward. A man six-eight started playing, dribbling in his backyard. Said, I can do these things. Now look. Everybody's trying to get a six-nine point guard.

JW: For me, the real creativity of the game begins with the playground. Like last night, watching young guys play, playing with them, that's where the new stuff is coming from. Then the basketball establishment names it and claims it.

MJ: They claim it. But they can't. The game today is going away from the big guy, the old idea everybody's got to have a Jabbar, Chamberlain. Game today is going toward a versatile game. Players who rebound, steal, block, run the court, score, the versatile player who can play more than one position. Which Magic started. Or maybe he didn't start it, but he made it famous. This is where the game's going now.

JW: Other people name it and claim it. That kind of appropriation's been a problem for African-American culture from the beginning. Music's an obvious example. What kind of music do you like?

MJ: I love jazz. I love mellow music. I love David Sanborn. Love Grover Washington Jr. Rap . . . it's okay for some people. But huh-uh. Not in my house.

JW: Do you listen to Miles Davis?

MJ: Yeah.

JW: He talks about his art in a new biography he wrote with Quincy Troupe. When Miles relates jazz to boxing, I also hear him talking about writing, my art, and basketball, yours.

MJ: I know what you're saying.

JW: Right. There's a core of improvisation, spontaneity in all African-American arts.

MJ: I'm always working to put surprises, something new in my game. Improvisation, spontaneity, all that stuff.

What's in a name: *Michael*—archangel, conqueror of Satan. "Now war arose in heaven. Michael and his angels fighting against the dragon; and the dragon and his angels fought, but they were defeated" (Revelation 12:7); *Jordan*—the foremost river in Palestine, runs from the Lebanons to the Dead Sea, 125 miles, though its meanderings double that length. "Jordan water's bitter and cold . . . chills the body, won't hurt the soul . . ." (African-American traditional spiritual). *Michael Jordan*—a name worth many millions per annum. What's in that name that makes it so incredibly valuable to the people who have millions to spend for advertising what they sell, who compete for the privilege of owning, possessing Michael Jordan's name to adorn or endorse their products? In a country where Willie Horton's name and image helped win (or lose) a presidential election, a country in which one out of every four young black males is in prison, on parole or probation, a country where serious academics convene to consider whether the black male is an endangered species, how can we account for Michael Jordan's enormous popularity? Because MJ is an American of African descent, isn't he? Maybe we're more mixed up about race than we already know we are. Perhaps MJ is proof there are no rules about race, no limits to what a black man can accomplish in our society. Or maybe he's the exception that proves the rule, the absence of rules. The bedrock chaos and confusion that dogs us. At some level we must desire the ambiguity of our racial thinking. It must work for us, serve us. When one group wants something bad enough from the other, we reserve the right to ignore or insist upon the inherent similarities among all races, whichever side of the coin suits our purposes. One moment color-blind, the next proclaiming one group's whiteness, the other's blackness, to justify whatever mischief we're up to. It's this flip-flopping that defines and perpetuates our race problem. Our national schizophrenia and disgrace. It's also the door that allows MJ entry to superstardom, to become a national hero, our new DiMaggio, permits him to earn his small fraction of the billions we spend to escape rather than confront the liabilities of our society.

Sports Illustrated offers a free Michael Jordan video if you subscribe right away. Call today. In this ad, which saturates prime time on the national sports network, a gallery of young people, male and female, express their wonder, admiration, awe, and identification with Michael Jordan's supernatural basketball prowess. He can truly fly. The chorus is all white, good-looking, clean cut, casually but hiply dressed. An audience of consumers the ad both targets and embodies. A very calculated kind of wish fulfillment at work. A premeditated attempt to bond MJ with these middle-class white kids with highly disposable incomes.

In other ads, black kids wear fancy sneakers, play ball, compete to be a future Michael Jordan. There's a good chance lots of TV viewers who are white will enter the work force and become dutiful, conspicuous consumers, maybe even buy themselves some vicarious flight time by owning stuff MJ endorses. But what future is in store for those who intend to *be* the next MJ? Buy Jordan or be Jordan. Very different messages. Different futures, white and black. Who's zooming who?

In another national ad, why do we need the mediating figure of an old, distinguished-looking, white-haired, Caucasian gentleman in charge, giving instructions, leading MJ into a roomful of kids clamoring for MJ's magic power?

The Palace at Auburn Hills, the Detroit Pistons' home, contrasts starkly with Chicago Stadium. Chicago, the oldest NBA arena; the Palace one of the newest. Chicago Stadium is gritty, the Palace plush. In the Auburn Hills crowd an even greater absence of dark faces than in Chicago Stadium. But they share some of the same fight songs. *We will, we will, rock you.* And the Isley Brothers' classic "Shout." On a massive screen in the center of the Palace, cuts from the old John Belushi flick *Animal House* drive the Detroit fans wild. "Shout" is background music for an archetypal late-Fifties, early-Sixties frat party. White college kids in togas twist and shout and knock themselves out. Pre-Vietnam American Empire PG-rated version of a Roman orgy. A riot of sloppy boozing, making out, sophomoric antics to the beat of a jackleg, black rhythm-and-blues band that features a frenzied, conk-haired singer, sweating, eyes rolling, gate-mouthed, screaming, "Hey-ay, hey-ay. Hey-ay, hey-ay, shout! C'mon now, shout." Minstrel auctioneer steering the action higher, higher. Musicians on the screen performing for their audience of hopped-up, pampered students fuse with the present excitement, black gladiators on the hardwood floor of the Palace revving up their whooping fans. Nothing is an accident. Or is it? Do race relations progress, or are we doomed to a series of reruns?

JW: What's the biggest misconception that is part of your public image? What's out there, supposedly a mirror, but doesn't reflect your features?

MJ: I'm fortunate that there are no big misunderstandings. My biggest concern is that people view me as being some kind of a god, but I'm not. I make mistakes, have faults. I'm moody, I've got many negative things about me. Everybody has negative things about them. But from the image that's been projected of me, I can't do any wrong. Which is scary. And it's probably one of the biggest fears I have. And I don't know how to open people's eyes. I mean, I'm not going to go out and make a mistake so that people can see I make mistakes. Hey, you know, I try to live a positive life, love to live a positive life, but I do have negative things about me and I do make mistakes. And I'm so worried that if I make a mistake today, it can ruin the positive things I try to project. It's a day-in, day-out, nine-to-five job.

JW: A lot of pressure.

MJ: Pressure I didn't ask for, but it was given to me and I've been living, living with it.

JW: A kind of trap, isn't it, because you say, "I don't want everybody to think I'm a paragon of virtue. I'm a real person." But you also know in the back of your mind being a paragon is worth X number of dollars a day. So you don't like it but you profit from it.

MJ: Right. It has its advantages as well as disadvantages. Advantages financially. I'm asked to endorse corporations that are very prestigious as well as very wealthy. I have the respect of many, many kids as well as parents, their admiration. So it's not *just* the financial part. You said the financial part, but the respect that I earn from the 350 kids in this camp and their parents, friends, equals the financial part of it. The respect I get from those people—that's the pressure.

JW: Not to let them down.

MJ: Not to let them down.

Postgame Chicago Stadium. Oldest arena in the league. Old-fashioned bandbox. Exterior built on monumental, muscle-flexing scale. Inside you have to duck your head to negotiate a landing that leads to steep steps descending to locker rooms. Red painted walls, rough, unfinished. Overhead a confusion of pipes, wires—the arteries of the beast exposed. Ranks of folding chairs set up for postgame interviews. MJ breaks a two-day silence with the media. Annoyed that the press misinterpreted some animated exchanges between teammates and himself.

None of the usual question-and-answer interplay. MJ says his piece and splits, flanked by yellow-nylon-jacketed security men, three of them, polite but firm, benign sheep dogs guarding him, discouraging the wolves.

In MJ's cubicle near the door hangs a greenish suit, a bright tropical-print shirt, yellows, black, beige, oranges, et cetera. He's played magnificently, admonished the press, clearly weary, but the effort of the game's still in his eyes, distracting, distancing him, part of him still in another gear; maybe remembering, maybe savoring, maybe just unable to cut it loose, the flow, the purity, the high of the game when every moment counts, registers, so as he undresses, the yellow jacket assigned to his corner has to remind him not to get naked, other people are in the room.

A man chatting up the security person screening MJ's cubicle holds a basketball for MJ to sign. As MJ undresses he's invited to a reporter's wedding. The soon-to-be groom is jiving with another member of the press, saying something about maybe having a kid will help him settle down, improve his sense of responsibility. MJ, proud father of two-year-old Jeffrey Michael, interrupts. "You got to earn the respect of kids. Responsibility and respect, huh-uh. You don't just get it when you have a kid. Or a couple kids."

Word's sent in that Whitney Houston and her entourage are waiting next door for a photo session. Celebrity hugging and mugging. I say hi to a man hovering near MJ's corner. Thought he might be MJ's cut buddy or an older brother. Turns out to be MJ's father. Same dark, tight skin. Same compact, defined physique. "Yes, I think I'm Mister Jordan. Hold on a minute, let me check my social security card." A kidder like his son. Like his son, he gives you friendly pats. Or maybe it's son like father. In the father's face, a quality of youthfulness and age combined, not chronological age but the timeless serenity of a tribal elder, a man with position, authority, an earned place in a community. In the locker room of the Spectrum in Philly, I'd been struck by the same mix in MJ's face as he addressed reporters. Unperturbed by lights, cameras, mikes, the patent buzz and jostle of media rudeness swarming around him, he sits poised on a shelf in a dressing stall, his posture unmistakably that immemorial high-kneed, flex-thighed, legs-widespread, weight-on-the-buttocks squat of rural Africans. Long hands dangling between his knees, head erect, occasionally bowing as he retreats into a private, inner realm to consider a question, an answer before he spoke. Dignified, respectful. A disposition of body learned how many grandfathers ago, in what faraway place. Passed on, surviving in this strange land.

From the shower MJ calls for slip-ons. Emerges wrapped in a towel. A man, an African-American man in a suit of dark skin, tall, broad-shouldered, long-limbed, narrow-waisted, bony ankles and wrists, his body lean-muscled, sleek, race cars, cheetahs, a computer-designed body for someone intended to sprint and leap, loose and tautly strung simultaneously, but also, like your body and mind, a cage. MJ is trapped within boundaries he cannot cross, you cannot cross. No candid camera needs to strip him any further. Why should it? Whose interests would be served? Some of his business is not ours. Are there skeletons in his closet? Letters buried in a trunk, sealed correspondence? What are we seeking with our demands for outtakes, for what's X-rated in public figures' lives? In the crush of the locker room, one reporter (a female) whispers to another; we build these guys up so we can be around to sell the story when they fall.

Naked MJ. A price on his head. He pays it. We pay it. Hundreds of thousands of fans plunk down the price of a ticket to catch his act live. Millions of dollars are spent to connect products with the way this body performs on a basketball court. What about feedback? If body sells products, how do products affect body? Do they commodify it, place a price on it? Flesh and blood linked symbolically with products whose value is their ability to create profit. If profit's what it's all about—body, game, product—does profit-making displace ballplaying? Are there inevitable moments when what's required of MJ the ballplayer is different from what's required of the PR Jordan created by corporate interests for media consumption?

The PR Michael Jordan doesn't need to win a ring. He's already everything he needs to be without a ring. Greatest pressure on him from this perspective is to maintain, replicate, duplicate whatever it is that works, sells. It's an unfunny joke when MJ says wryly, "Fans come to see me score fifty and the home team win." The PR Jordan doesn't really lose when he has a spectacular game and his teammates are mediocre. He's still MJ. But if he puts forth a kamikaze, all-or-nothing, individual effort and fails by forcing or missing shots, by coming up short, the blame falls squarely on his shoulders. If he plays that tune too often, will the public continue to buy it?

Can a player be bigger than the game? Is Jordan that good? Does he risk making a mockery of the game? (Recall John Lennon. His lament that the Beatles' early, extraordinary success pressured them to repeat themselves, blunted artistic innovation, eventually pushed them into self-parody, the songs they'd written taking over, consuming them.)

The young man from Mississippi, baby of eleven children, speaks with a slow, muddy, down-home drawl. We're both relaxing in the unseasonably warm sun, outside Hartford, the Bradley International Airport B Terminal. My destination: Chicago, Game Six of last spring's NBA Eastern Championship. He's headed for his sister's home in Indiana. A nice place, he hopes. Time to settle down after five, six years of roaming, but decent work's hard to find. "I sure hope Michael wins him a ring. Boy, I want to see that. Cause my man Michael's the best. Been the best awhile. He's getting up there a little bit in age, you know. Ain't old yet but you know, he can't do like he used to. Used to be he could go out anytime and bust sixty-three. He's still good, still the best now but he better go on and get him his ring."

JW: I'm jumping way back on you now. Laney High School, Wilmington, N.C., the late Seventies, early Eighties. How did it feel to sit on the bench?

MJ: I hated it . . . you can't help anybody sitting on the bench. I mean, it's great to cheer, but I'm not that type of person. I'm not a cheerleader.

JW: You couldn't make the team?

MJ: I was pissed. Because my best friend, he was about six six, he made the team. He wasn't good but he was six six and that's tall in high school. He made the team and I felt I was better. . . . They went into the playoffs and I was sitting at the end of the bench and I couldn't cheer them on because I felt I should have been on the team. This is the only time that I didn't actually cheer for them. I wanted them to lose. Ironically, I wanted them to lose to prove to them that I could help them. This is what I was thinking at the time: You made a mistake by not putting me on the team and you're going to see it because you're going to lose. Which isn't the way you want to raise your kids . . . but many kids now do think that way, only because of their desire to get out and show that they can help or they can give something.

I think to be successful, I think you have to be selfish, or else you never achieve. And once you get to your highest level, then you have to be unselfish. When I first came to the league, I was a very selfish person in the sense I thought for myself first, the team second . . . and I still think that way in a sense. But at the same time, individual accolades piled up for me and were very soothing to the selfishness that I'd had in myself. They taught me how, you know, to finally forget about the self and help out the team, which is where I am now. I always wanted the team to be successful but I felt, selfishly, I wanted to be the main cause.

Phi Gamma Delta was assailed Monday with charges of racism,
becoming the second fraternity to face such accusations stemming from
activities during Round-Up last weekend.
At the root of the newest charges is a T-shirt sold and distributed by the
fraternity—often known as the Fijis—during its annual "low-hoop" basketball
tournament Saturday. On the T-shirt is the face of a "Sambo" caricature atop
the body of professional basketball player Michael Jordan.
Meanwhile, Delta Tau Delta continued its internal investigation into Friday's
incident in which FUCK COONS and FUCK YOU NIGS DIE were spray-painted
on a car destroyed with sledgehammers on fraternity property. . . .
—*The Daily Texan*, University of Texas, Austin, 4/10/90.

We're slightly lost. My wife and I in a rental car on the edge of Shreveport, Louisiana, leading two rented vans carrying the Central Massachusetts Cougars. We're looking for the Centenary College Gold Dome, where soon, quite soon, opening ceremonies of the AAU Junior Olympic Girls Basketball national tourney will commence. Suddenly we cross Jordan Street, and I know we'll find the Gold Dome, be on time for the festivities, that my daughter, Jamila, and her Cougar teammates will do just fine, whatever. Renoir women everywhere, Jordans everywhere.

Next day, while girls of every size, shape, color, creed, and ethnic background, from nearly every state in the Union, are playing hoop in local high school gyms, about three miles from the Cougars' motel, at the Bossier City Civic Center, Klansmen in hoods and robes distribute leaflets at a rally for former Klan leader David Duke, who's running for the U.S. Senate.

MJ: Well, I think real often in terms of role models, in terms of positive leaders in this world . . . Nelson Mandela, Bill Cosby. . . . We're trying to show there are outlets, there are guidelines, there are positive things you can look for and achieve. I mean, we're trying to give them an example to go for. I think that's the reason I try to maintain the position I have in the corporate world as well as in the community. That we can do this, prove that success is not limited to certain people, it's not limited to a certain color. . . . Grab a hand and pull someone up. Be a guide or a role model. Give some type of guidelines for other people to follow.

JW: What ways do you have of controlling this tidal wave of public attention? How do you remain separate from the Michael Jordan created "out there"?

MJ: Stay reachable. Stay in touch. Don't isolate. I don't try to isolate myself from anybody. I think if people can feel that they can touch or come up and talk to you, you're going to have a relationship and have some influence on them. My old friends, who I try to stay in touch with at all times, I think they always keep me close to earth.

About six years ago I was only forty-three, so I couldn't understand why the jumper was falling short every time, banging harmlessly off the front of the iron. After a summer-camp game my wife, Judy, had watched mainly because our sons, Don and Jake, were also playing, I asked her if she'd noticed anything unusual about my jump shot. "Well, not exactly," she offered, "except when you jumped your feet never left the ground."

JW: When you're playing, what part of the audience is most important to you?

MJ: Kids. I can notice a kid enjoying himself. On the free-throw line, *bing*, that quick, I'll wink at him, smile, lick a tongue at him, and keep going and still maintain the concentration that I need for the game. That's my personality. I've always done it. I can catch eye-to-eye a mother, a father, anybody . . . kid around with them as I'm playing in a serious and very intense game. That's the way I relax, that's the way I get my enjoyment from playing the game of

JOHN EDGAR WIDEMAN

basketball. Seeing people enjoying themselves and relating to them like I'm enjoying myself. Certainly letting them know they're part of the game.

The game. I am being introduced to a group of young African-American men, fifteen or so high school city kids from Springfield, Massachusetts, who are attending the first-ever sessions of a summer camp at Hampshire College, an experiment intended to improve both their basketball scores and SAT scores. My host, Dennis Jackson (a coach, coincidentally, at Five-Star hoop camp back when Michael Jordan, still a high schooler, made his debut into the national spotlight), is generously extolling my credentials: Author, professor, college ballplayer, Rhodes scholar, but it isn't till Dennis Jackson says this man is working on an article about MJ that I know I have everybody's attention. I tell them that I haven't received an interview with MJ yet, he's cooling out after the long season, but they're eager to hear any detail of any MJ moment I've been privy to so far. An anecdote or two and then I ask them to free-associate. When I say MJ what comes to mind first? *Air, jam, slam-dunk, greatest, wow* are some of the words I catch, but the real action is in faces and bodies. No one can sit still. Suddenly it's Christmas morning and they're little boys humping down the stairs into a living room full of all they've been wishing for. Body English, *ohhs* and *ahhs*. Hey man, he can do anything, anything. DJ assures me that if Mike promised, I'll get my interview. *As good a player as MJ is, he's ten times the person.* We're all in a good mood, and I preach a little. Dreams. The importance of believing in yourself. My luck in having a family that supported me, instilled the notion I was special, that I could do anything, be anything. Dreams, goals. Treasuring, respecting the family that loves you and stands behind you.

What if you don't have no family?

The question stops me in my tracks. Silences me. I study each face pointed toward me, see the guys I grew up with, my sons, brothers, Sekou, MJ, myself, the faces of South African kids *toi-toing* in joy and defiance down a dirt street in Crossroads. I'd believed the young men were listening, and because I'd felt them open up, I'd been giving everything I had, trying to string together many years, many moments, my fear, anger, frustration, the hungers that had driven me, the drumbeat of a basketball on asphalt a rhythm under everything else, patterning the crazy-quilt chaos of images I was trying to make real, to connect with their lives. What if there's no family, no person, no community out there returning, substantiating the fragile dream a young man spins of himself? Silenced.

Michael said he didn't like politics. I'll always stand up for what I think is right, but. . . . Politics, he said, was about making choices. And then you get into: This side's right and that side's wrong. Then you got a fight on your hands. Michael's friends say he naturally shies away from controversy. He's mellow. Middle-of-the-road. Even when the guys are just sitting around and start arguing about something, Michael doesn't like it. He won't take sides, tries to smooth things out. That's Michael.

Finally I respond to the young man at the circle's edge leaning back on his arms. He doesn't possess an NBA body. He may be very smart, but that can be trouble as easily as salvation. You have me, I want to say. I support you, love you, you are part of me, we're in this together. But I know damn well he's asking for more. Needs more. Really, he's asking for nothing while he's asking everything.

Find a friend. I bet you have a cut buddy already. Somebody to hang with and depend on. One person who won't let you fall. And you won't let him fall. Lean on each other. It's hard, hard, but just one person can make a difference sometimes.

They look at the books I've written. Ask more questions. Mostly about Michael again. Some eyes are drifting back to the court. This rap's been nice, but it's also only a kind of intermission. The game. I should have brought my sneaks. Should be thirty years younger. But why, seeing the perils besetting these kids, would anyone want to be thirty years younger? And why, if you're Peter Pan playing a game you love and getting paid a fortune for it and adored and you can fly too, why would you ever want to grow a minute older?

The young men from Springfield say hello.

Nate, the historian from the court at Mill River, said: "Tell the Michael I say hello."

Be Like Mike?
Michael Jordan and the
Pedagogy of Desire

(1994)

MICHAEL ERIC DYSON

. . . .

For Michael Eric Dyson, Michael Jordan is a new type of cultural figure: the public pedagogue. Dyson describes Jordan's body as a cultural text with several levels of meaning to be read. Jordan's private pursuit of self-expressive glory is also a public pursuit of communal goals. Yet the nature of community in America is such that Jordan embodies conflicting desires and contradictory impulses. Dyson suggests that even as Jordan symbolizes a contemporary culture of consumption, he transcends and resists it by "expressing black cultural style," which Dyson defines as the will to spontaneity (improvisation), the stylization of the performed self (individual or trademark move), and edifying deception (another form of stylization). Dyson is a professor of communications at the University of North Carolina, 1992 winner of the National Association of Black Journalists National Magazine Award, and has published several collections of essays.

Michael Jordan is perhaps the best and most well-known athlete in the world today. He has attained unparalleled cultural status because of his extraordinary physical gifts, his marketing as an icon of race-transcending American athletic and moral excellence, and his mastery of a sport which has become the metaphoric center of the black cultural imagination. But the Olympian sum of Jordan's cultural meaning is greater than the fluent parts of his persona as athlete, family man, and marketing creation. There is hardly cultural precedence for the character of his unique fame which has blurred the line between private and public, between personality and celebrity, and between substance and symbol. Michael Jordan stands at the breach between perception and intuition, his cultural meaning perennially deferred from closure because his

Copyright © 1993. From *Between Borders* by Henry Giroux and Peter McLaren. Reproduced by permission of Routledge, Inc.

career symbolizes possibility itself, gathering into its unfolding narrative the shattered remnants of previous incarnations of fame and yet transcending their reach.

Jordan has been called "the new DiMaggio" (Boers 1990, 30) and "Elvis in high tops," indications of the Herculean cultural heroism he has come to embody. There is even a religious element to the near worship of Jordan as a cultural icon of invincibility, as he has been called a "savior of sorts" (O'Brien 1990–91, 82), "basketball's high priest" (Bradley 1991–92, 60), and "more popular than Jesus," except with "better endorsement deals" (Vancil 1992, 51). But the quickly developing canonization of Michael Jordan provokes reflection about the contradictory uses to which Jordan's body is put as a cultural text and ambiguous symbol of fantasy, and the avenues of agency and resistance available especially to black youth who make symbolic investment in Jordan's body as a means of cultural and personal possibility, creativity, and desire.

I understand Jordan in the broadest sense of the term to be a public pedagogue, a figure of estimable public moral authority whose career educates us about the convergence of productive and disenabling forms of knowledge, desire, interest, consumption, and culture in three spheres: the culture of athletics, which thrives on skill and performance; the specific expression of elements of African-American culture, and the market forces and processes of commodification expressed by, and promoted in, advanced capitalism. By probing these dimensions of Jordan's cultural importance, we may gain a clearer understanding of his function in American society.

Athletic activity has shaped and reflected important sectors of American society. First, it produced communities of common athletic interest organized around the development of highly skilled performance. The development of norms of athletic excellence evidenced in sports activities cemented communities of participants who valorized rigorous sorts of physical discipline in preparation for athletic competition and in expressing the highest degree of athletic skill. Second, it produced potent subcultures that inculcated in their participants norms of individual and team accomplishment. Such norms tapped into the bipolar structures of competition and cooperation that pervade American culture. Third, it provided a means of reinscribing Western frontier myths of exploration and discovery-as-conquest onto a vital sphere of American culture. Sports activities can be viewed in part as the attempt to symbolically ritualize and metaphorically extend the ongoing quest for mastery of environment and vanquishing of opponents within the limits of physical contest.

Fourth, athletic activity has served to reinforce habits and virtues centered in the collective pursuit of communal goals which are intimately connected to the common good, usually characterized within athletic circles as "team spirit." The culture of sport has physically captured and athletically articulated the mores, folkways, and dominant visions of American society, and at its best it has been conceived as a means of symbolically embracing and equitably pursuing the just, the good, the true, and the beautiful. And finally, the culture of athletics has provided an acceptable and widely accessible means of white male bonding. For much of its history, American sports activity has reflected white patriarchal privilege, and it has been rigidly defined and socially shaped by rules that restricted the equitable participation of women and people of color.

Black participation in sports in mainstream society, therefore, is a relatively recent phenomenon. Of course, there have existed venerable traditions of black sports such as the Negro Baseball Leagues, which countered the exclusion of black bodies from white sports. The prohibition of athletic activity by black men in mainstream society severely limited publicly acceptable forms of displaying black physical prowess, an issue that had been politicized during slavery and whose legacy extended into the middle of the twentieth century. Hence, the potentially superior physical prowess of black men, validated for many by the long tradition of slave labor that built American society, helped reinforce racist arguments about the racial regimentation of social space and the denigration of the black body as an inappropriate presence in traditions of American sport.

Coupled with this fear of superior black physical prowess was the notion that inferior black intelligence limited the ability of blacks to perform excellently in those sports activities which required mental concentration and agility. These two forces—the presumed lack of sophisticated black cognitive skills and the fear of superior black physical prowess—restricted black sports participation to thriving but financially handicapped subcultures of black athletic activity. Later, of course, the physical prowess of the black body would be acknowledged and exploited as a supremely fertile zone of profit as mainstream athletic society finally cashed in on the symbolic danger of black sports excellence.

Because of its marginalized status within the regime of American sports, black athletic activity often acquired a social significance that transcended the internal dimensions of game, sport, and skill. Black sport became an arena not only for testing the limits of physical endurance and forms of athletic excellence—while reproducing or repudiating ideals of American justice, goodness, truth, and beauty—but it also became a way of ritualizing racial achievement against socially imposed barriers to cultural performance.

In short, black sport activity often acquired a heroic dimension, as viewed in the careers of figures such as Joe Louis, Jackie Robinson, Althea Gibson,

Wilma Rudolph, Muhammad Ali, and Arthur Ashe. Black sports heroes transcended the narrow boundaries of specific sports activities and garnered importance as icons of cultural excellence, symbolic figures who embodied social possibilities of success denied to other people of color. But they also captured and catalyzed the black cultural fetishization of sport as a means of expressing black cultural style, as a means of valorizing craft as a marker of racial and self-expression, and as a means of pursuing social and economic mobility.

It is this culture of black athletics, created against the background of social and historical forces that shaped American athletic activity, that helped produce Jordan and help explain the craft that he practices. Craft is the honing of skill by the application of discipline, time, talent, and energy toward the realization of a particular cultural or personal goal. American folk cultures are pervaded by craft, from the production of cultural artifacts that express particular ethnic histories and traditions, to the development of styles of life and work that reflect and symbolize a community's values, virtues, and goals. Michael Jordan's skills within basketball are clearly phenomenal, but his game can only be sufficiently explained by understanding its link to the fusion of African-American cultural norms and practices, and the idealization of skill and performance that characterize important aspects of American sport. I will identify three defining characteristics of Jordan's game that reflect the influence of African-American culture on his style of play.

First, Jordan's style of basketball reflects the *will to spontaneity*. I mean here the way in which historical accident is transformed into cultural advantage, and the way acts of apparently random occurrence are spontaneously and imaginatively employed by Africans and African-Americans in a variety of forms of cultural expression. When examining Jordan's game, this feature of African-American culture clearly functions in his unpredictable eruptions of basketball creativity. It was apparent, for instance, during game two of the National Basketball Association 1991 championship series between Jordan's Chicago Bulls and the Los Angeles Lakers, in a shot that even Jordan ranked in his all-time top ten (McCallum 1991, 32). Jordan made a drive toward the lane, gesturing with his hands and body that he was about to complete a patent Jordan dunk shot with his right hand. But when he spied defender Sam Perkins slipping over to oppose his shot, he switched the ball in midair to his left hand to make an underhanded scoop shot instead, which became immediately known as the "levitation" shot. Such improvisation, a staple of the will to spontaneity, allows Jordan to expand his vocabulary of athletic spectacle, which is the stimulation of a desire to bear witness to the revelation of truth and beauty compressed into acts of athletic activity.

Second, Jordan's game reflects the *stylization of the performed self*. This is the creation and projection of a sport persona that is an identifying mark of diverse African-American creative enterprises, from the complexly layered jazz experimentation of John Coltrane, the trickstering and signifying comedic routines of Richard Pryor, and the rhetorical ripostes and oral significations of rapper Kool Moe Dee. Jordan's whole game persona is a graphic depiction of the performed self as flying acrobat, resulting in his famous moniker "Air Jordan." Jordan's performed self is rife with the language of physical expressiveness: head moving, arms extending, hands waving, tongue wagging, and legs spreading.

He has also developed a resourceful repertoire of dazzling dunk shots which further specify and articulate his performed self, and which have garnered him a special niche within the folklore of the game: the cradle jam, rock-a-baby, kiss the rim, lean in, and the tomahawk. In Jordan's game, the stylization of a performed self has allowed him to create a distinct sports persona that has athletic as well as economic consequences, while mastering sophisticated levels of physical expression and redefining the possibilities of athletic achievement within basketball.

Finally, there is the subversion of perceived limits through the use of *edifying deception*, which in Jordan's case centers around the space/time continuum. This moment in African-American cultural practice is the ability to flout widely understood boundaries through mesmerization and alchemy, a subversion of common perceptions of the culturally or physically possible through the creative and deceptive manipulation of appearance. Jordan is perhaps most famous for his alleged "hang time," the uncanny ability to remain suspended in midair longer than other basketball players while executing his stunning array of improvised moves. But Jordan's "hang time" is technically a misnomer, and can be more accurately attributed to Jordan's skillful athletic deception, his acrobatic leaping ability, and his intellectual toughness in projecting an aura of uniqueness around his craft than to his defiance of gravity and the laws of physics.

No human being, including Michael Jordan, can successfully defy the law of gravity and achieve relatively sustained altitude without the benefit of machines. As Douglas Kirkpatrick points out, the equation for altitude is $\frac{1}{2}g \times t^2 = VO \times t$ (Editors 1990, 28). However, Jordan appears to hang by *stylistically* relativizing the fixed coordinates of space and time through the skillful management and manipulation of his body in midair. For basketball players, "hang time" is the velocity and speed a player takes off with combined with the path her/his center of gravity follows on her/his way up. At the peak of a player's vertical jump, the velocity and speed are close to, or at, zero; hanging motionless in the air is the work of masterful skill and illusion (Editors 1990, 28).

Michael Jordan, through the consummate skill and style of his game, only appears to be hanging in space for more than the one second that human beings are capable of remaining airborne.

But the African-American aspects of Jordan's game are indissolubly linked to the culture of consumption and the commodification of black culture.[1] Because of Jordan's past mastery of basketball, his squeaky-clean image, and his youthful vigor in pursuit of the American Dream, he has become, along with Bill Cosby, the quintessential pitch man in American society. Even his highly publicized troubles with gambling, his refusal to visit the White House after the Bulls' championship season, and a book which purports to expose the underside of his heroic myth have barely tarnished his All-American image.[2] Jordan eats Wheaties, drives Chevrolets, wears Hanes, drinks Coca-Cola, consumes McDonalds, guzzles Gatorade, and, of course, wears Nikes. He and his shrewd handlers have successfully produced, packaged, marketed, and distributed his image and commodified his symbolic worth, transforming cultural capital into cash, influence, prestige, status, and wealth. To that degree, at least, Jordan repudiates the sorry tradition of the black athlete as the naif who loses his money to piranhalike financial wizards, investors, and hangers-on. He represents the New Age athletic entrepreneur who understands that American sport is ensconced in the cultural practices associated with business, and that it demands particular forms of intelligence, perception, and representation to prevent abuse and maximize profit.

From the very beginning of his professional career, Jordan was consciously marketed by his agency, Pro-Serv, as a peripatetic vehicle of American fantasies of capital accumulation and material consumption tied to Jordan's personal modesty and moral probity. In so doing, Pro-Serv skillfully avoided attaching to Jordan the image of questionable ethics and lethal excess that plagued inside traders and corporate raiders on Wall Street during the mid-1980s, as Jordan began to emerge as a cultural icon. But Jordan is also the symbol of the spectacle-laden black athletic body as the site of commodified black cultural imagination. Ironically, the black male body that has been historically viewed as threatening and inappropriate in American society (and remains so outside of sports and entertainment) is made an object of white desires to domesticate and dilute its more ominous and subversive uses, even symbolically reducing Jordan's body to dead meat (McDonald's McJordan hamburger), that can be consumed and expelled as waste.

Jordan's body is also the screen upon which is projected black desires to emulate his athletic excellence and replicate his entry into reaches of unimaginable wealth and fame. But there is more than vicarious substitution and the projection of fantasy onto Jordan's body that is occurring in the circulation

MICHAEL ERIC DYSON

and reproduction of black cultural desire. There is also the creative use of desire and fantasy by young blacks to counter, and capitulate to, the forces of cultural dominance that attempt to reduce the black body to a commodity or text that is employed for entertainment, titillation, or financial gain. Simply said, there is no easy correlation between the commodification of black youth culture and the evidences of a completely dominated consciousness.

Even within the dominant cultural practices that seek to turn the black body into pure profit, disruptions of capital are embodied, for instance, in messages circulated in black communities by public moralists who criticize the exploitation of black cultural creativity by casual footwear companies. In short, there are instances of both black complicity and black resistance in the commodification of the black cultural imagination, and the ideological criticism of exploitative cultural practices must always be linked to the language of possibility and agency in rendering a complex picture of the black cultural situation. As Henry Giroux observes,

> The power of complicity and the complicity of power are not exhausted simply by registering how people are positioned and located through the production of particular ideologies structured through particular discourses. . . . It is important to see that an overreliance on ideology critique has limited our ability to understand how people actively participate in the dominant culture through processes of accommodation, negotiation, and even resistance. (Giroux 1992, 194–95)

In making judgments about the various uses of the black body, especially Jordan's symbolic corporeality, we must specify how both consent and opposition to exploitation are often signalled in expressions of cultural creativity.

In examining his reactions to the racial ordering of athletic and cultural life, one can see that the ominous specificity of the black body creates anxieties for Jordan. His encounters with the limits of culturally mediated symbols of race and racial identity have occasionally mocked his desire to live beyond race, to be "neither black nor white" (Patton 1986, 52), to be "viewed as a person" (Vancil 1992, 57). While Jordan chafes under indictment by black critics who claim that he is not "black enough," he has perhaps not clearly understood the differences between enabling versions of human experience that transcend the exclusive gaze of race and disenabling visions of human community that seek neutrality.

The former is the attempt to expand the perimeters of human experience beyond racial determinism, to nuance and deepen our understanding of the constituent elements of racial identity and to understand how race, along with class, gender, geography, and sexual preference shape and constrain human experience. The latter is the belief in an intangible, amorphous, nonhistorical, and raceless category of "person," existing in a zone beyond not simply the negative consequences of race, but beyond the specific patterns of cultural and racial identity that constitute and help shape human experience. Jordan's unclarity is consequential, weighing heavily on his apolitical bearing and his refusal to acknowledge the public character of his private beliefs about American society and the responsibility of his role as a public pedagogue.

Indeed, it is the potency of black cultural expressions which have not only helped influence his style of play, but which have also made the sneaker industry in which he lucratively participates a multibillion-dollar business. Michael Jordan has helped seize upon the commercial consequences of black cultural preoccupation with style, and the commodification of the black juvenile imagination at the site of the sneaker. At the juncture of the sneaker, a host of cultural, political, and economic forces and meanings meet, collide, shatter, and are reassembled to symbolize the situation of contemporary black culture.

The sneaker reflects at once the projection and stylization of black urban realities linked in our contemporary historical moment to rap culture and the underground political economy of crack, and reigns as the universal icon for the culture of consumption. The sneaker symbolizes the ingenious manner in which black cultural nuances of cool, hip, and chic have influenced the broader American cultural landscape. It was black street culture that influenced sneaker companies' aggressive invasion of the black juvenile market in taking advantage of the increasing amounts of disposable income of young black men as a result of legitimate and illegitimate forms of work.

Problematically, though, the sneaker also epitomizes the worst features of the social production of desire, and represents the ways in which the moral energies of social conscience about material values are drained by the messages of undisciplined acquisitiveness promoted by corporate bastions of the culture of consumption. These messages, of rapacious consumerism supported by cultural and personal narcissism, are articulated on Wall Street and are related to the expanding inner-city juvenocracy, where young black men rule over black urban space in the culture of crack and illicit criminal activity, fed by desires to "live large" and to reproduce capitalism's excesses on their own terrain. Also, sneaker companies make significant sums of money from the illicit gains of drug dealers.

Moreover, while sneaker companies have exploited black cultural expressions of cool, hip, chic, and style, they rarely benefit the people who both consume the largest quantity of products and whose culture redefined the sneaker companies' raison d'être. This situation is severely compounded by the presence of spokespeople like Jordan, Spike Lee, and Bo Jackson, who are either ineffectual, defensive about, or indifferent to the lethal consequences (especially in urban black-on-black violence over sneaker company products) of black juvenile acquisition and consumption of products that these figures have helped make culturally desirable and economically marketable.

Basketball is the metaphoric center of black juvenile culture, a major means by which even temporary forms of cultural and personal transcendence of personal limits are experienced. Michael Jordan is at the center of this black athletic culture, the supreme symbol of black cultural creativity in a society of diminishing tolerance for the black youth whose fascination with Jordan has helped sustain him. But Jordan is also the iconic fixture of broader segments of American society who see in him the ideal figure: a black man of extraordinary genius on the court and before the cameras, who by virtue of his magical skills and godlike talents symbolizes the meaning of human possibility while refusing to root it in the specific forms of culture and race in which it must inevitably make sense or fade to ultimate irrelevance.

Jordan also represents the contradictory impulses of the contemporary culture of consumption, where the black athletic body is deified, reified, and rearticulated within the narrow meanings of capital and commodity. But there is both resistance and consent to the exploitation of black bodies in Jordan's explicit cultural symbolism, as he provides brilliant glimpses of black culture's ingenuity of improvisation as a means of cultural expression and survival. It is also partially this element of black culture that has created in American society a desire to dream Jordan, to "Be like Mike."

The pedagogy of desire that Jordan embodies, although at points immobilized by its cultural contexts, is nevertheless a remarkable achievement in contemporary American culture: a six-foot-six American man of obvious African descent is the dominant presence and central cause of athletic fantasy in a sport that twenty years ago was denigrated as a black man's game and hence deemed unworthy of wide attention or support. Jordan is therefore the bearer of meanings about black culture larger than his individual life, the symbol of a pedagogy of style, presence and desire that is immediately communicated by sight of his black body before it can be contravened by reflection.

In the final analysis, his big black body—graceful and powerful, elegant and dark—symbolizes the possibilities of other black bodies to at least remain safe long enough to survive within the limited but significant sphere of sport, since Jordan's achievements have furthered the cultural acceptance of at least the black athletic body. In that sense, Jordan's powerful cultural capital has not been exhausted by narrow understandings of his symbolic absorption by the demands of capital and consumption. His body is still the symbolic carrier of racial and cultural desires to fly beyond limits and obstacles, a fluid metaphor of mobility and ascent to heights of excellence secured by genius and industry. It is this power to embody the often conflicting desires of so many that makes Michael Jordan a supremely instructive figure for our times.

NOTES

1. I do not mean here a theory of commodification that does not accentuate the forms of agency that can function even within restrictive and hegemonic cultural practices. Rather, I think that, contrary to elitist and overly pessimistic Frankfurt School readings of the spectacle of commodity within mass cultures, common people can exercise "everyday forms of resistance" to hegemonic forms of cultural knowledge and practice. For an explication of the function of everyday forms of resistance, see Scott, *Domination and the Arts of Resistance.*

2. For a critical look at Jordan behind the myth, see Smith, *The Jordan Rules.*

WORKS CITED

Boers, Terry. 1990. "Getting Better All the Time." *Inside Sports*, May, 30–33.

Bradley, Michael. 1991–92. "Air Everything." *Basketball Forecast*, 60–67.

Editors. 1990. "How Does Michael Fly?" *Chicago Tribune*, February 27, 28.

Giroux, Henry. 1992. *Border Crossings: Cultural Workers and the Politics of Education.* New York: Routledge.

McCallum, Jack. 1991. "His Highness." *Sports Illustrated*, June 17, 28–33.

Patton, Paul. 1986. "The Selling of Michael Jordan." *New York Times Magazine*, November 9, 48–58.

Scott, James. 1990. *Domination and the Arts of Resistance.* New Haven: Yale University Press.

Smith, Sam. 1992. *The Jordan Rules.* New York: Simon and Schuster.

Vancil, Mark. 1992. "Playboy Interview: Michael Jordan." *Playboy Magazine*, May, 51–164.

African-American Festive Style

(1996)

WILLIAM D. PIERSEN

. . . .

Adopting a comparative approach to festivals throughout the African Diaspora, historian William D. Piersen outlines some aesthetic principles of African American cultural expression, the "raucous processions, idiophonic music, and energetic competitive dancing" of early African American festivals that have come to dominate American holiday traditions. An important element of such festivals is the back-and-forth interaction between spectators and performers, which Piersen calls the "principle of the second line," characteristic of the vernacular tradition Bertram D. Ashe describes in jazz performances.

The holiday occasions for major African-American festivals in North America were not consistent across the geographical and cultural boundaries of our nation's colonial and early national eras, for African-American holiday traditions had to adapt to the windows of activity permitted by the white elite's calendars. This did not inhibit black celebration because in North America it was far easier for arrivals from hundreds of separate African nationalities to create new syncretised festivals from a variety of African and Euro-American elements than to maintain more narrow old-world national and ethnic holidays. As a result, African-American festivals not only illuminate the formation of our national culture, but they also offer important insight into the aesthetic principles of African-American cultural expression.

The major occasions for slave festivities in what is now the United States ranged from Negro Election Day in New England to Pinkster in New York and New Jersey, and Jon Koonering[1] in southern Virginia and North Carolina; corn huskings and Christmas Day also provided opportunities for a variety of holiday celebrations, especially in the southern region. There were also black festivities at various times in most urban areas—especially noteworthy being those in New Orleans, Mobile, and Philadelphia. While all these occasions were framed within essentially European-American holidays, in each region black styles of celebration especially marked by raucous processions, idiophonic music, and energetic competitive dancing soon dominated despite the original holiday traditions of each area's majority white population.

Why did nominally dominant forms of the Euro-American occasions so quickly give way before African-American styles of amusement? To what degree did these African-influenced festive styles shape later white holiday traditions? What do the differences between African-American and European-American styles of celebration suggest about the interrelationship between the individual and the community in both black and white America? How does all this shape our understanding of African-American culture? To answer these questions, it is best to start by examining some specifics of black festive style.

Musical parading activities strutted to the center of many of the festive occasions celebrated by antebellum African Americans. Though these boisterous Afro-American processions were commonly interpreted as black imitations of more stately European-American political and mumming activities, so many features of the African-American parades are paralleled elsewhere throughout the Americas that their commonness suggests an African essence to the form.

The African-American parade typically featured a raucous improvised style of music and a back-and-forth interaction between spectators and parade performers; these features were not typical of white parades and processions of the era but they were prevalent in black rites in both West Africa and the nearby Caribbean. Certainly, the "showy" Negro Election parades of eighteenth-century New England, to take one example, did not try to approximate the region's European-American regard for uniformity. Typically, a group of musicians dressed in "somewhat fantastic" unmatched articles of clothing escorted the region's black kings and governors; sometimes parade participants were even more outlandishly bedecked with ribbons and feathers. The musicians carried whatever assortment of banjos, brass horns, tambourines, drums, fifes, clarinets, and "sonorous metals" they could find to serenade the accompanying crowd of revelers.[2]

In early New England, the features that distinguished black processions escorting black governors and kings from parallel white escorts for the region's incumbent white governors were the random firing of salutes, the raucous style of music, and the playfulness of the black paraders. In New England, it was African Americans who first developed inaugural parades, and, therefore, our contemporary inaugural and other political parades may be more African-American than we suspect.[3]

Elsewhere throughout the Americas, and in West Africa, observers had noticed the black preference for a noisy and random firing of holiday gun-

WILLIAM D. PIERSEN

powder salutes. According to Philip Fithian's journal entry of December 24, 1773, "Guns are fired this Evening in the Neighborhood [Westmoreland County, Virginia], and the Negroes seem to be inspired with new Life."[4] The tradition of firing off weapons around Christmas has been maintained in the South and eventually expanded northward since that time.[5] A firing of salutes like those that marked the New England parades was also found in the Christmas festivals of Jamaica,[6] and by the middle of the nineteenth century fireworks had become an emblem of most West Indian Christmas celebrations.[7]

African-American processions in the South displayed a parade style much like New England's. In the Jon Koonering celebrations of the eighteenth century, for example, a half-dozen secondary performers typically followed in the train of the principal actors; and much like some of the New England musicians of the same era, these celebrants were described as "arrayed fantastically in ribbons, rags, and feathers, and bearing between them several so-called musical instruments." The makeshift Jonkonnu bands were followed by noisy cheering crowds of black spectators of all ages who continually interacted with the processions as they moved from house to house.[8]

It was reported in Edenton, North Carolina, in 1824 that the "John Canno" festival was "a sport common in this part of the state with slaves on Holy-days," with the blacks "serenading and exhibiting" until late at night on Christmas Eve.[9] Similar Jonkonnu traditions were also widespread in the West Indies and the accompanying forms of the pageant had antecedents widely spread across West Africa.[10]

Activities similar to those normally associated with Jon Koonering also appeared, but without the principal African-style maskers, in eighteenth-century funeral "plays" and the nineteenth-century Christmas activities on southern plantations. As James Murray reported from Cape Fear, North Carolina, in 1755, "the Negroes . . . are at a great loss this Christmas for want of a death to play for."[11] Large groups of blacks attended African-American funeral rites, parts of which they treated as festive occasions or "plays" in honor of the deceased's triumphal entry into the world of the ancestral spirits, and the Jonkonnu rites which have been associated with ancestral maskers typical of West African secret societies may only be, therefore, specific forms of an already ongoing and widespread institution.[12]

Black festivals or "plays" required both free time and an excuse for merry-making. In New England it was Election Day, and in the South it was often funerals or the Christmas holidays.[13] But the activities were much the same. Consider the street dancing activities, so similar to Jon Koonering, that appeared in New Orleans in the 1820s; Timothy Flint reported that slaves there were given the liberty to "dance through the streets" as "merry Bachanaliars" whose antics "convulsed even the masters of the negroes with laughter." These events, where the central character—whom Flint called a "king"—wore "a series of oblong, gilt-paper boxes on his head, tapering upwards, like a pyramid" from which hung two huge tassels, strongly suggest the Jonkonnu ceremonies of the West Indies in the style of the masks, the role of a festive "king," and the associated humorous processional activities.[14] All the characters that followed the performers were said to have "their own peculiar dress, and their contortions. They dance, and their streamers fly, and the bells that they have hung about them tinkle."[15]

Jonkonnu-like processions, such as those that wandered the streets of New Orleans, were also probably far more common during the southern Christmas holidays than we have previously thought. Consider the black parade observed in Saint Marys, Georgia, on December 27, 1843, which had aspects of Election Day, Pinkster, Jon Koonering, and Mobile Mardi Gras: the blacks paraded during the last day of their feast "with a corps of staff officers with red sashes, mock epaulets & goose quill feathers, and a band of music." They were followed by others, some dancing, some walking & some hopping, others singing, all as lively as lively can be." With "music enough to deafen" observers, the black merrymakers went about "levying small contributions on all the whites," who in turn appeared as maskers in their own right on the next day.[16]

Similarly, the first so-called "Mardi Gras" activities in Mobile among whites, which took place in 1830 on Christmas Eve when the drunken Michael Krafft appeared in Jonkonnu-like garb, was followed on New Years by fifty "cowbellion" maskers who made up "as weird as they could." These white maskers who boisterously roamed the streets shouting and singing and making a rowdy spectacle, stopped to serenade at the houses of certain important citizens who furnished them with liquid refreshments just like so many Jon Kooners. It seems unnecessary to search far afield for white sources for these events in obscure Nova Scotian or Pennsylvania German activities when so many similar African-American processions were to be found along the Gulf Coast and the nearby Caribbean.[17]

In early New York, where Pinkster becomes the holiday of choice, African-American style again quickly asserts itself, and in Albany "a motley group of thousands" was said to have followed the local black "king" as he and his attendants wandered the streets "calling at one door after another and demand[ing] tribute, which demand he enforce[d] by . . . a horrid noise and frightful grimaces."[18] This ceremony recognizing local authorities has often been interpreted in the Jonkonnu festival as an imitation of European-style mumming. But since we have few, if any, examples of white English-style mumming groups queting throughout the Americas and hundreds of parallel

WILLIAM D. PIERSEN

African-American examples (including the grimaces) it would seem more reasonable to connect the house-to-house queting for gifts and liquor offerings that were featured in Pinkster, Mobile, the North Carolina coast, and the Caribbean to West African holiday traditions such as that described as typical by Kenneth Little:

A spirit, escorted by a number of attendants and followers, usually visits every big man in the town and squats in various grotesque poses in front of his house. It then proceeds to parade about the town attracting spectators and causing amusement wherever it goes. Bystanders with a position of social standing to maintain hand over a "dash" of money to the spirit's followers.[19]

Because similar "dashing" or queting traditions were found across West Africa and were also ubiquitous in the West Indies during Christmas, it should not be surprising that they appeared in a less exotic guise, without the central masker, in the "Christmas gift" activities of the southern United States. What looked to southern whites like a simple feudal homage of peasants or slaves to masters was in reality for the blacks an African-style custom that cut two ways in alternating potential praise of important personages with veiled social criticism, a form of performance that honored those who gave generously to the visiting party but also, in the veiled criticisms of the celebrants, reinforced the ultimate authority of the community in establishing social repute.

Crucial to the humor of the African-American celebrations was the role of black spectators who were at once observers and participants. Edward Warren in 1829 recorded just such audience and performer interchange between the two central characters in the Jon Koonering festivities in Washington County, North Carolina, and the following "motley crowd of all ages, dressed in their ordinary working clothes, which seemingly come as a guard of honor to the performers."[20] When the Jonkonnu masker improvised a song asking a white honoree for a gift, "the whole crowd joined in the chorus, shouting and clapping their hands in the wildest glee."[21]

This interaction between performer and audience is an essential principle of African-American festive style that we might call the principal of the second line. In New Orleans, the term "second line" has traditionally referred to "the friends and neighbors who dance with the [black Mardi Gras Indians or funeral society bands] along streets and sidewalks."[22] As trumpeter Bunk Johnson described those who followed the jazz funeral bands: "We would have a second line there that was 'most equivalent to King Rex parade—Mardi Gras Carnival parade. The police were unable to keep the second line back—all in the street, all on the sidewalks, in front of the band. . . . We'd have some immense crowds following. They would follow the funeral up to the cemetery just to get this ragtime music comin' back."[23]

Audience and performers also interacted when bands of African-American musicians played for white militias in the antebellum South. As northern schoolteacher Emily Burke noted in her journal of life in 1840s Georgia, "this performance [of the black musicians] also calls out all the servants that can obtain permission to attend the training, and it is not a few of them that not only follow but go before the companies whenever they march. They are excessively fond of such scenes, and crowds of men, women, and children never fail of being present on all such occasions, some carrying their masters children on their heads and shoulders. . . ."[24]

What was going on between performers and audience was usually not clearly spelled out in early reports of North American black parades, but the probable style of interaction can be illuminated by reference to more detailed observations of African-American dance. An interactive exchange between black audience and performers was observed in Haiti by African-American dancer Katharine Dunham, who described the back-and-forth feedback between performers and audience: "[The crowd] may stop to watch the dance of competition, cheering the more agile and ridiculing the loser, or they may go into a frenzy of dancing alone or with random partners."[25] African-American spectators never remained passive observers either in processional second lines or as members of the dance circle.

Samuel Kinser offers a suggestive trope for our thinking in his analysis of the dance structures of New Orleans Mardi Gras Indians when he compares black dance interaction with the musical improvisations and exchanges of jazz:

Each performer when he gets the feeling takes a riff, struts, moves to the center and does his stuff. That will stimulate somebody else, they may play then together. But it's all done with a guiding rhythm. . . . A challenge is a break in the rhythm, making strong dance moves, getting the tambourines to follow your moves, stopping the rap of the other. . . . As the confrontation gathers, people who are standing around, letting their bodies move with the tambourines, start throwing up fists, flail their arms, open wide their bodies, go away and go back toward the conflict. . . . Challenge is talking about yourself, boasting. You talk 'till you're cut.[26]

Roger Abrahams suggested the uniqueness of the black style of audience/performer interaction in his detailed study of Southern corn huskings by pointing out that when whites began to imitate black dance styles they took up the competitive "showing off," but they failed to duplicate, or even appreciate, the important interactive role of the "second line": "Through this imitation,

WILLIAM D. PIERSEN

whites seized license to dance alone, each dancer simply responding to the rhythms of the music. This is a white interpretation of the 'apart-playing' of the slave ring play or dance, without adopting or recognizing the black convention in which the dancer at the center of these show-off occasions relied on the support of the circle of dancers."[27] To avoid being cut from the circle, black dancers had to win the active and interactive support of their audience and fight off the challenges of competitors; those who were best also forced changes in the beat of the music, for the musicians in black dance, as in black parades, responded to and interacted with both spectators and fellow performers.

It is useful to compare Andrew Burnaby's description of a white Virginia jig, which he felt lacked the method and regularity of European dancing, with black examples. In the white imitation "a gentleman and a lady stand up, and dance about the room, one of them retiring, the other pursuing, then perhaps meeting in an irregular manner. After some time, another lady gets up, and then the first lady must sit down, she being, as the term is, cut out; the second lady acts the same part which the first did, till somebody cuts her out. The gentlemen perform in the same manner."[28] Black dances of this type were both far more competitive and far more suggestive: Nicholas Cresswell, reporting black dancing in Virginia at the same period put it this way: "[a] couple gets up and begins to dance a jig (to some Negro tune) others comes and cuts them out." The effect of these dances, he said, was "more like a Bacchanalian dance than one in polite company."[29]

More modern observers stated these points more explicitly. In viewing a Trinidadian dance, Katherine Dunham observed: "Then [the dancers] would shuffle again, and spurred by remarks from the sidelines, the center couple would come closer and the emphasis would move from the feet well into the central torso, becoming unmistakably sexual in intention."[30] As Roger Abrahams explained in the context of ring play dancing: "Each player is encouraged to show off in some way, either through some kind of individualized dance step ('show me your motion'), or through strutting, teasing, flirting, and wiggling, with everyone else clapping, commenting, and joking in support. This is the point. For while the player is at the center he or she is never alone; rather there is constant commentary and support by the ring."[31]

One of the appeals commonly made to African-American festive audiences was to their appreciation of a satiric takeoff. In many antebellum celebrations the central target for African-American humor was the pretentiousness of the master class. The use of satire directed against people in power during holiday festivities had long been traditional in West African societies where song lyrics, in general, targeted moral and ethical pretensions in whatever form these unsociable qualities appeared. Such critical songs came to serve the same purpose in America as they had in Africa—to mobilize and affirm the ultimate authority of community values.[32]

Less formal occasions for satire lampooning members of the local communities also used the same mechanisms. Typically African satire involved both physical humor and accompanying song lyrics; consider the experiences of two early nineteenth-century European visitors to West Africa, Renè Cailliè and Thomas Edward Bowdich: The Mandingo, said Cailliè, "ridiculed my gestures and my words, and went about the village mimicking me";[33] and the Ashanti, bemoaned Bowdich, "used to entertain themselves with mimicking our common expressions and our actions, which they did inimitably."[34] Throughout the Americas, as in Africa, whites quickly became favorite targets for black humor.[35]

Such satiric entertainment appeared in the informal gatherings called plays by the slaves as well as in more formal festive occasions such as corn-huskings, election parades, and militia training. Typical of the satiric plays is the example noted in the *South Carolina Gazette* of 1772 where a local black entertainment was described as being opened "by men copying (or *taking off*) the manners of their masters, and the women their mistresses, and relating some highly curious anecdotes, to the inexpressible diversion of that company."[36]

Black militias who trained and paraded in the early nineteenth century also featured satiric performances. Pointed humor appeared as part of the New England Negro Election festivities when it was said, "masters did not interfere until the utmost verge of decency had been reached, good-naturedly submitting to the hard hits leveled against themselves, and possibly profiting a little by some shrewd allusion."[37] When black governor Eben Tobias of Derby, Connecticut, drilled his escort, his troops responded to the command "Fire and fall off!" literally, sprawling comically to the ground.[38] The English visitor James Boardman clearly understood that the black militiamen, wearing a set of motley uniforms to their 5th of July parade, the day after white New Yorkers' July 4th festivities, were "a parody upon the shopkeeper colonels of the previous day."[39] William Cullen Bryant had noticed the same phenomenon in the South where "from the dances [of the blacks] a transition was made to a mock military parade, a sort of burlesque of our militia trainings, in which the words of command and evolutions were extremely ludicrous."[40]

One of the aspects of African-American festive style that most annoyed Euro-American observers was the indefatigable nature of the celebrations. This was as true at a funeral—"At a half past five I was dressed and out. The hymns of the Negroes, which had continued through the night, were still to be heard on all sides"[41] as at a play—"The party at Pierce's continued their jollification until broad daylight, when I returned to my master's house; somewhat wearied with the loss of rest . . ."[42]—or during a formal holiday event—"The [Christmas Day] entertainment was kept up till nine or ten o'clock in the evening . . . [when the blacks] at last retired, apparently quite satisfied with their saturnalia, to dance the rest of the night at their own habitations."[43]

Celebrations in West Africa ran far into the night in part to avoid the stultifying noontime heat of the tropics, but white Americans whose cultural roots were adapted to cooler climes found such late celebrations much too much; similarly, the noise level of black festivities, customarily held out-of-doors in Africa, was far too excessive for Euro-American sensibilities better adapted to their own indoor lives.[44]

We tend to think of African culture as communalist and Western European culture as individualist, yet in the aesthetics of festive dance and music these characterizations in crucial ways must be reversed. African-style dancing in the Americas was marked by individual competition and solo improvisations among both dancers and musicians. Where Euro-Americans swirled to traditional tunes in communal established patterns featuring prescribed sets of notes, steps, and movements, Afro-Americans leaped into and out of the dancing rings to perform original variations to a constantly changing music. Whites might take lessons from dancing masters, but blacks had to improvise anew using their basic skills with each succeeding performance; for among Europeans there was a right and wrong way to dance, but among blacks standards changed with each audience and each improvised piece of music.

African-American festive occasions were at base social occasions. The point may be obvious, but it is important to emphasize that in the African-American style both the performer and the audience were essential, complementary, and interacting elements—as Gena Caponi puts it, "Euro-Americans often miss the balancing act in African-American artistic expression altogether; they see only the tightrope walker and ignore the crowd standing in a circle around the performer, not only cheering him on, but holding up the rope, as well."[45]

We can see the same cultural emphasis on individual showmanship within a community context in American sports. Black athletes—such as defensive linemen, broken-field runners, basketball stars—tend to admire individual performance, the ability to break the pattern in displays of joyful showmanship; whereas, white athletes—offensive linemen, quarterbacks, basketball coaches—like to emphasize teamwork and the precise adherence to plan. Black athletes see their competitions as heroic, improvised, and personal; whereas, in the Anglo cultures, whites more often see themselves as humble, faceless components in a well-oiled communal team.

In basketball, whites pick-and-roll and screen while blacks fake, drive, and slam-dunk. These are cultural, not racial, choices. Compare the marching bands of any two historically white and historically black educational institutions; admittedly their styles are blending but we can still see the cake-walking heroic (and comedic) quality of the black musicians in comparison to the rigid patterning and martial seriousness of the white. Even today we can still feel the cultural collisions; American football commentators have generally recoiled in horror at the unbridled showmanship of black athletes who emphasize individual improvisation, showmanship, and strutting dance routines in a sport where formerly there was "no I in 'team'."

The African-style individualism we see in modern sports carries the old cultural coding of African-American festive style and, as such, is quite different from socially alienated individualism that characterizes more European forms. Although Afro-American performers in traditional artistic situations were expected to display individual showmanship, such performers were not expected to be impervious to, or isolated from, the social pressures of the group; in fact, the black performers responded directly to audience feedback. Where white dancers, for example, followed the scripting of the music and the particular dance, blacks interacted with the music so as to change the beat and the flow; the rhythms responded to the dancers as much as the dancers signified on the performance of the musicians.

Scholars of early African-American festivals, noting the humorous role reversals common in the holiday festivities, remind us that many European festivals centered on symbolic representations of class differentiation and "lords of misrule" activities. In a similar way, African-centered performance styles also attacked social barriers, but in the black cultural world the aggression was mirrored in the interaction and shifting focus between the apparently dominant performers and the actually controlling audience, an exchange that was purposefully subversive to artificial distinctions of power and prestige.

This interaction again raises the question of how we distinguish between activities that were primarily African in inspiration and those that were imitations of European traditions. By now, the extreme position of E. Franklin Frazier and Richard Dorson that not enough African cultural influence survived the brutal filter of the slave trade to affect African-American life in any influential way seems overstated. Probably most scholars would feel more comfortable proposing that African-American festive style was a result of a cultural blending—to one degree or another—of both African and European-American traditions. Among current writers Sterling Stuckey and Roger Abrahams lean southward, as I do, in emphasizing African influence while, to one degree or another, Shane White, Samuel Kinser, and Geneviève Fabre remind us not to neglect the importance of European precedents. Among the Africanists, Stuckey emphasizes the Yoruba heritage that shaped western Nigeria and

WILLIAM D. PIERSEN

nearby Dahomey while my own work gives as much attention to the lower Windward Coast and the festive traditions of the Senegambia as to Nigeria. For his part, Roger Abrahams prudently uses a more generalized West Africa as the source culture.

On the side of European influences, the French scholar Geneviève Fabre in her work on African-American festive style offers interesting and suggestive speculation as to the origins of the Jonkonnu ceremonies found across the West Indies and on the North Carolina coast. Her Eurocentric ideas can serve as a case study of the difficulties of separating out the African and European components within a particular ceremony. Fabre is well aware that Jonkonnu existed in a multicultural setting. She concedes to the theories of earlier scholars that the feast bore the name of a resident of the Gold Coast, John Coony, and that it continued to memorialize the man who, she believes, remained its main figure. But, that said, Fabre emphasizes that in North Carolina the festival was clearly set within a European time frame—"always associated with the Christmas and New Year's period," and, more important, Fabre asserts that the key rites were also European: the slaves, she says, "appropriated the [English] mumming tradition of visiting wealthy houses, setting themselves on an equal footing with their masters and white neighbors, [and] demand[ing] gifts as a just retribution, deriding in songs those not generous enough to accede to their requests."

Fabre believes "this reinterpretation of mumming, of the Roman Saturnalia custom of masters serving their slaves during the festival, and of the visiting and gift-giving rituals enabled the slaves to make statements on their condition as well as claims to greater social justice." For Fabre the costuming was "in mock imitation of the European masquerading tradition, the rags reminiscent of jesters' garments," with the whip as "both a magical instrument and, in mock imitation of the driver's lash, a tool to chastise and enforce order."[46]

Yet African-American parades in colonial Cuba on The Day of Kings, for example, also featured parallel queting processions but these were certainly not Celtic mummers. As the Cuba scholar Fernando Ortiz notes: The Day of Kings was when the transplanted African groups allowed their secret society maskers, described as "little devils," to be seen on the streets of Havana.[47] As the ceremony was described by contemporary observer F. W. Wurdeman:

The central object in the group was an athletic negro, with a fantastic straw helmet, an immensely thick girdle of strips of palm-leaves around his waist, and other uncouth articles of dress. Whenever they stopped, their banjoes struck up one of their monotonous tunes, and this frightful figure would commence a devil's dance, which was the signal for all his court to join in a general fandango, a description of which my pen refuseth to give. Yet when these parties stopped at the doors of the houses, which they frequently did to collect money from their inmates, often intruding into the very passages, the ladies mingled freely among the spectators.[48]

None of the Cuban observers thought they were watching an imitation of European customs.

Fernando Ortiz says an associated dance, called "kill the snake," "was very much popular among the negroes, so much so that the writers of the day say that it was 'the dance of the mob.' One dancing group of negroes jumping, dancing and singing, carried on their shoulders a huge artificial snake several meters long through the streets of Havana, stopping in front of the large houses where they gave them gifts. [On] The Day of Kings, after traveling through all of Havana, such a pantomime was done in the patio of the captain generals, before the supreme authority."[49] In analyzing these activities, Cuban scholars have not felt the compelling need of their English counterparts to look first to Europe for parallels for what seemed clearly to the contemporary observers to be African-style practices.

I suspect the Jonkonnu maskers of North America were modeling their performances on West African maskers from both hunting and ancestral societies. The anthropologist Martha Beckwith was told by a Myal priest, a specialist in counteracting the evil magic of obeah, that the key John Canoe mask was essentially an ancestral spiritual object:

Before building the house-shaped structure worn in the dance, a feast must be given consisting of goat's meat boiled without salt, together with plenty of rum. As the building progresses other feasts are given. On the night before it is brought out in public, it is taken to the cemetery, and there the songs and dances are rehearsed in order to "catch the spirit of the dead," which henceforth accompanies the dancer until, after a few weeks of merriment during which performances are given for money at the great houses and at village crossroads, it is broken up entirely. For "as long as it stays in the house the spirit will follow it."[50]

In upper North America the secular elements of the Jonkonnu ceremonies quickly replaced the spiritual aspects. Perhaps, in the end, the question of ultimate origins is not as productive as exploring the aesthetic design of the performances. In this we might be helped by the many scholars who have studied the West African and African-American arts; these humanists have been trying to put their fingers on essential aesthetic patterns that differentiate Afrocultural from Eurocultural elements and emphases.[51] African and African-

WILLIAM D. PIERSEN

influenced arts, they suggest, have a primarily social purpose, as opposed to the intrinsic and individual search for beauty and intellectual stimulation that are said to define European art. Black music and dance emphasize improvisation and personal stylization, a rhythmically complex dialogue between artist and audience usually described as a "call-and-response" effect. In both music and dance, performer and musician must see beyond the apparent multiplicity of beats to an unstated but unifying rhythmic center. The black artistic tradition fosters individual improvisation but within a communal tradition and collective setting. Competitive personal stylization such as "apart playing" is crucial but always operates within a communally approving context.

Early African-American performances typically occurred in permeable circular formations that reflected the communal, interactive, and nonliterate nature of African-style performances. Sterling Stuckey has seen African-American ring dances as symbolic of the very circle of African-American culture.[52] Certainly, black artistic performers were usually infused with a joyful communal spirit even while they moved off on their own improvised commentary, or signification,[53] on the shared realities of American life.

Such generalizations about an African-American aesthetic illuminate many of the characteristics that mark black festive style in antebellum North America. Certainly, most black celebrations can be characterized as long, loud, satiric, and joyful. Typically the central celebrants or performers interacted with a participatory audience. When the events took place in a stable location the spectators usually circled the action and the principal performers would move into and out of the circle on the basis of both personal initiative and audience feedback; when the celebrants were moving, as in a parade, there was usually special costuming for at least some of the central performers, and the interacting audience moved along with the procession forming a kind of second line.

Performers in African-American festive occasions usually competed individualistically for audience approval; improvisation and stylistic embellishment were the necessary marks of artistry, yet the individual performers had to stay within the social bounds of audience approval. At one and the same time, African-American performers were both more individualistic and innovative than corresponding Euro-Americans, yet they were also far more controlled by the immediate social context.

When black parades of the various urban societies in the nineteenth-century North became more bourgeois and European in order to appeal to both white observers and the black elite, *Freedom's Journal* caught the widening class and cultural divisions within African-American society as it castigated the older African forms of a Brooklyn march: "Nothing is more disgusting to the eyes of a reflecting man of colour than one *of these grand processions, followed by the lower orders of society.*"[54] That is, nothing was more disgusting than the controlling effect of the second line that required individual, elitist antisocial pretensions be punctured and communally approved "get-down" showmanship be flaunted.

By the nineteenth century, the circle of culture was coming full round as blacks took up European-American styles; but at the same time, in blackface minstrelsy, the mummers parades in Philadelphia, and the festive performances of Mardi Gras whites were also drinking deeply of long-established African-American patterns of performance. It was becoming harder and harder in America to say where one ethnic culture began and another ended.

NOTES

1. The spelling of this festival varies, it almost seems, with each observer. The first North Carolina account from Edenton called the celebration "John Canno"; six years later the term as used in Somerset was "John Koonering," Marvin L. Michael Kay and Lorin Lee Cary, *Slavery in North Carolina, 1748–1775* (Chapel Hill: University of North Carolina Press, 1995), 183–84. Other references from rites both in the Caribbean and the United States have used the terms "John Connú," "John Canoe," "Jon-canoe," "JonKanoo," "Jon-konnu," "John Kunering." For consistency I will use John Koonering and Jonkonnu without getting into the argument about which should be the standard terms.

2. William D. Piersen, *Black Yankees: The Development of an Afro-American Subculture in Eighteenth-Century New England* (Amherst: University of Massachusetts Press, 1988), 121–22.

3. Ibid., 122.

4. Philip Vickers Fithian, *Journal & Letters of Philip Vickers Fithian 1773–1774: A Plantation Tutor of the Old Dominion*, ed. Hunter Dickinson Farish (Williamsburg: Colonial Williamsburg, Inc., 1957), 39.

5. Ibid., 244, n. 79.

6. Anonymous, "Characteristic Traits of the Creolian and African Negroes in Jamaica, &c. &c.," *Columbian Magazine* (April–October 1797), as quoted in *After Africa: Extracts from British Travel Accounts and Journals of the Seventeenth, Eighteenth, and Nineteenth Centuries concerning the Slaves, Their Manners, and Customs in the British West Indies*, ed. Roger D. Abrahams and John F. Szwed (New Haven: Yale University Press, 1983), 233.

7. William G. Sewell, *The Ordeal of Free Labor in the British West Indies* (London, 1862), 216–17, as quoted in Abrahams and Szwed, *After Africa*, 271.

8. Kay and Cary, *Slavery in North Carolina*, 185–86.

9. Elizabeth A. Fenn, "'A Perfect Equality Seemed to Reign': Slave Society and Jon Konnu," *North Carolina Historical Review* 65 (April 1988), 130–33.

10. Kay and Cary, *Slavery in North Carolina*, 184–85.

11. James Murray to Sister Clark, December 26, 1755, as quoted in Sylvia R. Frey, *Water from the Rock: Black Resistance in a Revolutionary Age* (Princeton: Princeton University Press, 1991), 41.

12. Martha Warren Beckwith, *Black Roadways: A Study of Jamaica Folk Life* (Chapel Hill: University of North Carolina Press, 1929), 151.

13. Early black funerals in New England probably were close in style to those of their southern cousins, but we do not have as much evidence; see Piersen, *Black Yankees*, 77.

14. See, for comparison to the New Orleans mask, a very similar West Indian mask or crown pictured in J. M. Belasario, *Sketches*, reprinted in Lynne Fauley Emery, *Black Dance in the United States from 1619 to 1970* (Palo Alto: National Press Books, 1972), 31. On the role of the black "king" as a central character in early Jonkonnu rites see Robert Dirks, *The Black Saturnalia* (Gainesville: University of Florida Press, 1987), 174–75.

15. Timothy Flint, *Recollections of the Last Ten Years, Passed in Occasional Residences and Journeyings in the Valley of the Mississippi* . . . (Boston, 1826), 140.

16. Lester B. Shippee, ed., *Bishop Whipple's Southern Diary, 1843–1844* (Minneapolis, 1937), 51. On the red ribbon as an African-American holiday marker, Solomon Northrup noted: Christmas morning was "the happiest day in the whole year for the slave. . . . The time of feasting and dancing had come. . . . That day the clean dress was to be donned—the red ribbon displayed." See Solomon Northrup, *Twelve Years a Slave* (Cincinnati, 1853), as quoted in *Readings in Black American Music*, ed. Eileen Southern, 2d ed. (New York: W. W. Norton, 1983), 101.

17. On this subject compare the hypothesis for European origins developed by Samuel Kinser, *Carnival American Style: Mardi Gras at New Orleans and Mobile* (Chicago: University of Chicago Press, 1990), 80–81, 88–89, with the African-American emphasis given by William D. Piersen, *Black Legacy: America's Hidden Heritage* (Amherst: University of Massachusetts Press, 1993), 121–31.

18. *Albany Centinel*, as quoted in Shane White, "Pinkster: Afro-Dutch Syncretization in New York City and the Hudson Valley," *Journal of American Folklore* 102 (403) (January–March, 1989): 70.

19. Kenneth Little, "The Role of the Secret Society in Cultural Specialization," *American Anthropologist* 51 (1949), 208–209.

20. Edward Warren, *A Doctor's Experiences on Three Continents* (Baltimore: Cushings and Baily, 1885), 201.

21. Ibid., 202.

22. Samuel Kinser's description of the second line among Mardi Gras Indian tribes, in *Carnival American Style: Mardi Gras at New Orleans and Mobile* (Chicago: University of Chicago Press, 1990), 213.

23. Album notes, "New Orleans Parade," American Music Records, nos. 101–103, as quoted in Marshall W. Stearns, *The Story of Jazz* (Oxford: Oxford University Press, 1956), 61.

24. Emily Burke, *Pleasure and Pain: Reminiscences of Georgia in the 1840's* (Savannah: Beehive Press, n.d.), 26–27, as quoted in Roger D. Abrahams, *Singing the Master: The Emergence of African American Culture in the Plantation South* (New York: Pantheon Books, 1992), 193.

25. Katharine Dunham, *Dances of Haiti* (New York: 1937), 34, as quoted in Kinser, *Carnival American Style*, 227.

26. Kinser, *Carnival American Style*, 185–88.

27. Abrahams, *Singing the Master*, 139.

28. Andrew Burnaby, *A Concise Historical Account of All the British Colonies in North America* (Dublin: Printed for C. James, 1776), 213.

29. Nicholas Cresswell, *The Journal of Nicolas Cresswell: 1774–1777* (New York: Dial, 1924), 52–53.

30. Katherine Dunham, "Ethnic Dancing," *Dance Magazine* 20 (September 1946): 34.

31. Abrahams, *Singing the Master*, 104.

32. John Miller Chernoff, *African Rhythm and African Sensibility: Aesthetics and Social Action in African Musical Idioms* (Chicago: University of Chicago Press, 1981), 71, as quoted in Abrahams, *Singing the Master*, 112. See especially the chapter on satire in Piersen, *Black Legacy*, 53–73, reprinted in this volume.

33. Renè Cailliè, *Journal d'un voyage à Temboctu et à Jenne dans l'Afrique Centrale* (Paris, 1830), as quoted in Christopher Hibbert, *Africa Explored: Europeans in the Dark Continent, 1769–1889* (New York: W. W. Norton, 1983), 169.

34. T. Edward Bowdich, *Mission from Cape Coast Castle to Ashantee* (1819; rpt. ed., London, 1966), 292.

35. Piersen, *Black Legacy*, 60–73, reprinted in this volume.

36. *South Carolina Gazette*, September 17, 1772, as quoted in Peter H. Wood, *Black Majority: Negroes in Colonial South Carolina from 1670 through the Stono Rebellion* (New York: W. W. Norton, 1974), 342; likewise, see Marshall Stearns and Jean Stearns, *Jazz Dance* (New York: Macmillan, 1968), 22; Kinser, *Carnival American Style*, 73; and the many similar examples from around the Americas cited in Piersen, *Black Legacy*, 63–64, reprinted in this volume.

37. James R. Newhall, *The History of Lynn* (Lynn, 1883), 236, as quoted in Piersen, *Black Yankees*, 139. Compare Newhall's description with that of the associated satire of the Christmas "gombayers" in Jamaica in 1826: "The slaves sang satirical philippics against their master, communicating a little free advice now and then; but they never lost sight of decorum." Cynric R. Williams, *A Tour through the Island of Jamaica* (London, 1826) as quoted in Abrahams and Szwed, *After Africa*, 250.

38. Jane de Forest Shelton, "New England Negro: A Remnant," *Harpers New Monthly Magazine* 88 (March 1894): 536, as quoted in Piersen, *Damn Yankees*, 138.

39. James Boardman, *American and the Americans* (London, 1833), 310, as quoted in Shane White, " 'It was a Proud Day': African Americans, Festivals and Parades in the North, 1741–1834," *The Journal of American History* 81 (1) (June 1994): 45–46.

40. William Cullen Bryant, *Letters of a Traveller* (New York, 1850), 87, as quoted in Abrahams, *Singing the Master*, 194.

41. Fredricka Bremer, quoted in Southern, *Readings in Black American Music*, 106.

42. Solomon Northup, *Twelve Years a Slave* (Cincinnati, 1853), as quoted in Southern, *Readings in Black American Music*, 102.

43. Williams, *A Tour through . . . Jamaica*, 21–23. Compare this to the typical African reference of Richard Burton: They "sing, drum, and dance all the day. . . . [They] seem hardly to take natural rest; the drum and dance may be heard . . . until dawn." Richard Burton, *A Mission to Gelele King of Dahome* (New York, 1966), 196, 215.

44. On the noise level of black festivals see M. G. Lewis's typical observation from Jamaica: "In the negro festivals . . . the chief point lies in making as much noise as possible." Matthew Gregory Lewis, *Journal of a West India Proprietor* (London, 1834), 27. Similarly, see Charles William Day, *Five Years Residence in the West Indies* (London, 1852), vol. 1, 289, and James Kelly, *Voyage to Jamaica* (Belfast, 1838), 20–21.

45. Gena Dagel Caponi, "The Case for an African American Aesthetic." See Introduction to this volume.

46. Geneviève Fabre, "Festive Moments in Antebellum African American Culture," in

The Black Columbiad: Defining Moments in African American Literature and Culture, ed. Werner Sollors and Maria Diedrich (Cambridge: Harvard University Press, 1994), 58–62.

47. Fernando Ortiz, *Los Bailes y el Teatro de los Negros en el Folklore de Cuba* (Havana: Cardenas y cia, 1951), 195.

48. F. W. Wurdeman, *Notes on Cuba, Containing an Account of Its Discovery and Early History; a Description of the Face of the Country, Its Institutions, and Manners and Customs of Its Inhabitants.* (Boston: James Munroe and Company, 1844), 83–84.

49. Ortiz, *Los Bailes y el Teatro de los Negros*, 192.

50. Beckwith, *Black Roadways*, 151.

51. Caponi, in "The Case for an African American Aesthetic," suggests we might start with John Miller Chernoff, Olly Wilson, Samuel A. Floyd, Jr., and Portia Maultsby in music; Henry Louis Gates, Jr., Houston Baker, and Toni Morrison in literature; Robert Farris Thompson in visual arts and dance; Marshall Stearns in dance; and I would add Roger Abrahams and John Michael Vlach for folklore. See Introduction to this volume.

52. Sterling Stuckey, *Slave Culture: Nationalist Theory and the Foundations of Black America* (New York: Oxford University Press, 1987), 3–97.

53. I am expanding here on the insights of scholars who have emphasized the coded messaging of African-American verbal performance to suggest that most festive performances were also "signifying." For an introduction to this topic see Theophus H. Smith, *Conjuring Culture* (New York: Oxford University Press, 1994), 148–52.

54. *Freedom's Journal*, July 11, 18, 1828, as quoted in White, " 'It Was a Proud Day,' " 40.

From "Strolling, Jooking, and Fixy Clothes"

(1998)

SHANE WHITE & GRAHAM WHITE

. . . .

Shane White and Graham White, both historians at the University of Sydney, look at clothing and movement on the street, in juke halls, and in churches as opportunities for expressive freedom. Noting the competitive nature of this creative display, White and White suggest that such cultural characteristics as love of display, an "opulent color sense," and the "near constant physical movement" of religious expression create an alternative reality and enhance and display the black body in ways that challenge stereotypes by re-presenting the body as an instrument of pleasure, not of work. The authors note differences of gender, class, and generation in approaches to self-presentation, which also varies according to performance site.

In July 1881, a reporter from the *Atlanta Constitution*, curious as to the character of lower-class African American life, ventured into less salubrious sections of his city. Traversing Decatur, Ivy and Collins Streets, he surveyed such entertainment venues as the Beaver Slide and the Ant Hole before moving on to examine the condition of the communities of Ellis Row, Happy Hollow, Bone Alley, and Pigtail Alley. The newspaperman's verdict on the character of black Atlanta was a negative one. Not only were the people's residences in a deplorable condition, but "worthless negroes" congregated on street corners, and several commercial premises were little more than "nests where the worst forms of crime are born and bred." Concerned citizens, the writer concluded, "must hope that these dens, some of poverty and some of vice, . . . will be choked out of existence" as the expansion of the city brought more respectable people into the area.

But for all the *Constitution* man's evident distaste, there is enough ambiguity in his account to permit an alternative reading. His description of Ivy Street, which he reached just at sundown, hints at the presence not merely of poverty and crime but also of a vibrant street life. Ivy Street was "packed with colored people of every size and class—big, little, old, young, black, yellow, mad, happy, sad, men, boys, women, girls, all together in such a squirm of confusion as to require an expert to make his way along the sidewalk in anything like a satisfactory manner."[1] There was no room here for the daily humiliations that Jim Crow exacted; no need to walk with head bowed, or eyes averted, or to step off sidewalks to allow whites to pass. Freed from hostile white oversight and in the company of their own people, African Americans on Ivy Street could dress, move about, and comport themselves pretty much as they pleased.

A correspondent for another city newspaper, the *Journal Magazine*, who explored black areas in Atlanta in 1912, was more prepared than was the *Constitution*'s reporter to acknowledge the positive aspects of black urban life. To him, Decatur Street east of Pryor appeared a "paradise for . . . negroes," a "kaleidoscope of light, noise and bustle from dawn to dawn." On Decatur, "the negro is found in his element of fried fish and gaudy raimant," and African Americans were able to "meet old friends, and talk and gossip to their hearts' content." On Saturday afternoons, "people flock up and down in shoals." It was hopeless to try to move quickly through this throng, this observer conceded, "nothing to do but fall in with the shiftless tread of the carefree colored folk who make up a vast part of the crowds."[2] Though obviously romanticized, this description of the black section of Decatur Street suggests a degree of expressive freedom uncommon in African Americans' contemporary world. Counter images of such spaces exist, of course; for example, black bluesman Perry Bradford commented that "it was a tame Saturday night in the notorious Decatur Street section if there were only six razor operations performed, or if only four persons were found in the morgue on Sunday morning,"[3] but what is important here is the recognition by both of these white journalists of the significance of African American street life.

Blacks' descriptions of Memphis's Beale Street bear the point out. W. C. Handy, who settled in Memphis in 1905, first heard stories of this famous thoroughfare as a boy in Florence, Alabama, and those stories enchanted him. Life on Beale, violin player Jim Turner told him, was "a song from dawn to dawn." Turner spoke of "darktown dandies and high-brown belles" and of "the glitter and finery of their latest fashions," alluring images that "planted in [Handy's] heart a seed of discontent, a yearning for Beale Street and the gay universe that it typified."[4] To bluesman Muddy Waters, who traveled to Beale from Mississippi on Saturdays to earn money in the jukes, "Beale Street was the street. Black man's street." On Saturday nights, everyone was on the sidewalks, "somebody over here playing guitar, somebody singing gospel. . . . Walter Horton . . . , he's out there blowing the harp, and Honey Boy [David] Edwards, used to play guitar, and little midget, Buddy Doyle, he could sing good."[5] Much later, musician Rufus Thomas claimed to have said to a white man: "Hey man, if you were black for one Saturday night on Beale Street, never would you want to be white again."[6]

The same bifurcation of images that occurred in relation to Decatur is found in descriptions of Beale. Black musicians might eulogize Beale Street, but to Shields McIlwaine, a long-time white resident of Memphis, this concourse signified very differently. After midnight on a Saturday, McIlwaine warned, "nobody, white or black, who thinks much of his life should be around." During these hours, Beale "swarms with drunks, hop-heads, and hussies," and "blacks begin to slash each other with anything that will cut."[7] Like every other site where black people congregated, then, Beale Street carried many meanings, and the character of African American life there comes to us refracted through a variety of highly selective lenses.

What is clear, however, is that, for African Americans, streets such as Decatur and Beale served as performance sites, readily accessible urban stages for prideful or leisurely strolling and creative sartorial display. W. C. Handy has written of "powerfully built roustabouts saunter[ing] along [Beale Street's] pavement," of "fashionable browns in beautiful gowns," and of pimps in "box-back coats and undented stetsons," all of whom contributed to Beale's "color and spell."[8] The "Saturday night stroll" on Beale, African American George W. Lee declared, was "a thrilling adventure which the cooks in the kitchens and the men at the big plants on the Wolf River looked forward to all week." On that night, "golden browns, high yellows and fast blacks, some gorgeously dressed and others poorly clad, move together down the old thoroughfare. The working folks are on parade; going nowhere in particular, just out strolling just glad of a chance to dress up and expose themselves on the avenue after working hard all the week."[9]

The streets of black New Orleans offered similar prospects, a chance for the city's young black men, in particular (for the street, as Evelyn Brooks Higginbotham has pointed out, "signified *male* turf"),[10] to exhibit their distinctive clothing and movement styles. By Jelly Roll Morton's account, many of these "tremendous sports" dressed spectacularly, but no matter how unpromising his circumstances, each sport strove to acquire "at least one Sunday suit, because, without that Sunday suit, you didn't have anything." To avoid being thought "way out of line," the sport had to make sure that his coat and pants did not match. Blue coats were favored, and trousers that were striped and worn tight. "They'd fit um like a sausage. I'm telling you it was very seldom you could button the top button of a person's trousers those days in New Orleans." Suspenders, while not functionally important, were essential, and needed to be "very loud." To ensure visibility, one strap was invariably left "hanging down." The swells made every effort to maintain their carefully constructed appearance: "If you wanted to talk to one of these guys, he would find the nearest post, stiffen his arm and hold himself as far away as possible from the post he's leaning on. That was to keep those fifteen, eighteen dollar trousers of his from losing their press." Morton himself habitually dressed in what jazzman Pops Foster described as a "very flashy" style, displaying "gold on his teeth and a diamond in one." "Those days, myself," Morton has acknowledged, "I thought I would die unless I had a hat with the emblem Stetson in it and some Edwin Clapp shoes."[11]

Their preferred style of walking contributed to the sports' visual impact. As a sport moved down the street, Morton has related, his shirt "busted open" to reveal a "red flannel undershirt," he displayed a "very mosey" style of walking called "shooting the agate." When one shot the agate, "your hands is at your sides with your index fingers stuck out and you kind of struts with it," a type of movement inconceivable, of course, in white-controlled public space.[12] This style of dress and movement was attractive to certain African American women: "if you could shoot a good agate and had a highclass red undershirt with the collar turned up," Morton explained, "I'm telling you you were liable to get next to that broad. She'd like that very much."[13] Here again, then, is the salience of performance; in the theater of the street, before an appreciative African American audience, these visually exciting and coolly moving actors placed an alternative aesthetic on ostentatious, competitive display.

Dressing well on the street was tremendously important to middle-class blacks as well, as the recollections of former residents of Atlanta's Auburn Avenue show. "You didn't find people coming to Auburn in their shirttails like they do now, and just kind of loosely dressed," long-time resident Dan Stephens declared when interviewed in the 1970s. "They had a lot of pride and [when] they'd come to Auburn Avenue, they would be dressed up." Kathleen Adams, who was born in 1890 in a house that fronted Auburn Avenue, remembered that on Sundays women churchgoers wore "their taffetas" and the grandmothers their "alpacas and even their brocades," and how the women's bellback skirts "gave you that flow, and as they walked down the street those skirts had a certain bounce to them." Men who escorted women to church wore "striped britches, two-button cutaway coats." Kathleen Adams's father, a lawyer, "walked down Auburn Avenue in his striped britches, his Prince Albert, his Stetson hat and his walking cane and, in winter, his tan gloves." The clothing of former slaves, now storekeepers in Auburn, was also formal, and their bearing grave. "They had a certain pride and dignity," Kathleen Adams remembered, "as they stood in their store doors or . . . walked the streets."[14] As Robin Kelly has perceptively commented, for African Americans, "seeing oneself and others 'dressed up' was enormously important in terms of constructing a collective identity based on something other than wage work." No less than the donning of flashy attire, the re-presenting of the black body through neat, elegant clothing constituted "a public challenge to the dominant stereotypes of the black body . . . reinforcing a sense of dignity that was perpetually being assaulted."[15] Seeing oneself and others moving about confidently, even proudly, on streets such as Auburn Avenue must have had a similar effect.

Like major streets, the jukes, clubs, and dancehalls in black neighborhoods were sites for pleasure and performance. "By the light of a few smoky oil lamps," the *Atlanta Constitution*'s reporter had written back in 1881, describing the premises on Decatur Street known as the Beaver Slide, "and to the soul-harrowing music of a string band, the colored beaux and dusky damsels . . . trip the light fantastic toe, not forgetting to refresh themselves at the saloon counter when each dance is ended."[16] What we glimpse here, through this witness's not wholly disapproving eyes, is a club, tonk, or juke joint, roughly appointed certainly, but a place where, in a familiar cultural ambiance and without serious hindrance, black people could dress up, socialize, listen to music, and dance. Through distinctive clothing and movement styles, but also through a range of gestural interactions that have largely gone unrecorded—facial expressions, eye-to-eye exchanges, rituals of touching (as in distinctive handshakes)—African American working people who congregated in such venues reconfirmed their identity as members of a cultural community.[17]

In New Orleans, establishments such as the Big 25, Funky Butt Hall, Carrington's Saloon at 818 Rampart (described in one police report as "a Negro dive of the lowest type"),[18] and Animule Hall afforded working-class blacks similar opportunities. By Danny Barker's account, the patrons of Animule Hall—stevedores, field hands, steel-driving men, washer-women, female factory hands—who came each Saturday evening, dressed smartly, the men in "box-back suits, high, broad-rimmed Stetson hats, yellow shoes (called yellow yams), and the women mostly [in] common gingham dresses, starched and ironed stiff." Well into the early hours of the morning, Animule's patrons danced to the blues music of Long Head Bob's Social Orchestra, a music that, as Albert Murray points out, is a "good-time music" that "almost always induces dance movement that is the direct opposite of resignation, retreat, or

SHANE WHITE & GRAHAM WHITE

defeat." In these ways, hardships could be forgotten and the blues driven away, if only for a time.[19]

For New Orleans's black middle class, more "worthwhile" premises were available, or so, at any rate, declared the *Louisiana Weekly* of January 16, 1926, in the first installment of a regular feature to be known as the "Folly Column." Readers of this African American publication were informed that the city's Parisian Roof Garden, the "most beautiful Roof Garden for Colored people in the United States" and a veritable "palace of pleasurable dances," was open "Monday, Wednesday, Friday and Sunday, . . . from 9 to 12," and that, for any "who ha[d] not stilled the irresistable [*sic*] desire to dance at such an hour as 12 a.m. . . . the Dreamland Cafe should fill the bill." " 'Tis folly to listen long to the song of the Goddess Jazzmania," the writer added in mock apology, "but this is the Folly Column and the most righteous of us must admit that such folly is indeed enjoyable"—which is to say that, though elegantly clad and "respectable," the clientele of Dreamland Cafe danced to music that was hot. In its next edition, the *Weekly* announced that the Pelican, on Gravier and South Rampart, the city's "newest and largest dance hall," was about to open to the public. This venue would be "class A1, up to date in every way," with "a rest room for ladies, with a lady attendant," "choice lounges and dressing tables," a "free telephone," and a modern smoking room. In such settings, more well-to-do African Americans, their bodies clothed pridefully in fashionable evening wear, staged their own kind of glittering social parade.

Descriptions of clothing and dance styles feature in accounts of Beale Street's entertainment venues as well. Pianist Red (John Williams) described the patrons of the Monarch, the "classiest" club in town, as "real dressed up, gambling men with diamond rings on and suits of clothes." As for the pimps, "you'd thought it was a preacher or lawyer, the way they dressed then. . . . They had tailor-made suits, nice gray and blue serge, and brown broadcloth, Manhattan shirts, and Stacy Adams shoes, and Knox hats and stetsons." Not infrequently, the pimps would exchange one clothing ensemble for another during the day. "Yes, Lord," Williams declared, "they were nice dressers. Wear two-and-a-half-dollar gold pieces in his cuff links, five dollar gold piece for a stickpin."[20] At Pee Wee's, which served as headquarters for W. C. Handy's bands, and many other black musicians, one could see "glittering young devils in silk toppers and Prince Alberts."[21]

The dance scene on Beale was lively too. Early in the evening, long-time resident Nat D. Williams remembered, patrons of Beale Street's black working-class clubs would dance in the manner of whites, but later, when the "drink got to hitting just right, then people would do the type of dancing that suited them. You did what the spirit told you. If it said, 'Jump up and kick,' you jumped up and kicked. If it said, 'Turn around,' you'd turn around." African Americans could easily execute the "polite movements" characteristic of white dancing styles, Williams explained, but "when they got to the place where they felt they could release, just go on and enjoy themselves, they'd give a show." Better-educated blacks were not supposed to attend clubs of this type, but "sometimes if you took a notion to go native, . . . you'd be there jumping yourself and look over in the corner and there's another friend over there doing the same thing."[22] That sort of vigorous dancing could prove expensive. "At that time," Piano Red (John Williams) recalled, "women shoes costed one dollar and thirty-nine cents. And the next morning, they be in there 'catching the tiger' and doing the 'scratch' and be just as barefooted as a goose. Had nothing but the tops; done danced the soles plumb out."[23]

From W. C. Handy comes another striking, if more decorous, image of African American dance, this time at Memphis's Dixie Park. Here, the more than one thousand dancers resembled "a monstrous pin wheel, blazing with color and spinning magically," the whole scene becoming "an extravaganza, a pageant, a sea of gliding figures . . . ebony hands, brown hands, yellow hands, ivory hands, all moving in coordination with nimble dancing feet," and "gay smiling faces that had forgotten yesterday and never heard of tomorrow."[24] In such Memphis venues, and similar sites of night-time entertainment throughout the South, the African American body, so often the object of racist distortion, was proudly displayed and, in Paul Gilroy's words, "celebrated as an instrument of pleasure rather than an instrument of labor."[25]

Black clubs were not always as peaceful as these accounts suggest. New Orleans's Animule Hall received its name from the behavior of its patrons, who, as the night wore on and the cheap liquor took its toll, could become, in Danny Barker's words, "very antagonistic, belligerent, nasty, vulgar and provocative." As a result, challenges were issued and fights broke out. When violence erupted, Joe Baggers, the bouncer, allowed the contestants to settle the matter, using only their bare hands, while he kept the cheering crowds at bay by wielding an iron pipe. He would then eject the loser from the hall. In these fights, Danny Barker says, "men battled like bears and women like wildcats. . . . Most times the women fought until they were naked on the floor." In the early hours of the morning, at a signal from Joe Baggers, Long Head Bob's Social Orchestra would play the slow, slow drag and couples would begin dancing to the "sexy, body-twisting blues." But as dancers were discovered belly-rubbing with someone else's lover, the fighting would intensify. At a signal from Joe Baggers to the policeman on duty, Animule would be raided, and the rioters arrested and charged with disturbing the peace. Closing time at Animule was

3 a.m., but the evening's events never lasted that long.[26] Zora Neale Hurston also told of the violence that often seemed just below the surface at black entertainment sites. During a folklore-collecting expedition in 1927, Hurston and a woman called Big Sweet, who acted as her protector, attended a juke at a Florida lumber camp; when Big Sweet became involved in a fierce argument with two other women, knives were drawn and bloodshed was averted only by the intervention of a quarter boss, armed with two pistols.[27]

The contrast between New Orleans's Animule Hall on the one hand and its Parisian Roof Garden on the other signals once again the existence of class differences within the black community. Patrons of the Parisian Roof Garden and similar venues, who wore elegant clothing by night, were likely, by day, to have dressed in a "respectable," understated fashion, eschewing the more showy garments often favored by less well-off blacks. Hortense Powdermaker, who studied African American life in Indianola, Mississippi, in the late 1930s, noted that the "chief distinction" between the clothing of lower- and higher-class blacks was that "women of higher social status deliberately avoided bright colors" and were "offended if clerks in the stores assume that they want something 'loud.' " Not only were these better-off African Americans "pained by the Negro's reputation for wearing gaudy clothes," but "[a] few [were] sensitive about the insistence of some Negroes on having sound front teeth adorned with gold, when they cannot pay for dentistry needed on their back teeth." Disdaining such ostentatious display, middle-class blacks dressed with "quiet good taste."[28]

This understated style was certainly adopted by the African Americans depicted by the black photographer, Richard Samuel Roberts, in Columbia, South Carolina, in the 1920s. Roberts's studies plainly announce the desire of his subjects—dressmakers, morticians, nurses, barber-shop proprietors, physicians, pastors, teachers, college professors, grocers, cabinet makers, government officials, and members of their respective families—to present themselves as dignified, respectable and serious, certainly not flamboyant in any sense. Roberts's subjects are formally posed, often against a painted backdrop of plush drapery, flower-bedecked pillars, and "a stylized cathedral window." They are conservatively dressed, usually in tailor-made gowns or suits, and their erect posture and firm gaze registers cool self-possession and pride in their hard-won social status.[29] The dress of these African Americans would easily have been distinguishable, by night as well as by day, from that of the working-class clientele of Animule Hall or of the glittering denizens of Beale Street's night spots.

Class differences were encoded in hairstyles as well, though here the picture is more blurred. Many of the women in Richard Samuel Roberts's studies have their hair styled in what, in the 1920s, was considered the modern way. By the time Roberts took his photographs, the use of new hair treatment techniques, notably those associated with the Madam C.J. Walker and Poro systems, was widespread in the South, and large beauty salons, operating in urban centers, were busily catering to a predominantly middle-class clientele. In the hairdressing department of Madame Eve B. White's Beauty Parlor and College in New Orleans, the *Louisiana Weekly* told its readers in February 1926, "twelve operators are constantly turning out practically twelve patrons at once." Specialties of Madame White's establishment included hair bobbing, curling, and marcelling, and trade was brisk: "Two thousand regular semi-monthly patrons are booked, beside the drop-ins." This "modernly equipped" salon—a large photograph on the *Weekly*'s front page offered a view of its plush interior—was open from early in the morning and operated six days a week.[30]

Middle-class African American women, however, were not the only patrons of commercial hairdressing establishments. After observing that the beauty industry was thriving in Indianola, as in many other cities throughout the South, Hortense Powdermaker noted that even very poor women "got to a hair-dresser regularly, to have their hair greased and 'pressed.' " If money was short, a chicken might be offered as payment for these coiffures.[31] So popular among black women of all classes were commercial hair treatments that some Georgia towns, concerned that burgeoning employment levels in the cosmetics industry were depleting the supply of rural and domestic labor, imposed punitive taxes on hairdressing businesses, hoping thereby to ruin them.[32]

As a supplement to this commercial hair-styling activity, Southern black women from across a broad spectrum of income levels, and working from their homes, frequently dressed the hair of neighbors and friends. In his autobiography, *Colored People*, Henry Louis Gates, Jr., includes a wonderfully evocative account of his mother's hair-styling activities in the kitchen of the family home in Piedmont, West Virginia, a description that recalls the communal nature of slave hair-grooming practices.

> But the most important thing about our gas-equipped kitchen was that Mama used to do hair there. She had a "hot comb"—a fine-toothed iron instrument with a long wooden handle—and a pair of iron curlers that opened and closed like scissors: Mama would put them into the gas fire until they glowed. You could smell those prongs heating up.
>
> I liked what that smell meant for the shape of my day. There was an intimate warmth in the women's tones as they talked with my mama while she did their hair. I knew what the women had been through to get their hair ready to be "done," because I would watch Mama do it to herself. How

that scorched kink could be transformed through grease and fire into a magnificent head of wavy hair was a miracle to me. Still is.[33]

Among many rural women, however, there was some sturdy class and generational resistance to anything that smacked of modern cosmetic methods. These women continued to wrap, braid, and cornrow their hair in the time-honored manner and also to dress young black girls' hair in the same way.[34] When Mamie Garvin Fields introduced new hair-styling techniques to the girls at the James Island school at which she taught, one mother, whose own hair was "wrapped the traditional way, with multicolor thread and a bandanna on top," berated her the following morning: "I ain' sen' my chile ya fo' to fix he-yah. I sen' em fo' *lun*. You let ee he-yuh stay like I hahv 'em!"[35] The former slave Jane Michens Toombs also appears to have regarded modern hair-processing techniques with uniform disdain. Recalling her early years in Georgia, she informed her W.P.A. interviewer that "ef a nigger wanted ter git de kinks out'n dey hair dey combed hit wid de cards. Now dey puts all kinds ov grease on hit, an' buy straightenin' combs. . . . Old fashion cards'll straighten hair jess as well as all dis high smellin' stuff dey sells now."[36] Ex-slave Mary Williams, of Arkansas, was equally dismissive. "I don't think nothin' of this here younger generation," she asserted. "They say to me, 'Why don't you have your hair straightened' but I say 'I've got along this far without painted jaws and straight hair! And I ain't goin' wear my dresses up to my knees or trail 'em in the mud, either.' "[37]

The usual interpretation placed on much of this hair-straightening activity (and black men, with their preference for close-clipped hair and their use of grease, stocking caps, pomades, and processes, are taken to have been similarly engaged) is that it was a dubiously successful attempt by African Americans to make their hair look more like that of whites. Subjected over a long period of years to derogatory references to, and distorted images of, their physical appearance, blacks, so the argument goes, had internalized whites' conceptions of beauty. By straightening their hair and lightening their skin, they hoped more nearly to approximate white standards. The wording of advertisements for hair treatments, and, more obviously, those for preparations promising a lighter complexion (not to mention the sheer volume of such advertisements in the African American press) certainly supports these assumptions. So, unforgettably, does the fantasy of revenge created by a young Maya Angelou, embarrassed before the other children in her church because of her appearance: "I was going to look like one of the sweet little white girls who were everybody's dream of what was right with the world. . . . Wouldn't they be surprised when one day I woke out of my black ugly dream, and my real hair, which was long and blond, would take the place of the kinky mass that Momma wouldn't let me straighten? My light-blue eyes were going to hypnotize them."[38]

Without denying the force of these imperatives, it is possible to see other meanings in the early twentieth-century vogue for hair straightening. Straightening of the hair, which is to say, removing the knots and some of the kinkiness from it, was nothing new in African American life. It had been an important part of African American, indeed African, cosmetic activity long before Madam C.J. Walker or any of her rivals in the cosmetics industry were born. Whether accomplished by traditional or modern methods, straightening was a practical necessity if some sort of styling were to be accomplished, a preliminary to styling, not its end point. Once that is recognized, advertisements for hair-straightening compounds appear in a somewhat different light. To Mamie Garvin Fields, the main significance of the improved, modern methods of hair straightening was that they broadened the opportunities for creative display; they "made it possible for black women to straighten their hair and then style it in whatever way they wanted to."[39] If those women then chose to borrow from prevailing white styles, that would hardly be a first in African American history, or necessarily an admission of perceived inferiority. Straightening the hair may be seen not as a sign of a defective black consciousness but as an integral part of a time-honored creative process. As Gates's discussion of his mother's hair-straightening and styling activities (and of his own deep admiration for Nat King Cole's "process") suggests, to dismiss such practices as "slavish copying" of whites omits virtually everything that is interesting about them.[40]

Although streets and entertainment venues in black neighborhoods allowed African Americans rich opportunities for self-expression, it was within the welcoming sanctuary of the black church, as well as during their Sunday journeys to and from it, that they discovered their most frequent opportunity for aesthetic display. In the world outside the church, the everyday clothing of many blacks was often rudimentary. Arthur F. Raper, who surveyed African American life in the Georgia Black Belt counties of Green and Macon in the early 1930s, reported that "most of the farm Negroes . . . literally live in overalls, in winter wearing one or more pairs of old pants under them, in summer wearing them 'agin de skin.'" Raper heard from black schoolteachers that some children were unable to attend school because their clothing was inadequate, and he himself saw children going barefoot in the middle of winter. It was only rarely that rural women or their daughters obtained a new dress, and when they did such garments were likely to be cut from cheap materials. The few items of clothing possessed by very young children were often made from feed-

or salt-sacks.[41] Sacking was utilized by adults as well. Describing conditions in Mississippi in the 1930s, Ruth E. Bass stated that older African American women wore bandanna handkerchiefs made from "checked or flowered cotton, or a white flour sack," and, except on Sundays, "starched cotton aprons, many of them fashioned from well-washed and sometimes dried fertilizer sacks." Though canvas shoes were becoming more common among both the old and the young, it was not unusual for rural blacks to go barefoot for part of the year.[42] Loyle Hairston, born in Mississippi in 1926, remembers how poorly dressed the country children were who came to his mother's school classes, the boys in their "faded overalls, often patched at the knees and seat and denim jumpers and brogan shoes or rubber boots," the girls in "homemade gingham dresses and ragged ill-fitting coats."[43] Charles Evers, who was born in Decatur, Mississippi, in 1922, and his brother Medgar went barefoot every spring and summer. Every two years their father would buy each child two pairs of shoes, one pair (always two sizes too big to allow for growth) for Sunday wear, and the other, "heavy, lace-up brogans," for winter. In summer, the boys removed their Sunday shoes immediately after church; in winter, they exchanged them for brogans as soon as they reached home. "If Daddy caught us playing in our Sunday shoes," Charles Evers has recalled, "he'd whip us good." The family practiced similar economies with clothing. "We'd have to go pull off our Sunday clothes, too. We had one pair of green tweed pants for Sunday, and we'd pull them off as soon as we came back from church or come from a funeral. We'd put on coveralls, Medgar and me; or an old pair of blue jeans. And blue jeans, even to this day, remind me of how poor we were. It's a personal thing now. I just can't put blue jeans on to save my life."[44]

As description after description makes clear, however, the freedom that blacks had won in slavery times to dress up for weekly religious observances continued into the postslavery period, and throughout the South, even during Jim Crow's most oppressive years, African Americans continued to exchange their tattered, faded, functional weekday apparel for showy Sunday attire. South African Maurice Evans, who studied race relations in the American South in the early twentieth century, thought the dress of African American urban congregations "more fashionable, with apparently more spent on gewgaws and frippery, than that of a middle-class English congregation probably ten times as wealthy." Young black male and female churchgoers were "often adorned in ultra fashionable attire" and were "obviously conscious of their finery." Evans surmised that "love of display enter[ed] largely into the attractiveness of church attendance."[45] In rural areas, the contrast between everyday and Sunday attire was even more striking. Lura Beam, who, as a superintendent of schools, traveled through the South in the second decade of the twentieth century, wrote that "[a] shack on the edge of nowhere would send to Sunday church two well-dressed children and a teenager with daisies on her hat."[46] Anthropologist Hortense Powdermaker, investigating conditions in the deep South in the late 1930s, was surprised by the standards of dress observed by members of a rural black Baptist church. "Men, women, and children are all in their best clothes," she wrote, and "on the hottest Sunday in August, the men wear their coats and the women their hats."[47] An African American rural storekeeper in Clairborne County, Mississippi, told Allison Davis that white people often complained that local blacks dressed better than they did. "And it's really the truth," the woman said. "You see these poor farm people and tenants goin' by here to church, and the men have on good well-cared-for suits, and nice ties and shirts and hats, and the women will have on good dresses they buy in Old City, and shoes, you know, and they'll have their hair all fixed and curled!" The storekeeper recalled for Davis an occasion on which, not wishing to embarrass local folk, a visiting churchwoman of some importance had worn everyday clothing to a local service, only to discover that the women of that small rural congregation dressed better than did those in Natchez.[48]

Sunday was "the best day of the week," plantation owner and writer Julia Peterkin decided after studying African American life in rural South Carolina in the early 1930s. On that day "Christians and sinners dress up in their best clothes, whether they expect to go to church or not." On Sunday mornings, women whose hair had been "wrapped all week in small tight rolls wound with ball thread" unwrapped it, combed it, rewrapped it, and covered it with a brightly colored bandanna. Those with short hair treated it with a relaxing compound and straightened it with an iron. As women donned their "finery," the men "walk around, looking and feeling important in their store-bought clothes and shoes." With hats "cocked jauntily on the side of their heads," they "visit . . . neighbors or gather in groups along the roads to talk." Young women appeared "very smart" in dresses and hats bought from local stores or obtained through mail-order catalogues, and while most men dressed conservatively, some left price tags on their suits to indicate that the suits were new and had been bought rather than made at home. Some of the young men were, however, "inclined to be gaudy" and wore "purple or green 'peg-top' trousers, with square-cut box coats of another color, along with bright tan shoes and fancy socks and loud ties."[49] "Colored people," white Mississippi resident Willa Johnson declared, "are very fond of fixy clothes and seldom do we find one who has not at least one dress-up outfit." Though blacks might "go about during the week in raggedness," Sunday was "a day of dress."

As in slavery times, the aggressive color combinations preferred by southern blacks attracted whites' attention. African Americans, Willa Johnson averred, showed a "decided taste for vivid colors," so that, "without hesitation, green, yellow and red are clashed together" and a "wild colored sash" was often added for effect. Black women, Johnson declared, would "spend [their] last dime for a color-crazy effect."[50] Lura Beam called the "color combinations" in African American clothing "exciting." "Negroes put red and pink and orange together before Matisse did," she observed. "Women who could wear only gray and blue in slavery came out in yellow, orange, cerise, green, scarlet, magenta and purple. Matrons in their best clothes displayed an opulent color sense, topped by hats that were extravaganzas. They had a characteristic style."[51] The preference for strong, vibrant colors was also noted by English artists Jan and Cora Gordon, who watched female students attending a religious service at Atlanta's Spelman College in 1927, even if its cultural significance eluded them. The Gordons decided that the young women "had not yet that touchy sense of white folks' ridicule which has made the northern Negro so self-conscious." The students "did not know that, because the traditional Mammy wore bright colours, therefore bright colours were taboo; so they wore what colours they liked and made a pretty bouquet as they filed into chapel on a morning."[52]

The African American church, to which countless well-dressed blacks throughout the rual and urban South made their way each Sunday, gave its members a sense of self-esteem customarily denied them. In black churches, "field hands were deacons, and maids were ushers, mothers of the church, or trustees," positions of respect and authority often signified by the wearing of special uniforms or accessories. The young women who showed members and visitors to their seats in a rural Baptist church that Powdermaker visited "[wore] around their heads stiff bands of white on which the word 'Usher' [was] embroidered," and white cotton gloves.[53] In the Rock Hill Baptist Church at Chapel Hill, North Carolina, which Agnes Brown attended in the late 1930s, the choir was attired in black robes, set off, in the case of women members, with large white collars; female ushers wore black dresses with white buttons, collars and cuffs, and male ushers dark suits, white shirts, black bow ties, and "at least one white glove." Senior ushers displayed distinctive metal badges, their junior colleagues small felt flags.[54] But the manner in which African American churchgoers constructed their appearance has a more general significance. By abandoning shabby work clothes, or such negative signifiers as mob caps and bib-aprons, for more dignified Sunday attire—clothes which, as Arthur Raper expressed it, were "not made to work in"[55]—black churchgoers were repudiating white society's evaluation of the black body as an instrument of menial labor. They were declaring, in effect, that there was more to life than work, and that a sense of dignity and self-worth could survive the depredations of an avowedly racist society. Work clothes—nondescript and uniform—tended to erase the black body; Sunday clothing enhanced and proclaimed it.

In this private world of African Americans' own making, meanings were conveyed not merely through dress but through a range of culturally distinctive bodily movements that characterized religious celebrations. When R. Emmet Kennedy visited a number of black churches in the rural South in the early 1930s for the purpose of recording spirituals and other religious songs, the sense of cultural difference he experienced related, in significant degree, to the near-constant physical movement of the various congregations. Everywhere, singing was accompanied by "the rhythmic clapping of hands and patting of feet." Among members of the Sanctified Church, "dancing before the altar [was] an important feature of their ritual." After one of the churches Kennedy visited had filled, a "mournful humming" began, in response to which the congregation began "to sway like an undulating wave." Testimonies given by church members were "accentuated at times with hand clapping and boisterous stamping." As the congregation began to sing a holy song, adults and children stood up and began to dance. Before long they moved into the aisles and, as Kennedy related, "advance slowly towards the altar platform, where they continue to express themselves with joyful abandon," though "no two of them appear to be doing the same step." Deacons, their Bibles put aside, "join the celebration, doing fantastic steps and contortions on either side of the rostrum." An elder "walks back and forth, encouraging the harmonious tumult with loud hand clapping and vociferous singing."[56] During an evangelist's address to a revival meeting at a Chapel Hill church in 1938, Agnes Brown reported, the preacher vigorously acted out the biblical events with which he illustrated his sermon, such as the release of Paul from prison and the raising of Lazarus from the dead. As he moved energetically from side to side in the pulpit, the congregation "swayed with him."[57] During the prayers and the sermon at a small Baptist church near Natchez, which Hortense Powdermaker attended, the congregation beat time with their feet, and during the otherwise unaccompanied singing, Powdermaker observed, "many wave their hands in rhythm, and clap out the beats."[58]

In offering a scriptural justification for his congregation's dancing, an elder from the church which R. Emmet Kennedy attended referred to the fifteenth chapter of the Book of Exodus, which told "how Aaron sister took a cymbal in her hand, an' all the women went after her with cymbals an' with dancin'." Holy dancing was altogether different from the kind of dancing indulged in by unbelievers at frolics and balls, the elder declared, and "the kind of gladness that makes these people want to dance in the house of Gawd, ain't the same kind of feelin' *a-tall* them pleasure-seekin' people has when you see 'um get up an' strut in the common dance-hall."[59] Zora Neale Hurston's explanation was cultural rather than theological. Referring to the Sanctified Church, which she contrasted with more highbrow black Protestant congregations that were prone to adopt white ways, Hurston noted that "the service is really drama with music," and that "since music without motion is unnatural among Negroes there is always something that approaches dancing—in fact *IS* dancing—in such a ceremony." "Negro songs," Hurston declared, "are one and all based on a dance-possible rhythm."[60]

Hurston's reference to the all-but-inevitable confluence of music and movement in black life points to a deeper cultural influence. West African religions knew nothing of the dualism in Western culture between mind and body, or, in religious parlance, between spirit and flesh. Whereas, as Sheila Walker has observed, in most Christian worship "the activity of the body is suspended," in West African cultures dancing was integral to religious celebrations. As J. H. Kwabena Nketia tells us, "in the [Akan] dancing ring, participants . . . mime and interpret the rhythms of drummers . . . and mime the dramatic actions of storytellers," "especially attractive rhythms" being "accompanied by shoulder and head movements, foot stamping and hand clapping, and vocal shouts from spectators, dancers, and singers."[61] So essential are music and dance to West African religious expression," Albert Raboteau has written, "that it is no exaggeration to call them 'danced religions.' " Though the complex syncretic process that blended West African and European religious observances in the New World obviously produced many variants, rhythmic bodily movements, ranging from the ecstatic dancing impelled by the Spirit to gentle swaying and (as a replacement for the drums) the rhythmic patting of hands or feet, remained a distinctive element of African American religious services.[62]

Again, the general pattern of clothing and movement styles described above, a pattern which depicts religious practices in rural and poorer urban black churches, was modified by class differences within the African American community. Broadly speaking, the higher up the socio-economic scale black congregations were, the more likely they were to disdain "ostentation" in dress or manner of worship, the so-called "gaudy" clothing and ecstatic behavior of working-class congregations. At the very top of the social order, it was not uncommon for the black elite to seek and achieve membership in white churches, where the bold clothing ensembles and degree of enthusiastic participation common in many black Baptist, African Methodist Episcopal, or Sanctified Church congregations would have had no conceivable place.

In the culture-affirming, interactive space of most Southern black churches, however, and particularly within the numerically dominant working-class congregrations, African Americans reaffirmed their sense of cultural identity. Smart clothes, distinctive uniforms, and often vividly colored official robes communicated a sense of dignity and pride, and the expressive movement of the saints' bodies—in off-beat clapping and swaying, in holy dancing, in the synchronic waving of outstretched hands, in the rhythmic patting of feet— gave collective expression to the passion and joy they felt. In a world largely of their own making, these African Americans framed an alternative reality.[63] Rejecting evaluations of themselves by white society, they made strong visual statements about their identity and worth, and, free of white oversight and control, displayed the cultural forms that allowed them to transcend, for a time, the harsh circumstances of their everyday lives.

NOTES

1. Quoted in Franklin M. Garrett, *Atlanta and Environs: A Chronicle of Its People and Events*, 3 vols. (1954; Athens, Ga., 1969), vol. 2, 25–28.

2. Quoted in Garrett, *Atlanta and Environs*, vol. 2, 607–609.

3. Perry Bradford, *Born with the Blues: The True Story of the Pioneering Blues Singers and Musicians in the Early Days of Jazz* (New York, 1965), 18.

4. W. C. Handy, *Father of the Blues: An Autobiography*, ed. Arna Bontemps (1941; New York, 1991), 15, 16.

5. Quoted in Margaret McKee and Fred Chisenhall, *Beale Black and Blue: Life and Music on Black America's Main Street* (Baton Rouge, La., 1981), 233.

6. Statement by Rufus Thomas in *All Day and All Night: Memories from Beale Street Musicians*, videocassette, Center for Southern Folklore, Oxford, Miss., 1990.

7. Shields McIlwaine, *Memphis Down in Dixie* (New York, 1948), 327–28.

8. Handy, *Father of the Blues*, 118.

9. George W. Lee, *Beale Street: Where the Blues Began* (New York, 1934), 63–64.

10. Quoted in Robin D. G. Kelley, *Race Rebels: Culture, Politics, and the Black Working Class* (New York, 1994), 46 (emphasis added).

11. Alan Lomax, *Mister Jelly Roll* (1950; London, 1991), 18–19; Pops Foster, *Pops Foster: The Autobiography of a New Orleans Jazzman* (Berkeley, 1971), 93–94.

12. Robert Farris Thompson provides exciting hints as to the relationship between African American modes of walking and physical attributes prized in West and Central African societies. For example, Thompson notes the importance of "moving with flair" in order to display one's beauty and attract the attention of others and of "modes of phrasing the body [that] transform the person into art." Robert Farris Thompson, *African Art in Motion: Icon and Act* (Los Angeles, 1974), 16, xii.

13. Lomax, *Mister Jelly Roll*, 19.

14. Clifford H. Kuhn, Harlon E. Joye, and Bernard E. West, *Living Atlanta: An Oral History of the City, 1914–1918* (Athens, Ga., 1990), 39, 55–56.

15. Kelley, *Race Rebels*, 50.

16. Quoted in Garrett, *Atlanta and Environs*, vol. 2, 25–28.

17. Compare Charles W. Joyner, *Down by the Riverside: A South Carolina Slave Community* (Urbana, Ill., 1984), 126. Robin Kelley provides an example of this kind of cultural

creativity and affirmation in his recent study of African American working-class culture and politics. Employed, in the late 1970s, at a McDonald's establishment in Pasadena, he and other African Americans subverted the rigid system of discipline by "stylizing" their work, not only through their "verbal circus and collective dialogues" and subtle modifications to their uniforms, but by "looking cool," "gangster limpin'," and "brandishing a spatula like a walking stick or a microphone." By such means, they "turned work into performance." See Kelley, *Race Rebels*, 1–3.

18. Quoted in Donald M. Marquis, *In Search of Buddy Bolden: First Man of Jazz* (Baton Rouge, La., 1978), 52.

19. Danny Barker, *A Life in Jazz* (New York, 1986), 12–16; Albert Murray, *Stomping the Blues* (1976; New York, 1982), 16–17, 45, 258; Jacqui Malone, *Steppin' on the Blues: The Visible Rhythms of African American Dance* (Urbana, Ill., 1996), 27.

20. Quoted in McKee and Chisenhall, *Beale Black and Blue*, 136–37.

21. Handy, *Father of the Blues*, 92.

22. Quoted in McKee and Chisenhall, *Beale Black and Blue*, 34–35.

23. Ibid., 136–37.

24. Handy, *Father of the Blues*, 97.

25. Quoted in Kelley, *Race Rebels*, 48.

26. Danny Barker, *A Life in Jazz* (New York, 1986), 12–16.

27. Zora Neale Hurston, "Mules and Men," in Hurston, *Folklore, Memoirs, and Other Writings*, ed. Cheryl A. Wall (New York, 1995), 140–48.

28. Hortense Powdermaker, *After Freedom: A Cultural Study in the Deep South* (New York, 1939), 70. The liking for gold teeth provoked generational opposition as well. "Niggers dese days . . . is so uppity," former Alabama slave Mary Rice complained to her WPA interviewer, "callin' derselves 'cullud fokes' an havin' gold teeth. Dey sez de mo' gold teeth dy has, de higher up in church dey sets. Huh!" George P. Rawick, ed., *The American Slave: A Composite Autobiography* (Westport, Conn., 1976), vol. 6, Alabama Narratives, 330.

29. Thomas L. Johnson and Phillip C. Dunn, eds., *A True Likeness: The Black South of Richard Samuel Roberts, 1920–1936* (Columbia, S.C., and Chapel Hill, N.C., 1986). The reference to the "stylized cathedral window" is on p. 27.

30. *Louisiana Weekly*, February 13, 1926.

31. Powdermaker, *After Freedom*, 180.

32. Gwendolyn Robinson, "Class, Race, and Gender: A Transcultural Theoretical and Sociohistorical Analysis of Cosmetic Institutions and Practices to 1920," Ph.D. diss., University of Illinois at Chicago, 1984, 453.

33. Henry Louis Gates, Jr., *Colored People: A Memoir* (New York, 1994), 40–41.

34. Ruth E. Bass, "Cull'rd Folks," Works Progress Administration, Record Group 60, Mississippi State Archives, Jackson, Mississippi, n.d., 16. See also North Carolina Photographic Archives, Wooten-Moulton Collection, Celia Eudy Group, Wilson Library, University of North Carolina, Chapel Hill, for examples of hair stylings worn by African American women and girls.

35. Mamie Garvin Fields with Karen Fields, *Lemon Swamp and Other Places: A Carolina Memoir* (New York, 1983), 218–19.

36. Rawick, *The American Slave*, vol. 13, Georgia Narratives, pt. 4, 36.

37. Rawick, *The American Slave*, vol. 11, Arkansas and Missouri Narratives, Arkansas Narratives, pt. 7, 185.

38. Maya Angelou, *I Know Why the Caged Bird Sings* (London, 1984), 4.

39. Fields, *Lemon Swamp*, 187.

40. Gates Jr., *Colored People*, 40–49.

41. Arthur Raper, *A Preface to Peasantry* (1936; New York, 1968), 45–46.

42. Bass, "Cull'rd Folks," 16, 19.

43. Loyle Hairston, "Growing Up in Mississippi," in Abbott, ed., *Mississippi Writers*, vol. 2, 317.

44. Charles Evers, *Evers* (New York, 1971), 38.

45. Maurice S. Evans, *Black and White in the Southern States: A Study of the Race Problem in the United States from a South African Point of View* (London, 1915), 89, 119.

46. Lura Beam, *He Called Them by the Lightning: A Teacher's Odyssey in the Negro South, 1908–1919* (Indianapolis, 1967), 39–40.

47. Powdermaker, *After Freedom*, 236.

48. Alison Davis, Burleigh B. Gardner, and Mary R. Gardner, *Deep South: A Social Anthropological Study of Caste and Class* (Chicago, 194X), 388–89.

49. Julia Peterkin, *Roll, Jordan, Roll* (New York, 1933), 75–76.

50. Willa Johnson, "Characteristic Ways of Colored People," n.d., Works Progress Administration, Mississippi State Archives, Record Group 60, Jackson, Mississippi, 1.

51. Beam, *He Called Them by the Lightning*, 39–40.

52. Alton Hornsby, Jr., ed., *In the Cage: Eyewitness Accounts of the Freed Negro in Southern Society, 1877–1919* (Chicago, 1971), 75.

53. Quoted in James C. Cobb, *The Most Southern Place on Earth: The Mississippi Delta and the Roots of Regional Identity* (New York, 1992), 165; Powdermaker, *After Freedom*, 236.

54. Agnes Brown, "The Negro Churches of Chapel Hill: A Community Study," M.A. thesis, Sociology, University of North Carolina, Chapel Hill, 1939, 47.

55. Raper, *Preface to Peasantry*, 45.

56. R. Emmet Kennedy, *More Mellows* (New York, 1931), 7–8, 10. The Church of God in Christ, also known as the Sanctified Church, was founded in Memphis, Tennessee, in 1895 by a black Baptist, C. H. Mason, and won a large following in the South. The church was charismatic, its members believing in the possibility of sanctification, as evidenced by the possession of such spiritual gifts as the ability to speak in tongues, and services were characterized by enthusiastic participation and expressions of spiritual ecstasy. See Powdermaker, *After Freedom*, 233–34.

57. Brown, "Negro Churches of Chapel Hill," 56–57.

58. Powdermaker, *After Freedom*, 244–45.

59. Kennedy, *More Mellows*, 13.

60. Zora Neale Hurston, *The Sanctified Church: The Folklore Writings of Zora Neale Hurston* (Berkeley, 1981), 104, 83.

61. Quoted in Samuel A. Floyd, Jr., *The Power of Black Music: Interpreting Its History from Africa to the United States* (New York, 1995), 21.

62. Henry H. Mitchell, *Folk Beliefs of Blacks in America and West Africa* (New York, 1975), 146; Albert J. Raboteau, *Slave Religion: The "Invisible Institution" in the Antebellum South* (New York, 1978), 15.

63. The idea of framing an alternate reality comes from Earl Lewis; see his *In Their Own Interests: Race, Class, and Power in Twentieth-century Norfolk, Virginia* (Berkeley, 1991), 90.

Bibliography

Abrahams, Roger D. *Deep Down in the Jungle: Negro Narrative Folklore from the Streets of Philadelphia*. Hatboro, Pa.: Folklore Associates, 1964; Chicago: Aldine, 1970.

Abrahams, Roger D. *Singing the Master: The Emergence of African American Culture in the Plantation South*. New York: Pantheon Books, 1992.

Abrahams, Roger D., and John F. Szwed. *After Africa: Extracts from British Travel Accounts and Journals of the Seventeenth, Eighteenth, and Nineteenth Centuries Concerning the Slaves, Their Manners, and Customs in the British West Indies*. New Haven, Conn.: Yale University Press, 1983.

Adamson, Joe. *Bugs Bunny: Fifty Years and Only One Grey Hare*. New York: Henry Holt, 1990.

Appiah, Kwame Anthony. *In My Father's House: Africa in the Philosophy of Culture*. New York: Oxford University Press, 1992.

Ashe, Arthur R., Jr. *A Hard Road to Glory: A History of the African-American Athlete*. New York: Warner Books, 1988.

Baker, Houston A., Jr. *Afro-American Poetics: Revisions of Harlem and the Black Aesthetic*. Madison: University of Wisconsin Press, 1988.

———. *Black Studies, Rap, and the Academy*. Chicago: University of Chicago Press, 1993.

———. *Blues, Ideology, and Afro-American Literature: A Vernacular Theory*. Chicago: University of Chicago Press, 1984.

———. *Long Black Song: Essays in Black American Literature and Culture*. Charlottesville: University Press of Virginia, 1972.

Baraka, Imamu Amiri [as LeRoi Jones]. *Blues People: Negro Music in White America*. New York: William Morrow, 1963.

———. *Home: Social Essays*. New York: William Morrow, 1966.

Baraka, Amiri [as LeRoi Jones], and Larry Neal, eds. *Black Fire: An Anthology of Afro-American Writing*. New York: William Morrow, 1968.

Basie, Count. *Good Morning Blues: The Autobiography of Count Basie As Told to Albert Murray*. New York: Random House, 1985.

Bechet, Sidney. *Treat It Gentle*. New York: Hill and Wang, 1960.

Bigsby, C. W. E. *The Second Black Renaissance: Essays in Black Literature*. Westport, Conn.: Greenwood Press, 1980.

Blacking, John. *How Musical Is Man?* Seattle: University of Washington Press, 1973.

Blassingame, John W. *The Slave Community: Plantation Life in the Antebellum South*. New York: Oxford University Press, 1972.

Bogle, Donald. *Toms, Coons, Mulattoes, Mammies, and Bucks: A History of Blacks in American Films*. 3d ed. New York: Continuum, 1994.

Boime, Albert. *The Art of Exclusion: Representing Blacks in the Nineteenth Century*. Washington, D.C.: Smithsonian Institution Press, 1990.

Chernoff, John Miller. *African Rhythm and African Sensibility: Aesthetics and Social Action in African Musical Idioms.* Chicago: University of Chicago Press, 1979.

Chilton, John. *Let the Good Times Roll: The Story of Louis Jordan and His Music.* New York: Quartet Books, 1992.

Cockrell, Dale. *Demons of Disorder: Early Blackface Minstrels and Their World.* New York: Cambridge University Press, 1997.

Courlander, Harold. *Negro Folk Music, U.S.A.* New York: Columbia University Press, 1963.

Crawford, Richard. *The American Musical Landscape.* Berkeley: University of California Press, 1993.

Crouch, Stanley. *Notes of a Hanging Judge: Essays and Reviews, 1979–1989.* New York: Oxford University Press, 1990.

Cunard, Nancy. *Negro: An Anthology 1931–1933.* London: Wishnart, 1934.

Dahl, Linda. *Stormy Weather: The Music and Lives of a Century of Jazzwomen.* New York: Pantheon Books, 1984.

Dance, Stanley. *The World of Count Basie.* New York: Charles Scribner's Sons, 1980.

Davis, Angela Yvonne. *Blues Legacies and Black Feminism: Gertrude "Ma" Rainey, Bessie Smith, and Billie Holiday.* New York: Pantheon Books, 1998.

Davis, F. James. *Who Is Black? One Nation's Definition.* University Park: Pennsylvania State University Press, 1991.

De Lerma, Dominique-René. *Black Music in Our Culture: Curricular Ideas on the Subjects, Materials, and Problems.* Kent, Ohio: Kent State University Press, 1970.

Desmangles, Leslie G. *The Faces of the Gods: Vodou and Roman Catholicism in Haiti.* Chapel Hill: University of North Carolina Press, 1992.

Deveaux, Scott. "Constructing the Jazz Tradition: Jazz Historiography." *Black American Literature Forum* 25 (fall 1991): 525–60.

Dillard, J. L. *Black English: Its History and Usage in the United States.* New York: Random House, 1972.

———. *A History of American English.* New York: Longman, 1992.

Dodge, Roger Pryor. *Hot Jazz and Jazz Dance: Collected Writings 1929–1964.* New York: Oxford University Press, 1995.

Douglas, Ann. *Terrible Honesty: Mongrel Manhattan in the 1920s.* New York: Farrar, Straus and Giroux, 1995.

Drucker, Peter Ferdinand. *Managing in a Time of Great Change.* New York: Truman Talley Books/Dutton, 1995.

Dyson, Michael Eric. *Between God and Gangsta Rap: Bearing Witness to Black Culture.* New York: Oxford University Press, 1996.

———. *Making Malcolm: The Myth and Meaning of Malcolm X.* New York: Oxford University Press, 1995.

———. *Race Rules: Navigating the Color Line.* Reading, Mass.: Addison-Wesley Publishing Co., 1996.

———. *Reflecting Black: African-American Cultural Criticism.* Minneapolis: University of Minnesota Press, 1993.

Early, Gerald Lyn. *Culture of Bruising: Essays on Prizefighting, Literature, and Modern American Culture.* Hopewell, N.J.: Ecco Press, 1994.

———. *Lure and Loathing: Essays on Race, Identity, and the Ambivalence of Assimilation.* New York: Penguin Press, 1993.

————. *Tuxedo Junction: Essays on American Culture.* New York: Ecco Press, 1989.

Ellington, Duke. *Music is My Mistress.* Garden City, N.Y.: Doubleday, 1973.

Ellison, Ralph. *Going to the Territory.* New York: Random House, 1986.

————. *Shadow and Act.* New York: Random House, 1964.

Emery, Lynne Fauley. *Black Dance in the United States from 1619 to 1970.* Palo Alto, Calif.: National Press Books, 1972.

Epstein, Dena J. *Sinful Tunes and Spirituals: Black Folk Music to the Civil War.* Urbana: University of Illinois Press, 1977.

Erenberg, Lewis A. *Steppin' Out: New York Nightlife and the Transformation of American Culture, 1890–1930.* Westport, Conn.: Greenwood Press, 1981.

————. *Swingin' the Dream: Big Band Jazz and the Rebirth of American Culture.* Chicago: University of Chicago Press, 1998.

Fisher, Miles Mark. *Negro Slave Songs in the United States.* American Historical Association, 1953; New York: Citadel Press, 1990.

Fishkin, Shelley Fisher. *Was Huck Black? Mark Twain and African-American Voices.* New York: Oxford University Press, 1993.

Floyd, Samuel A., Jr. *The Power of Black Music: Interpreting Its History from Africa to the United States.* New York: Oxford University Press, 1995.

Gabbard, Krin, ed. *Jazz Among the Discourses.* Durham, N.C.: Duke University Press, 1995.

Gates, Henry Louis, Jr. *Figures in Black: Words, Signs, and the "Racial" Self.* New York: Oxford University Press, 1987.

————. *The Signifying Monkey: A Theory of African-American Literary Criticism.* New York: Oxford University Press, 1988.

Gayle, Addison, ed. *The Black Aesthetic.* Garden City, N.Y.: Doubleday, 1971.

————, ed. *Black Expression: Essays by and about Black Americans in the Creative Arts.* New York: Weybright and Talley, 1969.

Gennari, John. "Jazz Criticism: Its Development and Ideologies," *Black American Literature Forum* 25 (fall 1991): 449–523.

Genovese, Eugene D. *Roll, Jordan, Roll: The World the Slaves Made.* New York: Pantheon Books, 1974.

George, Nelson George. *Elevating the Game: Black Men and Basketball.* New York: Harper Collins, 1992.

————. *Hip Hop America.* New York: Viking, 1998.

Gillespie, Dizzy, with Al Fraser. *To Be, or not . . . to Bop: Memoirs.* Garden City, N.Y.: Doubleday, 1979.

Gilroy, Paul. *The Black Atlantic: Modernity and Double Consciousness.* New York: Verso, 1993.

Gottschild, Brenda Dixon. *Digging the Africanist Presence in American Performance: Dance and Other Contexts.* Westport, Conn.: Greenwood Press, 1996.

Guerrero, Edward. *Framing Blackness: The African American Image in Film.* Philadelphia: Temple University Press, 1993.

Harrison, Daphne Duval. *Black Pearls: Blues Queens of the 1920s.* New Brunswick, N.J.: Rutgers University Press, 1988.

Hazzard-Gordon, Katrina. *Jookin': The Rise of Social Dance Formations in African-American Culture.* Philadelphia: Temple University Press, 1990.

Henderson, Stephen Evangelist. *Understanding the New Black Poetry: Black Speech and Black Music as Poetic References.* New York: William Morrow, 1973.

Herskovits, Melville J. *The Myth of the Negro Past.* New York: Harper and Brothers, 1941; Boston: Beacon, 1958.

Hill, Errol, ed. *The Theater of Black Americans: A Collection of Critical Essays.* Englewood Cliffs, N.J.: Prentice-Hall, 1980; New York: Applause, 1987.

Holloway, Joseph E., ed. *Africanisms in American Culture.* Bloomington: Indiana University Press, 1990.

Holloway, Joseph E., and Winifred K. Vass. *The African Heritage of American English.* Bloomington: Indiana University Press, 1993.

Honour, Hugh. *The Image of the Black in Western Art.* New York: William Morrow, 1976.

hooks, bell. *Black Looks: Race and Representation.* Boston: South End Press, 1992.

———. *Outlaw Culture: Resisting Representations.* New York: Routledge, 1994.

Huggins, Nathan Irvin. *Black Odyssey: The Afro-American Ordeal in Slavery.* New York: Pantheon Books, 1977.

Hurston, Zora Neale. *The Sanctified Church: The Folklore Writings of Zora Neale Hurston.* Berkeley: Turtle Island, 1981.

Jackson, Irene V., ed. *More Than Dancing: Essays on Afro-American Music and Musicians.* Westport, Conn.: Greenwood Press, 1985.

Jackson, Phil, with Charles Rosen. *Maverick: More Than a Game.* Chicago: Playboy Press, 1975.

Johnson, James Weldon, and J. Rosamond Johnson. *The Books of American Negro Spirituals.* New York: Viking Press, 1969 (reissue: New York, 1925, 1926).

Jones, A. M. *Studies in African Music.* London: Oxford University Press, 1959.

Jones, Bessie, and Bess Lomax Hawes. *Step It Down: Games, Plays, Songs, and Stories from the Afro-American Heritage.* Athens: University of Georgia Press, 1972.

Keil, Charles. *Urban Blues.* Chicago: University of Chicago Press, 1966.

Keil, Charles, and Steven Feld. *Music Grooves: Essays and Dialogues.* Chicago: University of Chicago Press, 1994.

Kochman, Thomas. *Rappin' and Stylin' Out: Communication in Urban America.* Urbana: University of Illinois Press, 1972.

Kofsky, Frank. *Black Nationalism and the Revolution in Music.* New York: Pathfinder Press, 1970.

Korall, Burt. *Drummin' Men: The Heartbeat of Jazz, the Swing Years.* New York: Schirmer Books, 1990.

Kramer, Lawrence. *Music as Cultural Practice, 1800–1900.* Berkeley: University of California Press, 1990.

Lees, Gene. *Cats of Any Color: Jazz Black and White.* New York: Oxford University Press, 1994.

Levine, Lawrence W. *Black Culture and Black Consciousness: Afro-American Folk Thought from Slavery to Freedom.* New York: Oxford University Press, 1977.

Lhamon, W. T., Jr. *Raising Cain: Blackface Performance from Jim Crow to Hip Hop.* Cambridge: Harvard University Press, 1998.

Lincoln, C. Eric, and Lawrence H. Mamiya. *The Black Church in the African American Experience.* Durham: Duke University Press, 1990.

Lipsitz, George. *Time Passages: Collective Memory and American Popular Culture.* Minneapolis: University of Minnesota Press, 1990.

Lomax, Alan. *The Land Where the Blues Began.* New York: Pantheon Books, 1993.

Lott, Eric. *Love and Theft: Blackface Minstrelsy and the American Working Class.* New York: Oxford University Press, 1993.

Major, Clarence, ed. *Juba to Jive: Dictionary of African-American Slang.* New York: Penguin Books, 1994.

——. *The New Black Poetry.* New York: International Publishers, 1969.

Malone, Jacqui. *Steppin' on the Blues: The Visible Rhythms of African American Dance.* Urbana: University of Illinois Press, 1996.

Mbiti, John S. *African Religions and Philosophy.* New York: Praeger, 1969.

McElroy, Guy C. *Facing History: The Black Image in American Art, 1710–1940.* San Francisco: Bedford Arts, 1990.

Mercer, Kobena. *Welcome to the Jungle: New Positions in Black Cultural Studies.* New York: Routledge, 1994.

Miller, Norma with Evette Jensen. *Swingin' at the Savoy: The Memoir of a Jazz Dancer.* Philadelphia: Temple University Press, 1996.

Mintz, Sidney W., and Richard Price. *The Birth of African-American Culture.* Boston: Beacon Press, 1976.

Mitchell, Henry H. *Black Preaching.* Philadelphia: J. B. Lippincott Co., 1970.

Morrison, Toni. *Playing in the Dark: Whiteness and the Literary Imagination.* Cambridge: Harvard University Press, 1992.

Murray, Albert. *The Blue Devils of Nada: A Contemporary American Approach to Aesthetic Statement.* New York: Pantheon Books, 1996.

——. *The Hero and the Blues.* Columbia: University of Missouri Press, 1973.

——. *The Omni-Americans.* New York: Vintage, 1970.

——. *Stomping the Blues.* New York: McGraw-Hill, 1976.

Novak, Michael. *The Joy of Sports: End Zones, Bases, Baskets, Balls, and the Consecration of the American Spirit.* New York: Basic Books, 1976.

Otis, Johnny. *Upside Your Head! Rhythm and Blues on Central Avenue.* Hanover, N.H.: Wesleyan University Press, 1993.

Piersen, William D. *Black Legacy: America's Hidden Heritage.* Amherst: University of Massachusetts Press, 1993.

——. *Black Yankees: The Development of an Afro-American Subculture in Eighteenth-Century New England.* Amherst: University of Massachusetts Press, 1988.

Pieterse, Jan Nederveen. *White on Black: Images of Africa and Blacks in Western Popular Culture.* New Haven: Yale University Press, 1992.

Porter, Lewis. *Lester Young.* Boston: Twayne Publishers, 1985.

——. *A Lester Young Reader.* Washington, D.C.: Smithsonian Institution Press, 1991.

Raboteau, Albert J. *Slave Religion: The "Invisible Institution" in the Antebellum South.* New York: Oxford University Press, 1978.

Rainwater, Lee, ed. *Black Experience: Soul.* New Brunswick, N.J.: Transaction Books, 1973.

Ramsey, Frederick, Jr., and Charles Edward Smith, eds. *Jazzmen.* New York: Harcourt Brace, 1939.

Reagon, Bernie Johnson. *We'll Understand It Better By and By: Pioneering African American Gospel Composers.* Washington, D.C.: Smithsonian Institution Press, 1992.

Riis, Thomas L. *Just before Jazz: Black Musical Theater in New York 1890–1915.* Washington, D.C.: Smithsonian Institution Press, 1989.

Roberts, John Storm. *Black Music of Two Worlds.* New York: Praeger Publishers, 1972.

Roediger, David R. *Towards the Abolition of Whiteness: Essays on Race, Politics, and Working Class History*. New York: Verso, 1991.

———. *The Wages of Whiteness: Race and the Making of the American Working Class*. New York: Verso, 1991.

Rose, Tricia. *Black Noise: Rap Music and Black Culture in Contemporary America*. Hanover, N.H.: Wesleyan University Press, 1994.

Russell, Bill, and Taylor Branch. *Second Wind: The Memoirs of an Opinionated Man*. New York: Random House, 1979.

Russell, Ross. *Jazz Style in Kansas City and the Southwest*. Berkeley: University of California Press, 1971.

Sacks, Howard L., and Judith Rose Sacks. *Way up North in Dixie: A Black Family's Claim to the Confederate Anthem*. Washington, D.C.: Smithsonian Institution Press, 1993.

Schuller, Gunther. *Early Jazz: Its Roots and Musical Development*. New York: Oxford University Press, 1968.

———. *The Swing Era*. New York: Oxford University Press, 1988.

Shapiro, Nat, and Nat Hentoff, eds. *Hear Me Talkin' to Ya: The Story of Jazz as Told by the Men Who Made It*. New York: Rinehart and Co., 1955.

Sidran, Ben. *Black Talk*. New York: Holt, Rinehart and Winston, 1971.

Small, Christopher. *Music of the Common Tongue: Survival and Celebration in Afro-American Music*. London: J. Calder, 1987.

Sobel, Mechal. *The World They Made Together: Black and White Values in Eighteenth-Century Virginia*. Princeton: Princeton University Press, 1987.

Southern, Eileen. *The Music of Black Americans: A History*. 3d ed. New York: W. W. Norton and Co., 1997.

Southern, Eileen, ed. *Readings in Black American Music*. 2d ed. New York: W. W. Norton and Co., 1983.

Smitherman, Geneva. *Black Talk: Words and Phrases from the Hood to the Amen Corner*. Boston: Houghton Mifflin, 1994.

Spencer, Jon Michael. *Blues and Evil*. Knoxville: University of Tennessee Press, 1993.

Stearns, Marshall Winslow. *The Story of Jazz*. New York: Oxford University Press, 1956.

Stearns, Marshall, and Jean Stearns. *Jazz Dance: The Story of American Vernacular Dance*. New York: Macmillan, 1968.

Stowe, David W. *Swing Changes: Big-Band Jazz in New Deal America*. Cambridge: Harvard University Press, 1994.

Stuckey, Sterling. *Going through the Storm: The Influence of African American Art in History*. New York: Oxford University Press, 1994.

———. *Slave Culture: Nationalist Theory and the Foundations of Black America*. New York: Oxford University Press, 1987.

Szwed, John F., ed. *Black America*. New York: Basic Books, 1970.

Thompson, Robert Farris. *Flash of the Spirit: African and Afro-American Art and Philosophy*. New York: Random House, 1983.

Thompson, Robert Farris, and Joseph Cornet. *The Four Moments of the Sun: Kongo Art in Two Worlds*. Washington, D.C.: National Gallery of Art, 1981.

Toll, Richard C. *Blacking Up: The Minstrel Show in Nineteenth-Century America*. New York: Oxford University Press, 1974.

Tucker, Mark, ed. *The Duke Ellington Reader*. New York: Oxford University Press, 1993.

Van der Merwe, Peter. *Origins of the Popular Style: the Antecedents of Twentieth-Century Popular Music.* New York: Oxford University Press, 1989.

Watkins, Mel. *On the Real Side: Laughing, Lying and Signifying—the Underground Tradition of African American Humor that Transformed American Culture, from Slavery to Richard Pryor.* New York: Simon and Schuster, 1994.

West, Cornel. *Keeping Faith: Philosophy and Race in America.* New York: Routledge, 1993.

——. *Race Matters* Boston: Beacon Press, 1993.

White, Shane, and Graham White. *Stylin': African American Expressive Culture from Its Beginnings to the Zoot Suit.* Ithaca, N.Y.: Cornell University Press, 1998.

Whitten, Norman E., Jr., and John F. Szwed, eds. *Afro-American Anthropology: Contemporary Perspectives.* New York: Free Press, 1970.

Williams, Melvin D. *On the Street Where I Lived.* New York: Holt, Rinehart and Winston, 1981.

Wood, Peter H. *Black Majority: Negroes in Colonial South Carolina from 1670 through the Stono Rebellion.* New York: Alfred A. Knopf, 1974.

Wright, Josephine, ed., with Samuel A. Floyd, Jr. *New Perspectives on Music: Essays in Honor of Eileen Southern.* Warren, Mich.: Harmonie Park Press, 1992.

Index

jam session, 98, 252, 255–56
jazz, 6, 18, 19, 28, 60, 91, 96–109, 135, 137, 141, 142, 157, 167, 172, 176, 177, 182, 239–76, 417, 421; jazz dance, 93, 225, 231; jazz moment, 5, 232; performance aesthetic of, 281, 285, 286
Jerk, 88
jitterbug, 24, 88, 89, 90, 205
John Canoe. *See* Jon Koonering
John Henry, 106, 299
Johnson, Bunk, 103, 108, 421
Johnson, Jack, 2, 380, 386
Johnson, James P., 17, 230, 257
Johnson, James Weldon, 13–14, 15, 17, 45–71
Johnson, J. Rosamond, 45, 67, 69, 71
Johnson, Magic, 389, 396, 397
Jones, A. M., 78, 79, 92
Jones, Jo, 251, 266
Jonkonnu. *See* Jon Koonering
Jon Koonering (John Canoe, Jonkonnu), 359, 362, 417, 419, 420, 421, 427, 428
jook (juke), 303–7, 434, 438, 441
Jordan, Michael, 2, 4, 5, 240, 373, 388–406, 407–16
jubilee quartets, 175, 181
jump, 30, 82–83, 139, 375, 396, 428, 440; jump blues, 16, 108; jumps (children's play), 28
Jump for Joy, 260
jump shot, 3–4, 6, 376, 192

Kansas City style, 98, 108, 247
Kerouac, Jack, 253
King, B. B., 73
King, Martin Luther, Jr., 29–30, 343
King Sailor, 88
Kirk, Andy, 98
Kochman, Thomas, 142, 310, 321, 322
Krehbiel, H. E., 17, 18, 48, 51, 69, 137

Lee, Spike, 411
Legba, 139
Lindy Hop, 24, 30, 88, 89, 138, 205, 257
Lomax, Alan, 15, 27
loud-talking, 323–37

Louis, Joe, 2, 4, 379–87, 409
Lunceford, Jimmie, 245, 248

Malcolm X, 73, 248
Malone, Jaqui, 25
mambo, 88, 90
management philosophy, 6–7
Maravich, "Pistol" Pete, 6
march, 89, 141, 167, 228, 425–26, 429
Mardi Gras, 420, 421, 422, 430
marking, 310, 327–30
Marsalis, Branford, 279, 283, 284, 285, 286
Mbiti, John S., 9, 113
McLuhan, Marshall, 73
melody, 52, 58, 59, 67, 68; melismatic, 173, 185
Merriam, Alan P., 75, 81, 117
metaphor and simile, 293–96, 320, 330, 415
metronome sense, 11, 117
Middle Passage, 14
Miley, "Bubber," 168
Miller and Lyles, 62
mimicry, 301–2, 309, 354–55, 357, 358, 424
Mingus, Charles, 264, 277
Minns, Al, 24, 87–89
minstrelsy, 28, 48, 66, 165, 229, 243, 246, 247, 430
Mitchell-Kernan, Claudia, 145, 146
Moe, Orin, 147, 151–53
Monk, Thelonious, 262
Morrison, Toni, 22
Morton, Jelly Roll, 103, 147, 230, 436–37
Moten, Bennie, 98
multidimensionality, 222, 228
Murray, Albert, 8, 21, 26, 96, 139, 145, 146–47, 151, 153, 223, 226, 232, 267, 386, 438
music, 21; African, 10–12, 17–20, 45, 51, 55–59, 61, 62, 65; 110–134; industry, 172–190; Spanish, 52, 62; *See also* aesthetics, African; aesthetics, African American; audience-performer relations; bebop; blues; call-and-response; dance; drums; falsetto; gospel music; harmony; heterogeneous sound ideal; improvisation; jazz; percussive dominance; melody;

music (*cont.*)
  rhythm; ring shout; soul; timbre, timbral
    variations
musical theater, 229

Nanton, "Tricky Sam," 168
Nketia, J. H. K., 110, 118, 161

Oleke, 88
Oliver, King, 101, 103, 108, 247
oral traditions, 21; transmission of, 130
Ortiz, Fernando, 88
Osgood, Henry O., 18
Otis, Johnny, 1, 241, 267

Pachanga, 90
parade, 418–21, 424, 429
Parker, Charlie, 18, 22, 23, 101, 108, 109, 168,
    239, 250, 262, 263, 266, 281–82, 283, 284,
    286
pecking, 88, 90
pelvic thrust, 25, 91, 225
percussive dominance, 20, 75, 76–77, 99,
    117, 159, 185, 258
percussive performance concept, 12–13
Peterson, Oscar, 256
philosophy: African, 9, 72; black, 174
Pinkster, 417, 420, 421
play, 109, 226, 419
pop music, 172, 173, 174, 182, 185
postindustrial culture, 6–7
preachers and preaching, 21, 29–30, 55, 184,
    227, 331–47
Presley, Elvis, 25, 88
Primus, Pearl, 89

quadrille, 93
quartet, 65–66; barbershop singing, 66. *See
    also* jubilee quartet

radio, 174, 175, 177, 178, 178–81
ragtime, 28, 48, 138, 141, 157
Rainey, Ma, 103, 104, 108, 230
rap, 26, 141, 188, 191–221; women in, 211–13
Redman, Don, 168
religion, rituals and practices: African, 9,

15–16, 72–86, 113, 115, 331, 343, 449; African American, 15, 29–30, 45, 99, 106, 124,
  127, 172–90, 224–25, 331–47, 434, 448–50;
  role of women in, 45, 53, 54–55, 62, 339
rhythm, 52, 53, 59–62, 63, 231, 234, 250, 254,
  298, 422; propulsive, 26, 92, 231, 254, 256,
  289, 449; rhythmic and metric complexity, 10, 13, 16, 17, 18, 20, 26, 45, 52, 53, 62,
  74, 75, 77, 78, 79, 91, 92–93, 96, 105, 115,
  117, 119, 159, 162, 173, 256
rhythm and blues, 16, 138, 141, 173, 177, 180,
  182, 183, 184, 186, 187
riff, 96, 98, 100, 101, 149, 168, 422
ring shout, 13–17, 23, 26, 45, 63–65, 88, 135–
  39, 143, 144, 154; and ring dancing, 5, 9, 88,
  423; shout songs, 62, 63–64, 139, 142, 149
Roach, Max, 266
Robeson, Paul, 61, 62, 69
Robinson, Bill Bo-Jangles, 233, 298, 307
Robinson, Jackie, 4, 409
Robinson, Sugar Ray, 4
rock and roll, 30, 45, 72, 141; dancing, 91
Rollins, Sonny, 266
rumba, 90
Runnin' Wild, 62

samba, 90
Sanctified Church (Church of God in
    Christ, Holiness Church), 16, 29, 72, 178,
    185, 448–49
Sand, 90
satire, 10, 13, 17, 18, 22, 26, 27–28, 30, 139,
    191, 309, 348–66, 373, 423–24, 429; in
    songs, 348–66, 423–24
Savoy Ballroom, 24, 87, 257, 259
scat vocal, 103
Schuller, Gunther, 19, 147–49, 153, 239
sculpture (African), 83, 114
second line, principle of, 417, 421, 422, 430
sermonizing. *See* preaching
sexuality, 139
sexual orientation, 31
Shake, 88
Shango, 99
Shika, 88
shimmy, 24, 88, 89, 90